HERITAGE RESOURCES LAW
Protecting the Archeological and Cultural Environment

Sherry Hutt
Caroline M. Blanco
Ole Varmer

JOHN WILEY & SONS, INC.
New York, Chichester, Weinheim, Brisbane, Singapore, Toronto

Library of Congress Cataloging-in-Publication Data

Heritage resources law : protecting the archeological and cultural
    environment / the National Trust for Historic Preservation.
       p.   cm.
    Includes index.
    ISBN 0-471-25158-5 (cloth : alk. paper)
    1. Cultural property--Protection--Law and legislation--United
States.   2. Historic preservation--Law and legislation--United
States.   3. Archaeology--Law and legislation--United States.
I. National Trust for Historic Preservation in the United States.
KF4310.H47   1999
344.73'094--dc21   98-34684

FOREWORD

We all stand in awe of this nation's heritage resources, the treasures of our historic and prehistoric past. These precious artifacts tell us not only about the peoples who have gone before us, but—*if we can preserve them*—they can inform countless future generations. Today they are important to us on so many different levels: providing our scientists with information which is both fascinating and important to us all; and giving ordinary modern peoples a sense of respect and kinship with ancient peoples who found the means of eloquently expressing themselves in their everyday lives. Their structures, their art, their tools, their designs for living and dying, all tell us about the strength of the human spirit; about the great resilience of the human race; about the ingenuity and creativity of our ancestors. Our heritage resources serve as the ultimate model of what we are capable of accomplishing, regardless of hardship and circumstance.

The universal fascination with traces of our past is evident in every community in the nation. Americans from all walks of contemporary life agree that we must defend our heritage resources as fiercely as we defend our natural resources. The law is one of our most powerful tools. I am proud to say that the Department of Justice is working throughout the country with the Department of the Interior, other state and federal agencies, federally recognized Indian tribes, and the Congress to ensure that we do all we can to protect and preserve the rich evidence of our past. I urge each American to work in your community for the same goal.

Janet Reno, Attorney General of the United States

(The Attorney General serves, by operation of law, as an *ex officio* member of the Board of Trustees of the National Trust for Historic Preservation. The National Trust provides leadership, education and advocacy to save America's diverse historic places, and revitalize our communities.)

PREFACE

The law of heritage resources is an interdisciplinary undertaking involving some of the most important fields of substantive law, ranging from land management and property law to criminal justice and civil rights law. It also is a topic characterized by strongly held views and long-debated tensions between individual and public rights, and between federal and state interests. Heritage resources law is fascinating for the legal mind because it intersects statutory and regulatory law, and requires the reader to consider congressional and executive policy-making and politics. Also, it involves aspects of the legal process from sources as diverse as the United States Constitution and the federal Administrative Procedure Act.

Archeological resources are the physical evidence of past human habitation, occupation, or activity, including the site, location, or context of this evidence. Through controlled observation and collection, contextual measurement, analysis, and interpretation, archeological resources provide an understanding of past human behavior or cultural adaptation. Heritage resources are the parent set for archeological resources. They also contain places and items of ongoing historical, traditional, or cultural significance for a district, the nation, or a living culture. The U.S.S. *Constitution*, Plymouth Rock, Ebenezer Baptist Church, and Hopi Yei B'Chei jish are all examples of heritage resources.

Heritage resources cannot regenerate or be replaced, and even machine-made heritage resources are irreplaceable given that their contextual disposition within a site is unique and contributes to their value. In fact, the nexus between heritage resources and their environments is so important that the law considers these resources under the rubric of "environmental law" by including them in statutes such as the National Environmental Policy Act, the Coastal Zone Management Act, and the National Forest Management Act.

Heritage resources are part of the environment, making the Antiquities Act of 1906 one of this country's first environmental laws. Enacted in response to the destruction of archeological sites and structures that accompanied the settlement of the American Southwest in the second half of the nineteenth century, the Antiquities Act provided a means for setting aside and protecting particularly important places with historic, prehistoric, and commemorative value. It also established a permitting system whereby excavation, removal, recording, and curation of objects of antiquity would be undertaken only by properly qualified agents of recognized scientific or educational institutions. Thus, the United States, through the Antiquities Act, recognized the role of science—embodied in the discipline of archeology—in preserving and protecting for long-term public benefit the values represented by sites and objects of antiquity.

If the perception that the West was "closing" precipitated a legal initiative to preserve, protect, and scientifically recover antiquities for the public benefit, the view of the American Indian as "the vanishing American" only served to rationalize the collection and removal of native peoples' cultural heritage, sometimes in the name of science but generally without right of possession. Of course, American

Indians, Alaska Natives, and Native Hawaiians did not disappear, but not until the passage of the Native American Graves Protection and Repatriation Act (NAGPRA) in 1990 did the United States codify the civil rights of native peoples to possess the remains of their ancestors and the objects placed with the deceased, the sacred objects they need for religious practices, and the objects that constitute their collective cultural heritage. NAGPRA, then, in addition to being a civil rights law, also might be this country's first "environmental justice" law.

This book examines how the law has come to view archeological and other heritage resources. Although it addresses heritage resources mainly within the context of federal law, readers also will learn about aspects of state law and American Indian tribal law that sometimes constitute supplementary or controlling authority.

The four chapters in this book that deal substantively with the law are titled "Federal Compliance Statutes," " Federal Enforcement Statutes," "Native American Heritage Resources Law," and "Heritage Resources Law in the Marine Environment." Each chapter begins with an overview and a review of the historical and legislative development of the law, followed by a detailed discussion of the applicable statutes, regulations, cases, and other authorities. The "Notes" and "Issues for Discussion" provide further legal analysis, current issues in the law, and discussion about the law's direction.

The chapter on compliance addresses federal laws that, among other things, require adherence to a process that considers heritage resources in the context of federal undertakings in particular and land management in general. The chapter on enforcement deals with laws that regulate the use of heritage resources and provide criminal and civil sanctions for violations of law. Because the history and evolution of American Indian law and admiralty/maritime law have produced distinctive doctrines and analyses, they usually are studied as discrete law courses. Consequently, Native American heritage resources and heritage resources in the marine environment are given separate treatment in this book.

To our knowledge, this is the first legal text that brings the study of heritage resources law both to the law school classroom and the legal practitioner, and we hope it will bring some order and philosophical perspective to this important area of environmental law. The matrix of law and policy, combined with universal interest in cultural heritage, provides the educator with a unique platform from which to teach law and lawyering skills. Thus, we also hope that more law schools—as well as graduate programs in such areas as public affairs, environmental policy, and public archeology—will consider heritage resources law in their curricula.

Anthony Antonellis
David Tarler

Contributing Editors

ACKNOWLEDGMENTS

ACKNOWLEDGMENT BY
THE NATIONAL TRUST FOR HISTORIC PRESERVATION

The National Trust for Historic Preservation thanks the many persons and organizations who have contributed, directly or indirectly, to this important environmental law book. First and foremost, the National Trust wishes to publicly acknowledge the extraordinary efforts of Sherry Hutt, Caroline M. Blanco, and Ole Varmer. These three principal authors dedicated and volunteered hundreds of hours of their time to produce this book, and have unselfishly committed all royalties to the National Trust for Historic Preservation. Their spouses, family members, and friends also provided tremendous support for the production of this book.

The National Trust would also like to express its appreciation to Anthony Antonellis and David Tarler, who played instrumental roles in the book's creation and who served as contributing editors; and Richard Waldbauer, Jo Ann Harris, Francis P. McManamon, Julia H. Miller, Elizabeth S. Merritt; the Environment and National Resources Division of the Department of Justice; the National Oceanic and Atmospheric Administration; the National Park Service; Suffolk University Law School, American University's Washington College of Law; and John Wiley & Sons, Inc.

Paul W. Edmondson

General Counsel
National Trust for Historic Preservation

ABOUT THE AUTHORS

Sherry Hutt serves as a Maricopa County, Arizona, Superior Court Judge and a White Mountain Apache Tribal Appellate Court Judge. Since 1983, Judge Hutt has lectured throughout the country and has written extensively in the area of cultural resources protection law for federal land managing agencies, law schools, and for Heritage Resources Management Program of the University of Nevada, Reno. Judge Hutt, a recipient of the Department of the Interior Conservation Service Award, was formerly an Assistant U.S. Attorney prosecuting ARPA cases. She co-authored (with Elwood Jones and Martin McAllister) *Archeological Resource Protection* (Preservation Press, John Wiley & Sons 1992).

Caroline M. Blanco is a Trial Attorney in the General Litigation Section of the Environment and Natural Resources Division of the United States Department of Justice, where she specializes in heritage resources law and, in particular, historic shipwreck litigation. Ms. Blanco, a recipient of the Attorney General's Award for Distinguished Service, frequently lectures in the field of heritage resources law at law schools and government training seminars throughout the country. In addition, Ms. Blanco serves as a Professorial Lecturer on heritage resources law at the American University's Washington College of Law. Prior to her government service, Ms. Blanco was a litigation associate at the law firm of McCutcheon Doyle Brown & Enerson, San Jose, California.

Ole Varmer is an international environmental law attorney with the U.S. Department of Commerce, National Oceanic and Atmospheric Administration (NOAA). Mr. Varmer provides legal advice and assistance on marine environmental and historic preservation laws including the National Marine Sanctuaries Act, the Abandoned Shipwreck Act, and salvage law issues, and assists in cases involving claims by treasure salvors. He has represented NOAA's environmental and historic preservation interests in various state, national and international forums, including the U.S. 1998 delegation to the "Meeting of Experts" for UNESCO's draft Convention on the Protection of the Underwater Cultural Heritage. He has also written and lectured extensively on heritage resources law, including at Suffolk Law School, the American University's Washington College of Law, and at law courses offered by the Department of Justice Office of Legal Education.

TABLE OF CONTENTS

CHAPTER THREE

TABLE OF CONTENTS

CHAPTER ONE

AN INTRODUCTION TO HERITAGE RESOURCES LAW

WHAT ARE HERITAGE RESOURCES AND WHY ARE THEY PROTECTED?

Francis P. McManamon*

INTRODUCTION: HERITAGE RESOURCES DEFINED

"Heritage resources" (also known as "cultural resources") is a general term frequently used to refer to a wide range of archeological sites, historic structures, museum objects, historic shipwrecks, and traditional cultural places. Usually included within these categories are "archaeological resources," as defined by the Archaeological Resources Protection Act and its regulations; "historic properties," as defined by the National Historic Preservation Act and its regulations; and other resources not defined in statute or regulation.

Archeological Resources

The legal definition of "archaeological resources" is found in the Archaeological Resources Protection Act (ARPA) (Sec. 3(1)) and the uniform regulations implementing it, as required by Section 10 of the statute (43 C.F.R. Part 7 (Interior); 36 C.F.R. Part 296 (Agriculture); 18 C.F.R. Part 1312 (Tennessee Valley Authority); and 32 C.F.R. Part 229 (Defense)). For purposes of ARPA, archeological resources include any material remains of human life or activities that are at least 100 years of age and of archeological interest. The definitions section of the regulations is extensive, and contains illustrative examples of "material remains" and "archaeological interest." Essentially, material remains are "of archaeological interest" if they are "ca-

---

*Francis P. McManamon, Ph.D., is Chief Archeologist of the National Park Service, and Departmental Consulting Archeologist, Department of the Interior.

pable of providing scientific or humanistic understandings of past human behavior… through the application of scientific or scholarly techniques…"(Sec. __.3(1)). Material remains are "physical evidence of human habitation, occupation, use, or activity, including the site, location, or context in which such evidence is situated" (Sec. __.3(2)). The latter definition is followed by nearly an entire text column of small print listing examples of "material remains," such as domestic structures, baskets, and earthworks.

Historic Properties

NHPA- Registered historic places

Title I of the National Historic Preservation Act established the National Register of Historic Places as a national listing of "historic properties" comprising districts, sites, buildings, structures, and objects significant in American history, architecture, archeology, engineering, and culture. The statute and the regulations and procedures that govern the National Register of Historic Places have been written to include historic and prehistoric archeological sites within the definition of "historic properties." This inclusive approach and broad definition have enabled professionals working in public archeology and archeological preservation to operate under the umbrella of the national historic preservation program. Title I also expanded the level of federal concern beyond nationally significant resources, as expressed in the 1935 Historic Sites Act, to include the preservation of historic properties of local or state significance.

WHY ARE HERITAGE RESOURCES PROTECTED?

Knowledge, community, tourism, economy

Heritage resources define our culture in space and time. Since material cultural remains existed before written records, they are often the only remnants of people, historical processes, or traditional events, but they also amplify the record in historical times. Scientifically retrieved items have rendered information about such important events as the Little Bighorn Battle and the American Revolution, as well as the daily events in ancient Cahokia. Heritage resources possess the potential to transmit even greater knowledge, as future discoveries are made and new scientific and analytical techniques are developed.

The benefits to be derived from heritage resources include increased opportunities for education and tourism, and a strengthened sense of community identity, cohesion, and pride. Heritage resources impart knowledge of the past as they fascinate schoolchildren and other visitors to national, state, and local sites. These visitors, in turn, fuel a sizeable tourism economy, which sustains a large number of local communities. In serving to impart a feeling of connectedness to a place in time, the greatest benefit bestowed by heritage resources—which may be harder to quantify—is the enhancement of our environment.

History of Public Concern and Protection

In 1996, we celebrated the anniversaries of two very important preservation statutes: the 90th anniversary of the Antiquities Act (1906) and the 30th anniversary of the National Historic Preservation Act (1966). From the beginnings of the United States as a nation, there has been public interest in heritage resources. Early focus was directed at one of our national icons, George Washington, who, as first president of the United States and military leader of the Revolutionary War, came to embody the young country. Consequently, places and things associated with Washington became the objects of commemoration and study. By the late nineteenth century, however, the national government was being petitioned by concerned citizens and newly activist politicians to move into the arena of archeology and historic preservation out of concern for archeological resources on public lands in the western states.

As the final quarter of the 1800s began, much of the interest in American archeological sites was focused on the Southwest. Some of the interest came from people who had, themselves, plundered the prehistoric ruins there, and had taken ancient artifacts, including ancient building stone and roof beams, for personal use or commercial sale. Other interest came from investigators belonging to museums or archeological organizations, who wanted to examine and study ancient sites, and assemble collections for their institutions and the public they served.

As investigators visited and documented prominent ruins, they noted the destruction that was occurring. Their descriptions impelled early advocates of government action to protect the archeological sites. Thus, for example, when the issue of government action to protect archeological sites was debated in the United States Senate, Adolph Bandelier's 1881 report on the looting and destruction of ruins and archeological deposits at the site of Pecos, in New Mexico, was quoted (Lee 1970:7–12). One notable success along the path to legislation was the setting aside of Casa Grande Ruin as the first national archeological reservation in 1892.

During the 1890s, major public exhibitions, such as the World's Columbian Exposition in Chicago and the Louisiana Purchase Exposition in St. Louis, exposed even more of the American public to the antiquities of the United States, and municipal and university museums in large cities throughout the country featured American Indian antiquities in their displays. At the same time, explorers who had reached the Southwest's ruins, and archeological sites in other parts of the country and the hemisphere, published popular accounts of their exploits recalling the ancient sites they had visited. The growing popular appeal of American archeology was accompanied by a commercial demand for authentic prehistoric antiquities. Consequently, the unsystematic removal of artifacts from archeological sites for private use increased, especially in the Southwest, where the advancing railroads had facilitated accessibility to antiquities.

The legislative and political history of the Antiquities Act shows that the issue of protecting and managing archeological resources first was raised in the United States Senate by Massachusetts Senator George F. Hoar in 1882 (Lee 1970). Then, and subsequently, debates between the advocates of preservation and the advocates of commercial use of the public lands laced the issue. Interestingly, objections to conservation and preservation did not include statements that such efforts were unnecessary. There was general acknowledgment that looting and vandalism were occurring with increasing frequency. Instead, detractors of the protection and preservation effort argued that the government could not possibly protect all resources. Some of these people already were alarmed by the creation of the federal forest reserves, which by 1901 totaled 46 million acres, and they objected to creating another means by which the president could set aside large areas of the public domain for conservation or preservation, thereby further reducing the public land available for economic activity. Eventually, public sentiment in favor of remedying the problem of increased archeological site destruction in the Southwest, and the wholesale removal of artifacts, overcame these objections. After frequent and widespread efforts to protect specific archeological sites, such as Mesa Verde and Chaco Canyon, the 25-year effort to protect places and objects of antiquity culminated in the Antiquities Act.

On June 8, 1906, President Theodore Roosevelt signed the Antiquities Act into law. The law was intended to protect archeological sites on the public lands of the United States as resources of significance and value to every American, and to preserve historic, scientific, commemorative, and cultural values embodied in archeological sites for present and future generations of citizens.

The Antiquities Act served, and continues to serve, three important functions. First, it established basic public policies dealing with archeological resources in the United States. Through subsequent statutes and regulations, these policies have been extended to cover other kinds of heritage resources. Second, the Act also provided the president with the means of setting aside particularly important places for special preservation, commemoration, and interpretation. This function has been used by presidents throughout the twentieth century to establish National Monuments that preserve nationally important archeological, historic, and natural areas. Third, the Antiquities Act established the requirement of professionalism and a scientific approach to excavation, removal, or other investigation of archeological resources on the public lands. In so doing, the government of the United States endorsed the young discipline of archeology and the careful examination and recording of archeological sites. This professional and scientific approach to archeology now is accepted widely as the appropriate treatment of archeological resources, but in 1906, it was only beginning.

Preserving National Monuments

Prior to the Antiquities Act, specific areas had been set aside as parks or reserves, such as Hot Springs, Arkansas (1832), Yellowstone National Park (1872), and Casa Grande Ruin, Arizona (1892). However, creation of each of these parks or reserves required an Act of Congress, as well as presidential approval. The Antiquities Act made the establishment of National Monuments into administrative actions that were quicker and far more simple to execute. Section 2 of the Act gives the president the authority to set aside for protection "historic landmarks, historic and prehistoric structures, and other objects of historic or scientific interest that are situated upon the lands owned or controlled by the Government of the United States...." These protected areas were then designated as "National Monuments," and the federal agencies assigned to oversee them were required to afford them proper care and management. This section of the statute provided Progressive politicians and their supporters with an additional tool for determining the uses of public lands and resources in the rational, conservation-oriented manner they favored (see Rothman 1989:52–71).

Between 1906 and 1909, President Roosevelt proclaimed as National Monuments El Morro, Montezuma's Castle, Chaco Canyon, Gila Cliff Dwellings, Tonto, Tumacacori, Devil's Tower, Petrified Forest, Lassen Peak, Cinder Cone, Muir Woods, Grand Canyon, Pinnacles, Jewel Cave, Natural Bridges, Lewis and Clark, and Olympic. Since then, Section 2 of the Act has been used to protect dozens of other archeological sites and places of outstanding scientific or natural importance. Many National Monuments, in turn, have been designated as units of the National Park system or have been entrusted for special care to other land managing agencies. Presidents Taft, Wilson, Harding, Coolidge, Franklin D. Roosevelt, Truman, Eisenhower, Kennedy, Johnson, Carter, and Clinton have all established National Monuments by presidential proclamations.

Support for Professional and Scientific Methods and Techniques

An additional broad policy established by the Antiquities Act was that investigation and removal of archeological resources must be conducted by appropriately qualified and trained experts using the best contemporary methods and techniques. This policy has made professional and scientific approaches the standard practice for the examination and treatment of other cultural resources, including historic structures, museum objects, and cultural landscapes.

The Act prohibited individuals from digging haphazardly into ancient or historic sites, disturbing whatever caught their fancy, and removing artifacts for personal use or commerce. Section 3 of the Antiquities Act required that "the examination of ruins, the excavation of archaeological sites, or the gathering of objects of antiquity" on lands administered by the Departments of Interior, Agriculture, or War be carried out only after a permit to do so had been issued by the secretary of the department responsible for the land in question. Permits were to be issued only to institutions "properly qualified to conduct such examinations, excavations, or gatherings...." Any excavation, collection, or removal of artifacts or other archeological remains had to be directed by qualified specialists using up-to-date archeological methods and techniques. Only organizations with appropriate expertise, equipment, commitment, and proper facilities to care for the recovered artifacts and information were permitted to undertake these studies. In emphasizing those specific requirements, the federal government supported the professionalization of the young discipline of archeology. Careful excavation and removal of artifacts required by Antiquities Act permits also were necessary for the development of typological and stratigraphic description and analysis that would become the methodological and technical standards for professional archeology in the United States in the last decade of the nineteenth century and the first decades of the twentieth century (Willey and Sabloff 1993:38–95).

In requiring that approved investigations of antiquities result in public education and benefit, the Antiquities Act permitting system strove to ensure "the benefit of reputable museums, universities, colleges, or other recognized scientific or educational institutions, with a view to increasing the knowledge of such objects." As one means of ensuring these public benefits, Section 3 of the Act also required that the materials collected from investigations be deposited in public museums for preservation.

The Antiquities Act and Subsequent Historic Preservation Statutes

The Antiquities Act is recognized widely as the first general statute addressing archeological and historic preservation concerns in the United States (D. Fowler 1986:140–143; J. M. Fowler 1974:1473–1474; Lee 1970:1; McGimsey 1972:111). The increased role for the federal government created by the Act is characteristic of the laws and programs enacted at the turn of the twentieth century under the influence of the Progressive Movement. Progressive politicians championed new ways of looking after the public good within a federal system staffed by professional civil servants who were able to provide technical assistance to the public and support for the public resources.

The Act established basic public policies for archeological preservation that would, during the course of the twentieth century, expand to include other types of historic properties and cultural resources. Also, during this century, the application of these policies would grow to encompass archeological and historic resources beyond those found on federal and American Indian lands.

Enactment of the Antiquities Act constituted a recognition that archeological sites and their artifacts are most valuable as sources of historic and scientific information about the past, and as commemorative places; that careful archeological excavation, analysis, and interpretation reveal ancient events and long-term cultural, economic, and social developments; that antiquities tell the unwritten stories of people and places; and that these benefits must be shared through schools, parks, museums, and other public venues and programs, and through books, articles, videos, and other interpretive media. Implicit in the Act was also a general policy that digging archeological sites for a few commercially valuable artifacts was improper and wasteful.

Approaching archeological resources as noncommercial was the most basic public policy established by the Antiquities Act. A second aspect of national preservation policy initiated by the Antiquities Act was nearly as fundamental. By placing special requirements on who may excavate or remove archeological remains, how the excavation or removal will be accomplished, and what will happen to the objects excavated or removed, the statute acknowledged that archeological sites have a sufficiently important public value to be treated in a special way, and merit special consideration and protection. Like clean water and air, preserving these resources and learning from the information they contain contribute to the public good.

The policies of the Antiquities Act regarding protection and preservation of archeological resources apply to lands owned or controlled by the government of the United States. During the twentieth century, the policies of noncommercial and public value and benefit have been extended to additional types of historic properties and cultural resources and, in certain circumstances, to nonfederal land. The broader application of these policies came in two increments.

Nearly thirty years after the Antiquities Act, the Historic Sites Act of 1935 asserted a responsibility of the national government to recognize and provide technical assistance to historic American sites, buildings, objects, and antiquities of national significance, no matter where they were located within the United States. In testifying on behalf of the bill that served as the basis for the Historic Sites Act, Secretary of the Interior Harold L. Ickes noted that the Antiquities Act provided protection for archeological and historic resources on publicly owned land, but that we have never faced squarely the whole great problem of a definite governmental policy for the preservation of historic sites and buildings of transcendent national significance... the need for governmental action along these lines is urgent and immediate.... (Ickes 1935:4)

The policy expressed in the 1935 Historic Sites Act flows from the non-commercial and public value policies established by the Antiquities Act. Section 1 of the 1935 law states that

it is a national policy to preserve for public use historic sites, buildings, and objects of national significance for the inspiration and benefit of the people of the United States.

The first expansion of public policy toward heritage resources following the Antiquities Act thus extended to additional kinds of historic properties without regard to federal ownership or control, as long as they were nationally significant. The law does not, however, assert a regulatory or ownership interest of the federal government in these properties. Rather, it authorizes technical assistance, education, and interpretive services for them.

Developments in the 1960s and 1970s

The flood of postwar development that swept the United States in the 1950s resulted in substantial destruction of heritage resources that, at the time, were seen as obstructions to modern progress. Archeologists and historic preservationists fought this destruction in a variety of ways, but a national focus on the importance of heritage resources and the need to consider them in a serious and consistent manner during public projects would not achieve national attention until the mid-1960s, with the enactment of the National Historic Preservation Act of 1966, which is the second expansion of the basic policies set forth in the Antiquities Act.

The National Historic Preservation Act (NHPA) (Pub. L. No. 89-665 and the amendments thereto, 16 U.S.C. § 470 *et seq.*) is a very broadly written statute that has been expanded through major amendments in 1980 and 1992. It embraces a wider range of historic property types than either the Antiquities Act or the Historic Sites Act, and is more inclusive than the Historic Sites Act in that it considers historic properties that are of local or state significance. The extent to which the NHPA applies, however, varies with the extent of ownership and federal involvement in an undertaking that may affect specific resources.

Like the Antiquities Act and the Historic Sites Act, the NHPA adheres to the public policy that historic properties have a value to all of the public. Section 1(a)(4) states that the preservation of this irreplaceable heritage is in the public interest so that its vital legacy of cultural, education, aesthetic, inspirational, economic, and energy benefits will be maintained and enriched for future generations of Americans.

In addition, the noncommercial value of historic properties, and the need to consider their importance in deciding how they are treated, is recognized in the statement of purpose. As described in Section 1(a)(5):

[I]n the face of ever-increasing extensions of urban centers, highways, and residential, commercial, and industrial developments, the present governmental and nongovernmental historic preservation programs and activities are inadequate to insure future generations a genuine opportunity to appreciate and enjoy the rich heritage of our Nation.

The policy espoused by the NHPA calls for the consideration of historic properties within the context of our modern development and economy. Section 2(1), for example, calls for the federal government

in partnership with States, local governments, Indian tribes, and private organizations and individuals to… use measures, including financial and technical assistance, to foster conditions under which our modern society and our prehistoric and historic resources can exist in productive harmony and fulfill the social, economic, and other requirements of present and future generations.

This subsection highlights two important aspects of historic preservation policy in the United States. First, historic preservation, including public archeology and archeological preservation, is an activity that occurs at all levels of government—federal, state, and local—and involves private organizations and individuals. It is not the province of a single national government agency or national museum. Although the involvement of a multitude of public and private parties sometimes makes a comprehensive description of archeological and historic preservation in the United States abstruse, its value lies in giving many organizations and individuals some responsibility for preserving archeological and historic sites, structures, and historic properties. Another key aspect of preservation in the United States embodied in this subsection is that, as a component of contemporary development and economic activity, preservation is considered an aspect of modern life, even if it is not an assured outcome of these activities.

The NHPA establishes State Historic Preservation Officers (SHPO) as partners in the national historic preservation program. It also describes how the SHPO function, or portions of it, can be assumed by local governments or Indian tribes in certain circumstances.

Although only one paragraph long, section 106 of the Act has had a major impact on the structure and function of archeology and archeological preservation in the United States. This section requires that all federal agencies provide the Advisory Council on Historic Preservation—established in Title II of the statute—an opportunity to comment on any undertaking for which an agency has direct or indirect jurisdiction, when that undertaking has an effect on a historic property listed, or eligible for listing, in the National Register of Historic Places. In practice, Section 106 means that federal agencies, or state, local, and private organizations that are involved in federal undertakings, are required to identify archeological and other historic sites and assess the effect of their planned actions on them. This requirement has resulted in tens of thousands of archeological investigations since the mid-1970s, when the procedures for implementing Section 106 were established in regulation (36 C.F.R. Part 800). In some cases, federal agencies responsible for complying with the NHPA have hired archeologists and created their own professional staffs to comply with the law. In other cases, federal agencies have contracted with consulting firms or universities to undertake studies necessary for Section 106 compliance. Over the past twenty years, professional archeologists have come to be employed by public agencies or private consulting and engineering firms as frequently as they have been employed by academic institutions. Hundreds of millions of dollars in government funds have paid for tens of thousands of archeological investigations, including general archeological overviews, site discovery and evaluation studies, and extensive excavation of individual or multiple sites that were subject to destruction by public undertakings (e.g., Haas 1998; McManamon, et al. 1993).

The NHPA envisions that all federal agencies should develop their own programs to care for historic resources under their jurisdiction or control, or affected by their undertakings. Section 110, which was expanded and enhanced by the 1992 amendments, includes the identification, evaluation, nomination to the National Register of Historic Places, and protection of historic resources as federal responsibilities. Although agencies generally have been far more active in complying with Section 106 than with Section 110, the amended text of Section 110 perhaps will provoke greater attention to the responsibilities it describes.

Title II of the NHPA established the Advisory Council on Historic Preservation, an independent federal agency composed of twenty members, including the Secretaries of the Interior and Agriculture, and four other departments. Also on the Council are elected officials and citizens appointed by the president. The Council and its staff play an important role in the national historic preservation program, especially in the day-to-day implementation of Section 106, but also by providing both programmatic advice to federal agencies and training in historic preservation methods, techniques, and procedures.

Title IV of the statute, added in the 1992 amendments, established the National Center for Preservation Technology and Training. In so doing, Congress recognized "the complexity of technical problems encountered in preserving historic properties and the lack of adequate distribution of technical information to preserve such properties" (Section 401). The Center was established to "coordinate and promote research [in historic preservation], distribute information, and provide training about preservation skills and technologies...." (Section 401)

In the 1970s, the threats to American archeological resources from looting had reached notorious proportions, especially in the Southwest. In response, the Archaeological Resources Protection Act (ARPA) was drafted, debated, and enacted relatively quickly in the late 1970s, when difficulties in enforcing the Antiquities Act, and weaknesses in the penalties provided by that law, became critical [see articles in Friedman (1985)]. ARPA was envisioned as a means of affirming the basic policies of the Antiquities Act and, at the same time, providing a more effective law enforcement tool to prosecute looters of public archeological resources. Provisions for effective law enforcement and careful, detailed definitions, the two most apparent weaknesses of the Antiquities Act, were the aspects of ARPA that received the most attention during its enactment and early years of enforcement. ARPA provides a very strong basis for archeological protection on public and American Indian lands, and its antitrafficking provision also makes it an effective tool for discouraging illegal excavation or removal of archeological resources from state, local, or private lands throughout the United States. However, several sections of the law, including the 1988 amendments, also make ARPA an important part of the overall statutory basis for effective archeological resources management.

ARPA (Pub. L. No. 96-95 and amendments thereto, 16 U.S.C. §§ 470aa–470mm) was enacted

> to secure, for the present and future benefit of the American people, the protection of archaeological resources and sites which are on public lands and Indian lands, and to foster increased cooperation and exchange of information between governmental authorities, the professional archaeological community, and private individuals having collections of archaeological resources and data which were obtained before the date of enactment of this Act (Sec. 2(4)(b)).

Thus, the law recognizes that archeological resources are an irreplaceable part of America's heritage, and that, increasingly, they are endangered because of the escalating commercial value of a small component of archeological sites. At the same time, ARPA also notes that in order to better protect and learn about the archeological record of the United States, cooperation is needed among government authorities, professional archeologists and organizations, and interested individuals.

Section 4 of ARPA, and Sections 5 through 12 of the ARPA uniform regulations, describe the requirements that applicants must meet before federal authorities can issue a permit to excavate or remove any archeological resource on federal or American Indian lands. The curation requirements for artifacts and other materials excavated or removed, and the records related them, are described in Section 5 of the Act. Section 5 also authorizes the Secretary of the Interior to issue regulations describing in more detail the management and curation of collections. These regulations, which affect all federally owned or administered archeological collections, were issued in 1990 (36 C.F.R. Part 79).

The primary impetus behind ARPA was the need to provide more effective law enforcement to protect public archeological sites. ARPA improved on the Antiquities Act by providing a definition of the resources covered by the law, a list of the prohibited activities, monetary penalties up to the value of the resources in question, and both felony and misdemeanor sanctions. Section 6 of the statute describes the prohibited actions, and includes damage or defacement, in addition to unpermitted excavation or removal, as well as selling, purchasing, and other trafficking activities in either the United States or internationally. Section 6(c) prohibits interstate or international sale, purchase, or transport of any archeological resource excavated or removed in violation of a state or local law, ordinance, or regulation. It was used as the basis for the successful prosecution of an artifact dealer and collector in Indiana, Arthur Gerber. Gerber was convicted of transporting and selling in Kentucky artifacts obtained from a site on private land, but in violation of Indiana's trespass and conversion law. The conviction was upheld by the United States Court of Appeals for the Seventh Circuit, and is an important case because it shows that ARPA can be used to protect archeological resources located on private land if they are obtained illegally and moved across state lines.

The main focus of ARPA is on the regulation of legitimate archeological investigation on public lands, and the enforcement of penalties against looters and vandals of archeological resources. However, the statute has provided federal officials with the authority to better manage archeological sites on public land. Section 9, for example, requires managers who are responsible for protecting archeological resources to keep information concerning the locations and nature of these resources confidential, unless, by providing the information, they would further the purpose of the statute and not create a risk of harm to the resources. The statute also authorizes the Secretary of the Interior to cooperate with avocational and professional archeologists and organizations in exchanging information about archeological resources, in order to improve knowledge about the archeological record of the United States:

the Secretary [of the Interior] shall... make efforts to expand the archaeological data base for archaeological resources of the United States through increased cooperation between private individuals... and professional archaeologists and organizations. (Sec. 11)

The 1988 amendments to ARPA focused more attention on management actions to improve the protection of archeological resources (McManamon 1991). Section 10(c) required each federal land manager to:

establish a program to increase public awareness of the significance of the archaeological resources located on public lands and Indian lands and the need to protect such resources.

The objective in adding this section to the law was to impart the message to visitors using public lands that archeological resources are valuable to everyone; that, consequently, they must be properly investigated and cared for; and that, when they are located on public lands, they are protected under law. Anecdotal evidence from federal officials in the field indicates that public education and outreach have been effective, and that casual or unknowing destruction and vandalism have been reduced substantially.

Section 14, also added by the 1988 amendments, requires the major federal land managing departments (Interior, Agriculture, Defense, and the Tennessee Valley Authority) to plan and schedule archeological surveys of the lands under their control. The aim of this section is to emphasize the need for better knowledge of the locations and nature of archeological resources so they can be better protected.

CONCLUSIONS

In the years since the Antiquities Act became law, the means of preserving and interpreting America's archeology have expanded and improved, in particular through the Historic Sites Act and the National Historic Preservation Act. Although the Antiquities Act proved to be a means of overseeing and coordinating educational and scientific archeological investigations on federal and American Indian lands, it did not effectively prevent or deter looting of archeological sites on those lands. This problem became critical in the 1970s, when several attempts by federal land managing agencies and prosecutors in the Southwest to convict looters under the Antiquities Act resulted in judicial decisions holding that the terms of the Antiquities Act were unconstitutionally vague (Collins and Michel 1985). The response to these cases was a concerted effort by archeologists and preservationists, their allies in the law enforcement community, and several essential supporters in Congress to strengthen the legal protection of archeological resources, and the eventual outcome was a new statute, the Archaeological Resources Protection Act of 1979.

The Antiquities Act is important for many reasons. It asserted broad and general public interest in, and control over, archeological resources on federal and American Indian lands. This interest and concern continues today, and is the basis for public agency efforts to protect archeological sites from looting and vandalism. The Act also provided for the protection and preservation of specific areas of importance for their archeological, historical, and scientific resources. In addition, it remains an important achievement in the progress of conservation and preservation efforts in the United States. Its passage involved

> a whole generation of dedicated effort by scholars, citizens, and members of Congress... More important, this generation, through its explorations, publications, exhibits, and other activities, awakened the American people to a lasting consciousness of the value of American antiquities, prehistoric and historic. This public understanding, achieved only after persistent effort in the face of much ignorance, vandalism, and indifference, was a necessary foundation for many subsequent conservation achievements. Among them were several of great importance to the future National Park Service, including the establishment of many National Monuments, development of a substantial educational program for visitors, and eventually the execution of a far-reaching nationwide program to salvage irreplaceable archaeological objects threatened with inundation or destruction by dams and other public works and their preservation for the American people. (Lee 1970:86)

Widespread support for archeological preservation and interpretation is essential for better understanding the depth and variety of American history and prehistory. Today, many public agencies, such as the National Park Service, Bureau of Land Management, Bureau of Reclamation, Fish and Wildlife Service, Forest Service, State Historic Preservation Officers, State Archeologists, universities, museums, Indian tribes, and local governments, play important roles in archeological and historic preservation. State programs, for example, provide models for public-private partnerships, as the relationship between the Arkansas Archeological Survey and the Arkansas Archaeological Society demonstrates. Likewise, private, professional, and advocacy organizations, such as the Society for American Archaeology, Society for Historical Archeology, the Archeological Conservancy, the Archaeological Institute of America, and the National Trust for Historic Preservation, are important preservation partners.

The world is more complicated than it was in 1906. We continue to denounce, as did the Antiquities Act, those who pillage archeological sites for personal or commercial gain. Such behavior destroys the public benefit that can be derived from careful study of archeological sites and objects. At the same time, contemporary perspectives regarding the treatment of archeological resources exist which were not envisioned by the promoters and supporters of the Antiquities Act. For example, those of us who work at archeological protection, preservation, and interpretation seek to develop consensus about appropriate treatments of our shared heritage that take into account a multitude of perspectives. We have come to recognize as legitimate the traditional uses of cultural and natural resources, and to value ethnographic approaches in developing consultation about, and treatment of, these resources. Thus, the traditional uses and views of American Indians, Alaska Natives, Native Hawaiians, and other Pacific Islanders, as well as other ethnic groups with close associations to particular archeological sites, must be taken into account through appropriate consultation and treatment. These are the goals of modern archeological protection, preservation, and interpretation.

References

Collins, R. B., and M. P. Michel. 1985. Preserving the Past: Origins of the Archaeological Resources Protection Act of 1979. *A History of the Archaeological Resources Protection Act: Law and Regulations.* Assembled and edited by J. L. Friedman, *American Archeology* 5(2):84–89.

Fowler, Don D. 1986. Conserving American Archaeological Resources. In *American Archaeology Past and Future: A Celebration of the Society for American Archaeology, 1935-1985*, ed. David J. Meltzer, Don D. Fowler, and Jeremy A. Sabloff, pp. 135–162. Smithsonian Institution Press, Washington, DC.

Fowler, John M. 1974. Protection of the Cultural Environment in Federal Law. *In Federal Environmental Law,* ed. Erica L. Dolgin and Thomas G.P. Guilbert, pp. 1466–1517. Environmental Law Institute, West Publishing Company, St. Paul, Minnesota.

Friedman, J. L., editor. 1985. A History of the Archaeological Resources Protection Act: Laws and Regulations. *American Archeology* 5(2): 82–119.

Glass, James A. 1990. *The Beginnings of a New National Historic Preservation Program, 1957 to 1969.* American Association for State and Local History, Nashville, Tennessee.

Haas, D. 1998. *Federal Archeology Program: Secretary of the Interior's Report to Congress, 1994–95.* National Park Service, Department of the Interior, Washington, DC.

Ickes, Harold L. 1935. Statement by Hon. Harold L. Ickes, Secretary of the Interior. In *Preservation of Historic American Sites, Buildings, Objects, and Antiquities of National Significance.* Hearings Before the Committee on the Public Lands, House of Representatives, on H.R. 6670 and H.R. 6734, April 1,2, and 5, 1935. Government Printing Office, Washington, DC.

King, Thomas, F., Patricia Parker Hickman, and Gary Berg. 1977. *Anthropology in Historic Preservation: Caring for Culture's Clutter.* Academic Press, New York, New York.

Lee, R. F. 1970. *The Antiquities Act of 1906.* National Park Service, Department of the Interior, Washington, DC.

McGimsey, Charles R. 1972. *Public Archeology.* Seminar Press, New York and London.

McManamon, F. P. 1991. The Federal Government's Recent Response to Archaeological Looting. In *Protecting the Past,* ed. G.S. Smith and J.E. Ehrenhard, pp. 261–269. CRC Press, Boca Raton, Florida.

McManamon, Francis P., Patricia C. Knoll, Ruthann Knudson, George S. Smith, and Richard C. Waldbauer. 1993. *Federal Archeological Programs and Activities: The Secretary of the Interior's Report to Congress.* National Park Service, Department of the Interior, Washington, DC.

Rothman, H. 1989. *Preserving Different Pasts: The American National Monuments.* University of Illinois Press, Urbana and Chicago.

Willey, Gordon R., and Jeremy A. Sabloff. 1993. *A History of American Archaeology,* Third Edition. W. H. Freeman and Company, New York.

HISTORIC AND CULTURAL RESOURCES PROTECTION UNDER HISTORIC PRESERVATION LAWS

Julia H. Miller [**]

Historic preservation and archeology have long been viewed as two separate disciplines. Traditionally, the term "historic preservation" has been used to refer to the act of protecting buildings and sites associated with significant historic events and persons. Historically, archeology has focused on the study of structures and artifacts from historic and prehistoric life and culture, primarily through systematic recovery.

In more recent years, however, the distinction between "historic preservation" and "archeological protection" has become less apparent. Historic preservation has become more comprehensive in approach, focusing not only on important buildings, but also, for example, on traditional cultural property, archeological sites and artifacts, historic shipwrecks, and objects significant in engineering and culture. It involves not only the preservation of individual sites, but also neighborhoods, districts, and, in some cases, entire communities. Archeology has broadened in focus, too. It includes a wider range of resources (often collectively referred to as "cultural" or "heritage" resources) with increasing emphasis on "in place" protection over study through recovery.

Many people attribute the blurring of historic resource protection, archeology, other forms of cultural resource protection, and indeed environmental protection, to the passage of the National Historic Preservation Act (NHPA). [1] In 1966, these disciplines were linked together through the establishment of the National Register of Historic Places, which includes historic buildings, structures, sites, objects, and districts. Areas of significance broadened in scope, ranging from architecture to social history and from prehistoric settlements to space exploration.

Protection for historic, archeological, and other cultural resources is provided under the National Historic Preservation Act (NHPA), along with a substantial number of other historic preservation laws enacted at the federal, state, and local levels. Under Section 106 of the NHPA, for example, a fed-

---

[**]Julia H. Miller is the Editor in Chief of the *Preservation Law Reporter*, published by the National Trust for Historic Preservation.

[1]16 U.S.C. § 470 *et seq.*

eral agency must determine whether proposed actions will adversely affect archeological resources and, if so, consider alternative actions that would avoid or mitigate those adverse affects.[2] While federal and state preservation laws generally afford protection for historic and cultural resources from governmental actions only, an increasing number of communities regulate private actions affecting historic resources and, to a much lesser extent, cultural resources, through historic preservation ordinances and other types of land use laws.

This essay provides a basic overview of the structure of historic preservation laws and programs. It explains the various approaches to historic preservation and how protection for historic and cultural resources is provided under each of those approaches.[3] Students of either discipline, whether archeology or historic preservation, need to understand how these laws work independently and in tandem.

Historic preservation may be accomplished in several ways, including direct acquisition of historic and cultural properties by organizations and governmental entities, regulation (or procedural protection) against harmful public and/or private actions at the federal, state, and local levels, and private investment in historic structures spurred by tax incentive programs. No single approach works in every situation, and in many cases it may be necessary to draw from, and rely on, a blend of private and regulatory solutions to accomplish preservation goals.

PRIVATE AND PUBLIC OWNERSHIP

Historic preservation, in its earliest form, relied on private or public ownership to protect important historic or cultural resources. The usefulness of this approach in today's world as a tool for preservation depends, to a great extent, on the resource being protected. With respect to archeological or cultural resources, public ownership may be the only viable solution, particularly where the resource is extremely fragile or important not only for the information it contains, but also for its location. Places like Mesa Verde and Jamestown clearly belong in the protective hands of the federal government. Public or private ownership also may be utilized to preserve as muse-

---

[2]16 U.S.C. § 470f.

[3]For purposes of this discussion, the term "historic resources" refers to historic buildings, structures, and districts, while "cultural resources" refers to archeological sites and artifacts, traditional cultural sites, Native American burial grounds, cemeteries, and other areas.

ums places associated with important people or significant historic events, such as Mount Vernon or Independence Hall.[4]

While preservation through acquisition may be necessary in some instances, the purchase and restoration of historic properties on an *ad hoc* basis often proves to be a prohibitively costly solution and is adhered to only in situations where funding is available and no other alternative exists. Thus, historic preservation techniques tend to be far more sophisticated, relying on an array of regulatory and incentive programs.

PROPERTY IDENTIFICATION AND LISTING

The first step in developing preservation programs, under either a regulatory or incentive approach, is to identify what properties are considered to be "historic or cultural resources." In most cases, this is accomplished through an official process of identification that lists buildings, structures, districts, objects, and sites as resources based on specific criteria.

Historic or cultural resources may be listed in any of three types of registers: The National Register of Historic Places, a state register of historic places, or a local listing of historic landmarks and districts. To be eligible for listing, properties must meet certain statutory criteria generally based on historical, architectural, archeological, or cultural significance. Properties tend to be listed on historic registers only after they have been researched, photographed, and evaluated by a preservation professional (such as an architectural historian or archeologist).

Special concerns arise with respect to cultural resources buried under sediment or water, or properties regarded as "traditional cultural sites," which include religious and cultural sites important to Native Americans. Because the existence of these sites may not be known until archeological assessments or other information gathering is conducted, these resources, although significant, tend not to be included on historic registers until they are actually threatened.[5]

---

[4]Archeology is often a key component of this approach, as property owners seek to find more information or locate historical objects once associated with the site.

[5]For example, archeological sites may be discovered as part of a "Section 106 Review," which requires that federal agencies identify and consider the effect of federally funded or licensed projects on properties, including cultural sites, that are listed or eligible for listing on the National Register of Historic Places. 16 U.S.C. § 470f. See below the discussion on "Federal Preservation Laws."

National Register of Historic Places

Established under the Historic Sites Act of 1935[6] and expanded by the National Historic Preservation Act of 1966, as amended,[7] the National Register is the official list of historic and cultural resources at the national level and serves as a primary resource for significant historical, architectural, and archeological resources today. The Register includes districts, sites, buildings, structures, and other objects that are significant in American history, architecture, archeology, engineering, and culture.[8]

Designed primarily as a planning tool for federal agencies,[9] the National Register's principal purpose is to identify the historical and cultural resources of our nation. While listing on the National Register does not regulate the private use of land,[10] the National Register plays a central role in the federal protection scheme (which is largely procedural),[11] enables property owners to qualify for federal tax benefits,[12] and often helps to trigger protection at the state and local levels as well.

The National Register of Historic Places is maintained by the Secretary of the Interior through the National Park Service. The Keeper of the National Register within the Park Service is responsible for actually listing and determining eligibility for listing in the National Register. A cumulative listing of the National Register of Historic Places is published every few years.[13] The

---

[6]16 U.S.C. § 461 *et seq.*

[7]16 U.S.C. § 470a *et seq.*

[8]36 C.F.R. § 60.1. As of 1994, the National Register included more than 62,000 listings, comprising more than 900,000 resources. Approximately 4.7 percent of these listings include prehistoric sites. See National Trust for Historic Preservation, *National Register of Historic Places: 1966 to 1994.*

[9]36 C.F.R. § 60.2(a).

[10]36 C.F.R. § 60.2.

[11]16 U.S.C. § 470f. Under Section 106 of the National Historic Preservation Act, federal agency actions affecting property listed or eligible for listing on the National Register are subject to a review and comment process administered by the Advisory Council on Historic Preservation.

[12]See 26 U.S.C. §§ 48(g)(3); 170(f)(3)(B)(iii) and (h)(4)(B).

[13]See, *e.g.,* National Trust for Historic Preservation, *National Register of Historic Places 1966-1994.* The Interagency Resources Division of the National Park Service also publishes a series of National Register Bulletins which provide guidance on a variety of topics relating to the National Register. The National Park Service also maintains a "National Archeological Data Base" that includes information on federal agency projects involving archeological work, as well as references to other non-federal archeological projects and data bases.

National Park Service also publishes an annual compilation of newly listed National Register properties in the *Federal Register*.

State Registers

Several states maintain a state register of historic places that may be more or less inclusive than the National Register of Historic Places. In many cases, the composition of a state register has more to do with a particular state's commitment towards historic preservation than with differences in criteria for nomination. As with the National Register, listing on a state register is primarily honorific. However, in some cases, it may trigger regulatory or procedural protection, or govern whether a property owner may qualify for favorable tax treatment.

Locally Designated Landmarks and Historic Districts

Historic buildings, structures, and sites may also be designated as individual landmarks or as contributing structures within a historic district, pursuant to a local historic preservation ordinance. Unlike listing on the National Register, designation under local ordinances generally serves as a means of identifying properties subject to regulations governing the issuance of permits for demolitions, alterations, removals, or new construction.[14] In some cases, properties designated under local ordinances may be eligible for significant tax benefits, including federal tax benefits if the local government program has been "certified" by the federal government.[15]

REGULATION AND PROCEDURAL PROTECTION

The identification and listing (or designation) of properties is central to all regulatory schemes governing historic properties. Owners of properties identified as historic or cultural resources may be prevented from taking actions

---

[14]Special restrictions may apply to cultural resources. For example, a permit may be required before any ground breaking activity that could affect the site may occur, such as building a house or road, or installing underground pipes.

[15]Historic property located within locally designated historic districts may qualify for tax benefits if the designating ordinance is "certified." See I.R.C. § 48(g)(3)(A). The qualifications for certification are set forth in the Secretary of the Interior's regulations at 36 C.F.R. Part 67.

that would adversely affect those properties until they receive approval from a preservation review board or other administrative body. However, the degree and nature of the restrictions imposed on such properties vary widely. In some cases, historic preservation controls are essentially "advisory," while in other cases such controls afford historic resources meaningful protection.

Federal Preservation Laws

The NHPA of 1966, amended in 1980, and again in 1992, establishes a national preservation program and a system of procedural protection, which together encourage the identification and protection of historic and cultural resources at the federal, state, and local levels through the use of a federal-state-local partnership. In addition to providing for the systematic identification of historic and cultural resources through the National Register of Historic Places, the NHPA also encourages their protection by requiring federal agencies to consider the potential impact proposed actions may have on such resources.[16]

The key statutory tool for protecting historic and cultural resources under the NHPA is the Section 106 review process. Section 106 of the NHPA, codified at 16 U.S.C. § 470f, directs federal agencies to consider the effects of their activities on properties which are listed or are eligible for listing in the National Register.[17] No federal agency may proceed with a proposed activity adversely affecting any such properties until the agency has taken into account the effects of its actions, consulted with the State Historic Preservation Officer (SHPO) and other interested parties to identify measures that would mitigate any harm, and afforded the Advisory Council on Historic Preservation an opportunity to comment on the undertaking.[18]

In the majority of cases, the Section 106 review process culminates in the execution of a Memorandum of Agreement (MOA), which is a legally bind-

---

[16]For an interesting discussion of the developments that led to the passage of the NHPA, see National Trust for Historic Preservation, *With Heritage So Rich.*

[17]In many cases, this entails taking affirmative measures to identify historic and cultural resources. Under the Advisory Council on Historic Preservation's regulations governing the section 106 process, federal agencies must make a "reasonable and good faith effort" to identify historic properties. 36 C.F.R. § 800.4(b). For example, an agency may be required to conduct an archeological survey or consult with Native American tribal leaders regarding the existence of traditional cultural sites before making a determination that no historic properties will be affected by a proposed undertaking.

[18]The Advisory Council on Historic Preservation is an independent federal agency created by the NHPA. Regulations promulgated by the Advisory Council that govern the section 106 review process are set forth at 36 C.F.R. Part 800.

NEPA = all aspects of env.
NHPA = Historic properties

ing document that identifies specific measures an agency will undertake to mitigate or avoid harm to historic or cultural resources. With respect to archeological resources, for example, an MOA may allow for the excavation of all or part of a site in cases where the site is important only for the information it contains. It may then prescribe particular responsibilities regarding the methodology to be employed and the ultimate disposition of any artifacts that have been recovered.

Other major tools for protecting historic and cultural resources at the national level include the National Environmental Policy Act (NEPA) and Section 4(f) of the Department of Transportation Act.[19] NEPA is broader in scope than the NHPA in that it protects all aspects of the environment, not just historic properties. NEPA requires that federal agencies consider the harmful impact of "major federal actions" on the environment. Section 4(f) governs actions undertaken by the Department of Transportation that affect historic and cultural properties, as well as park lands, recreational areas, and wildlife and waterfowl refuges. The Secretary of Transportation may not proceed with a project unless "there is no feasible and prudent alternative," and then only if the project "includes all possible planning to minimize harm to such... historic site resulting from such use."

Together, the NHPA, NEPA, and Section 4(f) are helpful in compelling federal agencies to identify and consider the impact of their actions on historic or cultural resources. They provide a useful and sometimes critical mechanism for developing workable solutions that accomplish both agency and preservation objectives. Nonetheless, it is important to recognize that these laws are simply procedural safeguards that do not guarantee that historic or cultural resources will be protected. The NHPA and NEPA require federal agencies to consider the impact of their actions on such properties. However, they do not mandate that such properties be protected. While Section 4(f) provides stronger protection for historic or cultural resources in that it prohibits harm to such properties unless there is no reasonable alternative, it applies only to Department of Transportation actions. In addition, none of

Consider impacts, but does not mandate protection to CR

---

[19] 42 U.S.C. §§ 4321–4347; 49 U.S.C. § 303. Several other federal laws provide protection for historic and cultural resources. These laws include the Antiquities Act of 1906, 16 U.S.C. §§ 431–433; the Historic Sites Act of 1935, 16 U.S.C. §§ 461–467; the Archeological and Historic Preservation Act of 1974, 16 U.S.C. §§ 469–469c-1; the Archaeological Resources Protection Act of 1979, 16 U.S.C. §§ 470aa–mm; the Surface Mining Control and Reclamation Act of 1977, 30 U.S.C. § 1272; the Abandoned Shipwreck Act of 1987, 43 U.S.C. §§ 2101–2106; and the Public Buildings Cooperative Use Act, 40 U.S.C. §§ 601–606. Executive orders addressing federal agency responsibilities with respect to historic and cultural properties also have been adopted. See, *e.g.*, Executive Order No. 13006, 61 Fed. Reg. 26071–26072 (May 24, 1996), which encourages federal agencies to locate their facilities in historic properties.

these federal laws has any effect on private actions in the absence of some degree of federal involvement, such as funding or licensing. Generally speaking, the strongest measures for ensuring the protection of historic, and in some cases, cultural, properties are substantive regulatory controls found at the state and local levels.

State Preservation Laws

State involvement in historic preservation activities historically has concentrated on the administration of federal government programs. Pursuant to the NHPA, each state has established a State Historic Preservation Office for the purpose of administering federal preservation programs, such as nominating properties for listing in the National Register of Historic Places, or reviewing projects seeking certification for federal tax benefits. However, an increasing number of states have expanded their role in historic preservation by adopting a comprehensive preservation program which includes regulatory protection for historic and cultural resources, rehabilitation incentives, and educational and technical support.

The regulation of historic properties at the state level varies considerably. Most states have enacted state enabling laws that grant specific powers and authority to local governments to pass ordinances for the protection and preservation of historic structures. Unless a local government operates under home rule authority, the degree of protection afforded to historic resources by an enabling act can be critical to the extent that the act defines the regulatory scope of a local preservation ordinance. An increasing number of states also regulate governmental actions affecting historic and cultural property through state environmental protection laws,[20] archeological protection laws,[21] burial and cemetery laws,[22] historic shipwreck laws,[23] and other laws spe-

---

[20]See, *e.g.*, California Environmental Quality Act (CEQA), Cal. Pub. Res. Code § 21000 *et seq.*, which requires state agencies to consider the impact of their actions in making decisions that could adversely affect the environment, including historic resources, and the Alaska Coastal Management Program (ACMP), Alaska Stat. § 46.40.040–210, which sets forth specific requirements that agencies must follow to protect environmental and cultural resources within Alaska's coastal zone.

[21]Indiana, through its Historic Preservation and Archeology Act, Ind. Code § 14.3-3.4, for example, regulates actions affecting archeological resources on both private and public property.

[22]Section 381 *et seq.* of the Nevada Revised Statutes, for example, prohibits the excavation of Native American burial sites, and it imposes both civil and criminal penalties for violations.

[23]See, *e.g.*, Mass. Regs. Code tit. 312, § 2, which regulates activity affecting underwater archeological resources.

cific to historic preservation. Some states have enacted laws patterned after the Section 106 review process under the NHPA and Section 4(f) of the Department of Transportation Act.[24]

Local Preservation Laws

The strongest protection for historic properties generally occurs at the local level—not federal or state—where laws are more likely to regulate actions affecting privately owned property. Through historic preservation ordinances, local jurisdictions regulate changes to historic resources that would otherwise irreparably change or destroy their character. Today, an estimated 2,000 historic preservation ordinances have been enacted across the country.

Preservation ordinances vary widely from jurisdiction to jurisdiction, depending on a variety of factors ranging from limitations on permissible regulatory action imposed at the state level to the degree of support for preservation within a given community. While a number of jurisdictions extend protection for cultural resources in local preservation ordinances, only a handful of communities have developed specific measures to protect those resources.[25] Several jurisdictions, for example, include archeological resources among other sites qualifying for designation, but they provide little guidance as to how these sites are to be protected in individual circumstances.[26]

Local historic preservation laws generally empower historic preservation commissions to review and deny requests to alter, demolish, or remove property designated as a historic landmark or included in historic districts. Other jurisdictions confer ultimate regulatory authority to a zoning board of appeals or, in some cases, a legislative body, limiting the authority of the preservation commission to making recommendations to the decision-making body.

Most jurisdictions designate both historic districts and individual landmarks. While designations generally include entire historic structures, many

---

[24]See, *e.g.*, Minnesota Environmental Rights Act, Minn. Stat. § 116B.02 (historic resource may not be demolished unless there is "no prudent and feasible alternative site") and New Mexico Prehistoric and Historic Sites Preservation Act, New Mex. Stat. Annot. § 18-8-1–18-8-8 (State must undergo "all possible planning to preserve and protect and to minimize harm" to historic resources).

[25]Section 35-432.2 of the San Antonio Historic Districts and Landmarks Zoning Ordinance requires owners to prepare a "determination of effect," and to explore alternative ways to reduce or avoid any adverse effects.

[26]See, *e.g.*, the Wasco County, Oregon, Historic Preservation Ordinance, which provides for the designation of archeological resources and artifacts, but is silent with respect to how those resources are to be protected.

communities extend protection only to the exteriors of such properties, and in a few cases, only to façades visible from a public way. However, some communities protect both the interior and exterior of historic properties.

Although the scope of protection afforded to individual structures varies from place to place, most jurisdictions regulate both proposed alterations and demolitions of historic structures and new construction within a historic district. Many communities allow for the demolition of historic properties only in cases where a property owner establishes "economic hardship" or the property poses a safety threat to the community. Some communities only regulate alterations, allowing property owners to demolish historic properties after a waiting period, during which private preservation groups may attempt to purchase the property. An increasing number of communities also impose affirmative maintenance requirements on property owners to prevent structural damage through "demolition by neglect" provisions, and they authorize preservation commissions to make limited repairs to landmarked properties and recoup expenses, when necessary, through the imposition of liens.

In addition to "stand alone" preservation ordinances, local zoning and planning laws are increasingly used to meet broader preservation goals, often through the inclusion of specific preservation elements in the local land use regulatory scheme. Cultural resource protection may be addressed through other land use laws that deal with "land disturbing" activity. For example, protection for archeological resources might be provided through conditional zoning or incentive zoning, which allows for preservation in exchange for more intensive development on another part of the same site or elsewhere. Cultural resources also may be protected through subdivision laws and/or site plan review, by requiring that an archeological assessment be performed as a condition to approval, and directing applicants to avoid or mitigate the destruction of such resources in delineating the size and location of buildings, and the design and location of streets and lots.[27]

Many jurisdictions also develop preservation plans, either as a stand-alone measure or in conjunction with the comprehensive planning process, to en-

---

[27]Ledyard, Connecticut, requires, through its subdivision regulations, the preparation of archeological assessments when "there is a likelihood that significant cultural resources or undetected human burials will be adversely impacted by construction activities associated with the proposed development." When archeological resources are found, a management plan must be prepared that identifies measures to be taken to avoid or minimize any adverse effects on those resources. Alexandria, Virginia, requires a preliminary archeological assessment and, in some cases, also the development of a resource management plan as part of its site plan review process.

sure citywide consistency in preservation policy.[28] Strong policy statements in favor of preservation can help a decision-maker act favorably toward preservation in instances where historic or cultural resources might otherwise be harmed, such as in conducting a site plan review or acting upon a zoning request.

OTHER LAWS AFFECTING THE REGULATION OF HISTORIC AND CULTURAL PROPERTIES

In addition to the more broadly termed "historic preservation laws," there are a few laws which focus on specific types of resources or a specific aspect of preservation, such as the Archaeological Resources Protection Act (ARPA),[29] the Native American Graves Protection and Repatriation Act (NAGPRA),[30] and the Abandoned Shipwreck Act.[31]

ARPA prohibits the removal, excavation, or alteration of any archeological resource from federal or Indian lands in the absence of a permit issued by the federal land manager. The law also prohibits the selling, purchasing, exchanging, transporting, and trafficking of archeological resources illegally removed from public and Indian lands, as well as the interstate and international trafficking of archeological resources in violation of state or local law. Violations are subject to civil and criminal penalties.

NAGPRA establishes a process for protecting and disposing of Native American cultural items found on federal or tribal lands through "intentional excavation" or "inadvertent discovery." Among other things, the law seeks to place ownership or control of such items in the appropriate Indian tribe or Native Hawaiian organization and imposes specific requirements on how to resolve competing claims. NAGPRA also imposes special requirements on museums and federal agencies (excluding the Smithsonian Institution) to assist Indian tribes and Native Hawaiians in the identification and eventual repatriation of items within their collections.

The Abandoned Shipwreck Act clarifies the authority of states to enact and enforce laws and regulations to protect abandoned shipwrecks in state territorial waters (generally defined as three miles from the coast or islands off the coast of the state). The Act governs abandoned shipwrecks that are:

---

[28]See Bradford J. White and Richard J. Roddewig, "Preparing a Historic Preservation Plan," PAS Report No. 450 (APA 1994).

[29]16 U.S.C. §§ 470aa–mm.

[30]25 U.S.C. §§ 3001–3013.

[31]43 U.S.C. §§ 2102–2106.

(1) embedded in submerged lands of a state; (2) embedded in coralline formations protected by a state on submerged lands of a state; or (3) on submerged lands of a state and included in, or determined eligible for inclusion in, the National Register of Historic Places.

There are also a number of other laws that may or may not address historic preservation matters *per se*, but nonetheless affect historic resources in significant ways. Laws falling within this category include transportation laws;[32] aesthetic regulations, such as sign control and scenic highway laws; state and local environmental laws; land use and planning laws; certain nonregulatory programs that can be used to encourage historic resource preservation in specific situations, such as land banking; and laws governing what accommodations must be made to meet the needs of the disabled.[33]

TAX INCENTIVES FOR THE REHABILITATION OF HISTORIC PROPERTY

Tax incentive programs generally address three important objectives: they provide financial benefits to owners otherwise burdened by preservation laws; they counter private and public land use policies favoring demolition and new construction, or the destruction of cultural resources; and they encourage the rehabilitation of historic structures. While no one incentive program accomplishes all three objectives, meaningful tax incentives have been adopted at the federal, state, and, increasingly, the local, levels.

Federal Rehabilitation Tax Credit

Perhaps the best-known incentive to preserve historic property is the rehabilitation tax credit. This incentive gives property owners either a 10 or 20 percent tax credit on rehabilitation expenses, depending on the classification of the building at issue. Certified historic structures are eligible for a 20 percent credit, and noncertified, nonresidential property placed in service

---

[32]See, *e.g.*, Intermodal Surface Transportation Efficiency Act of 1991 (ISTEA), 23 U.S.C. §§ 133–135, which focuses on transportation planning requirements, and provides opportunities to protect historic and cultural sites through a special enhancements program; see also Transportation Equity Act for the 21st Century ("TEA 21"), Pub. L. No. 105-178 (June 9, 1998), which reauthorizes the federal transportation enhancements program.

[33]See Americans with Disabilities Act, 42 U.S.C. § 12204. For a discourse on specific provisions relating to historic preservation, see David Battaglia, "Americans with Disabilities Act: Its Impact on Historic Buildings and Structures," 10 PLR 1169 (Nov. 1991).

before 1936 is eligible for a 10 percent credit.[34] Several specific conditions must be satisfied in order to qualify for the credit, including: the building must be income-producing, not an owner-occupied residence; rehabilitation costs must exceed the adjusted basis of the building or $5,000; and the work performed must meet preservation standards. The National Park Service administers the tax certification process.[35]

conditions (handwritten annotation)

Federal Tax Benefits Relating to Preservation Easements

Owners of historic and cultural properties who donate preservation or conservation easements to qualified organizations also may be eligible for a charitable contribution deduction under Section 170 of the Internal Revenue Code.[36] With respect to historic structures, eligibility generally entails the relinquishment of rights to demolish or alter a property and the gift of such rights, in perpetuity, to a qualified historic preservation organization. Thereafter, the property owner and all subsequent owners will not be able to alter or demolish the property without the express permission of the recipient organization. In situations involving cultural resources, an owner will be required to refrain from any land disturbing activity that would jeopardize the resource. In some cases, this would preclude development altogether.

The value of the easement is the difference between the property's fair market value before donation of the easement and its fair market value afterward. In order to obtain the charitable deduction, the taxpayer must retain a qualified appraiser to value the donated easement if its value exceeds $5,000.[37]

State and Local Incentives for Rehabilitation

Several states and local jurisdictions provide special incentives to encourage the maintenance and rehabilitation of historic properties, typically in the form of property tax freezes or income tax credits on rehabilitation expenditures. Georgia, for example, provides an eight-year freeze on property tax

---

[34]I.R.C. §§ 46(b) and 48(g).

[35]See I.R.C. § 48(g), and Treas. Reg. § 1.46 *et seq*. It should be noted that since 1986, passive activity loss rules have restricted the tax credit a taxpayer can use in any given year. For a thorough discussion of the tax credit program, see "A Guide to Tax Advantaged Rehabilitation," (National Trust for Historic Preservation Information Series 1994).

[36]I.R.C. §§ 170(h), 2055(f), and 2522; Treas. Reg. § 1.170A *et seq*.

[37]For further information, see Janet Diehl and Thomas S. Barrett, *The Conservation Easement Handbook* (Trust for Public Land and the Land Trust Alliance 1989).

assessments of substantially rehabilitated buildings, and Rhode Island permits owners of historic residential property to claim a 10 percent credit against state income taxes.[38] San Antonio provides a 10-year property tax freeze at prerehabilitation levels to taxpayers who substantially rehabilitate residential historic structures. Owners of rehabilitated commercial historic buildings may qualify for a five-year city property tax exemption, and then a property tax freeze at half the property's value during the subsequent five-year period.[39]

SUMMARY

Historic preservation law, to those who only rarely deal with its intricacies, may appear to be a confusing web of federal, state, and local legal requirements, overlapping designation systems, and varying sets of incentives. This complex framework nonetheless provides a range of important legal protection that has ensured the preservation of thousands of significant properties across the United States.

As efforts to preserve historic and cultural resources continue into the future, perhaps some of these intricacies will start to disappear. The distinction between historic preservation laws, archeological laws, environmental laws, and other laws is already starting to blur. The objective of all these laws is resource protection, and over time, this single objective may be dealt with in a more comprehensive, cohesive fashion.

---

[38]For a comprehensive listing of state tax incentive programs, see "State Tax Incentives for Historic Preservation: A State-by-State Summary" (National Trust for Historic Preservation, Center for Preservation Policy Studies 1992).

[39]See "Local Incentives for Historic Preservation" (National Trust for Historic Preservation, Center for Preservation Policy Studies 1991).

CHAPTER TWO

FEDERAL COMPLIANCE STATUTES

SECTION A.   AN OVERVIEW AND BRIEF HISTORY

Approximately one-third of the land in the United States is owned and managed by the federal government. In addition to its responsibilities for the lands it owns in fee simple, the federal government also has management responsibility for lands over which it has "control." This responsibility, carried out by agencies such as the Bureau of Land Management, the National Park Service, the National Forest Service, and the National Oceanic and Atmospheric Administration, includes the protection and management of both natural and heritage resources for present and future generations.

Since the late 1960s, several major pieces of federal environmental legislation have been enacted that provide for the management of both natural and heritage resources. In addition to other procedural requirements, these statutes specifically require federal agencies to consider the effects of federal or federally assisted "undertakings" on heritage resources before they take final action. Among these statutes are the National Historic Preservation Act [16 U.S.C. § 470, *et seq.* (1994)], the National Environmental Policy Act of 1969 [42 U.S.C. § 4321, *et seq.* (1994)], the Federal Land Policy and Management Act of 1976 [43 U.S.C. § 1701, *et seq.* (1994)], the Coastal Zone Management Act [16 U.S.C. § 1451, *et seq.* (1994)] and Section 4(f) of the Department of Transportation Act of 1966 [49 U.S.C. § 303 (1994)]. The mandates set forth in these and other environmental statutes are clear, and failure to comply with them may result in liability.

In addition to complying with their obligations under these statutes, federal agencies also must determine how and whether federal permits to conduct activities affecting heritage resources are to be issued to third parties under statutes such as the Antiquities Act of 1906 [16 U.S.C. §§ 431–33 (1994)], the Archaeological Resources Protection Act of 1979 [16 U.S.C. §§ 470aa–mm (1994)], and the National Marine Sanctuaries Act [16 U.S.C. § 1431, *et seq.* (1994)]. If permits are issued, federal agencies must then ensure that the permittees comply with the terms and conditions of those permits, as well as the federal statutes and regulations that govern them. If no

31

oversight by the relevant agency is exercised, that agency may be liable for failure to fulfill its responsibility to manage heritage resources.

Most of the environmental statutes cited in this chapter do not allow for a private right of action to be brought directly against the United States for noncompliance with their requirements. Instead, an action typically can be brought against a federal agency through the Administrative Procedure Act [5 U.S.C. § 701, *et seq.* (1994)], which provides a waiver of sovereign immunity for challenging final agency actions in certain circumstances. The Administrative Procedure Act also dictates the scope and standard of review which courts must follow in resolving challenges to final agency action, such as claims that the agency has failed to comply with its statutorily mandated management responsibilities over natural and heritage resources.

SECTION B.   FEDERAL LAWS THAT SPECIFICALLY REQUIRE MANAGEMENT OF HERITAGE RESOURCES

1.   National Historic Preservation Act

One of the most important pieces of legislation enacted to protect and preserve heritage resources is the National Historic Preservation Act of 1966, as amended [NHPA, 16 U.S.C. §§ 470–70x-6 (1994)].[1] The NHPA is a very inclusive statute that provides for consideration of the value of a variety of heritage resources, including resources of federal, state, and local significance, and recognizes the ever-increasing growth of the nation's urban centers [16 U.S.C. § 470(b)(5) (1994)]. As defined by the statute itself, the purpose of the NHPA is to recognize that our nation is "founded upon and reflected in its historic heritage" [16 U.S.C. § 470(b)(1) (1994)].[2] The statute also declares that "the preservation of this irreplaceable heritage is in the public interest so that its vital legacy of cultural, educational, aesthetic, inspirational, economic, and energy benefits will be maintained and enriched for future generations of Americans" [16 U.S.C. § 470(b)(4) (1994)]. In Congress's declaration of policy behind the NHPA, the mandate to federal resource management agencies is clear:

---

[1]The NHPA was substantially amended in 1980, by the National Historic Preservation Act Amendments of 1980, Pub. L. No. 96-515, and again in 1992, by the National Historic Preservation Act Amendments of 1992, Title XL of Pub. L. No. 102-575.

[2]For a comprehensive discussion of the legislative history of the NHPA, see *WATCH (Waterbury Action to Conserve Our Heritage Inc.) v. Harris*, 603 F.2d 310, 319–26 (2nd Cir. 1979).

It shall be the policy of the Federal Government, in cooperation with other nations and in partnership with the States, local governments, Indian tribes, and private organizations and individuals to—

(1) use measures, including financial and technical assistance, to foster conditions under which our modern society and our prehistoric and historic resources can exist in productive harmony and fulfill the social, economic, and other requirements of present and future generations;

(2) provide leadership in the preservation of the prehistoric and historic resources of the United States and of the international community of nations and in the administration of the national preservation program in partnership with States, Indian tribes, Native Hawaiians, and local governments;

(3) administer federally owned, administered, or controlled prehistoric and historic resources in a spirit of stewardship for the inspiration and benefit of present and future generations;

(4) contribute to the preservation of nonfederally owned prehistoric and historic resources and give maximum encouragement to organizations and individuals undertaking preservation by private means;

(5) encourage the public and private preservation and utilization of all usable elements of the Nation's historic built environment; and

(6) assist State and local governments, Indian tribes and Native Hawaiian organizations and the National Trust for Historic Preservation in the United States to expand and accelerate their historic preservation programs and activities.

    16 U.S.C. § 470-1 (1994).

In essence, by enacting the NHPA, Congress mandated that federal agencies: (1) consider the impact of federal undertakings on historic resources of national significance [Sec. 106, 16 U.S.C. § 470f (1994)]; and (2) assume responsibility for the preservation of historic resources that they own or control [Sec. 110, 16 U.S.C. § 470h-2 (1994)]. Failure to comply with these mandates may give rise to a lawsuit against the agency.

The center of federal agency responsibilities under the NHPA can be found in sections 106 and 110 of the Act. Section 106 sets forth the responsibilities of a federal agency having direct or indirect jurisdiction over a proposed federal or federally assisted "undertaking:"

The head of any federal agency having direct or indirect jurisdiction over a proposed federal or federally assisted undertaking in any State and the head of any federal department or independent agency having authority to license any undertaking shall, prior to the approval of the expenditure of any federal funds on the undertaking or prior to the issuance of any license, as the case may be, take into account the effect of the undertaking on any district, site, building, structure, or object that is included in or eligible for inclusion in the National Register. The head of any such federal agency

shall afford the Advisory Council on Historic Preservation established under Title II of this Act a reasonable opportunity to comment with regard to such undertaking.
16 U.S.C. § 470f (1994).[3]

For a discussion of the definition of "federal undertaking," see *McMillan Park Committee v. National Capital Planning Comm'n*, 968 F.2d 1283 (D.C. Cir. 1992). The requirements under section 106 are essentially procedural in nature [see *Preservation Coalition, Inc. v. Pierce*, 667 F.2d 851 (9th Cir. 1982)]. Section 106 clearly requires agency decision-makers to consider specified information concerning the effects of a federal undertaking on heritage resources prior to the agency's issuance of a final decision. In essence, agencies must comply with the mandates of the NHPA only when they are carrying out discretionary duties. Ministerial acts do not invoke compliance with the NHPA [see *Lee v. Thornburgh*, 877 F.2d 1053, 1056–58 (D.C. Cir. 1989), finding that the NHPA does not apply against Congress, and does not apply where the federal agency "lacks the right to approve or disapprove" of the project].

VIEUX CARRE PROPERTY OWNERS, RESIDENTS & ASSOCIATES, INC. v. BROWN

875 F.2d 453 (5th Cir. 1989), *cert. denied,* **493 U.S. 1020 (1990)**

GARWOOD, Circuit Judge:

This dispute focuses the Court's attention on a private plaintiff's enforcement of the National Historic Preservation Act (NHPA) against the United States Army Corps of Engineers (the Corps). Vieux Carre Property Owners, Residents & Associates, Inc. (the Vieux Carre), the plaintiffs–appellants in this case, is made up of landowners within the Vieux Carre National Historic Landmark District—popularly referred to as the French Quarter—on the Mississippi River in New Orleans, Louisiana. The Vieux Carre ultimately seeks to arrest the construction of an aquarium and riverfront park currently being erected on and just landward of the Bienville Street Wharf at the foot of Bienville Street. This appeal comes from the district court's summary dismissal of the Vieux Carre's suit on jurisdictional grounds.

---

[3]The National Register of Historic Places is maintained by the Secretary of the Interior, and is comprised of "districts, sites, buildings, structures, and objects significant in American history, architecture, archaeology, engineering, and culture" [16 U.S.C. § 470a (1994)]. The criteria applied to evaluate objects for inclusion in the National Register, including the requirement that the object be at least 50 years old, can be found at 36 C.F.R. § 60.4 (1997).

The Vieux Carre first claims that the Rivers and Harbors Act, 33 U.S.C. § 403(RHA) and the Corps' regulations found in 33 C.F.R. §§ 320 through 330 (1987), require the Corps to issue a permit for the aquarium phase of the project, and that such permitting in turn requires the Corps to submit the project to the NHPA historic impact review process dictated by 16 U.S.C. §§ 470f and 470h-2(f). The Vieux Carre then claims that the park phase required an individual permit, but that even if it complied with the Corps' nationwide permit that itself triggered section 470f and required the Corps to follow the historic impact review procedures detailed in 36 C.F.R. §§ 800 *et seq*. The Corps failed to submit any of the project to the NHPA review process. Thus, the Vieux Carre sued for a declaratory judgment against the Corps and an injunction against those developing or otherwise authorizing the project, namely, the Audubon Park Commission, the City of New Orleans, the Board of Commissioners of the Port of New Orleans, and the Board of Commissioners of the Orleans Levee District. We find that the dismissal of the Vieux Carre's aquarium phase claim was proper, though for different reasons than those stated by the district court. We reverse the court's dismissal of the Vieux Carre's riverfront park claim against the Corps and remand for further legal and factual findings in relation to that claim. We affirm the court's dismissal of the Vieux Carre's request to enjoin the other appellees from proceeding with the project.

* * *

CONSIDERATION OF AQUARIUM PLANS

The Vieux Carre argues that the Corps' May 14, 1987, response to inquiries about necessary permits for the Audubon Park project triggered the historical impact evaluation procedures of the NHPA, 16 U.S.C. § 470f, in four different ways: through the Corps' continuing supervision over the aquarium phase of the project even if no license was required; through the allegedly erroneous determination that no license was necessary for the aquarium despite the requirements of the RHA; because an individual license should have been issued for the park phase; and, even if no new license were necessary, by its determination that the park fell under a nationwide permit. The proper interpretation of section 470f is therefore relevant to all four assertions. This provision of the NHPA provides:

> "*The head of any Federal agency* having direct or indirect jurisdiction over a proposed Federal or federally assisted undertaking in any State and the head of any Federal department or independent agency having authority to license any undertaking shall, *prior to the approval of the expenditure of any Federal funds on the undertaking or prior to the issuance of any license*, as the case may be, *take into account* the effect of the undertaking on any district, site, building, structure, or object that is included in or eligible for inclusion in the National Register. The head of any such Federal agency *shall afford* the Advisory Council on Historic Preservation established under sections 470i to 470v of this title *a reasonable opportunity* to comment with regard to such undertaking." (Emphasis added.)

In effect, the Vieux Carre claims that the Corps' reserved final approval of plans for the aquarium phase constitutes indirect jurisdiction requiring the Corps to subject the project to the requirements of section 470f. We disagree. This is simply too attenuated.

Regardless of the projects arguably included in the first clause of the first sentence of section 470f, the second clause thereof makes it clear that the agency need not act unless it is about to approve an expenditure of federal funds or issue a license. The scant legislative history verifies this understanding of the scope of section 470f: "The committee agreed that Federal agencies having direct or indirect jurisdiction over various undertakings, either through Federal funding or through their licensing powers, should recognize these [preservation] values." H.R. No. 1916, *reprinted in* 1966 U.S.Code Cong. & Admin.News, 3307, 3310. Although no cases have been found that interpret section 470f federal assistance as broadly as the Vieux Carre proposes, at least one gives it a very restrictive meaning. See *Ringsred v. Duluth*, 828 F.2d 1305, 1309 (8th Cir. 1987), (equating section 470f federal assistance with the explicit triggering requirement for action under the NEPA—"major federal undertaking").

We conclude that section 470f is not triggered by either the Corps' instructions for the project developers to submit final plans of the aquarium phase, or by its surveillance of the project to ensure that no permits become necessary. Significantly, circuit courts have ruled that federal environmental protection statutes do not enlarge the Corps' jurisdiction. See, *e.g., Riverside Irrigation Dist. v. Andrews*, 758 F.2d 508, 512 (10th Cir. 1985) (stating that the Endangered Species Act does not enlarge the jurisdiction of the Corps under the Clean Water Act); *United States v. Stoeco Home, Inc.*, 498 F.2d 597, 607 (3d Cir. 1974), *cert. denied*, 420 U.S. 927, 95 S.Ct. 1124, 43 L.Ed.2d 397 (1975) (such statutes do not enlarge the Corps' jurisdiction under the RHA).

* * *

PERMITTING THE RIVERSIDE PARK

The Corps admits that the park phase of the project comes under a nationwide permit, but maintains that such a permit is not subject to the historical impact review procedures of 16 U.S.C. §§ 470f and 470h-2(f).[1] The Vieux Carre contends that (1) the park is not permitted by a nationwide permit and therefore requires an individual permit; (2) if a nationwide permit covers the park, making an individual permit unnecessary, that nationwide permit is a "license" triggering section 470f's historic impact review procedures.

---

[1][*Orig. fn.*] The Vieux Carre has asserted that all of the challenged Corps decisions trigger the NHPA's section 470h-2(f) in addition to section 470f. Section 470h-2(f) states:

"Prior to the approval of any Federal undertaking which may directly and adversely affect any National Historic Landmark, the head of the responsible Federal agency shall, to the maximum extent possible, undertake such planning and actions as may be necessary to minimize harm to such landmark, and shall afford the Advisory Council on Historic Preservation a reasonable opportunity to comment on the undertaking."

Because we find that this section is inapplicable when a federal agency no more than issues a license or permit, we will not address this provision again.

The original Bienville Street Wharf, permitted by the Corps in 1930, could itself come within only one nationwide permit, that under the provisions of 33 C.F.R. § 330.3(b) for "[s]tructures or work completed before December 18, 1968, or in waterbodies over which the district engineer had not asserted jurisdiction at the time the activity occurred provided, in both instances, there is no interference with navigation." The Corps stipulated that the reconstruction of the wharf pursuant to the 1930 permit affected the navigability of the Mississippi River. Thus, the original wharf structure does not fall under a nationwide permit.

That does not mean, however, that the park phase cannot fall under such a permit. Section 330.5(a)(3) grants nationwide permits for:

"The repair, rehabilitation, or replacement of any previously authorized, currently serviceable, structure or fill, or of any currently serviceable structure or fill constructed prior to the requirement for authorization, provided such repair, rehabilitation, or replacement does not result in a deviation from the plans of the original structure or fill, and further provided that the structure or fill has not been put to uses differing from uses specified for it in any permit authorizing its original construction. Minor deviations due to changes in materials or construction techniques and which are necessary to make repair, rehabilitation, or replacement are permitted."

This nationwide permit is subject to the section 330.5(b)(9) requirement that the district engineer give the advisory council an opportunity to comment if he determines that historic properties may be adversely affected by the repair, rehabilitation, or replacement.

If the riverfront park does not fit within this section 330.5(a)(3) nationwide permit, it must be individually permitted because its location riverward of the box levee—the OHWL— places it within the navigable waters of the United States and the Corps' jurisdiction under the second clause of RHA section 10. If an individual permit is necessary, the NHPA section 470f historic impact review procedures would concededly be triggered. Before discussing whether the park falls within the section 330.5(a)(3) permit, however, we address the relationship between nationwide permits and section 470f.

The Vieux Carre asserts that even if we find that the park project is covered by the section 330.5(a)(3) nationwide permit, "a permit is a permit," and nothing in the wording of section 470f indicates that some federal agency licensing is exempt from its requirements. The Corps' regulations in fact state that permits are either "in the form of individual permits or general permits." 33 C.F.R. § 325.5(a). A "nationwide permit" is simply "a type of general permit." See 33 C.F.R. §§ 325.5(c)(2) and 330.1.

Interpreting the Clean Water Act (CWA), similar in relevant part to the NHPA, the Tenth Circuit, in *Andrews*, 758 F.2d at 512–13, held that by allowing a party to proceed under a nationwide permit the Corps had triggered provisions of the CWA requiring agencies to issue environmental impact statements. In so holding, the court distinguished the CWA from the NEPA, which explicitly states that it is triggered by "major federal actions." As noted above, however, the Eighth Circuit recently approved the parties' treatment of the NHPA's section 470f "undertaking" requirement as "coterminous" with the NEPA's "major Federal actions" triggering event. *Ringsred*, 828 F.2d at 1309; *cf. Lee*, 742 F.2d at 901 (referring throughout to activities falling under a nationwide permit as "exempt" from permitting requirements).

The Tenth Circuit's *Andrews* interpretation, if adopted for the NHPA, reflects the NHPA's statutory purpose, which contemplates widespread agency responsibility for the protection of historic interests. See, *e.g.*, 16 U.S.C. § 470(b)(4); H.R.Rep. No. 1916, 89th Cong., 2d Sess. 7, *reprinted in* 1966 U.S. Code Cong. & Admin. News 3307, 3309. It is also true to the NHPA statutory language itself.

Section 330.5(b)'s incorporation of an accelerated historic review procedure as a precondition to a project falling under a section 330.5(a)(3) nationwide permit does not seem to help the Corps' case. In addition to the fact that the Corps concedes that it did not evaluate the historic impact of either phase of the project, we note that through correspondence the Advisory Council has warned the Corps that section 330.5(b)(9) does not satisfy section 470f requirements. Indeed, regulations promulgated under the NHPA provide for counterpart regulations only under specific circumstances:

"In consultation with the Council, agencies may develop counterpart regulations to carry out the section 106 process. When concurred in by the Council, such counterpart regulations shall stand in place of these regulations for the purposes of the agency's compliance with section 106." 36 C.F.R. § 800.15 (1987).

The Corps' position that nationwide permits do not trigger section 470f, however, has great practical appeal, especially in relation to the nationwide permit described in 33 C.F.R. § 330.5(a)(3), which unquestionably covers such activities as repainting and rerooting original structures. Congress clearly did not intend to require the Corps to subject such truly inconsequential projects to the procedural complexities of section 470f. See National Historic Preservation Act Amendments of 1980, H.R. No. 96-1457, 1980 U.S. Code Cong. & Admin. News 6378, 6408; *cf. 162.20 Acres of Land*, 639 F.2d at 302 n. 3. Such a literal construction of section 470f is unreasonable and unintended, and as such is a result we must endeavor to avoid. See, *e.g.*, *United States v. Mendoza*, 565 F.2d 1285, 1288, *on reh'g*, 581 F.2d 89 (5th Cir. 1978) (citing "the celebrated" *Rector of Holy Trinity Church v. United States*, 143 U.S. 457, 12 S.Ct. 511, 36 L.Ed. 226 (1892), as the seminal case approving judicial avoidance of absurd but literal statutory constructions). Moreover, the applicability of section 470f should not be at the whim of the Corps' subsequent "permit" label; such labeling does not alter congressional intent.

And, as pointed out by the Corps, the nationwide permits of 33 C.F.R. § 330 are specifically designed to expedite activities with inconsequential effects on the RHA concerns. See 33 C.F.R. § 330.1 (stating that nationwide permits "are designed to allow certain activities to occur with little, if any, delay or paperwork"). Indeed, "[t]he purpose of the nationwide permit system is to allow certain types of [activities to go forward] without prior Corps approval." *Lee*, 742 F.2d at 909; see also *Andrews*, 758 F.2d at 511. Consequently, 33 C.F.R. § 330.1 notes that some of its chapter's nationwide permits require notification to the district engineer prior to commencement of the activity in question. Presumably, these are the more significant projects—those more likely to have measurable impacts on navigation. We hold that nationwide permits authorizing truly inconsequential activities are not triggering "licenses" under section 470f.

We now turn to whether section 330.5(a)(3) authorizes such inconsequential activities, for we find that the regulation's failure to require notification by the "permittee" to the Corps is not dispositive of the issue. This nationwide permit has not previously been interpreted by a federal court in a published opinion. The Corps apparently determined that the park constitutes a "rehabilitation" or "replacement" of the wharf, that the park plans do not deviate from the 1930 plans of the wharf except for minor deviations due to changes in materials or construction techniques that are necessary for the rehabilitation or replacement, and that the park is not a use differing from uses specified in the 1930 wharf permit. The reviewing court must determine whether the Corps' interpretation of its own regulation is reasonable and consistent with the regulations themselves. *Lyng v. Payne*, 476 U.S. 926, 106 S.Ct. 2333, 90 L.Ed.2d 921 (1986). Because the district court did not address this issue, we remand for an interpretation of the scope of section 330.5(a)(3); a determination of whether the Corps' finding that the riverfront park is covered by this nationwide permit (as the district court defines it) was arbitrary or capricious; and if the park is covered by section 330.5(a)(3), a ruling on whether the project is so inconsequential that it escapes section 470f's historic impact review requirements.

Finally, if the district court finds that the riverfront park does fall under section 330.5(a)(3) and is inconsequential, it must also address the Vieux Carre's argument that this nationwide permit is invalid because the Corps did not evaluate the park's impact on historic properties as is required by the Corps' own regulation—section 330.5(b)(9). The Audubon Park Commission notified the Corps (so as to apparently trigger that regulation) when it submitted plans for the project and asked whether permits would be necessary.

CONCLUSION

Because we find that the Vieux Carre has no private right of action under the RHA, and that the APA grants judicial review only of federal agency actions, we affirm the district court's dismissal of the Vieux Carre's claims against all defendants except the Corps. We further hold that the Corps' determination that the aquarium phase of the project was outside its RHA section 10 permitting jurisdiction reflects a reasonable interpretation of the statute and an evaluation of these specific facts that is neither arbitrary nor capricious. Finally, we remand to the district court for a ruling on whether the park phase falls within the nationwide permit in 33 C.F.R. § 330.5(a)(3). If the district court determines that the Corps' interpretation of this nationwide permit regulation, or its finding that the park is within the regulation, is arbitrary and capricious, the project must be individually permitted because it is within the Corps' RHA jurisdiction, and thus is subject to section 470f review. If, however, the district court sustains the Corps' determination that the park phase does fall within this nationwide permit regulation, the court is to go on to determine whether the project is so inconsequential that it nevertheless escapes the historic preservation review requirements of NHPA section 470f; and if it does thus escape section 470f, the district court must address section 330.5(b)(9).

Accordingly, the judgment of the district court is AFFIRMED in part and REVERSED in part, and the cause is REMANDED for further proceedings consistent herewith.

Note

Consider the types of activities that might be deemed to be "inconsequential" under a nationwide permit such that an agency need not comply with Section 106.

Because the NHPA creates essentially procedural obligations, it "neither...
forbid[s] the destruction of historic sites, nor... command[s] their preservation" [*United States v. 162.20 Acres of Land*, 639 F.2d 299, 302 (5th Cir.
1981), *cert. denied*, 454 U.S. 828 (1981)]. Section 106 merely requires a
federal agency with jurisdiction over a federally approved undertaking to
take into account the effects of the undertaking on properties included in, or
eligible for inclusion in, the National Register of Historic Places. The agency
also must afford the Advisory Council on Historic Preservation (Advisory
Council or ACHP)[4] a reasonable opportunity to comment on the undertaking
before approving the funding, licensing, or execution of that undertaking
[see *McMillan Park Committee v. National Capital Planning Comm'n*, 968
F.2d 1283 (D.C. Cir. 1992); *WATCH (Waterbury Action to Conserve Our
Heritage) v. Harris*, 603 F.2d 310 (2d Cir. 1979); and *National Trust for
Historic Preservation v. United States Army Corps of Engineers*, 552 F. Supp.
784 (S.D. Ohio 1982). But see *City of Grapevine, Texas v. Department of
Transportation*, 17 F.3d 1502, 1508–509 (D.C. Cir. 1994), holding that the
FAA did not violate the NHPA by issuing approval of an airport runway
project before compliance with Section 106 of the NHPA had been completed, as approval was conditioned upon such compliance, and no approval
for the expenditure of federal funds was made.].

In addition to the requirements set forth under section 106 of the NHPA,
agencies must comply with the regulations promulgated by the Advisory.
Council [see 36 C.F.R. Part 800 (1997)].[5] For example, the regulations require federal agencies to identify heritage resources[6] within the geographic
area or areas within which an undertaking may cause changes to the character or use of those heritage resources [36 C.F.R. §§ 800.2, 800.4 (1997)].
The agency must review existing information, request the views of the State
Historic Preservation Office (SHPO), and, in accordance with the planning
processes of the agency, seek information and input from local governments,
Indian tribes, and other entities or persons likely to have knowledge of, or

---

[4]The Advisory Council is an independent federal agency whose composition is listed at 16
U.S.C. § 470i (1994). The Council's duties are prescribed in the NHPA at 16 U.S.C. §
470j (1994). The State Historic Preservation Officer coordinates state participation in
the implementation of the NHPA and "is a key participant in the Section 106 process"
[36 C.F.R. § 800.1(c)(ii) (1997)].

[5]As this book goes to press, the Advisory Council is in the process of considering revisions
to its regulations. Readers should consult the regulations themselves for potential amendments.

[6]The NHPA and Advisory Council use the term "historic property" [16 U.S.C. § 470w(5);
36 C.F.R. § 800.2(e)]. The authors use the term "heritage resources" throughout this
book. However, the meaning of the two terms is equivalent.

seek council from other agencies
3 impact

concerns about, heritage resources in the area [36 C.F.R. § 800.4(a) (1997)]. Criteria for locating potentially affected heritage resources and evaluating their historical significance are set out in 36 C.F.R. § 800.4(b)-(c) (1997). If no heritage resources are found, the agency will document that finding to the SHPO and notify designated interested persons [36 C.F.R. § 800.4(d) (1997)], thereby completing the "Section 106 process." The determination of a resource's National Register eligibility is the responsibility of the federal agency and the SHPO, and, absent an abuse of discretion, their application of the regulations to the facts must be sustained [*Wilson v. Block*, 708 F.2d 735, 755 (D.C. Cir. 1983), *cert. denied*, 464 U.S. 956 (1983)].

If National Register-eligible properties are located, but the agency makes a "no effect" determination, the agency must notify the SHPO and interested persons who have made their concerns known to the agency of this determination. The agency is not required to take any further steps unless the SHPO objects within 15 days of notification. If the SHPO does object, the agency then must follow the procedures set forth in 36 C.F.R. § 800.5(c) (1997), which are the same ones used for a finding of an effect [36 C.F.R. § 800.5(b) (1997)].

When an effect of an undertaking on heritage resources is found, the agency, in consultation with the SHPO, applies the criteria set forth in 36 C.F.R. § 800.9(b) (1997) to determine whether the effect of the undertaking should be considered "adverse" [36 C.F.R. § 800.5(c) (1997)]. If a "no adverse effect" determination is made, the agency must: (1) obtain the concurrence of the SHPO; and (2) notify the Advisory Council. If the Advisory Council does not object to the finding within 30 days of notification, the agency official is not required to take any further steps in the "Section 106 process." If the Advisory Council does object within the 30-day time frame, and the agency does not agree with the changes proposed by the Advisory Council, then the effect of the undertaking is to be considered "adverse" [36 C.F.R. § 800.5(d)(2) (1997)].

After applying the criteria set forth in 36 C.F.R. § 800.9(b) (1997), if a determination is made that the effect of the undertaking should be considered "adverse," the agency must inform the Advisory Council and then consult with the SHPO to "seek ways to avoid or reduce the effects on" the heritage resources. The Advisory Council may, at the request of either the agency or the SHPO, or on its own initiative, participate in this consultation process. In addition, interested parties such as local governments, Indian tribes, affected landowners, and applicants for, or holders of, grants, permits, or licenses must be invited to participate if they so request. Documentation developed in the course of consultation must be provided to all interested parties, and the public must be provided with an adequate opportunity to receive information and express their views. When the agency and the SHPO agree on how the effects will be mitigated, the consultation process culminates in a Memorandum of Agreement, which, under Section 106, is binding [36 C.F.R. § 800.5(e)(1997); see 16 U.S.C. § 470h-2(1); *West Branch Valley Flood Protection Ass'n v. Stone*, 820 F. Supp. 1, 10 (D.D.C. 1993); and *Tyler v. Cisneros*, 136 F.3d 603 (9th Cir. 1998)].

ATTAKAI v. UNITED STATES

746 F. Supp. 1395 (D. Ariz. 1990)

CARROLL, District Judge:

Defendants, officials of the United States Department of the Interior (DOI) and the Bureau of Indian Affairs (BIA), are involved in construction of fences and livestock watering facilities on portions of the Hopi Indian Reservation as part of a range restoration and management program. Plaintiffs, individual members of the Navajo Tribe, filed this action on behalf of a class of all members of the Navajo Tribe who practice the traditional Navajo religion, seeking to enjoin defendants from continuing current and proposed fencing and construction projects on the Hopi Reservation. The case has not been certified as a class action.

Plaintiffs, who continue to reside upon or use the land in the vicinity of the projects, allege that the construction activities are interfering with their ability to practice their religion, in violation of the Free Exercise Clause of the First Amendment and the American Indian Religious Freedom Act, and are irreparably disturbing and destroying sites and objects of religious, historical, and archaeological significance in violation of the National Historic Preservation Act, the Historic and Archaeological Data Preservation Act, the Archaeological Resources Protection Act, the National Environmental Policy Act and the Administrative Procedure Act.

BACKGROUND

This action arises out of the long-standing dispute between the Hopi and Navajo Tribes over title and interest in reservation lands in northeastern Arizona. The construction activities involved in this action affect a portion of the 1882 Executive Order Reservation established for use by the Hopi Indians and "such other Indians as the Secretary of the Interior may see fit to settle thereon," which became a Joint Use Area (JUA) of the Navajo and Hopi Tribes as a result of the decision in *Healing v. Jones*, 210 F. Supp. 125 (D. Ariz. 1962), *affirmed per curiam*, 373 U.S. 758, 83 S.Ct. 1559, 10 L.Ed.2d 703 (1962). The specific portions of the JUA involved in this action were subsequently partitioned to the Hopi Tribe on April 18, 1979 pursuant to provisions of the Navajo-Hopi Land Settlement Act, Pub.L. 93-531, 25 U.S.C. § 640d *et seq*. See *Sekaquaptewa v. MacDonald*, 575 F.2d 239 (9th Cir. 1978); *Sekaquaptewa v. MacDonald*, 626 F.2d 113 (9th Cir. 1980). The Settlement Act, as amended by the Navajo and Hopi Indian Relocation Amendments Act of 1980, Pub.L. 96-305, provides for the relocation of members of one tribe residing on lands partitioned to the other tribe. The plaintiffs in this action continue to use portions of the land partitioned to the Hopi Tribe (Hopi Partitioned Lands or HPL) near their residences. Most of the plaintiffs continue to reside on the HPL in the vicinity of the construction projects and are subject to relocation from the HPL. The construction activities of which plaintiffs complain are part of an ongoing range restoration and management program throughout the HPL required by Court Orders and the Settlement Act.[1] The particular construction projects which are the subject of this action involve separate projects in two different parts of the HPL. The first involves the construction of fences to restrict livestock movements in Range Unit 562, in the vicinity of Star Mountain. This fencing project includes three fence lines, one of which stops at the base of Star Mountain, one which continues about half-way up the mountain, and a third which would rise to near the top of the mountain. The second project involves the construction of a pipeline and earthen stock tank to provide a watering facility for livestock in Range Unit 257. Both projects are funded by defendants, but have been approved by the Hopi Tribe and are actually being accomplished by the Hopi Tribe through contracts with defendants pursuant to the Indian Self Determination Act.

At the hearing on the Motion for a Preliminary Injunction the Court recommended that the defendants provide seven days notice of proposed projects on the HPL to the Navajo Tribe and plaintiffs to reduce tensions and the possibilities for conflict in the area while this matter was being considered. The defendants agreed to provide such notice.

Defendants have filed a motion to dismiss the complaint on various procedural grounds and for failure to state claims. The Court has reviewed the briefs relating to the Application for a Preliminary Injunction and the Motion to Dismiss, the evidence presented at the hearing, and documents incorporated into this action from a related action before this Court, *Manybeads v. United States*, 730 F. Supp. 1515 (D. Ariz.) (Order of Dismissal filed October 20, 1989). This order will address plaintiffs' Motion for a Preliminary Injunction and the defendants' Motion to Dismiss.

* * *

II. PRELIMINARY INJUNCTION AND MOTION TO DISMISS

In the Ninth Circuit, the criteria for granting a preliminary injunction requires plaintiffs to establish either: (1) a combination of probable success on the merits and possibility of irreparable injury; or (2) that serious questions are raised and the balance of hardships tips sharply in its favor. *Johnson Controls, Inc. v. Phoenix Control Systems, Inc.*, 886 F.2d 1173 (9th Cir. 1989).

---

[1][*Orig. fn.*] The restoration project began in 1972 when the Court, in response to a request for a Writ of Assistance from the Hopi Tribe to enforce the Hopi rights to equal use of the JUA, ordered the Secretary of the Interior to begin range restoration and conservation measures on the JUA, which was at that time found to be severely overgrazed by the more populous Navajos. In 1974, Congress specifically directed the Secretary to restore the grazing potential of the former JUA to the "maximum extent feasible." 25 U.S.C. § 640d-18(a). In the 1980 amendments, Congress further directed that conservation activities be conducted with the concurrence of the Tribe to which the particular land was partitioned. 25 U.S.C. § 640d-9(e)(1)(A).

The claims asserted by plaintiffs in support of their request for a preliminary injunction do not specifically include their equal protection and breach of fiduciary duty claims alleged in the complaint, although these claims were occasionally raised in argument or examination. However, based on a review of the record in regard to these claims, the Court finds that plaintiffs' have not made the necessary showing to obtain a preliminary injunction on the basis of these claims. The remaining claims will be discussed separately.

* * *

B.   National Historic Preservation Act (NHPA)

Plaintiffs allege that prior to construction on these projects, defendants did not (1) engage in consultation with the State Historic Preservation Officer and Advisory Council on Historic Preservation in either the decision making process or implementation of the range management projects as required by sections 106 and 110 of the National Historic Preservation Act, 16 U.S.C. §§ 470f and 470h-2, Executive Order 11593, and the applicable regulations, and (2) did not provide the Advisory Council a reasonable opportunity to comment. A substantial portion of the testimony and argument at the preliminary injunction hearing related to the parties' interpretations of what procedures are required by law, and what the government actually did in regard to compliance with these requirements for the specific construction projects at issue.

1.   Section 106

Section 106 of the NHPA provides that the head of any federal agency having jurisdiction over a federally assisted undertaking, shall, prior to approval of the expenditure of funds or issuance of a license, take into account the effect of the undertaking on any site or object included in or eligible for inclusion in the National Register and shall provide the Advisory Council on Historic Preservation a reasonable opportunity to comment with regard to the undertaking. See 16 U.S.C. § 470f. The Advisory Council has established regulations for federal agencies in regard to compliance with Section 106. See 36 CFR Part 800 (1987).[5] The process established by the regulations is designed to accommodate historic preservation concerns and the needs of federal undertakings, principally through consultation among the Agency Official, the State Historic Preservation Officer (SHPO), the Advisory Council and other interested persons, to provide efficient identification and adequate consideration of historic properties. § 800.1(b).

The section 106 process, set out in sections 800.4 through 800.6 of the regulations, consists of the identification of historic properties which may be affected by the federal undertaking, an assessment of the historical significance of the property, a determination of whether there will be an adverse effect on the property, consideration of ways to reduce or avoid any adverse effect on such historic property, and review and comment by the Advisory Council

---

[5][*Orig. fn.*] All subsequent references herein to the regulations are to 36 CFR Part 800 (1987) unless otherwise specified.

on the procedures and conclusions of the Agency Official and SHPO. Under this regulatory scheme, formal consideration of adverse effects and ways to avoid or reduce these effects is required for an undertaking which affects "historic properties", defined as properties included in or which meet the criteria and are eligible for inclusion in the National Register of Historic Places. § 800.2(e). Accordingly, the initial steps in the process, the identification of historic properties that may be affected and the determination of the eligibility of these properties for inclusion in the National Register, is of considerable importance, and is the focus of the violations alleged by plaintiffs.

Section 800.4 sets out the procedures for identification of historic properties and evaluation of eligibility for inclusion in the National Register. Paragraph (a) provides that the Agency Official "shall": (i) review existing information on historic properties potentially affected by the undertaking; (ii) request the views of the SHPO on further actions to identify historic properties which may be affected; and (iii) seek information in accordance with agency planning processes from local governments, Indian tribes, and other parties likely to have knowledge of or concerns with historic properties in the area. On the basis of this information, the Agency Official is to determine the need for further actions to identify historic properties, such as field surveys. § 800.4(a)(2). In consultation with the SHPO, the Agency Official is required to make a reasonable and good faith effort to identify historic properties which may be affected, and gather sufficient information to evaluate the eligibility of these properties for inclusion in the National Register. § 800.4(b). Paragraph (c) provides that in consultation with the SHPO, the Agency Official shall apply the National Register Criteria to these properties and make a determination as to eligibility for inclusion in the National Register. "If the Agency Official determines in accordance with paragraphs (a) through (c) that there are no historic properties that may be affected by the undertaking, the Agency Official shall provide documentation of this finding to the SHPO," and no further steps are required in the section 106 process. § 800.4(d). If the Agency Official determines that there are historic properties that may be affected, the effects are to be assessed in accordance with section 800.5.

Plaintiffs' principal claim is that the defendants did not engage in consultation with the SHPO in determining the existence of historic properties as required by section 800.4 of the regulations. Defendants contend that they substantially complied with the implementing regulations, and determined that there were no properties which meet the criteria for inclusion in the National Register which would be affected by the projects.

In regard to the procedures actually followed by the BIA as to section 106 compliance on these projects, the Court heard testimony from the BIA Range Conservationist, the Area Archaeologist for the Phoenix Area Office of the BIA, who is responsible for compliance with section 106, and a Soil Technician from the BIA Hopi Agency who now conducts section 106 surveys on the HPL and oversees construction with regard to historic preservation concerns after archaeological clearance. The evidence shows that the following occurred with respect to compliance with section 106 on the undertakings at issue.

In attempting to identify historic properties which might be affected by the projects, none of the procedures described in section 800.4(a)(1) of the regulations were followed. The testimony indicated that such procedures are rarely if ever utilized by the BIA Phoenix Area Office. Rather, the standard practice of the Phoenix office is to complete a field survey on each project prior to archaeological clearance and final approval, purportedly pursuant to section 800.4(a)(2) of the regulations. The survey consists of a walkover of the entire project line, which has been surveyed and staked prior to this section 106 survey, to inspect the area for cultural or archaeological remains which lie in the project line, or sufficiently close that incidental impact might be expected.

Field surveys were completed for both projects involved in this action. In 1986, the Area Archaeologist, accompanied by the Soil Technician of the Hopi Agency surveyed the proposed locations for the pipeline and earthen stock tank in Range Unit 257. In April 1988, the Soil Technician surveyed the proposed fence lines in Range Unit 562. In each project, potential historic properties were located and, pursuant to standard practice of the Phoenix office, the Soil Technician and Area Archaeologist recommended that portions of the projects be moved to new alignments to avoid any potential effect on the resources. New alignments were proposed and incorporated into the project.

Based on the realignment of the project away from the cultural or archaeological remains a sufficient distance to satisfy the Area Archaeologist that there would be no effect, the Area Director determined that the project would have no effect, and issued archaeological clearance for both projects. Although the Area Archaeologist further testified that it is the standard practice of the Phoenix office to then send documentation of the "no effect" or no properties finding to the SHPO in the form of a copy of the archaeological clearance from the Director to the Superintendent, the testimony and records of the SHPO do not show that this was done on either project in this instance.

Plaintiffs argue that these procedures violate the Act and regulations in several respects. First, plaintiffs assert that consultation with the SHPO is required by section 800.4(a)(1). It is clear that there was no consultation between the SHPO and Agency in any manner. Section 800.4(a)(1) states that the agency official shall consult with the SHPO in assessing information needs to identify historic properties which may be affected. Defendants contend however, that section 800.4(a)(2) reflects that the purpose of section 800.4(a)(1) and the consultation is to determine the need for a survey of the area. Defendants therefore contend that since they conducted a survey, they are in substantial compliance with section 800.4(a). The Court disagrees.

Section 800.4(a)(2) states that based on the information gathered through consultation and the procedures in paragraph (a), the Agency Official is to determine the need for further actions, such as surveys or predictive modeling. Without consultation with the SHPO or reference to other available information, the Agency Official has no reasonable basis under the regulations to determine what additional investigation aside from a survey may be warranted, or the reasonable scope of the survey. Paragraph (b) requires the agency official to make a reasonable and good faith effort to identify historical properties, in consultation with the SHPO. Thus, the regulations clearly require consultation with the SHPO. The procedures of the Phoenix Area Office in this instance were not sufficient under paragraphs (a) or (b) of section 800.4.

Nevertheless, defendants contend that they substantially complied with the regulations by moving the projects away from any cultural or historical resources in the project areas, permitting a determination by the Agency Official that there are no historic properties that will be affected by the undertaking. The defendants argument in this regard is based on section 800.3(b) of the regulations, which provides that they may be implemented by the Agency Official in a flexible manner reflecting differing program requirements, as long as the purposes of section 106 and the regulations are met.

Paragraph (d) provides that if the Agency Official determines in accordance with paragraphs (a) through (c) that there are no historic properties that will be affected, the Agency Official shall provide documentation to the SHPO and is not required to take further steps in the section 106 process. Here, as discussed, the Agency Official did not reach such a determination in accordance with paragraphs (a) through (c). Further, the Agency Official, in this instance, did not provide any required documentation to the SHPO. The procedures of the BIA in this instance essentially substitute for a determination through consultation with the SHPO, a unilateral determination by the Area Archaeologist, based on his own survey, or in the case of Range Unit 562, one by a non-archaeologist, that a realignment of a project is sufficient to avoid any effect on potential historic properties. Although the SHPO testified that the actions taken here may constitute proper avoidance of a historic property, the SHPO testified to an understanding of the regulations that the SHPO must be consulted for all undertakings. The Court finds that the procedures of the BIA Phoenix office in this instance are contrary to the letter and spirit of the regulations, which rely on consultation, particularly with the SHPO, as the principal means of protecting historical resources. See § 800.1(b). Accordingly, I find that there is a substantial probability of success on the merits as to the alleged violation of section 106 of the Act and the applicable regulations with regard to the failure to consult with the SHPO.

Plaintiffs also contend that the defendants are required to consult with plaintiffs or the Navajo Tribe, including cultural leaders, in the section 106 process.

Section 800.1(c) of the regulations identifies the intended participants in the section 106 process. The participants are divided into two classes—consulting parties and interested persons. Consulting parties may include the Agency Official, SHPO, and the Advisory Council. § 800.1(c)(1). Interested persons are defined as "those organizations and individuals that are concerned with the effects of an undertaking on historic properties," and may include local governments, Indian tribes and the public. § 800.1(c)(2). Certain portions of the regulations require that interested persons be invited to be consulting parties, while the Agency Official, SHPO and Council may agree to invite others to become consulting parties where it will advance the objectives of section 106.

With respect to Indian tribes, section 800.1(c)(2)(iii) provides:

> The Agency Official, the State Historic Preservation Officer, and the Council should be sensitive to the special concerns of Indian tribes in historic preservation issues, which often extend beyond Indian lands to other historic properties. When an undertaking will affect Indian lands, the Agency Official shall invite the governing body of the responsible tribe to be a consulting party and to concur in any agreement.... When an undertaking may affect properties of historic value to an Indian tribe on non-Indian lands, the consulting parties shall afford such tribe the opportunity to participate as interested persons. Traditional cultural leaders and other Native Americans are considered to be interested persons with respect to undertakings that may affect historic properties of significance to such persons.

The regulations clearly require that an Indian Tribe participate as a consulting party and that it must concur in any agreement regarding undertakings which affect its lands. The undertakings involved in this action are located on the Hopi Reservation, and the Hopi Tribe must concur in any agreement. As to these projects, the Hopi Tribe approved the range management program, and is actually completing the work on these projects. These projects do not affect Navajo lands, and the regulations do not require participation by the Navajo Tribe as a consulting party, or that it concur in any agreement. However, the plaintiffs argue that consultation must still take place with the Navajo tribe and cultural leaders because these projects affect properties of interest to Indians on non-Indian lands.

While the lands in question are in fact "Indian lands", being part of the Hopi Reservation, they are not Navajo lands and the Navajo Tribe is not the "responsible" tribe and is not required to concur in any agreement. Nevertheless, the regulations clearly contemplate participation by Indian tribes regarding properties beyond their own reservations. The conclusion of the defendants that the Navajo tribe is to be afforded no participation since the lands in question are Hopi lands and not "non-Indian lands" is contrary to the language and evident intent of the regulations, and the facts concerning the history of these two tribes in relation to these lands.

The regulatory scheme depends on consultation with appropriate persons to gather information concerning historic properties to facilitate the identification and adequate consideration of historic preservation in the face of new undertakings. Navajos still reside in the areas affected by these projects awaiting relocation. Under these circumstances, it is clear that input from the Navajo tribe would advance the objectives of section 106. Accordingly, I find that the regulations require that the Navajo tribe be afforded the opportunity to participate as interested persons. This conclusion does not extend to consultation with the plaintiffs, as interested persons or otherwise, or other individual members of the Navajo Tribe.

This conclusion does not infringe on the right of the Hopi Tribe to develop or use its lands, as the Navajo Tribe is not entitled to be a consulting party or to concur in any agreement. It merely assures, as the regulations contemplate, that decisions regarding historic properties will be made upon reasonably adequate information. Further, since each tribe has sites of historic significance that are now located on the reservation of the other tribe, it is in their mutual interests that they reciprocate in the consideration of the historic preservation interests of the other tribe on their respective reservations.

Based on these regulations, I find that the defendants did not adequately take into account the effect of the undertakings on historic properties and that the plaintiffs have made the necessary showing and the motion for a preliminary injunction as to violations of section 106 of the NHPA will be granted.

* * *

Accordingly, for the reasons stated herein,

* * *

IT IS FURTHER ORDERED granting plaintiffs' motion for a preliminary injunction as to Count V, for violations of section 106 of the National Historic Preservation Act, 16 U.S.C. § 470f and the regulations promulgated thereunder. Defendants are enjoined from continuing construction of the range management and restoration projects in Range Units 257 and 562 and on the remainder of the Hopi Partitioned Lands without compliance with section 106 and the applicable regulations.

IT IS FURTHER ORDERED that plaintiffs' motion for a preliminary injunction and defendants' motion to dismiss are otherwise denied.

PUEBLO OF SANDIA v. UNITED STATES

50 F.3d 856 (10th Cir. 1995)

SEYMOUR, Chief Judge:

The Pueblo of Sandia and various environmental groups brought suit for declaratory and injunctive relief against the United States and a National Forest Service supervisor, alleging that the Forest Service failed to comply with the National Historic Preservation Act (NHPA), 16 U.S.C. § 470 *et seq.*, in its evaluation of Las Huertas Canyon in the Cibola National Forest. The Pueblo asserts that the New Mexico canyon contains numerous sites of religious and cultural significance to the tribe, qualifying the canyon as a "traditional cultural property" eligible for inclusion in the National Register of Historic Places. The Forest Service, however, concluded that the canyon did not constitute a traditional cultural property and instituted a new management strategy for it. The district court granted summary judgment for the Forest Service, finding that it had made a reasonable and good faith effort to identify historic properties. Because we conclude that the Forest Service's efforts were neither reasonable nor in good faith, we reverse and remand.

I.

Las Huertas Canyon is located in the Sandia Mountains northeast of Albuquerque, New Mexico. Lying within the Cibola National Forest, the canyon is under the supervision of the Forest Service. The Sandia Pueblo reservation is nearby, and tribal members visit the canyon to gather evergreen boughs for use in significant private and public cultural ceremonies. Aplt. App. at 109-11. They also harvest herbs and plants along the Las Huertas Creek which are important for traditional healing practices. *Id.* at 111. The canyon contains many shrines and ceremonial paths of religious and cultural significance to the Pueblo. *Id.* at 108–11.

In July 1988, the Forest Service released a Draft Environmental Impact Statement (DEIS) detailing eight alternative management strategies for Las Huertas Canyon. After an extended comment period, the Forest Service selected a ninth alternative, Alternative I, as the preferred strategy. Alternative I required the realignment and reconstruction of the Las Huertas Canyon Road and additional improvements to the area, including the rehabilitation and expansion of several picnic grounds and the installation of sanitary facilities at other locations. Aplt. App. at 48.

Voicing concerns that the strategy would adversely impact traditional cultural properties and practices in the canyon by encouraging additional traffic and visitation to the area, the Pueblo filed an administrative appeal of the decision. The Deputy Regional Forester affirmed the decision, altering the snow plowing and road closure provisions of Alternative I in response to complaints from other appellants. The decision became administratively final in January 1990 when the Chief of the Forest Service declined to review it.

The Pueblo filed this suit in federal court, alleging numerous statutory violations.[1] The Pueblo subsequently amended the complaint to plead a violation of the NHPA, 16 U.S.C. § 470 *et seq.* The Pueblo alleged that the Forest Service failed to comply with section 106 of the NHPA when it refused to evaluate the canyon as a traditional cultural property eligible for inclusion on the National Register.

The parties filed cross motions for summary judgment on the issue of NHPA compliance. By the time the district court heard the motions, the State Historic Preservation Officer (SHPO) had concurred in the Forest Service's conclusion that certain specific sites near the roadway and picnic grounds were not eligible for the National Register. In a Memorandum Opinion and Order entered April 30, 1993, the district court noted that "[t]he administrative record is silent as to whether any of the sites found were evaluated [by the Forest Service] against the National Register Criteria as required by [the NHPA], and whether the sites met the criteria." Memorandum Opinion and Order (April 30, 1993) at 11 (Order). The court accepted the SHPO's concurrence as "evidence that the Forest Service met the substantive requirements with respect to the roadway and the picnic area." *Id.*

Although concerned that the Forest Service "does not appear to have taken the requirements of [the NHPA] very seriously," the court relied on the agency's assertion that it would diligently pursue information on the potential historic value of other individual sites within the canyon. *Id.* at 12. On that basis, the court granted summary judgment for defendants, and plaintiffs filed this appeal.

On May 13, 1993, the SHPO concurred in the Forest Service's final conclusion that "there is no evidence that there are Pueblo Indian traditional cultural properties in Las Huertas Canyon." Aplee. Br., Addendum at 1, 3. Plaintiffs filed this appeal on June 19, 1993. Significantly, nine months later the SHPO withdrew his concurrence upon receiving evidence suggesting that traditional cultural properties existed in Las Huertas Canyon. Aplt. Supp. Br., Addendum 1. The SHPO stated:

We were surprised to see the [affidavits of Dr. Elizabeth Brandt and Phillip Lauriano] since we had been informed that the Cibola National Forest had received no comments on [Traditional Cultural Properties] from the [All Indian Pueblo Council] or from any pueblos (cf. Report 1993-03-054, prepared by Dr. Joseph A. Tainter, dated April 29, 1993). Our previous consultations on this undertaking were based on Dr. Tainter's report. This documentation is relevant to our consultations on this undertaking. I am concerned that our not having received the affidavits has affected our ability to consult appropriately under Section 106 of the National Historic Preservation Act.

---

[1][*Orig. fn.*] Sandia Pueblo alleged that the Forest Service's approval of the Final Environmental Impact Statement (FEIS) violated the National Environmental Policy Act, 42 U.S.C. § 4321, *et seq.* (NEPA); the National Forest Management Act, 16 U.S.C. § 1600, *et seq.* (NFMA); the Clean Water Act, 33 U.S.C. § 1251, *et seq.* (CWA); the American Indian Religious Freedom Act, 42 U.S.C. § 1996 (AIRFA); and the Administrative Procedure Act, 5 U.S.C. §§ 701, *et seq.* (APA). The Pueblo abandoned the NFMA, AIRFA, and CWA claims and does not appeal the district court's grant of summary judgment for defendants on the NEPA and APA claims.

Id. The SHPO concluded that the withheld information had a substantial impact on the inquiry into the canyon's eligibility for the Historic Register. He wrote:

> Much of our consultation, dating back to September of 1992, concentrated on determining what would represent a "reasonable" attempt to identify [Traditional Cultural Properties] that may be affected by the project. *Bulletin 38...* states that "a 'reasonable' effort depends in part on the likelihood that such properties may be present." Mr. Lauriano's statement, supported by the ethnographic overview provided by Dr. Brandt, indicates that Las Huertas Canyon is used for ceremonial purposes, contains plants and soils used in traditional ceremonies and contains traditional trails that lead to other [traditional cultural properties]. This information suggests that properties that may be eligible to the National Register of Historic Places may be affected by the proposed improvements to the Las Huertas Canyon Road and recreational facilities. It is my opinion that we do not have enough information to make a determination of eligibility.

Id. Consequently, the SHPO recommended an ethnographic analysis of the canyon to further evaluate the possibility that it contained traditional cultural properties.

> Consistent with *Bulletin 38*, this analysis should include interviews with appropriate Pueblo representatives, field inspections and documentation. I recommend that the Forest Service hire a professional ethnographer to conduct this analysis. An independent professional is most likely to be able to work out any impasse that may have developed between the Pueblos and the Forest Service. I also believe that this procedure will give the Pueblos a reasonable opportunity to provide us with enough documentation to conduct a formal determination of eligibility as outlined in *Bulletin 38*.

Id. (citations omitted).

We review the district court's summary judgment de novo. Housing Authority v. United States, 980 F.2d 624, 628 (10th Cir. 1992).

II.

The NHPA requires the Forest Service to "take into account the effect of [any] undertaking on any district, site, building, structure, or object that is included in or eligible for inclusion in the National Register." NHPA, § 106, 16 U.S.C. § 470f (1993). Section 106 also mandates that the agency afford the Advisory Council on Historic Preservation "a reasonable opportunity to comment" on the undertaking. *Id.*

The Advisory Council has established regulations for federal agencies to follow in complying with section 106. See 36 C.F.R. § 800. The process is designed to foster communication and consultation between agency officials, the SHPO, and other interested parties such as Indian tribes, local governments, and the general public.

First, the Agency Official must review all existing information on the site, request the SHPO's views on ways to identify historic properties, and seek information from interested parties likely to have knowledge about historic properties in the area. 36 C.F.R. § 800.4(a). In light of this information, the agency determines any need for further investigation.

In consultation with the SHPO, the agency then must make a "reasonable and good faith effort to identify historic properties that may be affected by the undertaking and gather sufficient information to evaluate the eligibility of these properties for the National Register." 36 C.F.R. § 800.4(b). Finally, for each property identified, the agency official and the SHPO must evaluate the property on the basis of the National Register criteria to determine its eligibility for inclusion. 36 C.F.R. § 800.4(c).

The Pueblo claims that the sites within the Las Huertas Canyon are traditional cultural properties which are thus eligible for inclusion in the National Register.[2] The Pueblo asserts that the Forest Service's conclusion to the contrary stems from that agency's failure to make a "reasonable and good faith effort" to identify historical properties.

A.   Reasonable Effort

The Forest Service contends that it engaged in reasonable efforts to identify historic properties in Las Huertas Canyon. The record reveals that the Forest Service did request information from the Sandia Pueblo and other local Indian tribes, but a mere request for information is not necessarily sufficient to constitute the "reasonable effort" section 106 requires. Because communications from the tribes indicated the existence of traditional cultural properties and because the Forest Service should have known that tribal customs might restrict the ready disclosure of specific information, we hold that the agency did not reasonably pursue the information necessary to evaluate the canyon's eligibility for inclusion in the National Register.

During the assessment phase of the section 106 process, the Forest Service mailed letters to local Indian tribes, including the Sandia Pueblo, and individual tribal members who were known to be familiar with traditional cultural properties. Aplt. App. at 159–65. The letters requested detailed information describing the location of the sites, activities conducted there, and the frequency of the activities. *Id.* They also asked tribes to provide maps of the sites, drawn at a scale of 1:24,000 or better, as well as documentation of the historic nature of the property. *Id.*

In addition to mailing form letters to the tribes and individuals, Forest Service officials also addressed meetings of the All Indian Pueblo Council and the San Felipe Pueblo. Aplt. App. at 177, 181. The officials informed the groups that traditional cultural properties are eligible for inclusion in the National Register and requested the same specific information required in the letters. *Id.*

None of the tribes or individuals provided the Forest Service with the type of information requested in the letters and meetings. We conclude, however, that the information the tribes did communicate to the agency was sufficient to require the Forest Service to engage in further investigations, especially in light of regulations warning that tribes might be hesitant to divulge the type of information sought.

---

[2][*Orig. fn.*] The National Register Bulletin 38 provides that a traditional cultural property is "eligible for inclusion in the National Register because of its association with cultural practices or beliefs of a living community that (a) are rooted in that community's history, and (b) are important in maintaining the continuing cultural identity of the community." Aplt. App. at 82.

Prior to its final determination on April 29, 1993 that Las Huertas Canyon contained no traditional cultural properties, the Forest Service was aware of numerous claims to the contrary. As early as January 5, 1987, the Governor of the Sandia Pueblo informed the Forest Service that the Las Huertas Canyon was an area "of great religious and traditional importance to the people of Sandia Pueblo." Aplt. App. at 130. The minutes of a Las Huertas Canyon Work Group meeting on March 10, 1987 reveal that the group knew that Native Americans used the canyon area for a number of ceremonial, religious, and medicinal purposes. *Id.* at 133. During the period of public comment on the eight alternatives, the Sandia Pueblo supported alternative C, which it believed would be most likely "to permit the Sandia members to perform secret, traditional activities in more seclusion." *Id.* at 135.

On August 9, 1989, the Regional Forester took the affidavit of Philip Lauriano, an elder and religious leader of the Sandia Pueblo. Mr. Lauriano listed several "long-standing religious and traditional practices" which take place in the canyon and alluded to sacred sites which it contains. Aplt. App. at 108–09. In 1992, Dr. Elizabeth Brandt, a highly qualified anthropologist who is an expert on the Sandia Pueblo, provided a detailed ethnographic overview of the tribe's religious and cultural connections to the canyon.[3] Dr. Brandt noted the canyon's significance to the Pueblo as a source of herbs and evergreen boughs, which have been an integral part of certain Pueblo ceremonies for at least 60 years.[4] *Id.* at 110–11. She also described certain ceremonial paths and sites in the canyon which "serve as gateways for access to the spirit world," concluding that

> [t]hese sites and their functions would be significantly impaired if not totally destroyed as a result of the planned development of the Canyon, thus cutting off spiritual access for religious leaders and those responsible for the actions which occur at these shrines. These sites are critical to the religious practice, cultural identity, and overall well-being of the Pueblo.

Id. at 111. Noting the secrecy which is crucial to Pueblo religious and cultural practices, Dr. Brandt expressed concern that the proposed development would allow the outside world to intrude upon and negatively impact these practices.[5] Based on these factors, she concluded

---

[3][*Orig. fn.*] Although the record indicates that Dr. Brandt gave her affidavit on April 13, 1992, it is unclear when it was given to the Forest Service. The agency, however, refers to the Brandt affidavit in its brief, Aplee. Br. at 28 n. 11, and does not claim that it did not have the affidavit at the time it made its final decision that Las Huertas Canyon contained no traditional cultural properties. Therefore, we presume that the Brandt affidavit was a part of the record upon which the Forest Service based its April 29, 1993, decision.

[4][*Orig. fn.*] Oral testimony establishes that the Pueblo have gathered evergreen boughs in Las Huertas Canyon for at least 60 years. Dr. Brandt notes, however, that the canyon has probably played a role in tribal religious and cultural practices for centuries as archeological evidence reveals that the Pueblo village has remained at essentially the same site since the 1300s. Aplt. App. at 112.

[5][*Orig. fn.*] Dr. Brandt asserted that the safety of the Pueblo members might be implicated, stating that Pueblo members reported having been "placed at gunpoint by persons while gathering evergreens." Aplt. App. at 112. She also pointed to examples of shrines in other areas having been overrun or desecrated as a result of increased traffic and visitation. *Id.*

that "Las Huertas Canyon constitutes a Traditional Cultural District with multiple Sites for the Sandia Tribe." *Id.* at 112.

Furthermore, the Forest Service received communications clearly indicating why more specific responses were not forthcoming. At the meeting with the San Felipe Pueblo, tribal members indicated that "[t]hey did not want to disclose any specific details of site locations or activities." Aplt. App. at 177. A representative of the Sandia Pueblo made the same claim at the All Indian Pueblo Council meeting. *Id.* at 181. Dr. Brandt also commented upon the Pueblo people's general unwillingness "to divulge any information regarding their religious practices." *Id.* at 113.

This reticence to disclose details of their cultural and religious practices was not unexpected. National Register Bulletin 38 warns that "knowledge of traditional cultural values may not be shared readily with outsiders" as such information is "regarded as powerful, even dangerous" in some societies. Aplt. App. at 88. Joseph Tainter, an archeologist for the Forest Service, "acknowledged that [P]ueblos are often reluctant to provide such information" and promised confidential treatment of any communications. *Id.* at 181. The Work Study Group also noted that "[k]nowledge of Native American attitudes towards divulging information regarding Forest use and past experience by Forest Service cultural resources personnel indicates [sic] that general requests of tribes for information... will go unanswered." *Id.* at 134.

Determining what constitutes a reasonable effort to identify traditional cultural properties "depends in part on the likelihood that such properties may be present." National Bulletin 38, Aplt. App. at 86. Based on the information contained in the Lauriano and Brandt affidavits, the SHPO ultimately concluded that the "properties [ ] may be eligible to the National Register of Historic Places" but "we do not have enough information to make a determination of eligibility." Aplt. Supp. Br., Addendum 1.[6] We agree. The information communicated to the Forest Service as well as the reasons articulated for the lack of more specific information clearly suggest that there is a sufficient likelihood that the canyon contains traditional cultural properties to warrant further investigation.[7] We thus hold that the Forest Service did not make a reasonable effort to identify historic properties.

---

[6][*Orig. fn.*] Although the letters containing the SHPO's concurrence and subsequent withdrawal of that concurrence were not a part of the record below, we take judicial notice of them on this appeal. See *Clemmons v. Bohannon*, 956 F.2d 1523, 1532 & n. 2 (10th Cir. 1992) (Seymour, J., dissenting) (en banc) (judicial notice of government reports); see also *Clappier v. Flynn*, 605 F.2d 519, 535 (10th Cir. 1979) (judicial notice of official governmental publications).

[7][*Orig. fn.*] The SHPO has recommended that the Forest Service conduct an ethnographic analysis of Las Huertas Canyon.

> Consistent with *Bulletin 38*, this analysis should include interviews with appropriate Pueblo representatives, field inspections and documentation.... An independent professional [ethnographer] is most likely to be able to work out any impasse that may have developed between the Pueblos and the Forest Service.

Aplt. Supp. Br., Addendum 1; see Aplt. App. at 88. We note that it is the role of the SHPO to recommend further actions to identify historic properties. See 36 C.F.R. § 800.4(a)(1)(ii).

B.   Good Faith Effort

The Pueblo also claims that the Forest Service failed to make the requisite good faith effort to identify traditional cultural properties in Las Huertas Canyon. It bases this assertion on the fact that the Forest Service withheld relevant information from the SHPO during the required consultation process. The district court expressed concern about the Forest Service's commitment to the section 106 process and placed great weight upon the SHPO's concurrence in granting summary judgment. Thus, the withdrawal of that concurrence upon discovery of the withheld information suggests that the Forest Service did not put forth a good faith effort to identify historic properties.

The regulations require that "[i]n consultation with the [SHPO], the Agency Official shall make a reasonable and good faith effort to identify historic properties." 36 C.F.R. § 800.4(b). Indeed, consultation with the SHPO is an integral part of the section 106 process. See *Attakai v. United States*, 746 F. Supp. 1395, 1407 (D. Ariz. 1990) ("[T]he regulations clearly require consultation with the SHPO.") Affording the SHPO an opportunity to offer input on potential historic properties would be meaningless unless the SHPO has access to available, relevant information. Thus, "consultation" with the SHPO mandates an informed consultation.

The Forest Service did not provide the SHPO copies of the Lauriano and Brandt affidavits until after the consultation was complete and the SHPO had concurred. See Aplt. Supp. Br., Addendum 1. In fact, the Forest Service informed the SHPO during consultation that "[c]onsultations with pueblo officials and elders, and other users of the Las Huertas Canyon area, disclosed no evidence that the... area contains traditional cultural properties." Aplt. App. at 152. The SHPO's initial concurrence was based on this report. Aplt. Supp. Br., Addendum 1. Once the SHPO acquired access to the withheld information, he withdrew his concurrence, noting the relevance of the documents and his concern that "our not having received [them] has affected our ability to consult appropriately under Section 106 of the [NHPA]." *Id.*

Moreover, the regulations require that once the agency concludes that no historic properties are present, it must provide the SHPO documentation of that finding. 36 C.F.R. § 800.4(d). The Forest Service rendered its final decision that no traditional cultural properties exist in Las Huertas Canyon on April 29, 1993. Aplee. Br., Addendum. The report was sent to the SHPO on May 4, 1993, prompting the SHPO's concurrence nine days later. The relevant documents, *i.e.,* the Lauriano and Brandt affidavits, were not communicated to the SHPO until January 14, 1994. Aplt. Supp. Br., Addendum 1. Thus, the Forest Service failed to provide documentation of its decision to the SHPO in a timely manner.

Prior to the SHPO's letter revealing that the Forest Service withheld relevant information, the district court expressed reservations about the Forest Service's approach to the section 106 process. The court noted its concern "that the Forest Service does not appear to have taken the requirements of this Act very seriously." Order at 12. Those reservations were partially alleviated by the fact that the SHPO had concurred, at that time, with part of the Forest Service's new management plan. *Id.* at 11. By withholding relevant information from the SHPO during the consultation process, however, the Forest Service further undermined any argument that it had engaged in a good faith effort. We thus hold that the Forest Service did not make a good faith effort to identify historic properties in Las Huertas Canyon.

Because we conclude that the Forest Service did not make a reasonable and good faith effort in its evaluation of Las Huertas Canyon, we REVERSE the judgment of the district court and REMAND for further proceedings in accordance with this opinion.

Note

Compare and contrast the consultation with the Indian tribes initiated by the federal agencies pursuant to Section 106 of the NHPA in *Attakai* and *Pueblo of Sandia*.

The other core section that sets forth the management responsibilities of federal agencies under the NHPA is Section 110 [16 U.S.C. § 470h-2 (1994)]. Pursuant to Section 110, a federal agency is responsible for the preservation of heritage resources that are owned or controlled by the agency. In addition, the agency must, in consultation with the Secretary of the Interior, establish a preservation program to identify, evaluate, protect, and nominate to the National Register of Historic Places heritage resources under their ownership or control.

Section 110 was originally added to the NHPA in 1980 to "'clarif[y] and codif[y] the minimum responsibilities expected of federal agencies in carrying out the purposes of th[e] Act'" [*Lee v. Thornburgh*, 877 F.2d 1053, 1057 (D.C. Cir. 1989), quoting H.R. Rep. No. 1457, 96th Cong., 2d Sess. 36 (1980), *reprinted in* 1980 U.S. Code Cong. & Admin. News 6378, 6399]. Section 110 codified a previous Executive Order signed by President Nixon in 1971 (Executive Order 11573), and therefore it was not intended to:

> change the preservation responsibilities of Federal agencies as required by any other laws, executive orders or regulations, nor limit the President's authority to specify additional responsibilities. [Rather,] [s]ection 110(a)(1) requires a Federal agency to assume preservation responsibilities for properties owned or under the control of the agency. It is intended that the degree of preservation responsibility be commensurate with the extent of the agency's interest in or control of a particular property....
>
> Section 110(d) requires that, consistent with their missions and mandates, all federal agencies will carry out their programs... so that historic preservation interests are affirmatively addressed.... It is recognized that most federal agencies have a primary purpose other than historic preservation; however, it is reasonable to expect that they also view themselves as multiple resource managers responding to diverse economic, social and environmental concerns—including the concerns of historic preservation....
>
> H.R. Rep. No. 1457, 96th Cong., 2d Sess. 36 (1980), reprinted in 1980 U.S. Code Cong. & Admin. News 6378, 6399.

Section 110 was substantially amended in 1992 to further clarify and strengthen federal stewardship of heritage resources. Federal managers, therefore, must address historic preservation concerns as part of their ongoing responsibility to carry out and develop their own historic preservation programs.

NATIONAL TRUST FOR HISTORIC PRESERVATION v. BLANCK

938 F. Supp. 908 (D.D.C. 1996)

FRIEDMAN, District Judge:

This case concerns the extent of the federal government's obligation to spend scarce funds to preserve historic buildings under the National Historic Preservation Act ("NHPA"), 16 U.S.C. § 470 *et seq.* Plaintiffs, the National Trust for Historic Preservation and Save Our Seminary at Forest Glen, seek declaratory and injunctive relief to compel the Army to expend substantial sums of money in long-term preservation activities that, plaintiffs argue, are not only necessary to preserve the National Park Seminary Historic District, a community of historic buildings located at the Walter Reed Army Medical Center, but are statutorily mandated. The government asserts that it has in fact expended significant resources in order to preserve the Historic District consistent with the Department of the Army's spending priorities and mission, that it has complied with the requirements of the NHPA, and that the Act does not contemplate the kind of relief plaintiffs seek. Both sides moved for summary judgment, and plaintiffs subsequently filed a motion for a preliminary injunction, supplemented by affidavits, photographs and other evidence of deterioration, to force the Army to undertake emergency repairs and stabilization measures to the historic buildings in the Historic District in order to preserve the status quo during the pendency of this litigation. See Pls.' Mot. for Temporary Restraining Order and Preliminary Injunction (Jan. 22, 1996) and Appendix A.[1]

In this case, the availability of preliminary injunctive relief turns on whether plaintiffs have demonstrated a likelihood of success on the merits entitling them to relief under the

---

[1][*Orig. fn.*] Plaintiffs filed a supplemental memorandum in support of their request for a preliminary injunction on May 22, 1996; they filed a second supplemental memorandum on July 5, 1996, and a third on August 5, 1996. In the second submission, plaintiffs advised the Court that on or about June 24, 1996, the Pergola Bridge had collapsed after a severe thunderstorm and now is totally destroyed. The Pergola Bridge was the last remaining historic bridge in the National Park Seminary Historic District. They reported that the Pergola Bridge was the second contributing structure in the Historic District to be completely destroyed by the Army's neglect of the property; the Odeon Theater had been destroyed by fire in September 1993. They assert that other buildings in the Historic District—most notably, the Gymnasium, the Main Building, the Castle, and the Dining Hall—are also at risk.

statute. The Court will address plaintiffs' request for a preliminary injunction as a part of its discussion of the ultimate disposition of the case and what relief, if any, is appropriate.[2]

I. FACTUAL BACKGROUND

Walter Reed Army Medical Center ("Walter Reed" or "WRAMC") is a medical care, research and teaching facility; Forest Glen, one of three geographically separate sections of Walter Reed, is an auxiliary service, support and research area in Silver Spring, Maryland. The National Park Seminary Historic District consists of 29 buildings spread over 23 acres of the Forest Glen section. The Maryland Historical Trust determined that twenty-four of those buildings contribute individually to the historic character of the Historic District while five other buildings do not. Plaintiffs' Statement of Material Facts As to Which There is No Genuine Dispute ("Pls.' Statement of Material Facts") p. 7; Cultural Resource Management Plan ("CRMP") at IV-3, Pls.' Ex. 2, Administrative Record ("A.R.") at 947. Walter Reed currently uses some of the 24 historic buildings for administrative purposes. The majority of the buildings, however, are not used at all. Interim Stabilization Plan (Apr. 13, 1994), A.R. at 1713.

A.   The Buildings of the Historic District

The National Park Seminary Historic District has been listed in the National Register of Historic Places since 1972. Built in the 1880s, Ye Forest Inne is the oldest building in the District. It was originally constructed as a resort and now serves as the Main Building (Building 101) of the National Park Seminary. The Odeon Theater (Building 104) was constructed in 1901, the Gymnasium (Building 118) in 1907, Aloha House (Building 116) in 1898, and the Villa (Building 199) in 1907. The Pergola Bridge spanned the glen and connected the Villa to the Practice House (Building 112). See note 1, *supra*. In the late 1890s and early 1900s, eight eclectic sorority houses were built, each in a different architectural style, which also are among the 29 buildings in the Historic District. In addition, the District contains formal gardens, foot bridges, retaining walls, walkways, trails, garden ornaments and statuary. Pls.' Statement of Material Facts ¶¶ 8–13.

The parties agree that there has been significant damage to and deterioration of the buildings in the Historic District over the years, although they disagree about the extent of the damage and deterioration. At least the following facts are not in dispute. By 1989, Building 101, the largest building in the complex, showed some rotten wood joints, mortar loss and deterioration. Walter Reed Survey of Historical Buildings on the 26 Acre Forest Glen Historic District, Maryland ("1989 Survey") (April 1989), Pls.' Ex. 4, A.R. at 280–301.5, 1122–1193. The foundation walls of Senior House were badly deteriorated. The Pergola Bridge was "in a deteriorating condition and might well be considered unsafe. Maintenance [on the

---

[2][*Orig. fn.*] Plaintiffs have persuaded the Court on the irreparable harm prong of the test for preliminary injunctive relief. See *Sea Containers Ltd. v. Stena AB*, 890 F.2d 1205, 1208 (D.C. Cir. 1989).

Bridge] has been stopped." A.R. at 1145. See also note 1, *supra*. Building 109 needed a new roof; Building 112 had water infiltration in all basement areas and serious wall damage; and Building 107 had a deteriorating structural condition. The Army subsequently reported in 1992 that the south wall of the dining room of Building 101 had partially collapsed and one of the columns in the west portico of the library wing had rotted and dropped eight to ten inches. CRMP at V-7, A.R. at 951.

In 1990, KFS Historic Preservation Group, a paid consultant, prepared a "Section 106 Report" for the Army Corps of Engineers. Pls.' Ex. 27, A.R. at 3077.[3] The report found that the structures of the Historic District had "suffered serious and in some instances irreversible damage from long-term deferred maintenance. Several buildings have been condemned... [and] abandoned and are rapidly falling into ruinous condition." *Id.* at 31–32, A.R. at 3114–15. The report described a wide variety of damage and concluded that "[w]hile the appropriate mitigation measure would be to develop a Historic Preservation Plan, as specified by Army Regulation 420-40, at this time funds are not available for WRAMC to undertake such an action." *Id.* at 47, A.R. at 3132. The Army does not dispute that its failure to expend more resources to maintain the District caused at least some of the significant damage. See CRMP at V-6, A.R. at 950.

B.   Walter Reed's Efforts in the Historic District

Since acquiring the Historic District in 1942, the Army has made some efforts to account for and preserve the historic value of the buildings, primarily through the development of Master Plans and, in 1992, a Cultural Resource Management Plan.[4] In 1967, the Army prepared a Master Plan that proposed demolishing the old buildings and erecting new ones; this plan was approved by the Maryland National Capital Parks and Planning Commission ("MNCPPC"). A.R. at 2003. A 1972 revised Master Plan retained the demolition proposal. At that time, however, MNCPPC raised concerns about the historic value of the buildings, and the Army delayed demolition. A.R. at 3975, 3979. On July 10, 1972, the Maryland Historical Trust ("MHT") nominated the property for inclusion in the National Register of Historic Places and, on September 14, 1972, the National Park Seminary Historic District was officially entered in the Register. A.R. at 1564-73. Walter Reed developed a further Master Plan in 1977, which was approved by the National Capitol Planning Commission ("NCPC"). A.R. at 586, 601, 608, 618.

In 1979, the General Services Administration proposed that Walter Reed "excess" the Historic District. See Executive Order 11954 Real Property Survey (Jan. 10, 1978) at 3,

---

[3][*Orig. fn.*] The reference is to section 106 of the National Historic Preservation Act, 16 U.S.C. § 470f.

[4][*Orig. fn.*] According to the Army, "the expressed purpose of the master plan is to establish a plan for the orderly and comprehensive development of the installation to satisfy immediate as well as long-range mission requirements in the most efficient and economical manner." A.R. at 2545; see Defs.' Mot. at 10 n. 3. A Master Plan "typically addresses maintenance concerns and contains such things as Architectural Surveys, Stabilization and Maintenance Guidelines, and a Cultural Resource Management Plan." Defs.' Mot. at 21.

Pls.' Ex. 13.[5] Walter Reed rejected that proposal, opting to retain the property, even while acknowledging that the buildings were underutilized at that time and that their fate was uncertain. U.S. Army Health Services Command Memorandum (July 6, 1979), Pls.' Ex. 14, A.R. at 4351; see also Unclassified Memorandum (Sept. 1981), A.R. at 2222. In the ensuing years, however, Walter Reed apparently continued to consider declaring the property to be excess and selling it off in order to redirect maintenance funds toward its medical mission. See Letter from Colonel Gerald D. Allgood to Maryland State Historic Preservation Office (May 14, 1984), A.R. at 1574 ("From a monetary standpoint, the Walter Reed Facilities Engineer would like to be relieved from the responsibilities for these 19 [historic] buildings as they use a disproportionate amount of his limited operation and maintenance budget."); see also Installation Survey Report (Apr. 17, 1984), A.R. at 2131-77 (identifying potential areas of Forest Glen for sale). In 1984, however, the Army abandoned the idea of excessing the property "as a result of the limited monetary return and expected time required (8–12 years) to excess the property." Defs.' Statement of Facts Identified By Plaintiffs to Which There is A Genuine Issue ("Defs.' Statement of Facts in Dispute") at 1 p 28; see Pls.' Statement of Material Facts p 30; see also 1989 Survey at 3, A.R. at 287.

In 1989, the Army completed another survey of historic buildings in the District in compliance with its own historic preservation regulation, Army Regulation 420-40. 1989 Survey, A.R. at 287. The 1989 Survey noted that "[h]istoric preservation was not a consideration to the Army at this site" until Army Regulation 420-40 became effective in 1984. It further stated that the Army's mission at Walter Reed and historic preservation were "in conflict," and that the underutilization of the old buildings on the site put "these facilities on a lower priority for maintenance funds when competition for funding direct medical facilities is severe." *Id.*

In 1991, the Commander of Walter Reed, Major General Richard D. Cameron, again recommended that the Historic District be excessed. As part of his recommendation, Major General Cameron noted that "the current condition of the buildings to be excessed is deteriorating to the point that it is hazardous to life and property and cannot be repaired or maintained at our justifiable cost." Memorandum to Headquarters of the Department of the Army ("HQDA") from Major General Richard Cameron (April 26, 1991), Pls.' Ex. 28, A.R. at 316.

In 1991, Walter Reed consulted with the National Capital Planning Commission ("NCPC"), the Montgomery County Planning Board ("MCPB"), the Maryland Historical Trust and the Maryland State Historic Preservation Officer ("SHPO"). A new proposed Master Plan was submitted to the MCPB on September 12, 1991. At a meeting on October 15, 1991, the MCPB and the NCPC raised 19 items of concern about the Master Plan, seven of which directly concerned the Historic District. A.R. at 586–89. On April 30, 1992, the NCPC approved the proposed Master Plan, as modified, and specifically noted that certain concerns relating to historic preservation had been resolved. A.R. at 601, 608, 618. See also A.R. at 355 (letter from the MNCPPC reflecting cooperation with Walter Reed on Master Plan); A.R. at 1611–1618 (letter from the MNCPPC to Senator Paul Sarbanes dated September 22, 1993, stating that Walter Reed had "fully cooperated" with the MNCPPC). The

---

[5][*Orig. fn.*] The Army has established procedures to decide when real property over which it has control is surplus to its needs and is no longer required and the various ways in which such surplus or excess property may be disposed of. See 32 C.F.R. §§ 644.326–644.329.

1992 Master Plan approved by the NCPC stated several times that the Historic District would be excessed. Master Plan Report (March 1992) ("1992 Master Plan") at ES-5, 12-2, Pls.' Ex. 6, A.R. at 697, 808.

As part of the 1992 Master Plan, KFS Historic Preservation Group prepared a report for the Army Corps of Engineers providing recommendations for stabilization and maintenance of the Historic District. These recommendations were adopted by Walter Reed as the "Forest Glen Section WRAMC Stabilization and Maintenance Guidelines" in accordance with the Secretary of the Interior's Standards for Rehabilitation Guidelines. Forest Glen Section WRAMC Stabilization and Maintenance Guidelines (Aug. 14, 1992), Pls.' Ex. 38, A.R. at 3836-50; see 36 C.F.R. pt. 68.[6] In December 1992, Army consultants prepared a "Roof Repair and Replacement Study," documenting damage to various roofs and windows and recommending immediate maintenance. Pls.' Ex. 36, A.R. at 3207. In October 1993, the Army commissioned a Stabilization Report from Ward Bucher to identify emergency stabilization measures. Pls.' Ex. 39, Attachment B.

The Army also commissioned a Cultural Resource Management Plan ("CRMP") in 1992. A.R. at 922. The Plan, prepared by KFS Historic Preservation Group, is dated August 14, 1992, but it was held out by the Army as having been formally adopted by Walter Reed as early as April 27, 1992. A.R. at 302, 305, 320. The Maryland Historical Trust never approved the CRMP, although the parties dispute the reason for the non-approval. See Letter from Maryland Historical Trust to Lt. Colonel Roy D. Quick (June 4, 1992), A.R. at 345 (describing the CRMP as "a comprehensive approach for the protection of the National Park Seminary" that "includes the necessary components as outlined in the Section 110 regulations" but raising several issues requiring resolution before the MHT would approve the plan). In the Section 106 Coordination documents, issued in April 1992, the Army described the CRMP as satisfying the requirements of Army Regulation 420-40 as well as Section 110 of the NHPA. A.R. at 305.[7]

On August 20, 1992, Walter Reed initiated formal consultations with the Advisory Council on Historic Preservation ("ACHP") under Section 106 of the NHPA with regard to the deci-

---

[6][*Orig. fn.*] Under the NHPA, the Secretary of the Interior is responsible for promulgating standards and guidelines governing the placement of properties in the National Register, professional standards for the preservation of federally owned or controlled properties, and federal agency responsibilities under the NHPA. 16 U.S.C. §§ 470a(a)(6), (a)(7), (b), (f), (g).

[7][*Orig. fn.*] The summary of Army Regulation 420-40 (May 15, 1984), describes that regulation as follows:

> [It] prescribes management responsibilities and standards for the treatment of historic properties... on land controlled by the Army. It describes the steps for locating, identifying, evaluating, and treating historic properties in compliance with the [NHPA]. It explains how these steps can be done through a Historic Preservation Plan (HPP) and, as required, in consultation with the Advisory Council on Historic Preservation and the appropriate State Historic Preservation Officer.

Army Regulation 420-40 at i. The entire Army Regulation is contained in Plaintiffs' Exhibit 46.

sion to excess the District. A.R. at 302-04, 312. A Cooperative Agreement between Walter Reed and Montgomery County was signed and a consulting firm was selected to perform an Alternative Use Study which was completed in May 1995. Declaration of Major General Ronald R. Blanck ("Blanck Decl.") p. 10 (July 8, 1996), Exhibit 1 to Defs.' Supp. Mem. (Aug. 5, 1996). Defendants now represent that Walter Reed has decided not to excess the District but rather will retain and reuse it and has or intends to initiate consultation procedures regarding repairs. Blanck Decl. pp 10, 12; Defs.' Supp. Mem. (Aug. 5, 1996) at 3.

Plaintiffs assert that although the 1992 Master Plan committed $2 million toward immediate repair and renovation activities, no such activities have taken place. They also claim that the Army failed to implement any of the October 1993 Bucher Report's recommendations, while defendants state that repairs were undertaken in response to the Bucher Report. A.R. at 1661–62. The parties also disagree about the Army's commitment to undertake future repairs: Plaintiffs characterize the Army as refusing to fund future measures, while defendants state that Walter Reed has expended millions of dollars in maintenance, repair and preservation of the Historic District—including recent expenditures of $367,468 in FY 1992; $508,151 in FY 1993; $290,527 from October 1993 to August 1994, A.R. at 1712; and $46,000 from January through July 1996, Blanck Decl. p 7—and that certain projects have yet to be funded but that funding has been or is being sought.[8]

Defendants acknowledge that the facilities in the Historic District are a lower priority for maintenance funds than the direct medical care facilities, such as the hospital, since the Historic District buildings for the most part have no function and are not being used. Defs.' Mot. at 27. Walter Reed has an annual maintenance and repair budget of approximately $5 million for all three of its sections, including Forest Glen; that budget was cut by $500,000 in 1994. A.R. at 1649, 1659. Walter Reed also has a backlog of $80 million worth of work orders. A.R. at 1649, 1659.

* * *

III. THE NATIONAL HISTORIC PRESERVATION ACT

Section 106 of the National Historic Preservation Act is a procedural provision and the provision under which almost all NHPA cases are prosecuted. It provides:

---

[8][*Orig. fn.*] The record reflects approximately $2,915,508 spent on repairs, maintenance and preservation in the Historic District since 1989: A.R. at 1712 (1989–1993 expenditures of $2,080,300); Declaration of Henry J. Henley (Feb. 1, 1996) pp. 11–14 (nearly $500,000 spent on roof repair in April 1994, $60,000 spent from October 1, 1994, to December 31, 1995, on outside contractors performing repairs, $191,894 spent in FY 1995 on maintenance, and $83,314 spent in the first quarter of FY 1996), Exhibit 1 to Defs.' Memorandum in Opposition to Pls.' Motion for Preliminary Injunction; A.R. at 1896–1966 (chronicling ongoing daily, weekly and annual maintenance program). See also Defs.' Statement of Material Facts in Dispute p. 41; Blanck Decl. p. 8; Defs.' Supp. Mem. (Aug. 5, 1996) at 5. The record does not reflect expenditures made between 1984 and 1989. Plaintiffs argue that the Army has not demonstrated that the bulk of these expenditures were made on maintenance and repair items that are material to the legal issues in this case, Pls.' Response to Defs.' Statement of Material Facts Not in Genuine Dispute pp. 40, 44, 50, 51, 53, 54, but they do not dispute that such sums were expended.

The head of any Federal agency having direct or indirect jurisdiction over a proposed Federal or federally assisted undertaking in any State... shall, prior to the approval of the expenditure of any Federal funds on the undertaking..., take into account the effect of the undertaking on any district, site, building, structure, or object that is included in or eligible for inclusion in the National Register. The head of any such Federal agency shall afford the Advisory Council on Historic Preservation... a reasonable opportunity to comment with regard to such undertaking.

16 U.S.C. § 470f. The majority of NHPA cases that have reached the courts concern instances where a federal agency is alleged to have failed to comply with the consultation provisions of Section 106.

Section 110 of the NHPA was added to the NHPA in 1980 to "clarif[y] and codif [y] the minimum responsibilities expected of Federal agencies in carrying out the purposes of th[e] Act." *Lee v.Thornburgh*, 877 F.2d 1053, 1057 (D.C. Cir. 1989) (quoting H.R.REP. NO. 1457, 96th Cong., 2d Sess. 36 (1980), reprinted in 1980 U.S.C.C.A.N. 6378, 6399). Although the language of the section is broad, it was not "intended to change the preservation responsibilities of Federal agencies as required by any other laws, executive orders or regulations...." *Id.* Section 110 provides in relevant part:

(a)(1) The heads of all Federal agencies shall assume responsibility for the preservation of historic properties which are owned or controlled by such agency.... Each agency shall undertake, consistent with the preservation of such properties and the mission of the agency and the professional standards established pursuant to section 470a(g) of this title, any preservation, as may be necessary to carry out this section.[11]

(2) Each Federal agency shall establish... in consultation with the Secretary, a preservation program for the identification of, evaluation, and nomination to the National Register of Historic Places, and protection of historic properties. Such program shall ensure...

* * *

(B) that such properties under the jurisdiction or control of the agency as are listed or may be eligible for the National Register are managed and maintained in a way that considers the preservation of their historic, archaeological, architectural, and cultural values in compliance with section 470f [Section 106] of this title....

* * *

(d) Consistent with the agency's missions and mandates, all Federal agencies shall carry out agency programs and projects... in accordance with the purposes of this subchapter and give consideration to programs and projects which will further the purposes of this subchapter....

* * *

---

[11][*Orig. fn.*] 16 U.S.C. § 470a(g) provides: "In consultation with the Advisory Council on Historic Preservation, the Secretary [of the Interior] shall promulgate guidelines for Federal agency responsibilities under section 470h-2 of this title." The guidelines are located at 53 Fed. Reg. 4729 (Feb. 17, 1988) ("Section 110 Guidelines"). See also Secretary of the Interior's Standards and Guidelines for Archeology and Historic Preservation, 48 Fed. Reg. 44716 (Sept. 29, 1983). 16 U.S.C. § 470w(8) defines "preservation" to "include[ ] identification, evaluation, recordation, documentation, curation, acquisition, protection, management, rehabilitation, restoration, stabilization, maintenance and reconstruction, or any combination of the foregoing activities."

(f) Prior to the approval of any Federal undertaking which may directly and adversely affect any National Historic Landmark, the head of the responsible Federal agency shall, to the maximum extent possible, undertake such planning and actions as may be necessary to minimize harm to such landmark, and shall afford the Advisory Council on Historic Preservation a reasonable opportunity to comment on the undertaking.

16 U.S.C. § 470h-2(a)(1), (a)(2), (d), (f) (as amended 1992).

In this case, plaintiffs assert that the Army's actions in permitting the decay and deterioration of the Historic District violate the mandate of Section 110. Plaintiffs would have the Court interpret Section 110(a)(1) as creating an independent substantive requirement that agencies engage in minimal preservationist activities so long as such activities are consistent with the agency's mission. Under such an interpretation, whether Walter Reed violated the NHPA by permitting the buildings of the Historic District to deteriorate would be a question separate and apart from whether it also violated the procedural provisions of the Act contained in Section 106 and other subsections of Section 110. Only one court has come close to ruling on this interpretive question. See *North Oakland Voters Alliance v. City of Oakland*, 1992 WL 367096, (N.D. Cal. 1992) (finding that plaintiffs stated a claim under the NHPA based on Oakland's failure to maintain and preserve historic property while engaging in the Section 106 consultation process).

Defendants reply that all of the requirements of the NHPA, including those in Section 110, are procedural, that the NHPA is designed to ensure that federal agencies merely take into account or consider the effect of their actions on historic places as part of the planning process for those properties, that there is no substantive requirement that agencies undertake particular preservationist activities at all, and that Congress intended the provisions of Sections 106 and 110 to have a limited reach. Defendants' underlying premise is that the statute does not mandate preservation but merely encourages it, citing this Circuit's opinion in *Lee v. Thornburgh*, 877 F.2d at 1056. They also rely on *Waterford Citizens' Assoc. v. Reilly*, 970 F.2d 1287, 1290 (4th Cir. 1992) ("Congress did not intend [Section 106] to impose general obligations on federal agencies to affirmatively protect preservation interests."); *Connecticut Trust for Historic Preservation v. ICC*, 841 F.2d 479, 483–84 (2d Cir. 1988) ("NEPA and NHPA require only that agencies acquire information before acting."); *United States v. 162.20 Acres of Land, More or Less, Etc.*, 639 F.2d 299, 302 (5th Cir.) ("[Section 106] neither... forbid[s] the destruction of historic sites nor command[s] their preservation."), *cert. denied*, 454 U.S. 828, 102 S.Ct. 120, 70 L.Ed.2d 103 (1981). Each of these cases, however, focuses on the language of Section 106 and does not address the effect, if any, of the seemingly more substantive language of Section 110. Indeed, most courts discuss the obligations of Section 106 and the Act as a whole as if they were interchangeable.

A. The Section 106 Consultation Process

Section 106 of the NHPA requires that agencies give the Advisory Council on Historic Preservation a reasonable opportunity to comment on any "undertaking" that will "adversely affect" a listed property. 16 U.S.C. § 470f; see *McMillan Park Committee v. National Capital Planning Comm'n*, 968 F.2d at 1284–85; *Lee v. Thornburgh*, 877 F.2d at 1056. The

NHPA defines "undertaking," in relevant part, as "a project, activity, or program funded in whole or in part under the direct or indirect jurisdiction of a Federal agency" if carried out by a federal agency, with federal financial assistance or requiring a federal permit, license or approval. 16 U.S.C. § 470w(7). 36 C.F.R. § 800.2(o) defines an "undertaking" as

> any project, activity or program that can result in changes in the character or use of historic properties.... The project, activity or program must be under the direct or indirect jurisdiction of a Federal agency. Undertakings include new and continuing projects, activities, or programs and any of their elements not previously considered under section 106.

36 C.F.R. § 800.9(b)(4) defines an "adverse effect" of an undertaking as including but not limited to "[n]eglect of a property resulting in its deterioration or destruction."

Different circuits describe the Section 106 process as imposing more or less stringent or limited obligations upon agencies. Compare *United States v. 162.20 Acres of Land, More or Less, Etc.*, 639 F.2d at 302 ("While the [NHPA] may seem to be no more than a 'command to consider,' it must be noted that the language is mandatory and the scope is broad.") with *Waterford Citizens' Association v. Reilly*, 970 F.2d at 1290–91 ("[T]he scope of the obligations imposed upon federal agencies by the enactment of section 106 is quite narrow."). Nevertheless, Section 106 is universally interpreted as requiring agencies to consult and consider and not to engage in any particular preservation activities per se. The issue here is when the Army became obligated to consult with the Advisory Council on Historic Preservation and whether it did so at that time.

The Historic District was listed in the National Register in 1972. The Army decided not to excess the Historic District as early as 1979 and cemented that initial decision in 1984 despite having acquired additional information. Yet, no "Section 106 Report" was prepared until 1990, and that was done in connection with the preparation of a revised Master Plan in 1991.[12] Furthermore, there were no consultations with the relevant boards, commissions and historic trusts until 1991, and the revised Master Plan was not finally modified and approved until 1992. The question is whether any of these actions—or lack of action—violated the NHPA. The Army argues that until it affirmatively decided to excess the District in 1991 there was no "undertaking" on which to comment. Plaintiffs assert that the Army's failure to maintain the Historic District since at least 1984, when the Army made its decision not to excess the District, constitutes "demolition by neglect" that warrants relief.

It is clear that "an agency need not satisfy the Section 106 process at all... unless it is engaged in an undertaking." *McMillan Park Committee v. National Capital Planning*

---

[12][*Orig. fn.*] Master Plans are general planning documents, see *supra* note 4, and do not trigger the section 106 consultation process. The Maryland Historical Trust itself has stated that the preparation of a Master Plan does not constitute an undertaking. A.R. at 590. Although plaintiffs do not expressly concede this point, see Pls.' Response to Defs.' Statement of Material Facts Not in Genuine Dispute p 42, plaintiffs do not assert that Master Plans are cognizable undertakings but rather dismiss them as mere proposals that do not satisfy the Army's obligations to engage in historic preservation. See Pls.' Mem at 23–24; Pls.' Opp'n at 20–24; Pls.' Reply at 17–19.

Comm'n, 968 F.2d at 1289. Although the regulations consider neglect of a property that results in deterioration or destruction to be a cognizable "adverse effect" of an undertaking, not every instance of neglect or destruction can be said to flow from a cognizable undertaking. As a general matter, the APA defines "agency action" to include "failure to act," 5 U.S.C. § 551(13), and, where an agency maintains a policy of inaction in the face of an explicit statutory mandate, generally a court may set that policy aside. *NAACP v. Secretary of Housing and Urban Development*, 817 F.2d at 160. The explicit terms of Section 106, however, require a finding not just of agency "action" but of an "undertaking—that is, "a project, activity, or program." 16 U.S.C. § 470w(7).

An agency's failure to act, without more, is not an "undertaking" under Section 106; indeed, if it were there would be a constant and ongoing requirement for ACHP comment and consultation. See *Sheridan Kalorama Historical Assoc. v. Christopher*, 49 F.3d at 754 (State Department's failure to disapprove Turkish Embassy's plan to demolish building was not an undertaking where no federal funds or approval were involved). On the other hand, an undertaking includes any "activity... that can result in changes in the character or use of historic properties" and may include not only new but also "continuing" projects. 36 C.F.R. § 800.2(o). Thus, the NHPA contemplates a certain level of agency vigilance even in the absence of a specific new project. For example, Section 106 procedures must be "applied to ongoing Federal actions as long as a Federal agency has opportunity to exercise authority at any stage of an undertaking where alterations might be made to modify its impact on historic preservation goals." *Vieux Carre Property Owners v. Brown*, 948 F.2d 1436, 1444–45 (5th Cir. 1991); see *Morris County Trust for Historic Preservation v. Pierce*, 714 F.2d 271, 280 (3d Cir. 1983); *WATCH v. Harris*, 603 F.2d 310, 326 (2d Cir.), *cert. denied*, 444 U.S. 995, 100 S.Ct. 530, 62 L.Ed.2d 426 (1979). Even the Army recognizes that such ongoing and routine activities as maintenance and repair may rise to the level of undertakings. Army Regulation 420-40, Glossary-3 (May 15, 1984), Pls.' Ex. 46. Accordingly, the analysis turns on the nature of the projects, activities and decisions that properly trigger Section 106 review.

In this regard, it is instructive to examine case law decided under the National Environmental Policy Act ("NEPA"), 42 U.S.C. §§ 4321–4361. While Section 106 of the NHPA and NEPA are not identical, many courts fruitfully compare them, and their similarities shed light on the issue of agency action and inaction. See *McMillan Park Committee v. National Capital Planning Comm'n*, 968 F.2d at 1290 (Randolph, J., concurring). In passing the NHPA, Congress inserted historic preservation concerns into all aspects of agency decision making by requiring agency heads to "take into account the effect of [any] undertaking" on historic buildings and structures, 16 U.S.C. § 470f, much as NEPA injects environmental concerns into all major federal actions. Both statutes require the government to conduct certain procedural and informational activities before embarking on projects that might affect, respectively, historic sites or the environment. Neither NEPA nor Section 106 mandates a particular outcome of governmental decisions; rather each defines the processes by which those decisions must be made. See *Apache Survival Coalition v. United States*, 21 F.3d 895, 906 (9th Cir. 1994); *Colorado River Indian Tribes v. Marsh*, 605 F. Supp. 1425, 1440 & n. 11 (C.D. Cal. 1985).

The obligation to prepare an environmental impact statement under NEPA is triggered by the proposal of a "major federal action," 42 U.S.C. § 4332(2)(C), which the court of appeals for this Circuit has interpreted as requiring either federal action or some "overt act" by the federal government that furthers the project of another sovereign or non-federal entity. *Defenders of Wildlife v. Andrus*, 627 F.2d 1238, 1244–45 (D.C. Cir. 1980) [citing *Kleppe v. Sierra Club*, 427 U.S. 390, 401, 96 S.Ct. 2718, 2726, 49 L.Ed.2d 576 (1976)]. In *Defenders of Wildlife*, the court ruled that the Secretary of the Interior's inaction—specifically, his failure to exercise his power to prevent the State of Alaska from killing 170 wolves—did not constitute a "federal action" requiring the preparation of an environmental impact statement. *Id.* at 1245. See also *Cross-Sound Ferry Services, Inc. v. ICC*, 934 F.2d 327, 334 (D.C. Cir. 1991) (describing *Defenders of Wildlife* as holding that an "agency's mere refusal to exercise its statutory authority to act" does not constitute a federal action).

In 1984, the Army decided not to excess the Historic District because the costs were too high and the process would take too long. Defs.' Statement of Facts in Dispute at 1 p. 28; Pls.' Statement of Material Facts p 30; 1989 Survey at 3, A.R. at 287. This was not a mere failure to prevent another entity from taking action, *cf. Sheridan Kalorama Historical Assoc. v. Christopher*, 49 F.3d at 754; *Defenders of Wildlife v. Andrus*, 627 F.2d at 1244–45, but a considered, affirmative decision by Walter Reed about how to allocate its limited resources. That decision had the sort of serious and long-term consequences for the Historic District that the NHPA requires be undertaken in consultation with the ACHP. Indeed, the record is replete with evidence attesting to the consideration given over the years to the decision whether to excess the District,[13] and defendants acknowledge that an affirmative decision was made in 1984 not to do so. Defs.' Statement of Facts in Dispute at 1 p. 28. Yet there were no Section 106 consultations with the Advisory Council on Historic Preservation, the National Capital Planning Commission or the various Maryland state agencies about the overall disposition of the Historic District until 1991. The Court concludes that the 1984 decision not to excess the District was an undertaking under Section 106. It therefore should have been made in consultation with the Advisory Council on Historic Preservation.

B.   Section 110, The Secretary's Section 110 Guidelines and the Army's Regulations

Plaintiffs contend that Walter Reed not only disregarded the Section 106 consultation process but also violated the substantive mandate contained in Section 110 to repair and maintain the buildings in the District. Agency obligations under Section 110, however, are far less defined than those under Section 106, and the parties vigorously disagree as to their scope and effect.

---

[13][*Orig. fn.*] See Memorandum from Major Franklin Goriup, WRAMC (July 6, 1979) (rejecting GSA proposal to excess Historic District), A.R. at 4351; Unclassified WRAMC Memorandum (July 2, 1979) (same), A.R. at 2225; Letter from Colonel Gerald D. Allgood, Army Health Services Command, to Maryland SHPO, (May 14, 1984), A.R. at 1574; Letter from Maryland Historical Trust to Colonel Allgood (June 21, 1984), A.R. at 1577; Letter from Major General Lewis Mologne to Army Medical Research and Development Command (July 27, 1984) (noting that the Historic District was to be sold), A.R. at 2853.

1. Section 110

The contested language of Section 110 reads as follows: "Each agency shall undertake, consistent with the preservation of such [historic] properties and the mission of the agency and the professional standards established pursuant to section 470a(g) of this title, any preservation, as may be necessary to carry out this section." 16 U.S.C. § 470h-2(a)(1). In addition, each agency "shall ensure" that properties listed in or eligible for the National Register of Historic Places "are managed and maintained in a way that considers the preservation of their historic [and] architectural... values in compliance with Section 470f [Section 106] of this title." 16 U.S.C. § 470h- 2(a)(2)(B). In this case, the District was listed in the National Register in 1972 and the Army's most significant decision was taken in 1984 when the Army decided not to excess the District but rather to retain control over it. That 1984 decision, and the ongoing policy thereafter to treat the historic preservation of the District's buildings as a low priority, gave rise to much of the deterioration now complained of by plaintiffs. See 1989 Survey at 3, A.R. at 287.

The meaning of Section 110 is not clear on its face. On the one hand, the use of the word "shall" in Sections 110(a)(1) and (2) suggests that agencies have a mandatory obligation to engage in preservation, separate and apart from their obligations under Section 106. On the other hand, the section refers several times to the Section 106 consultation process and uses the word "consider" three times in describing an agency's responsibilities. 16 U.S.C. § 470h-2(a)(2)(B) & (C), (d). It also provides that the agency must act consistent with its "missions and mandates." 16 U.S.C.§ 470h-2(d). Reading the section as a whole, this suggests that Section 110 represents an elucidation and extension of the Section 106 process but not its replacement by new and independent substantive obligations of a different kind.

Although the District of Columbia Circuit has interpreted the NHPA on several occasions, none of its decisions has addressed the scope of Section 110(a) or the federal government's obligations thereunder. Rather, the cases that have reached our court of appeals have either primarily concerned the scope of Section 106 or dealt with projects undertaken by non-federal entities. In *Lee v. Thornburgh*, 877 F.2d 1053 (D.C. Cir. 1989), the court held that Section 106 and subsections (b) and (d) of Section 110 did not apply to a project undertaken by the District of Columbia because no federal agency had authority to license or approve expenditures for the project. The court concluded that the requirements of the Act "are triggered only when approval or financial assistance from a federal agency are involved." *Id.* at 1056. The court recognized that "Congress intended these provisions to have a limited reach; they are aimed solely at discouraging federal agencies from ignoring preservation values in projects they initiate, approve funds for or otherwise control." *Id.* While the court construed two subsections of Section 110 (although not subsection (a) at issue here), it did so specifically in order to answer the question of whether the statute applied to the District of Columbia project at all. As a result, the court did not describe what the federal government's obligations would have been under Section 110(a) if that section of the statute had in fact been implicated.

In *McMillan Park Committee v. National Capital Planning Comm'n*, 968 F.2d 1283 (D.C. Cir. 1992), the court decided that the act of amending a comprehensive plan governing the commercial development of McMillan Park did not constitute an "undertaking" under Section 106 because the possible adverse effects of the amendments had previously been considered; the court did not discuss Section 110 at all. In *Sheridan Kalorama Historical Ass'n. v. Christopher*, 49 F.3d 750 (D.C. Cir. 1995), the court decided that the Secretary of State's failure to disapprove the Republic of Turkey's proposal to demolish its chancery building did not constitute an "undertaking" for Section 106 purposes; again the court did not discuss Section 110. While each of these decisions might be read to imply that the only obligations imposed by the NHPA flow from Section 106 because the court did not mention any obligation arising under Section 110, the Court declines to infer such a sweeping conclusion from the mere absence of discussion.

The legislative history of Section 110, which was added to the NHPA in 1980, provides limited guidance as to the section's purposes. See H.R.REP. NO. 1457, 96th Cong., 2d Sess. 36 (1980), *reprinted in* 1980 U.S.C.C.A.N. 6378, 6399 ("House Report"). The House Report describes the aims of Section 110 in relevant part as follows:

> The new Section 110 clarifies and codifies the minimum responsibilities expected of Federal agencies in carrying out the purposes of this Act.... It is not intended to change the preservation responsibilities of Federal agencies as required by any other laws, executive orders or regulations, nor limit the President's authority to specify additional responsibilities.
>
> Section 110(a)(1) requires a Federal agency to assume preservation responsibilities for properties owned or under the control of the agency. It is intended that the degree of preservation responsibility be commensurate with the extent of the agency's interest in or control of a particular property.... Agencies are further directed to undertake such preservation as may be necessary (including rehabilitation, documentation, etc.) in accordance with the Secretary's standards....
>
> * * *
>
> Section 110(d) requires that, consistent with their missions and mandates, all Federal agencies will carry out their programs... so that historic preservation interests are affirmatively addressed.... It is recognized that most Federal agencies have a primary purpose other than historic preservation; however, it is reasonable to expect that they also view themselves as multiple resource managers responding to diverse economic, social and environmental concerns—including the concerns of historic preservation....
>
> Section 110(f) establishes a higher standard of care to be exercised by Federal agencies when considering undertakings that may directly and adversely affect National Historic Landmarks. Agencies are directed to undertake, to the maximum extent possible, such planning and actions as may be necessary to minimize harm to such a landmark and to provide the Advisory Council on Historic Preservation a reasonable opportunity to comment on such proposed actions.... This section does not supersede Section 106, but complements it by setting a higher standard for agency planning in relationship to landmarks before the agency brings the matter to the Council....
>
> House Report at 36–38, *reprinted in* 1980 U.S.C.C.A.N. at 6399–6401.

The Court concludes that Section 110(a) cannot be read to create new substantive preservationist obligations separate and apart from the overwhelmingly procedural thrust of the NHPA as described by every court that has considered the Act. In interpreting other subsections of Section 110, the D.C. Circuit has reasoned that "the legislative history of § 110, though scant, supports [ ] reading [ ] that section in conjunction with § 106." *Lee v. Thornburgh*, 877 F.2d at 1057. The court pointed out that when Section 110 was added to the NHPA in 1980, Congress made clear that the new section "is not intended to change the preservation responsibilities of Federal agencies as required by any other laws, executive orders or regulations." *Id.* Plaintiffs' interpretation would create vast new preservationist responsibilities unrelated to the consultation provisions of Section 106 to which the rest of Section 110 constantly refers. Indeed, under plaintiffs' theory, Section 110 would replace Section 106 as the heart and soul of the NHPA, requiring an agency to spend money on historic preservation regardless of whether it was engaged in or contemplating an undertaking. Nothing in the statute or the legislative history suggests that Congress intended to alter the nature of the NHPA in such a fashion when it amended it in 1980, and the Court finds that Congress had no such intention.

2.   The Secretary's Guidelines and the Army's Regulations

The guidelines promulgated by the Secretary of the Interior support this interpretation. See Guidelines for Federal Agency Responsibilities Under Section 110 of the National Historic Preservation Act ("Section 110 Guidelines"), 53 Fed. Reg. 4728 (Feb. 17, 1988); see also Secretary of the Interior's Standards and Guidelines for Archeology and Historic Preservation, 48 Fed. Reg. 44716 (Sept. 29, 1983).[14] The Section 110 Guidelines state that "[t]he basic purpose of section 110(a)(1) is to cause agencies when planning or carrying out their programs, to consider whether there are ways that the use of historic properties can be effectively integrated into such programs so as to advance program purposes while preserving or even enhancing the integrity of the properties." Section 110 Guidelines, 53 Fed. Reg. at 4731. The Guidelines further explain:

> Section 110(a)(1) also requires agencies to "undertake, consistent with the preservation of such properties and the mission of the agency... any preservation as may be necessary to carry out this section."... Preservation plans should be developed for historic property types that the agency knows it has under its jurisdiction or control.... In managing historic properties, agencies should consider a variety of factors in addition to, but not in lieu of, the significant element or elements of the properties which qualify them for inclusion in the National Register.
>   Section 110 Guidelines, 53 Fed. Reg. at 4732.

The Section 110 Guidelines require the development by agencies of historic preservation plans and list a variety of factors that agencies "should consider" in establishing such plans and in managing historic properties. Nowhere, however, do they state that agencies have an affirmative obligation to spend money to preserve historic buildings. Rather, the entire thrust of the Guidelines is to channel agency decisionmaking in an informed preservationist direction consistent with the agency's mission. Since the NHPA expressly delegates the responsibility for promulgating such guidelines to the Secretary of the Department of the Interior, the Secretary's interpretation of Section 110 is entitled to substantial deference from the Court. *Lyng v. Payne*, 476 U.S. 926, 939, 106 S.Ct. 2333, 2341–42, 90 L.Ed.2d 921 (1986); *Orengo Caraballo v. Reich*, 11 F.3d 186, 192–93 (D.C. Cir. 1993).

---

[14][*Orig. fn.*] 16 U.S.C. § 470a(g) requires "the Secretary [of the Interior] [to] promulgate
    guidelines for Federal agency responsibilities under section 470h-2 of this title."

Walter Reed's obligations under Section 110 are further defined by the Army's own regulations. Army Regulation 420-40, promulgated in 1984 in compliance with the NHPA and various of the Secretary of the Interior's regulations and guidelines for historic preservation, provides in detail for the preparation of a Historic Preservation Plan ("HPP") as the main mechanism by which the Army is to comply with the requirements and implementing regulations of Sections 106 and 110 of the NHPA. Pls.' Ex. 46. Army Regulation 420-40 also provides guidelines for the programming, staffing, contracting, information management and disposal procedures pertaining to historic properties. Plaintiffs assert that the Army violated Army Regulation 420-40 both by neglecting the Historic District and by failing to prepare a Historic Preservation Plan and that, in so doing, it violated the NHPA. The Army replies that the Cultural Resource Management Plan ("CRMP"), A.R. at 922, adopted in 1992, serves as the HPP for the Historic District and therefore that Walter Reed is in compliance with its own regulations and with Sections 106 and 110 of the NHPA.[15]

The Court finds that the CRMP was the Historic Preservation Plan for the Historic District and that it satisfies the requirements of Army Regulation 420-40. The CRMP contains an extensive discussion of the history, condition and present needs of the Historic District. It proposes a detailed protection plan outlining the procedures for maintaining the historic properties, including the procedures to be followed under Section 106. A.R. at 941–62.[16] Indeed, plaintiffs concede that the CRMP "provide[s] very specific and detailed guidance for the treatment and protection of the Historic District." Pls.' Mem. at 16 n. 6.[17] Accordingly, the Court finds that the Army has been in compliance with the Section 110 Guidelines and its own regulations since 1992 when the CRMP was created and officially adopted.

Plaintiffs argue, however, that even if the CRMP for the Historic District serves as a valid HPP, Walter Reed has not carried out the preservation and maintenance activities required by the CRMP, Army Regulation 420-40 and Section 110, and that the Army therefore is still out of compliance. For their part, defendants point to nearly three million dollars that have been spent on the Historic District since 1989, nearly two million of which was spent since 1992 when the CRMP was promulgated. See note 8, *supra*. While it is true that the CRMP calls for two million dollars to be spent specifically on roof repair and mainte-

---

[15][*Orig. fn.*] While an agency is entitled to substantial deference when it interprets statutes and regulations whose enforcement is committed to that particular agency, *Orengo Caraballo v. Reich*, 11 F.3d at 192–93, the NHPA delegates to the Army no particular interpretive or enforcement authority. Thus, the Army's interpretation of the NHPA is not entitled to the deference accorded to the Secretary of the Interior.

[16][*Orig. fn.*] By contrast, the 1992 Master Plan, like the earlier Master Plans, devotes a single general section to the Historic District and does not reflect the substantial level of consideration and analysis required by the Section 110 Guidelines. 1991 Master Plan at 3–7, A.R. at 726.

[17][*Orig. fn.*] Plaintiffs assert that the CRMP was only a draft and was never formally approved or adopted by the Army, but the portions of the record to which they cite do not support that assertion. Deposition of Henry Henley ("Henley Dep.") at 262 (Excerpts from Jan. 18, 27, Feb. 1, 1995), Pls.' Ex. 49; Letter from William Pencek, Deputy SHPO, Maryland Historical Trust, to Lt. Colonel Quick, WRAMC, at 4–6 (June 4, 1992), A.R. at 348–50.

nance, money that does not appear to have been allocated, the Army has explained that those funds, while originally available, were diverted to other Army projects and that Walter Reed continues to seek funding. A.R. at 1669–70. The Court concludes that since Walter Reed has formally complied with Army Regulation 420-40 by creating and adopting the CRMP, has spent substantial sums of money on repair, maintenance and preservation activities (although obviously not enough to avoid significant deterioration) and continues to make efforts to obtain additional funding to carry out its obligations under the CRMP, Walter Reed has complied with the Secretary's Guidelines and its own regulations. Its manner of doing so cannot be said to be arbitrary and capricious. It therefore has not violated Section 110 of the NHPA, at least since 1992.

From 1984 until 1992, however, Walter Reed was in compliance neither with Section 110 nor with its own regulations.[18] Defendants have identified no documents in the administrative record that demonstrate that Walter Reed engaged in a deliberate, considered decisionmaking process to assess, consider and plan for the preservation needs of the Historic District during that period. Until the CRMP was adopted in 1992, the only planning document to make any reference to the historic needs of the District at all was the Master Plan of 1977, A.R. at 581, and between 1977 and 1992 no Master Plans were developed. See Def.'s Statement of Material Facts pp. 36–40. It was not until 1991, when Major General Cameron proposed to excess the District and triggered a series of assessments by Walter Reed, that Walter Reed began seriously to assess its obligations under the NHPA. Accordingly, on this record, the Court finds that Walter Reed violated Section 110 and its own Army Regulation 420-40 beginning in 1984. These violations lasted until 1992 when the considered decisionmaking process finally produced the CRMP.

IV.   CONCLUSION

From 1984, when Army Regulation 420-40 formalized the Army's obligations under Section 110 of the NHPA, until 1992, the Army violated Section 110 and its own regulations by neglecting the buildings in the Historic District without considering how to undertake, consistent with its mission, their preservation or alternative use. The Army also violated Section 106 of the NHPA in 1984 by failing to initiate consultation procedures with the Advisory Council on Historic Preservation when it decided not to excess the District, even though it was clear that the decision would cause further deterioration of the historic buildings.

Plaintiffs acknowledge that the Army undertook the proper Section 106 consultation procedures with respect to Major General Cameron's 1991 proposal to excess the District. The Army now represents to the Court that it is presently or is about to be engaged in further Section 106 consultation procedures because it has decided not to excess the District after

---

[18][*Orig. fn.*] Walter Reed might arguably have been in violation of section 110 as early as 1980 when Section 110 was added to the NHPA. Since the Secretary of the Interior's Section 110 Guidelines were not promulgated until 1988, and Army Regulation 420-40 not until 1984, it is disputable whether the Army was properly on notice of its obligations prior to 1984. From 1984 onward, however, Walter Reed's obligations were clearly defined by Army Regulation 420-40 interpreting Section 110.

all. Blanck Decl. p. 7, 10–12; Defs.' Supp.Mem. at 3–6 (Aug. 5, 1996). The Court concludes that no purpose would be served by ordering the Army to engage in Section 106 consultation with respect to decisions made years ago. Similarly, Walter Reed's 1992 Cultural Resource Management Plan, while belated, rectifies the procedural and informational harm done by the Army's failure to prepare a Historic Preservation Plan between 1984 and 1992. Accordingly, the Court will not order the Army to undertake the consultations and assessments contemplated by Sections 106 and 110 of the NHPA and Army Regulation 420-40 since the Army has represented to the Court that it is in the process of doing so.

This leaves the very serious issue of the deterioration and damage that has resulted from the Army's neglect and failure to expend adequate resources on the preservation of the Historic District. Plaintiffs do not ask the Court, as in the typical NHPA case, to require the Army to halt a proposed undertaking such as the demolition or construction of a building, but rather to repair existing buildings to bring them back to a former level of integrity that pre-dates the Army's neglect. Plaintiffs argue that the Army's noncompliance with the NHPA and its own regulations caused significant harm to the buildings in the Historic District and that the Army is now obligated to make the District whole.

Plaintiffs are clearly correct that the Army's noncompliance has caused real harm. On the other hand, Walter Reed currently spends significant funds on repairing and maintaining the District and it is now in compliance with Sections 106 and 110 and its own regulations. The Court having concluded that Section 110 was not intended to create new substantive preservationist obligations, it follows that the NHPA does not give the Court the authority to order the Army to turn back the hands of time, or even to spend more money to halt further deterioration while the Army completes its plans for the Historic District.

This conclusion flows from the limited nature of Section 110 itself. The NHPA requires the Army to undertake the level of preservation necessary to carry out Section 110, consistent with its mission. 16 U.S.C. § 470h-2(a)(1). Section 110 is to be read in conjunction with Section 106 which constitutes the main thrust of the NHPA. The case law in this and other circuits holds that an agency's duty to act under the NHPA is triggered only when there is an undertaking and that that obligation, once triggered, is procedural in nature. Section 110 itself does not require anything more, since the addition of Section 110 to the statute was not intended to expand the preservationist responsibilities of federal agencies beyond what the NHPA already required. Moreover, the Section 110 Guidelines demonstrate that the Secretary of the Interior has interpreted Section 110 to embody the requirement that agencies thoroughly consider preservationist goals in all aspects of agency decisionmaking but that Section 110 does not itself affirmatively mandate the preservation of historic buildings or other resources. The Court therefore concludes that Section 110, read in conjunction with Section 106, the statute as a whole and the case law, did not require Walter Reed to undertake any preservation beyond what was necessary to comply to the fullest extent possible with, and in the spirit of, the Section 106 consultation process and with its own Historic Preservation Plan. While the Army could and, in a perfect world, should have done more to preserve the Historic District, the APA does not permit this Court to substitute its judgment for that of the agency with respect to resource allocations, so long as those allocations are not arbitrary or capricious, an abuse of discretion or contrary to law. See *Citizens to Preserve Overton Park v. Volpe*, 401 U.S. at 415, 91 S.Ct. at 823. While the Court may disagree with the Army's decisions—individual and cumulative—to permit the buildings of the Historic District to deteriorate, the Court finds that the Army's expenditure of nearly two million dollars in repairs and maintenance since 1992 was not insignificant, consistent with

Walter Reed's mission and mandate.[19] The Court concludes that the Army's level of expenditure, although low in relation to the expensive preservation needs of the Historic District, did not constitute an abuse of discretion or an arbitrary and capricious response to the dictates of Section 110, the Secretary of the Interior's Guidelines and Army Regulation 420-40. The Army's course of conduct since 1992 therefore was permissible under the NHPA and the Court finds no basis in law on which to require the Army to invest any more funds in the District.

It may seem ironic for the Court to find that Walter Reed violated the NHPA and its own regulations for over eight years and nevertheless to conclude that the Army cannot now be ordered to fix what it undoubtedly broke. Congress has decided as a legislative matter, however, to institutionalize the national commitment to historic preservation by creating certain planning, consultation and decisionmaking procedures to assure adequate consideration of preservationist concerns and not, as plaintiffs would have it, by requiring federal agencies to spend the taxpayers' money on historic preservation when it is not earmarked for such purposes.

Lest this conclusion be misunderstood as somehow diminishing the Army's obligations under the NHPA or excusing its derelictions over the years, it should be emphasized that merely because a statutory requirement is described as "procedural" does not render it any less meaningful or mandatory. As the Fifth Circuit has observed, "[w]hile the [NHPA] may seem to be no more than a 'command to consider,' it must be noted that the language is mandatory and the scope is broad." *United States v. 162.20 Acres of Land, More or Less, Etc.*, 639 F.2d at 302. Merely because "it is impossible for us to know with any degree of certainty just what the end result of the NHPA process would be[, it would be] inappropriate to pre-judge those results...," or to relieve an agency from its obligation to engage in the process. *Vieux Carre Property Owners v. Brown*, 948 F.2d at 1446–47. Historic preservation by its very nature demands action to stem the otherwise inevitable wear and tear of time itself, and in obeying the NHPA's "command to consider," agencies necessarily will consider taking actions that they might not otherwise even have contemplated. While courts may not be authorized under the NHPA to order a recalcitrant agency to rebuild decaying historic treasures, it is their duty to declare what the agency's statutory obligations are and what the agency's procedural course should be.

As Judge Gasch aptly put it over twenty years ago:

"A nation is an entity in many senses beside the political. Shared beliefs and experiences provide the flesh and sinew which cover and unite the bones of political organization. These common beliefs and experiences are nourished, sustained and, indeed, sometimes created by history. Historical knowledge, then, is the life's blood of a people. To cut it off is to assure the eventual disintegration of the political entity. Congress has wisely recognized this and has provided, in the statutes here involved, for a careful consideration of historical values before a project which may destroy

---

[19][*Orig. fn.*] See A.R. at 1712 (1992–1993 expenditures of $875,619); Henley Decl. p. 11–14 (identifying $835,208 spent from April 1994 to first quarter of FY 1996 on repairs and maintenance); A.R. at 1896–1966 (chronicling ongoing daily, weekly and annual maintenance program); see also Defs.' Statement of Material Facts pp. 53–55.

those values is begun. This is not to say, of course, that contemporary needs should be utterly subordinated to the remnants of the past. That would indeed be to crush the present under the detritus of antiquity. All that is required is that the Government agency concerned take into consideration the historical values which may be affected by any planned project. The Congress has provided a procedure whereby this may be done."

Don't Tear It Down, Inc. v. GSA, 401 F. Supp. 1194, 1198–99 (D.D.C. 1975).

Accordingly, defendants' motion for summary judgment is granted and plaintiffs' motion for summary judgment is denied. The merits having been decided in this fashion, plaintiffs' motion for preliminary injunctive relief necessarily also is denied.

An Order consistent with this Opinion will be entered this same day.

SO ORDERED.

---

2. National Environmental Policy Act of 1969

The National Environmental Policy Act of 1969 [NEPA, 42 U.S.C. § 4321 *et seq.* (1994)] mandates federal agencies to consider the impacts of their activities—including the issuance of federal permits, federal funding, and other federal agency actions—on the environment, and to ensure that information about these environmental impacts is available to the public before final decisions are made. In addition to requiring federal agencies to consider the consequences of their activities on natural resources, NEPA specifically mandates agencies "to use all practical means, consistent with other essential considerations of national policy, to improve and coordinate federal plans, functions, programs, and resources to the end that the Nation may... preserve important historic, cultural, and natural aspects of our national heritage, and maintain, wherever possible, an environment which supports diversity and variety of individual choice..." [42 U.S.C. § 4331(b)) 1994)].

The Council on Environmental Quality, established by NEPA, promulgated regulations that implement the Act (CEQ Regulations, 40 C.F.R. Parts 1500–08). Specifically, the purpose of the CEQ Regulations is "to tell federal agencies what they must do to comply with the procedures and achieve the goals of the Act" [40 C.F.R. § 1500.1(a) (1997)]. The heart of NEPA is the development and analysis of a proposed action and alternatives to carrying out that course of action for the purpose of informing the agency decision-maker [40 C.F.R. § 1502.14 (1997)]. As part of the analysis of alternatives, agencies must include discussions of "... historic and cultural resources..." [40 C.F.R. § 1502.16(g) (1997)]. Further, in analyzing the impacts of each alternative on the environment, agencies are to consider direct, indirect, and cumulative effects of a historical and cultural nature [40 C.F.R. § 1508.8 (1997); see *Colorado River Indian Tribes v. Marsh*, 605 F. Supp.

1425, 1429–34 (C.D. Cal. 1985*); Friends of the Payette v. Horseshoe Bend Hydroelectric Co.*, 811 F. Supp. 524, 533 (D. Idaho 1992), holding that issuance of a Clean Water Act permit by the Army Corps of Engineers did not violate NEPA, as it was issued contingent upon the permittee's evaluation of "any historic or prehistoric properties" in conjunction with the Idaho SHPO; and *Warm Springs Dam Task Force v. Gribble*, 378 F. Supp. 240 (N.D. Cal. 1974)].

COLORADO RIVER INDIAN TRIBES v. MARSH

605 F. Supp. 1425 (C.D. Cal. 1985)

TAKASUGI, District Judge:

The Colorado River Indian Tribes ("Tribes") and the Sierra Club (jointly "plaintiffs") have filed a complaint for declaratory and injunctive relief and petition for writ of mandamus against the heads of a number of federal agencies (collectively "Federal Defendants"), heads of state agencies, and River City Development Co. ("Developer") (jointly "defendants"). The prayer seeks a declaration that the defendants have acted in violation of the first amendment rights of the members of the Tribes; an injunction enjoining the Army Corps of Engineers ("Corps") from issuing a permit for the placement of riprap (large boulders to stabilize shorebanks from erosion); an injunction enjoining the Developer and his agents from any construction activities; and a writ of mandamus directing the Corps to vacate the permit.

The plaintiffs essentially alleged that the construction of the River City project ("Development") and the permit for placement of riprap on the Development violate the National Environmental Policy Act of 1969 (42 U.S.C. § 4321 *et seq.*) ("NEPA"), the National Historic Preservation Act of 1966 (16 U.S.C. § 470 *et seq.*) ("NHPA"), the American Indian Religious Freedom Act (42 U.S.C. § 1996), executive orders and regulations promulgated to implement these statutes, and the first amendment to the United States Constitution.[1]

The pertinent background facts are as follows: The proposed Development is a 156-acre residential and commercial development proposed to be built on the west side of the Colorado River. The site of the Development is directly across the river from the Colorado River Indian Reservation and also immediately south of other portions of the reservation which lie on the west side of the river. The Development site spans Highway 95, with most of the site lying between the highway and the river. The Developer proposes to subdivide the parcel into approximately 447 lots for single-family homes, mobile homes, and commercial

---

[1][*Orig. fn.*] Plaintiffs seek this judicial review pursuant to the Administrative Procedure Act, 5 U.S.C. § 701 *et seq.* Any contention that plaintiffs, as organizations, lack standing to seek this equitable relief can be put to rest in the light of *Sierra Club v. Morton*, 405 U.S. 727, 92 S.Ct. 1361, 31 L.Ed.2d 636 (1972). In *Morton*, the Supreme Court recognized organizational standing where members thereof were in fact threatened by defendant's acts.

facilities. The land abutting the Development site on the west is owned by the United States Government and administered by the Bureau of Land Management ("BLM") of the United States Department of the Interior. The BLM land, an archeological district, includes several recorded significant cultural and archeological sites.

In connection with this proposed Development, the Developer has proposed to stabilize 4050 feet of the western shore of the Colorado River (the eastern boundary of the project site) by placing riprap along the river bank. The proposal calls for approximately two cubic yards of rock along every linear foot of the river bank. The purpose of the riprap is to stabilize the bank and to establish a permanent boundary line enabling the property to be subdivided and developed. The Developer must obtain a permit from the Corps in order to stabilize the river bank. Without bank stabilization, the approval for the development cannot be obtained from the County of Riverside.

In April, 1978, the Developer applied to the Corps for a permit to allow placement of riprap along the west river bank on the Development site. In November, 1978, the Corps prepared an environmental assessment of the permit application and concluded that because significant impact upon the environment would result from the Developer's proposed project, an environmental impact statement ("EIS") would be prepared.

A Draft EIS was prepared and published in September 1979. On January 11, 1981, the Corps informed the Developer that the Draft EIS was "lacking only an adequate treatment of cultural resources," and stated that a "thorough cultural resources survey" of resources on and near the proposed development site was "essential" before the Corps could complete a Final EIS. The Corps proposed a detailed scope of work for a "systematic intensive cultural resources survey of lands surrounding the proposed River City Development."

In June, 1981, however, before the preparation of the survey, the Corps announced its retraction of the Draft EIS as a result of changes in Corps policy regarding its jurisdictional authority, and stated that no EIS was required.

The Corps' decision to retract the draft EIS was apparently in conformity with its proposed cultural resource regulations, 33 C.F.R. § 325, Appendix C, 45 Fed. Reg. 22112 (1980). Those regulations have never been finally adopted and incorporated into the Code of Federal Regulations.

In response to the Corps' notice retracting the Draft EIS, the Tribes wrote to the Corps noting that issuance of the requested Corps permit without preparation of an adequate EIS fully analyzing potential impact of the project on cultural and archeological resources would violate NEPA and NHPA. The Tribes also pointed out that another potentially significant effect of the project was an adverse impact upon the opposite shore of the river. On April 15, 1982, the Corps responded to the Tribes' comments, asserting that under its proposed regulations, no further evaluation or protection of cultural resources was required. Also, the Corps concluded that the riprap would cause no significant impact on the eastern side of the river. On May 21, 1982, the Corps issued a permit to the Developer authorizing it to place the riprap along the west bank of the Colorado River.

The County of Riverside approved the tract maps for the project on June 19, 1984. Plaintiffs herein have challenged that action and the County's December, 1982 approval of the specific plan for the project in two separate Superior Court actions. *Colorado River Indian Tribes and Sierra Club v. County of Riverside, et al.*, Riverside County Superior Court, Indio Nos. 37230 and 41515. Both actions are pending in the trial court.

Tribes filed this complaint for injunctive and declaratory relief on September 28, 1982. On October 27, 1982, pursuant to a stipulation and order of the court, Tribes and the Developer agreed that the Developer would provide the Tribes at least 45 days' notice before beginning any construction or riprapping at River City. On May 27, 1983, pursuant to stipulation of the parties and order of the court, a First Amended Complaint was filed naming the Sierra Club as an additional plaintiff.

On August 13, 1984, the Developer formally gave plaintiffs the 45-day notice of its intent to commence riprapping activities pursuant to the Corps' permit, thus giving rise to the instant motion. Plaintiffs seek a preliminary injunction to enjoin the placement of riprap, arguing essentially that the Corps improperly issued a permit for the riprap without an EIS, in contravention of NEPA; that the Federal Defendants have failed to take the required measures to protect the cultural and archeological resources on the BLM land as mandated by NHPA; and that the balance of harm weighs heavily in favor of the Tribes.

PRELIMINARY INJUNCTION

The traditional factors which must be present in order for preliminary injunctive relief to be granted are (1) a strong likelihood of success on the merits, (2) the possibility of irreparable injury to plaintiff if the preliminary relief is not granted, (3) a balance of hardships favoring the plaintiff, and (4) advancement of the public interest. *Los Angeles Memorial Coliseum Commission v. NFL*, 634 F.2d 1197, 1200 (9th Cir. 1980); *Sierra Club v. Hathaway*, 579 F.2d 1162, 1167 (9th Cir. 1978). In this circuit, two different formulations of this test have been applied. The moving party must show either (1) probable success on the merits and possible irreparable injury, or (2) sufficiently serious questions going to the merits to make them a fair ground for litigation and a balance of hardships tipping decidedly toward the party requesting the preliminary relief. *Aguirre v. Chula Vista Sanitary Serv.*, 542 F.2d 779, 781 (9th Cir. 1976), quoting *Gresham v. Chambers*, 501 F.2d 687, 691 (2nd Cir. 1974). See *Benda v. Grand Lodge of the Int'l Ass'n of Machinists & Aerospace Workers*, 584 F.2d 308, 315 (9th Cir. 1978), *cert. dismissed*, 441 U.S. 937, 99 S.Ct. 2065, 60 L.Ed.2d 667 (1979); *Wm. Inglis & Sons Baking Co. v. ITT Continental Baking Co.*, 526 F.2d 86, 88 (9th Cir. 1975). These are not separate tests, but the outer reaches "of a single continuum." *Benda v. Grand Lodge*, 584 F.2d at 315. In effect, the standard provides that the more probability of success on the merits that a plaintiff establishes, the less he or she must show in the way of irreparable harm. See *Benda v. Grand Lodge, Id.*[2]

---

[2][*Orig. fn.*] Developer raises two equitable defenses, laches and "unclean hands," to the action for injunctive relief arguing that plaintiffs should be estopped from seeking equitable relief for not objecting to the Development when first advised; and that the propriety of the action should be questioned in light of the Tribes' own development in the area. Plaintiffs take issue with the factual allegations that Developer raises, and presents its set of facts and interpretations. While the Developer might establish the sufficiency of these defenses at trial, the court after a careful examination of the facts presented is unable to agree with Developer's position at this stage of the proceedings.

SUCCESS ON THE MERITS

A. NEPA

This issue focuses upon statutory and regulatory interpretations of NEPA, which requires an EIS to be prepared for "major Federal actions significantly affecting the quality of the human environment." 42 U.S.C. § 4332(2)(C).[3] The standard for determining whether a project would significantly affect the quality of the human environment is whether "the plaintiff has alleged facts which, if true, show that the proposed project may significantly degrade some human environmental factor." *Foundation for North American Wild Sheep v. U.S. Department of Agriculture*, 681 F.2d 1172, 1178 (9th Cir. 1982) (*quoting Columbia Basin Land Protection Association v. Schlesinger*, 643 F.2d 585, 597 (9th Cir. 1981) (emphasis in original). A determination that significant effects on the environment will in fact occur is not necessary. *City of Davis v. Coleman*, 521 F.2d 661, 673 (9th Cir. 1975). "If substantial questions are raised whether a project may have a significant effect on the human environment, an EIS must be prepared." *Foundation for North American Wild Sheep*,

---

[3][*Orig. fn.*] Federal defendants argue that NEPA focuses on the effects on the physical environment, such as water, air, and ecosystems; cultural impacts by themselves are insufficient to require an EIS. They rely on *Goodman Group, Inc. v. Dishroom*, 679 F.2d 182 (9th Cir. 1982) wherein this Circuit held that appellant's claim that the Federal government's plan to convert the Goodman Building to low income housing would displace local artists who inhabit the Goodman Building, and thus irreparably damage the character of the area, was not in and of itself sufficient to require preparation of an EIS. Categorizing appellant's alleged harm as a "cultural threat," the Court stated that it would be doubtful that effects to the aesthetic and cultural environment, would alone, necessitate an EIS. *Id.* at 185.

Federal Defendants' assertion that the decision in Goodman is controlling in this case misconstrues the decision. The present case does not deal strictly with claims of future harm to the aesthetic and cultural environment. Aside from plaintiffs' claim of possible physical injury to the Tribes' riverbank from the Development, they claim that the Development threatens sites of historical and cultural significance because of influx of people that would reside and use the Development. The Court in Goodman recognized the distinction between the facts before the Court and the type of case before this court. After citing cases where the courts had demanded an EIS, the Court stated: "The federal action in each of these cases either threatened the physical resources of the area, by posing significant traffic, population-concentration, or water-supply problems, or proposed the irreversible alteration of the historic attributes of rare sites." 679 F.2d at 185.

Aside from misinterpreting the case, Federal Defendants' argument overlooks the plain language of NEPA which imposes upon the Federal Government the responsibility to "preserve important historic, cultural and national aspects of our national heritage and maintain, whenever possible, an environment which supports diversity and variety of individual choices." 42 U.S.C. § 4331(b)(4) (emphasis added). Additionally, the regulations provide that "Effects include ecological..., aesthetic, historical, cultural, economic, social, or health, whether direct, indirect, or cumulative." 40 C.F.R. § 1508.8.

681 F.2d at 1178 (emphasis in original); *City and County of San Francisco v. U.S.*, 615 F.2d 498, 500 (9th Cir. 1980).

Where an agency has determined that no EIS need be prepared, a court will review the reasonableness of the agency's determination. *City of Davis v. Coleman*, 521 F.2d at 673. If the court finds that the agency's conclusion that the project will have no significant adverse environmental consequences is unreasonable, it will require that an EIS be prepared in connection with the project. *Foundation for North American Wild Sheep v. U.S. Department of Agriculture*, 681 F.2d at 1178; *Portela v. Pierce*, 650 F.2d 210, 213 (9th Cir. 1981); *City and County of San Francisco v. United States*, 615 F.2d 498, 500; *City of Davis v. Coleman*, 521 F.2d at 673.

Developer and Federal Defendants contend that an EIS was unnecessary because federal involvement in the project was minimal and therefore "major federal action" triggering NEPA was lacking. In support of their contention, both rely upon *Save the Bay, Inc. v. U.S. Corps. of Eng.*, 610 F.2d 322 (5th Cir.), *cert. denied*, 449 U.S. 900, 101 S.Ct. 269, 66 L.Ed.2d 130 (1980), and *Winnebago Tribe of Nebraska v. Ray*, 621 F.2d 269 (8th Cir.), *cert. denied*, 449 U.S. 836, 101 S.Ct. 110, 66 L.Ed.2d 43 (1980). These cases suggest that NEPA reaches only "major federal actions" and that the degree of federal involvement controls the scope of an agency's review of potential impact. Their holdings give independent significance to the word "major" and suggest that the degree of federal involvement is a threshold question in ascertaining the reasonableness of the federal agency's decision not to issue an EIS. This court disagrees with *Save the Bay, Inc.* and *Winnebago* insofar as their rulings stress that "major federal action" is an element that must be met to trigger NEPA and that "major federal action" has significance independent from the element of "significantly affecting the quality of the human environment" in 42 U.S.C. § 4332(2)(C).

Furthermore, conclusions reached in *Save the Bay* and *Winnebago* are in conflict with the Ninth Circuit ruling in *City of Davis v. Coleman*, 521 F.2d 661. In *City of Davis*, the Court was faced with the allegation that a federal agency had failed to prepare and file an EIS as mandated by NEPA in connection with a joint state and federal project to build a freeway interchange. The Court rejected the requirement for purposes of an EIS that the federal involvement must be "major," and instead focused its attention upon the significance of the environmental impact of the freeway interchange:

> The circuits have split on the question of whether federal action that significantly affects the environment must also be "major" in an economic or some other nonenvironmental sense to trigger the EIS requirement. We incline to the views expressed in *Minnesota Public Interest Research Group v. Butz*, 8 Cir. *in banc*, 1974, 498 F.2d 1314, 1321–22:
>
>> To separate the consideration of the magnitude of federal action from its impact on the environment does little to foster the purposes of the Act, i.e., to 'attain the widest range of beneficial uses of the environment without degradation, risk to health and safety, or other undesirable and unintended consequences.' By bifurcating the statutory language, it would be possible to speak of a 'minor federal action significantly affecting the quality of the human environment,' and to hold NEPA inapplicable to such an action. Yet if the action has a significant effect, it is the intent of NEPA that it should be the subject of the detailed consideration mandated by

> NEPA; the activities of federal agencies cannot be isolated from their
> impact upon the environment." (Citations omitted.)

Thus, we confine ourselves on this appeal to determining whether the defendants
reasonably concluded that the Kidwell project will have no significant environmental
effects.
>   521 F.2d at 673 n. 15.

The holding in *City of Davis* is supported by the regulations promulgated under NEPA.
As defined by 40 C.F.R. § 1508.18: " '[M]ajor Federal action' includes actions with effects
that may be major and which are potentially subject to Federal control and responsibility.
Major reinforces but does not have a meaning independent of significantly (§ 1508.27)...."
(Emphasis added.) Finally, NEPA's declaration of national environmental policy suggests a
concern for the effects of development upon the environment and a commitment to restore
and preserve environmental quality:

> The Congress, recognizing the profound impact of man's activity on the interrela-
> tions of all components of the natural environment, particularly the profound influ-
> ences of population growth, high-density urbanization, industrial expansion, resource
> exploitation, and new and expanding technological advances and recognizing further
> the critical importance of restoring and maintaining environmental quality to the overall
> welfare and development of man, declares that it is the continuing policy of the Fed-
> eral Government, in cooperation with State and local governments, and other con-
> cerned public and private organizations, to use all practicable means and measures,
> including financial and technical assistance, in a manner calculated to foster and pro-
> mote the general welfare, to create and maintain conditions under which man and
> nature can exist in productive harmony, and fulfill the social, economic, and other
> requirements of present and future generations of Americans.

42 U.S.C. § 4331(a). To limit the scope to only "major" federal involvement, ignoring the
potential for significant impact, seems incongruous to the avowed intent of NEPA to maintain environmental quality. It is not the degree of federal involvement that influences the
standard of living of our society, but is instead, the potential and degree of impact from
development that bears upon the overall welfare and enjoyment of our society.
     Turning to the question of significant impact, the federal agency's decision that there
will be no significant impact will not be disturbed unless the agency's decision was unreasonable. *City of Davis*, 521 F.2d at 673. This, of course, presupposes that the scope of the
inquiry was proper. Should a federal agency unduly narrow the scope of inquiry in contravention to the edicts of NEPA, the test of reasonableness would be inapplicable because the
factors that a federal agency should have considered and which could have affected the
agency's decision, would have been improperly ignored. Had the Corps duly considered the
impact and concluded that the Development's impact was not significant or too speculative,
the inquiry would be circumscribed around the question of "reasonableness." The evidence
presented, however, suggests that the Corps' scope of inquiry in deciding that an EIS was
unnecessary, was limited to the Corps' jurisdiction, *i.e.,* the river and its banks. This seems
evident from the change in position in June, 1981. Prior to that date, the Corps had prepared
an environmental assessment of the permit and concluded that because significant impacts

upon the environment would result from the Developer's proposed project, an EIS would be prepared. Plaintiffs' Exhibit 8. In or about June, 1981, the Corps announced its retraction of the Draft EIS. The Corps Public Notice No. 78-112-TM (June 3, 1981) provided that

> Due to the recent change in policy regarding jurisdictional authority under Sections 10 and 404, the Los Angeles District of the Corps of Engineers is retracting the EIS currently under preparation entitled Bank Stabilization near Blythe, Riverside County, California. The District has determined that the impact assessment of features outside of jurisdictional boundaries, and not physically dependent upon activities within Corps jurisdiction, is not appropriate. Therefore, the scope of the environmental assessment has been limited to the portion of the project requiring authorization (*i.e.* bank stabilization activities only). *Id.* at 2 (Plaintiffs' Exhibit 20).

It is evident from this statement that the Corps had not merely reassessed its previous decision, but redefined its scope, narrowing the parameters of the word "impact." Instead of assessing the possible impacts of a future development which was dependent upon the placement of riprap, it circumscribed the inquiry solely to the bank stabilization activities. Any doubt as to the change of policy by the Corps is put to rest upon examining the Corps' Public Notice which invited the public to comment on the riprap permit and its impact on cultural resources. The Corps' statement was: "[D]irect impacts from placement of riprap, and indirect impacts from haul roads and movement of equipment will have no impact on any known cultural resources." *Id.* at 3 (Plaintiffs' Exhibit 20). The failure to consider the environmental impacts outside the Corps' jurisdiction is further evidenced by its Memorandum for Record (January 19, 1982), Plaintiffs' Exhibit 21, which stated:

> 2. Although significant cultural resources do exist just beyond the boundary of the proposed River City Development, those sites are located outside of the jurisdictional boundary of the Corps of Engineers. River City Development Company has applied for a Department of the Army permit to stabilize its property boundary along the Colorado River.
> 3. An environmental assessment of the proposed bank stabilization project disclosed that no significant impacts upon the human environment are expected as a result. Therefore, no Environmental Impact Statement (EIS) is being prepared. A review of the comments received during the comment period failed to produce any new information which indicate that an EIS should be prepared.[4]

In limiting the scope of its inquiry, the Corps acted improperly and contrary to the mandates of NEPA. The Corps' decision to assess only those impacts physically dependent

---

[4][*Orig. fn.*] In a letter from the Corps to the Tribe (April 15, 1982), Plaintiffs' Exhibit 6, there is language that the impact from the Development are speculative, which suggests that this was truly considered. However, any claim by the Corps that the Development's impact was considered is at odds with its avowed change in policy to only ascertain the impact of the bank stabilization activities. Additionally, it would not account for its prior position before the policy change in June, 1981, wherein it held that there would be a significant impact on the environment as a result of the proposed Development.

upon activities within its redefined jurisdiction, *i.e.,* the river and its immediate banks, was tantamount to limiting its assessment to primary impacts. The Corps proceeded to assess the project with tunnel vision. In *City of Davis*, the Ninth Circuit strongly stressed that direct, indirect (secondary) and cumulative impacts of proposed major federal action must be assessed. 521 F.2d at 676–77. The regulations promulgated under NEPA fortify such an approach. 40 CFR § 1508.8 defines effects as:

(a) Direct effects, which are caused by the action and occur at the same time and place.

(b) Indirect effects, which are caused by the action and are later in time or farther removed in distance, but are still reasonably foreseeable. *Indirect effects may include growth inducing effects and other effects related to induced changes in the pattern of land use, population density or growth rate, and related effects on air and water and other natural systems, including ecosystems.* Effects and impacts as used in these regulations are synonymous. Effects includes ecological (such as the effects on natural resources and on the components, structures, and functioning of affected ecosystems), aesthetic, historic, cultural, economic, social, or health, whether direct, indirect, or cumulative. Effects may also include those resulting from actions which may have both beneficial and detrimental effects, even if on balance the agency believes that the effect will be beneficial. (Emphasis added.)

Furthermore, 40 C.F.R. § 1508.7 defines cumulative impact as:

the impact on the environment which results from the incremental impact of the action when added to other past, present, and reasonably foreseeable future actions regardless of what agency (Federal or non-Federal) or person undertakes such other actions. Cumulative impacts can result from individually minor but collectively significant actions taking place over a period of time.

It is within these guidelines that the Corps should have attempted to assess the consequences of the issuance of the permit. The Corps should have analyzed the indirect effects of the bank stabilization on both "on site" and "off site" locations, *i.e.,* the growth-inducing effects related to the changes in the pattern of land use and population growth. It would appear that the Corps failed to consider the cumulative impact associated with the bank stabilization project when it may have been reasonably foreseeable that the placement of the ripraps was just a stepping stone to major development in the area.

The indirect impact of a project and the cumulative effects thereof are equally as important as the direct or primary effects of the proposed action. The Federal Defendants are in error when they contend that because there was minimal federal involvement, there was no need to examine each and every effect, direct or indirect, "on site" or "off site."

Impact statements usually analyze the initial or primary effects of a project, but they very often ignore the secondary or induced effects. A new highway located in a rural area may directly cause increased air pollution as a primary effect. But the highway may also induce residential and industrial growth, which may in turn create substantial pressures on available water supplies, sewage treatment facilities, and so forth.

For many projects, these secondary or induced effects may be more significant than the project's primary effects.

* * *

While the analysis of secondary effects is often more difficult than defining the first-order physical effects, it is also indispensable. If impact statements are to be useful, they must address the major environmental problems likely to be created by a project. Statements that do not address themselves to these major problems are increasingly likely to be viewed as inadequate. As experience is gained in defining and understanding these secondary effects, new methodologies are likely to develop for forecasting them, and the usefulness of impact statements will increase. *Fifth Annual Report of the Council on Environmental Quality*, 410–11 (December 1974).
  City of Davis, 521 F.2d at 676–77.

Defendants contend that the indirect effects of harm to archeological and historical resources caused by the Development are too speculative to consider as potential impacts of the granting of the permit.[5] While effects which are not reasonably foreseeable may be disregarded, an agency should not attempt to travel the easy path and hastily label the impact of the Development as too speculative and not worthy of agency review. The purpose of an EIS is to evaluate the possibilities regarding a project in light of current and future plans and contingencies in order to produce an informed estimate of the environmental consequences.

It must be remembered that the basic thrust of an agency's responsibilities under NEPA is to predict the environmental effects of proposed action before the action is taken and those effects fully known. Reasonable forecasting and speculation is thus implicit in NEPA, and we must reject any attempt by agencies to shirk their responsibilities under NEPA by labeling any and all discussion of future environmental effects as "crystal ball inquiry."

City of Davis, 521 F.2d at 676 citing, *Scientists' Institute for Public Information v. A.E.C.*, 481 F.2d 1079, 1092 (D.C. Cir. 1973). This court finds that the defendants' position regarding the speculative nature of the effects of the Development may be untenable given the grave concerns which the Corps expressed in the Draft EIS. In light of the holding that the

---

[5][*Orig. fn.*] Additionally, because of unprecedented flooding in 1983 which caused extensive erosion of Developer's property, Developer claims that pursuant to 33 C.F.R. § 323.4, it is exempted from the permit requirement. Developer's reliance upon 33 C.F.R. § 323.4 is misguided. Section 323 deals with "Permits for discharges of dredged or fill material into waters of the United States," and section 323.4, upon which Developer relies, deals with certain discharges that are exempt from a permit requirement. This case, of course, does not deal with discharges. The permit in question is for a structure, i.e., riprap, in or affecting navigable waters of the United States, which is covered in 33 C.F.R. § 322. Even assuming that section 323 were applicable, 33 C.F.R. § 323.4(a)(iii)(E)(2) exemptions are limited discharges caused by emergency *reconstruction of currently serviceable structures*. The present case does not involve reconstruction of a previously installed man-made structure.

Corps impermissibly narrowed the scope of their responsibility under NEPA, the question of whether the indirect effects of the Development and its impact are "reasonably foreseeable" need not be addressed.

* * *

IRREPARABLE INJURY

As noted earlier, the standard to be met in obtaining a preliminary injunction is the showing of

(1) a strong likelihood of success on the merits, (2) the possibility of irreparable injury to plaintiff if the preliminary relief is not granted, (3) a balance of hardships favoring the plaintiff, and (4) advancement of the public interest (in certain cases). [Citations.] In this circuit, the moving party may meet its burden by demonstrating either (1) a combination of probable success on the merits and the possibility of irreparable injury or (2) that serious questions are raised and the balance of hardships tips sharply in its favor. [Citation.] These are not separate tests, but the outer reaches "of a single continuum." [Citation.]

Los Angeles Memorial Coliseum Commission v. NFL, 634 F.2d at 1200–1201.

When dealing with NEPA violations, this Circuit appears to take a decidedly different approach. It has applied more liberal standards upon a showing of likelihood of success on the merits by the party seeking the enforcement of NEPA. See *American Motorcyclist Ass'n v. Watt*, 714 F.2d 962, 965–966 (9th Cir. 1983); *Warm Springs Dam Task Force v. Gribble*, 565 F.2d 549, 552 n. 2 (9th Cir. 1977). Instead of imposing an affirmative responsibility upon the plaintiff to show harm or injury, irreparable damage may be implied from the failure of responsible authorities to evaluate thoroughly the environmental impact of a proposed federal action. *Friends of the Earth, Inc. v. Coleman*, 518 F.2d 323, 330 (9th Cir. 1975); *American Motorcyclist Ass'n v. Watt*, 714 F.2d at 966. Once a substantial NEPA violation has been shown, an injunction should issue without detailed consideration of traditional equity principles, because the injunction in aid of NEPA enforcement is the execution of a congressional policy mandate. *California v. Bergland*, 483 F. Supp. 465, 498 (E.D. Cal. 1980), *mod. sub nom. California v. Block*, 690 F.2d 753 (9th Cir. 1982); See also *Lathan v. Volpe*, 455 F.2d 1111, 1116 (9th Cir. 1971); Grad's Treatise on Environmental Law, Vol. 2, § 9.04[2][b].[10]

---

[10][*Orig. fn.*] In "unusual circumstances," the court must balance the equities, despite a finding of a NEPA violation. See *American Motorcyclist Ass'n v. Watt*, 714 F.2d 962, 966 (9th Cir. 1983); *Forelaws on Board v. Johnson*, 743 F.2d 677, 685 (9th Cir. 1984), *modified* (9th Cir. Jan. 21, 1985). See *also, Grad's Treatise on Environmental Law*, Vol. 2, § 9.04 [2][b]. Additionally, irreparable damages will not be implied in an action to enforce NEPA if movant shows little likelihood of prevailing on their claim. *Friends of the Earth, Inc. v. Coleman*, 518 F.2d 323, 330 (9th Cir. 1975). These limitations, however, are inapplicable to the present case. Plaintiffs have established a likelihood of success and there are none of the "unusual circumstances" which prompted the courts in the cases cited above, to compel a different holding.

> The rationale for this NEPA injunction rule is clear. NEPA represents a declared Congressional policy requiring assessment of environmental concerns. As such, Congress has weighed the equities and determined that failure to examine environmental issues represents irreparable injury. If having established a violation of NEPA, plaintiffs are not allowed to enjoin further activities until the agency complies with NEPA, then NEPA would be an "exercise in futility."

California v. Bergland, 483 F. Supp. at 498–499. (Citations omitted.) The purpose of enjoining government action pending preparation of the environmental impact statement is, generally, to maintain the status quo while additional environmental data is obtained, in order to preserve the decision makers' opportunity to choose among policy alternatives. *Forelaws on Board v. Johnson*, 743 F.2d 677, 685 (9th Cir. 1984), *modified*, (9th Cir. Jan. 21, 1985).[11]

Even assuming that the question of irreparable injury must be considered, the conclusion herein that a preliminary injunction should issue would remain unchanged.

Plaintiffs in this case, having established probable success on the merits (i.e., that NEPA and NHPA have been violated), would only need to show the possibility of irreparable injury under the traditional standard. That irreparable injury must be causally connected to the violation of NEPA and/or NHPA. In the case of both NEPA and NHPA, that violation is, essentially, the failure of the Federal defendants to consider the reasonable foreseeability of the Development upon the granting of the riprap permit and the potential harm that the Development poses to the historical and archeological sites. The granting of the permit without such consideration forecloses the taking of any steps to alleviate potential harm.

The evidence submitted regarding the historical and archeological sites on or near the proposed Development, in the form of letters, studies, evaluations, and declarations, unquestionably suggests the importance of at least some of these sites. The importance of these sites transcends their spiritual value to the Tribes and, instead, evidences their cultural significance to the general public. While there seems to be some dispute as to the degree of impact that the Development poses, there seems to be a general consensus among the parties that the Development will necessarily exert pressures that threaten the integrity of the cultural and archeological resources. The frailty of the resources and the fact that the Development would increase the number of "off-road-vehicles," which represents the greatest threat to these resources, suggest, at a minimum, the possibility of irreparable harm. The court is also mindful of the advancement of the public interest in preserving these resources. They represent a means by which to better understand the history and culture of the American Indians in the past, and hopefully to provide some insight and understanding of the present day American Indians.

Defendants urge this court to consider only the direct impact of the riprap, limiting inquiry of the effects of the riprap to the river and its banks. However, defendants' focus is misdirected. The injury that must be focused upon in a motion for preliminary injunction

---

[11][*Orig. fn.*] While the holdings of the cases cited so far dealt with NEPA, the guidelines expounded would also be applicable to NHPA, since the rationale underlying the relaxation of the traditional standards for a preliminary injunction for NEPA violations would seem to have the same force and substance for NHPA violations.

must be the injury that is threatened by the defendant's improper conduct. In this case the improper conduct, the violation of NEPA and NHPA, poses a possibility of irreparable injury to the historical and archeological sites. This court does not pass on the reasonableness of the Corps' finding that impact on the opposite riverbank is insignificant. As such, any impact on the riverbanks is not within the scope for which irreparable injury should be measured.

While this court is mindful that one of the reasons Developer seeks to riprap the bank is to mitigate further river erosion,[12] and that the Developer must, in addition to the riprap permit, seek the two additional permits from federal agencies, it cannot ignore the fact that the primary reason the Developer sought a federal permit for the riprap was that said riprap was required by the County as a pre-condition to the development of the land. To then say that the Development is not a reasonably foreseeable event and therefore its impact should not be considered because Developer has other reasons in seeking to riprap the bank or that other permits are necessary before development begins, overlooks the primary motivating force behind the application for the permit. This court is of the opinion that irreparable harm to the cultural and archeological resources as a result of the Development is possible.

As such, under either the traditional or the NEPA standard, this court finds that plaintiffs are entitled to a preliminary injunction.[13] IT IS SO ORDERED.

NATIONAL INDIAN YOUTH COUNCIL v. ANDRUS

501 F. Supp. 649 (D. N.M. 1980), *aff'd*, 664 F.2d 220 (10th Cir. 1981)

CAMPOS, District Judge:

This litigation ensues from a surface mining (strip mining) project proposed for a tract in northwestern New Mexico on the Navajo Reservation. Plaintiffs consist of the National Indian Youth Council (NIYC), a nonprofit organization headquartered in Albuquerque, New Mexico, which characterizes its purpose as "preserving and protecting the traditional life-styles of Native American people";[1] and twelve individual members of the Navajo Tribe residing on the Reservation at Burnham, New Mexico.

---

[12][*Orig. fn.*] Developer states that it has a common law right to protect its property from erosion by flooding, relying upon *Beach Colony II v. California Coastal Com.*, 151 Cal. App. 3d 1107, 199 Cal. Rptr. 195 (1984) as authority. The decision is clearly inapposite as the case dealt with California statutory and common law interpretation. Additionally, the decision did not hold that the concept of "self-help" was absolute, but was, instead, subject to reasonable conditions imposed by agencies with regulatory jurisdiction over the area. *Id.* at 1118, 199 Cal. Rptr. 195.

[13][*Orig. fn.*] In reaching this conclusion as to the issue of irreparable harm, this court is painfully aware of the damage in terms of lost acreage suffered by the Developer in 1983 due to the unprecedented release of water into the Colorado River and is sympathetic to Developer's legitimate desire to develop his land. Nevertheless, plaintiffs have been successful in showing the required possibility of irreparable harm.

[1][*Orig. fn.*] Amended Complaint, para. 4.

Federal Defendants are officials of the United States Department of the Interior and include Cecil D. Andrus, Secretary of the Interior (Secretary), and Forrest J. Gerard, Assistant Secretary of the Interior for Indian Affairs.[2] Intervenor-Defendants are El Paso Natural Gas Company (El Paso) and Consolidation Coal Company (Consol).[3]

Plaintiffs have petitioned this Court for declaratory and injunctive relief based upon allegations that Defendants' approvals of (1) a mining lease executed in 1976 between Intervenors and the Navajo Tribe, and (2) a subsequent mining plan violate the National Environmental Policy Act of 1969 (NEPA), 42 U.S.C. Section 4321 *et seq.*; the National Historic Preservation Act of 1966 (NHPA), 16 U.S.C. Section 470 *et seq.*; Exec.Order No. 11593, 3 C.F.R. Part 154 (1971 Compilation); the Historic and Archeological Data Preservation Act of 1974 (HADPA), 16 U.S.C. Section 469 *et seq.*; 36 C.F.R. Part 800 *et seq.*; and 40 C.F.R. Part 1501 *et seq.* Plaintiffs have also alleged that the approval of the lease by Defendants constitutes a breach of a fiduciary duty owed by Defendants to the individual Plaintiffs.[4]

At the close of the evidence on Plaintiffs' motion for a preliminary injunction, the parties indicated that there would be no further evidence to present at a hearing on the merits. Thus, this Court is able to bypass the preliminary injunction issues and decide the case on its merits pursuant to Rule 65(a)(2), Federal Rules of Civil Procedure, 28 U.S.C.[5]

BACKGROUND.

In 1959, the Navajo Tribe granted a coal prospecting permit to El Paso for exploration of 85,760 acres on the Navajo Reservation. As a result of coal discoveries El Paso and Consol, as joint venturers, entered into a lease with the Navajo Tribe in 1968 for the extraction of an estimated 678,000,000 tons of coal on 40,286 acres located on the Burnham Chapter of the

---

[2][*Orig. fn.*] The other Defendants are R. Keith Higginson, Commissioner of the Bureau of Reclamation; Vincent E. McKelvey, Director of the United States Geological Survey; and William T. Whalen, Director of the National Park Service.

[3][*Orig. fn.*] For clarification of further references, "Defendants" denotes only the federal Defendants and "Intervenors" denotes El Paso and Consol.

[4][*Orig. fn.*] A cause of action based upon the allegation that the Secretary's approval of the mining lease was "arbitrary, capricious and an abuse of discretion" was voluntarily withdrawn by Plaintiffs prior to the preliminary injunction hearing.

[5][*Orig. fn.*] Rule 65(a)(2) provides that "(b)efore or after the commencement of the hearing of an application for a preliminary injunction, the court may order the trial on the merits to be advanced and consolidated with the hearing of the application...." This consolidation can be consummated even after the preliminary injunction hearing has concluded, especially when the parties agree to such a consolidation, as did the parties in this case. *Raymond Motor Transp., Inc. v. Rice*, 417 F. Supp. 1352, 1354, n.2 (W.D. Wisc. 1976), *rev'd on other grounds*, 434 U.S. 429, 98 S.Ct. 787, 54 L.Ed.2d 664 (1978); *Wood v. National Railroad Passenger Corp.*, 341 F. Supp. 908, 914 (D. Conn. 1972); see, 11 Wright & Miller, Federal Practice and Procedure: Civil Section 2950 (1973 ed.).

Reservation.[6] The 1968 Lease was approved by the Secretary in December 1968.[7] This was prior to the passage of NEPA in 1969.

During 1970 El Paso evaluated the potential of utilizing the leasehold for a coal gasification project and in 1973 proposed to the Tribe that two coal gasification facilities be installed on the leasehold.[8] During 1973 and 1974 the Bureau of Reclamation (Reclamation), pursuant to NEPA, made environmental studies and analyses of the impacts of the proposed gasification project and alternatives. On July 16, 1974, Reclamation submitted its draft environmental statement, DES 74-77,[9] to the Council on Environmental Quality (CEQ). DES 74-77 was also presented to other federal and state agencies and the public for review and comment. DES 74-77 addressed the environmental impacts associated with the proposed gasification project and the attendant surface mining and support activities.

In 1975, El Paso and Consol revised the proposed project, eliminating one of the gasification complexes. This revised plan divided the leasehold into two distinct mining areas. The northernmost 9,000 acres of the leasehold was designated as a thermal mine (Northern Mine), the coal from which was proposed to be used for direct commercial sale. The remaining acreage was designated as a gasification mine (Southern Mine). The production from this mine is intended to supply the coal requirements of the gasification facility.

In December 1975, Consol submitted a Mining and Reclamation Plan (1975 Mining Plan) to the United States Geological Survey (USGS), the Bureau of Indian Affairs (BIA), and the Navajo Tribe, in accordance with 25 C.F.R. Part 117. This mining plan described the revised project (ConPaso Project) and its environmental implications. The plan included, among other detail, descriptions of the proposed mining operations, the existing environment on the leasehold, potential impacts of strip mining, and measures to mitigate those impacts, including reclamation and revegetation associated with the ConPaso Project.

In 1976, the 1968 Lease was renegotiated between the Tribe and Intervenors. The revised lease (1976 Lease) encompassed the identical 40,286 acres of its predecessor but increased the Tribe's control over the operations, increased the financial benefits accruing to the Tribe, guaranteed preferential employment on the project for Tribe members, and designated certain procedures to be followed to protect the environment and paleontological and archeological resources on the leasehold. The 1976 Lease was executed on August 26, 1976.

On February 8, 1977, Reclamation issued its final environmental statement on the project, FES 77-03. FES 77-03 mentioned, but did not discuss, the changes in the proposed project

---

[6][*Orig. fn.*] During the interval between 1959 and 1968, El Paso had entered into a lease with the Navajo Tribe to mine 8,762 acres and obtained an option to lease an additional 13,880 acres of tribal lands. Both of these leases terminated without mining activity.

[7][*Orig. fn.*] The Secretary's approval of mining leases for unallotted Indian lands within a reservation is required by 25 U.S.C. § 396a.

[8][*Orig. fn.*] This proposed gasification project encompassed the entire leasehold area.

[9][*Orig. fn.*] Entitled "El Paso Coal Gasification Project."

that had occurred since the filing of DES 74-77.[10] Reclamation did note in FES 77-03 that a subsequent environmental impact statement (EIS) would be prepared by BIA which would address the 1976 Lease and the 1975 Mining Plan and the environmental impacts of the ConPaso Project as revised.

The draft environmental statement issued by BIA, DES 77-04,[11] was submitted to CEQ on February 9, 1977. DES 77-04 was issued as a supplement to FES 77-03.[12] Following circulation for review and comment among the federal and state agencies and the public, BIA filed the final environmental statement, FES 77-13, on May 11, 1977.[13] On July 1, 1977, the Tribe approved the 1975 Mining Plan. Shortly thereafter, the Secretary gave the Office of Surface Mining (OSM) the assignment of reviewing the 1975 Mining Plan and making recommendations as to its approval.[14]

On August 31, 1977, the Secretary approved the 1976 Lease based upon the information contained in FES 77-03 and FES 77-13. On October 23, 1978, Consol submitted a Restructured Mining and Reclamation Plan (1978 Mining Plan) to OSM. This revised mining plan was required by OSM after its examination of the 1975 Mining Plan. The 1978 Mining Plan addressed only the proposed mining operations and impacts for the Northern Mine. This Plan was subsequently approved by the New Mexico Coal Surface Mining Commission, the Tribe, USGS and BIA. On August 27, 1979, OSM issued an Environmental Assessment (EA) of the Plan. The EA was revised and reissued on November 2, 1979.

On January 11, 1980, Assistant Secretary Gerard issued a "Finding of No Significant Impact" (FONSI) with regard to the 1978 Mining Plan. The 1978 Mining Plan was given final approval that same day.

In Count One, Plaintiffs allege that the two FESs prepared in this case are inadequate, thereby violating NEPA. The four specific deficiencies propounded by Plaintiffs are (1) failure to adequately discuss the potential for unsuccessful land reclamation, (2) failure to adequately discuss other alternatives to the proposed action, (3) failure to adequately investigate and discuss the significance of archeological and paleontological resources on the leasehold, and (4) the failure to adequately discuss the human impacts upon the residents of the Burnham area.

* * *

---

[10][*Orig. fn.*] FES 77-03 differed from its draft version, DES 74-77, in that FES 77-03 discussed the environmental impacts of gasification for the project as revised in 1975. However, the scope of FES 77-03 was confined to the gasification phase of the revised project and the Southern Mine. It did not address the environmental impacts expected from the operation of the Northern Mine.

[11][*Orig. fn.*] Entitled "Navajo-El Paso/Consolidation Coal Lease and Mining Plan, Navajo Reservation, San Juan County, New Mexico."

[12][*Orig. fn.*] DES 77-04 discussed the environmental impacts associated with both the Southern and Northern Mines, the 1975 Mining Plan, and the 1976 Lease.

[13][*Orig. fn.*] FES 77-13 had the identical scope of DES 77-04.

[14][*Orig. fn.*] On August 3, 1977, the Surface Mining Control and Reclamation Act of 1977 (SMCRA), 30 U.S.C. § 1201 *et seq.* was enacted. SMCRA created the Office of Surface Mining Reclamation and Enforcement and invested it with the responsibility of supervising surface mining and reclamation in the United States.

ARCHEOLOGICAL AND PALEONTOLOGICAL RESOURCES.

The third alleged deficiency in the EIS record is the failure to describe the nature, extent and importance of archeological and paleontological resources on the leasehold, and to properly survey those resources and take mitigating measures prior to approval of the lease and mining plan.

The EIS record contains a detailed description of the nature and type of archeological and paleontological resources which could be expected to be encountered on the leasehold. See FES 77-03, Vol. I at pp. 3-87 through 88; FES 77-13 at pp. 2-39 through 40. Secondly, although Plaintiffs stated in one of their briefs that "(n)o estimate is given of the number of archeological sites on the leasehold (in the EIS record)," this simply is not true. The density of archeological sites expected to be discovered was ten sites per square mile. This estimate was based upon an archeological survey that was conducted on land immediately north of the ConPaso Project. FES 77- 03, Vol. I at p. 3-87; FES 77-13 at p. 3-44. Also, the EIS record estimates that the total number of archeological sites in the entire leasehold was between 600 and 650 sites. *Id.* The accuracy of these estimates has been verified by surveys conducted subsequent to the filing of the FESs.[50] The potential importance of these resources is also expressed in the statements. FES 77-03, Vol. I at pp. 2-184 through 2-185 and 3-187 through 3-188; FES 77-13 at pp. 2-39 through 2-40.

Plaintiffs have also contended that there should have been surveys conducted on the entire leasehold for archeological and paleontological resources and that all discovered resources should have been studied and evaluated in the FESs before approval of either the lease or the mining plan. There was only one preliminary archeological survey and no paleontological survey made prior to the filing of the FESs. However, statements made in the FESs relative to archeological and paleontological resources were based upon surveys and findings which occurred within the immediate vicinity of the ConPaso Project. These findings were deemed to be sufficient to allow a "reasonable" discussion of the impacts of the proposed actions upon those resources. In addition, the FESs specifically set forth ongoing controls over this phase of the project which include the conducting of surveys, inventorying, mitigating and clearance before any mining activities can commence on a particular sector of the project. FES 77-03, Vol. I at p. 3-88.

Based upon the data available, the discussions included in the FESs, and the ongoing controls over this segment of the project, the Court concludes that in relation to archeological and paleontological resources the EIS record was in "good faith compliance" and represents a "reasonable discussion" so as to provide the Secretary and the Assistant Secretary the means to take a "hard look" at the environmental consequences of approvals of the Lease and Mining Plan.

* * *

The Court's Findings of Fact and Conclusions of Law consist of those included in this Opinion and those filed by the Court on May 9, 1980, in conjunction with Plaintiffs' Motion for an Injunction Pending Appeal. See Fed.R.Civ.P. 52(a).

---

[50][*Orig. fn.*] See n.38, *supra.*

IT IS, THEREFORE, THE ORDER OF THIS COURT that the First, Second, Third, and Fourth Causes of Action be, and they are hereby, dismissed, with prejudice.

IT IS THE FURTHER ORDER OF THIS COURT that the Sixth Cause of Action be dismissed for failure to join an indispensable party under Fed.R.Civ.P. 19(b).

IT IS THE FURTHER ORDER OF THIS COURT that Plaintiffs' request for a Permanent Injunction be, and it is hereby, denied.

PRESERVATION COALITION, INC. v. PIERCE

667 F.2d 851 (9th Cir. 1982)

SNEED, Circuit Judge:

The Preservation Coalition, Inc. (Coalition) filed this action contending that the Secretary of the Department of Housing and Urban Development (HUD), the Mayor of Boise, Idaho, and the Boise Redevelopment Agency (BRA) violated the National Environmental Policy Act (NEPA) by failing to prepare an environmental impact statement (EIS) in 1979 for the Boise Downtown Center Redevelopment Project. The Coalition also contended that the defendants violated the National Historic Preservation Act (NHPA) by deciding to demolish or substantially alter seven buildings in the project that are currently listed on the National Register of Historic Places.

The district court found that laches barred the NEPA claims, and, in the alternative, that the BRA reasonably concluded that an EIS was not necessary. It further found that defendants did not violate the NHPA. The Coalition appeals the NEPA findings. The National Trust for Historic Preservation (National Trust) has filed an amicus brief raising issues under the NHPA. The BRA insists that these issues are not properly before the court. HUD, on the other hand, in its brief addresses the NHPA issues on the merits.

We hold that laches does not bar the NEPA claims but that under the circumstances of this case there was no violation of NEPA. Finally, we hold the NHPA issues are not properly before this court.

I.
FACTS

In July 1969 HUD and the BRA entered into a loan and grant contract to fund an urban renewal project covering several blocks in downtown Boise (the R-4 contract). NEPA became effective January 1, 1970. On June 28, 1971 the defendants signed a similar loan and grant contract for additional downtown blocks (the R-5 contract). The BRA prepared environmental clearances on both the R-4 and R-5 contracts finding that the project would have no significant environmental impact; thus, no EIS was needed. HUD approved the BRA finding.

Portions of the project site were cleared between 1972 and 1978, but no construction took place. In 1973 the area was reviewed to determine if buildings were eligible to be placed on the National Register. Seven buildings were placed on the National Register in

1974. In 1978, the Eastman Building was added to the Register. The BRA signed Memoranda of Agreement with the Advisory Council on Historic Preservation regarding the listed buildings in 1974 and 1979, respectively.

In 1979, the BRA converted the funding for the project from urban renewal loan and grant funds to Community Development Block Grant (CDBG) funds by signing a "financial settlement" with HUD. At the same time, the BRA prepared a lengthy environmental assessment (EA) on the entire project. The study found that the project would have no significant environmental impact. HUD approved the finding, and the Coalition filed the instant action.

* * *

III.
NEPA

A. Funding Conversion as a "Major Federal Action" Under NEPA

NEPA requires Federal agencies to make detailed reports on "major Federal actions significantly affecting the quality of the human environment." 42 U.S.C. § 4332(2)(C). We have held this standard met whenever substantial questions are raised as to whether a project may significantly degrade some human environmental factor. If an agency determines not to file an EIS, the reviewing court must consider whether the agency has reasonably concluded that the project will have no significant adverse environmental consequences. *City and County of San Francisco v. United States*, 615 F.2d 498, 500 (9th Cir. 1980); *City of Davis v. Coleman*, 521 F.2d 661, 673 (9th Cir. 1975); see *Portela v. Pierce*, 650 F.2d 210, 213 (9th Cir. 1981). The district court here found that the financial settlement that the BRA signed with HUD was not a major federal action.

1. Funding Conversion as Equivalent to Authorizing Construction of a Parking Garage

The Coalition contends otherwise. It argues that since block grant funds will be used to build a 3000-car parking facility, for which purpose the urban renewal funds could not have been used, the conversion has caused all the environmental effects that ordinarily would be associated with construction of the parking garage. Thus, the conversion has, as would have had the construction of the garage, a significant environmental impact.

This overstates the matter. While the urban renewal funds could not have been used for parking construction, a parking facility was nevertheless part of the original plan. Under that plan the BRA committed itself to raise funds for the parking facility to satisfy the state matching requirement. This had not been accomplished by 1978. The funding conversion simply removed a limit on the use of the federal money, but did not alter the planned scope of the project.

A funding change does not resemble changing an industrial park to a neighborhood development, *San Francisco Tomorrow v. Romney*, 472 F.2d 1021, 1025–26 (9th Cir. 1973). Instead, like a grant of additional funds to cover increased land acquisition and relocation costs, *id.*, the shift from urban renewal funds to CDBG funds does not affect the fundamental nature of the project, nor inject into it a new aspect which has never been considered. To the contrary, the parking facilities for whose construction CDBG funds will pay have always been considered essential. Any potential degradation of the environment flows, not from the funding conversion, but from the initial plans which included the parking facility.

2. Funding Conversion as a "Major Federal Action" Pursuant to HUD Regulations

The Coalition next argues that the funding conversion from urban renewal to CDBG funds requires an EIS under HUD regulations. To evaluate this contention properly it is necessary to analyze HUD's then-applicable environmental review procedures for the CDBG program which appear in Title 24, C.F.R. Part 58 (1979). Two sections of Part 58, §§ 58.19 and 58.20, are directly relevant.

Section 58.19 covers environmental review of continuations of previous activities. Section 58.19(a) states that a project which is a continuation of a previously commenced activity for which previously conducted environmental reviews "are insufficient due to changed circumstances, including the availability of additional data..., must be subjected to an... updated environmental review under this Part." This review "shall be carried out with respect to the entire project to the extent that the entire project or portions of it could still be altered in light of environmental considerations." 24 C.F.R. § 58.19(a) (1979). Section 58.19(c) provides, however, that if environmental review has been completed and circumstances, including available data, have not changed significantly, no new environmental review is required.

Section 58.20 pertains to financial settlement of urban renewal projects. It makes additional requirements, beyond those for CDBG funding in general, applicable to applications for financial settlement of an urban renewal project prior to substantial completion thereof. Every such application becomes a "project" requiring environmental review. Section 58.20(a)(1) makes section 58.19(c), which permits, as indicated, forgoing of environmental review with respect to some continuations of previous activities, inapplicable to such applications. Furthermore, the environmental review must include an assessment of the environmental consequences of the financial settlement. See 24 C.F.R. § 58.20(a)(2).

Taken together, these provisions require that we recognize that HUD erred in concluding that the BRA complied with HUD regulations by filing a statement that the funding conversion itself had no significant environmental impact. See Affidavit of Ryomi Tanino, Clerk's Record Vol. II, Appendix E. The first paragraph of section 58.20 clearly states that it imposes additional requirements. Its requirements are additional to, but do not oust, those imposed by section 58.19 governing continuation of previous activities with respect to which changed circumstances, including additional data, have made a prior review insufficient. Thus, both section 58.20 and section 58.19 are applicable here. HUD regulations require not only an account of the impact of the financial settlement itself, 24 C.F.R. § 58.20, but also an updating of the environmental review where changed circumstances, totally independent of the financial settlement, make it desirable, see 24 C.F.R. § 58.19(a). That appellee's environmental reviews in 1971 and 1975 were adequate under the regulations then in effect in no way renders the 1979 regulations inapplicable to appellee's application for financial settlement.

It cannot be denied that by 1979 the circumstances had changed from what they were in 1971 and 1975. See 24 C.F.R. § 58.19(a). The Eastman Building was added to the National Register in 1978. It also cannot be denied that the project in 1979 "could still be altered in light of environmental considerations." *Id.* And, of course, it cannot be denied that there was a "financial settlement" with HUD in 1979. See 24 C.F.R. § 58.20. It follows that the procedures outlined by sections 58.19 and 58.20 must be followed.[1]

BRA indeed followed these procedures in preparing its 1979 environmental assessment, which it assumed was required by applicable federal regulations, HUD's contrary interpretation notwithstanding. These procedures, however, do not lead irresistibly to imposing upon BRA the duty of preparing an EIS with respect to the 1979 funding conversion. The updated environmental review required by section 58.19(a) contemplates a new "clearance finding" that will take into account the information theretofore developed and the new factors. 24 C.F.R. § 58.19(b)(1). Preparation of the clearance finding is described in section 58.15 which is captioned "Steps to commence environmental review process." Section 58.16 governs completion of the environmental review process where a clearance finding under section 58.15 has determined that the request for release of funds for the project (and, necessarily, any related action whose review is required ancillary to the release of funds) is not an action which may significantly affect the environment. Under these circumstances, no EIS is required. 24 C.F.R. § 58.16. Here, BRA found precisely that the Boise project had no significant impact. Our task is to determine whether this finding under section 58.16 in the BRA's 1979 environmental assessment was reasonable. *Portela v. Pierce*, 650 F.2d 210, 213 (9th Cir. 1981); *City and County of San Francisco v. United States*, 615 F.2d 498, 500 (9th Cir. 1980); *City of Davis v. Coleman*, 521 F.2d 661, 673 (9th Cir. 1975).

a.   *Effect of Destruction of National Register Building.*

The Coalition takes the position that the contemplated destruction or significant alteration of buildings listed on the National Register, without more, imprints BRA's finding of no

---

[1][*Orig. fn.*] 24 C.F.R. Part 58 has since been substantially revised. However, it appears that under the new regulations supplementary review would still be required. See 24 C.F.R. § 58.19 (1980). If the regulations do not demand such supplementation, the statute itself probably requires it. *Cf. Warm Springs Dam Task Force v. Gribble*, 621 F.2d 1017, 1024 (9th Cir. 1980) (continuing duty to supplement). Current Council on Environmental Quality guidelines for agencies address only the need to update draft or final EISs, not environmental assessments. The guidelines now provide that agencies "(1) Shall prepare supplements to either draft or final environmental impact statements if:... (ii) There are significant new circumstances or information relevant to environmental concerns and bearing on the proposed action or its impacts." (emphasis added). 40 C.F.R. § 1502.9(c) (1981). However, logic would also require supplementation in the less frequent situation where significant new circumstances or information relevant to environmental concerns arises after an initial finding of no significant impact. Supplementation of an environmental assessment after designation of historic buildings in the project area to the National Register would not, of course, be required where applicable environmental review has been previously carried out in a timely and proper manner. See *Central Oklahoma Preservation Alliance v. Oklahoma City, etc.*, 471 F. Supp. 68 (W.D. Okl.) (1979).

significant impact on the environment with the mark of unreasonableness. It cites *WATCH (Waterbury Action, etc.) v. Harris*, 603 F.2d 310 (2d Cir. 1979), *cert. denied*, 444 U.S. 995, 100 S.Ct. 530, 62 L.Ed.2d 426 (1979), in support of its position. *WATCH* can be read in this fashion. *Id.* at 318, 326. We decline, however, to follow *WATCH* when read in this fashion.

We regard the adoption of such a rule as inconsistent with at least the spirit of *San Francisco Tomorrow v. Romney*, 472 F.2d 1021 (9th Cir. 1973). There we refused to regard amendatory contracts, which increased funding for the sole purpose of providing for the rising cost of land acquisitions and relocation of displaced residents, as "further major federal action" within the meaning of NEPA. Our refusal indicates that within this circuit federal action subsequent to the initiation of a project must be evaluated comprehensively and in terms of its relationship to the environmental effects of the entire project. Only then can it be determined whether the recent federal action amounted to "further major federal action."

Presently agencies prepare some 1,000 EISs and some 30,000 environmental assessments annually. U.S. Council on Environmental Quality, Environmental Quality-1976, pp. 123, 132. The environmental assessment is an established part of NEPA environmental review. See, *e.g., Hanly v. Kleindienst*, 471 F.2d 823 (2d Cir. 1972), *cert. denied*, 412 U.S. 908, 93 S.Ct. 2290, 36 L.Ed.2d 974 (1973), *and later appeal*, 484 F.2d 448 (2d Cir. 1973), *cert. denied*, 416 U.S. 936, 94 S.Ct. 1934, 40 L.Ed.2d 286 (1974); *Portela v. Pierce*, 650 F.2d 210, 213 (9th Cir. 1981) ("environmental clearance"); *City and County of San Francisco v. United States*, 615 F.2d 498, 500 (9th Cir. 1980); *City of Davis v. Coleman*, 521 F.2d 661, 674 (9th Cir. 1975) ("negative declaration"). As a screening device, the environmental assessment allows agencies with limited resources to focus on truly important federal actions. We decline to remove this screen by imposing a *per se* rule. See *Stewart & Krier, Environmental Law and Policy* 754 (2d ed. 1978).

Hart v. Denver Urban Renewal Authority, 551 F.2d 1178 (10th Cir. 1977), is not inconsistent with our approach in this case. There it was held that the loan and grant contract's provision that HUD approve all acquisitions and dispositions of property by the urban renewal authority established a continuing federal involvement sufficient to make the approval by HUD of the sale of a National Register building "further federal action." Our approach to the "continuing involvement" of HUD is guided by HUD's own regulations on CDBG funding rather than by a "continuing involvement" gloss on NEPA. Whether this gloss exists in this circuit need not detain us. HUD's own regulations, in this instance, embody its substance in any event. Neither, moreover, requires that we adopt the *per se* rule of *WATCH*.

It, therefore, becomes necessary to determine whether the district court erred in holding that the Boise project, at the time of the funding conversion, had "no significant impact" on the human environment under NEPA. The standard of review we must apply to an agency's failure to prepare an EIS is whether the agency's action was reasonable. See *Warm Springs Dam Task Force v. Gribble*, 621 F.2d 1017, 1024 (9th Cir. 1980) (updating prior review); *Portela v. Pierce*, 650 F.2d 210 (9th Cir. 1981); *City and County of San Francisco v. United States*, 615 F.2d 498 (9th Cir. 1980); *City of Davis v. Coleman*, 521 F.2d 661 (9th Cir. 1975). But *cf. Shea, The Judicial Standard for Review of Environmental Impact Statement Threshold Decisions*, 9 Boston College Envt'l Affairs L. Rev. 63 (1980) (Administrative Procedure Act requires "arbitrary and capricious" standard of review).

b. Reasonableness of BRA's Finding.

We commence our review by recognizing, as we must, that NEPA requires federal agencies to preserve important historic and cultural aspects of our nation's heritage. 42 U.S.C. § 4331(b)(4) (1976). See *Aluli v. Brown*, 437 F. Supp. 602, 607 (D. Haw. 1977), *reversed in part*, 602 F.2d 876 (9th Cir. 1979) (archaeological sites). Furthermore, judgments of historical significance made by the Advisory Council on Historic Preservation, the expert regulatory body concerned with preserving, restoring, and maintaining the historic and cultural environment of the Nation, Exec. Order No. 11,593, 36 Fed. Reg. 8921 (May 15, 1971), deserve great weight.[2] However, compliance with the NHPA, even when it exists, does not assure compliance with NEPA. Each mandates separate and distinct procedures, both of which must be complied with when historic buildings are affected.[3] *Cf. Stop H-3 Ass'n v. Coleman*, 533 F.2d 434, 444–45 (9th Cir. 1976), *cert. denied, Wright v. Stop H-3 Ass'n*, 429 U.S. 999, 97 S.Ct. 526, 50 L.Ed.2d 610 (1976) (NEPA compliance does not constitute NHPA compliance). Execution of a "Memorandum of Agreement" with the Advisory Council on Historic Preservation, on the other hand, does not relieve a federal agency of the duty of complying with the impact statement requirement "to the fullest extent possible," 42 U.S.C. § 4332.

There are, however, similarities between the demands and goals of NEPA and the NHPA. Both Acts create obligations that are chiefly procedural in nature; both have the goal of generating information about the impact of federal actions on the environment; and both require that the relevant federal agency carefully consider the information produced.[4] That

---

[2][*Orig. fn.*] Executive Order 11,593 requires federal agencies to institute procedures, in consultation with the Advisory Council on Historic Preservation, to assure that federal agencies carry out their responsibilities of historic preservation under NHPA. Thus, cooperation with the Advisory Council is a regulatory mandate. Of course, Advisory Council decisions are of greater weight for NHPA purposes, where their role is prescribed by statute, than for NEPA purposes. See generally *Rose, Preservation and Community: New Directions in the Law of Historic Preservation*, 33 Stan. L. Rev. 473 (1981).

[3][*Orig. fn.*] NEPA requires detailed statements on major federal actions significantly affecting the quality of the human environment, including the historic and cultural environment, 42 U.S.C. § 4332(C), whereas the NHPA requires federal agencies, prior to the approval of the expenditure of federal funds on any undertaking, to take into account the effect of the undertaking on National Register buildings, and to afford the Advisory Council on Historic Preservation a reasonable opportunity to comment. 16 U.S.C. § 470f. Thus, the NHPA mandate is much more narrowly focused.

[4][*Orig. fn.*] See note 3 *supra*. The U.S. Supreme Court recently emphasized the procedural character of NEPA in *Strycker's Bay Neighborhood Council, Inc. v. Karlen et al.*, 444 U.S. 223, 100 S.Ct. 497, 62 L.Ed.2d 433 (1980). In overruling the Second Circuit's finding that the EIS was insufficient, the Court held that a reviewing court is limited to ensuring that the agency has considered the environmental consequences of its action. The Supreme Court chided the court below for requiring HUD to "elevate environmental concerns over other, admittedly legitimate, considerations. Neither NEPA nor the APA provides any support for such a reordering of priorities by a reviewing court." *Id.* at 438.

is, both are designed to insure that the agency "stop, look, and listen" before moving ahead. NHPA compliance will often be relevant to a determination of whether a threshold finding of no significant impact on the historic environment was reasonable. Nonetheless, unless agency regulations specifically mandate otherwise,[5] each Act must be taken on its own terms.

(1) Impact on Historic Environment.

Turning to the particulars of this case, we find that the BRA carefully considered information about the Boise project's impact on the historic environment, as shown in the list of documents attached to Mayor Richard R. Eardley's July 27, 1979 letter to Gerald Huard, Acting Area Manager for HUD. With respect to the Eastman building, the BRA determined it to lack significance based on several factors: lack of a public perception of historic or other significance, the inadequacy of the comments and attached documents supporting the finding of significance in the Nomination Form, and the fact that the Eastman building's colorably significant features were better represented in other buildings that were being retained. In particular, the BRA relied on a report by architect Ernest Lombard assessing the impact on the historic environment. With respect to the other historic buildings in the project area, the BRA determined that no features integral to the historic, cultural, or architectural significance of the buildings will be affected. On balance, the careful manner in which the BRA considered historic information and the thoroughness of its statement explaining its decision not to require an EIS convinces us that the BRA's finding of no significant impact on the historic environment was reasonable. See *Gribble, supra*, at 1024–25....

V.
CONCLUSION

Although the Coalition's NEPA claims are not barred by laches, neither the conversion from urban renewal funds to CDBG funds in 1979, nor HUD regulations applicable to that conversion, nor the planned destruction of a building included on the National Register requires an EIS for the Boise project. Preparation of an environmental assessment in 1979 to evaluate new information leading to changed circumstances with respect to the project's impact on the historic and cultural environment was required by then-applicable HUD regulations. However, the 1979 environmental assessment's finding of no significant impact was reasonable. As modified by this opinion, the judgment of the court below is AFFIRMED.

---

[5][*Orig. fn.*] For example, HUD Handbook 1390.1, 38 Fed. Reg. 19182, which applies only to HUD's own projects, requires an EIS for "any project which has an adverse effect on a property listed on, or nominated to the National Register of Historic Places." *Id.* at 19189 (Appendix A-2).

ALL INDIAN PUEBLO COUNCIL v. UNITED STATES

975 F.2d 1437 (10th Cir. 1992)

HOLLOWAY, Circuit Judge:

Indian Pueblos and two environmental organizations challenge on procedural grounds and for alleged legal insufficiency an environmental impact statement (EIS) that the Bureau of Indian Affairs (BIA) prepared for the Ojo Line Extension Project, a proposed major electrical transmission line and associated substations to be built by the Public Service Company of New Mexico (PNM) and Los Alamos County, New Mexico. The plaintiff organizations present two principal issues on appeal: (1) whether the district court erred in upholding the decision by the Assistant Secretary of the Interior to deny the appellants an administrative appeal of the BIA's decision to issue the Record of Decision (ROD); and (2) whether, under the National Environmental Policy Act (NEPA), 42 U.S.C. § 4321, *et seq.*, the EIS adequately evaluated the proposed project, and alternatives to it. We affirm.

I

At the end of a major electric transmission line, Public Service Company of New Mexico's Norton Switching Station was designed to be a primary delivery point of power for the Santa Fe and Los Alamos areas. The Norton station currently is served by a single, 345 kilovolt (kV) transmission line. For several years PNM and Los Alamos County have proposed building a new 345 kV transmission line in order to link the Norton station to an existing 345 kV line, known as the San Juan-Ojo line, to the north. The new line would serve as an alternate major transmission source at the Norton Station in the event of an outage on the existing 345 kV line.

The proposed Ojo Line Extension (OLE) would consist of from 45 to 50 miles of overhead transmission line on a 150-foot right of way and associated substations. In and near the possible paths of the line are the Jemez Mountains, several Pueblos, and significant archeological sites, as well as tribal cultural and religious sites. Because of the possibility that federal agencies would be required to take action on the project to grant or approve rights of way, an environmental impact statement was prepared in compliance with NEPA. Acting as the lead agency for several federal agencies, see 40 C.F.R. § 1501.5 (1986), the Bureau of Indian Affairs formally began preparing an EIS for the project in late summer 1984. The BIA issued a draft EIS in October 1985. A comment period followed in late 1985 and early 1986. On August 15, 1986, the BIA issued a 242-page final environmental impact statement (FEIS) for the project.

The FEIS evaluated three major alternatives, including no action or "no approval of rights-of-way or construction." FEIS at xxii. The other alternatives discussed in the FEIS were two possible routes for the new transmission line: (1) a western route, upon which a line would be built in a generally northwesterly direction from the Norton station through the Los Alamos area and would intersect with the San Juan-Ojo line near Coyote, New Mexico; and (2) an eastern route, a path generally extending north of the Norton station through the Espanola area and connecting with the San Juan-Ojo line at the existing Ojo

Switching Station. In addition, the agency analyzed two variations of each of the two proposed routes. The BIA Albuquerque office issued a record of decision (ROD) on September 26, 1986, which selected one of the two western corridor alternatives known as "W-2" as the route for the project.

II

In late October 1986, the appellants and the State of New Mexico filed an administrative appeal of the ROD challenging the legal sufficiency of the EIS and arguing that the route adopted violated the protections guaranteed by the First Amendment and the American Indian Religious Freedom Act, 42 U.S.C. § 1996. In letters of March 19, 1987, and April 3, 1987, the Assistant Secretary for Indian Affairs dismissed the appeals from the ROD. The letters stated that since the ROD ultimately selected an alternative route which bypasses all Indian lands, there was no substantive decision to be made by a BIA official in reference to the proposed project; any appeal would lie to other agencies having administration of lands to be crossed. Following the administrative denial of their appeal by the Assistant Secretary, the appellants filed this action in June 1987 claiming federal question jurisdiction under 28 U.S.C. § 1331. See I R. Doc. 1.

This action was brought in part under the Administrative Procedure Act (APA), 5 U.S.C. §§ 701–06, seeking judicial review of the Assistant Secretary's decision to deny the administrative appeal. I R. Doc. 1, at 12 (First Claim). The appellants sought an order mandating the BIA to hear the administrative appeal, *id.* at 16, or an order setting aside the FEIS and directing the agencies to prepare a new environmental impact statement, *id.* at 17. Further, the appellants sought a judicial determination that the final EIS was inadequate as a matter of law under NEPA. *Id.* at 14 (Fourth Claim).[1]

The district court resolved both the issues of the denial of an administrative appeal and the NEPA issues in separate grants of summary judgment in favor of the defendants. On August 25, 1989, the district court granted partial summary judgment in favor of the defendants on the plaintiffs' claim that they were improperly denied an administrative appeal. I R. Doc. 122. The court explained that it viewed the agency's dismissal of the appeal as a final order, that the BIA "contemplates no further action" on the claims, and that the appellants had exhausted the available administrative remedies. *Id.* at 2. The court stated that: plaintiffs had other remedies, namely judicial review by the district court; the plaintiffs had not been cut off from presenting additional testimony and would be allowed to move its admission regarding adequacy of the EIS at a later stage of the proceedings; and the doctrines of exhaustion of administrative remedies and primary jurisdiction did not apply because the BIA had no special expertise to review adequacy of the FEIS. *Id.*

---

[1] *[Orig. fn.]* The appellants' Second and Third Claims alleged that the appellees' actions violated the Indian plaintiffs' rights under the First Amendment and the American Indian Religious Freedom Act. The plaintiffs consented to the entry of partial summary judgment in favor of the defendants on the Second and Third Claims in response to *Lyng v. Northwest Indian Cemetery Protective Association*, 485 U.S. 439, 108 S.Ct. 1319, 99 L.Ed.2d 534 (1988). See Appellants' Opening Br. at 4. No issue concerning these two claims is presented in this appeal.

After ruling on the APA claims, the district court on August 15, 1990, granted summary judgment in favor of the defendants on the NEPA issues by a written Memorandum Opinion and Order. I R. Doc. 128.[2] In addressing the appellants' claim that the FEIS inadequately analyzed alternatives to the project, the district judge applied the rule that "if the FEIS is sufficient to inform a decision maker of the major alternatives, it thereby enables the agency to put forth a reasonable determination of the best alternative." *Id.* at 15. The judge explained that in making the ruling he had considered the agency's discussion of the four alternative routes, as well as the "no action" alternative, and had considered the other alternatives that the agency in the ROD explained it had "eliminated from further consideration" after addressing them in "minor detail." Joint App. of PNM tab 2, at 14 (ROD); see I R. Doc. 128, at 15–17. In conclusion, the district judge reasoned that the discussion of alternatives was adequate because the FEIS and the ROD "contain an adequate amount of information for the agency to make its decision that the W-2 alternative would best meet the project needs." I R. Doc. 128, at 17.

Concerning the appellants' remaining NEPA contentions, the district judge ruled that the FEIS adequately analyzed the environmental impact of the project. Addressing specific issues, the court ruled that the EIS adequately dismissed the potential impact of the project on the habitat of the Jemez Mountain salamander by referencing a study completed after the statement was prepared. I R. Doc. 128, at 4–5. The court concluded that the EIS also adequately addressed the potential impact of the power line on visual resources. *Id.* at 7. The judge noted that the agency in addressing the issue had acknowledged that "some impairment to visual resources" would occur, and had included in the EIS a description of the methodology used to assess visual impact. *Id.*

Further, the judge rejected the appellants' contention that the discussion of the impact on paleontological and cultural resources was insufficient in part because of the use of tables and charts. The judge noted that the EIS contained a separate review of studies relevant to the issue, and that the condensation of the study data in the tables "reflects that the agency did in fact undertake some analysis of the paleontological and cultural resources within the W-2 corridor." *Id.* at 8. In sum, the district court ruled that the EIS was adequate under the mandate of NEPA and granted summary judgment for the defendants. This appeal followed.

After argument of this appeal, we were advised in an Emergency Application for Injunction Pending Appeal filed on August 31, 1992, that the New Mexico Public Service Commission (PSC or Commission) has held its hearings on the OLE project but has not determined whether to issue a Certificate of Convenience and Necessity for the project. In its proceeding the Commission issued a Preliminary Cease and Desist Order on May 18, 1992, against certain activities related to the construction of the OLE project. On August 3, 1992, the PSC, with one commissioner dissenting, issued an order vacating the cease and desist order in part. The order left in place the Commission's directive prohibiting PNM from conducting "intensive data recovery" as a part of "archaeological mitigation and site protection activities." In re Public Service Co. of New Mexico, No. 2382 (N.M.Pub.Serv.Comm'n Aug. 3, 1992) (order vacating in part preliminary cease and desist order). This order allowed PNM to initiate or to continue some activities preliminary to construction, including

---

[2][*Orig. fn.*] The parties agreed that the plaintiffs' claims were "appropriately suited to disposition on summary judgment motions." I R. Doc. 128, at 3.

nonintrusive "archaeological mitigation and site protection," geotechnical and centerline surveying, tree marking, and a "solid waste management unit survey." *Id.*[3]

The emergency application to this court of August 31 sought injunctive relief to restrain some activities related to the OLE project, including "archaeological material removal and data recording," tree cutting and painting as part of a centerline survey, and use of heavy equipment and drilling for core soil samples at proposed tower sites as part of a geotechnical survey. On September 1, 1992, this court granted a temporary injunctive order, directed prompt filing of responses, and later granted leave for a reply thereto.[4] In view of the conclusions we reach in this opinion, our temporary injunctive order of September 1 is being vacated forthwith upon the filing of this opinion.

* * *

IV

We turn now to the appellants' contentions challenging the sufficiency of the EIS.

A

Environmental impact statements are among the procedures that NEPA mandates in order to effect "a broad national commitment to protecting and promoting environmental quality." *Robertson v. Methow Valley Citizens Council*, 490 U.S. 332, 348, 109 S.Ct. 1835, 1844–45, 104 L.Ed.2d 351 (1989). NEPA requires all federal agencies to prepare an EIS for "every recommendation or report on proposals for legislation and other major Federal actions significantly affecting the quality of the human environment." 42 U.S.C.§ 4332(2)(C). An EIS serves the goals of NEPA in part by ensuring that the agency, in reaching its decision, will have available and will carefully consider detailed information concerning significant environmental impacts; it also guarantees that the relevant information will be made available to the larger audience that may also play a role in both the decisionmaking process and the implementation of that decision. *Robertson*, 490 U.S. at 349, 109 S.Ct. at 1845. An EIS must contain a detailed statement about

(i) the environmental impact of the proposed action,
(ii) any adverse environmental effects which cannot be avoided should the proposal be implemented,

---

[3][*Orig. fn.*] The New Mexico Attorney General petitioned the New Mexico Supreme Court for a writ of mandamus directing the Commission to vacate its order allowing activities in preparation for construction. On August 26, 1992, the New Mexico Supreme Court denied the petition for a writ of mandamus. *Attorney General v. New Mexico Pub. Serv. Comm'n*, No. 20,737 (N.M. Aug. 26, 1992) (order denying petition for a writ of mandamus).

[4][*Orig. fn.*] Our order enjoined PNM "from proceeding with construction of Ojo Line Extension 345 kV Transmission Project pending further order of the court." *All Indian Pueblo Council v. United States*, No. 90-2225 (10th Cir. Sept. 1, 1992).

(iii) alternatives to the proposed action,

(iv) the relationship between local short-term uses of man's environment and the maintenance and enhancement of long-term productivity, and

(v) any irreversible and irretrievable commitments of resources which would be involved in the proposed action should it be implemented.

    42 U.S.C.§ 4332(2)(C) (1988).

The discussion of alternatives that § 4332(2)(C)(iii) requires is "the heart of the environmental impact statement." 40 C.F.R. § 1502.14 (1986). NEPA requires a "detailed" EIS "to ensure that each agency decision maker has before him and takes into proper account all possible approaches to a particular project (including total abandonment of the project) which would alter the environmental impact and the cost-benefit balance." *Calvert Cliffs' Coordinating Comm., Inc. v. United States Atomic Energy Comm'n*, 449 F.2d 1109, 1114 (D.C. Cir. 1971) (emphasis added). As another court observed, "[i]t is absolutely essential to the NEPA process that the decisionmaker be provided with a detailed and careful analysis of the relative environmental merits and demerits of the proposed action and possible alternatives, a requirement that we have characterized as 'the linchpin of the entire impact statement.' " *Natural Resources Defense Council v. Callaway*, 524 F.2d 79, 92 (2d Cir. 1975) (emphasis added). We agree that a thorough discussion of the alternatives is imperative.

In addressing alternatives to a proposed action in an EIS, federal agencies must "[r]igorously explore and objectively evaluate all reasonable alternatives, and for alternatives which were eliminated from detailed study, briefly discuss the reasons for their having been eliminated." 40 C.F.R. § 1502.14(a) (1986). Concerning the requisite level of detail necessary, "[w]hat is required is information sufficient to permit a reasoned choice of alternatives as far as environmental aspects are concerned." *Natural Resources Defense Council, Inc. v. Morton*, 458 F.2d 827, 836 (D.C. Cir. 1972), quoted with approval in *Environmental Defense Fund, Inc.*, 619 F.2d at 1375. NEPA does not require agencies to analyze "the environmental consequences of alternatives it has in good faith rejected as too remote, speculative, or... impractical or ineffective." *City of Aurora v. Hunt*, 749 F.2d 1457, 1467 (10th Cir. 1984).

As the Supreme Court has noted, "it is now well settled that NEPA itself does not mandate particular results, but simply prescribes the necessary process." *Robertson*, 490 U.S. at 350, 109 S.Ct. at 1846; see also, *e.g., Environmental Defense Fund, Inc. v. Andrus*, 619 F.2d 1368, 1374 (10th Cir. 1980) (explaining "requirements of NEPA... apply to procedure and do not undertake to control decision making"). In reviewing a challenge to the adequacy of an EIS, then, our job is not to "second-guess the experts" in policy matters but rather it is to determine "whether the statement is a good faith, objective, and reasonable presentation of the subject areas mandated by NEPA." *Manygoats v. Kleppe*, 558 F.2d 556, 560 (10th Cir. 1977); see also, *e.g., Save Our Invaluable Land (SOIL), Inc. v. Needham*, 542 F.2d 539, 542– 43 (10th Cir. 1976) (explaining "an EIS is to be tested by the concepts of 'good faith' and a 'reasonable' discussion of the five mandated areas of subject matter"), *cert. denied*, 430 U.S. 945, 97 S.Ct. 1580, 51 L.Ed.2d 792 (1977).

Stated another way, in considering a challenge to the adequacy of an EIS a "court should 'ensure that the statement contains sufficient discussion of the relevant issues and opposing viewpoints to enable the decisionmaker to take a "hard look" at environmental factors, and to make a reasoned decision.' " *Natural Resources Defense Council, Inc. v. Hodel*, 865 F.2d 288, 294 (D.C. Cir. 1988) [quoting *Izaak Walton League of Am. v. Marsh*,

655 F.2d 346, 371 (D.C. Cir. 1981)]. Thus, we test the discussion of alternatives in an EIS under a "rule of reason" standard of review. See *Environmental Defense Fund, Inc.*, 619 F.2d at 1375 (noting, "test the agencies must meet in dealing with the environmental aspects of proposed action is anchored to the 'rule of reason'").

* * *

C

The appellants also challenge the adequacy of the BIA's evaluation of the potential environmental impact of the project. First, the appellants challenge the sufficiency of the analysis of cultural resources. The FEIS evaluates in general terms the potential impact of the possible corridors on historical and archeological sites. Addressing the impact on religious sites, the agency concluded that none of the possible routes would "physically impact any known religious sites and have been designed to avoid them by a sufficient buffer so that there should be no effect on the practice of Native American religion." FEIS at IV-22, IV-25. The agency quantified as "high," "medium," or "low" the possible environmental impacts on "resources" including archeology, biotic resources, land use, soils, threatened and endangered species, and visual resources; charts in the FEIS show, for each resource, the number of miles of each corridor alternative that the agency placed in each of the three categories.

The appellants contend in general that the analysis is inadequate, and in particular that the charts contain no analysis. We disagree. As the district judge noted, the FEIS contains

a review of the existing studies of the mountain and valley alternative areas, inventory data, the results of a vehicle [reconnaissance] of the study areas, a review of the site files at the Laboratory of Anthropology, and the results of an on-the-ground [reconnaissance] survey of the areas adjacent to the known concentration of archeological sites.

I R. Doc. 128, at 8. We agree with the district judge that the charts condensed the available information, and reflected that the BIA "did in fact undertake some analysis of the paleontological and cultural resources within the W-2 corridor." *Id.* at 8. We conclude the discussion in the FEIS of the potential environmental impacts on archeological sites, as well as on Pueblo Indian religious practices, was sufficient.

* * *

V

In sum, we are convinced that the district court properly upheld the actions of the BIA and the sufficiency of the EIS, and accordingly we AFFIRM the judgment and orders of that court. In light of this conclusion, the temporary injunction entered by this court on September 1, 1992, is VACATED effective upon the filing of this opinion.

NEPA's mandate to the federal agencies is, like the NHPA, essentially procedural [*Vermont Yankee Nuclear Power Corp. v. NRDC*, 435 U.S. 519, 558 (1978)]. "[I]t is now well settled that NEPA itself does not mandate particular results, but simply prescribes the necessary process.... Other statutes may impose substantive environmental obligations on federal agencies, but NEPA merely prohibits uninformed—rather than unwise—agency action" [*Robertson v. Methow Valley Citizens Council*, 490 U.S. 332, 350–51 (1989); and see also *Marsh v. Oregon Natural Resources Council*, 490 U.S. 360, 371 (1989), holding that "NEPA does not work by mandating that agencies achieve particular substantive environmental results"; and *Stryker's Bay Neighborhood Council, Inc. v. Karlen*, 444 U.S. 223 (1980)].

The goal of NEPA was clearly explained by the U.S. Supreme Court in *Baltimore Gas & Electric Co. v. NRDC*:

> NEPA has twin aims. First, it 'places upon an agency the obligation to consider every significant aspect of the environmental impact of the proposed action.' Second, it insures that the agency will inform the public that it has indeed considered environmental concerns in its decisionmaking process. Congress in enacting NEPA, however, did not require agencies to elevate environmental concerns over other appropriate considerations. Rather, it required only that the agency take a 'hard look' at the environmental consequences before taking a major action.
> 462 U.S. 87, 97–98 (1983) (citations omitted).

Federal agencies, therefore, need only take a "hard look" at the consequences to heritage resources as a result of their proposed actions in order to comply with the mandates of this aspect of NEPA. In sum, an agency has complied with the Act if it "adequately considered and disclosed the environmental impact of its actions and that its decision is not arbitrary or capricious" (*Baltimore Gas* at 97–98). Nothing further is required of the federal agency.

3.   Federal Land Policy and Management Act of 1976

The Federal Land Policy and Management Act of 1976 [FLPMA, 43 U.S.C. § 1701 *et seq.* (1994)] "vests the Secretary of the Interior with broad authority to manage the federal government's vast land holdings. The statute departs from the federal government's earlier policy of giving away public lands, in favor of a philosophy of retention and management to maximize the multitudinous interests in the lands" [*Sierra Club v. Hodel*, 848 F.2d 1068, 1078 (10th Cir. 1988)].

By enacting FLPMA, Congress delegated to the Secretary of the Interior, through the Bureau of Land Management (BLM), the responsibility to manage the public lands and their resources. As part of this responsibility, the BLM is required to manage the public lands:

> in a manner that will protect the quality of scientific, scenic, *historical*, ecological, environmental, air and atmospheric, water resource, and *archeological* values; that, where appropriate, will preserve and protect certain public lands in their natural condition; that will provide food and habitat for fish and wildlife and domestic animals; and that will provide for outdoor recreation and human occupancy and use;
> 43 U.S.C. § 1701(a)(8) (1994) (emphasis added).

Further, FLPMA dictates that the "management be on the basis of multiple use and sustained yield unless otherwise specified by law" [43 U.S.C. § 1701(a)(7) (1994)]. The statute defines the term "multiple use" as:

the management of the public lands and their various resource values so that they are utilized in the combination that will best meet the present and future needs of the American people; making the most judicious use of the land for some or all of these resources or related services over areas large enough to provide sufficient latitude for periodic adjustments in use to conform to changing needs and conditions; the use of some land for less than all of the resources; a combination of balanced and diverse resource uses that takes into account the long-term needs of future generations for renewable and nonrenewable resources, including, but not limited to, recreation, range, timber, minerals, watershed, wildlife and fish, and natural scenic, scientific and <u>historical</u> values; and harmonious and coordinated management of the various resources without permanent impairment of the productivity of the land and the quality of the environment with consideration being given to the relative values of the resources and not necessarily to the combination of uses that will give the greatest economic return or the greatest unit output.

43 U.S.C. § 1702(c) (1994) (emphasis added).

Thus, FLPMA's mandate to the BLM, the United States' largest terrestrial land manager, is clear: management of the public lands must be carried out in a manner that provides for multiple uses, yet protects heritage resources.[7]

4.   National Forest Management Act

The National Forest System (NFS)[8] is administered by the United States Forest Service under various statutes, including the National Forest Management Act [16 U.S.C. § 1600, *et seq.* (1994)] and the Multiple-Use Sustained-Yield Act of 1960 [16 U.S.C. §§ 528–31 (1994)], which states that "the National Forests are established and shall be administered for outdoor recreation, range, timber, watershed, and wildlife and fish purposes." Under these statutes, the Secretary of Agriculture, through the Forest Service, is directed to develop, maintain and revise land and resource management plans (LRMP) for units of the National Forest System. In developing LRMPs, the Forest Service is required to "use a systematic interdisciplinary approach to achieve integrated consideration of physical, biological, economic, and other sciences," and to provide for public participation [16 U.S.C. §§ 1604(b) and (d) (1994)]. In addition, the Forest Service is required to assure that LRMPs provide for multiple-use and sustained-yield of the products and services

---

[7]Although the provisions of FLPMA, as they pertain to the protection and management of heritage resources, are rarely, if ever, litigated, the BLM must nevertheless comply with FLPMA's requirements.

[8]The term "National Forest System" (NFS) is defined in 16 U.S.C. § 1609(a) (1994). Generally, this term encompasses all lands and interests administered by the Forest Service.

and include coordination of outdoor recreation, range, timber, watershed, wildlife and fish, and wilderness [16 U.S.C. § 1604(e) (1994)].

At Congress's direction, and following public notice and comment, the Forest Service promulgated regulations setting forth the LRMP planning process, in 1979,[9] which are codified as amended at 36 C.F.R. Part 219 (1997).[10] The regulations state that the purpose of LRMPs is to "provide for multiple-use and sustained-yield of goods and services from the National Forest System in a way that maximizes long-term net public benefits in an environmentally sound manner," and also provide that forest planning be based on several principles, including the "preservation of important historic, cultural, and natural aspects of our national heritage" [36 C.F.R. § 219.1(a) and (b)(5) (1997)].

The process for integrating cultural resources into forest planning is set out in 36 C.F.R. § 219.24 (1997):[11]

> Forest planning shall provide for the identification, protection, interpretation, and management of significant cultural resources on National Forest System lands. Planning of the resource shall be governed by the requirements of federal laws pertaining to historic preservation, and guided by paragraphs (a)(1) through (a)(3) of this section.
>
> (a) Forest planning shall
>
> (1) Provide an overview of known data relevant to history, ethnography, and prehistory of the area under consideration, including known cultural resource sites;
>
> (2) Identify areas requiring more intensive inventory;
>
> (3) Provide for evaluation and identification of appropriate sites for the National Register of Historic Places;
>
> (4) Provide for establishing measures for the protection of significant cultural resources from vandalism and other human depredation and natural destruction;
>
> (5) Identify the need for maintenance of historic sites on, or eligible for inclusion in, the National Register of Historic Places; and
>
> (6) Identify opportunities for interpretation of cultural resources for the education and enjoyment of the American public.

---

[9]44 Fed. Reg. 53,928. The regulations have been amended twice [47 Fed. Reg. 43,037 (1982) and 48 Fed. Reg. 29,122 (1983)].

[10]The regulations set forth the requirements for an interdisciplinary approach [36 C.F.R. § 219.5 (1997)] and for public participation [36 C.F.R. § 219.6 (1997)]. General procedure, content, and process requirements for forest planning are provided in 36 C.F.R. §§ 219.10, 219.11, and 219.12 (1997).

[11]Integrated resource direction for forest planning of all forest resources is set forth at 36 C.F.R. §§ 219.13 to 219.26 (1997).

(b) In the formulation and analysis of alternatives, interactions among cultural resources and other multiple uses shall be examined. This examination shall consider impacts of the management of cultural resources on other uses and activities and impacts of other uses and activities on cultural resource management.

(c) Formulation and evaluation of alternatives shall be coordinated to the extent feasible with the State cultural resource plan and planning activities of the State Historic Preservation Office and State Archaeologist and with other State and Federal agencies.

   36 C.F.R. § 219.24 (1997).

Consequently, in order for the Forest Service to be in compliance with federal law, the Forest Service *must* consider the protection and management of heritage resources in its planning of LRMPs.

5. Section 4(f) of the Department of Transportation Act

Section 303 of the amended Department of Transportation Act [49 U.S.C. § 303 (1994), formerly cited as 49 U.S.C. § 1653(f), and commonly referred to as "Section 4(f)"] directs the Secretary of Transportation to use "special effort[s]" to preserve public parks, recreation lands, wildlife and waterfowl refuges and historic sites in the development of transportation plans and programs. Specifically, this statute provides that:

(a) It is the policy of the United States Government that special effort should be made to preserve the natural beauty of the country-side and public park and recreation lands, wildlife and waterfowl refuges, and historic sites.

* * *

(c) The Secretary may approve a transportation program or project (other than any project for a park road or parkway under section 204 of title 23) requiring the use of publicly owned land of a public park, recreation area, or wildlife and waterfowl refuge of national, State, or local significance, or land of an historic site of national, State, or local significance (as determined by the federal, State, or local officials having jurisdiction over the park, area, refuge, or site) only if —

   (1) there is no prudent and feasible alternative to using that land; and

   (2) the program or project includes all possible planning to minimize harm to the park, recreation area, wildlife and waterfowl refuge, or historic site resulting from the use.

   49 U.S.C. § 303(a) (1994). See also 23 U.S.C. § 138.

In contrast to NEPA, the NHPA, and other statutes that are procedural in nature, Section 4(f) has substantive requirements that *mandate* protection of historic sites. Specifically, federal approval of a program or project that uses land of a historically significant nature is *prohibited* unless it can be shown that the requirements of the statute's two-prong test have been met, by establishing that: (1) there is "no prudent and feasible alternative to using that land;" and (2) "all possible planning to minimize harm" to the historic site has been accomplished. Thus, Section 4(f) sets forth Congress's determination that properties defined in the statute are to be given paramount consideration in transportation programs or projects that are federally funded [see *Citizens to Preserve Overton Park, Inc. v. Volpe*, 401 U.S. 402, 412–13 (1971)].

The terms "feasible" and "prudent," contained in the first prong of the Section 4(f) test, were defined by the Supreme Court in *Citizens to Preserve Overton Park* (at 411–13). In that case, the Court determined that an alternative to a transportation project is "feasible" if it can be built as a matter of sound engineering. A "prudent" alternative is one where there are no "truly unusual factors present in a particular case or the cost or community disruption resulting from [the] alternative [route reaches] extraordinary magnitudes." An alternative route also is prudent if it does not present "unique problems" [*Citizens to Preserve Overton Park* at 413]. It is important to note, however, that an alternative can be "feasible" yet not "prudent," as was the case in *Conservation Law Foundation v. Federal Highway Administration*, 24 F.3d 1465, 1470 (1st Cir. 1994). In that case, the alternative, while feasible, was found not to be prudent, as it caused "a number of disruptive consequences" to the community in avoiding the historic district.

The second prong of the test, the requirement that "all possible planning to minimize harm" to the historic site be accomplished, was explained by the Eleventh Circuit in *Druid Hills Civic Association v. Federal Highway Administration*, 722 F.2d 700 (11th Cir. 1985). This prong:

> requires a simple balancing test which totals the harm caused by each alternative route to [the historic site] and selects the option which does the least harm. The only relevant factor in making a determination whether an alternative route minimizes harm is the quantum of harm to the park or historic site caused by the alternative. Considerations that might make the route imprudent, *e.g.,* failure to satisfy the project's purpose, are simply not relevant to this determination. If the route does not minimize harm, it need not be selected. The Secretary is free to choose among alternatives which cause substantially equal damage to parks or historic sites.
> *Druid Hills* at 716 (citations omitted).

The court in *Druid Hills*, made clear, however, that meeting the second prong of the test has no bearing on the first prong, which also must be met. "Thus, a route that does minimize harm can still be rejected if it is infeasible or imprudent. The determination whether the route is infeasible or imprudent is based on factors other than the route's impact on [historic sites]" (*Druid Hills* at 716).

DRUID HILLS CIVIC ASSOCIATION v.
FEDERAL HIGHWAY ADMINISTRATION

772 F.2d 700 (11th Cir. 1985)

HENDERSON, Circuit Judge:

Druid Hills Civic Association, Inc., *et al.*, in No. 84-8894 and National Trust For Historic Preservation in the United States in No. 84-8924 appeal the November 14, 1984 order of the United States District Court for the Northern District of Georgia denying their motions to enjoin construction of the Presidential Parkway (Parkway), a proposed 2.4 mile highway running east from the I-75/I-85 stub in downtown Atlanta to Ponce de Leon Avenue, an east-west arterial that is part of the Olmsted Park network in Atlanta's Druid Hills Historic District. On appeal, the appellants contend that the district court erred in finding that the named appellees complied with the requirements of the National Environmental Policy Act of 1969 (NEPA), 42 U.S.C. §§ 4321–4347 (1982), section 4(f) of the Department of Transportation Act of 1966, 49 U.S.C. § 303 (1982),[1] and section 18 of the Federal-Aid Highway Act of 1968, 23 U.S.C. § 138 (1982).[2]

---

[1][*Orig. fn.*] Section 4(f) of the Department of Transportation Act, 49 U.S.C. § 1653(f), was repealed in 1983 but was recodified without substantial change at 49 U.S.C.§ 303.

[2][*Orig. fn.*] Section 18 of the Federal-Aid Highway Act, 23 U.S.C.§ 138, is virtually identical to section 4(f) of the Department of Transportation Act, 49 U.S.C.§ 303. For purposes of this appeal, the statutes will be referred to collectively as "section 4(f)."

Section 4(f) states:

(a) It is the policy of the United States Government that special effort should be made to preserve the natural beauty of the country-side and public park and recreation lands, wildlife and waterfowl refuges, and historic sites.

(b) The Secretary of Transportation shall cooperate and consult with the Secretaries of the Interior, Housing and Urban Development, and Agriculture, and with the States, in developing transportation plans and programs that include measures to maintain or enhance the natural beauty of lands crossed by transportation activities or facilities.

(c) The Secretary may approve a transportation program or project requiring the use of publicly owned land of a public park, recreation area, or wildlife and waterfowl refuge of national, State, or local significance, or land of an historic site of national, State, or local significance (as determined by the Federal, State, or local officials having jurisdiction over the park, area, refuge, or site) only if

(1) there is no prudent and feasible alternative to using that land; and

(2) the program or project includes all possible planning to minimize harm to the park, recreation area, wildlife and waterfowl refuge, or historic site resulting from the use. 49 U.S.C. § 303 (1982).

FACTS AND HISTORICAL BACKGROUND[3]

For a better understanding of the current litigation, it is necessary to detail the history of the tract comprising the proposed Parkway. In the late 1960s and early 1970s, the Georgia Department of Transportation (GDOT) acquired approximately 219 acres as right-of-way for two multi-lane highways, one oriented north-south (I-485) and one extending east-west (Stone Mountain Tollway). The land, known locally as the Great Park, was cleared of dwellings and other structures and has been vacant ever since. In 1971, the United States District Court for the Northern District of Georgia enjoined construction of I-485 pending completion of an environmental impact statement (EIS) by the GDOT and the Federal Highway Administration (FHWA).[4] The GDOT prepared an EIS which was approved by the FHWA. The Secretary of the United States Department of Transportation (USDOT) nevertheless rejected the EIS in 1973 because it did not satisfy the requirements of section 4(f).

As a result of strong opposition to the Stone Mountain Tollway, Governor Jimmy Carter appointed a commission to examine the project and make recommendations. The commission recommended against building the Tollway until an assessment could be made on the effect of the impending construction of the MARTA[5] east rail line. Governor Carter accepted the commission's recommendation in December, 1972.

In 1973, the City of Atlanta withdrew its support for I-485 and the Atlanta Regional Commission (ARC) deleted the project from its Regional Transportation Plan in 1974. The State Transportation Board removed I-485 from the interstate highway system plan in 1974, which action was approved by the FHWA in 1975. In 1977, the GDOT began to dispose of all I-485 properties north of St. Charles Avenue but retained all the right-of-way south of that point for future transportation improvements in the east-west corridor.

Over the succeeding years, numerous alternatives for the use of the Great Park were developed. In 1974, Atlanta Mayor Maynard Jackson proposed the "Great Park" concept, a plan that included a variety of recreational and cultural facilities. In 1975, the City of Atlanta retained Arkhora Associates to prepare a reuse planning study for the Great Park. Arkhora's conceptual plan advocated a passive open space consisting of recreation areas, cultural facilities and housing. To meet transportation needs, the Arkhora proposal recommended that the I-75/I-85 stub be connected to DeKalb Avenue. The GDOT opposed the recommended action because it did not use the existing right-of-way to meet transportation needs and thereby failed to address the legal consequences of using the land for a non-transportation purpose. In 1977, the ARC adopted the Decatur Parkway Connector and Decatur Parkway, a road connecting the I-75/I-85 stub to an improved DeKalb Avenue, as part of its Regional Transportation Plan.

Atlanta Great Park Planning, Inc. (AGPP), a public nonprofit corporation, was formed in 1975 to study and plan for reuse of the property. AGPP's board of directors included representatives of ten neighborhoods, the Cities of Atlanta and Decatur, DeKalb County and the State of Georgia. A report published in 1977 acknowledged that the Great Park could serve

---

[3][*Orig. fn.*] This section is taken substantially from the district court opinion and from the purpose and need section of the environmental impact statement.

[4][*Orig. fn.*] *Morningside-Lenox Park Association, Inc. v. Volpe*, 334 F. Supp. 132 (N.D. Ga. 1971).

[5][*Orig. fn.*] The Metropolitan Atlanta Rapid Transit Authority.

not only as a major recreational area but also as a stimulus for economic development and cultural revitalization but withheld recommendation pending further study. In 1978, AGPP retained H. Randall Roark to study housing opportunities in the right-of- way. In addition to its housing proposals, Roark's study, published in 1979, adopted the transportation, open space and economic development recommendations contained in the Arkhora plan and the AGPP's 1977 report. The GDOT did not support the Roark plan for the same reasons that it opposed the earlier Arkhora proposal.

In 1978, the GDOT retained Evan L. Marbut and Associates, Inc. to prepare a park and road development project for the area. The Marbut Plan consisted of four-lane north-south and east-west roadways through the existing right-of-way, with the east-west road terminating at Moreland Avenue. Remaining right-of-way was to be developed as a park. The GDOT approved the plan, but the City of Atlanta and AGPP opposed it because it was excessively oriented to transportation.

John C. Portman, Jr., developed a land use plan for the Great Park in 1979 at the request of Governor George Busbee. Alan M. Voorhees & Associates, a transportation planning firm retained by Portman, recommended that the I-75/I- 85 stub be connected to DeKalb Avenue by way of a tunnel. The plan also called for housing units and cultural, recreational and open space uses, including the proposed Carter Presidential Library.

In 1980, the Georgia General Assembly created the Great Park Authority to examine the various proposals and to develop a master plan for use of the property. The Great Park Authority retained Howard, Needles, Tammen & Bergendoff for transportation advice. The authority report presented to the 1981 General Assembly incorporated the firm's recommendation that the I-75/I-85 stub be connected to DeKalb Avenue along one of three proposed connecting routes and also included a park and housing facilities. The General Assembly took no specific action on this proposition.

The current design came into existence in the early 1980s. After leaving office in 1981, President Jimmy Carter began to formulate plans for a presidential library, museum and policy center (the Complex). President Carter regarded the Great Park property as an ideal location for the Complex because of its proximity to the central business district and metropolitan Atlanta universities, its relative seclusion and its accessibility to the interstate highway network.

In 1981, Andrew Young sought election as mayor of Atlanta. He ran in part on a platform of opposition to any roadway through the Great Park. After his election, Mayor Young reversed his position and in 1982 supported the so-called Mayor's Plan, the basic proposal sought to be enjoined in this litigation. The Mayor's Plan includes the Jimmy Carter Complex, a thirty-acre park surrounding the Complex, and a 2.4 mile highway consisting of a pair of two-lane roadways, one eastbound and one westbound, which circumscribe the Complex and park. In addition, the City of Atlanta is developing a housing plan for use of the remaining acreage. The Complex and roadside park would be located on existing right-of-way but further land acquisition would be necessary to build the highway.

Throughout the first half of 1982, the Mayor's office presented the plan to the Great Park Authority, the ARC, various neighborhood organizations, neighborhoods and concerned citizens. On July 6, 1982, the Atlanta City Council approved the Parkway plan by a vote of ten to nine. The plan was then analyzed by the ARC to determine if it should become part of the Regional Transportation Plan. In September, 1982, the ARC voted to amend its Regional Transportation Plan by replacing the proposed Decatur Parkway Connector and the

Decatur Parkway with the Presidential Parkway. The ARC nonetheless acknowledged that the Decatur Parkway provided better traffic distribution by encouraging alternative routing.

In August, 1982, the FHWA placed a notice of intent to prepare an EIS in the Federal Register. On April 21, 1983, the FHWA, the lead agency for the Parkway project, signed the draft EIS. Approximately 1,000 copies of the draft statement were distributed to agencies, organizations and individuals. The draft EIS allocated four pages to a discussion of the building of the Parkway, but only two sentences to the alternative of not building it. Other alternatives, including previous plans for the area, a road extending only to the presidential library, a road terminating at Moreland Avenue, intersection improvements on existing streets, a two-lane Parkway and traffic improvements in the Ponce de Leon Avenue/Scott Boulevard corridor were discussed in four pages of text. Additional discussion of alternatives, including the proposed Decatur Parkway, was incorporated into the section addressing impacts on properties protected by section 4(f).

The GDOT and the FHWA conducted three informal public information meetings between May 31 and June 2, 1983 in neighborhoods adjacent to the project. Court reporters were available to transcribe comments. A fourth public information meeting was held at the Atlanta Civic Center on June 7, 1983. A public hearing consisting of a formal presentation followed by a public comment session was held later that evening. Court reporters were available in the lobby and in the auditorium to receive oral and written comments. Approximately 1,500 to 3,000 people attended the hearing.

Several federal agencies commented on the draft EIS, including the Department of the Interior (DOI), the Environmental Protection Agency (EPA), the General Services Administration and the USDOT. DOI first recommended that the final EIS give consideration to whether the proposed Parkway would meet transportation needs. The comments noted that it was not clear that termination of the Parkway at Ponce de Leon Avenue, an east-west arterial, would substantially relieve traffic congestion and provide for future transportation needs in the east-west corridor. In addition, the DOI stated that discussion of alternatives in the draft EIS was inadequate and recommended that the final statement contain a more extensive discourse of the no-build and Moreland Avenue termination alternatives. Given these deficiencies, the DOI felt that the draft EIS failed to adequately address section 4(f) considerations. The EPA found that the draft statement did not adequately evaluate the impact on air quality. The USDOT took the position that the draft EIS adequately addressed the effects of the project and measures to minimize harm. The department's comments further stated, however, that the draft EIS did not contain sufficient information to support a determination that there was no feasible and prudent alternative to the use of lands protected by section 4(f). Furthermore, the draft statement did not demonstrate a need for the Parkway as opposed to improvements to existing facilities. Therefore, the USDOT suggested a more thorough investigation of the Decatur Parkway alternative. The department concluded that it appeared that the proposed project would aggravate, rather than alleviate, traffic conditions on Ponce de Leon Avenue. The FHWA and the GDOT held meetings with the various agencies to evaluate their comments.

On August 4, 1983, ten days after the expiration of the period for comment on the draft EIS, the GDOT made the decision to proceed with preparation of the final EIS around the build, *i.e.*, Parkway, option. The GDOT and FHWA also began preparation of a Preliminary Case Report (PCR) pursuant to section 106 of the National Historic Preservation Act of 1966, 16 U.S.C. § 470f, and 36 C.F.R. § 800 to evaluate the impact of the project on historic and archaeological resources. The PCR was forwarded to the Georgia Department of Natural Resources on October 25, 1983 and to the United States Advisory Council on Historic Preservation (ACHP) on November 3, 1983. Copies of the PCR were made available to the public for comment.[6]

After a review of this preliminary report, the ACHP recommended that the GDOT and FHWA give further consideration to the Moreland Avenue termination alternative in conjunction with other transportation improvements. The FHWA responded that the Moreland Avenue alternative and others had been adequatelyconsidered but were not feasible or prudent. The chairman of the ACHP referred the matter to the full Council for consideration at a public hearing in Atlanta on February 27, 1984. Council members heard from witnesses and made an on-site inspection of the property. By a twelve to four vote, the Council recommended that the Parkway not be built but that the Carter Complex should be constructed on the site. The Council's written findings, forwarded to the Secretary of the USDOT on March 13, 1984, were largely critical of the stated need for the project and of the attempt to link the Parkway and the Complex. The FHWA responded to the comments on April 17, 1984.

On May 22, 1984, the FHWA approved the final EIS. Copies of the statement were distributed to interested parties and notice of the approval was published in the Federal Register. In addition to alternatives raised in the draft EIS, the final EIS discussed MARTA, a light rail proposal, one-way pairings of streets, staggered work hours, and toll charges and provided a more detailed discussion of the Decatur Parkway alternative.

The DOI, EPA, individuals and organizations submitted comments on the final EIS. The DOI decided that the statement did not adequately respond to the department's comments on the draft EIS and was not responsive to the requirements of section 4(f). Accordingly, the department objected to section 4(f) approval of the project.

On June 25, 1984, the chairman of the ACHP filed a formal notice of referral with the Council on Environmental Quality (CEQ). The CEQ solicited written comments from the public on the national importance of the Parkway and held a public meeting on July 17, 1984. On September 20, 1984, the CEQ determined that the proposed Parkway was not of national importance and declined to further review the project. The CEQ requested the FHWA to resume its normal decisionmaking process. On September 21, 1984, the FHWA, acting through William Van Luchene, the designee of the Secretary of the USDOT, approved and executed a record of decision.

These actions for declaratory and injunctive relief were initiated on September 24 and September 28, 1984.[7] Carter Library, Inc., the entity responsible for developing the Carter Complex, obtained title to the 3.2 acres on which the Complex would be built via a landswap with the GDOT on October 2, 1984. Construction commenced the same day.

---

[6][*Orig. fn.*] The PCR is included as Volume II of the final EIS.

[7][*Orig. fn.*] The plaintiffs included the Druid Hills Civic Association, Inc.; Inman Park Restoration, Inc.; Candler Park Neighborhood Organization; CAUTION, Inc.; various named individuals; and the National Trust for Historic Preservation. The named defendants were the FHWA; USDOT; GDOT; EPA; R.A. Barnhart, the Administrator of the FHWA; D.J. Altobelli, Georgia State Division Director of the FHWA; Elizabeth Dole, Secretary of the USDOT; Thomas D. Moreland, Commissioner of the GDOT; and Carl Jeter, Regional Administrator of the EPA.

The district court consolidated the applications for preliminary injunction with the trial on the merits. The trial was held October 22-25, 1984. By order dated November 14, 1984, the district court denied the motion to enjoin construction of the Parkway. The appeal was ordered expedited by this court. Both the district court and a panel of this court denied the appellants' motions for injunction pending appeal.

* * *

II. SECTION 4(f)

A. Standard of Review

Section 4(f) evidences Congress' response to growing public concern over the preservation of our nation's parklands, recreation areas, wildlife and waterfowl refuges, and historic sites [also referred to as section 4(f) properties]. In enacting this section, Congress determined that section 4(f) properties should be accorded paramount consideration in connection with all federally financed transportation projects. *Citizens to Preserve Overton Park, Inc. v. Volpe*, 401 U.S. 402, 412–13, 91 S.Ct. 814, 821–22, 28 L.Ed.2d 136, 151 (1971). Thus, the Secretary of Transportation[16] can approve a federal highway project requiring the use of parklands or historic sites only if (1) no feasible and prudent alternative to the use of the land exists, and (2) the project includes all possible planning to minimize harm to the property. 49 U.S.C. § 303; 23 U.S.C. § 138.

The Supreme Court enunciated the standard of judicial review of the Secretary's section 4(f) determination in *Overton Park*. While the Secretary's decision is entitled to a presumption of regularity, that presumption does not "shield his action from a thorough, probing, in-depth review." 401 U.S. at 415, 91 S.Ct. at 823, 28 L.Ed.2d at 153. A reviewing court must first consider whether the Secretary acted within the scope of her authority. Under this facet of the review, the court must determine whether the Secretary properly construed her authority to approve the use of section 4(f) property as limited to situations where there are no feasible and prudent alternatives, and whether the Secretary could have reasonably believed that no such alternatives exist. *Id*. at 415–16, 91 S.Ct. at 823, 28 L.Ed.2d at 153. The court must next determine whether the Secretary's ultimate decision was arbitrary, capricious or an abuse of discretion. This assessment requires an evaluation of whether "the decision was based on a consideration of the relevant factors and whether there has been a clear error of judgment." *Id*. at 416, 91 S.Ct. at 823–24, 28 L.Ed.2d at 153. Although the judicial inquiry should be penetrating, the court is not empowered to substitute its judgment for that of the Secretary. *Id*. at 416, 91 S.Ct. at 824, 28 L.Ed.2d at 153. The third and final inquiry is whether the Secretary's action followed the necessary procedural requirements. *Id*. at 417, 91 S.Ct. at 824, 28L.Ed.2d at 154.

In reviewing the district court's decision affirming the Secretary's section 4(f) action, "the focal point for judicial review should be the administrative record already in existence [on the basis of which the administrator's determination was made], not some new record made

---

[16][*Orig. fn.*] William R. Van Luchene, acting as the Secretary of Transportation's designee, made the final determination to proceed with the Parkway project. For the sake of convenience, we use the term "Secretary" throughout this section.

initially in the reviewing court." *Louisiana Environmental Society, Inc. v. Dole*, 707 F.2d 116, 119 (5th Cir. 1983) (*LES III*) [quoting *Camp v. Pitts*, 411 U.S. 138, 142, 93 S.Ct. 1241, 1244, 36 L.Ed.2d 106, 111 (1973)]. Since the appellate court applies the same standard of review as the district court, we need accord no particular deference to the district court's conclusions as to whether the administrative record supports the Secretary's decision. *Id.* If the record fails to show a sufficient basis for the administrative decision, the 4(f) determination must be overturned. The reviewing court, in dealing with a determination or judgment which an administrative agency alone is authorized to make, must judge the propriety of such action solely by the grounds invoked by the agency. If those grounds are inadequate or improper, the court is powerless to affirm the administrative action by substituting what it considers to be a more adequate or proper basis. *Securities & Exchange Commission v. Chenery Corp.*, 332 U.S. 194, 196, 67 S.Ct. 1575, 1577, 91 L.Ed. 1995, 1999 (1947).

B. Analysis

The plaintiffs-appellants object to the district court's findings that the Secretary reasonably complied with the requirements of section 4(f). They do not voice any objections to the Secretary's compliance with procedural requirements. Rather, they first claim that the state and federal defendants violated section 4(f)(1) because there was no reasonable basis for the conclusion that there exists no feasible and prudent alternative to the use of parks and historic sites. Specifically, they assert that the appellees failed to examine several feasible and prudent alternatives that would avoid harm to section 4(f) areas and improperly rejected other alternatives. Second, the appellants contend that the agencies failed to incorporate all possible planning to minimize harm to protected areas as mandated by section 4(f)(2).

(1) Section 4(f)(1)

Section 4(f)(1) requires a finding of no feasible or prudent alternatives to the use of parklands and historic sites before the Secretary can approve the use of such property for highway purposes. An alternate route that also impacts upon parks and historic sites is not an "alternative to the use" of such property. *Louisiana Environmental Society, Inc. v. Coleman*, 537 F.2d 79, 85 (5th Cir. 1976) (*LES II*). Thus, in making the section 4(f)(1) assessment, the Secretary is concerned with those alternatives that do not also impact on parks and historic sites.

The Supreme Court defined "feasible" and "prudent" in *Overton Park*. An alternative is feasible if it can be built as a matter of sound engineering. 401 U.S. at 411, 91 S.Ct. at 821, 28 L.Ed.2d at 150. An alternative is prudent unless there are "truly unusual factors present in a particular case or the cost or community disruption resulting from alternative routes reache[d] extraordinary magnitudes," or the alternative routes present "unique problems." *Id.* at 413, 91 S.Ct. at 822, 28 L.Ed.2d at 151.

The section 4(f) statement contained in the EIS[17] discussed five alternatives to the Parkway project: the no-build option, the Decatur Parkway, two plans for roads terminating at

---

[17][*Orig. fn.*] The Preliminary Case Report, included as Volume II of the final EIS, also addresses alternatives to avoid the project's impact on historic properties. The information contained in the PCR essentially duplicates that found in the EIS.

Moreland Avenue and widening of Ponce de Leon Avenue with improved signalization. Of these, the no-build option is the only alternative to the use of section 4(f) areas because the other proposals contemplated the "use" of parklands and/or historic districts to some degree. *LES II*, 537 F.2d at 85. The district court examined the consequences of not building the highway and found that the Secretary could reasonably have concluded that the no-build option was not prudent because it failed to meet the need which the project was designed to address and because it might have resulted in loss of the Carter Complex or reduction in its scope.

Despite protestations to the contrary, the district court properly interpreted *LES II* to provide support for its conclusion that the Secretary could reasonably have rejected the no-build option as imprudent for failure to fulfill the need for a highway in Atlanta's east-west corridor. In *LES II*, the former Fifth Circuit Court of Appeals held that the Secretary could reasonably have determined that two alternatives, one of them the no-build option, were imprudent because they did not serve the project's purpose. *Id*. The appellants' reliance on the recent decision in *Stop H-3 Association v. Dole*, 740 F.2d 1442 (9th Cir. 1984), *cert. denied*, 471 U.S. 1108, 105 S.Ct. 2344, 85 L.Ed.2d 859 (1985), in an attempt to cast doubt on the correctness of the district court's determination ignores clear precedent binding on this circuit.[18] Accordingly, since the no-build alternative could reasonably have been found

---

[18][*Orig. fn.*] The district court in *Dole* found that rejection of the no-build alternative was reasonable because the need for the road had been sufficiently established. *Stop H-3 Association v. Lewis*, 538 F. Supp. 149, 180 (D. Hawaii 1982). In a footnote to its discussion of the no-build option, the Ninth Circuit Court of Appeals said:

> The mere fact that a "need" for a highway has been "established" does not prove that not to build the highway would be "imprudent" under *Overton Park*. To the contrary, it must be shown that the implications of not building the highway pose an "unusual situation," are "truly unusual factors," or represent cost or community disruption reaching "extraordinary magnitudes."

740 F.2d at 1455 n. 21 (citing *Overton Park*, 401 U.S. at 411–13, 91 S.Ct. at 821–22, 28 L.Ed.2d at 150–51). This footnote appeared in a portion of the opinion joined by only two judges. Judge Wallace, who did not concur in the majority's analysis of the no-build alternative, was of the opinion that a project-wide no-build option did not provide a prudent alternative to a highway for purposes of the section 4(f) analysis because section 4(f) deals with the manner of building the project rather than whether to undertake it in the first place. *Id*. at 1466–68 (emphasis added).

Even were we to agree that *Stop H-3 Association* offers a view more consistent with *Overton Park*, we would still be bound by our decision in *LES II*. See *Bonner v. City of Prichard*, 661 F.2d 1206 (11th Cir. 1981) (*en banc*). Only this court sitting en banc or the United States Supreme Court can overrule precedent binding on this court. *Julius v. Johnson*, 755 F.2d 1403, 1404 (11th Cir. 1985) (*per curiam*).

imprudent, we affirm this portion of the district court's order.[19]

(2)   Section 4(f)(2)

Section 4(f)(2) imposes the duty to utilize all possible planning to minimize harm to parks and historic sites before the Secretary can approve a route using section 4(f) property. Relocation of the highway through another portion of the section 4(f) area or through other section 4(f) properties must be considered as a means of minimizing harm. *LES II*, 537 F.2d at 85. As explained by the court in *LES II*, section 4(f)(2) requires a simple balancing process which totals the harm caused by each alternate route to section 4(f) areas and selects the option which does the least harm. *Id.* at 85–86. The only relevant factor in making a determination whether an alternative route minimizes harm is the quantum of harm to the park or historic site caused by the alternative. Considerations that might make the route imprudent, *e.g.*, failure to satisfy the project's purpose, are simply not relevant to this determination. *Id.* at 86. If the route does not minimize harm, it need not be selected. The Secretary is free to choose among alternatives which cause substantially equal damage to parks or historic sites. *Id.*

The court in *LES II* made it clear that the Secretary does not have to accept an alternate route which causes less harm to parks and historic sites. Rather, the court construed section 4(f)(2) to mean that the route must also be feasible and prudent. Thus, a route that does minimize harm can still be rejected if it is infeasible or imprudent. The determination whether the route is infeasible or imprudent is based on factors other than the route's impact on section 4(f) areas. *Id.*

Applying this legal standard to the proposed Decatur Parkway, Moreland Avenue and Ponce de Leon Avenue alternatives, the district court found that the Secretary's determination that the alternatives either did not minimize harm or were imprudent was reasonable. As pointed out above, section 4(f)(2) requires the Secretary to utilize a balancing process that totals the harm caused by each alternative so that an option can be selected which does the least harm. *Id.* at 85–86. From this it is evident that the administrative record must

---

[19][*Orig. fn.*] The district court concluded that loss of the Complex could constitute a truly unique or unusual factor. The court continued with the statement, "Thus, even if No-Build were prudent, the magnitude and uniqueness of the Carter Complex could justify an exception to the prudent requirement."

Given our disposition of the section 4(f)(1) claim, it is not necessary that we determine whether possible loss of the Complex or reduction in its scope is enough to render the no-build option imprudent. Indeed, it is not certain that such an occurrence would come to pass. See Final EIS, Vol. I, at 85 ("There would also be a possibility that the no-build might include a presidential library and policy center at or near its presently proposed location."). We do note, however, that Congress enacted no exceptions to the requirement that there be no prudent alternatives to the use of parks and historic sites before the Secretary can approve a project using protected properties. As such, possible loss of the Complex would be a factor to consider in determining whether no-build was imprudent, not an event warranting an exception to the prudence requirement.

contain adequate information to enable the Secretary to weigh the relative damage to protected properties which would result from building each of these roads. The record here is replete with references to the preferred route's impact on section 4(f) properties and to the efforts to minimize this harm. By comparison, the generalized and often contradictory attention directed to the section 4(f) impacts associated with the Decatur Parkway and Moreland Avenue routes is significantly deficient and is examined, for the most part, under the feasible and prudent standard. With the present record, it is difficult to see how the Secretary could have made the proper evaluation mandated by section 4(f)(2) of the harm caused by each of these options. A meaningful balancing of the damage done by the preferred route with that caused by the alternatives was therefore impossible. Accordingly, we are unable to review the correctness of the district court's findings as to the Decatur Parkway and Moreland Avenue plans because we conclude that the Secretary did not make the requisite findings necessary for an informed comparison of the relative harms anticipated by the construction of the various routes. It is the deficiency in this "testing" process that afflicts the integrity of the EIS. *Id.* at 86.[20]

The GDOT and the FHWA concluded that their five-lane version of the Decatur Parkway was not a feasible and prudent alternative because it would have used land from one or more historic districts, would have cost more than the preferred alternative, would have destroyed residences and businesses, and would have impacted an archaeological site and rapid transit facilities. Final EIS, Vol. I, at 199. The EIS generally describes the various historic sites which would be affected, either by acquisition of right-of-way or visually, and represents that a number of structures would have to be removed. The EIS also states, however, that many of these areas were physically and visually impacted by construction of MARTA's east rail line. *Id.* at 196. Indeed, with respect to possible effects on the Sycamore Street Historic District, the EIS states that "[b]oth the boundary and the eligibility of the district would need reevaluation before effects could be determined realistically." *Id.* at 197. In discussing the effect on the archaeological site, the EIS states that, according to procedures mandated by section 106 of the National Historic Preservation Act, 16 U.S.C. § 470f, a finding of no adverse impact could be anticipated. Moreover, measures to mitigate harm to the site were taken following evaluative testing. *Id.* at 198. This candid, albeit too limited, discussion of the characteristics of the property that would be taken by construction of the Decatur Parkway, when coupled with the lack of specificity about the quantity of the affected area, convinces us that the Secretary has not conformed to the requirement that all

---

[20][*Orig. fn.*] It is not entirely clear whether the Secretary rejected the various alternatives because they failed to minimize harm or because they were imprudent. The EIS states that the various alternatives are not feasible and prudent but then proceeds to list reasons that largely relate to the alternatives' impacts on parks and historic sites. As cautioned by the court in *LES II*, a route that minimizes harm may be rejected as imprudent only for reasons other than its impact on 4(f) properties. 537 F.2d at 86. On the remand, the Secretary must furnish a more specific analysis of the impact on 4(f) areas occasioned by the various alternatives. If this review results in the conclusion that the harm caused by an alternative is substantially equal to that caused by the preferred route, the Secretary is free to choose among the routes. If the alternative does minimize harm, however, it can be rejected as imprudent only for truly unusual reasons other than its impact on parks and historic sites.

possible planning to minimize harm be accomplished before the Secretary chooses a route impacting on 4(f) areas.[21]

The EIS discussed two road plans which would terminate at Moreland Avenue. The first, known as the Marbut Plan, consists of an east-west roadway terminating at Moreland Avenue with a related north-south road on existing right-of-way. The plan calls for a future extension eastward to Lullwater Road. The second proposal, which we will refer to as the Moreland Avenue Plan, entails construction of an east-west road ending at Moreland Avenue and the widening of Moreland and Ponce de Leon Avenue between Moreland and Clifton Road. The district court found that the Secretary could reasonably have determined that neither of the plans would minimize harm to section 4(f) areas and that the Moreland Avenue Plan was also imprudent because it did not fulfill the need for a road.

Again, we cannot evaluate the reasonableness of these conclusions because the EIS does not provide the predicate facts on which to make a reasoned judgment. Although discussion of the Marbut Plan's effect on parks and historic sites is lacking in substance, it would provide a more adequate basis for a finding that an alternative did not minimize harm than would the comments concerning the impact of the Moreland Avenue Plan.[22] The EIS acknowledges that the Moreland Avenue Plan would cause the same disruption as the Presidential Parkway up to its termination at Moreland. *Id.* at 204. The comments concerning this route's additional effects on historic sites bordering Moreland and Ponce de Leon Avenues are largely conclusory, however. For instance, the EIS states that widening of Moreland Avenue would adversely affect the North Highland/North Avenue Historic District but there is no mention of the type of impact, the characteristics of the property or the degree of harm that will accrue to the historic area.

Finally, the district court found that the Secretary could reasonably have concluded that widening Ponce de Leon Avenue, along with improved signalization, would have a greater effect on the Olmsted Park network and the Druid Hills Historic District. This alternative would impact on five of the Olmsted Parks and some land would be taken from the northern side of Ponce de Leon. The discussion of the quantum of harm caused to 4(f) areas by widening Ponce de Leon is the most acceptable of the 4(f) statements in the EIS. The Advisory Council on Historic Preservation is opposed to the Parkway but acknowledged that widening Ponce de Leon would undermine the integrity of the Druid Hills Historic District. *Id.*, Appendix B, at 333, 334. We agree with this portion of the district court's opinion.

In summary, the case must be remanded to the Secretary for adequate findings of the impact on 4(f) properties caused by the Decatur Parkway and the two Moreland Avenue plans. This review should encompass an accurate assessment of the characteristics of the

---

[21][*Orig. fn.*] The district court found that the Secretary could reasonably have rejected the Decatur Parkway as imprudent because it did not fulfill transportation needs in the east-west corridor. Under the proper section 4(f)(2) analysis, a conclusion that an alternative was imprudent could prevent its acceptance even if it was less harmful. If we followed the district court's reasoning, there would be no need for further inquiry into the minimization of harm issue.

[22][*Orig. fn.*] Our task of determining whether there was compliance with section 4(f) was made all the more difficult by the fact that consideration of the two Moreland Avenue plans was merged into one section with little to differentiate what discussion related to which plan.

property that will be affected by the alternative, *e.g.*, if the property is in a historic district, whether it has been previously impacted by commercial development and if so, to what extent. The Secretary's review must also address the quantity of harm that will accrue to the park or historic site and the nature of that harm, *e.g.*, visual impact or physical taking. It will not suffice to simply state that an alternative route would affect 4(f) properties without providing some rational, documented basis for such a conclusion. In short, the same consideration must be given to whether these alternative routes would minimize harm to the section 4(f) properties as was accorded the adopted route.

After reviewing the voluminous record in this case, we are mindful of the tremendous task confronting the Secretary in resolving these difficult issues. However, the magnitude of the problem does not diminish the need to follow the stringent requirements of section 4(f)(2). All of the proposed routes involved in this litigation will affect parklands and historic sites to some degree. It is important then that all of these options be carefully examined in an effort to minimize the damage to section 4(f) lands. This is the command of *Overton Park* and *LES II* and we are not free to ignore that directive.

For the foregoing reasons, we AFFIRM in part, REVERSE in part, and REMAND to the district court for proceedings consistent with this opinion.

Note

Town of Belmont v. Dole, 766 F.2d 28 (1st Cir. 1985) below, highlights an interesting interplay between the mandates of Section 4(f) and the application of Section 106 of the NHPA.

TOWN OF BELMONT v. DOLE

766 F.2d 28 (1st Cir. 1985), *cert. denied*, 474 U.S. 1055 (1986)

BREYER, Circuit Judge:

Section 4(f) of the Department of Transportation Act says in part that the Secretary of Transportation may not approve a project requiring the use of... land of an historic site of national, State, or local significance (as determined by the Federal, State or local officials having jurisdiction over the... site) unless there is no "prudent and feasible alternative to using that land." 49 U.S.C. § 303.... See also 23 U.S.C. § 138. In October 1980 the Secretary promulgated a set of regulations that, in part, concerns historic sites of archeological value. The relevant paragraph said that

archeological sites on or eligible for inclusion on the National Register [fall within the scope of § 4(f)'s definition]... unless the Administration, after consultation with the State Historic Preservation Officer and the Advisory Council on Historic Preservation, determines that the archeological resource is important chiefly for the information it contains and has minimal value for preservation in place.... [In that event the] archeological resouces... may be recovered in accordance with a resource recovery plan developed in compliance [with a different set of regulations, contained in 36 C.F.R. Part 800]

23 C.F.R. § 771.135(f)(1)(1984).... The issue in this case is whether this "archeological regulation" is consistent with the statute. The district court held that it was not, declared the regulation void, and issued an injunction based on that finding. Before this court, appellees have argued vigorously that the regulation departs from the "plain meaning" of the statute. Their argument is a strong one. Nonetheless, having looked into the matter in some depth, we conclude that the regulation does not conflict with the statute's language, properly understood, and that the "archeological regulation" in fact furthers the statute's preservationist goals. Hence, we reverse the district court's decision.

I

A.

Since the district court, in effect, declared the regulation invalid on its face, we shall examine it in light of the government's version of the facts. They include the following: The federal Department of Transportation (DOT) and the New Hampshire Department of Public Works and Highways wish to build a twelve-mile, four-lane bypass to relieve highway congestion along a corridor of U.S. 3-N.H. 11 between Franklin and Laconia, New Hampshire. The bypass route they have proposed runs through the towns of Tilton and Belmont. In 1977 they published a draft environmental impact statement. In 1976, 1978 and 1980 various federal and state officials involved with the highway project surveyed the proposed bypass route to determine whether it contained any "historic sites." As a result of the 1978 survey, New Hampshire found and created a special zone, the Lochmere Archeological District. The District consists of about 90 acres of land containing Indian and colonial settlement sites with buried artifacts but no historic buildings. As New Hampshire's State Preservation Officer wrote, when he successfully applied to have the National Park Service list the District in its National Register of Historic Places, the site's significance is "strictly archeological," consisting of the data it contains. DOT consulted relevant state and federal agencies, all of which have agreed with DOT about this characterization. DOT has agreed that

[The state and federal highway agencies] will develop an appropriate data recovery program, which meets the approval of the NH State Historic Preservation Office and Advisory Council on Historic Preservation, for any sites determined to be eligible for inclusion in the National Register.
[The state and federal highway agencies] will conduct the data recovery at the earliest possible date under the supervision of an archeologist whose qualifications have been determined acceptable by the State Historic Preservation Office.

Together with DOT, these agencies are now developing a satisfactory "retrieval" plan that will preserve significant data and artifacts, though not necessarily where now buried.

B.

In considering the "archeological regulation's" lawfulness, it is important to keep in mind the following "legislative" background: DOT promulgated the regulation pursuant to its general rulemaking power to implement Congressional transportation statutes, see 23 U.S.C. § 315. DOT intended the regulation to further, not only the purposes of § 4(f), but also those of a different statute [enacted the same day as § 4(f)], the National Historic Preservation Act of 1966, 16 U.S.C. § 470 *et seq.* Section 106 of that Act requires DOT (and other federal agencies) to "take into account the effect" of any "undertaking on any district, site, building, structure or object that is included in or eligible for inclusion in the National Register," and to give the "Advisory Committee on Historic Preservation... a reasonable opportunity to comment" on the "undertaking." *Id.* § 470f. (See Appendix for full text.) When promulgating its "archeological regulation," DOT explained how it reconciled and fulfilled the purposes of both § 4(f) and the Preservation Act, as follows:

> A related problem has arisen with respect to archeological sites which are treated as historic sites under both section 4(f) and the National Historic Preservation Act. Frequently, the consultation required by section 106 [of the NHPA, 16 U.S.C. § 470f] results in a determination that data recovery is the appropriate form of mitigation for the archeological site. Such determinations are typically made when the recovery of the material contained in or on the site renders more valuable information than leaving such material at the specific location. Applying section 4(f) to archeological sites where data recovery is appropriate would impose the section 4(f) test to sites for which all interested agencies have agreed that removal of the archeological material is in the best public interest. This regulation incorporates current DOT policy by applying section 106 and section 4(f) to archeological sites sequentially. If data recovery under section 106 is appropriate, then section 4(f) would not apply, since recovery results in the removal of materials which make the site significant for purposes of section 4(f). It should be noted that section 4(f) continues to apply to archeological sites on or eligible for the National Register where the site has significance for reasons other than the materials contained.

45 Fed. Reg. 71,976 (1980). The "archeological regulation" thus says in essence that DOT, in accordance with procedures set out elsewhere (in 36 C.F.R. Part 800) will consult with state and federal preservation officials, both to determine the applicability of its "archeological regulation" and to develop an appropriate retrieval plan. See 36 C.F.R. Part 800 (1984) (implementing the Preservation Act). DOT promulgated the initial version of this regulation in 1980, as part of a far larger proposed regulation dealing with § 4(f). DOT apparently received 196 comments from interested parties. 45 Fed. Reg. 71,968 (1980). DOT then summarized and discussed significant comments when promulgating the final regulation. Judging from this discussion, no environmental group or archeological group seriously opposed the "archeological regulation" subsection.

C.

Our task on this appeal is to determine the lawfulness of an agency's "legislative rule"— a rule that is lawful if "reasonable" and not "contrary" to the relevant statutes. *Schweiker v.*

Gray Panthers, 453 U.S. 34, 43–44, 101 S.Ct. 2633, 2639–40, 69 L.Ed.2d 460 (1981); *Batterton v. Francis*, 432 U.S. 416, 424–26, 97 S.Ct. 2399, 2404–06, 53 L.Ed.2d 448 (1977); *Mayburg v. Secretary of Health and Human Services*, 740 F.2d 100, 106 (1st Cir. 1984); see generally *2 K. Davis, Administrative Law Treatise* § 7:8 (1979). We consider that rule in light of the factual assumptions set forth in part IA, above, namely that DOT and others have fully complied with the rule and with related regulations. Indeed, we consider its lawfulness on the still more favorable assumption that the relevant State official "having jurisdiction" (the State Historic Preservation Officer), the relevant federal preservationist agencies (including the Advisory Committee on Historic Preservation established under the Preservation Act), and DOT all agree about both the regulation's applicability and the likely creation of a satisfactory "retrieval" plan. We also consider the rule in light of its history set forth in part IB above, namely that the regulation is aimed at serving the purposes of both § 4(f) and the Preservation Act.

II

Given our assumptions, we conclude that the "archeological regulation" is lawful. It is consistent with § 4(f), because neither the language nor the purpose of that section requires DOT to determine whether there exists a "prudent and feasible" alternative to use of the land that the regulation describes. Thus § 4(f) does not require DOT to choose any such alternative route instead of the land in question.

First, as a matter of language, we fail to find any necessary conflict between statute and regulation. The statute applies to "the use of... land of an historic site of national, State, or local significance." The regulation picks out those archeological sites whose significance lies only in the data they contain that will be at least equally well preserved outside the site. Once the data is removed, the land lacks the necessary "significance." The process of removal itself cannot be considered an adverse "use" of the site as long as it does not injure but preserves the objects in question. And, the word "use" in the statute refers to a use that is adverse in terms of the statute's preservationist purposes, a "use" that might "harm" the resources the statute seeks to protect, 49 U.S.C. § 303(c)(2) (emphasis added). See *Adler v. Lewis*, 675 F.2d 1085, 1092 (9th Cir. 1982) ("the term 'use' is... not limited to the concept of physical taking, but includes areas that are significantly, adversely affected by the project"); *D.C. Federation of Civic Associations v. Volpe*, 459 F.2d 1231, 1239 (D.C. Cir.) ("harm" to recreational park under § 4(f) encompasses "noise, air pollution and general unsightliness" that might "dissipate its aesthetic value, crush its wildlife [or] defoliate its vegetation") *cert. denied*, 405 U.S. 1030, 92 S.Ct. 1290, 31 L.Ed.2d 489 (1972); *Nashvillians Against I-440 v. Lewis*, 524 F. Supp. 962, 976 (M.D. Tenn. 1981) (constructive "use" of historic property under § 4(f) occurs only where "the claimed harm will affect the historic value or quality of the properties" and where "the purposes for which such properties are protected [are] threatened by the 'use'") (emphasis in original). Indeed, a contrary view of the word "use" would perversely forbid DOT from helping to preserve the environment in any instance in which a project helps, rather than hurts, the environment. (Imagine a DOT project planting trees along the edge of a port, or reconstructing a bridge so as to help free an estuary of pollution making it better fit for wildlife.) *Cf. Trans Alaska Pipeline Rate Cases*, 436 U.S. 631, 643, 98 S.Ct. 2053, 2061, 56 L.Ed.2d 591 (1978) ("in interpreting the words of a statute," courts have "some scope for adopting a restricted rather than a literal or usual meaning of words where acceptance of that meaning would lead to absurd results... or would thwart the obvious purpose of the statute").

Second, the regulation is consistent with the purpose of § 4(f)—a purpose described in its opening sentence as requiring the United States to make a "special effort... to preserve the natural beauty of the country-side and public parks and recreation lands, wildlife and waterfowl refuges, and historic sites." 49 U.S.C. § 303(a). See generally, *Gray, Section 4(f) of the Department of Transportation Act*, 32 Md.L.Rev. 327 (1973). As courts and commentators have noted, historic sites, particularly archeological sites, raise special problems, for unlike sea, parks and recreation lands, many of them are in private hands, see *Stop H-3 Association v. Coleman*, 533 F.2d 434, 442 n. 15 (9th Cir.), *cert. denied*, 429 U.S. 999, 97 S.Ct. 526, 50 L.Ed.2d 610 (1976); and private owners are not necessarily obligated to preserve the sites' historic or archeological value. See, *e.g., Lovis, "A Case Study of Construction Impacts on Archeological Sites in Michigan's Inland Waterway,"* Journal of Field Archeology (1978) (in area studied, only two percent of the destruction of all archeological sites was due to federal programs; thirty-eight percent, to commercial ventures; and the rest, to other private developers). Choosing an "alternative" route for a road in order to avoid a public park in all likelihood helps to preserve the park; choosing an "alternative" route for a road in order to avoid an archeological site may well harm the site, at least where the site's only value lies, say, in its buried artifacts, where road building is accompanied by a carefully designed plan to retrieve them, and where the alternative is to leave the site in the hands of private owners free to ignore, or even to harm, its archeological value.

Recognizing this fact, DOT, the Advisory Council on Historic Preservation, and state preservationist agencies have developed an archeological preservationist program, embedded in regulations promulgated pursuant to the Historic Preservation Act, see 36 C.F.R. Part 800 (1984) and the regulation at issue here. We are told by four states filing amicus briefs that this program works well. Pennsylvania, for example, in a brief signed by both counsel to its Department of Transportation and counsel to its Historical and Museum Commission, notes that the state contains over 11,000 archeological sites, and explains how the federal program has helped to advance archeological objectives. It concludes,

> The recovery program created by the Advisory Council Regulations [36 C.F.R. Part 800], which are necessarily triggered by [the "archeological regulation"] has operated successfully in Pennsylvania, fostering cooperation between the Department of Transportation and the Historical and Museum Commission and serving the needs and objectives of both agencies.

To strike down the "archeological regulation" as contrary to § 4(f) would have the perverse effect of interfering with § 4(f)'s preservationist objective, for it would forbid DOT to help retrieve and preserve the buried artifacts as long as the road could be put elsewhere. The state of Illinois, in its amicus brief, describes the possibility as follows:

> If the District Court's decision is upheld, the Department will, no doubt, be faced with the anomalous situation of discovering a significant site which should be salvaged so that the information it contains can be professionally collected, published, and displayed. Instead of completing this task and contributing to the body of knowledge associated with archeology, the Department will be faced with the mandate of Section 4(f) to avoid the site unless no feasible and prudent alternative exists. If such an

alternative is found, the site will then be abandoned. The site will be left, in most cases, in private ownership with no absolute restraints against total destruction or vandalism....

If the District Court's decision is not reversed, the Department will be required to shift the focus in its archeological program from its present standard of maximum preservation of valuable information to one of finding significant sites so that they can be avoided and possibly ruined. Instead of serving the historical preservation goal stated in Section 4(f), the Department would be assisting in the loss of irreplaceable archeological resources.

Even if this dismal picture is overdrawn, the vast number of archeological sites that may exist in some areas (Hawaii, for example) suggests that the district court's view, if generalized, could significantly delay or halt road building, improvement, or maintenance in at least some states without significantly furthering any preservationist value. (Here, for example, appellee townships, while anxious to stop the road, have no particular expertise or institutional interest in archeological preservation.)

Third, the "archeological regulation," viewed in the context of its accompanying and cross-referenced regulations promulgated under the Preservation Act, see 36 C.F.R. Part 800 (1984), contains, as we interpret it, sufficient substantive and procedural safeguards to prevent its being applied in a manner that would undercut its, and § 4(f)'s, preservationist goals. It does not apply and § 4(f) does apply, for example, if the archeological items give a particular site a special "in place" historical or archeological significance. (Consider, for example, the Civil War battle artifacts at Gettysburg.) The regulation also would not apply if it turns out that the related agencies cannot develop a "resource recovery plan" that would remove and preserve the significant items. Finally, we consider here the regulation as applied to a site where "all" state and federal officials with "jurisdiction" agree that site meets the regulation's definition. (DOT says that they are in agreement; and the district court struck down the regulation on that assumption). We need not now decide how, or whether, the regulation can apply should DOT, for example, believe the site's archeological elements lack "in place" value but the State Historical Preservation Officer or the Advisory Committee on Historic Preservation disagrees. (We note authority, however, for the proposition that a claim by one of the state or federal officials with jurisdiction that a particular site falls within § 4(f)'s scope is sufficient to invoke the protection of that statute, *Stop H-3 Association v. Coleman*, 533 F.2d at 441–42.)

III

We note that appellees seek to dispute one of our factual assumptions. They argue that DOT has not fulfilled the requirements laid down in the "archeological regulation" and related regulations. DOT replies that it has done so. The record is consistent with DOT's claim. Nonetheless, this is a matter the district court should consider in the first instance.

The decision of the district court is Reversed and the case is remanded for proceedings consistent with this opinion.

Note

Under *Town of Belmont*, if the Section 106 consultation process reveals that the value of the historic site will be better realized by removal of the artifacts rather than by applying the traditional policy of preservation in place, then the site does not fall within the scope of Section 4(f). In upholding the Department of Transportation regulation, the Court found no conflict between the regulation and Section 4(f), and further held that the regulation actually promotes preservation and contains enough procedural safeguards to protect the historic value of the site. [The authors note, however, that this regulation was subsequently amended.]

D.C. FEDERATION OF CIVIC ASSOCIATIONS v. VOLPE

459 F.2d 1231 (D.C. Cir. 1971), *cert. denied*, 405 U.S. 1030 (1972)

BAZELON, Chief Judge:

This appeal injects us back into the midst of a long and sometimes acrimonious imbroglio over the proposed construction of a bridge across the Potomac River from Virginia into the District of Columbia. In an earlier appeal we held that the so-called Three Sisters Bridge could not be built except in compliance with the hearing, environmental protection, safety, and other provisions of federal law applicable to the construction of federally-assisted highway projects.[1] That question, accordingly, is no longer open. We must now decide whether the Department of Transportation did, in fact and in law, heed the applicable federal statutes when it decided that the bridge should be built. On the basis of an extended factual inquiry, the District Court concluded that the Department had failed to comply with some of the provisions.[2] We affirm that part of the District Court's judgment. As to the provisions with

---

[1][*Orig. fn.*] *D.C. Federation of Civic Ass'ns, Inc. v. Volpe*, 140 U.S. App. D.C. 162, 434 F.2d 436 (1970), holding that "both the planning and building of the Three Sisters Bridge [must] comply with all applicable provisions of Title 23." *Id.*, at 447. In their complaint before the District Court on remand plaintiffs alleged that the Secretary had not complied with the following provisions: 23 U.S.C. §§ 102, 103, 128(a), 134, 138, and 317 (1970), and the regulations implementing § 128 (a), 23 C.F.R. Part 1, App. A (1970). Apart from alleged violations of title 23, plaintiffs also complained of violations of various sections of title 7 of the District of Columbia Code, and of 16 U.S.C. §§ 1, 470; 33 U.S.C. §§ 401, 403, 525; and 49 U.S.C. § 1655 (1970). At the commencement of trial, the District Court granted plaintiffs' motion to amend their complaint to allege also a violation of 23 U.S.C. § 109(a) (1970). The Court granted plaintiffs a hearing on each complaint under title 23, but not under any of the other statutory provisions. See pp. 1244, 1245, *infra*; *D.C. Federation of Civic Ass'ns, Inc. v. Volpe*, 316 F. Supp. 754, 761 & nn. 13–14 (D.D.C. 1970).

[2][*Orig. fn.*] 316 F. Supp. 754 (D.D.C. 1970).

which the District Court found compliance, however, we have concluded that the statutory requirements were not satisfied, and the case will therefore be remanded to afford the Secretary an opportunity to make appropriate determinations as required by the statute.

The factual background of this dispute has been described in detail in our earlier opinion[3] and in the opinion of the District Court.[4] Briefly stated, the controversy concerns a projected bridge between the Georgetown waterfront in the District of Columbia and Spout Run in Virginia. The bridge, which would be part of the Interstate Highway System and would be built largely with federal funds, would traverse the Three Sisters Islands, would "affect the Georgetown Historic District,"[5] and would use some parkland. The precise amount of harm to parkland and historic sites has not yet been determined, however, since the planning of the bridge—including the approaches and access roads—is not yet finalized.[6] A source of continuous controversy since its conception, the proposed bridge was deleted from the Interstate Highway System in January, 1969, when the National Capital Planning Commission, the official planning body for the District, adopted "a comprehensive transportation plan which did not include the Three Sisters Bridge."[7] The bridge was redesignated part of the Interstate System six months later after Representative Natcher, Chairman of the Subcommittee on the District of Columbia of the House Appropriations Committee, indicated unmistakably that money for construction of the District's subway system would be withheld if the bridge plan were not revived.[8] To satisfy the Chairman, it was necessary, first, for the District of Columbia City Council to reverse its earlier position,[9] and vote to approve the project. On August 9, 1969, the District government so voted, with the swing members loudly protesting that they would not have changed their votes but for the pressures exerted by Representative Natcher.[10] The second prerequisite of redesignation was a decision by Transportation Secretary Volpe that the project should go ahead as part of the Interstate System. He announced that decision on August 12, 1969, and the project sprang full-blown back to life on the following day.

On April 6, 1970, we held that the hearing and planning requirements of title 23 of the United States Code were fully applicable to this project notwithstanding a 1968 Act directing that construction of the bridge begin not later than thirty days after the Act's passage.[11] We remanded the case to the trial court for an evidentiary hearing to determine whether the Secretary had complied with the pertinent provisions in concluding that the project should be revived. The case is before us on appeal and cross-appeal from the trial court's decision.

---

[3][*Orig. fn.*] 140 U.S. App. D.C. 162, 434 F.2d 436 (1970).

[4][*Orig. fn.*] 316 F. Supp. 754 (D.D.C. 1970).

[5][*Orig. fn.*] *Id.* at 769.

[6][*Orig. fn.*] *Id.* at 774.

[7][*Orig. fn.*] *Id.* at 759.

[8][*Orig. fn.*] *Id.*

[9][*Orig. fn.*] On Jan. 17, 1969, the District's City Council had voted to approve the NCPC transportation plan which rejected the Three Sisters Bridge as unnecessary and undesirable. *Id.*

[10][*Orig. fn.*] *Id.* at 764, 767.

[11][*Orig. fn.*] Pub.L.No.90-495, 82 Stat. 827 (1968); *cf.* pp. 1244–1245 *infra.*

I.

Given our earlier decision, the Secretary's approval of the bridge must be predicated on compliance with a number of statutory provisions. Plaintiffs[12] challenged with two lines of argument the District Court's finding of compliance. First, they maintain that the Secretary's determinations under the statute were tainted by his consideration of extraneous factors unrelated to the merits of the questions presented. They allege, and argue, moreover, that the District Court specifically found that pressures exerted by Representative Natcher contributed to the decision to approve the bridge. Second, they argue that quite apart from the allegations of pressure, the record and applicable legal principles do not support a finding of compliance. The two strands of argument are plainly related, in plaintiffs' view, since the alleged shortcomings under each statutory provision illustrate and lend substance to the argument that the rational, impartial evaluation of the project envisioned by the statute was impermissibly distorted by extraneous pressures. We consider first plaintiffs' argument that the determinations could not stand even if there were no issue of extraneous pressure.

A.   Requirements of § 138

If a proposed federally-assisted highway project would encroach on parkland or historic sites, the Secretary of Transportation must determine before construction can begin that there is "no feasible and prudent alternative to the use of such land," and, assuming such a finding, that the "program includes all possible planning to minimize harm to such park... or historic site."[12a] The District Court concluded that Secretary Volpe had complied with each of these requirements.

In defending the Secretary's action, the government can hardly maintain that there was no "feasible" alternative to construction of the Three Sisters Bridge. This exemption applies, as the Supreme Court indicated in *Citizens to Preserve Overton Park, Inc. v. Volpe*, only if the Secretary finds that "as a matter of sound engineering it would not be feasible to build the highway along any other route."[13] It could still be argued, however, that the Secretary rejected each of the feasible alternatives because none of them was "prudent." In construing this second exemption, the Supreme Court pointed out that the very existence of the statute indicates that protection of parkland was to be given paramount importance. The few green havens that are public parks were not to be lost unless there were truly unusual factors present in a particular case or the cost or community disruption resulting from alternative routes reached extraordinary magnitudes. If the statutes are to have any meaning, the Secretary cannot approve the destruction of parkland unless he finds that alternative routes present unique problems....[14]

* * *

---

[12][*Orig. fn.*] For purposes of this opinion we refer to the D.C. Federation of Civic Associations, appellants (and cross-appellees) in this Court, as "plaintiffs," and to Secretary Volpe, the District of Columbia, and the other appellees (and cross-appellants) as "defendants."

[12a][*Orig. fn.*] 23 U.S.C.§ 138 (1970).

[13][*Orig.fn.*] 401 U.S. 402, 411, 91 S.Ct. 814, 821, 28 L.Ed.2d 136 (1971) (emphasis added).

[14][*Orig. fn.*] *Id.* at 412–413, 91 S.Ct. at 821.

Furthermore, an apparent misconception about our earlier decision may itself have distorted the Secretary's determination under § 138. The government has read our earlier opinion to mean that a bridge must be built, albeit in accordance with the provisions of title 23, somewhere in the vicinity of the proposed Three Sisters Bridge. Congress did direct, as we previously indicated, "that a bridge be built over the Potomac following the general configurations laid out in the cost estimates."[23] Viewed in context, however, the statement does not convey the meaning which the government suggests, for we held that "nothing in the statute indicates that Congress intended the Bridge to be built contrary to its own laws."[24] If the bridge cannot be built consistently with applicable law, then plainly it must not be built. It is not inconceivable, for example, that the Secretary might determine that present and foreseeable traffic needs can be handled (perhaps by expansion of existing bridges) without construction of an additional river crossing. In that case, an entirely prudent and feasible alternative to the Three Sisters Bridge might be no bridge at all,[25] and its construction would violate § 138. Thus, the Secretary may have disregarded one possible prudent and feasible alternative to the use of parkland and historic sites on the mistaken assumption that that alternative was foreclosed by our earlier decision.[26]

While these difficulties give rise to at least a substantial inference that the Secretary failed to comply with § 138, that inference ripens into certainty when one turns to the second determination required by § 138. Before the project can begin, the Secretary must determine that all possible planning has been done to minimize harm to the affected parkland and historic sites. Yet the District Court found, and the Secretary apparently concedes, that final design of the ramps and interchanges is not yet complete. Thus, when Secretary Volpe purportedly complied with § 138 in August, 1969, he could at best have been "satisfied... that the designs which would be developed based on the preliminary plans would result in a minimum taking of parkland,"[27] but he could not have concluded that the necessary planning had already been done. The District Court reasoned that the expectation of future planning could satisfy § 138. But that reasoning seems inconsistent with the Supreme Court's subsequent admonition that § 138 can be obeyed "only if there has been 'all possible planning to minimize harm' to the park."[28] Moreover, the District Court approved the § 138

---

[23][*Orig. fn.*] 140 U.S. App. D.C. at 172, 434 F.2d at 446.

[24][*Orig. fn.*] *Id.* at 447.

[25][*Orig. fn.*] Cf. *Environmental Defense Fund, Inc. v. Corps of Engineers*, 325 F. Supp. 749, 761 (E.D. Ark. 1971).

[26][*Orig. fn.*] Testifying before the District Court, Secretary Volpe did indicate that he "had considered several alternatives including the bridge, no bridge, the tunnel, various types of ramp connections etc...." (Tr. at 742) (emphasis added). It is possible, however, that the Secretary might have given that alternative (and the studies which seem to support it, see Brief for Appellants at 36 n. 2) more extensive consideration if his Department had not been convinced, judging by its representations before this Court, that "no bridge" was not a viable alternative in view of Section 23 of the Federal-Aid Highway Act of 1968.

[27][*Orig. fn.*] 316 F. Supp. at 775 (emphasis added).

[28][*Orig. fn.*] *Citizens to Preserve Overton Park, Inc. v. Volpe*, 401 U.S. 402, 405, 91 S.Ct. 814, 816, 28 L.Ed.2d 136 (emphasis added).

determination on the basis of the Secretary's testimony that a "minimum of parkland would be taken" for the ramps and interchanges.[29] More is at stake, however, than the "minimum taking" of parkland. Section 138 speaks in terms of minimizing "harm" to parkland and historic sites, and the evaluation of harm requires a far more subtle calculation than merely totaling the number of acres to be asphalted. For example, the location of the affected acres in relation to the remainder of the parkland may be a more important determination, from the standpoint of harm to the park, than determining the number of affected acres. The Secretary has not yet determined which acres will be taken. In addition, a project which respects a park's territorial integrity may still, by means of noise, air pollution and general unsightliness, dissipate its aesthetic value, crush its wildlife, defoliate its vegetation, and "take" it in every practical sense.[30]

Absent a finalized plan for the bridge, it is hard to see how the Department could make a meaningful evaluation of "harm." Furthermore, Secretary Volpe did not consult with other planning agencies to coordinate efforts to minimize harm to the park and historic sites.[31] He also made no studies of potential air pollution damage to the park. His approval of the project under § 138 was, in short, entirely premature, and we hold that he must make new determinations consistent with the statutory standards....

* * *

III.

We conclude that the case should be remanded to the District Court with directions that it return the case to the Secretary[87] for him to perform his statutory function in accordance with this opinion. It seems clear that even though formal administrative findings are not required by statute, the Secretary could best serve the interests of the parties as well as the reviewing court by establishing a full-scale administrative record which might dispel any doubts about the true basis of his action.[88] Accordingly, the District Court is directed to

---

[29][*Orig. fn.*] 316 F. Supp. at 775.

[30][*Orig. fn.*] Compare Brief for Federal Appellees at 11: "The park areas underneath the bridge would, in essence, remain available for park purpose uses...."

[31][*Orig. fn.*] 316 F. Supp. at 794.

[87][*Orig. fn.*] *Cf. id.* at 419 n. 33, 91 S.Ct. 814, 28 L.Ed.2d 136.

[88][*Orig. fn.*] While formal findings are not required by statute, they are compelled by one of the Department's own internal regulations, DOT Order 5610.1, issued on October 7, 1970. See generally *Citizens to Preserve Overton Park, Inc. v. Volpe*, 401 U.S. 402, 417–419, 91 S.Ct. 814, 28 L.Ed.2d 136 (1971). That Order was not in effect at the time the Secretary's determinations were made. Plaintiffs argue that the Order should be applied retrospectively, and that it should therefore constitute an independent basis for reversal. While the Supreme Court rejected a similar claim in Overton Park, *supra*, that decision may be distinguishable in that a full administrative record was available there to facilitate review. *Id.* at 419, 91 S.Ct. 814, 28 L.Ed.2d 136. While the proposed distinction would seem to have a good deal of force, we need not reach the question in view of our conclusion that the Secretary failed, irrespective of DOT Order 5610.1, to make the determinations required by statute. When the Secretary makes new determinations on remand, the Order will presumably apply.

enjoin construction of the bridge until the defendants have complied with the applicable statutory provisions as set forth in our opinion.

    Reversed and remanded.

As set forth above, the cases clearly illustrate that no federal approval of a program or project that uses land of a historically significant nature is permitted unless it can be established that no prudent and feasible alternative to using that land exists, and that all possible planning has been undertaken to minimize harm to the historic site. If these requirements cannot be demonstrated, the statute and the courts dictate that the program or project cannot proceed. For this reason, and to ensure the protection and preservation of potentially affected sites, compliance with Section 4(f) is essential.

6.   Coastal Zone Management Act of 1972

As declared by Congress, the primary policy of the Coastal Zone Management Act of 1972 [CZMA, 16 U.S.C. § 1451 *et seq.* (1994)] is "to preserve, protect, develop, and where possible, to restore or enhance, the resources of the Nation's coastal zone for this and succeeding generations." The Act declares the means of achieving this goal through declarations of policy and the requirement to comply with the "consistency provisions" of the Act [16 U.S.C. §§ 1452, 1456 (1994)].

    The CZMA provides for states to prepare coastal management plans (CMPs) to implement the law's provisions, including the development of "enforceable policies."[12] Among the various provisions of their CMPs, states must: (1) identify the boundaries of the coastal zone; (2) define permissible land and water uses within the coastal zone which have a direct and significant impact on coastal waters; (3) provide an inventory and designation of areas of particular concern within the coastal zone; (4) identify the means by which each state proposes to exert control over the land and water uses, including a list of relevant legal authority; (5) specify guidelines for determining priorities of uses in particular areas; (6) provide a description of the organizational structure proposed to implement their CMPs; and (7) define the term "beach" and provide a planning process for the protection of, and access to, public beaches and other public coastal areas of environmental, recreational, *historical*, esthetic, ecological, or *cultural* values [16 U.S.C. § 1455(d)(2) (1994) (emphasis added)]. In their CMPs, states also must include the identification of federal agency activities which, in their opinion,

---

[12]The term "enforceable policies" is defined in the statute as "State policies which are legally binding through constitutional provisions, laws, regulations, land use plans, ordinances, or judicial or administrative decisions, by which a State exerts control over private and public land and water uses and natural resources in the coastal zone" [16 U.S.C. § 1453 (6a) (1994)].

are reasonably likely to affect coastal uses or resources [15 C.F.R. § 930.35(a) (1997)].

Once completed, the CMPs are submitted to the Secretary of Commerce, through the National Oceanic and Atmospheric Administration (NOAA), for review and approval. If they meet the requirements set forth under 16 U.S.C. § 1455(d) (1994), they are afforded full protection under the CZMA, including the force of the federal "consistency provisions." These provisions require federal agencies proposing activities taking place either inside or outside of the coastal zone, and affecting any coastal use or resource, to carry out those activities in a manner that "is consistent to the maximum extent practicable with the enforceable policies of approved State management programs" [16 U.S.C. § 1456(c)(1)(A) (1994)]. The consistency provisions also apply to the issuance of licenses or permits by federal agencies [16 U.S.C. § 1456(c)(3)(A) (1994)]. Federal agencies demonstrate consistency with the enforceable policies of state CMPs by providing a "consistency determination" to the relevant state [16 U.S.C. § 1456(c)(1)(C) (1994)].[13] A consistency determination must include a description of the nature of the activity, its effects on the coastal zone, and whether the activity is consistent, to the maximum extent practicable, with the enforceable policies of the state's coastal management plan [see generally 16 U.S.C. § 1456 (1994) and 15 C.F.R. § 930.39(a) (1997)].[14] Responsibility for making this determination lies with the *federal agency engaging in the activity*, and *not* the state [15 C.F.R. §§ 930.33(a) and (b); 930.34(a); and 930.35(c) (1997)]. *No* federal activity is exempt from the requirements of the consistency provisions of the CZMA. In general, if the federal agency determines that its intended activity does not affect coastal resources or uses of the coastal zone, no consistency determination need be submitted to the state. However, the "effects test" still must first be applied to the activity before such a determination is made by the agency.

Through the application of the CZMA's requirements, heritage resources are to be identified, preserved, and protected as resources of the states' coastal zone environment. They are considered to be part of the coastal environment and, therefore, are afforded the protections set forth in the Act. The

---

[13] A "consistency certification," rather than a "consistency determination," is required for demonstrating that the issuance of a federal license or permit meets the consistency requirements.

[14] 16 U.S.C. § 1456(c)(1)(A) (1994) provides in full:

Each Federal agency activity within or outside the coastal zone that affects any land or water use or natural resource of the coastal zone shall be carried out in a manner which is consistent to the maximum extent practicable with the enforceable policies of approved State management programs. A Federal agency activity shall be subject to this paragraph unless it is subject to paragraph (2) or (3).

"Congressional Findings" section of the Act reiterates the need to protect and preserve these irreplaceable resources of the coastal zone: "Important ecological, cultural, historic, and esthetic values in the coastal zone which are essential to the well-being of all citizens are being irretrievably damaged or lost" [16 U.S.C. § 1451 (1994)]. Accordingly, through compliance with the mandates of the CZMA, federal agencies play an important role in the protection and preservation of heritage resources located in the coastal zone.

7.   National Marine Sanctuaries Act

The National Marine Sanctuaries Act [NMSA, 16 U.S.C. § 1431, *et seq.* (1994)] is a comprehensive management statute that confers authority to designate and manage marine sanctuaries on the Secretary of Commerce [16 U.S.C. §§ 1433–34 (1994)], and provides for preservation of sanctuary resources, while allowing for other uses of those resources by the public. The Secretary of Commerce, through the National Oceanic and Atmospheric Administration (NOAA), has the authority to designate and manage "certain areas of the marine environment possess[ing] conservation, recreational, ecological, *historical,* research, education, or aesthetic qualities which give them special national significance" [16 U.S.C. § 1431(a)(2) (1994) (emphasis added)]. The Act also contains civil enforcement mechanisms that can be imposed against persons who violate the requirements of the statute and its regulations.

Congress enacted the NMSA in response to a "growing concern about the increasing degradation of marine habitats." The Act:

> provides for the protection of important and sensitive marine areas and resources of national significance through the establishment of marine sanctuaries. The purpose of such sanctuaries is to preserve or restore such areas for their conservation, recreational, ecological, or aesthetic value.
> S. Rep. No. 100-595, 2d Sess. 1, reprinted in, 1988 U.S. Code Cong. & Admin. News 4387; and see also 16 U.S.C. § 1431 (1994).

The NMSA defines "sanctuary resource" broadly to mean "any living or nonliving resource of a National Marine Sanctuary that contributes to the conservation, recreational, ecological, historical, research, educational, or aesthetic value of the sanctuary" [16 U.S.C. § 1432(8) (1994)]; and see also

United States v. Fisher, 22 F.3d 262, 264 (11th Cir. 1994).[15] In enacting the NMSA, Congress intended that NOAA, as trustee for the public, protect and comprehensively manage historic and natural sanctuary resources [see 16 U.S.C. §§ 1431(a)(2) and 1432(8) (1994)]. In fact, the very first National Marine Sanctuary, designated in 1975, was established to protect the historic, Civil War-era shipwreck *USS Monitor* from any claims that might be asserted under the maritime law of salvage and common law of finds (explained in Chapter 5).

To date, NOAA's compliance with the management requirements of the NMSA has not been challenged. The only lawsuits implicating the NMSA and heritage resources have involved the Act's enforcement provisions. These cases are discussed in the chapter "Heritage Resources Law in the Marine Environment."

8.   Historic Sites Act of 1935

The Historic Sites Act of 1935 [16 U.S.C. §§ 461–67 (1994)] provides for the preservation of historic American sites, buildings, objects and antiquities of national significance. The Act's express declaration of national policy is "to preserve for public use historic sites, buildings and objects of national

---

[15]See also Florida Keys National Marine Sanctuary and Protection Act, Pub. L. No. 101-605, 104 Stat. 3089 (1990), 16 U.S.C. §§ 1433 note, 1444 (1994). The Florida Keys National Marine Sanctuary and Protection Act was the first marine sanctuary to be designated legislatively by Congress. The Sanctuary Act specifically recites Congress's determination that:

> (2) Adjacent to the Florida Keys land mass are located spectacular, unique, and nationally significant marine environments, including seagrass meadows, mangrove islands, and extensive living coral reefs.
> (3) These marine environments support rich biological communities possessing extensive conservation, recreational, commercial, ecological, *historical*, research, educational, and aesthetic values which give this area special significance.
> (4) These environments are the marine equivalent of tropical rain forests in that they support high levels of biological diversity, are fragile and easily susceptible to damage from human activities, and possess high value to human beings if properly conserved....

Sanctuary Act, section 2 (emphasis added).

The stated "purpose of this Act is to protect the resources of the Sanctuary" (*Sanctuary Act*, section 3). Accordingly, the statute provides that the area described in the statute "is designated as the Florida Keys National Marine Sanctuary under [the NMSA]. The Sanctuary shall be managed and regulations enforced under all applicable provisions of [the NMSA] as if the Sanctuary had been designated pursuant to [the NMSA]" (*Sanctuary Act*, Section 4).

significance for the inspiration and benefit of the people of the United States" [16 U.S.C. § 461 (1994)]. In order to carry out this policy, the law delegates to the Secretary of the Interior certain powers and responsibilities, among which are the duties to:

1. secure, collate and preserve data of heritage resources and sites, Section 2(a) of the Act;

2. complete "a survey of historic and archaeologic sites, buildings and objects for the purpose of determining which possess exceptional value as commemorating or illustrating the history of the United States";

3. make cooperative agreements with States, municipal subdivisions, corporations, associations or individuals "to protect, preserve, maintain, or operate any historic or archaeologic building, site, object or property used in connection therewith for public use, regardless as to whether the title thereto is in the United States";

4. "restore, reconstruct, rehabilitate, preserve, and maintain historic or prehistoric sites, buildings, objects, and property of national historical or archaeological significance and where deemed desirable establish and maintain museums in connection therewith";

5. "[o]perate and manage historic and archaeologic sites, buildings, and properties acquired [by the Secretary]" under the provision of the Act authorizing the Secretary to make such acquisitions; and

6. "develop an educational program and service for the purpose of making available to the public facts and information pertaining to American historic and archaeologic sites, buildings, and properties of national significance."
    16 U.S.C. § 462 (1994).

If these duties are not carried out properly, the Secretary may be subject to liability.

The Historic Sites Act is the legal basis for the creation of the National Historic Landmarks Program [16 U.S.C. § 462(b) (1994)]. In addition, it authorizes the Secretary of the Interior to seek and accept the technical and professional assistance of "any Federal, State, or municipal department or agency, or any educational or scientific institution, or any patriotic association, or any individual" [16 U.S.C. § 464(a) (1994)].[16]

---

[16]The Historic Sites Act also contains an enforcement provision [16 U.S.C. § 462(k) (1994)], which provides for the imposition of a fine plus costs for the violation of any of the rules and regulations authorized by the Act. This enforcement provision is discussed in the chapter "Federal Enforcement Statutes."

HISTORIC GREEN SPRINGS, INC. v. BERGLAND

497 F. Supp. 839 (E.D. Va. 1980)

MERHIGE, Jr., District Judge:

This case involves the controversy surrounding the designation of approximately 14,000 acres of land in Louisa County, Virginia, known as the Historic Green Springs District, as a National Historic Landmark, its listing in the National Register of Historic Places (hereinafter "National Register"), and the acceptance by the Secretary of the Interior of preservation easements over half of the District. An explanation of the posture of the case requires a review of the proceedings, both administrative and judicial, since this suit was filed on April 26, 1977.

This action was originally filed in this Court by Historic Green Springs, Inc. (hereinafter "HGSI"), a local organization dedicated to the preservation of the District's historical qualities. HGSI filed its complaint against Virginia Vermiculite, Ltd. (hereinafter "VVL"), Secretary of Agriculture Bob Bergland, the Farmers Home Administration, and United Virginia Bank. HGSI sought to prevent the Farmers Home Administration from guaranteeing a loan from United Virginia Bank to VVL, the proceeds of which loan were to be used by VVL to finance mining operations in the Historic Green Springs District (hereinafter "District"). The basis of the complaint was that the District's listing in the National Register required compliance with certain protective procedures before such a loan guarantee could be effected.

On May 4, 1977, VVL filed a counterclaim and third-party complaint against defendant Bergland, Secretary of the Interior Cecil Andrus, and Keeper of the National Register William Murtagh. VVL challenged the District's listing in the National Register on the basis of the allegedly defective nomination of the property to the National Register by the Virginia Historic Landmarks Commission. A similar challenge was asserted by intervenors Louisa County Board of Supervisors and various owners of land within the District. Shortly thereafter, the Secretary of the Interior conceded that the state nomination of the District to the National Register was defective due to inadequate notice, but determined that because of its national historic significance, the District would remain on the Register as a National Historic Landmark. Upon motion by HGSI on May 16, 1978, the Court dismissed HGSI's complaint.

VVL and the intervening landowners (hereinafter "plaintiffs") as well as the Louisa County Board of Supervisors supplemented and amended their pleadings in order to challenge the actions of the Department of the Interior taken since the filing of the counterclaim and third-party complaint. A trial in this matter was held, at which time the federal defendants' motion for summary judgment was denied. The parties filed post-trial memoranda with the Court addressing the issues raised at trial. After reviewing such memoranda and the administrative record submitted to the Court, and finding further argument in this matter unnecessary, the Court finds the matter ripe for disposition.

I. FACTUAL BACKGROUND

The factual background that follows, regrettably, is necessarily detailed. The Historic Green Springs District comprises an area of approximately 14,000 acres, described as roughly the size of New York's Manhattan Island. The District lies within Louisa County, Virginia, about midway between Richmond and Charlottesville. While the national significance of the District's historic qualities is disputed, the area does constitute a beautiful and remarkably well-preserved concentration of eighteenth and nineteenth century buildings of architectural merit. Most of its land is used for agricultural purposes, although some commercial development may be found there, such as a lumber company, motel, meat processing plant, and used car dealership. Most importantly, two mining companies, VVL and W. R. Grace Co., Inc., have acquired mining rights over much of the land in and around the District for the mining and processing of vermiculite. Vermiculite is used in the production of plaster and lightweight concrete construction materials, fertilizers, paints, and insulation in both residential and commercial structures. The extent of the vermiculite deposits in the District has been termed significant.

The instant controversy over the district's historic value began as early as 1972, when the Commonwealth of Virginia proposed the construction of a new prison in the District. HGSI, with the support of the District's residents, organized a successful effort to block the construction. HGSI's efforts at promoting the District's historical qualities to state officials resulted in its recognition as a Virginia Historic Landmark by the Virginia Historic Landmarks Commission. This state commission in February, 1973, nominated the District to the National Register. On March 1, 1973, the Department of the Interior (hereinafter "the Department") approved the state nomination and listed the District on the National Register.[1]

HGSI also acquired "preservation easements" over approximately half of the land in the District, which preserved the affected land by prohibiting new industrial and commercial development, limiting in some instances any construction around various historic structures, and requiring proper maintenance of historic buildings. Once acquired by HGSI, these preservation easements were offered in 1973 to the Department of the Interior. Although the Department initially rejected the proffered easements, the offer itself led to consideration of the adoption of a national program of acquiring preservation easements over national historic landmarks.

Despite the Department's rejection of the easements, its interest in the District continued. In 1974, the Secretary considered designating the District a National Historic Landmark. In April, 1974, the Department's Advisory Board on National Parks, Historic Sites, Buildings & Monuments had presented to it a report on the District by Benjamin Levy, a Department historian. Levy's report, after noting a modicum of historical events and persons associated with the District, focused on the District's architectural qualities. Replete with photographs and diagrams, the report discussed in detail the characteristics of the various manor houses and outbuildings said to "constitute a textbook of Virginia architecture up to the period following the Civil War." Based upon this report, the Secretary designated the District a National Historic Landmark in 1974.

After HGSI renewed its offer of the preservation easements to the Department, the Department made clear in a letter to HGSI that the easements would be accepted only as part of a national easements program then under consideration. By September, 1975, the Secretary had decided to proceed with such a national program for accepting easements on se-

---

[1] *[Orig. fn.]* This listing on The National Register by state nomination was later found to have been defective for lack of adequate notice to the affected landowners.

lected historic landmarks. Evidence of the Secretary's interest in accepting the Green Springs easements as part of that program can be found in his letter to the Chairman of the Board of W. R. Grace Company, Inc., in which he emphasized the Department's interest in the area in relation to the easements program and suggested that the mining company utilize its vermiculite holdings outside the District.

Although funding for a national easements program was ultimately denied, the Department proceeded with consideration of acceptance of the Green Springs easements. The Department assigned its Senior Historian, Benjamin Levy, to prepare an evaluation of the proffered easements. Levy's report, submitted in November, 1976, noted many flaws in the terms and extent of the easements, such as their failure to grant public use and access, and to prohibit in all cases subdivision and development of the land. Notwithstanding the incomplete protection facilitated by the preservation easements, Levy concluded that their acceptance was a necessary first step in preserving the District. This belief was shared by Assistant Secretary of the Interior Ronald Coleman, who by memorandum dated January 4, 1977, recommended a quick acceptance of the easements without the benefit of an environmental impact statement pursuant to the National Environmental Policy Act of 1969 (hereinafter "NEPA"), 42 U.S.C. § 4321 *et seq.*, or of the promulgation of regulations to govern easement acceptance.

On January 19, 1977, Assistant Secretary of the Interior Nathaniel Reed informed HGSI President Elizabeth Nolting that adoption of a policy of accepting the easements was underway. By notice in the Federal Register on March 18, 1977, the Department publicly announced the proposed acceptance of the Green Springs easements. The announcement gave notice of a public hearing on the merits of the proposal to be held on April 22, 1977, and provided for a fact sheet to be made available on request for that hearing. The hearing was held on April 22 in Louisa County at which both proponents and opponents of the proposal stated their respective positions.

Immediately following this hearing, Assistant Secretary of the Interior Robert Herbst requested that the Farmers Home Administration not guarantee a loan to VVL to finance mining operations until the Department could review the proposed mining and loan guarantee, and until the Farmers Home Administration could prepare an environmental impact statement for the operation. In addition, HGSI filed the original complaint in this action seeking to block the loan guarantee. Due to the resulting delay in the loan guarantee, VVL was forced to obtain alternate financing. In a further obvious effort to impede VVL's mining operation in the District, Assistant Secretary Herbst notified VVL on May 16, 1977, that the Department was reviewing the proposed mining pursuant to the Mining in the Parks Act, 16 U.S.C. § 1908, to determine whether the mining would cause irreparable loss or destruction to the District and, if so, how the government could mitigate such activity.

On May 18, 1977, the Department published a notice in the Federal Register announcing its procedure for acceptance of the Green Springs easements. The procedures consisted of departmental review of the easements, preparation of an environmental assessment of the proposal leading to either a negative declaration of significant environmental impact or the promulgation of an environmental impact statement, subsequent publication of such declaration or statement, a public hearing in the event a negative declaration is issued, and final decision by the Secretary. The May 18 notice stated that preparation of the departmental study as well as of the environmental assessment had been accomplished, and further that a public hearing had been held in connection with that assessment. Preparation of the environmental assessment, however, had not in fact been completed at that time.

On June 8, 1977, the Department issued its environmental assessment of the easements proposal. This twenty page document detailed the history of the easements offer, the nature and terms of the easements, the effect of federal acceptance of the easements, and the Department's plans for the District. Although the environmental assessment noted that acceptance of the easements would impede state, local, and industrial development of the District in several ways, the Department issued a negative declaration stating that acceptance of the easements was not a major federal action having a significant impact on the environment. A public hearing was then scheduled for the afternoon of July 27, 1977, to receive public comment on the negative declaration.

Prompted, at least in part, by the protests of Green Springs landowners and by plaintiffs' counterclaim and third-party complaint in this action, the Department announced in the Federal Register on June 29, 1977, that it would reconsider the District's listing on the National Register as a state nomination and the District's designation as a National Historic Landmark. A public hearing was announced for the morning of July 27, 1977, for the purpose of receiving public comment on the reconsideration. By Federal Register announcement of July 18, 1977, the Department defined "reconsider" as to "determine anew, without any presumptions based on prior actions," the issues concerning the District. The Department, however, announced that the reconsideration process would not entail resubmission of the District's landmark status to the Department's Advisory Board.

While the Department's reconsideration of the District's status was pending, Assistant Secretary Herbst again wrote the Farmers Home Administration on July 19, 1977, this time in response to a request for review of the loan proposal. Herbst renewed his suggestion that the Administration prepare an environmental impact statement for the proposal, as well as submit extensive documentation of the proposed mining operation. On the same day, Herbst wrote to the Virginia State Air Pollution Control Board requesting a delay in issuance of VVL's permits until completion of the Department's Mining in the Parks Act study.

On July 27, 1977, the Department held public hearings concerning the District's listing on the National Register and its landmark designation, as well as the negative declaration of environmental impact of the easements proposal. A transcript of the morning hearing concerning the reconsideration of the District's landmark status reveals that great confusion existed over the scope of the hearing and over the action being proposed by the Department. Department officials at the hearing did not, for the most part, respond to the public's questions. By Federal Register notice of September 20, 1977, the Department announced the issuance of, and summarized, an environmental assessment and negative declaration concerning the redesignation of the District as a National Historic Landmark. The September 20 notice also clarified for the first time that the District could remain a National Historic Landmark despite a defective state nomination to the National Register.

Inter-departmental memoranda of November and December, 1977, show that the Department of the Interior had recognized that the state nomination of the District to the National Register was defective and that it had been removed from such a listing. Finally, on December 13, 1977, the Secretary of the Interior decided to redesignate the District as a National Historic Landmark on his own authority, and to accept HGSI's offer of preservation easements. The District's designation as a National Historic Landmark automatically placed it back on the National Register. 36 C.F.R. § 60.2(d)(2). These decisions were announced in the Federal Register on January 24, 1978.

Plaintiffs attacked the Secretary's decisions to designate the District as a National Historic Landmark and to accept the preservation easements on several grounds. Initially, plaintiffs challenge the Secretary's authority to designate the District and to accept easements over it pursuant to the Historic Sites, Buildings and Antiquities Act of 1935, 16 U.S.C. § 461 *et seq.* Plaintiffs contend that the Department of the Interior confused the standards for national significance under the Historic Sites Act of 1935 with the less strict standards of historic importance under the National Historic Preservation Act of 1966, 16 U.S.C. § 470 *et seq.* Arguing that the District's historical significance does not meet a level of national importance, the plaintiffs question the Secretary's authority under the Historic Sites Act of 1935 to take the administrative action challenged here.

* * *

III.   THE SECRETARY'S SCOPE OF AUTHORITY

As heretofore noted, plaintiffs argue that the Secretary's designation of the District as a National Historic Landmark, and his acceptance of preservation easements in order to protect it, were actions beyond the scope of his authority under the Historic Sites Act of 1935 (hereinafter "the 1935 Act"), 16 U.S.C. § 461 *et seq.* Before addressing the allegations of unauthorized action, the Court must review the legislation that forms the basis of the Secretary's actions.

The policy underlying the 1935 Act is contained in § 461 of the Act: "It is (hereby) declared that it is a national policy to preserve for public use historic sites, buildings and objects of national significance for the inspiration and benefit of the people of the United States." 16 U.S.C. § 461. In order to effectuate that policy, the Secretary of the Interior is empowered, *inter alia*, to acquire on behalf of the government any historic site, building, or object by gift, purchase, or otherwise. 16 U.S.C. § 462. Further, the Secretary is authorized, in cooperation with state and local agencies and professional individuals, to recognize and study historic landmarks of national significance not owned by the federal government. To this end, the Secretary instituted the National Historic Landmark Program. Both the acceptance of the Green Springs preservation easements and the designation of the District as a National Landmark were accomplished pursuant to the 1935 Act.

In 1966, Congress passed the National Historic Preservation Act of 1966 (hereinafter "the 1966 Act"), 16 U.S.C.§ 470 *et seq.*, which provided for the recognition of historic places and objects of state and local importance in addition to those of national significance. The 1966 Act expanded the scope of the National Register to include not only National Historic Landmarks and historic properties of the National Park System, but properties of state and local importance nominated by the states. For the first time in such legislation, allowance was made for the recognition of historic "districts" in addition to the previously recognized sites, buildings and objects. Further, the 1966 Act added "cultural" significance as a valid subject of federal protective measures. As part of this expanded concept of cultural and historical significance, the 1966 Act added architectural and archeological importance to social and political importance as worthy of recognition.

In summary, the 1935 Act restricted its scope to the few properties possessing truly national historical significance. The Secretary is empowered thereunder to acquire property on behalf of the United States and to designate as National Historic Landmarks those exceptional properties of national importance. The 1966 Act broadened the scope of federal historical preservation by recognizing properties of state and local importance and by adding "districts" and "cultural" values as subjects of federal protective measures. The 1966 Act did not authorize acquisition of such properties but, rather, provided for the listing on the National Register with the protection inherent in such listing.

Plaintiffs argue that designation of the District as a National Historic Landmark and acceptance of the Green Springs easements, though authorized actions under the 1935 Act, were accomplished by applying the standards of the 1966 Act. As a threshold matter, the Court finds that plaintiffs' contention that the District lacks national significance and is therefore not a proper subject of recognition under the 1935 Act is more appropriately an attack on the merits of the Secretary's decision rather than on his authority; the Court finds that the Secretary regarded the District's historic qualities as possessing national importance and did not misapply a state or local standard to the District. This attack on the merits will be addressed in a later section. However, plaintiffs do raise some apparent inconsistencies between the Secretary's actions under the 1935 Act and the language of that Act.

First, the Secretary appears to have based the findings of the District's historical significance on its architectural qualities, yet recognition of "architecture" and "cultural" values is only mentioned in the 1966 Act. Further, recognition of a historic "district," as opposed to sites, buildings and objects, is likewise mentioned only in the 1966 Act. Plaintiffs also argue that because the Green Springs easements do not grant any right of public access to the affected land, and because the Department has consistently disavowed any intention of publicizing the District, the acceptance of the easements does not constitute acquisition of property "for public use," the stated policy of the 1935 Act. A further violation of the underlying policy of the 1935 Act is alleged in the fact that the easements provide incomplete protection to the District and therefore their acquisition does not in fact "preserve" the historic property. Finally, plaintiffs argue that the Department's acceptance of the easements before approval of any appropriations for the undertaking violates the 1935 Act requirement that no property be acquired thereunder "which will obligate the general fund of the Treasury for the payment of such property, unless or until Congress has appropriated money which is available for that purpose." 16 U.S.C. § 462(d).[2]

The Court has little trouble with most of these allegations. That the easements do not grant a right of public access to the property is not violative of the policy of preserving historic properties "for public use," as that term may encompass the "taking of land for commemorative purposes." *Barnidge v. United States*, 101 F.2d 295, 298 (8th Cir. 1939). Nor is it a violation of the Act's policy that the preservation easements in many instances allow for subdivision and development of the land or cover less than half of the District. It is clear from the administrative record that the Department viewed acceptance of the easements as merely an initial step towards preservation of the District and not as a final protective measure. The Court also finds that the acceptance of the easements did not "obligate the general fund of the Treasury for the payment of such property," (emphasis added) but simply entailed certain administrative costs for maintenance of the easements.

The Court admittedly is troubled, however, by the Department's assertion that a "district" the size of Manhattan can be a historic "site," in spite of the absence of any significant

---

[2][*Orig. fn.*] 16 U.S.C. § 462(d) includes the following proviso concerning the acquisition of property under the 1935 Act:

That no such property shall be acquired or contract or agreement for the acquisition thereof made which will obligate the general fund of the Treasury for the payment of such property, unless or until Congress has appropriated money which is available for that purpose.

commemorative event or historical person associated with it, and further that its architectural significance is covered by the term "historic" in the 1935 Act. A review of the legislative history of the 1935 Act and the 1966 Act reveals that the latter was necessitated by the narrow scope of the 1935 Act. In light of that fact, it strikes the Court as incongruous that the scope of the 1935 Act's protection should be expanded here so far beyond a literal reading of the Act's language.

In construing the extent of the Secretary's authority under the 1935 Act, the Court's task is made the more difficult by the absence of adequate substantive criteria for that which merits treatment as a National Historic Landmark or what constitutes national historic significance for purposes of acquiring property. Further, while the Court finds it possible that the Secretary's actions were authorized under the 1935 Act, the paltry statement of reasons for the Secretary's actions forces the Court to speculate about how the Secretary applied the Act's standards to the District. Because these and other procedural problems, in the Court's view, require a reversal and remand to the Secretary, as hereinafter discussed, the Court will not engage in speculation concerning the scope of the Secretary's authority.

* * *

VI. CONCLUSION

The Court thus finds the landmark designation invalid based on the Department's failure to promulgate substantive standards for national historic significance and its failure to prepare and publish rules of procedure to govern the designation process.[8] The Court finds further that the administrative record provides an inadequate insight into the reasons underlying the landmark designation, including but not limited to the District's historic values of national importance and the justification for drawing the boundaries as they now exist. As discussed above, the flaws in the Department's actions concerning the District are for the most part relevant only to the landmark designation. The Court finds that plaintiffs' due process rights are not implicated by the Department's acceptance of already-existing preservation easements over parts of the District. However, because the Secretary's powers of acquisition are contingent upon a property's landmark status, the easements acceptance is hereby invalidated irrespective of the procedural flaws associated with it.

The Court must, therefore, remand this matter to the Department for promulgation of both substantive and procedural regulations consistent with the Court's opinion. On remand, the Court urges the Secretary not simply to codify the criteria and procedures developed informally in the instant case, but to articulate meaningful standards in as much detail as possible so that the Department's efforts are channeled efficiently, the public may make a meaningful response, and, in the event further judicial review is necessary, a court may determine that the proper standards have been applied. In articulating substantive standards, the Department should be careful to develop criteria for landmark designation that are consistent with the language of the 1935 Act. With regard to the standards to be applied to historic districts, the Department should address the question of a district's inclusion under the term "site" and provide for the criteria relevant to setting the boundaries of such a site. To the extent that other comments of the Court have suggested additional clarifica-

---

[8][*Orig. fn.*] Because the Court finds these procedural flaws fatal to the landmark designation, it is unnecessary to address plaintiffs' allegations concerning improper notice and bias.

tion, the Secretary should respond thereto in the subsequent promulgation of regulations.

In addition, the Secretary should ensure, by means of a clear statement of reasons, that the public and, if necessary, a reviewing court, can understand the grounds for his exercise of discretion. See *Matlovich v. Secretary of the Air Force*, 192 U.S. App. D.C. 243, 248, 591 F.2d 852, 857 (D.C. Cir. 1978); *Environmental Defense Fund v. Ruckelshaus, supra*, 142 U.S. App. D.C. at 86, 88, 439 F.2d at 596, 598. No formal findings need be articulated, but the Secretary should indicate in as much detail as possible the reasoning supporting his ultimate decision.

ORDER

In accordance with the memorandum of the Court this day filed, and deeming it proper so to do, it is ADJUDGED and ORDERED that:

1. The designation of the Historic Green Springs District as a National Historic Landmark and its placement on the National Register of Historic Places be, and the same are hereby set aside as violative of plaintiffs' due process rights under the Fifth Amendment, U.S.Const. Amend. V, and of the Administrative Procedure Act, 5 U.S.C. § 552(a)(1);

2. The acceptance of the preservation easements over the District be, and the same is hereby set aside due to the defective landmark designation;

3. The Secretary shall remove the District from the National Register and any list of National Historic Landmarks; and

4. The Secretary shall develop and promulgate regulations setting out substantive criteria and procedural guidelines for landmark designation under The Historic Sites Act of 1935, 16 U.S.C § 461 *et seq.*, not inconsistent with the Court's memorandum.

The Court having found that counsel for the Secretary of the Interior has increased the costs unreasonably and vexatiously in connection with the interrogatories addressed to the defendants Andrus and Murtagh, it is ADJUDGED and ORDERED that said counsel pay unto Virginia Vermiculite, Ltd. the sum of Four Hundred and Eighty Dollars ($480.00), representing excess costs incurred.

This action stands dismissed.

Notes

1. Congress remedied the problem identified in the *Historic Green Springs* case through the 1980 amendments to the NHPA. [See 16 U.S.C. §§ 470a(a)(2)(A), 470a(a)(3)(B). See also 36 C.F.R. §§ 65.4-65.5 (National Park Service).]

2. Consider the reach of the Secretary of the Interior's responsibilities. Is that reach so great that it might have takings consequences under the Fifth Amendment to the U.S. Constitution?

---

9. Historic and Archeological Data Preservation Act of 1974

The Historic and Archeological Data Preservation Act of 1974 [HADPA, 16 U.S.C. §§ 469–69c (1994)], also known as the "Archeological Recovery

Act" or the "Moss-Bennett Act," provides for the preservation of historical and archeological data which might otherwise be lost as the result of alterations to the terrain caused by a federal or federally licensed activity or program. The primary purpose of HADPA is to extend the policy set forth in the Historic Sites Act of 1935 to all federal agency construction-related activities. Specifically, HADPA provides for:

> the preservation of historical and archeological data (including relics and specimens) which might otherwise be irreparably lost or destroyed as the result of (1) flooding, the building of access roads, the erection of workmen's communities, the relocation of railroads and highways, and other alterations of the terrain caused by the construction of a dam by any agency of the United States, or by any private person or corporation holding a license issued by any such agency or (2) any alteration of the terrain caused as a result of any Federal construction project or Federally licensed activity or program.
> 16 U.S.C. § 469 (1994).

HADPA also sets forth the procedure for executing the law:

> Whenever any Federal agency finds, or is notified, in writing, by an appropriate historical or archeological authority, that its activities in connection with any Federal construction project or Federally licensed project, activity, or program may cause irreparable loss or destruction of significant scientific, prehistorical, historical, or archeological data, such agency shall notify the Secretary [of the Interior], in writing, and shall provide the Secretary with appropriate information concerning the project, program, or activity. Such agency may request the Secretary to undertake the recovery, protection, and preservation of such data (including preliminary survey, or other investigation as needed, and analysis and publication of the reports resulting from such investigation), or it may, with funds appropriated for such project, program, or activity, undertake such activities. Copies of reports of any investigations made pursuant to this section shall be submitted to the Secretary, who shall make them available to the public for inspection and review.
> 16 U.S.C. § 469a-1(a) (1994).

Upon notification by any federal or state agency, or appropriate historical or archeological authority, of the possibility of an irrevocable loss or destruction of data, the Secretary of the Interior *shall*, upon determining that the data is significant, conduct or cause to be conducted a survey of the affected areas, and preserve such data [16 U.S.C. § 469a-2(a) (1994)]. HADPA further requires the Secretary to consult with any interested federal and state agencies, educational and scientific organizations, private institutions, and qualified individuals regarding the determination of ownership of, and the appropriate repository for, any relics and items recovered as a result of work performed under the Act [16 U.S.C. § 469a-3(b) (1994)]. These are *substantive* obligations and, if ignored, give rise to liability.

HADPA differs from statutes such as the NHPA in two significant ways. First, it is a *substantive* tool to protect and preserve heritage resources, as opposed to a procedural one. Specifically, HADPA "secures preservation of historic and archeological resources discovered *during* the construction phase of a project." The NHPA, on the other hand, is invoked at the *planning* stage and terminates when the construction phase begins. Second, HADPA differs from the NHPA in that it provides for the protection and preservation of paleontological resources, "which are categorically beyond the scope of NHPA's jurisdiction...." [*National Indian Youth Council v. Andrus*, 501 F. Supp. 649, 680 (D.N.M. 1980) (emphasis added)].

SIERRA CLUB v. MORTON

431 F. Supp. 11 (S.D. Tex. 1975)

OWEN D. COX, District Judge:

The Plaintiffs, on March 15, 1973, filed their complaint for injunctive and declaratory relief against the Defendants herein, Rogers C. B. Morton, Secretary of the Department of Interior of the United States of America; Gilbert Stamm, Commissioner of the Bureau; James A. Bradley, Regional Director of the Bureau of Reclamation, officing in Amarillo, Texas; and Norman Flagg, Area Planning Officer of the Bureau of Reclamation, Defendants. They allege the Defendants are acting unlawfully and without authority in their prosecution of the Palmetto Bend Project (called sometimes Palmetto Bend), and they seek to enjoin further development of it.

Plaintiff Sierra Club is a non-profit corporation organized and existing under the laws of the State of California; it is a national conservation organization having approximately 140,000 members, of whom several thousand are residents of the State of Texas. Plaintiff Palmetto Citizens Group claims to be a private, voluntary, unincorporated citizens' association whose members are citizens, residents, and, in some instances, landowners in the area to be affected by the Project. One of the affected landowners, Wayne L. Legro, is also a named Plaintiff. These environmental protection activists contend the government officials and agencies just named have not complied with applicable laws, regulations, executive orders and agencies' policies. On September 30, 1974, this cause came for trial before the Court without a jury, and continued intermittently through November 14, 1974.

BACKGROUND INFORMATION

Public Law 90-562, 43 U.S.C. § 616gggg, *et seq.*, by which the Congress of the United States determined the need for this project, was approved by the President on October 12, 1968. It authorized the construction of that portion of the Project which has been designated Stage One, and about which we are here primarily involved. It further authorizes the purchase of lands involved in Stage Two.

Testimony and exhibits presented reflect that as early as 1957 area residents contacted the Bureau of Reclamation in regard to the possible development of adequate surface water supplies. In 1967, the voters of Jackson County authorized the Lavaca-Navidad River Authority (L-N RA) to issue bonds in the amount of $3,770,000, to meet the Authority's financial obligations incurred in construction of the Palmetto Bend Dam. Stage One of the Project[1] will be an earth-filled dam with concrete spillway, multiple-level river outlet works, and dual-level outlet works for allowing municipal and industrial water releases. The 7.9-mile dam structure will be located on the Navidad River in Jackson County, Texas, near the two small cities of Edna and Ganado, and approximately four miles above the confluence of the Lavaca and Navidad Rivers. The Navidad River drains an area approximately 1,400 square miles above the dam site. Historically, the flows of this river have been very erratic.

The reservoir will extend approximately eighteen miles up the two principal tributaries, Sandy and Mustang Creeks. At the normal water surface elevation (also called the conservation pool level) of 44 feet above mean sea level, the reservoir will have approximately 125 miles of shorelines, will contain approximately 170,300 acre-feet, and have a surface area of approximately 11,000 acres, and when the water level reaches the maximum available, that is, 47 feet above mean sea level, the reservoir will contain 204,300 acre-feet and have a surface area of approximately 12,500 acres; subject to the estimated annual sedimentation rate of 215 acre-feet. The Project is to provide water for municipal and industrial purposes (an expected firm water yield of 75,000 acre-feet annually), as well as recreational, fish, and wildlife facilities. Congress has appropriated funds for the continued construction of Stage One every year[2] since the first appropriation in 1968, by Public Law 90-562, 43 U.S.C. § 616gggg, *et seq.*

There has been some consideration given to the possibility of constructing a Stage Two dam and reservoir[3] over Post Oak Creek and the Lavaca River. This would tie into the Stage One dam and reservoir. However, the Congress has acted regarding Stage Two only to the extent of authorizing land acquisition. Should the Secretary of the Interior issue a feasibility report concerning Stage Two, a complete environmental impact statement is to be made prior to initiation of actions seeking authorization for the construction of Stage Two. If Stage Two is not activated, Stage One can stand alone. Therefore, there is no reason for the Court to consider Stage Two at this time. *Sierra Club, et al. v. Callaway, Secretary of the Army*, 499 F.2d 982 (5th Cir. 1974).

In 1949, investigations were begun by the Bureau of Reclamation to study water supply problems of the Texas river basins draining into the Gulf of Mexico. This was commonly referred to as the Texas Basins Project. Various studies culminated with the publishing of

---

[1]*[Orig. fn.]* The following, as well as a more detailed, description of Stage One is contained in the Final Environmental Impact Statement (FEIS), Plaintiffs' and Defendants' Exhibit 3, at A-8 through A-25.

[2]*[Orig. fn.]* Public Law 91-144, December 11, 1969, 83 Stat. 323, $200,000. Public Law 91-439, October 7, 1970, 84 Stat. 890, $1,000,000. Public Law 92-134, October 5, 1971, 85 Stat. 365, $1,775,000. Public Law 92-405, August 25, 1972, 86 Stat. 621, $7,300,000. Public Law 93-97, August 16, 1973, 87 Stat. 318, $6,990,000. Public Law 94-393, August 28, 1974, 88 Stat. 782, $9,349,000.

[3]*[Orig. fn.]* See FEIS, at A-25; Defendants' Exhibit 15, Item R-5, House Document No. 279 at 25–29.

the Texas Basins Project report in February, 1965. The key element to part of the Texas Basins Project would be an Interbasin Canal extending a total length of 418 miles, from the Sabine River near Orange to its terminus near Raymondville in the Lower Rio Grande Valley. The canal would facilitate inter-basin transfer of water supplies from river basins having excess supplies to other areas to fulfill the needs of municipal and industrial, as well as irrigation, projects. At points where the proposed canal intersects a river, it would become necessary to either siphon the water under the river or else utilize a surface reservoir into which the incoming water is stored temporarily, then equalized in level and transported further along the canal.

Clearly, Palmetto Bend constitutes an integral part in the plans for the Texas Basins Project, since the Palmetto Bend reservoir would be utilized to transmit water across the Navidad River along the Interbasin Canal. Despite the possible integration of Palmetto Bend and the Texas Basins Project, if the latter is ever completed, Palmetto Bend has been authorized and dealt with as a separate entity and there is no justifiable reason to treat it otherwise; it will be examined accordingly. *Sierra Club v. Callaway, supra.*

The Texas Water Plan addresses the issues of management, development and redistribution of the state's water resources, as well as the possibility of importation of water from out of state. While the Texas Water Plan anticipates the future construction of the Texas Basins Project, the fact remains that the Plan is an inventory of existing and potential water sources, binding in no way upon the federal government.

On the 2nd day of February, 1972, the United States of America, acting through the Regional Director of the Bureau of Reclamation, entered into a written contract with the Texas Water Development Board and the Lavaca-Navidad River Authority, whereby the state contracting agencies agreed to repay certain portions of the costs of constructions and the costs of maintenance and operation of the dam and reservoir.[4] All of the water for municipal and industrial purposes to be produced by the reservoir (a firm yield of 75,000 acre-feet per year) is to be used or held by the state agencies after obtaining permits for such use from the Texas Water Rights Commission, which Commission must pass upon each of the areas of allocation.

* * *

ARCHEOLOGICAL-HISTORICAL

Plaintiffs believe that the Defendants are, at present, and will be in the future, in violation of the provisions of Public Law 86-523,[16] which call for the preservation of historical and archeological data which might be destroyed by construction of the project.

Testimony by the Acting Director of the Texas Archeological Survey, Dave Dibbell, revealed that the recovery of archeological data has been completed at seven of the nine sites located in the project area.[17] Completion of studies at the two sites will, in Dibbell's opinion, exhaust the recovery work on the project. The data gathered has not called for the utilization of any preservation techniques.

---

[4]Defendant's Exhibit No. 15, Item R-23.

[16][*Orig. fn.*] 74 Stat. 220; 16 U.S.C. § 469, *et seq., as amended*, Public Law 93-291; 88 Stat. 174.

[17][*Orig. fn.*] Recovery work funded jointly by Nat. Parks Services and University of Texas.

Alton Briggs, an architect with the Texas Historical Commission, participated in the inventory of the archeological data, and in the preparation of the Archeological Survey Report for the project. Briggs stated that, to date, no sites which would be affected by the project are eligible for inclusion in the National Register of Historical Sites, and that there is no reasonable probability that any eligible sites will be discovered. But, the Bureau has agreed, by its response to comment by the Texas Historical Commission, that if such a discovery be made during construction, work would be stopped in order to allow the necessary salvage to proceed.

* * *

This Court orders that the relief, injunctive and otherwise, prayed for by Plaintiffs, be, and such is hereby, denied. A final judgment will be signed by the Court in favor of the Defendants herein. IT IS SO ORDERED.

Note

Compare and contrast the procedural and substantive nature of the NHPA, NEPA, Section 4(f) of the Department of Transportation Act, and HAPDA.

---

10. Native American Graves Protection and Repatriation Act

The Native American Graves Protection and Repatriation Act [NAGPRA, 25 U.S.C. §§ 3000-13 (1994)] provides for the repatriation, disposition, and protection of Native American human remains and other defined cultural items. The Act, which is discussed in the chapter "Native American Heritage Resources," specifically requires federal agencies and federally funded museums to compile information on their collections of Native American cultural items, disseminate that information to culturally affiliated Indian tribes and Native Hawaiian organizations, and, following a process of consultation, repatriate defined cultural items to Native American lineal descendants and affiliated groups. NAGPRA also prohibits the intentional excavation and removal of Native American human remains and defined cultural property from federal or tribal lands without a permit issued under the Archaeological Resources Protection Act[17] and without consultation with, or (when necessary) permission from, Indian tribes or Native Hawaiian organizations.

In cases involving the inadvertent discovery of Native American human remains or defined cultural items during legal activities occurring on federal or tribal lands, NAGPRA requires that the activity be halted temporarily,

---

[17]A discussion of permits issued under the Archaeological Resources Protection Act is discussed in this chapter. NAGPRA's provisions also authorize the United States to bring criminal and civil (administrative) actions (see the chapter "Federal Enforcement Statutes.")

that the items be protected, and that the appropriate federal agency or tribal authority be notified of the discovery.

11.   Abandoned Shipwreck Act of 1987

In passing the Abandoned Shipwreck Act of 1987 [ASA, 43 U.S.C. §§ 2101–06 (1994)], Congress exercised the sovereign prerogative of the United States to assert title to certain abandoned shipwrecks and their cargo within the waters of the states and U.S. territories. Specifically, the ASA first asserts federal title to wrecks that are abandoned and either: (1) embedded in the submerged lands of states and territories, or (2) located on the submerged lands of states or territories and determined eligible for listing, or are listed, in the National Register of Historic Places. The Act then authorizes the transfer of title to those wrecks to the states and U.S. territories in or on whose submerged lands the wrecks are located. This transfer of title allows states and territories to manage these submerged heritage resources as part of their duty to manage living and non-living resources in state waters and submerged lands. The ASA also asserts federal title to abandoned wrecks located in or on the public lands of the United States. As to these wrecks, the federal government retains its management responsibility.

One important section of the ASA directs the Secretary of the Interior, through the National Park Service, to prepare and publish guidelines in the Federal Register that seek to:

(1) maximize the enhancement of cultural resources;
(2) foster a partnership among sport divers, fishermen, archeologists, salvors, and other interests to manage shipwreck resources of the States and the United States;
(3) facilitate access and utilization by recreational interests; [and]
(4) recognize the interests of individuals and groups engaged in shipwreck discovery and salvage.
      43 U.S.C. § 2104(a) (1994).

These guidelines [55 Fed. Reg. 50,116 (1990), *corrected*, 56 Fed. Reg. 7875 (1991)] are available to assist states, territories, and appropriate federal agencies in developing legislation and regulations to carry out their responsibilities under the ASA. It is important to note, however, that the Guidelines are only advisory, and, because they are not regulations, do not have the force and effect of law.[18]

---

[18]The ASA is discussed more extensively in Chapter 5, "Heritage Resources Law in the Marine Environment," but it is included in this chapter in order to underscore the federal management responsibility for abandoned shipwrecks located in or on the public lands of the United States, and to convey the purpose of the guidelines promulgated by the Department of the Interior, which is to advise the states and territories on how to carry out their management authority over wrecks within and on their submerged lands.

Note

Using the ASA and other heritage resources laws, consider the responsibilities, if any, of a National Seashore (a National Park unit) to manage abandoned historic shipwrecks located within its exterior boundaries, but in or on submerged lands owned and controlled by a state.

---

12. Curation Regulations of 1990 Promulgated Under the Archaeological Resources Protection Act

In addition to federal statutes enacted by Congress, regulations have been promulgated by each federal agency to carry out their management responsibilities to protect heritage resources under their ownership and/or control. The regulations concerning the curation of collections [36 C.F.R. Part 79 (1997)], however, apply to all federal agencies, and their purpose is to establish definitions, standards, procedures, and guidelines to govern federal agencies in their preservation of collections of prehistoric and historic material remains, and associated records recovered under the authority of the Antiquities Act [16 U.S.C. §§ 431–33 (1994)], the Historic and Archeological Data Preservation Act of 1974 [16 U.S.C. §§ 469–69c (1994)], section 110 of the National Historic Preservation Act [16 U.S.C. § 470h-2 (1994)], or the Archaeological Resources Protection Act of 1979 [16 U.S.C. §§ 470aa–mm (1994)]. By setting out the methods to secure and fund curatorial services, as well as the standards for long-term curatorial services, the curation regulations provide for proper management and preservation of preexisting and new collections [36 C.F.R. § 79.5–79.11 (1997)].

The section of the regulations dealing with the management and preservation of collections calls for the demonstration of long-term curatorial services that include initial processing of "material remains" (defined as "artifacts, objects, specimens and other physical evidence that are excavated or removed in connection with efforts to locate, evaluate, document, study, preserve, or recover a prehistoric or historic resource" [36 C.F.R. § 79.4(a)(1) (1997)]) and the preparation and organization of associated records. That section also sets forth the requirement to record the disposition of the collection in the associated records, and to retain those records.

In providing for methods to secure curatorial services, the regulations authorize agencies to place collections in a repository that is federally owned, leased, or otherwise operated by a federal agency, or in another suitable repository with which the federal agency has entered into an agreement for curatorial services [36 C.F.R. § 79.6(a) (1997)]. When selecting a repository, a federal agency must consider whether the potential repository is located in the state where the collection was recovered, is storing and maintaining other collections from the same site or project as the collection to be deposited, or is housing collections from a similar geographic or cultural area. Furthermore, in order to maintain the integrity and research value of the collection, the agency may not subdivide and deposit the collection at more than a single repository, unless a subdivision is necessary to meet special storage, conservation, or research needs [36 C.F.R. § 79(b) (1997)]. To help insure that the needs of the collection are properly met, the regulations encourage federal agencies to consult with persons having expertise in the management and preservation of collections prior to selecting a repository [36 C.F.R. § 79(c) (1997)].

Methods of funding curatorial services also are specified in the regulations. Curatorial services may be funded through annual appropriations of funds by Congress to federal agencies. In addition, section 110(g) of the NHPA [16 U.S.C. § 470h-2(g) (1994)] and section 208(2) of the NHPA Amendments [16 U.S.C. § 470p (1994)] authorize federal agencies to charge licensees and permittees reasonable costs for curatorial services associated with identification, surveys, evaluation, and data recovery as a condition to the issuance of a permit. Yet another source of funding identified in the regulations might be for a repository to provide curatorial services at no cost to the federal government. In addition, if data recovery costs exceed the one percent limitation contained in HADPA, the regulations authorize a way to waive this limitation in order to obtain additional funding [36 C.F.R. § 79.7 (1997)].

Standards for long-term curatorial services are specified in the regulations, and they include a description of professional museum and archival practices, standards affecting the nature and content of collections, a directive guiding the use of collections, and a provision specifying how inspections and inventories are to be conducted. Among the several articulated standards dictating the nature, content, and use of collections are the requirements that federal agencies:

1. Maintain complete and accurate records;
2. Dedicate facilities to properly store, study, and conserve the collection;
3. Physically secure the collections;
4. Require managers of collections to be qualified museum professionals;
5. Handle, store, clean, and conserve the collection;
6. Protect stored records from theft and fire;
7. Inspect for possible deterioration and damage to material remains and, if needed, stabilize;
8. Conduct inventory to verify location of collections, records and other property; and
9. Provide access for scientific, educational and religious uses.
   36 C.F.R. § 79.9 (1997).

The curation regulations are mandatory and have the force and effect of law. Accordingly, if they are not followed, the federal agency may be subject to liability.

SECTION C. PERMITS ISSUED BY FEDERAL AGENCIES THAT AFFECT HERITAGE RESOURCES

As part of their responsibility to manage heritage resources, federal land managing agencies issue permits, at their discretion, to qualified individuals or organizations to undertake certain activities. Two federal heritage resources statutes, the Antiquities Act of 1906 [16 U.S.C. §§ 431–433 (1994)] and the Archaeological Resources Protection Act of 1979 [ARPA, 16 U.S.C. §§ 470aa–mm (1994)], contain specific permitting provisions authorizing federal land managers to issue permits for examination, study, and/or excavation of heritage resources located on lands within their jurisdiction. The Antiquities Act applies to activities occurring on lands owned *or* controlled by the United States, while ARPA applies *only* to activities occurring on lands *owned* by the United States.

Other federal statutory and regulatory authorities provide for the examination and excavation of heritage resources in limited situations. For example, regulations found at 15 C.F.R. Part 922 (1997), which implement the National Marine Sanctuary Act [16 U.S.C. § 1434 (1994)], provide for the issuance of permits for activities otherwise prohibited by statute (such as the removal of historical sanctuary resources), on condition that these activities promote research and educational goals that are compatible with the establishment of the sanctuary in question. Also, section 10 of the Rivers and Harbors Act of 1899 [33 U.S.C. § 403 (1994)] and its implementing regulations require persons wishing to conduct dredge and fill activities on submerged lands within the jurisdiction of the Army Corps of Engineers (for the purpose of removing submerged heritage resources) to first obtain a permit.

The issuance of permits affecting heritage resources by federal land managers is discretionary. Discretion, however, must not be exercised in either an arbitrary or capricious manner. Rather, federal land managers must consider whether the issuance of these permits is within their jurisdiction and is compatible with the way in which the resources under their jurisdiction are to be managed. In this manner, issuance of permits constitutes one of the ways in which federal land managers comply with federal law.[19]

1.   Antiquities Act of 1906

The Antiquities Act of 1906 [16 U.S.C. §§ 431–433 (1994)] was the first statute enacted to protect heritage resources. It has two main components: (1) a criminal enforcement component providing for the prosecution of persons who appropriate, excavate, injure, or destroy any historic or prehistoric ruin or monument, or any object of antiquity on lands owned or controlled by the United States; and (2) a component that authorizes, through the issuance of a permit, the examination of ruins, the excavation of archeological sites, and the gathering of objects of antiquity on lands owned or controlled by the United States. Only the permitting provision of the Antiquities Act is discussed in this chapter, as the issuance of Antiquities Act permits is a component of the federal government's land management responsibilities. The criminal enforcement provision is discussed in Chapter 3, "Federal Enforcement Statutes."

The Antiquities Act specifically provides:

> That permits for the examination of ruins, the excavation of archaeological sites, and the gathering of objects of antiquity upon the lands under their respective jurisdictions may be granted by the Secretaries of the Interior, Agriculture, and War to institutions which they may deem properly qualified to conduct such examination, excavation, or gathering, subject to such rules and regulations as they may prescribe: *Provided*, That the examinations, excavations, and gatherings are undertaken for the benefit of reputable museums, universities, colleges, or other recognized scientific or

---

[19]Because most permits to conduct archeological research and recovery on federally owned or controlled lands are issued pursuant to either the Antiquities Act or (more commonly) ARPA, only the permitting provisions of these two statutes are discussed in this section. The permitting provisions contained in the regulations implementing the National Marine Sanctuaries Act are discussed more thoroughly in the chapter "Heritage Resources Law in the Marine Environment." In addition to permits issued under these three authorities, which specifically regulate archeological research and recovery under certain circumstances, federal agencies issue a plethora of other permits, albeit not for the specific purpose of conducting archeological research and recovery. The issuance of those permits is subject to the requirements of the NHPA and NEPA, and, in that respect, affords consideration of impacts on heritage resources [see, e.g., *Indiana Coal Council v. Lujan*, 774 F. Supp. 1385 (D.D.C. 1991) (NHPA applies to permits issued under the Surface Mining Control and Reclamation Act, 30 U.S.C. § 1272) (note, however, that this case was partially vacated as moot)].

educational institutions, with a view to increasing the knowledge of such objects, and that the gatherings shall be made for permanent preservation in public museums.
16 U.S.C. § 433 (1994) (emphasis provided in original).

While almost every legal case implicating the Antiquities Act has been brought under its criminal enforcement provision, the Act's permitting provision was litigated and upheld in two cases involving the marine environment.

LATHROP v. UNIDENTIFIED, WRECKED & ABANDONED VESSEL

817 F. Supp. 953 (M.D. Fla. 1993)

SCHLESINGER, District Judge:

This cause is before the Court on Plaintiff Randy L. Lathrop's Motion for Preliminary Injunction (Doc. No. 66) filed in Case No. 88-37 (*in rem* action). The United States has filed an Amicus Curiae Response in Opposition to Plaintiff's Motion for Preliminary Injunction (Doc. No. 81, filed on April 6, 1992).

I
PROCEDURAL BACKGROUND

These two consolidated cases involve a dispute over an alleged unidentified shipwreck located within 2,500 yards of a point with coordinates 80 degrees, 41.5' west longitude and 28 degrees, 44' north latitude. This dispute originated in November 1984, when Plaintiff was exploring the shallow coastal area north of Cape Canaveral, Florida. While diving, Plaintiff found several Spanish coins, covered in green from immersion in salt water, which he believes are part of the remains of a sunken eighteenth century Spanish galleon. These coins were milled in Mexico City, Mexico, from 1777 through 1782, and they bore the bust of King Charles III.

Because the coins were all minted in Mexico City within the same time period, Plaintiff postulates that the coins were part of a larger shipment, a mint shipment, which sank before reaching its final destination. Plaintiff hypothesizes that an eighteenth century ship lay submerged in the Cape Canaveral National Seashore and off the coast of Florida for over two hundred years.[1] Believing this to be true, Plaintiff filed a complaint *in rem* in January 1988 seeking ownership of the alleged unidentified vessel or a salvage award for his services.

---

[1]For centuries, Cape Canaveral, Florida has been known for its numerous navigational hazards. Historical records indicate many ships—possibly in the hundreds—have been lost on the Cape's treacherous shoals.

The Court arrested the vessel on January 27, 1988, and appointed Plaintiff as substitute custodian.

After the alleged vessel was arrested, Plaintiff published notice of this *in rem* action in the Florida Today, a newspaper of general circulation in Brevard County, Florida, on March 10, 1988. No one either responded to this publication or asserted an interest in the alleged vessel. Plaintiff then filed a Motion for Entry of Default which the clerk entered on June 7, 1988.

Shortly thereafter, Plaintiff began to experience problems with the U.S. Park Service for conducting what he thought were legitimate salvage activities. Park rangers arrested Plaintiff's assistants for carrying metal detectors within the Cape Canaveral National Seashore. At that time, the park rangers were not aware that Plaintiff obtained an order arresting the alleged vessel. Thereafter, the charges were dismissed, and Plaintiff was allowed on the premises. For the remainder of the year, Plaintiff conducted very little salvage activities.

In August 1989, Plaintiff began organizing salvage activities. First, he employed James Sinclair, an archaeologist who specializes in historic shipwrecks and president of SAS, Inc., to document the archaeological history of the wreck. Sinclair helped to formulate a research design, produce a map of the wreckage, and verify that the magnetometer readings truly identified an historic shipwreck. Also, Plaintiff hired Shipwrecks, Inc., to assist in a preliminary magnetometer survey and excavation of the alleged vessel.

Salvage operations from August 1989 through September 1989 consisted mainly of magnetometer and remote sensing surveys of the alleged vessel. During this time, Cape Canaveral was preparing for a space shuttle launch carrying sensitive Jupiter Probes which required heightened security. Under these circumstances, extensive salvage operations became nearly impossible. Thus, Plaintiff's salvage activities were limited by security concerns and involved additional magnetometer surveys.

The information obtained from these surveys indicated a pattern of magnetic anomalies (or abnormalities beneath the ocean floor) which could be the scattered remains of an historic shipwreck. To confirm this finding, Plaintiff needed to pinpoint selected areas, excavate them, and examine any objects producing the anomalies. Only then would Plaintiff know whether objects causing the anomalies were the remains of an historic shipwreck or some other objects (such as coke cans and other debris). Plaintiff recovered various objects, but none were ancient artifacts or other items belonging to an eighteenth century Spanish galleon. In addition, these objects did not prove the existence of an historical shipwreck.

Salvage activity from October 1989 through December 1989 consisted of additional magnetometer and remote sensing surveys. There were no recoveries. Similarly, salvage activities from January 1990 through March 1990 remained similarly idle, but due to poor weather conditions.

While Plaintiff prepared to resume salvage activities in April, Plaintiff encountered a series of misfortunes. First, the State of Florida required Plaintiff to abide by its regulatory scheme and obtain a permit before conducting salvage operations. Although Plaintiff disagreed with the State's authority to impose its regulations on activity conducted within a federal domain, he applied for a state permit.

Plaintiff applied to the State of Florida Division of Historical Resources. After reviewing Plaintiff's application, James J. Miller, State Archaeologist and Chief of the Bureau of Archaeological Research, informed him (in a letter dated May 25, 1990) that a salvage contract would be inconsistent with the agreement specifying the land's proper use. Plaintiff's permit was, therefore, denied.

Plaintiff did not apply for a permit with the United States Park Service, but Plaintiff did discuss the matter with Assistant United States Attorney Gregory N. Miller. The United States Government took a similar position regarding salvage activities in the Cape Canaveral National Seashore. Miller opined (in a letter dated May 31, 1990) that the "terms of the dedication prohibit the United States of America from granting Mr. Lathrop permission to conduct salvage operations within the Canaveral National Seashore." Plaintiff's Motion for Preliminary Injunction, Exhibit C. Also, the letter stated that if the Park were used contrary to the dedication's purpose, the reverter clause would terminate the United States' interest, causing the land to revert to the State of Florida. The United States fearing that it would lose an important National Park reaffirmed its adherence to park regulations requiring a permit. See 36 C.F.R. § 2.1.

One month later, Plaintiff filed a Motion for Preliminary Injunction (the first motion), seeking to invoke this Court's admiralty jurisdiction and to enjoin the United States from interfering with Plaintiff's maritime right of salvage. Plaintiff alleged that imposing a federal requirement to obtain a permit from the United States before conducting salvage activities—primarily excavation—in the Cape Canaveral National Seashore interfered with his right of salvage. The Court conducted a hearing on Plaintiff's Motion on July 23, 1990. The United States filed an *amicus curiae* brief opposing Plaintiff's Motion and appeared at the hearing.[2]

On August 6, 1990, Judge G. Kendall Sharp granted Plaintiff's Motion for a Preliminary Injunction,[3] and enjoined the United States for ninety days from interfering with the Court's *continuing in rem* jurisdiction over the alleged vessel and with Plaintiff's ongoing salvage operations. In granting that injunction, the Court determined that the United States did not have "constructive possession" which would establish its claim of ownership and thereby defeat Plaintiff's claim. Moreover, the Court held that general admiralty law principles award ownership to a salvor or finder who locates abandoned property and then exercises dominion and control over the found property. According to the Court, applying an "embeddedness" theory would conflict with admiralty law. Therefore, federal statutes could not be construed to displace general admiralty law because those statutes conflict with established maritime principles. The Court did not address the State's claim of title.

With the injunction firmly in place, Plaintiff resumed salvage operations. Plaintiff had contracted with Cobb Coin Company, Inc. ("Cobb"), and its Operations Manager, John Brandon, to help salvage the vessel. During August 1990, Cobb conducted a preliminary magnetometer survey twenty-two miles south of Ponce de Leon Inlet. The objective of this survey was to determine the presence of ferrous or other objects within the area thought to contain a sunken shipwreck.

A seven-person crew led by Kim Fisher, Captain and Vice President of Cobb, was dispatched to the alleged vessel site. This crew conducted preliminary magnetometer surveys. The crew's analysis of the preliminary survey led them to conclude that no identifiable correlation existed between the anomalies. The area, which Plaintiff believed to contain an

---

[2]Counsel for the State of Florida and the United States appeared at the hearing, but did so as non-parties.

[3]The issue raised in that previous injunction by the United States was ownership of the alleged shipwreck.

historic shipwreck, instead, could be a natural trap for metallic debris washed in from the sea. Without acquiring additional knowledge of the depth of the sand and shell overburden covering the bedrock, it was impossible to calculate the size of the objects producing the magnetic fluctuations or anomalies.

After the surveys were completed, Plaintiff began excavating selected areas in search of the alleged vessel. Cobb's crew would anchor the boat and utilize the boat's prop-wash deflectors to steer prop-wash into the ocean floor and excavate a pinpoint area. Although this was an effective technique, it created large craters in the soil. These craters were examined carefully for clues that may prove the existence of a shipwrecked vessel; and should the vessel's remains be found, Plaintiff could then determine its size and location. While Plaintiff vigorously pursued the alleged vessel, his salvage activities created large craters that were damaging the Cape Canaveral National Seashore.

After Plaintiff had resumed salvage activities, and two days after Judge G. Kendall Sharp issued the preliminary injunction, the State of Florida filed a separate action in state court. In that complaint, the State of Florida sought to protect Cape Canaveral National Seashore's submerged lands from damage, trespass or unlawful use. Under Florida law, it is a violation to use state-owned lands to dredge, or to excavate and remove historic artifacts without a permit. Counsel for Florida requested a temporary restraining order to protect its claim of title and ownership to the alleged vessel embedded in submerged lands located within its territorial waters. See Fla. Stat. Ann. § 267.061 (1990). The State of Florida sought an order prohibiting Plaintiff from dredging or excavating until title could be adjudicated.

Plaintiff removed that state action to federal court on August 13, 1990, and the two cases were subsequently consolidated. Plaintiff then renewed his earlier motion for Preliminary Injunction to include the State of Florida and its agencies. The Court granted that motion, and enjoined the State of Florida from interfering with Plaintiff's ongoing salvage operations. Thereafter, the State filed a Motion to Remand the newly removed action, arguing that the Eleventh Amendment barred such a suit. The Court denied the State's motion.[4]

On October 22, 1990, Plaintiff filed a Motion to Modify the Preliminary Injunction. Plaintiff requested that the injunction remain in effect beyond the original expiration date and until October 1, 1991. Plaintiff requested this extension because he was unable to conduct salvage operations when the injunction was first issued in August 1990. One reason for his inability to conduct salvage activities during this period was the meteorological conditions. Another reason was the earlier delay caused by the State of Florida. The Court denied the motion on January 11, 1991, because the 1990 salvage season had ended.

For the next six months, Plaintiff did not conduct any salvage operations. Plaintiff refrained from conducting salvage activities because the State of Florida was processing Plaintiff's application to excavate. Eric J. Taylor, an Assistant Attorney General, notified Plaintiff in December 1990 that the Florida Department of State had approved a settlement, in principle, authorizing Plaintiff to conduct salvage activities. There were two reservations: He declared that additional time was necessary to obtain final approval and prepare a written agreement. After receiving approval from Florida, Plaintiff would be required to obtain permission from the United States.

Although Plaintiff edged closer to obtaining the State's permission, a new problem emerged shortly before the 1991 salvage season began. As regulator of the Cape Canaveral

---

[4]See *infra* note 9 and text accompanying note.

National Seashore, the United States asserted its paramount role in protecting the land from further excavation. William A. Baxter, Assistant District Counsel for the Corps of Engineers, informed Plaintiff's Counsel on July 8, 1991, that the Court's admiralty jurisdiction would not preclude the United States from regulating salvage activities that occurred within their dredge-and-fill jurisdiction. Counsel for the Corps of Engineers urged that it had jurisdiction over dredging activities occurring in tidal water that extended from the mean high water line to the outer limits of the continental shelf. The Corps of Engineers did not recognize the Preliminary Injunction as affecting its jurisdiction.

Although the United States insisted that Plaintiff obtain a federal permit before resuming salvage activities, Plaintiff began operations without the Corps' approval. On September 9, 1991, Counsel for the United States, Caroline M. Zander, notified Plaintiff's Counsel that the Chief Ranger of the Canaveral National Seashore had seen a plume coming from an area where Plaintiff's ships were anchored. The presence of a plume indicated dredging, and Zander urged that Plaintiff's salvage activities were unlawful in the Cape Canaveral National Seashore without first obtaining a permit from the Army Corps of Engineers.[5]

A week later the Army Corps of Engineers issued a cease and desist order. In that order, the Corps of Engineers stated that Plaintiff must comply with the Rivers and Harbors Act before dredging in navigable waters of the United States. If Plaintiff failed to comply, the Corps of Engineers would seek legal action.

While the Corps of Engineers was asserting its jurisdiction and ordering Plaintiff to cease and desist salvage activities, there was some confusion between the United States and the State of Florida concerning each sovereign's regulatory responsibilities. To clarify each sovereign's role, Robert M. Baker, National Director of the U.S. Park Service, wrote Secretary Smith concerning his views on the problem. In a letter dated September 20, 1991, Secretary Smith, who is a member of the Board of Trustees with review authority over Plaintiff's application, responded to Baker's assertion that the dedication vested in the United States administrative and regulatory authority over the Cape Canaveral National Seashore:

> I agree with your legal analysis concluding that the State's interest in the subject land is subordinate to the interest conveyed to the United States by the dedication instrument of April 1, 1980, wherein the Board of Trustees conveyed exclusive use of the lands to the United States for 'wilderness/preservation purposes' and the administration of said lands as part of the Canaveral National Seashore.... In view of the rights already conveyed to the federal government, I agree that it would be inappropriate for the Department of State to issue a contract to conduct salvage within Canaveral National Seashore, and no such permission will be given.

United States Opposition to Plaintiff's Motion for Preliminary Injunction, Exhibit C (emphasis added). Secretary Smith agreed that through the dedication the United States' regulatory interest became paramount.[6]

The Court held a status conference addressing this problem on September 27, 1991. All parties were represented at the hearing. After the hearing, the Magistrate Judge issued an

---

[5]The United States took the position that Plaintiff must comply with the Rivers and Harbors Act of 1899 (codified at 33 U.S.C. § 403).

[6]See *infra* note 21.

Order requiring the United States, a non-party to the litigation, to file a separate action requiring Plaintiff to comply with the permitting process which would be consolidated with the pending cases.

The United States never filed a separate action. During this time, the parties conducted settlement negotiations, and Plaintiff agreed to comply with the permitting procedures. From these negotiations, Plaintiff agreed, therefore, to cease all dredging and salvaging activities within the boundaries of the Canaveral National Seashore, including the use of a metal detector or magnetometer. Plaintiff refrained from any further salvage activities for the remainder of 1991, awaiting a response from the State of Florida and the Army Corps of Engineers on his permits.

By January 1992, Plaintiff had made little, if any, progress on obtaining the State of Florida's consent to use state-owned submerged lands.[7] Likewise, the Army Corps of Engineers notified Plaintiff on March 5, 1992, that it had denied his permit [1991-01016(IP-eb)] because the State of Florida Department of Environment Regulation had denied a similar request. On February 24, 1992, Plaintiff filed a Second Motion for Preliminary and Permanent Injunction, which is presently pending before the Court.[8] The State of Florida has filed no response to the request for an injunction.[9] On April 6, 1992, the United States of America filed an *amicus curiae* brief in opposition to Plaintiff's request for an injunction. The Court conducted a hearing on Plaintiff's request for an injunction on May 14, 1992.

This controversy presents two complex issues involving principles of jurisdiction, federalism and comity, and Congress' power to alter substantive admiralty law, namely: (1) whether the Court has *in personam* jurisdiction to issue an injunction against the United States and its agents where the United States is not a party to this litigation and has not been served with process and (2) whether Congress can constitutionally supplement substantive admiralty law by regulating salvage activities; and if so, whether the United States can require a potential salvor of an alleged historical shipwreck to comply with federal law requiring a permit before conducting salvage activities in a National Park.

* * *

III
PRELIMINARY INJUNCTION

Although the Court has determined that it lacks *in personam* jurisdiction over the United States, and therefore is without authority to enjoin it, the Court will address the merits of Plaintiff's motion in the event the United States has been properly served.

---

[7]There remains confusion over ownership of the submerged lands. The State of Florida maintains that the dedication did not convey title to the submerged lands. Thus, the State of Florida asserts ownership over the alleged wreck, presumably leaving the United States with exclusive authority to manage the Cape Canaveral National Seashore.

[8]This case was reassigned to the undersigned on January 2, 1992.

[9]The State of Florida is not a party to the *in rem* action, but argues that its removed action is an *in personam* action to adjudicate title to the alleged vessel binding only the State of Florida and Plaintiff. The State claims that the Eleventh Amendment bars this Court from adjudicating its interest in the vessel since it has not waived sovereign immunity.

In order for the Court to issue an injunction, a Plaintiff must establish four essential elements: (1) a substantial likelihood of prevailing on the merits; (2) a substantial threat that Plaintiff will suffer irreparable injury if the injunction is not granted; (3) that the threatened injury to Plaintiff outweighs the threatened harm; and (4) that granting the preliminary injunction will not disserve the public interest. *Jupiter Wreck, Inc. v. Unidentified Sailing Vessel*, 691 F. Supp. 1377, 1383 (S.D. Fla. 1988). *Canal Authority of the State of Florida v. Callaway*, 489 F.2d 567, 572 (5th Cir. 1974).

A
Substantial Likelihood of Success

Plaintiff presents two claims in this *in rem* action: (1) a right of salvage and (2) ownership of the vessel. Distinguished from the law of finds, the law of maritime salvage is concerned not with title to the property, but rather with successful recovery and possession of lost property from the oceans and waterways. See *MDM Salvage v. Unidentified W & A Sail Vessel*, 631 F. Supp. 308, 312 (S.D. Fla. 1986). Salvage involves the right to possess another's property and to save it from destruction, danger or loss, allowing a salvor to retain it until being compensated by the owner. *Id.* Once in possession, no other person can lawfully intrude upon that possession, including the salved vessel's master or owner. 3A M. Norris, *Benedict on Admiralty: The Law of Salvage* § 151 (7th ed. 1983).

1. Salvage Claim

In order to establish a claim for salvage, three elements must be proven: (1) a "marine peril"; (2) service voluntarily rendered; and (3) success—either wholly or partly—in recovering the imperiled property. *Id.* The alleged historic shipwreck is in marine peril, *Treasure Salvors, Inc. v. Wrecked and Abandoned Sailing Vessel*, 569 F.2d 330 (5th Cir. 1978), *aff'd in part and rev'd in part, on other grounds, sub nom. Florida Dep't of State v. Treasure Salvors, Inc.*, 458 U.S. 670, 102 S.Ct. 3304, 73 L.Ed.2d 1057 (1982). But see *Klein v. Wrecked and Abandoned Sailing Vessel*, 758 F.2d 1511, 1515 (11th Cir. 1985) (stating that vessel was not lost or suffering any marine peril), and Plaintiff has voluntarily rendered his services to rescue its remains. Plaintiff has been only slightly successful in recovering its remains. To date, he has recovered approximately eight silver coins and a nail.

Although Plaintiff has established these elements of salvage (the last element in part), this case presents an additional problem: The vessel is located in a National Park, and the State of Florida conveyed exclusive use of those lands to the United States for a single purpose—to preserve and protect the wildlife. As the protector of the Cape Canaveral National Seashore, the United States requires Plaintiff to obtain a permit before *lawfully* excavating the alleged vessel.[12] Simply put, the United States argues that several Congressional

---

[12][*Orig. fn.*] Unlike *Jupiter Wreck, Inc. v. Abandoned Sailing Vessel*, 691 F. Supp. 1377 (S.D. Fla. 1988), in which a salvor sought an injunction against state officials, Plaintiff seeks an injunction against the United States because the United States Park Rangers have threatened to arrest Plaintiff if he attempts further excavation in the Cape Canaveral National Seashore's seabed.

enactments have modified the *substantive law* of admiralty. By these enactments—the Rivers and Harbors Act, the Antiquities Act, and several U.S. Park Service Regulations[13]— Congress has restricted the *manner* in which a potential salvor can excavate abandoned shipwrecks located on federal lands. According to the United States, these enactments restricting Plaintiff's manner of salvaging the alleged shipwreck do not conflict with the underlying principles of salvage; namely, that the law of salvage was developed to offer economic incentives to seamen observing cargo in immediate marine peril to undertake rescue efforts. *Zych v. Wrecked and Abandoned Vessel*, 941 F.2d 525, 531 (7th Cir. 1991). The Court agrees.

The Constitution has extended the judicial power to all cases of admiralty and maritime jurisdiction. See U.S. Const. Art. III, § 2. Congress has implemented statutorily the Constitutional grant of jurisdiction and made it exclusive. See 28 U.S.C. § 1333. Courts have held that Congress may constitutionally "alter, qualify, or supplement the substantive admiralty law [presumed to be in existence at the writing of the Constitution]." *Panama R.R. Co. v. Johnson*, 264 U.S. 375, 386, 44 S.Ct. 391, 393, 68 L.Ed. 748 (1924) (alteration in original). There are limits, though, to Congressional power to supplement or alter admiralty law. The Supreme Court noted these limitations:

> One is that there are boundaries to the maritime law and admiralty jurisdiction which inhere in those subjects and cannot be altered by legislation, as by excluding a thing falling clearly within them or including a thing falling clearly without. Another is that the spirit and purpose of the constitutional provision require that these enactment… shall be co-extensive with and operate uniformly in the whole of the United States.
> *Id.* at 386–87, 44 S.Ct. at 394.[14]

Congressional enactments restricting the *manner* in which a potential salvor excavates property located on federally owned or managed lands does not offend these sound constitutional limitations. The State of Florida dedicated the Cape Canaveral National Seashore to the United States for a specific purpose which is "to preserve and protect the outstanding natural, scenic, scientific, ecologic, and historic values of certain lands, shoreline, and waters of the State of Florida, and to provide for public outdoor recreation use and enjoyment of the [park]." 16 U.S.C. § 459j. The dedication contains a reverter clause allowing the State of Florida to reenter and reclaim possession if the land is used for an improper purpose.[15] To prevent against the land's reversion, Congress has enacted legislation allowing

---

[13][*Orig. fn.*] The Abandoned Shipwreck Act of 1987, [codified at 43 U.S.C. §§ 2102(a), 2105(a)(1)], does not apply. It only applies to actions brought prior to April 28, 1988.

[14][*Orig. fn.*] The Supreme Court has implied that the uniformity doctrine is only "properly invoked to strike down state legislation when it purports to regulate commercial navigation." *Zych*, 941 F.2d at 533 n. 11. [construing *Askew v. American Waterways Operators, Inc.*, 411 U.S. 325, 93 S.Ct. 1590, 36 L.Ed.2d 280 (1973)].

[15][*Orig. fn.*] The reverter clause states: "Should the United States of America cease for any reason, to use these lands for the herein stated purposes, title to said lands shall revert to said Board of Trustees." United States' Amicus Curiae Opposition, Defendant's Exhibit A, at 2, ¶ 2.

the Secretary to terminate a right of use and occupancy retained by an owner of improved property in the park if the land is being used in a *manner inconsistent* with its specified *purpose*. See 16 U.S.C. § 459j-2(b).

In order to protect National Parks, such as the Cape Canaveral National Seashore from being endangered, Congress has passed various laws which prohibit the appropriation of historic artifacts,[16] or excavation[17] on federal lands without first obtaining a permit from the Corps of Engineers. The permitting process is comprehensive, but it considers the effects of the proposed activity on the public interest as well as the effect on the environment, wildlife, and historical and cultural resources. 33 C.F.R. § 320.4. See *Zable v. Tabb*, 430 F.2d 199 (5th Cir. 1970), *cert. denied*, 401 U.S. 910, 91 S.Ct. 873, 27 L.Ed.2d 808 (1971). Such laws, however, do not deprive a federal court of admiralty jurisdiction. Nor do they necessarily prohibit a potential salvor from conducting salvage activities, although they might. Rather, these statutes supplement admiralty law by providing substantive rules for lawfully conducting salvage operations on federally owned or managed lands.

The requirement that a salvor act lawfully while salvaging a vessel is consistent with general admiralty law. By itself, possession of abandoned property is not sufficient to establish a salvage claim. *Martha's Vineyard Scuba HQ. v. Wrecked and Abandoned Steam Vessel*, 833 F.2d 1059 (1st Cir. 1987). Before a valid claim can be established, a salvor must acquire possession lawfully. Otherwise, as one court noted, "buccaneering would again flourish on the high seas." *Id.* It is for Congress—through appropriate legislation—to substantively supplement admiralty law and determine the lawfulness of certain salvage activities.

In instances such as the case at bar, restrictions are necessary. Without any restrictions, Plaintiff's salvage activities could not only destroy the alleged vessel and its historic artifacts, but also could disrupt the delicate marine life living on the seabed. An example illustrates the need for such restrictions. Salvors could conceivably block an international shipping route by anchoring a salvage vessel in the channel while attempting to rescue a sunken shipwreck. See *id.* at 1067. Certainly, the United States Coast Guard could exercise its jurisdiction and prevent placement of salvage vessels that would interrupt the flow of maritime traffic. Although this restriction would interfere with salvage activities, it is a necessary restriction to ensure the safety of both salvors and the public. Legislation which supplements admiralty jurisdiction by imposing necessary restrictions on salvage activities is an important legislative function properly reserved to Congress.[18]

In sum, it appears to the Court that Plaintiff would not prevail on a salvage claim because he cannot lawfully gain possession of the alleged vessel without first obtaining a permit from the United States. The United States Congress has the legislative power to regulate a National Park such as the Cape Canaveral National Seashore, even though the State of Florida may retain ownership of the submerged lands. Thus, Plaintiff must comply with the permitting process. When Plaintiff obtains a permit, Plaintiff's salvage activities and recovery of artifacts will be deemed lawful. The Court concludes, therefore, that Plaintiff has failed to demonstrate a substantial likelihood of prevailing on his salvage claim.

---

[16][*Orig. fn.*] Antiquities Act of 1906, (codified at 16 U.S.C. § 433).

[17][*Orig. fn.*] Rivers and Harbors Act of 1899, (codified at 33 U.S.C. § 403).

[18][*Orig. fn.*] The Eleventh Circuit has recognized Congress' broad powers over "all public lands pursuant to the Property Clause of the United States Constitution." *Klein, supra*, at 1514 [construing *Kleppe v. New Mexico*, 426 U.S. 529, 96 S.Ct. 2285, 49 L.Ed.2d 34 (1976)].

There is another aspect of salvage law that further demonstrates Plaintiff cannot establish a substantial likelihood of prevailing on the merits. Potential salvors do not have an inherent right to save distressed vessels. *Jupiter Wreck*, 691 F. Supp. at 1377. Instead, a salvage award may be denied if a salvor forces its services on a vessel despite rejection by the owner or by a person with authority. *Platoro Ltd., Inc. v. Unidentified Remains*, 695 F.2d 893 (5th Cir. 1983) [construing *The Indian*, 159 F. 20, 25 (5th Cir. 1908)]. The doctrine of rejection normally applies when the master of a distressed vessel directly and unequivocally rejects a salvor's services. In cases where the vessel has sunk, the master can communicate rejection of salvage services through a sign, buoy, marker or public advertisement. When the master does so, a salvor who continues efforts to rescue the vessel will not be entitled to a salvage award.

There exists a similarly related doctrine—constructive rejection—which would allow a state[19] to reject a salvor's services. See *Platoro*, 695 F.2d at 902. The constructive rejection of salvage services bars an award if the rejection was reasonably understood by a salvor. In this context, the United States must demonstrate that various federal laws put Plaintiff on notice that his services have been rejected. This doctrine then requires a fact finder to determine Plaintiff's understanding of relevant federal laws.

Typically, a salvor acts as an agent for a vessel's owner. A salvor acquires the right to possess an abandoned shipwreck, but he does not acquire title. Title remains with the owner as does the right to refuse salvage. Yet in cases involving an historic shipwreck, it may be unclear to a salvor who the owner actually is.[20] If a salvor does not know whether it is the

---

[19][*Orig. fn.*] States not only have laid claim to ownership of wrecked property located within their territorial waters, but also have attempted to preclude salvage activities by potential salvors. These claims have been viewed by salvors as state interference in an area which is predominantly controlled by Federal law, and which is "essentially a Federal problem." M. Norris, *Benedict on Admiralty, supra*, at 11–14.

[20][*Orig. fn.*] The Eleventh Circuit applies the law of finds in determining ownership of an abandoned vessel. *Klein*, 758 F.2d at 1513. See also *Treasure Salvors*, 569 F.2d at 337 n. 11 (stating that "the primary difference between the two doctrines is that under the law of salvage the claim of the finder of abandoned property is satisfied by proceeds from the sale of the property paid into court"). According to the law of finds, title vests in the person who reduces the property to his or her possession. *Id.*

There are two exceptions to the law of finds. When the abandoned property is embedded in the soil, it belongs to the soil's owner. Second, the law considers the owner of the land who has "constructive possession" of the property to have never lost the property. If either exception applies, a salvor cannot prevail on his or her claim of ownership. See *Zych*, 941 F.2d at 530 n. 7 ("Embeddedness" [ ] is to be 'consistent with the recognized exception from the law of finds for shipwrecks embedded in the submerged lands of a state.").

Although ownership of the alleged vessel is an unresolved question, a salvor who knows that a shipwreck is submerged on federal or state lands also should know that a State has a colorable claim of ownership. As such, a salvor should investigate the State's laws to see if the sovereign has rejected salvage services. Here, Plaintiff should have examined either Florida law (if the State has retained ownership of the submerged lands), or federal law. Under *Klein*, an owner can refuse salvage services.

United States or the State of Florida which has a valid claim of ownership, a salvor will not know which sovereign's laws apply. This assumes, of course, that whichever law applies, it provides a clear statement rejecting salvage services.

At this stage, the Court must determine whether Plaintiff has demonstrated a substantial likelihood of prevailing on the merits of his salvage claim. For the reasons that follow, the Court concludes Plaintiff has not demonstrated a substantial likelihood of prevailing. In this case, Plaintiff knew the alleged vessel was located on land owned by the State of Florida and dedicated to the United States for preservation as a National Park. It is unquestioned that the State of Florida has, by virtue of its police powers, the right to regulate the use of its land and to refuse salvage services when those services will endanger its natural and historical resources.

Because the State of Florida dedicated its land to the United States to establish a National Park, the United States has the authority to manage and protect the land, its marine life, and historic artifacts from damage caused by dredging or excavating.[21] Thus, Plaintiff should have known that the State of Florida, the presumed owner of the submerged lands and any property embedded in the soil, might refuse Plaintiff's offer to excavate the alleged vessel.

While this Court does not decide the ownership of the alleged shipwreck, the Court concludes that it is likely that Plaintiff must have reasonably known that the State of Florida, the alleged vessel's likely owner, rejected his offer of salvage services. *Jupiter Wreck, Inc. v. Abandoned Sailing Vessel*, 691 F. Supp. 1377 (S.D.Fla1988) (denying injunctive relief because the court concluded that the State of Florida was not required to allow the property salved, and the State's statutory scheme reflected the owner's rejection of salvage services). The Court concludes that Plaintiff has not demonstrated a substantial likelihood of prevailing on the merits of his salvage claim.

* * *

B
Plaintiff's Irreparable Injury

The question of Plaintiff's irreparable injury is inextricably intertwined with the question of ownership and the right to refuse salvage. If the United States is declared owner and has refused Plaintiff's salvage services, Plaintiff has suffered no irreparable injury. Plaintiff alleges, however, that if the injunction is not granted, he will lose his right to pursue a salvage claim, and his employees will face arrest, and criminal and civil penalties. If Plaintiff prevails then on its claim of ownership or salvage, Plaintiff will be entitled to either take

---

[21][*Orig. fn.*] There remains to be resolved a question regarding the United States' authority to regulate the submerged lands. Because the State of Florida alleges that it retained ownership of the submerged lands, it is unclear whether the dedication allows the United States to exercise sole regulatory authority over the Cape Canaveral National Seashore, including the submerged lands. The Court does not decide this question, but proceeds under the assumption that State of Florida retained ownership of the submerged lands, and that the dedication allows the United States to regulate the submerged lands.

possession of the vessel[24] or receive a salvage award for his services. If he does not prevail, the harm Plaintiff alleges is purely theoretical.

C
Balancing of the Harm

For the reasons that follow, any harm to the public and the United States would outweigh any harm suffered by Plaintiff if the injunction were granted. At stake is the continued preservation of a National Park dedicated by the State of Florida. As the dedication itself states, these lands are dedicated to preserve the waters of the State of Florida for the public's outdoor recreational use. The public's use and enjoyment is deeply rooted in the preservation of the seashore's natural, scenic, scientific, ecologic, and *historic* value.[25] Because the dedication includes a reverter clause, the land could revert to the State of Florida if the injunction were granted. The consequences of that reversion would be severe indeed.

The United States and its citizens would lose a National Park of unparalleled beauty and historical significance. Americans have always possessed a deep affection for America's National Parks and its environment. The United States establishes National Parks primarily to protect precious lands from being damaged and to promote the well-being of marine life by preserving its habitat. Yet National Parks serve another important function—their creation allows citizens to enjoy the beauty, peacefulness and uninterrupted solitude of the outdoors.

Cape Canaveral is a popular tourist attraction which is visited by thousands annually, and the National Seashore adds to the magnificence and enchantment of this well-known attraction. Similar to the environment, Americans have held a deep affection for the space program. To many, it personifies America's love for freedom, science, and adventure. As representative of those ideals, Cape Canaveral has become a well-endowed sanctuary for those who journey to Florida to watch shuttle launches or to visit the space museum. Presumably, the State of Florida dedicated this land to the United States because it would be in a better position financially to maintain the park and its shores. By granting this injunction,

---

[24][*Orig. fn.*] This assumes of course that Plaintiff files for and receives a permit. A question that may conceivably arise is whether the United States could impose its regulatory scheme on Plaintiff should Plaintiff prevail as owner of the alleged wreck. Plaintiff's present status is that of a potential salvor. The Court finds that the United States may, consistent with admiralty principles, impose regulations on a potential salvor, but does not decide the extent of its regulatory authority.

[25][*Orig. fn.*] The United States included two affidavits in support of its motion. Affiant Tyrell A. Henwood, Ph.D., a Fishery Biologist employed by the United States Department of Commerce, stated that Plaintiff's salvage operations increase the turbidity and alteration of nearshore bottom characteristics that could adversely affect turtles. Affidavit of Tyrell A. Henwood at 2.

Larry Murphy, an Archeologist with the Submerged Cultural Resources Unit, a division of the United States Department of Interior, asserts that Plaintiff's salvage activities are contrary to standard archeological procedures and unnecessarily endanger any artifacts that might exist. Affidavit of Larry Murphy at 3.

it appears with certainty that the land comprising the National Park could revert to the State of Florida, and the future of this National Park would be greatly jeopardized.

D
Disservice to the Public

The last requirement that must be satisfied is that by granting an injunction the public interest would not be disserved. In this case, Plaintiff's continued efforts to excavate the alleged shipwreck would disserve the public by bringing about two severe consequences: (1) the Cape Canaveral National Seashore would revert to the State of Florida, and (2) the marine life and artifacts would be damaged.[26] Many of the issues in this case depend on resolution of a critical question—ownership of the alleged vessel. Essentially, the resolution of this entire matter requires the presentation of evidence during trial. Until the Court has an opportunity to adjudicate title[27] to the shipwreck, the Court finds that the best way to adequately protect the rights of the salvor and the public is by denying the injunction.

Clearly, there are two important interests to be preserved: the right to salvage and the preservation of a National Park. On the one hand, Plaintiff asserts that his maritime right of salvage has been impeded. The United States asserts that it will lose the Cape Canaveral National Seashore if Plaintiff prevails. During trial, it is clear that both parties cannot prevail on their claims. For this reason—both parties cannot prevail on their claims—an injunction is an extraordinary remedy which should not be granted unless Plaintiff can establish a substantial likelihood of prevailing on the merits of his claims. Plaintiff has failed to meet his burden.

Because it is unclear that during trial Plaintiff could establish either entitlement to a salvage award or ownership of the alleged vessel, an injunction is not a proper remedy. If the Court granted an injunction improvidently, the United States could lose the Cape Canaveral National Seashore. The reason for this austere result is the dedication agreement's reverter provision. The purpose of having a reverter clause, such as the one in the dedication, is to ensure usage consistent with a specified purpose. Here, the purpose advocated by the United States is the land's preservation. Should the land be used for other purposes that endanger its preservation, the State of Florida then can reenter, oust the United States of any ownership interest, and reclaim the land. If this were to occur, the United States and its citizens would lose an important National Park. Moreover, the future of the park's land, its artifacts, and its marine life also would be jeopardized. The Court concludes that Plaintiff cannot meet his burden on this element because an injunction would disserve the public.

Accordingly, it is ORDERED AND ADJUDGED that Plaintiff's Motion for Preliminary Injunction (Doc. No. 66) is DENIED.

DONE AND ORDERED.

---

[26][*Orig. fn.*] See *supra* note 25 and text accompanying note.

[27][*Orig. fn.*] The State of Florida contends that title to the alleged vessel must be adjudicated in state court. See *supra* note 9. Shortly after removal, the state filed a Motion to Remand which was denied on August 22, 1990. Before ruling on Removed Plaintiff's Motion for Summary Judgment, the Court may wish to reconsider the State's request for remand in order to decide the alleged vessel's ownership.

Notes

1.   In a second case involving the marine environment and underwater heritage resources, the permitting authority under the Antiquities Act again was recognized and upheld. In *United States v. Fisher*, 977 F. Supp. 1193 (S.D. Fla. 1997) (see Chapter 5), the United States brought an enforcement action against treasure hunter Melvin Fisher, his son, and others (collectively referred to as "the Fishers") after they created approximately 600 holes in the seabead of the Florida Keys National Marine Sanctuary in their search for treasure. In that case, the United States took the position that the Fishers failed to obtain a permit from NOAA, the trustee of the Florida Keys National Marine Sanctuary, pursuant to the Antiquities Act and other statutes that would have regulated their treasure hunting activities and prevented them from damaging sanctuary resources. The United States prevailed on this point; the Fishers have appealed. In ruling in favor of NOAA on partial summary judgment, the Court, citing the *Lathrop* case, held that compliance with statutes such as the Antiquities Act and the National Marine Sanctuaries Act does not offend traditional admiralty/maritime law principles:[20]

> Congress has the right to modify general admiralty law. *Panama R.R. Co. v. Johnson*, 264 U.S. 375, 386 (1924); *Lathrop v. Unidentified, Wrecked & Abandoned Vessel*, 817 F. Supp. 953, 962 (M.D. Fla 1993). The *Lathrop* court rejected the argument that the Defendants make here. In that case, the plaintiff was salvaging in the Cape Canaveral National Seashore. He argued that the federal law requiring him to get a salvage permit unconstitutionally infringed on preexisting maritime salvage law. In finding against that claim, the Court held that 'Congressional enactments restricting the manner in which a potential salvor excavates property located on federally owned or managed lands does not offend' the Constitution. *Lathrop*, 817 F. Supp. at 962.
>
> This Court agrees. Common law principles do not automatically bar Congress from exercising its legislative prerogative to protect federal lands from potentially damaging activity. [fn.5 See the Antiquities Act of 1906, prohibiting the appropriation of historic artifacts on federal land without a permit, the Rivers and Harbors Act of 1899, prohibiting excavation on federal land without a permit, and the Property Clause of the U.S. Constitution. U.S. Const., art. 4, § 3, cl. 2.] And the requirement that a salvor act lawfully while salvaging does not offend admiralty law principles. *Id.* at 963. Other courts have upheld challenges to laws restricting salvage activities in National Parks. *Klein v. Unidentified Wrecked and Abandoned Sailing Vessel*, 758 F.2d 1511 (11th Cir. 1985) (holding that salvager was not entitled to award for artifacts recovered from shipwreck in Biscayne National Park); *Craft v. National Park*

---

[20]A thorough discussion of admiralty/maritime law and its interplay with heritage resources law can be found in Chapter 5, "Heritage Resources Law in the Marine Environment."

Serv., 34 F.3d 918 (9th Cir. 1994) (upholding fine against divers who used hammers and chisels to excavate a shipwreck located in a marine sanctuary).

Fisher Summary Judgment Order (unpublished) at pages 11–12 (Case No. 92-10027 Civ.-Davis (S.D. Fla. filed April 21, 1992)).

Lathrop and *Fisher* uphold the rule that where the United States has ownership or control of the lands in or on which heritage resources are located, the Antiquities Act permitting provision can be used to regulate excavation of heritage resources.

2. Confusion remains over the meaning of the term "control" in reference to lands "owned or *controlled*" for purposes of requiring an Antiquities Act permit. This confusion derives from another case involving treasure hunter Melvin Fisher, *Treasure Salvors v. The Unidentified Wrecked and Abandoned Sailing Vessel*, 569 F.2d 330 (5th Cir. 1978). In that case, the Fifth Circuit denied the United States' attempt to use the Antiquities Act as a basis for claiming ownership to the sunken seventeenth century Spanish Galleon, the *Atocha*, located beyond state waters on the outer continental shelf of the United States. Specifically, the Fifth Circuit rejected the United States' argument that Congress, through enactment of the Outer Continental Shelf Lands Act [43 U.S.C. § 1331, *et seq.* (1994)], sought to extend jurisdiction and control of the United States to the outer continental shelf and that, accordingly, the Antiquities Act (which applies to lands owned and *controlled*) gave the United States "control" over the *Atocha*. The confusion was created because the Fifth Circuit, in rejecting the United States' argument, did not clarify whether it meant that the Antiquities Act requires the United States to have "control" over the submerged lands *for the specific purpose of protecting heritage resources* in order for the Act to apply. Moreover, the Court's interpretation of "control" remains an issue as far as applying the Antiquities Act's permitting provision is concerned, as *Treasure Salvors* did not involve the application of that provision. *Lathrop* likewise cannot provide any clarity on this point, as the interpretation of the term "control" was not an issue raised in that case. Had the meaning of "control" been an issue in *Lathrop*, the United States still would have prevailed because the National Park Service has exclusive management authority and control over the submerged lands located within Canaveral National Seashore for the express purpose of protecting heritage and other resources. In *Fisher*, the application of the Antiquities Act's permitting provision was also not an issue with respect to "control" because the United States, through NOAA, has control over the submerged lands located within the Florida Keys National Marine Sanctuary for the express purpose of protecting historical sanctuary resources. Consequently, the confusion over what is meant by "control" is confined to the question of whether the reach of the Antiquities Act's permitting provision applies only in or on lands in which the United States has express authority to regulate activities affecting heritage resources.

2.   Archaeological Resources Protection Act of 1979

The Archaeological Resources Protection Act [ARPA, 16 U.S.C. §§ 470aa–mm (1994)] is a management statute that also addresses looting and destruction of archeological resources. Like the Antiquities Act, ARPA has both enforcement and permitting components. The enforcement provision, providing for the imposition of both criminal and civil (administrative) penalties against violators of the Act, is discussed in Chapter 3, "Federal Enforcement Statutes." A noteworthy difference between ARPA and the Antiquities Act is that ARPA only applies to lands *owned* in fee title by the United States. In addition, ARPA explicitly does *not* apply to activities occurring on the outer continental shelf. As the Antiquities Act covers all lands that are covered by ARPA *plus* lands that are under the control of the United States, the territorial reach of ARPA is more limited than that of the Antiquities Act. Nevertheless, where both ARPA and the Antiquities Act apply, ARPA is the statute of preference, even though it does not expressly supersede the Antiquities Act.

ARPA's permitting component allows for recovery of certain resources consistent with the standards and requirements of the federal government's archeology program. In pertinent part, the ARPA permitting process is comprised of the following components:

(a) Application for permit
Any person may apply to the federal land manager for a permit to excavate or remove any archaeological resource located on public lands or Indian lands and to carry out activities associated with such excavation or removal. The application shall be required, under uniform regulations under this chapter, to contain such information as the federal land manager deems necessary, including information concerning the time, scope, and location and specific purpose of the proposed work.
(b) Determinations by federal land manager prerequisite to issuance of permit
A permit may be issued pursuant to an application under subsection (a) of this section if the federal land manager determines, pursuant to uniform regulations under this Act, that
(1) the applicant is qualified to carry out the permitted activity,
(2) the activity is undertaken for the purpose of furthering archaeological knowledge in the public interest,
(3) the archaeological resources which are excavated or removed from public lands will remain the property of the United States, and such resources and copies of associated archaeological records and data will be preserved by a suitable university, museum, or other scientific or educational institution, and
(4) the activity pursuant to such permit is not inconsistent with any management plan applicable to the public lands concerned.
(c) Notification to Indian tribes of possible harm to or destruction of sites having religious or cultural importance

If a permit issued under this section may result in harm to, or destruction of, any religious or cultural site, as determined by the federal land manager, before issuing such permit, the federal land manager shall notify any Indian tribe which may consider the site as having religious or cultural importance.

* * *

(d) Terms and conditions of permit

Any permit under this section shall contain such terms and conditions, pursuant to uniform regulations promulgated under this chapter, as the federal land manager concerned deems necessary to carry out the purposes of this chapter.

(e) Identification of individuals responsible for complying with permit terms and conditions and other applicable laws

Each permit under this section shall identify the individual who shall be responsible for carrying out the terms and conditions of the permit and for otherwise complying with this chapter and other law applicable to the permitted activity.

(f) Suspension or revocation of permits; grounds

Any permit issued under this section may be suspended by the federal land manager upon his determination that the permittee has violated any provisions of section (a), (b), or (c) of section 470ee [Prohibited Acts and Criminal Penalties] of this title. Any such permit may be revoked by such federal land manager upon assessment of a civil penalty under section 470ff [Civil Penalties] of this title against the permittee or upon the permittee's conviction under section 470ee of this title.

(g) Excavation or removal by Indian tribes or tribe members; excavation or removal of resources located on Indian lands

> (1) No permit shall be required under this section or under the Act of June 8, 1906 (16 U.S.C. § 431) [the Antiquities Act], for the excavation or removal by any Indian tribe or member thereof of any archaeological resource located on Indian lands of such Indian tribe, except that in the absence of tribal law regulating the excavation or removal of archaeological resources on Indian lands, an individual tribal member shall be required to obtain a permit under this section.

> (2) In the case of any permits for the excavation or removal of any archaeological resource located on Indian lands, the permit may be granted only after obtaining the consent of the Indian or Indian tribe owning or having jurisdiction over such lands. The permit shall include such terms and conditions as may be requested by such Indian tribe.

16 U.S.C. § 470cc (1994).

Federal land managers are charged with ensuring that the requirements of the permitting regime are followed, and failure to do so can result in liability of the land managing agency, which is separate and distinct from criminal liability for conducting excavation or removal of archeological resources either without a permit or in violation of the terms or conditions of a permit.[20]

SECTION D.   CHALLENGES TO AGENCY ACTION BASED ON NON-COMPLIANCE

Plaintiffs who sue federal agencies for failure to comply with the statutes cited in this chapter typically bring causes of action founded on several statutes. For example, a plaintiff might sue a federal agency on the grounds that it violated both the NHPA and NEPA. This approach to litigation is very common in heritage resources lawsuits based on agency noncompliance. Problems may arise, however, when plaintiffs fail to assert a proper jurisdictional basis for bringing these actions. Most of the statutes cited in this chapter do not authorize plaintiffs to bring private rights of action, nor do they contain an express waiver of sovereign immunity to sue the United States. Consequently, plaintiffs must invoke the Administrative Procedure Act [APA, 5 U.S.C. § 701, *et seq.* (1994)] as a basis for conferring jurisdiction on federal district courts to hear these challenges to agency action or inaction. In order to invoke the APA, plaintiffs must allege a violation of the APA and establish that the challenged action or inaction of the federal agency constitutes "final agency action" for purposes of the APA. Once invoked, judicial review of the federal agency action at issue is usually limited to the "administrative record," including documents created by the agency that led up to the challenged action, including the final decision document itself. The reviewing court must then determine whether the decision is supported by the administrative record, or whether the agency was arbitrary or capricious in reaching its decision.

The goal of many plaintiffs who challenge federal agency actions is to enjoin the action. Accordingly, plaintiffs almost always will seek injunctive relief as a remedy.

---

[20]Liability resulting from failure either to follow the terms or conditions of an ARPA permit, or to obtain an ARPA permit prior to conducting excavation or removal of archeological resources on public or Indian lands, is discussed in Chapter 3, "Federal Enforcement Statutes."

1.   Jurisdictional Basis for Bringing Suit
Against Federal Agencies

As a sovereign, the United States is immune from suit except when it consents to be sued, and consent must be found in a clear, unequivocal, specific jurisdictional statement found in a statute enacted by Congress [*Lehman v. Nakshian*, 453 U.S. 156 (1981); *United States v. Testan*, 424 U.S. 392 (1976); and *United States v. Sherwood*, 312 U.S. 584, 590 (1941)]. This waiver of sovereign immunity "cannot be implied but must be unequivocally expressed" [*Army and Air Force Exchange Service v. Sheehan*, 456 U.S. 728, 734 (1982), quoting *United States v. Testan*, 424 U.S. 392, 399 (1976)] and generally will be "strictly construed in favor of the United States" [*United States v. Idaho*, ex rel. Dir., Dept. of Water Res., 508 U.S. 1, 7 (1993); and *United States v. Nordic Village*, Inc., 503 U.S. 30, 33–34 (1992)]. This principle of narrow construction of waivers of sovereign immunity applies with full force to environmental statutes [see *United States Dep't of Energy v. Ohio*, 503 U.S. 607 (1992), finding no waiver of federal sovereign immunity for civil penalties under either the Clean Water Act or the Resource Conservation and Recovery Act, and stating that courts should presume "congressional familiarity" with the "common rule" that immunity waivers must be "unequivocal"].

The Federal Rules of Civil Procedure require that a plaintiff bringing suit against the United States allege both a basis for the court's jurisdiction and a specific statute containing a waiver of the government's sovereign immunity from suit [Fed. R. Civ. P. 8(a)(1); see *United States v. Clarke*, 33 (8 Pet.) U.S. 436 (1900); and *Reeves v. United States Dept. of Treasury*, 809 F. Supp. 92 (N.D. Ga. 1992)]. This requirement is based upon the principle that federal courts are courts of limited jurisdiction, and that there is no presumption that they possess subject matter jurisdiction to adjudicate any particular case [see *General Atomic Co. v. United Nuclear Corp.*, 655 F.2d 968–69 (9th Cir. 1981)]. Accordingly, the burden of proving the proper jurisdictional basis for any particular suit is on the party invoking the district court's jurisdiction [*Data Disc., Inc. v. Systems Tech. Ass'n, Inc.*, 557 F.2d 1280, 1285 (9th Cir. 1977); and *Williams v. United States*, 711 F.2d 893, 895 (9th Cir. 1983)].

The statutes cited in this chapter do not contain an express waiver of sovereign immunity from suit or private right of action that otherwise would authorize the commencement of an action against federal agencies for noncompliance. Instead, the waiver of sovereign immunity is provided by the

Administrative Procedure Act [APA, 5 U.S.C. §§ 701–706 (1994)].[21] By itself, the APA does not create a private right of action to sue federal agencies for non-compliance. A private right of action is permissible only if the plaintiff invokes both the APA and a separate, relevant statute (such as NEPA, NFMA, or FLPMA) "…to demonstrate that the claimant has suffered a 'legal wrong,' such that there is federal jurisdiction to address that wrong" [*Califano v. Sanders*, 430 U.S. 99, 104 (1977); and *Pinar v. Dole*, 747 F.2d 899 (4th Cir. 1984), *cert. denied*, 471 U.S. 1016 (1985)].[22]

2.   Requirement of "Final Agency Action"

An action under the APA for failure to comply with the requirements of one or more of the statutes discussed in this chapter presupposes "final agency action" as defined by the APA. "Review is sought not pursuant to specific authorization in the substantive statute, but only under the general review provisions of the APA[.] [T]he 'agency action' in question must be '*final agency action*'" [*Lujan v. National Wildlife Federation*, 497 U.S. 871, 882 (1990) (emphasis added), citing 5 U.S.C. § 704 (1994)]. "Final agency action" is defined by the APA as "the whole or part of an agency rule, order, license, sanction, relief or the equivalent, or denial thereof, or failure to act" [5 U.S.C. § 551(13) (1994); see also *CWWG v. U.S. Dept. of the Army*, 111

---

[21]Several courts have found, however, that the NHPA does create an implied private right of action. [See *Boarhead Corp. v. Erickson*, 923 F.2d 1011 (3d Cir. 1991); *Vieux Carre Property Owners, Residents & Assoc's v. Brown*, 948 F.2d 1436 (5th Cir. 1989), *cert. denied*, 493 U.S. 1020 (1990); and *Tyler v. Cisneros*, 136 F.3d 603 (9th Cir. 1998). But see *National Trust for Historic Preservation v. Blanck*, 938 F. Supp. 908 (D.D.C. 1996); and *Carson v. Alvord*, 487 F. Supp. 1049 (N.D. Ga. 1980).]

[22]It is well-established that NEPA does not provide an independent basis for jurisdiction (see *Public Citizen v. Office of United States Trade Rep.*, 970 F.2d 916, 918 (D.C. Cir. 1992), holding that "NEPA does not create a private right of action.…"; *City of Blue Ash v. McLucas*, 596 F.2d 709, 712 (6th Cir. 1979), holding that "It is clear that there is no explicit provision… [creating a private right of action] in NEPA"; *and Mountainbrook Homeowners Ass'n, Inc. v. Adams*, 492 F. Supp. 521, 527–29 (W.D.N.C.1979), *aff'd*, 620 F.2d 294 (4th Cir. 1980), holding that "[i]t is difficult to see how any court could read into 'NEPA' any implied private remedy…," and citing *Cort v. Ash*, 422 U.S. 66 (1975); and *Public Citizen v. Office of United States Trade Rep.*, 970 F.2d at 918–19, holding that, because NEPA does not create a private right of action, plaintiffs must seek judicial review under the APA). Likewise, claims brought under the NFMA, FLPMA, ARPA, and other similar statutes are not free-standing claims. Therefore, a plaintiff must also allege that the federal agency failed to comply with the APA, which provides the jurisdictional basis for judicial review of the actions in question [5 U.S.C. § 706(2)(A) (1994); see also *Carson v. Alvord*, 487 F. Supp. 1049 (N.D. Ga 1980)].

F.3d 1485 (10th Cir. 1997)]. In *Abbott Laboratories v. Gardner* [387 U.S. 136, 148 (1967)], the U.S. Supreme Court set forth the basis for the APA requirement of final agency action before judicial review is available.[23] The Court explained that the "basic rationale" for this requirement, as applied to review of administrative actions:

> is to prevent the courts, through avoidance of premature adjudication, from entangling themselves in abstract disagreements over administrative policies, and also *to protect the agencies from judicial interference until an administrative decision has been formalized and its effects felt in a concrete way by the challenging parties.*
> *Abbott Laboratories* at 148–49 (emphasis added).

Examples of "final agency action" include the issuance of: (1) a Finding of No Significant Impact or a Record of Decision under NEPA; (2) a federal license or permit; and (3) a Record of Decision to issue federal funds. In addition, an agency's decision to undertake a project without completing its consultation responsibilities under section 106 of the NHPA would be a "final agency action" that could be challenged [see *National Trust for Historic Preservation v. U.S. Army Corps of Engineers*, 552 F. Supp. 784 (S.D. Ohio 1982)].

3.   The APA Standard and Scope of Review

Once a plaintiff properly brings an action based on non-compliance with one or more of the statutes cited in this chapter, by invoking the APA as a basis for federal district court jurisdiction, the court reviews the action using the APA standard for judicial review [5 U.S.C. § 706 (1994)]. Under this standard, an agency's decision will be upheld unless found to be arbitrary, capricious, an abuse of discretion, or otherwise not in accordance with law, or contrary to statutory right or authority [5 U.S.C. §§ 706(2)(A) and (C) (1994)].

In applying the APA standard of review to an agency's decision, courts are to accord deference to the agency's construction of the statutory scheme it administers [*Chevron U.S.A., Inc. v. Natural Resources Defense Council*, 467 U.S. 837, 842–45 (1984); *and Environmental Coalition of Broward County, Inc. v. Meyers*, 831 F.2d 984, 986 (11th Cir. 1987)]. Specifically, "the question for the [reviewing] court is whether the agency's [decision] is based on a permissible construction of the statute" [*Chevron* at 842–43; see also *Amoco Production Co. v. Lujan*, 877 F.2d 1243, 1248 (5th Cir. 1989),

---

[23]*Abbott Laboratories* was overruled on other grounds by *Califano v. Saunders*, 430 U.S. 99 (1976).

cert. denied, 493 U.S. 1002 (1989), holding that an agency's interpretation of law must be honored so long as it is a reasonable one]. Courts are also to give substantial deference to an agency's interpretation of its regulations. An agency's interpretation of its own regulations controls unless plainly erroneous or inconsistent with the regulation itself. [*Udall v. Tallman*, 380 U.S. 1, 17 (1965); *Robertson v. Methow Valley Citizens Council*, 490 U.S. 332, 359 (1989); and *McMillan Park Committee v. National Capital Planning Comm'n*, 968 F.2d 1283 (D.C. Cir. 1992)].

Agency decisions are also entitled to a presumption of validity [*Wilderness Public Rights Fund v. Kleppe*, 608 F.2d 1250, 1254 (9th Cir. 1979), *cert. denied*, 446 U.S. 982 (1982)]. Further, courts should generally defer to an agency's technical expertise, and are not to substitute their judgment for that of the agency [*Baltimore Gas & Elec. Co.* 462 U.S. at 98; *Citizens to Preserve Overton Park v. Volpe*, 401 U.S. 402, 416 (1971)].

As stated above, the scope of judicial review of an agency's final action is generally limited to the administrative record that was before the agency at the time it made its decision [*Citizens to Preserve Overton Park* at 419–20, holding that judicial review of agency action must be based on "the 'whole record' compiled by the agency"; *Camp v. Pitts*, 411 U.S. 138 (1973), which overturned a lower court decision permitting additional fact-finding in court as part of the review of an agency decision; and *Pollgreen v. Morris*, 770 F.2d 1536, 1545 (11th Cir. 1985)]. The reviewing court, then, should uphold the agency action if the administrative record demonstrates that the agency has "considered the relevant factors and articulated a rational connection between facts found and the choice made" [*Baltimore Gas* at 105]. However, the presumption of regularity accorded to agency decisions "is not to shield [the agency's] action from a thorough, probing, in-depth review" by the reviewing court [*Citizens to Preserve Overton Park* at 415]. If the agency's decision is not sustainable on the administrative record when subjected to this standard of review, the matter must be remanded back to the agency for further consideration [*Vermont Yankee Nuclear Power Corp. v. NRDC*, 435 U.S. 519, 549 (1978); *Camp* at 143; *and Avoyelles Sportsmen League, Inc. v. Marsh*, 715 F.2d 897 (5th Cir. 1983)].

4. Discovery Generally Prohibited

In APA cases, discovery is generally prohibited [see *Region 8 Forest Service Timber Purchasers Council v. Alcock*, 736 F. Supp. 267, 275 (N.D. Ga. 1990), *aff'd*, 993 F.2d 800 (11th Cir. 1993), *cert. denied*, 510 U.S. 1040, 114 S.Ct. 683 (1994), holding that "[t]he general rule in administrative review cases is that, absent certain exceptions, discovery is not permitted."); *United States v. Seymour Recycling Corp.*, 679 F. Supp. 859, 865 (S.D. Ind. 1987), holding that "[a]s a general rule, review of the administrative record eliminates the need for discovery, as the administrative record contains all that is relevant to the decision at issue." Further, the Supreme Court set the tone long ago when it observed that, "in cases where Congress has simply provided for review [under the Administrative Procedure Act],... [judicial] consideration is to be confined to the administrative record and... no *de novo* proceeding may be held" [*United States v. Carlo Bianchi & Co.*, 372 U.S. 709, 715 (1963)]. This judicial restraint, expressed in numerous Supreme Court opinions interpreting the APA, stems from the characteristics of the administrative process, whereby expertise, such as the management of a forest, has been delegated by Congress to federal agencies, and not to the reviewing federal district courts. Courts are not to supplant the agency's judgment as to what would be the wisest administrative decision with their own [see *Bowman Transportation, Inc. v. Arkansas-Best Freight System, Inc.*, 419 U.S. 281, 283 (1974); and *Citizens to Preserve Overton Park* at 416]. Instead, the judicial function is an inquiry into whether the agency's action is reasonable, a question the court must answer based on the administrative record. "The grounds upon which an administrative order must be judged are those upon which the record discloses that [the] action was based" [*Securities and Exchange Comm'n v. Chenery Corp.*, 318 U.S. 80, 87 (1943)]. "[T]he focal point for judicial review should be the administrative record already in existence, not some new record made initially in the reviewing court" [*Camp* at 142; see also *Florida Power & Light Co. v. Lorton*, 470 U.S. 729, 743 (1985)].

Courts may generally inquire outside the administrative record when one of the following circumstances is present:

1) an agency's failure to explain its action effectively frustrates judicial review;[24]
2) it appears that the agency has relied on documents or materials not included in the record;
3) supplementation of the record is necessary to explain technical terms or complex subject matter involved in the agency action; or
4) the plaintiffs make a showing of agency bad faith.
Animal Defense Council v. Hodel, 840 F.2d 1432, 1436–37 (9th Cir. 1988).[25]

---

[24]This outside inquiry is limited to determining, either through affidavit or testimony of the agency, whether the agency has considered all relevant factors or has explained its course of conduct or grounds for decision [*Animal Defense Council*, 840 F.2d at 1436].

[25]See also *National Trust for Historic Preservation v. Blanck*, 938 F. Supp. 908, 916 n.10 (D.D.C. 1996) (court permitted supplementation of the administrative record to establish whether agency decision was correct).

The party seeking discovery beyond the administrative record has the burden of demonstrating that its request falls within one of these exceptions [*Animal Defense Council* at 1436].

If the administrative record is "facially deficient" in relation to a particular issue, no further inquiry is necessary, and the proper recourse for the court is to remand it to the agency for further consideration [*Florida Power & Light Co. v. Lorion*, 470 U.S. 729, 743–44 (1985), holding that "the proper course, except in rare circumstances, is to remand to the agency for additional investigation or explanation"... "[t]he reviewing court is not generally empowered to conduct a *de novo* inquiry into the matter being reviewed and to reach its own conclusions based on such an inquiry"].

5. Injunctive Relief Often Sought

In lawsuits brought under the APA, plaintiffs often will seek the remedy of injunctive relief. The issuance of injunctive relief, however, "does not issue as of course" [*Amoco Production Co. v. Gambell*, 480 U.S. 531, 542 (1987); see also *Cuomo v. United States Nuclear Regulatory Commission*, 772 F.2d 972, 978 (D.C. Cir. 1985)]. There are three types of injunctive relief: (1) a temporary restraining order (TRO); (2) a preliminary injunction; and (3) a permanent injunction. If granted, a TRO will enjoin the agency action temporarily until the court schedules a hearing on the plaintiffs' motion for preliminary injunction, which usually occurs within ten days. In order to obtain a TRO, plaintiffs must demonstrate: (1) a likelihood of success on the merits of the lawsuit; (2) that they will suffer irreparable injury if the TRO is not issued; (3) that, when balancing the hardship the plaintiffs will suffer if a TRO is not granted against the hardship the federal agency will suffer if a TRO is granted, the plaintiffs' hardship is greater; and (4) the issuance of a TRO is in the public interest. The most important of the four elements for plaintiffs to prove at the TRO stage is the second one, namely that they will suffer irreparable injury if a TRO is not granted.

The elements for obtaining a preliminary injunction are identical to those for obtaining a TRO. The showing of irreparable injury at the preliminary injunction stage also is very important [*Weinberger v. Romero-Barcelo*, 456 U.S. 305, 312 (1982); C. Wright and A. Miller, *Federal Practice and Procedure*, section 2948 at 431 (1973)]. In order to obtain injunctive relief, however, plaintiffs must establish irreparable injury that *is certain, actual, imminent, and not theoretical* [*Connecticut v. Massachusetts*, 282 U.S. 660, 674 (1931), holding that injunctive relief is only appropriate to "prevent existing or presently threatened injuries" and "will not be granted against something merely feared as liable to occur at some indefinite time in the future"; *Wisconsin Gas Co. v. F.E.R.C.*, 758 F.2d 669 (D.C. Cir. 1985); *Hous-*

ing Study Group v. Kemp, 736 F. Supp. 321 (D.D.C. 1990); and *Ashland Oil, Inc. v. F.T.C.*, 409 F. Supp. 297 (D.D.C. 1976), *aff'd*, 548 F.2d 977 (D.C. Cir. 1977)]. Neither generalized allegations of injury, mere conjecture, nor theoretical predictions of harm constitute irreparable injury sufficient to warrant the issuance of preliminary injunctive relief [see *Connecticut* at 674; *Wisconsin Gas Co.* at 669; *Ashland Oil, Inc. v. F.T.C.*, 409 F. Supp. 297, 307 (D.D.C. 1976), holding that "[i]njunctive relief is appropriate only to 'prevent existing or presently threatened injuries' and 'will not be granted against something merely feared as liable to occur at some indefinite time in the future,'" quoting *Connecticut* at 674; and *Housing Study Group* at 330, holding that "[i]n order to establish irreparable injury justifying preliminary injunctive relief, plaintiff must establish injury that is certain, great and actual, not theoretical"]. Although the showing of irreparable injury must be made, plaintiffs must be able to demonstrate their heavy burden of establishing that *all* four requirements have been sufficiently met in order to warrant the issuance of a preliminary injunction. If granted, a preliminary injunction will enjoin the agency action until the reviewing court decides the merits of the case or, in other words, decides whether the agency action should be permanently enjoined.

The standard for entry of a permanent injunction is similar to the standard for entry of a preliminary injunction, except that the moving party must show *actual* success on the merits rather than a likelihood of success. A permanent injunction constitutes a final determination of the merits of the plaintiffs' lawsuit in favor of the plaintiffs, and, permanently enjoins the agency's action [see, e.g., *National Trust for Historic Preservation v. Army Corps of Engineers*, 552 F. Supp. 784 (S.D. Ohio 1982)].

CHAPTER THREE

FEDERAL
ENFORCEMENT STATUTES

SECTION A. AN OVERVIEW AND BRIEF HISTORY

Archeological resources are the nonrenewable and irreplaceable material remains of past human existence. Often, they are the only evidence of people who lived within the United States. These heritage resources serve the public welfare both intellectually and emotionally. At the same time, they stimulate the desire to recover as much of the past as possible, and as soon as possible. This temptation to exploit archeological sites, however, must be tempered by the realization that all excavation, even if scientifically sound, is also a form of destruction, and that the amount of information obtainable from a site today is only a fraction of what will be possible in the future. Consequently, one of the purposes of the federal government's archeology program is to fight looting and preserve the archeological record in place [Secretary of the Interior, *A National Strategy for Federal Archeology* (Oct. 24, 1991) (available from Dept. of the Interior, Off. of the Departmental Consulting Archeologist, Washington, DC)].

Because archeological resources contribute to our understanding of the forces and people that shaped our world, public policy has deemed them important for both science and the general public welfare, and worthy of protection by civil and criminal laws. These laws protect archeological, historical, and other heritage resources on federal, tribal, state, and private lands.

Specific nationwide protection and regulation of archeological resources in the United States began in 1906, with the passage of the Antiquities Act. The Act functioned well as both a means to establish National Monuments and a permitting process for excavation on federally owned or controlled land, but it was less effective in deterring criminal activity. In the mid-1970s, the Antiquities Act was struck down by the Ninth Circuit Court of Appeals as unconstitutionally vague because it failed to define "antiquity." Thereafter, federal prosecutors used more general criminal statutes in the United States Code to charge persons who looted and injured archeological sites. Those criminal laws respecting property, in fact, always had protected heritage resources, but the denuding of vast areas of archeological and historic interest and significance notwithstanding, preservation of heritage resources through criminal prosecution was not a priority for federal prosecutors. In 1979, the Archaeological Resources Protection Act (ARPA) was enacted to provide a comprehensive means of managing archeological resources by standardizing and expanding on the permitting process, improving the ability of federal prosecutors to deter destructive activity, and preserving collections for scientific and public benefit. It also considered the interests of hobbyists and the public, whose level of fascination with the past might be less technical than that of scientists. Although Native American concerns were referenced by the 1979 legislation, they really were not an integral part of ARPA.

SECTION B.   FEDERAL LAWS THAT SPECIFICALLY PROHIBIT DAMAGE TO HERITAGE RESOURCES

1.   Antiquities Act of 1906

In the late nineteenth century, with the cessation of wars between the United States and the Indian tribes, and the opening of vast territories through the expansion of the railroads, pristine archeological sites in the West became accessible to vandals, commercial looters, and anyone with a curiosity about the past. As a result, the public felt that its heritage was in danger of being lost, and agitated for Congressional action to address this issue. Finally, on June 8, 1906, the Antiquities Act was enacted [Pub. L. No. 59-209, 34 Stat. 225 (1906), 16 U.S.C. §§ 431–433 (1994). For a detailed history of the Antiquities Act, see Ronald F. Lee, *The Antiquities Act of 1906* (1970)].

The components of the Act are: (1) regulation through permits for excavation, examination, and study of archeological sites on lands owned or controlled by federal land managing agencies (which, in 1906, were comprised of the Departments of the Interior, Agriculture, and War); (2) authority of the president to establish National Monuments, and authority of the Secretary of the Interior to accept the relinquishment to the government of private land for this purpose; and (3) punishment of anyone who destroys archeological sites through vandalism or theft. Of these provisions, only the authority to proclaim National Monuments has not been affected by subsequent legislation or case law. The requirements for obtaining a permit have been superseded by ARPA, and the criminal provision of the Antiquities Act—to the extent a criminal act is redressed by a minor offense penalty—can no longer be used in the Ninth Circuit.

It is a violation of the Antiquities Act for any person to "appropriate, excavate, injure, or destroy any historic or prehistoric ruin or monument, or any object of antiquity" on federally owned or controlled land without a permit [16 U.S.C. § 431 (1994)]. The original punishment of a fine of not more than $500 and/or imprisonment for up to 90 days was a substantial sentence in 1906. It has been updated to a fine of not more than $5,000 and/or incarceration of up to six months [Criminal Fines Improvement Act of 1987, 18 U.S.C. § 1 (1994); Comprehensive Crime Control Act of 1984, 18 U.S.C. § 3623 (1994)].

The Antiquities Act was the only specific statute providing a criminal sanction for injury to historic and prehistoric (before European contact) sites until it was challenged in 1974. In *United States v. Diaz*, 368 F. Supp. 856 (D. Ariz. 1973), *rev'd*, 499 F.2d 113 (9th Cir. 1974), the Ninth Circuit Court of Appeals held that the term "object of antiquity" was vague, and that the failure of the Antiquities Act to provide notice of what the law prohibited rendered it void. The same claim subsequently was used by the defendants in *United States v. Smyer*, 596 F.2d 939 (10th Cir.), *cert. denied*, 444 U.S. 843 (1979). In *Smyer*, however, the Tenth Circuit Court of Appeals found that the defendants were commercial looters, and that they had sufficient notice that their actions violated the Antiquities Act. Consequently, the Tenth Circuit upheld the convictions, and denied the constitutional challenge. The Antiquities Act's criminal sanctions never have been tested in the other circuits (mainly because they have been overshadowed by the Archaeological Resources Protection Act), and they still are viable everywhere except in the Ninth Circuit.

UNITED STATES v. DIAZ

499 F.2d 113 (9th Cir. 1974)

MERRILL, Circuit Judge:

Appellant was charged in 1973 with appropriating "objects of antiquity situated on lands owned and controlled by the Government of the United States without the permission of the Secretary of Interior," contrary to 16 U.S.C. § 433.[1]

---

[1][*Orig. fn.*] That section provides: "Any person who shall appropriate, excavate, injure, or destroy any historic or prehistoric ruin or monument, or any object of antiquity, situated on lands owned or controlled by the Government of the United States, without the permission of the Secretary of the Department of the Government having jurisdiction over the lands on which said antiquities are situated, shall, upon conviction, be fined in a sum of not more than $500 or be imprisoned for a period of not more than ninety days, or shall suffer both fine and imprisonment, in the discretion of the court."

The items appropriated were face masks found in a cave on the San Carlos Indian Reservation. They were identified by a San Carlos medicine man as having been made in 1969 or 1970 by another medicine man personally known to him. A professor of anthropology at the University of Arizona testified as an expert on the religious systems of the Western Apache in the State of Arizona. He testified that artifacts such as those appropriated by appellant were used by the Apache Indians in religious ceremonies and that after the conclusion of ceremonies the artifacts traditionally were deposited in remote places on the reservation for religious reasons; that the artifacts are never allowed off the reservation and that they are considered sacred and may not be handled by anyone except the medicine man once they are stored in a cave. He further testified that in anthropological terms "object of antiquity" could include something that was made just yesterday if related to religious or social traditions of long standing. In his opinion the artifacts in the instant case were antiquities despite the fact that they were no more than three or four years old.

We have no doubt as to the wisdom of the legislative judgment (made close to seventy years ago and reinforced by experiences of the present in the despoliation of public lands) that public interest in and respect for the culture and heritage of Native Americans requires protection of their sacred places, past and present, against commercial plundering.

Protection, however, can involve resort to terms that, absent legislative definition, can have different meanings to different people. One must be able to know, with reasonable certainty, when he has happened on an area forbidden to his pick and shovel and what objects he must leave as he has found them.

Nowhere here do we find any definition of such terms as "ruin" or "monument" (whether historic or prehistoric) or "object of antiquity." The statute does not limit itself to Indian reservations or to Indian relics. Hobbyists who explore the desert and its ghost towns for arrowheads and antique bottles could arguably find themselves within the Act's proscriptions. Counsel on neither side was able to cite an instance prior to this in which conviction under the statute was sought by the United States.

In *Connally v. General Const. Co.*, 269 U.S. 385, 391 (1926), the Court, in discussing the due process requirement of legislative specificity, stated:

> That the terms of a penal statute creating a new offense must be sufficiently explicit to inform those who are subject to it what conduct on their part will render them liable to its penalties, is a well-recognized requirement, consonant alike with ordinary notions of fair play and the settled rules of law. And a statute which either forbids or requires the doing of an act in terms so vague that men of common intelligence must necessarily guess at its meaning and differ as to its application, violates the first essential of due process of law.

In *Grayned v. City of Rockford*, 408 U.S. 104, 108–109 (1972), it was stated:

> Vague laws offend several important values. First, because we assume that man is free to steer between lawful and unlawful conduct, we insist that laws give the person of ordinary intelligence a reasonable opportunity to know what is prohibited, so that he may act accordingly. Vague laws may trap the innocent by not providing fair warning. Second, if arbitrary and discriminatory enforcement is to be prevented, laws must provide explicit standards for those who apply them. A vague law impermissibly delegates basic policy matters to policemen, judges, and juries for resolution on an ad

hoc and subjective basis, with the attendant dangers of arbitrary and discriminatory application.

Here there was no notice whatsoever given by the statute that the word "antiquity" can have reference not only to the age of an object but also to the use for which the object was made and to which it was put, subjects not likely to be of common knowledge.

In our judgment the statute, by use of undefined terms of uncommon usage, is fatally vague in violation of the due process clause of the Constitution.

Judgment REVERSED.

Note

Diaz could have been charged under general criminal statutes for theft or embezzlement, which carry more severe penalties. By 1973, the maximum penalty under the Antiquities Act (90 days and/or $500) was a minor cost of doing business considering the substantial market value of the masks. As a result of *Diaz*, federal prosecutors used the general crimes statutes to charge more serious offenses. The gravamen of these offenses is not that the stolen object is an object of antiquity or a heritage resource, only that the item is federal property, and that it was taken without permission. If the masks in *Diaz* had been several hundred years old, might the result have been different?

UNITED STATES v. SMYER

596 F.2d 939 (10th Cir. 1979)

BREITENSTEIN, Circuit Judge:

After trial to the court without a jury, the defendants-appellants were found guilty of each count of an eleven-count information charging violations of 16 U.S.C. § 433 which relates to American antiquities. They received 90-day concurrent sentences on each count.

The offenses occurred in the Mimbres Ranger District, Gila National Forest, New Mexico. Count I charges that, without permission from the Secretary of Agriculture, the defendants excavated a prehistoric Mimbres ruin at an archaeological site, herein designated as 250, which was inhabited about 1000–1200 A.D. Count II charges excavation of a ruin at a site designated as 251. Counts III through XI charge the appropriation from the ruins of specified objects of antiquity, 800–900 years old.

The two sites are about 300 yards apart and may be approached either from the north or the south. Forest Rangers had observed "very wide, deep-lugged" tire tracks at the sites. On October 29, 1977, a Forest Service Recreation Officer, Roybal, discovered that a vehicle with "wide, deep-lugged" tires had entered the northern road leading to the sites and had passed a Forest Service sign warning that the area was protected by the American Antiquities Act. Upon his request for assistance, Ranger Bradsby and Enforcement Officer Dresser came and the three followed the tire tracks to the ruins. They found freshly dug holes at each ruin, shovels, picks, a sifting screen, and a small pottery bowl. In an arroyo between the sites they found a four-wheel drive truck, the tires on which matched the earlier discovered tire marks. No one was present at the sites. The officers inventoried the contents of the truck and had it towed away. That evening defendant May came to Ranger Bradsby's home and said that "he had been scouting for deer and that his truck had been stolen." A few days later federal officers interviewed, and obtained statements from, both May and Smyer. The officers took some artifacts from Smyer's home without objection and later, on the execution of a search warrant, seized other pieces of Indian bowls.

Defendants urge that the Antiquities Act is unconstitutional because it is vague and uncertain. The Act, which was passed in 1906, provides:

> Any person who shall appropriate, excavate, injure, or destroy any historic or prehistoric ruin or monument, or any object of antiquity, situated on lands owned or controlled by the Government of the United States, without the permission of the Secretary of the Department of the Government having jurisdiction over the lands on which said antiquities are situated, shall, upon conviction, be fined in a sum of not more than $500 or be imprisoned for a period of not more than ninety days, or shall suffer both fine and imprisonment, in the discretion of the court.

The claim of vagueness and uncertainty is based on the use in the statute of the words "ruin," and "object of antiquity." In *United States v. Diaz*, the Ninth Circuit held that "the statute, by use of undefined terms of uncommon usage, is fatally vague in violation of the due process clause of the Constitution." We respectfully disagree. In *Diaz* the charge was appropriation of objects of antiquity consisting of face masks found on an Indian Reservation. The masks had been made in 1969 or 1970. The government evidence was that "'object of antiquity' could include something that was made just yesterday if related to religious or social traditions of long standing." Id. at 114. Those facts must be contrasted with the instant case where the evidence showed that objects 800–900 years old were taken from ancient sites for commercial motives. We do not have a case of hobbyists exploring the desert for arrow heads. See, id. at 114. Defendants admitted visiting the sites on several occasions and May had sold Mimbres bowls to an archaeologist.

The charges here were the excavation of two ruins and the appropriation of several objects of antiquity. The defendants' attack can go only to "ruin" and "antiquity." A ruin is the remains of something which has been destroyed. Webster's New International Dictionary, 2d Ed., 1960, p. 2182, ruin (4). Antiquity refers to "times long since past." Id. p. 119, antiquity (1). When measured by common understanding and practice, the challenged language conveys a sufficiently definite warning as to the proscribed conduct. *United States v. Petrillo*, 332 U.S. 1, 8 (1877); see also *United States v. Goeltz*, 10 Cir., 513 F.2d 193, 196–197, *cert. denied*, 423 U.S. 830.

The case under consideration is not a "sit-in" case like *Bouie v. City of Columbia*, 378 U.S. 347, a vagrancy case like *Papachristou v. City of Jacksonville*, 405 U.S. 156, nor an antipicketing case like *Grayned v. City of Rockford*, 408 U.S. 104. We are not concerned with the deprivation of any First Amendment right. In their briefs defendants charge selective enforcement, but their claim has no support in the record. The statute in question was designed for the protection of American antiquities. It affects the property of the United States and is well within the power over public lands given to Congress by the federal Constitution. Art. IV, § 3, cl. 2.

In assessing vagueness, a statute must be considered in the light of the conduct with which the defendant is charged. See *United States v. National Dairy Products Corp.*, 372 U.S. 29, 32–33. The Antiquities Act gives a person of ordinary intelligence a reasonable opportunity to know that excavating prehistoric Indian burial grounds and appropriating 800–900-year-old artifacts is prohibited. See *Grayned v. City of Rockford*, 408 U.S. 104, 108. We find no constitutional infirmity in § 433.

The Gila National Forest was established in 1899. *United States v. New Mexico*, 438 U.S. 696–699. The Secretary of Agriculture has jurisdiction over historic sites within forest reserves. 43 C.F.R. § 3.1(a). To bolster their claim that they did not know they were in the National Forest, defendants argue that the Department gave inadequate notice that the two sites were on government land. The tire tracks of the vehicle went by an Antiquities Act sign. When the defendants saw the forest officers, one of whom was in uniform, they fled. Each defendant in his statement to officer Dresser admitted that he had been to the site several times. Mimbres bowls were found in Smyer's home. The trial court rejected the defendants' claim that they believed they were on private property. The overwhelming evidence shows violations of § 433.

* * *

Defendants assert that the government did not comply with Rule 16, F.R. Crim. P., relating to discovery and inspection. At the trial much controversy arose over the government's compliance with a defense motion for discovery. One dispute related to a map of the area in which the antiquity sites were located. The defense claimed that they did not know that they were on government property. A land surveyor presented an area map. The defense claims that they did not receive an exact copy and that the evidence given by the surveyor included scientific tests or experiments within the purview of Rule 16(a)(1)(D). We are not impressed. We are convinced that the government complied with Rule 16. The record sustains the government's contention that the defendants knew they were on government land. If there was any misunderstanding about the map, the defendants were not prejudiced.

* * *

The next objection goes to the receipt in evidence of the tangible objects which are the bases of Counts III to XI. During his interview with officer Dresser, May admitted digging at the ruins and selling two bowls. May offered to return the artifacts. At Smyer's home, May selected a number of artifacts from a collection and turned them over to the officer. Later the officer returned to Smyer's home with a search warrant and seized 31 bowls. A government expert testified that certain bowls were "all Mimbres classic or Mimbres Black on White Bowls." A shard found at the site fitted one of the bowls. A government expert placed the value of the artifacts taken by the defendants at about $4,000. The sites were prehistoric ruins inhabited by Mimbres Indians, a sub-group of the Mogollon culture, from about 1000–1200 A.D., and the bowls were made sometime during that period. The questioned evidence was either given voluntarily to the officer or obtained by a search warrant of unquestioned validity. The bowls were adequately identified with the site, both by physical evidence and the admissions of the defendants. The evidence was properly received.

Defendants object to the receipt in evidence of a photograph of defendant May, seized by the officers during an inventory search of the truck. The photo showed May standing with a skull on his head and on each shoulder. He was holding skeletal bones in his hands. The evidence showed the presence of skeletal bones at the sites. On cross-examination May said that the photo was of him.

After the officers found the truck, they investigated the surrounding area and found no one. They decided to impound the truck and made a routine inventory of its contents. While doing so, officer Roybal lowered a sun visor, and the questioned photo fell down. The routine inventory protected the owner's property while in police custody, protected the officers against claims and disputes and against potential danger. *South Dakota v. Opperman*, 428 U.S. 364, 368–372, sustains the actions of the officers. They had reasonable cause to connect the truck with the excavations at the sites, and it had been abandoned. The seizure of the photo was proper. The evidence showed that the picture had been taken at site 250. The picture connected May with the site and was properly received in evidence.

Ranger Bradsby testified that the special-use permits, which authorized exploration of antiquity sites, were kept in his office and that neither May nor Smyer had a permit. The government introduced a computer print-out which named those who had the necessary permits. The introduction of the print-out is said to violate the Rules of Evidence, particularly Rule 802 (hearsay) and 602 (witnesses—lack of personal knowledge). The government says that the print-out is admissible under Rule 803(6) (Records of regularly conducted activity). The controversy need not be decided because other evidence showed that defendants did not have a permit, and they did not claim to have one. The government did not need to offer the print-out to prove its case, and the defendants were not prejudiced by its receipt.

AFFIRMED.

Note

The Tenth Circuit did not find the Ninth Circuit's reasoning in *Diaz* relevant in *Smyer*. Instead, the court used the dictionary definition, or plain meaning, of "object of antiquity" to hold that the items clearly were objects of antiquity by "common understanding and practice." How clearly must a statute state its terms in order to withstand constitutional scrutiny? The facts in *Smyer* were compelling. To what extent do the facts, rather than the stated principle, guide case law? The defendants claimed they believed they were on private property. By what standard is general intent determined? As the defendants questioned every aspect of their conviction, the *Smyer* decision provides a good discussion of each element of proof of the criminal case.

---

2. Archaeological Resources Protection Act of 1979

In the 1970s, archeologists, mindful of the court decisions affecting heritage resources, were concerned that commercial looters of archeological sites located on federal land were not being deterred by existing laws. Looters were emboldened by the ineffectiveness of the Antiquities Act in *Diaz*, and, in any case, the threat of a $500 fine under the Antiquities Act was dwarfed by the tremendous profit from sales to specialist customers. Thus, archeologists foresaw that the rate of site destruction would outstrip the ability of scientific institutions to collect data and recover the past. The Society for American Archaeology, the largest professional association devoted to the archeology of the Americas, took their concerns to Congress, and nine months later the Archaeological Resources Protection Act was passed [ARPA, Pub. L. No. 96-95, 93 Stat. 721 (1979), codified as amended at 16 U.S.C. §§ 470aa–mm (1997)].

ARPA replaced the permitting procedures of the Antiquities Act, and standardized this process for all federal land managing agencies. It also established criminal sanctions for various resources crimes, and went further than the Antiquities Act by adding civil (administrative) enforcement and forfeiture provisions. In addition, to ensure that archeological information, wherever found, would not be lost to science, the Act articulated the public's role in land management as interested parties and possessors of archeological resources.

Legislative Background

ARPA was introduced in the House of Representatives on February 1, 1979, and in the Senate on February 26, 1979. These "companion measures" received strong cross-party support, which virtually ensured swift passage of the Act [see Beaty, *ARPA Enacted: the Legislative Process*, 5 American Antiquity 90 (1985)]. Nevertheless, rock hunting clubs and manufacturers of metal detectors expressed concern that this law would infringe on their activities. Also, the senators from Alaska, responding to President Carter's 1978 proclamation creating National Monuments on 56 million acres of federal land in Alaska, sought to use the legislation in order to weaken the Antiquities Act provision giving the president authority to declare National Monuments. By the time it was passed, ARPA contained numerous compromises affecting rock, coin, bullet, and arrowhead collectors. It did not, however, address National Monument designations, leaving the Antiquities Act provision in effect.

Following the passage of ARPA on October 31, 1979, the process of promulgating regulations began. Whereas criminal prosecution under ARPA could begin immediately after passage of the Act (for violations occurring after the effective date of ARPA), civil enforcement could not begin until the regulations were promulgated more than four years later. The Departments of the Interior, Agriculture, and Defense, and the Tennessee Valley Authority were responsible for implementing the law, with the Department of the Interior being the lead agency. After substantial agency and public input, final uniform regulations were published on January 6, 1984.

Purpose

> The purpose of this Act is to secure, for the present and future benefit of the American people, the protection of archaeological resources and sites which are on public lands and Indian lands, and to foster increased cooperation and exchange of information between governmental authorities, the professional archaeological community, and private individuals having collections of archaeological resources and data which were obtained before the date of the enactment of this Act.
> [16 U.S.C. § 470aa(b) (1997)].

It was not the purpose of ARPA to make criminals of persons who historically collected archeological items from the public lands, even though laws against theft of and injury to property always had prohibited this activity. In fact, compromises inherent in the Act reflected hobbyist groups' special interests, as well as the general public's mores about archeological resources in 1979. Instead, ARPA focused on stemming the destruction of sites caused by looting and vandalism, and eliciting existing information about archeological resources from all sources.

ARPA's enforcement provisions provide options for prosecuting injurious conduct toward archeological resources, so that the government may choose only the level of action necessary to protect the resource. Thus, overzealous collectors might have their metal detector seized, while commercial looters might be charged with a felony.

Criminal Enforcement

Understanding ARPA (or any criminal law) begins with an examination of the elements of the offense. ARPA requires jurisdiction to impose the law, a protected item or victim, a prohibited act, and lack of permission. The perpetrator also must possess the requisite *mens rea*, or mental intent, in order to be in violation of the law. Under ARPA, jurisdiction is tied to the land (except in specified circumstances); the protected item is an archeological resource; the enumerated, prohibited acts fall under the broad categories of injury, removal, attempted injury or removal, and trafficking of that resource; and lack of permission is the absence of an ARPA permit or other government authorization. ARPA is a general intent law.

Jurisdiction

ARPA protects resources on "public lands" [16 U.S.C. § 470bb(3) (1997)], which include the National Park system, National Wildlife Refuge system, the National Forest system, and all other lands which the United States holds in fee. Exempted from coverage are lands on the outer continental shelf and under the jurisdiction of the Smithsonian Institution. Since the ARPA exemption preserves the Smithsonian's own right to control compliance, it must rely on general criminal statutes for enforcement purposes. ARPA also was drafted not to impact the 1872 Mining Act, and its compliance section does not control permitted mining activities [16 U.S.C. § 470kk(a) (1997)]. Whether ARPA's criminal sanctions may apply to these activities is an issue that remains unresolved.

Indian lands belonging to tribes or individuals fall within the jurisdiction of ARPA if they are held in trust by the United States or are subject to a restriction from alienation, that is, transfer of ownership. Lands owned in fee and subsurface interests not controlled by Indian tribes are outside the land-based jurisdiction of the Act [16 U.S.C. § 470bb(4) (1997)]. For purposes of ARPA, "Indian tribe" means particular, organized groups of American Indians and Alaska Natives.

There is a component of ARPA that protects resources on state (including the District of Columbia, Puerto Rico, Guam, and the Virgin Islands) or private lands by imposing federal jurisdiction where there is a violation of a state or local law or regulation involving an archeological resource, and the resource is placed in interstate or international commerce [16 U.S.C. § 47ee(c) (1997)]. Jurisdiction to apply ARPA to prohibited acts occurring on private lands was addressed in *United States v. Gerber*, 999 F.2d 1112 (7th Cir. 1993), *cert. denied*, 510 U.S. 1071 (1994). In *Gerber*, the defendant removed archeological resources from private land without permission of the landowner, and then took the items across state lines. He entered into a plea agreement which required him to plead guilty to a criminal violation of ARPA, with the reservation that he could attack jurisdiction on appeal.

UNITED STATES v. GERBER

999 F.2d 1112 (7th Cir. 1993), *cert. denied*, 510 U.S. 1071 (1994)

POSNER, Circuit Judge:

Arthur Joseph Gerber pleaded guilty to misdemeanor violations of the Archaeological Resources Protection Act of 1979, 16 U.S.C. § 470aa *et seq.*, and was sentenced to twelve months in prison, reserving however his right to appeal on the ground that the Act is inapplicable to his offense. What he had done was to transport in interstate commerce Indian artifacts (*note omitted*) that he had stolen from a burial mound on privately owned land in violation of Indiana's criminal laws of trespass and conversion. The section of the Archaeological Resources Protection Act under which he was convicted provides that "no person may sell, purchase, exchange, transport, receive, or offer to sell, purchase, or exchange, in interstate or foreign commerce, any archaeological resource excavated, removed, sold, purchased, exchanged, transported, or received in violation of any provision, rule, regulation, ordinance, or permit in effect under State or local law." 16 U.S.C. § 470ee(c). Gerber argues that despite the references in this section to state and local law, the Act is inapplicable to archaeological objects removed from lands not owned either by the federal government or by Indian tribes. His back-up argument is that the provisions, rules, regulations, and so forth of state or local law to which the Act refers are limited to provisions expressly protecting archaeological objects or sites, as distinct from laws of general application such as those forbidding trespass and theft. The issues are novel because this is the first prosecution under the Act of someone who trafficked in archaeological objects removed from lands other than either federal or Indian lands.

More than fifteen hundred years ago in the American midwest Indians built a series of large earthen mounds over prepared mound floors containing human remains plus numerous ceremonial artifacts and grave goods made of silver, copper, wood, cloth, leather, obsidian, flint, mica, quartz, pearl, shells, and drilled, carved, or inlaid human and bear teeth. This mound culture, the product of a civilization that included the beginnings of settled agriculture, an elaborate ceremonialism, and far-flung trading networks, has been dubbed the "Hopewell phenomenon." N'omi B. Greber & Katharine C. Ruhl, *The Hopewell Site: A Contemporary Analysis Based on the Work of Charles C. Willoughby* (1989); Warren K. Moorehead, *The Hopewell Mound Group of Ohio* (Field Museum of Natural History, Publication No. 211, 1922). In 1985 farmers sold General Electric a piece of untillable land in southwestern Indiana adjacent to one of its factories. The land contained a prominent knob on top of a ridge. Unbeknownst to anyone this knob was a Hopewell burial mound some 400 feet long, 175 feet wide, and 20 feet high. The mound and its contents (which included two human skeletons) were intact—even the perishable materials such as wood and leather artifacts were well preserved—and when discovered it would prove to be one of the five largest Hopewell burial mounds known.

A highway was planned to run through the ridge on which the knob was located. In the course of construction, in 1988, earth was removed from the knob to stabilize the roadbed. Workmen engaged in this removal discovered in the knob curious objects—turtleback-shaped rocks—which they showed to a heavy-equipment operator on the project, named Bill Way, who happened to be a collector of Indian artifacts. Recognizing the significance of the find, Way nosed his bulldozer into the knob and quickly discovered hundreds of artifacts, including copper axeheads, inlaid bear canines, and tooled leather. He loaded these items into his pickup truck and covered up the excavation he had made. An acquaintance put him in touch with Arthur Joseph Gerber, a well-known collector of Indian artifacts and promoter of annual Indian "relic shows." Gerber paid Way $6,000 for the artifacts and for revealing to Gerber the location of the mound. Way took Gerber to the site the same night, encountering other people digging for Indian artifacts. Gerber returned to the site several more times, excavating and removing hundreds of additional artifacts, including silver earspools, copper axeheads, pieces of worked leather, and rare silver musical instruments, some with the original reeds preserved. On Gerber's last visit to the site he was detected by a General Electric security guard and ejected. Shortly afterward Gerber sold some of the artifacts at his annual "Indian Relic Show of Shows" in Kentucky. He acknowledges that in entering upon General Electric's land without the company's permission and in removing, again without its permission, Indian artifacts buried there, he committed criminal trespass and conversion in violation of Indiana law. He also acknowledges having transported some of the stolen artifacts in interstate commerce.

The preamble of the Archaeological Resources Protection Act of 1979 states that "archaeological resources on public lands [defined elsewhere in the Act as federal public lands] and Indian lands are an accessible and irreplaceable part of the Nation's heritage" and that the purpose of the Act is "to secure, for the present and future benefit of the American people, the protection of archaeological resources and sites which are on public lands and Indian lands." 16 U.S.C. §§ 470aa(a)(1), (b). Consistent with this preamble, most of the Act is given over to the regulation, in the form of civil and criminal penalties, permit requirements, forfeiture provisions, and other regulatory devices, of archaeological activities *on federal and Indian lands*. The criminal penalties are for archaeological activities conducted on those lands without a permit and for trafficking in archaeological objects that have been removed from them in violation either of the Act's permit requirements or of any other federal law. 16 §§ 470ee(a), (b). Gerber did not remove Indian artifacts from federal or Indian lands, however, and was therefore prosecuted under the third criminal provision (§ 470ee(c), quoted earlier), which is not in terms limited to such lands.

The omission of any reference in subsection (c) to federal and Indian lands was, Gerber argues, inadvertent. Not only the preamble of the Act, but its legislative history, shows that all that Congress was concerned with was protecting archaeological sites and objects on federal and Indian lands. This is indeed all that the preamble mentions; and a principal sponsor of the Act said that "it does not affect any lands other than the public lands of the United States and [Indian] lands." 125 Cong. Rec. 17,394 (1979) (remarks of Congressman Udall). The legislative history contains no reference to archaeological sites or objects on state or private lands. The Act superseded the Antiquities Act of 1906, 16 U.S.C. §§ 431–33, which had been expressly limited to federal lands. And if the Act applies to nonfederal, non-Indian lands, its provisions are at once overinclusive and underinclusive: overinclusive because the Act authorizes the federal court in which a defendant is prosecuted to order, in its discretion, the forfeiture of the archaeological objects involved in the violation to the United States (unless they were removed from Indian lands), §§ 470gg(b), (c); underinclusive because the provisions authorizing civil penalties and the payment of rewards to informers out of fines collected in criminal prosecutions under the Act are administered by officials who lack jurisdiction over nonfederal, non-Indian lands. §§470bb(2), 470ff, 470gg(a). (The artifacts stolen by Gerber were recovered and are being held by the United States as evidence in this case, but they have not been ordered forfeited.) Most scholarly commentators on the Act assume that it is limited to federal and Indian lands. *E.g.*, Kristine Olson Rogers, "Visigoths Revisited: The Prosecution of Archaeological Resource Thieves, Traffickers, and Vandals," 2 J. *Environmental Law & Litigation* 47, 72 (1987). Gerber reminds us of the rule of lenity in interpreting criminal statutes and of the implied constitutional prohibition against excessively vague criminal statutes. He adds that subsection (c) of section 470ee would not be a nullity if the Act were held to be limited to sites and objects on federal and Indian lands. A number of state laws prohibit trafficking in stolen Indian artifacts regardless of their origin, and it has not been suggested that these statutes are preempted by the federal Act even with respect to artifacts stolen from federal or Indian lands. A person who trafficked in Indian artifacts in violation of state law would be subject to federal prosecution only under subsection (c) even if the artifacts had been removed from federal or Indian lands, if the removal happened not to violate federal law.

We are not persuaded by these arguments. That the statute, the scholarly commentary, and the legislative history are all focused on federal and Indian lands may simply reflect the fact that the vast majority of Indian sites—and virtually all archaeological sites in the Western Hemisphere are Indian—are located either in Indian reservations or on the vast federal public lands of the West. Subsection (c) appears to be a catch-all provision designed to back up state and local laws protecting archaeological sites and objects wherever located. It resembles the Mann Act, the Lindbergh Law, the Hobbs Act, and a host of other federal statutes that affix federal criminal penalties to state crimes that, when committed in interstate commerce, are difficult for individual states to punish or prevent because coordinating the law enforcement efforts of different states is difficult. The reference to interstate commerce would be superfluous if the subsection were limited to artifacts taken from federal or Indian lands, since either source would establish federal jurisdiction with no need to require proof that the artifacts were transported in interstate commerce. Probably the subsection was added as an afterthought, so one is not surprised that it does not jibe perfectly with the surrounding provisions; but that does not make it invalid, and it certainly is not vague. And we cannot see how the purposes of the Act would be undermined by our giving subsection (c) the interpretation that its words invite.

An amicus brief filed by several associations of amateur archaeologists claims that such an interpretation will infringe their liberty to seek to enlarge archaeological knowledge by excavating private lands. But there is no right to go upon another person's land, without his permission, to look for valuable objects buried in the land and take them if you find them. At common law General Electric would have been the owner of the mound and its contents regardless of the fact that it was unaware of them. *Elwes v. Brigg Gas Co.*, 33 Ch D 562 (1886); *South Staffordshire Water Co. v. Sharman*, [1896] 2 QB 44. The modern American law is the same. *Klein v. Unidentified Wrecked & Abandoned Sailing Vessel*, 758 F.2d 1511, 1514 (11th Cir. 1985); *Ritz v. Selma United Methodist Church*, 467 NW2d 266, 269 (Ia 1991*); Favorite v. Miller*, 176 Conn. 310, 407 A2d 974, 978 (1978); *Bishop v. Ellsworth*, 91 Ill. App. 2d 386, 234 NE2d 49 (1968); *Allred v. Biegel*, 240 Mo. App. 818, 219 SW2d 665 (1949*); Chance v. Certain Artifacts Found & Salvaged*, 606 F. Supp. 801, 806–08 (S.D. Ga. 1984). *Allred* actually involved an Indian artifact. Although we have found no Indiana cases, we are given no reason to suppose that the Indiana courts would adopt a different rule. It would make no difference if they would. Whatever the rightful ownership of the mound and its contents under current American law, no one suggests that Way or Gerber obtained any rights to the artifacts in question. No doubt, theft is at the root of many titles; and priceless archaeological artifacts obtained in violation of local law are to be found in reputable museums all over the world. But it is almost inconceivable that Congress would have wanted to encourage amateur archaeologists to violate state laws in order to amass valuable collections of Indian artifacts, especially as many of these amateurs do not appreciate the importance to scholarship of leaving an archaeological site intact and undisturbed until the location of each object in it has been carefully mapped to enable inferences concerning the design, layout, size, and age of the site, and the practices and culture of the inhabitants, to be drawn. It is also unlikely that a Congress sufficiently interested in archaeology to impose substantial criminal penalties for the violation of archaeological regulations [the maximum criminal penalty under the Act is five years in prison plus a $100,000 fine, §470ee(d)] would be so parochial as to confine its interests to archaeological sites and artifacts on federal and Indian lands merely because that is where most of them are.

We conclude that section 470ee(c) is not limited to objects removed from federal and Indian lands, but we must consider Gerber's alternative argument, that the section is limited to removals in violation of state and local laws explicitly concerned with the protection of archaeological sites or objects. Gerber argues that if it is not so limited all sorts of anomalies are created. Suppose he had bought an Indian artifact from its rightful owner but had failed to pay the applicable state sales tax, and had transported the artifact across state lines. Then he would, he tells us, be transporting in interstate commerce an archaeological object purchased in violation of state law. And likewise if he transported such an object in interstate commerce in a vehicle that exceeded the weight limitations imposed by state law.

These are poor examples. It is unlikely in either case that the state would consider the transportation of a good to be in violation of state law merely because sales tax had not been paid or an overweight vehicle had been used. But we agree with the general point, that the Act is limited to cases in which the violation of state law is related to the protection of archaeological sites or objects. A broader interpretation would carry the Act far beyond the objectives of its framers and create pitfalls for the unwary. But we do not think that to be deemed related to the protection of archaeological resources a state or local law must be limited to that protection. A law that forbade the theft of Indian artifacts "and any other objects having historical or artistic value" could not reasonably be thought a law unrelated to the protection of such artifacts merely because it had broader objectives. That is essentially what Indiana's laws forbidding trespass and conversion have: objectives that include but are not exhausted in the protection of Indian artifacts and other antiquities. A law that comprehensively protects the owner of land from unauthorized incursions, spoliations, and theft could well be thought to give all the protection to buried antiquities that they need, making the passage of a law specially protecting buried antiquities redundant—and the passage of new laws is never costless and rarely easy. The interpretation urged by Gerber would, if accepted, compel states desiring federal assistance in protecting Indian artifacts in nonfederal, non-Indian lands within their borders to pass laws that might duplicate protections already adequate conferred on landowners sitting atop undiscovered archaeological sites by existing laws of general applicability. Granted, all fifty states have laws expressly protecting their archaeological sites; and in 1989, too late for this case, Indiana amended its law to forbid—redundantly—what Gerber had done. So the interpretation for which he contends might not actually impose a significant burden on the states. But Indiana may not have amended its law earlier because it thought its general criminal laws of trespass and conversion adequate—for all we know, it amended the law in response to Gerber's contention that the federal Act contains a loophole through which he and others like him might be able to squeeze.

We conclude that Gerber's conduct was forbidden by the Act.

* * *

AFFIRMED.

Note

The Court in *Gerber* clearly established the application of ARPA to acts occurring on private land, despite the absence of an express statement in the definition section of the law. Note, however, that while nothing in ARPA "shall be construed to affect the lawful recovery, collection, or sale of archaeological resources from land other than public or Indian land" [16 U.S.C. § 470kk(c) (1997)], Gerber acted unlawfully.

Since Gerber's crime began with activity on private land, the compliance section of the Act was not applicable to him, and the absence of an agency permit was not an element of the case. Instead, lack of permission from the landowner, which was a component of the state law dealing with theft and trespass, replaced the need for a permit and satisfied the permission element of the law. Was it necessary that Gerber first be prosecuted and convicted of theft in state court as a predicate to an ARPA prosecution? Would a prior conviction have placed Gerber in double jeopardy?

Protected Archeological Resources

ARPA was drafted to preserve and protect all archeological resources containing information about human beings, so that prehistoric (before European contact) and historic life can be scientifically investigated. "The term 'archaeological resource' means any material remains of past human life or activities which are of archeological interest," and are at least 100 years of age [16 U.S.C. § 470bb(1) (1997)]. Unlike the National Historic Preservation Act, which provides for the preservation of intact, "significant" examples of the past that are at least 50 years old, ARPA does not consider significance, as the significance of many archeological resources might not be determinable until a substantial amount of information from many sources is collected and synthesized over time. ARPA also differs from the National Historic Preservation Act in that it does not protect only resources in place.

All items of "archeological interest" that are at least 100 years old and not exempted by the statute are archeological resources for purposes of ARPA. The short, illustrative—and expressly nonexhaustive—list of protected archeological resources [16 U.S.C. § 470bb(1) (1997)] was defined further by uniform regulations. However, the four-year gap between the enactment of the statute and the promulgation of the uniform regulations created some confusion about what constituted material remains of archeological interest. As a result, at the first ARPA criminal trial (which preceded the promulgation of regulations), the judge instructed the jury that the area of disturbance, a midden, was not protected by ARPA because middens were not expressly listed as protected resources [see Green and Hanks, "Prosecuting Without Regulations: ARPA Successes and Failures," 5 *American Archeology* 103 (1985)]. The ARPA Uniform Regulations [Department of the Interior, 43 C.F.R. Part 7; Department of Agriculture, 36 C.F.R. Part 296; Tennessee Valley Authority, 18 C.F.R. Part 1312; Department of Defense, 32 C.F.R. Part 229 (1997)] sought to clarify any future uncertainty about what is protected by expanding the illustrative list of archeological resources in the statute to include resources such as middens [see 43 C.F.R. § 7.3(a)(3) (1997)]. However, this list, too, is only illustrative.

The term "'of archaeological interest' means capable of providing scientific or humanistic understandings of past human behavior, cultural adaptation, and related topics through the application of scientific or scholarly techniques..." [see 43 C.F.R. § 7.3(a)(1) (1997)]. Because context is of primary concern to archeologists, and even dirt piles or backfill at disturbed sites still retain some degree of contextual integrity, ARPA refrained from setting a qualitative threshold for "archeological interest." However, in deference to hobbyists and others who felt that ARPA might ban their activities on every inch of public land regardless of any actual scientific interest, the uniform regulations allow land managers to determine that certain material remains are not, or are no longer, of archeological interest, and are not to be considered archeological resources under ARPA [see 43 C.F.R. § 7.3(a)(5) (1997)]. In 1987, the Department of the Interior promulgated a supplemental regulation to provide their land managers with a procedure for making such a determination [43 C.F.R. § 7.33 (1997)], but to date, it never has been invoked.

Tactically, proof of archaeological interest requires testimony from an archeologist or other expert, who should be prepared for rigorous courtroom scrutiny. In 1988, Congress considered several amendments to ARPA, one of which would have deleted "archaeological interest" as an element of proof in a case. Perhaps it is fortuitous that the proposed amendment failed, because testimony concerning this element of proof often is the most compelling part of a trial. When the archeologist relates the story behind the site or item, the jury is drawn into the case both intellectually and emotionally as they learn about their shared past and about what may never be known due to the injury inflicted on their heritage by the accused.

Certain items fall outside ARPA's enforcement provisions, either because they are not archeological resources by definition, or because they were exempted as a result of political compromise. Rocks, coins, and bullets collected for private purposes are not subject to ARPA's compliance requirements and enforcement provisions because, generally, they are not archeological resources by definition [16 U.S.C. § 470kk(b) (1997)]. The Act's deference to metal detector enthusiasts, however, does not extend to the wholesale collection of artifacts, and the exemption for these items does not apply if they are within the context of an archeological site. For example, coins and bullets within the boundary of a battlefield site are objects that fall within the scope of ARPA, but they are not archeological resources if they are found at random, even though some archeological information could be gleaned from them.

Rocks and minerals that have been transformed by humans into an object or structure take on the characteristic of that item and become archeological resources subject to protection. Unworked rocks and minerals, however, are not archeological resources because they are not remains of past human existence. Similarly, paleontological resources are not archeological resources because they have not been affected by humans. While fossils are certainly of interest to science and are subject to excavation, removal, and commerce, pending the passage of specific legislation, they are protected only by general criminal statutes.

Arrowheads are archeological resources, but if they are located on the surface of the ground they expressly are exempt from ARPA's criminal sanction [16 U.S.C. § 470ee(g) (1997)]. Mining the subsurface for arrowheads, however, is a violation of ARPA. The arrowhead exception was enacted in direct deference to the numerous hobbyist collectors who otherwise would have been made criminals by the Act, and it exemplifies the evolution of a policy that recognizes the value of scientific inquiry and public knowledge about the past. While absolute protection for arrowheads evidently was compromised, ARPA, taken as a whole, sent a message that public lands, although open to many uses, are not available for removing pieces of the nation's history. Ironically, ARPA's arrowhead exception has no practical effect on the removal of arrowheads from Indian or public lands because this activity is proscribed by laws against theft of property.

UNITED STATES v. SHIVERS

96 F.3d 120 (5th Cir. 1996)

EDITH H. JONES, Circuit Judge:

Billy Ray Shivers found buried treasure at the site of an abandoned lumber mill company town. Unfortunately for Shivers, the site is located in the Angelina National Forest, and the federal government claimed ownership of and seized from Shivers some 50–70 metal tokens he uncovered with a metal detector. The district court denied his Fed. Rule Crim. Proc. 41(e) motion seeking return of the tokens, as it concluded Shivers did not own them pursuant to either the Archaeological Resources Protection Act ("ARPA"), 16 U.S.C. § 470ee, or the common law of finds. This court approves the district court's conclusion and therefore affirms.

BACKGROUND

The tokens that Shivers excavated from the Aldridge Lumber Company mill site were used by the saw mill as payment for workers 50–100 years ago. The tokens and other items were seized pursuant to a search warrant from Shivers's home when the government came to believe he had obtained them in violation of ARPA, which forbids the un-permitted excavation of archeological resources from federal lands.

When the government chose not to pursue criminal charges against Shivers, it eventually gave back the rest of the seized property, but refused to return the tokens to him. The district court's rebuff of Shivers's Fed. R. Crim. Proc. 41(e) motion for return of seized property gives rise to this appeal.

DISCUSSION

A. Standard of Review

As Shivers expressly concedes the factual findings of the district court, this court reviews the district court's conclusions of law *de novo. Palma v. Verex Assurance, Inc.*, 79 F.3d 1453, 1458 (5th Cir. 1996).

B. Ownership under the ARPA: 16 U.S.C. § 470kk

Shivers argues that the plain language of ARPA § 470kk vests him with ownership of the Aldridge tokens because he is a private collector of coins and other artifacts not defined by the ARPA as archaeological resources.

ARPA was enacted by Congress to protect "archaeological resources" found on public lands and to promote study and evaluation of these resources. See 16 U.S.C. § 470aa(b). An "archaeological resource" is statutorily defined as any material remains of past human life or activities which are of archeological interest, as determined under uniform regulations promulgated pursuant to this chapter. No item shall be treated as an archaeological resource under regulations under this paragraph unless such item is at least 100 years of age. 16 U.S.C. § 470bb(1). "Archaeological resources" so defined remain property of the United States if removed from public lands. See 16 U.S.C. § 470cc(b)(3); 36 C.F.R. § 296.6(b)(5); H.R. Rep. No. 311, 96th Cong., 1st Session, 7, 1979 *U.S. Code Cong. & Admin. News*, pp. 1709, 1710. Since the Aldridge tokens are between 50 and 100 years old, however, they are not "archaeological resources" for purposes of the ARPA.

Shivers's principal argument rests on a facile premise: because the tokens are not "archaeological resources," §470kk of the ARPA conveys an ownership interest to him as a private collector of coins. Section 470kk provides that [n]othing in this chapter applies to, or requires a permit for, the collection for private purposes of any rock, coin, bullet, or mineral which is not an archaeological resource, as determined under uniform regulations promulgated under section 470bb(1) of this title. 16 U.S.C. § 470kk(b). From this provision, Shivers infers that private individuals are authorized by ARPA to remove coins less than 100 years old from public land and to retain ownership.

Shivers also suggests that the purpose and policy of the ARPA support his conclusion. By encouraging private collection of non-"archaeological resources," the ARPA may actually help safeguard these resources, protecting them from further dislocation caused by either human or natural disturbances. To achieve such protection, Congress did not explicitly retain an ownership interest in non-"archaeological resources" found on public lands, though it did prevent private ownership of statutorily covered artifacts. Shivers urges that the asserted failure to retain ownership over non-"archaeological resources" evinces Congressional intent to cede their ownership to private collectors.

But the premise on which Shivers's argument rests is a faulty one, belied by the very passage on which he relies. Section 470kk(b) provides that "[n]othing in this chapter applies to... the collection for private purposes of any rock, coin, bullet, or mineral which is not an archaeological resource..." Because the ARPA does not apply to artifacts less than 100 years old, it does not regulate the private collection of such non-"archaeological resources." This statute cannot vest Shivers with an ownership interest in the tokens because it neither divests ownership interest from the United States or, indeed, says anything at all about "archaeological resources" it does not cover.

Even assuming arguendo that the ARPA regulates private collection of non-"archaeological resources," however, § 470kk(b) does not transfer to or vest ownership of the Aldridge tokens in Shivers. The statute merely provides that private collectors need not obtain a permit for the collection of certain artifacts. Shivers implies a transfer of property rights from this provision, arguing that since the statute allows for the private collection of non-"archaeological resources," it necessarily entitles the collector to retain or own what he has collected. This conclusion, however, is neither supported by the text of the statute nor is it a necessary implication of the right to collect non-"archaeological resources." Admittedly, the express statutory authorization to collect non-"archaeological resources" without a permit is much less valuable to a private collector if he may not retain what he collects; unless the collector enjoys collection for its own sake, ARPA furnishes little incentive to discover and gather non-"archaeological resources." But it would not be absurd to conclude that Congress dispensed with the cumbersome process of requiring permits for gathering non-"archaeological resources," even though it refused to transfer ownership of these less ancient artifacts.

Further, the ARPA is concerned with protecting the integrity of archaeological sites, presumably even more so if they are located in national forests. See, *e.g.*, 16 U.S.C. § 470cc(b)(1)-(b)(2) (requiring that those who apply for a permit to excavate archaeological resources be "qualified to carry out the permitted activity."); 36 C.F.R. § 296.8(a)(1); 1979 U.S.C.C.A.N. 1709, 1712 (recognizing the importance of protecting the unaltered integrity of archaeological sites). The record suggests that several hundred shovel holes found at the Aldridge site were attributed to Shivers's excavation activities.[1] Considering the resulting landscape alteration, Congress's intent to regulate digging or excavating on public archaeological sites is easy to understand, while Shivers's contrary position in favor of encouraging unregulated amateur collection is virtually incomprehensible.

Finally, the "arrowhead exception" to the ARPA discussed by Shivers is inapposite and irrelevant. This exception is not intended to encourage removal of arrowheads from public lands, but rather to exempt such removal from the civil and criminal penalty provisions of the ARPA. See 16 U.S.C. § 470ff(a)(3); 36 C.F.R. § 296.3(a)(3)(iii). Unlike the tokens excavated by Shivers, the arrowhead exception is limited to those found on the surface of public lands. See 16 U.S.C. § 470ff(a)(3) ("[n]o penalty shall be assessed... for the removal of arrowheads located on the surface of the ground."). Also, the ARPA expressly provides

---

[1][*Orig. fn.*] These figures are taken from a report relied upon by the district court and prepared by an Assistant Forest Archaeologist for the United States Forest Service. This report also concludes that many of the holes attributed to Shivers were not backfilled after excavation. Shivers does not challenge the accuracy or conclusions of the report.

that the removal of arrowheads can be penalized under other regulations or statutes. See, *e.g.*, 49 Fed. Reg. 1016, 1018 ["regulations under other authority which penalize (the removal of surface arrowheads) remain effective."] No inferences or implications helpful to Shivers are found in these provisions.

Because the ARPA does not vest Shivers with an ownership interest in the tokens, we need not discuss the Forest Service regulations, relied upon by the government, which go beyond ARPA and attempt to define as "archaeological resources," prohibited from excavation, artifacts that are at least 50 years old. See 36 C.F.R. §§ 261.2, 261.9(g). The asserted conflict between the Forest Service regulations and the ARPA does not need to be resolved in this case.

C. Ownership and the Federal Common Law of Finds

The district court concluded not only that the ARPA did not convey to Shivers an ownership interest in the Aldridge tokens, but also that in the absence of express or statutory title transfer, the federal common law of finds dictates that the United States, not Shivers, owns the tokens.

The federal common law of finds, including certain critical exceptions, is pertinent to this case. As the Eleventh Circuit explained, [t]he common law of finds generally assigns ownership of the abandoned property without regard to where the property is found. Two exceptions to the rule are recognized: First, when the abandoned property is embedded in the soil, it belongs to the owner of the soil; Second, when the owner of the land where the property is found (whether on or embedded in the soil) has constructive possession of the property such that the property is not "lost," it belongs to the owner of the land. *Klein v. Unidentified Wrecked & Abandoned Sailing Vessel*, 758 F.2d 1511, 1514 (11th Cir. 1985). In Klein, a vessel submerged beneath the waters of Biscayne National Park, Florida, had been rediscovered and salvaged by a private diver. Holding that the wreck was property of the government, not the diver, the court emphasized that the "ship is buried in the soil. The soil belongs to the United States as part of its National Park system... When the United States acquired title to the land from Florida in 1973, it also acquired title to the shipwrecks embedded in that soil... Thus the United States has never legally lost the subject shipwreck and, as the owner of the land on and/or water in which the shipwreck is located, it owns the shipwreck." Id. at 1514. Similarly, the Aldridge tokens excavated by Shivers were buried in the soil of the Angelina National Forest. As in Klein, this soil belongs to the United States, and with it the embedded tokens under the first exception to the federal common law of finds discussed in Klein.[2]

Shivers does not challenge this interpretation of the federal common law of finds. Indeed, his only retort is that the common law of finds is inapplicable because Congress expressly provided in §470kk(b) of the ARPA that private collectors enjoy ownership of the

---

[2][*Orig. fn.*] Analyzing the ARPA, Judge Posner has also explained that "there is no right to go upon another person's land, without his permission, to look for valuable objects buried in the land and take them if you find them." *United States v. Gerber*, 999 F.2d 1112, 1114–15 (7th Cir. 1993), *cert. denied*, 510 U.S. 1071 (1994).

non-archaeological resources that they discover on public lands. As already discussed, this contention is indefensible. The district court correctly held that the United States owns the tokens that Shivers discovered.

CONCLUSION

For the foregoing reasons, the judgment of the district court denying Shivers's 41(e) motion for the return of the Aldridge tokens is AFFIRMED.

Ten years after passage, ARPA faced a constitutional challenge. A person who was digging for artifacts in a cave in Oregon was apprehended and charged under ARPA. He appealed his conviction by attacking the definition of "archaeological resource" as vague, using the *Diaz* rationale. He also argued that, as a non-archeologist, ARPA prevented him from advancing his knowledge, in violation of the First Amendment.

UNITED STATES v. AUSTIN

902 F.2d 743 (9th Cir. 1990)

TANG, Circuit Judge:

After lengthy investigation in 1986 and 1987, and subsequent searches of appellant Bradley Owen Austin's abandoned car and his house trailer, government agents seized some 2,800 Native American artifacts, excavation implements, photographs, and documents, which implicated Austin in excavating a Native American archaeological site. In February 1988, the government indicted Austin on fourteen counts. The indictment included eight counts under two subsections of the Archaeological Resources Protection Act (ARPA), 16 U.S.C. § 470ee(a) and (d): No person may excavate, remove, damage, or otherwise alter or deface, or attempt to excavate, remove, damage, or otherwise alter or deface any archaeological resource located on public lands or Indian lands unless such activity is pursuant to a permit... [or] exemption... 16 U.S.C. § 470ee(a). The statute defines an archaeological resource as any material remains of past human life or activities which are of archeological interest, as determined under uniform regulations promulgated pursuant to this chapter. Such regulations containing such determination shall include, but not be limited to: pottery, basketry, bottles, weapons, weapon projectiles, tools, structures or portions of structures, pit houses, rock paintings, rock carvings, intaglios, graves, human skeletal materials, or any portion or piece of any of the foregoing items. 16 U.S.C. § 470bb(1). Any person who knowingly violates, or counsels, procures, solicits, or employs any other person to violate any prohibition contained in subsection (a), (b), or (c) of this section shall, upon conviction, be fined not more than $10,000 or imprisoned not more than one year, or both: Provided, however, that if the commercial or archaeological value of the archaeological resources involved and the cost of restoration and repair of such resources exceeds the sum of $500, such person shall be fined not more than $20,000 or imprisoned not more than two years, or both. 16 U.S.C. § 470ee(d). The indictment also included five counts under 18 U.S.C. § 641 (government property theft)[1] and one count under 21 U.S.C. § 844 (simple possession of a controlled substance).

Austin pleaded not guilty and moved for dismissal of the ARPA counts on the ground that ARPA is unconstitutionally vague. The government then filed a twenty-five count superseding indictment, which added three counts of government property theft under 18 U.S.C. § 641 and eight counts of government property depredation in violation of 18 U.S.C. § 1361.[2] Austin again pleaded not guilty and moved to dismiss on the ground of prosecutorial vindictiveness. The government subsequently filed a second superseding indictment adding six more counts under the same statutes.

Austin and the government agreed to a stipulated-facts bench trial on count 13 of the second superseding indictment, which charged Austin under ARPA with excavating "archaeological resources in an archaeological site, including obsidian weapon projectile points and tools such as scrapers." By agreement, the government dismissed the other counts. Austin was convicted. He appeals on the grounds that ARPA is unconstitutionally overbroad and vague and that he was vindictively prosecuted.

I.   IS ARPA UNCONSTITUTIONALLY OVERBROAD?

"'In a facial challenge to the overbreadth and vagueness of a law, a court's first task is to determine whether the enactment reaches a substantial amount of constitutionally protected conduct. If it does not, then the overbreadth challenge must fail.'" *Schwartzmiller v. Gardner*, 752 F.2d 1341, 1346 (9th Cir. 1984) [quoting *Hoffman Estates v. Flipside, Hoffman Estates*, 455 U.S. 489, 494 (1982)].

Austin's argument is creative. He argues that because curiosity motivated him, his activity was academic, and that academic freedom therefore protects him. Because academic freedom "long has been viewed as a special concern of the First Amendment," *Regents of the Univ. of Cal. v. Bakke*, 438 U.S. 265 (1978) (opinion of Powell, J.), Austin concludes that he may challenge ARPA as overbroad.

Academic freedom's aegis, however, does not protect Austin's excavating. Austin has not demonstrated that he is affiliated with any academic institution, nor has he posited how his own curiosity is otherwise academic.

To succeed on a claim of overbreadth where conduct and not merely speech is involved, Austin must argue that ARPA at least ambiguously reaches protected activities and that the

---

[1][*Orig. fn.*] Whoever embezzles, steals, purloins, or knowingly converts to his use or the use of another, or without authority, sells, conveys or disposes of any record, voucher, money, or thing of value of the United States or of any department or agency thereof.... shall be fined not more than $10,000 or imprisoned not more than ten years, or both.... 18 U.S.C. § 641.

[2][*Orig. fn.*] Whoever willfully injures or commits any depredation against any property of the United States, or of any department or agency thereof... shall be punished as follows: If the damage to such property exceeds the sum of $100, by a fine of not more than $10,000 or imprisonment for not more than ten years, or both. 18 U.S.C. §1361.

overbreadth is substantial. See *Broadrick v. Oklahoma*, 413 U.S. 601, 615 (1973). Not only does Austin not claim that the First Amendment actually protects any activity that ARPA reaches, he does not even suggest its relevance to any activity except his own excavating. Therefore, he has not shown that ARPA is unconstitutionally overbroad.

II. IS ARPA UNCONSTITUTIONALLY VAGUE?

After overbreadth analysis, the court should "examine the facial vagueness challenge and, assuming the enactment implicates no constitutionally protected conduct, should uphold the challenge only if the enactment is impermissibly vague in all of its applications. A plaintiff who engages in some conduct that is clearly proscribed cannot complain of the vagueness of the law as applied to the conduct of others." *Schwartzmiller*, 752 F.2d at 1346 (quoting *Flipside*, 455 U.S. at 494–95).

Whether Austin can successfully challenge ARPA as vague depends on whether defendants would have "had fair notice that the conduct that [he] allegedly engaged in was prohibited." *United States v. Mussry*, 726 F.2d 1448, 1454 (9th Cir.), *cert. denied*, 469 U.S. 855 (1984). Austin was charged with and convicted of excavating scrapers and arrow points. Although he contends that "weapons" and "tools" are ambiguous terms, we are not here concerned with the vagueness of the law as applied to the conduct of others. See *Schwartzmiller*, 752 F.2d at 1346. As to Austin, there can be no doubt nor lack of fair notice that the scrapers and arrow points for which he was convicted are indeed weapons and tools. The statute provided fair notice that it prohibited the activities for which Austin was convicted. His vagueness challenge therefore fails.

III. VINDICTIVE PROSECUTION

Austin argues that because the government twice added charges to his indictment after he challenged his initial indictment, he established a presumption of vindictive prosecution that the government had the burden of rebutting. We disagree. That the prosecution adds charges pretrial after a defendant asserts some right does not establish a presumption of vindictiveness. See *United States v. Goodwin*, 457 U.S. 368, 381 (1982).

Our inquiry, however, does not end there. As we understand it, Austin and the government do not disagree over the prosecutor's motives but rather dispute whether those motives are properly characterized as vindictive. Both agree that the prosecutor's discovery of new law occasioned the charge increase.[3] Austin contends that this implies vindictiveness. We disagree.

There may be a suggestion that the prosecution evinced an extralegal animus against Austin by continuing to prosecute him, and indeed adding charges, even when it came to

---

[3][*Orig. fn.*] Austin does not argue that the government added the charges partly to induce Austin to plead guilty. *Cf. Bordenkircher v. Hayes*, 434 U.S. 357, 363–65 (1978).

doubt the validity of the charges on which it based its original decision to prosecute. But the record indicates that the government did not doubt that its charges were valid. It did not try to convict Austin regardless of the merits of his challenges. Quite to the contrary, it agreed to a stipulated-facts trial on the ARPA count alone. If Austin's constitutional challenge had been valid, he would have been acquitted. The prosecution was not vindictive.

AFFIRMED.

Note

ARPA is responsive to the right of the public to know about archeological resources and the history of the nation. Much of the law is devoted to addressing the need for public involvement and education in the archeological sciences. The court in *Austin* put to rest definitional objections and arguments that the law is vague and overbroad. In *Austin, Gerber,* and *Smyer,* the appellants attacked the applicability or the constitutionality of the laws to their actions, but did not deny the activity. Their posture poses the question of whether our culture condones the destruction of its past, and whether the law reflects or prompts change in the public's attitude toward its heritage.

Prohibited Acts

ARPA prohibits destructive impact on archeological resources in various ways [16 U.S.C. § 470ee (1997)]. After the effective date of the Act, it is a violation of law to:

a. (E)xcavate, remove, damage, or otherwise alter or deface or attempt to excavate, remove, damage, or otherwise alter or deface any archaeological resource located on public lands or Indian lands unless such activity is pursuant to a permit." [16 U.S.C. § 470ee(a) (1997)].

b. (S)ell, purchase, exchange, transport, receive, or offer to sell, purchase, or exchange any archaeological resource if such resource was excavated or removed from public lands or Indian lands." [16 U.S.C. § 470ee(b) (1997)].

c. (S)ell, purchase, exchange, transport, receive, or offer to sell, purchase, or exchange, in interstate or foreign commerce, any archaeological resource excavated, removed, sold, purchased, exchanged, transported, or received in violation of any provision, rule, regulation, ordinance, or permit in effect under State or local law." [16 U.S.C. § 470ee(c) (1997)].

d. Knowingly violate, counsel, procure, solicit, or employ another to violate the Act. [16 U.S.C. § 470ee(d) (1997)].

Subsection (a) lists actions that may damage archeological resources. In 1988, it was amended to include attempt. Thus, ARPA also proscribes any voluntary substantial step in a course of conduct that would have resulted in damage to an archeological resource.

A person violates subsection (b) by selling a protected item after the effective date of ARPA, even if they obtained the item before the law was enacted. Moreover, funds do not necessarily have to change hands for a violation to occur. Proving that an item originated from federal or Indian lands may be difficult, however, when the perpetrator is not apprehended onsite, and it may require utilizing forensic and other law enforcement techniques, as well as archeological temporal and spatial data.

The interstate and international trafficking prohibition in subsection (c) is an extension of general criminal law to archeological resources. The federal law is invoked when a state or local law generally protecting archeological resources is violated, and protected items are taken across state lines or international borders. The state or local law need not be a criminal law; it might be a local regulation or zoning ordinance. Also, the violator need not be prosecuted in the state or local court as a predicate to an ARPA prosecution. The federal prosecution will include the violation of the state or local law as part of the proof of its case, and the federal jury, in essence, will have to find guilt of a crime within a crime.

In *Gerber,* the defendant entered land belonging to the General Electric Corporation and took items from a burial mound that had been uncovered during road construction. He did not have permission from General Electric to be on the premises (constituting trespass), and he did not have permission to remove the items and keep them for his benefit (constituting theft and conversion). Also, Gerber did not have a permit from the state for archeological investigation (if one was required) and he may have violated local health and burial laws, too. Violation of any of these state laws would have been an underlying offense for purposes of ARPA. When Gerber transported the items to another state for sale, he invoked federal jurisdiction by violating ARPA.

ARPA's last subsection dealing with prohibited acts focuses on persons who are steps removed from the resource, but who are complicit in supporting illegal activity. It may be applied to dealers or brokers in archeological resources who obtain items and fill orders through procurers; to persons who enlist "amateur archeologists" to excavate on public lands; or to magazine publishers and advertisers who counsel readers on how to violate the law without detection.

Absence of a Permit

Not all excavation of archeological sites is prohibited, only excavation undertaken without authority. There are three ways to obtain this authorization: (1) for federal employees, by performing within the scope of government employment; (2) for contractors, subcontractors, and their employees, by performing within the scope of a government contract; and (3) by obtaining an ARPA permit and complying with that permit. For Indian lands there exists a variation to the permit element. Tribes who control land may formulate their own permit requirements for tribal members, and such a permit would take the place of an ARPA permit. In the absence of tribal law or regulation, however, ARPA is controlling. Just as lack of permission is an element of theft, lack of a permit is an element of an ARPA violation. Thus, for purposes of ARPA enforcement, anyone excavating on federal land must have the permission of the land manager.

Criminal Intent

ARPA is a general intent offense. Congress indicated that the "knowing," or voluntary, commission of an act prohibited by ARPA meets the statute's *mens rea* threshold [H.R. Rep. No. 311, 96th Cong., 1st Sess., *reprinted in* 1979 *U.S. Code Cong. & Admin. News*, 1709, 1714: "This is a general intent crime..."]. As the United States Attorney for the District of Arizona (who later was appointed to the Ninth Circuit Court of Appeals) testified:

> A proof requirement that an individual acted "knowingly" will protect the innocent individual who acts out of mistake, accident, or other innocent reason. To change the standard and require the government to prove the defendant did act "willfully" or "intentionally" will impair the ability of federal prosecutors to adequately deal with the problem this legislation addresses.

[*Archaeological Resources Protection Act: Hearings on S. 490 Before the Comm. on Energy and Natural Resources*, 96th Cong., 1st Sess. 87 (1979) (statement of Michael D. Hawkins, U.S. Attorney for the District of Arizona)]. Requiring the prosecutor to prove that the perpetrator specifically intended to violate ARPA thus is beyond the requirement of the law. The prosecutor must show that the accused knew what they were doing, but not that they knew they were on federal or Indian land when they were doing it.

Criminal Penalties

If assessed damages do not exceed $500, a first ARPA offense carries a misdemeanor penalty of up to one year imprisonment and/or a fine of up to $10,000. Damages exceeding $500 meet the felony threshold, and carry a penalty of up to two years incarceration and/or up to $20,000 in fines. For second or subsequent ARPA violations, any damage to an archeological resource, regardless of the amount, is punishable by up to five years of confinement and a fine of up to $100,000.

When ARPA first became law, the threshold level for a felony offense was damages in excess of $5,000. Some legislators felt that a high threshold would protect hobbyists who were unaware of the law and the risk involved in damaging archeological resources. As a result, the cost of doing business to commercial looters and illegal traffickers was relatively modest, while the scientific information at risk of loss was substantial. Also, as misdemeanor offenses usually fail to attract priority attention from law enforcement agents, many potential ARPA cases went unattended. By 1988, however, ARPA had been used for almost ten years to instill the notion that cultural resources crimes should not be tolerated. That year, Congress amended ARPA by, among other things, lowering the felony threshold to $500. The lower felony threshold led to an upsurge of ARPA prosecutions throughout the country [LOOT Clearinghouse, National Park Service, Archeology and Ethnography Program, Washington, D.C.].

The penalty provisions in ARPA are subject to any general federal penalty provisions. The Criminal Fines Improvement Act of 1987 increased the maximum fine under ARPA to $100,000 for a misdemeanor and $250,000 for a felony [Pub. L. No. 100–185, 101 Stat. 1279 (1987), codified at 18 U.S.C. § 1 (1997)], and the Sentencing Reform Act of 1984, as amended [Title II of the Comprehensive Crime Control Act of 1984, Pub. L. No. 98-473, 98 Stat. 1987, codified at 18 U.S.C. §§ 3551, 3553, 3559(a), 3571, and 3582 (1997)] impacted the amount of time a person may be incarcerated. Among other things, the Sentencing Reform Act delegated broad authority to the United States Sentencing Commission to promulgate detailed guidelines prescribing the appropriate sentences for offenders convicted of federal crimes. These sentencing guidelines replaced the specific sentence range in the statutes with a determination that considers the type of offense, amount of damage, or severity of the offense [United States Sentencing Commission, Guidelines Manual (Nov. 1995)]. Because no specific guidelines exist for ARPA, prosecutors, by analogy, have used the factors under theft.

UNITED STATES v. SHUMWAY

112 F.3d 1413 (10th Cir. 1997)

BRORBY, Circuit Judge:

Appellant, Mr. Earl K. Shumway, appeals his conviction and sentence entered in the United States District Court for the District of Utah. We affirm in part, reverse in part, and remand for resentencing.

I. BACKGROUND

On November 16, 1994, Mr. Shumway was charged in a three-count indictment alleging: 1) violation of the Archaeological Resources Protection Act, 16 U.S.C. § 470ee(a) and 18 U.S.C. § 2; 2) a related charge of damaging United States property under 18 U.S.C. § 1361 and 18 U.S.C. § 2; and 3) felon in possession of a firearm under 18 U.S.C. § 922(g). Mr. Shumway pleaded guilty to all three felony counts.

On June 1, 1995, Mr. Shumway was charged in a four-count indictment. Counts one and three alleged violations of the Archaeological Resources Protection Act, 16 U.S.C. § 470ee and 18 U.S.C. § 2. Counts two and four alleged related charges of damaging United States property pursuant to 18 U.S.C. § 1361 and 18 U.S.C. § 2. After a trial, a jury convicted Mr. Shumway of all charges.

In a consolidated sentencing, the district court sentenced Mr. Shumway to seventy-eight months in prison, a three-year term of supervised release, restitution in the amount of $5,510.28, and a $350 special assessment. Mr. Shumway now appeals both his sentence and his jury conviction.

II. FACTS

Mr. Shumway's jury conviction stemmed from his unauthorized excavation of two Anasazi[1] archeological sites: Dop-Ki Cave and Horse Rock Ruin. Dop-Ki Cave is located on federal lands in Canyonlands National Park, and Horse Rock Ruin, also known as Cliffdwellers' Pasture or Jack's Pasture, is located on federal lands near Allen Canyon, Manti-LaSal National Forest.

At trial, the government introduced evidence to show Mr. Shumway met a helicopter mechanic, Michael Miller, at a lounge and pool hall in Utah and developed a social relationship with him. The two eventually began discussing Mr. Shumway's experience in finding archeological artifacts and his experience in making large amounts of money selling those artifacts. Mr. Shumway asked Mr. Miller if he could find a helicopter to fly them around to find archeological artifacts.

Enticed by the prospects of money and Mr. Shumway's apparent knowledge of the subject, Mr. Miller contacted his friend, John Ruhl, a helicopter pilot. Mr. Miller told Mr. Ruhl of the plan to find and sell artifacts and asked Mr. Ruhl to pilot the helicopter to fly Mr. Miller and Mr. Shumway around to look for artifacts. Mr. Ruhl agreed. Mr. Shumway then posed as a movie scout and called Mr. Ruhl's supervisor at the helicopter company claiming he needed the helicopter to look for movie sites. Mr. Shumway arranged to have Mr. Ruhl fly to Moab, Utah, to pick up Mr. Shumway and Mr. Miller.

Once airborne, Mr. Shumway directed Mr. Ruhl to fly to a particular archaeological site southeast of Moab, but Mr. Shumway had trouble locating the site. Unable to find the particular location, the group eventually landed at Dop-Ki Cave in Canyonlands National Park.

---

[1][*Orig. fn.*] Anasazi is the name assigned by archaeologists to a prehistoric culture living in the Four Corners area of Utah, Arizona, Colorado, and New Mexico during the Formative Period from 300 A.D. to 1300 A.D.

Mr. Shumway and Mr. Miller began digging in the area. While digging in the cave, Mr. Miller discovered the human remains of an infant wrapped in a burial blanket. Mr. Shumway explained to Mr. Miller he had found a burial site. Mr. Shumway then took over the digging. Mr. Shumway fully excavated the infant remains and removed the burial blanket leaving the infant remains on the ground. When the damage to the site was later assessed, the only portion of the infant's skeleton remaining was the skull on top of the dirt pile.

The group then attempted, a second time, to find Mr. Shumway's first intended site. Unable to locate it, Mr. Shumway directed Mr. Ruhl to land at Horse Rock Ruin. Mr. Miller testified that based on the directions Mr. Shumway had given, and based on his detailed knowledge of the site, it seemed Mr. Shumway had been to the Horse Rock Ruin site before. The next morning, after spending the night at the site, Mr. Shumway found sandals and a sleeping mat during the dig at the site.

In 1986, Mr. Shumway testified in court regarding his conduct at Horse Rock Ruin in 1984, the same site referred to in counts three and four of the 1995 indictment. The government attempted to admit evidence of Mr. Shumway's prior illegal activities at Horse Rock Ruin to establish identity, knowledge and intent, pursuant to Fed. R. Evid. 404(b). Mr. Shumway filed a motion in limine to preclude the government from introducing Rule 404(b) evidence. After the hearing, the district court deemed admissible the evidence relating to Mr. Shumway's 1984 activities in the Horse Rock Ruin.

Specifically, the district court admitted the following evidence: 1) a certified transcript of Mr. Shumway's sworn colloquy with the court in the 1986 case, redacted to include only admissions concerning his 1984 conduct at Horse Rock Ruin; 2) a redacted portion of a videotape of Mr. Shumway examining several artifacts he stated he excavated and removed from Horse Rock Ruin in 1984; 3) the 1986 testimony of United States Forest Service Special Agent Craig Endicott summarizing Mr. Shumway's statements about removing and selling artifacts from the Horse Rock Ruin site in 1984; 4) several photographs of artifacts Mr. Shumway removed from Horse Rock Ruin in 1984; and 5) a certified transcript of Mr. Shumway's sworn testimony in *United States v. Black*, No. CR 67-97 (D. Utah), a case related to the illegal sale of artifacts taken from the Horse Rock Ruin site in 1984. During the motion in limine hearing, Mr. Shumway's counsel informed the court his defense at trial would be that Mr. Shumway was not the person who committed the offenses. The district court therefore deemed this evidence admissible, yet limited the evidence's admissibility to the purpose of establishing Mr. Shumway's identity.

During trial, the government requested the district court to reconsider and broaden its previous ruling to allow the 404(b) evidence to prove knowledge and intent in addition to identity. The court determined that absent a stipulation by Mr. Shumway that identity was the only issue involved, the 404(b) evidence also would be admitted to prove knowledge and intent. Accordingly, the court instructed the jury as to the limited purpose of the 404(b) evidence to establish intent, knowledge and identity.

After the jury convicted Mr. Shumway on all four counts, the district court consolidated for purposes of sentencing the 1994 case that resulted in Mr. Shumway's guilty plea. At sentencing, the court enhanced Mr. Shumway's base offense level as follows: two points for the vulnerable victim adjustment, pursuant to United States Sentencing Guidelines Manual § 3A1.1(b) (1995) (hereinafter U.S.SG); two points for obstruction of justice, pursuant to U.S.SG § 3C1.1; and nine points for calculating the loss at $138,000 or more, pursuant to U.S.SG § 2B1.1. Relying on U.S.SG § 4A1.3, the court also departed upward from the

Guidelines by increasing Mr. Shumway's criminal history category from III to IV. After the adjustments, Mr. Shumway's total offense level was twenty-two and his criminal history level IV, which resulted in a sentencing range of 63 to 78 months. The district court sentenced Mr. Shumway to seventy-eight months incarceration.

On consolidated appeal we consider five issues: 1) whether the district court erred in admitting evidence of Mr. Shumway's prior acts at Horse Rock Ruin pursuant to Fed. R. Evid. 404(b); 2) whether the district court erred in enhancing Mr. Shumway's offense level by imposing a vulnerable victim adjustment pursuant to U.S.SG § 3A1.1(b); 3) whether the district court erred in enhancing the offense level for obstruction of justice pursuant to U.S.SG § 3C1.1; 4) whether the district court erred in calculating the loss sustained under U.S.SG § 2B1.1; and 5) whether the district court erred in departing upward from the Guidelines by increasing Mr. Shumway's criminal history category from III to IV under U.S.SG § 4A1.3.

III.   404(b) EVIDENCE

Mr. Shumway argues the district court erred in admitting the evidence regarding his 1984 acts in Horse Rock Ruin for purposes of identity, knowledge and intent. Specifically, Mr. Shumway argues the 1984 evidence lacked the "signature quality" necessary to show identity and was highly prejudicial to Mr. Shumway.

We review the district court's admission of evidence under Fed. R. Evid. 404(b) for an abuse of discretion. *United States v. Wilson*, 107 F.3d 774, 782 (10th Cir. 1997). "An abuse of discretion occurs when a judicial determination is arbitrary, capricious or whimsical." *United States v. Wright*, 826 F.2d 938, 943 (10th Cir. 1987). We will not overturn a discretionary judgment by the trial court where it falls within the "bounds of permissible choice in the circumstances." *United States v. Dorrough*, 84 F.3d 1309, 1311 (10th Cir.) [quoting *Moothart v. Bell*, 21 F.3d 1499, 1504 (10th Cir. 1994)], *cert. denied*, ___ U.S. ___, 117 S. Ct. 446 (1996).

Under Fed. R. Evid. 404(b):

Evidence of other crimes, wrongs, or acts is not admissible to prove the character of a person in order to show action in conformity therewith. It may, however, be admissible for other purposes, such as proof of motive, opportunity, intent, preparation, plan, knowledge, identity, or absence of mistake or accident....

In determining whether the admission of 404(b) evidence was proper, we apply a four-part test, which requires the following: 1) the evidence was offered for a proper purpose; 2) the evidence was relevant; 3) the trial court properly determined under Fed. R. Evid. 403 the probative value of the similar-acts evidence was not substantially outweighed by its potential for unfair prejudice; and 4) the trial court gave the jury proper limiting instructions upon request. *Huddleston v. United States*, 485 U.S. 681, 691–92 (1988); *United States v. Hill*, 60 F.3d 672, 676 (10th Cir.), *cert. denied*, ___ U.S. ___, 116 S. Ct. 432 (1995).[2] Because all

---

[2][*Orig. fn.*] To the extent Mr. Shumway argues this court's decision in *United States v. Harrison*, 942 F.2d 751, 759–60 (10th Cir. 1991) is inconsistent with Huddleston's four-part test, we disagree and reject the argument.

four parts of the *Huddleston* test are satisfied, we conclude the district court did not abuse its discretion in admitting evidence of Mr. Shumway's prior illegal acts at Horse Rock Ruin.

A.   Proper Purpose and Relevance

First, the government offered, and the district court admitted, the evidence of Mr. Shumway's prior activities at Horse Rock Ruin for proper purposes under Fed. R. Evid. 404(b): identity, knowledge, and intent. Second, the evidence was relevant as to each of these factors.

1.   Relevance—Identity

As stated, at a pretrial hearing on Mr. Shumway's motion in limine to exclude the evidence, Mr. Shumway's counsel stated his main defense would be that Mr. Shumway was not the person involved. After the hearing, the district court determined it would allow the prior evidence only to show identity. The court held, and we agree, the evidence of Mr. Shumway's 1984 prior activities at Horse Rock Ruin, the exact same site as that specified in two counts of the 1995 indictment, made more likely the inference the same person looted the same site on both occasions.

Mr. Shumway argues, however, the prior act evidence was not relevant under 404(b) because the prior act lacked the "signature quality" necessary to show identity. Specifically, Mr. Shumway argues the 1984 act was not sufficiently similar to the acts at issue in the present case to be probative of identity because the methods used to excavate the sites were not sufficiently similar. Additionally, Mr. Shumway argues the prior act is not probative of identity because it preceded the acts at issue in the trial by seven years. We disagree.

We have held that to prove identity, evidence of prior illegal acts need not be identical to the crime charged, so long as, based on a "totality of the comparison," the acts share enough elements to constitute a "signature quality." *United States v. Patterson*, 20 F.3d 809, 813 (10th Cir.), *cert. denied*, 513 U.S. 841 (1994); *United States v. Ingraham*, 832 F.2d 229, 233 (1st Cir. 1987); *United States v. Gutierrez*, 696 F.2d 753, 754 (10th Cir. 1982), *cert. denied*, 461 U.S. 909 and 461 U.S. 910 (1983).

Elements relevant to a "signature quality" determination include the following: geographic location, *United States v. Porter*, 881 F.2d 878, 887 (10th Cir. 1989) (fact that all crimes took place in small rural Kansas communities relevant to "signature quality" determination); *United States v. Stubbins*, 877 F.2d 42, 44 (11th Cir. 1989) (that both offenses occurred at the same premises was probative of identity); the unusual quality of the crime, *Patterson*, 20 F.3d at 813 (fact that hijacking is an unusual crime was a relevant factor in "signature quality" determination); the skill necessary to commit the acts, *United States v. Barrett*, 539 F.2d 244, 248 (1st Cir. 1976) (ability to bypass burglar alarm a "distinctive feature" of crime); *United States v. Garcia*, 880 F.2d 1277, 1278 (11th Cir. 1989) (defendant's skill in forging documents relevant to show identity); or use of a distinctive device, *United States v. Trenkler*, 61 F.3d 45, 55 (1st Cir. 1995) (defendant's prior use of distinctive remote-control car bombs relevant in determining whether same person built both bombs); *United States v. Andrini*, 685 F.2d 1094, 1097 (9th Cir. 1982) (defendant's description of distinctive incendiary devise used in crime "sufficiently distinctive to show identity").

These enumerated elements relevant to a "signature quality" determination are not inclusive. Furthermore, the weight to be given to any one element and the number of elements necessary to constitute a "signature" are highly dependent on the elements' uniqueness in the context of a particular case. In other words, a few highly unique factors may constitute a "signature," while a number of lesser unique factors "although insufficient to generate a strong inference of identity if considered separately, may be of significant probative value when considered together." *United States v. Myers*, 550 F.2d 1036, 1045 (5th Cir. 1977).

It is by this reasoning we are guided in making our "signature quality" determination. Here, the evidence of Mr. Shumway's prior activities at Horse Rock Ruin and the activities charged at trial share at least two distinctive features such that they demonstrate a "signature quality": the unique geographical location, and the skill and specialized knowledge necessary to commit both acts. See *United States v. Stubbins*, 877 F.2d 42 (11th Cir.), *cert. denied*, 493 U.S. 940 (1989); *United States v. Barrett*, 539 F.2d 244, 248 (1st Cir. 1976).

First, Mr. Shumway visited Horse Rock Ruin to loot its contents once before. In *Stubbins*, the defendant was tried for conspiracy and distribution of crack cocaine. His main defense at trial was mistaken identity. 877 F.2d at 43. The prosecution attempted to admit evidence of a prior similar drug sale that took place at the same address as the location of the offense at issue during trial. Id. The court held the prior acts evidence was admissible and relevant to show identity under Fed. R. Evid. 404(b). Id. at 44. Specifically, the court held one distinctive feature of both offenses was that they occurred at the same address, a factor "sufficiently unusual and distinctive" as to be probative of identity. Id. at 44. The same is true here. An expert testified during Mr. Shumway's trial there are approximately 22,000 documented archaeological sites located within San Juan County, Utah, alone; however, Mr. Shumway chose the exact same site once before to search for artifacts. Consequently, while the methods employed at the Horse Rock Ruin site may not have been identical, given the context of this case, both acts share as a distinctive element the exact same location.

Also, Mr. Shumway's prior activities and the acts charged share a second distinctive feature: the skill and specialized knowledge necessary to commit both acts. *Barrett*, 539 F.2d at 248. In *Barrett*, the defendant was charged with crimes arising from the theft of a collection of postage stamps from a museum. Id. at 245. During the investigation it was discovered the burglars had bypassed the alarm system using sophisticated methods requiring skill and specialized knowledge. Id. at 246, 248. The circuit court affirmed the district court's decision to allow testimony portraying the defendant as one knowledgeable in the workings of burglar alarms. Id. at 247–49. In so holding, the court explained because the knowledge and expertise necessary to commit the crime was "so distinctive a feature" of the crime, evidence of the defendant's knowledge was relevant to establish identity. Id. at 248.

We find Barrett's reasoning persuasive here. The existence of 22,000 sites in San Juan County alone, the remoteness of the location, the difficulty of access, and the varying concentration of artifacts, all suggest the person who committed both the prior act and the charged acts was one possessing distinctive, unique and unusual skills necessary to locate and excavate the artifacts. Extensive testimony was introduced showing that Mr. Shumway's statements and actions demonstrated substantial specialized knowledge and prior visits to the site. Mr. Miller testified Mr. Shumway had detailed knowledge as to how to get to the site and had a high degree of familiarity with the Horse Rock Ruin site. Particularly, Mr.

Miller testified Mr. Shumway knew precisely where at the Horse Rock Ruin site to find artifacts. The prior acts evidence Mr. Shumway had looted the Horse Rock Ruin site once before therefore is probative to show he was one with specialized skill and knowledge sufficient to commit the acts charged. The fact Mr. Shumway not only looted before, but looted the Horse Rock Ruin once before, shows he had knowledge of the site's location and means of access, as well as the artifacts to be found there.

Therefore, we hold the two features shared by the prior and charged acts—location and skill—are sufficient under the circumstances of this case to constitute a "signature quality" such that commission of the prior act was relevant to show identity.

Mr. Shumway also argues because the first occurrence at Horse Rock Ruin was seven years prior to the second, it was not probative of identity. However, "[t]here is no absolute rule regarding the number of years that can separate offenses. Rather, the court applies a reasonableness standard and examines the facts and circumstances of each case." *United States v. Franklin*, 704 F.2d 1183, 1189 (10th Cir.) [quoting *United States v. Engleman*, 648 F.2d 473, 479 (8th Cir. 1981)], *cert. denied*, 464 U.S. 845 (1983). Here, the district court considered the seven-year time span when deciding whether the evidence was probative; Mr. Shumway fails to convince us the district court abused its discretion in reaching its conclusion the evidence was probative as to identity.

2. Relevance—Intent and Knowledge

As stated, the district court initially allowed the prior acts evidence only to show identity. However, during trial, the court reconsidered its decision and admitted the evidence also to show knowledge and intent. The district court held since knowledge and intent were required elements, and since Mr. Shumway had not stipulated that the only contested issue was identity, the 404(b) evidence was admissible to show knowledge and intent as well as identity. We agree.

The 404(b) evidence was relevant to show intent. Mr. Shumway was charged with violating 18 U.S.C. § 1361, which requires the government prove the accused acted "willfully." Therefore, Mr. Shumway's intent was an essential element of the crime charged. By standing on his not guilty plea, and by failing to give enforceable pretrial assurances he did not intend to dispute criminal intent, the government may "'include such extrinsic offense evidence as would be admissible if intent were actively contested.'" *Franklin*, 704 F.2d at 1188 [quoting *United States v. Webb*, 625 F.2d 709, 710 (5th Cir. 1980)]. See also *Hill*, 60 F.3d at 676. Prior acts evidence is "clearly" relevant to show an essential element of the charged offense. *Hill*, 60 F.3d at 676. Therefore, the 404(b) evidence was relevant to show the essential intent elements of 18 U.S.C. § 1361.

The 404(b) evidence was also relevant to show "knowledge" as to the charged violation of 16 U.S.C. § 470ee(a). Under § 470ee(a), no person may excavate, remove, etc. any archaeological resource located on public lands. 16 U.S.C. § 470ee(a) (1994). Here, the 404(b) evidence tended to show Mr. Shumway knew the objects he was excavating were archaeological resources. See *Hill*, 60 F.3d at 676 (evidence of prior cocaine possessions admissible to show the defendant knew the substance he possessed was cocaine). Consequently, we hold the prior acts evidence was relevant to show identity, knowledge, and intent, as well as identity.

B. Probative Value Versus Prejudice

Mr. Shumway argues admission of the 404(b) evidence was highly prejudicial under Fed. R. Evid. 403 and therefore the district court erred in admitting the 404(b) evidence under *Huddleston's* second prong. However, the district court explicitly found the probative value of the 404(b) evidence was not substantially outweighed by its potential for prejudice. The trial court is vested with broad discretion in determining whether evidence's probative value is substantially outweighed by its potential to cause prejudice. *Patterson*, 20 F.3d at 814. "Evidence of prior bad acts will always be prejudicial, and it is the trial court's job to evaluate whether the guaranteed risk of prejudice outweighs the legitimate contribution of the evidence." Id. Mr. Shumway makes no more than conclusory statements the district court admission of the 404(b) evidence was prejudicial to his defense. However, "we are required to give the trial court 'substantial deference' in Rule 403 rulings." Id. In light of the district court's explicit findings the 404(b) evidence's probative value was not substantially outweighed by its potential for prejudice, and because Mr. Shumway fails to convince us otherwise, we find no abuse of discretion. Therefore, we affirm the district court's determination the probative value of the 404(b) evidence was not substantially outweighed by its potential for prejudice.

C. Limiting Instruction

Huddleston's fourth prong requires the district court, upon request, to instruct the jury that the 404(b) evidence is to be considered only for the proper purpose for which it was admitted. 485 U.S. at 691–92. Here, the district court properly gave such a limiting instruction to the jury that the 404(b) evidence was to be considered only for the purposes of intent, knowledge, and identity. Having therefore determined the admission of the 404(b) evidence satisfied every element of *Huddleston*, 485 U.S. at 69–92, we hold the district court did not abuse its discretion in admitting the prior acts evidence under Fed. R. Evid. 404(b).

IV. SENTENCING—BASE LEVEL ENHANCEMENTS

A. Vulnerable Victim

At sentencing, the district court enhanced Mr. Shumway's base offense level by two points under U.S.SG § 3A1.1(b), which provides: If the defendant knew or should have known that a victim of the offense was unusually vulnerable due to age, physical, or mental condition, or that a victim was otherwise particularly susceptible to the criminal conduct, increase by 2 levels. We must now decide whether the human skeleton of an Anasazi infant is a "vulnerable victim" for purposes of § 3A1.1(b) of the Sentencing Guidelines.

Normally, a district court's determination of a "vulnerable victim" for purposes of U.S.SG § 3A1.1(b) is a question of fact reviewable for clear error. *United States v. Hardesty*, 105 F.3d 558, 559 (10th Cir. 1997). Here, however, the question is not so clear-cut; rather, the question is whether U.S.SG § 3A1.1(b) properly is interpreted to include skeletal remains as "vulnerable victims." This question deals with the district court's interpretation of the Guidelines, which we review de novo. *United States v. Frazier*, 53 F.3d 1105, 1111 (10th Cir. 1995). We hold U.S.SG § 3A1.1(b) does not apply to prehistoric human skeletal remains.[3] We are convinced that to interpret "vulnerable victim" to include skeletal remains would stretch the imagination, and would render application of U.S.SG § 3A1.1(b) potentially absurd.

The status of "vulnerable victim" hinges on the idea that some characteristic renders a victim "particularly susceptible" to the criminal conduct. In other words, the "vulnerable victim" is someone who is unable to protect himself or herself from criminal conduct, and is therefore in need of greater societal protection than the average citizen. *United States v. Brunson*, 54 F.3d 673, 676 (10th Cir.), *cert. denied*, ___ U.S.___, 116 S. Ct. 397 (1995). Skeletons certainly are completely unable to defend against criminal conduct. However, to illustrate the absurdity of applying the "vulnerable victim" status to a skeleton, consider for example, a pile of cremated remains, or a pile of dirt that was once a pile of bones; if skeletal remains are "vulnerable victims," certainly, then, these types of remains also should qualify. These types of human remains are undoubtedly no more able to guard against criminal harm than a buried infant skeleton, yet can they qualify as a victim? Our answer is an unqualified no. These examples illustrate the untenable results application of the Guidelines to skeletal remains would have, and this we refuse to justify.

In support of the proposition the infant skeleton qualifies as a "vulnerable victim" under U.S.SG § 3A1.1(b), the government relies on *United States v. Roberson*, 872 F.2d 597 (5th Cir.), *cert. denied*, 493 U.S. 861 (1989), and *United States v. Quintero*, 21 F.3d 885 (9th Cir. 1994). In *Roberson*, the defendant's eighty-four-year-old roommate died after falling and hitting his head on a table. 872 F.2d at 599. The defendant feared the police would think he killed the man, so he put the body in his car and drove around Texas for several days. Id. During this time, the defendant charged several thousands of dollars on the dead man's credit card. Id. After a few days, the defendant put the body in a garbage dumpster, doused it with diesel fuel, and burned it beyond recognition. Id. The defendant was convicted of credit card fraud. Id. at 600. The district court enhanced the defendant's offense level pursuant to U.S.SG § 3A1.1's "vulnerable victim" provision, id., and departed upward from the guideline range finding his conduct constituted "extreme conduct" pursuant to U.S.SG § 5K2.8.[4] Id. at 602.

---

[3][*Orig. fn.*] This is not to say, however, that we do not recognize the special import of this case's context. We are aware of the increasing need for the protection of Native American burial sites, and we in no way intend to diminish the cultural importance of those sites nor the importance of a commitment to the preservation of those sites. Nevertheless, we are left with somewhat of a conundrum. Grave robbing, especially grave robbing the sacred objects of Native Americans, is undoubtedly detestable conduct worthy of severe castigation; however, such castigation cannot come at the expense of reason and common sense. Certainly, better means exist to deter the loathsome conduct of grave robbers than to drain the term "vulnerable victim" of any reasonable meaning.

[4][*Orig. fn.*] U.S.SG § 5K2.8 (1995), which has remained unchanged since its original effective date, provides:

If the defendant's conduct was unusually heinous, cruel, brutal, or degrading to the victim, the court may increase the sentence above the guideline range to reflect the nature of the conduct. Examples of extreme conduct include torture of a victim, gratuitous infliction of injury, or prolonging of pain or humiliation.

On appeal, the Fifth Circuit held the district court did not err in applying either provision to the defendant's sentencing calculation. Id. at 608, 612. However, the circuit court did not specifically address the defendant's argument that the body could not be a "victim." Id. at 604. Rather, the circuit court focused on rejecting the defendant's argument the owner of the credit card could not be a "victim" for purposes of the Guidelines if he was not a "victim" of the crime of conviction. Id. at 605, 608-09. The court held the Guidelines required no such nexus—U.S.SG § 5K2.8 and s 3A1.1 did not require the "victim" for purposes of the sentencing departure to be the "victim" for purposes of the crime. Id. at 609. The court glossed the issue of whether a victim must be alive or dead. Consequently, Roberson is not particularly helpful to our "vulnerable victim" analysis.

We have a similar problem applying Quintero. In Quintero, after the defendant's two-year-old daughter died, to avoid discovery, the defendant burned the body, removed the head with a shovel, and left it at a different location several miles away. 21 F.3d at 889. At sentencing, the district court departed upward from the sentencing range finding the defendant's conduct after the girl's death constituted "extreme conduct" for purposes of U.S.SG s 5K2.8. Id. at 893. On appeal, the defendant argued U.S.SG § 5K2.8 applied only to live victims. Id. at 894. The Ninth Circuit affirmed the "extreme conduct" departure holding "[t]he section focuses on the defendant's conduct, not the characteristics of the victim." Id. The court went on to explain the term "victim" as used in U.S.SG § 5K2.8 was meant simply to modify "degrading," and was not meant to distract from the provision's focus on the offender's conduct. The phrase "to the victim" appears to modify the term "degrading," making the point that the Sentencing Commission was not concerned about conduct that might be degrading to the offender. By contrast, the terms "heinous," "cruel," or "brutal" conduct need no such clarification. Id. at 894 n. 8. The Quintero analysis does not apply here. It is true the Guideline's "vulnerable victim" provision does, as do all the provisions, deal generally with the offender's conduct; the evident purpose of the guideline is "to punish more severely conduct that is morally more culpable and to protect such victims by adding more deterrence." *United States v. Gill*, 99 F.3d 484, 488 (1st Cir. 1996). However, unlike the "extreme conduct" provision, which focuses on the nature of the offender's conduct, the "vulnerable victim" enhancement focuses heavily on the characteristics of the crime's victim. This, we find, is a compelling distinction, for in provisions such as the U.S.SG § 5K2.8 "extreme conduct" provision, the state of the victim, living or dead, is of far less consequence. As a result, our holding here is not intended to limit the application of provisions such as s 5K2.8, which focus on the offender's conduct. We leave for another day the question whether the "extreme conduct" provision, or like provisions, could properly apply to this case, or any case where the supposed "victim" is no longer among the living.

For all these reasons, we hold the skeletal remains in this case could not constitute a "vulnerable victim" for purposes of sentencing enhancement under s 3A1.1(b). Consequently, we remand this case for resentencing without the "vulnerable victim" two-point enhancement.[5]

---

[5][*Orig. fn.*] Mr. Shumway also makes the following two arguments the "vulnerable victim" enhancement was in error: the "vulnerable victim" enhancement was improper because there was no evidence Mr. Shumway "targeted" the victim, and the enhancement was improper because the skeletal remains did not constitute an "unusually vulnerable victim." See, *e.g.*, *Hardesty*, 105 F.3d at 560; *Brunson*, 54 F.3d at 677. Because we reverse the district court's application of the enhancement to Mr. Shumway's sentence on other grounds, we need not address these arguments.

B.   Calculation of Loss

Mr. Shumway argues the district court erred in its method of calculating loss. On appeal, while we review the district court's factual findings for clear error, we review de novo questions of what factors the district court may consider in assessing loss under the Guidelines. *United States v. Williams*, 50 F.3d 863, 864 (10th Cir. 1995).

The district court applied U.S.SG § 2B1.3 when it calculated Mr. Shumway's offense level. Section 2B1.3(b)(1) directs the court to § 2B1.1 to calculate loss. The district court calculated loss at "[m]ore than $120,000," which, pursuant to U.S.SG § 2B1.1(b)(1)(J), increased Mr. Shumway's offense level by nine points.

Application note 2 of § 2B1.1 explains that when property is taken or destroyed, "loss is the fair market value" of the property taken, and when property is damaged, "loss is the cost of repairs, not to exceed the loss had the property been destroyed." Application note 2 also provides: "Where the market value is difficult to ascertain or inadequate to measure harm to the victim, the court may measure loss in some other way." U.S.SG § 2B1.1 comment. (n. 2). Specifically relying on this second provision, the district court turned to the regulations promulgated pursuant to the Archaeological Resources Protection Act to calculate loss. 16 U.S.C. § 470ii; 43 C.F.R. § 7.14. Section 470ee of the Archaeological Resources Protection Act, the statute under which Mr. Shumway was convicted and which he admitted violating, identifies archaeological value and cost of repair as relevant factors in determining the violation's severity. 16 U.S.C. § 470ee(d). 43 C.F.R. § 7.14 defines both "archaeological value" and "cost of repair."[6] During Mr. Shumway's trial, two archaeologists testified as to both "archaeological value" and "cost of restoration and repair," as determined under 43 C.F.R. § 7.14, and estimated the total damage to both the Dop-Ki Cave and Horse Rock Ruin at about $96,500. Also, an archaeological damage assessment report was prepared for the two additional sites damaged in the counts to which Mr. Shumway pleaded guilty. The damage report estimated damage to those additional sites at about $40,700. Because the sentencing was consolidated to sentence Mr. Shumway both for the results of his conviction and for the results of his guilty plea, the district court added these two estimates of loss as calculated pursuant to 43 C.F.R. § 7.14 to enhance Mr. Shumway's sentence.

---

[6][*Orig. fn.*] Specifically, 43 C.F.R. § 7.14 provides:

§ 7.14 Determination of archaeological or commercial value and cost of restoration and repair (a) Archaeological value.... [T]he archaeological value of any archaeological resource involved in a violation of the prohibitions in section 7.4... shall be the value of the information associated with the archaeological resource. This value shall be appraised in terms of the costs of the retrieval of the scientific information which would have been obtainable prior to the violation. These costs may include, but need not be limited to, the cost of preparing a research design, conducting field work, carrying out laboratory analysis, and preparing report as would be necessary to realize the information potential.... (c) Cost of restoration and repair.... [T]he cost of restoration and repair of archaeological resources damaged as a result of a violation of prohibitions or conditions... shall be the sum of the costs already incurred for emergency and restoration or repair work, plus those costs projected to be necessary to complete restoration and repair...

Mr. Shumway argues the court should have relied solely on the cost of repairs to the sites and the fair market value of the artifacts taken to calculate a loss of $9,122. Mr. Shumway argues the court's method of calculation was not one contemplated by the Guidelines and resulted in an incorrect standard of measure. We disagree.

For purposes of determining an appropriate offense level under the Guidelines, "loss" is not simply intended to be a measure of net monetary damage. "Loss" also serves to "gauge the severity of a particular offense." *United States v. Lara*, 956 F.2d 994, 999 (10th Cir. 1992). Here, the district court quoted part of U.S.SG § 2B1.1's application note 2, and specifically relied on the language stating where the market value of the property at issue is "inadequate to measure harm to the victim," the court may determine loss some other way. By expressly relying on this language, the district court implicitly found the fair market value of the artifacts inadequately reflected the level of harm Mr. Shumway inflicted. As a result, the district court turned to the objective measure of damage as reflected in regulations specific to the statute Mr. Shumway was convicted of violating—43 C.F.R. § 7.14.

Congress enacted the Archaeological Resources Protection Act to ensure for the present and future benefit of the American people, irreplaceable aspects of Native American history and culture. 16 U.S.C. § 470aa(a), (b). We agree with the district court the paltry sum of $9,122, the asserted cost of the artifact's fair market value and cost of restoration and repair, fails to reflect adequately the extent of damage Mr. Shumway inflicted. The fair market value and cost of repair calculation was grossly insufficient to quantify the devastating and irremediable cultural, scientific, and spiritual damage Mr. Shumway caused to the American people in general and to the Native American community in particular. The Guidelines provided the district court could calculate loss in some way other than fair market value and cost of repair, if those calculations were inadequate. U.S.SG § 2B1.1 comment. (n. 2). The district court relied on this flexible provision and used a reasonable and objective measure specifically formulated to calculate damages under the statute Mr. Shumway was convicted of violating to calculate loss for purposes of sentencing. 43 C.F.R. § 7.14. We hold the district court's method of calculating loss for the purposes of sentencing was proper.

C.   Obstruction of Justice

Mr. Shumway argues the district court erred in enhancing his offense level for obstruction of justice pursuant to U.S.SG § 3C1.1. On appeal, we review the district court's factual findings on this issue for clear error and its legal conclusions de novo. *United States v. Pretty*, 98 F.3d 1213, 1221 (10th Cir. 1996), *petition for cert. filed* (U.S. Feb. 5, 1997) (No. 96-7768).

Under the Guidelines, the district court must enhance the defendant's offense level by two "[i]f the defendant willfully obstructed or impeded, or attempted to obstruct or impede, the administration of justice during the investigation, prosecution, or sentencing of the instant offense." U.S.SG § 3C1.1. Perjury can be the basis for such an enhancement. Id., comment. [n. 3(b)]. Under § 3C1.1, a defendant commits perjury if he or she "gives false testimony concerning a material matter with the willful intent to provide false testimony." *United States v. Dunnigan*, 507 U.S. 87, 94 (1993); *Pretty*, 98 F.3d at 1221.

The district court enhanced Mr. Shumway's offense level by two for obstruction of justice after finding Mr. Shumway committed perjury during the hearing in which he pleaded guilty to the 1994 three-count indictment. Specifically, the district court found Mr. Shumway perjured himself by testifying that his codefendant in the 1994 case, Mr. Verchick, did not assist him in any digging, and did not go into the alcoves at issue with him. Mr. Verchick later pleaded guilty to the charges against him and testified he entered the alcoves with Mr. Shumway. The district court found, therefore, Mr. Shumway had committed perjury and the two-level enhancement pursuant to § 3C1.1 was warranted.

Mr. Shumway argues the obstruction of justice enhancement was in error because the false statements were not "material" as defined by the Guidelines.[7] Specifically, Mr. Shumway argues because his testimony did not specifically exculpate his codefendant, Mr. Shumway's false statements were not "material" for purposes of § 3C1.1. Because we find no evidence the district court's findings are in clear error, and because we find the district court's application of the Guideline proper, we affirm the enhancement.

In *United States v. Bernaugh*, 969 F.2d 858, 862 (10th Cir. 1992), we affirmed the district court's obstruction of justice enhancement where, during his guilty-plea hearing, the defendant made false statements regarding his codefendant's illegal activities. We held the district court's obstruction of justice enhancement was proper because "the section 3C1.1 enhancement applies where a defendant attempts to obstruct justice in a case closely related to his own, such as that of a codefendant." *Bernaugh*, 969 F.2d at 861. The same is true here. Mr. Shumway made false statements regarding his codefendant's role in an apparent attempt to relieve his codefendant of criminal liability. Mr. Shumway argues that while his testimony regarding his codefendant was "less than forthcoming," the testimony was not "materially" perjurious because Mr. Shumway did not provide a story that fully exculpated his codefendant. However, to sustain a U.S.SG § 3C1.1 enhancement, a defendant need not provide a story that when believed, would fully exculpate his or her codefendant. Rather, it is enough that a defendant provides false information bearing on the extent of the codefendant's criminal liability. *Bernaugh*, 969 F.2d at 862. Therefore, because Mr. Shumway made false statements bearing on the criminal liability of his codefendant, we hold the district court properly enhanced his offense level pursuant to U.S.SG § 3C1.1.

V.   SENTENCING—UPWARD DEPARTURE

The presentence report assigned Mr. Shumway a criminal history category of III. Mr. Shumway's criminal history, combined with the enhanced offense level of 22, resulted in an applicable sentencing range under the Guidelines of 51 to 63 months. During sentencing, the district court relied on U.S.SG § 4A1.3, p.s., which suggests a district court adjust the criminal history category if "reliable information" convinces the court the criminal history category does not adequately reflect the seriousness of the defendant's past criminal conduct, or likelihood the defendant will commit future crimes. U.S.SG § 4A1.3, p.s. The district court looked to several factors and determined Mr. Shumway's criminal history category of III did not adequately reflect the seriousness of his past conduct, nor the likelihood he would commit future crimes. After determining the criminal history category of III

---

[7][*Orig. fn.*] For purposes of section 3C1.1, "material" is defined as: "evidence, fact, statement, or information that, if believed, would tend to influence or affect the issue under determination." U.S.SG § 3C1.1, comment. (n. 5).

was inadequate, the district court treated Mr. Shumway as if he had one additional felony conviction, which resulted in an adjusted criminal history category of IV. The court then referenced the sentencing range for a defendant with an offense level of 22 and a criminal history category of IV—63-78 months—and sentenced Mr. Shumway to seventy-eight months.

Mr. Shumway argues the district court's upward departure was in error for three reasons: 1) the district court did not adequately articulate its reasons for departure; 2) the district court was unclear as to whether it considered factors already taken into account by the Guidelines; and 3) the departure was not reasonable.

On appeal, we review the district court's decision to depart from the Sentencing Guidelines for an abuse of discretion. *Koon v. United States*, ___ U.S. ___, ___, 116 S. Ct. 2035, 2043 (1996); *United States v. Contreras*, 108 F.3d 1255, 1270 (10th Cir. 1997). A district court may depart from the applicable sentencing range if "the court finds that there exists an aggravating or mitigating circumstance of a kind, or to a degree, not adequately taken into consideration" by the Guidelines. 18 U.S.C. § 3553(b) (1994); *Koon*, ___ U.S. at ___, 116 S. Ct. at 2044. "Before a departure is permitted, certain aspects of the case must be found unusual enough for it to fall outside the heartland of cases in the Guideline." *Koon*, ___ U.S. at ___, 116 S. Ct. at 2046. The district court has an "institutional advantage" over appellate courts in making these sorts of determinations due to extensive experience in applying the Guidelines. Nevertheless, "[a] district court by definition abuses its discretion when it makes an error of law," such that "[t]he abuse of discretion standard includes review to determine that the discretion was not guided by erroneous legal conclusions." *Koon*, ___ U.S. at ___, 116 S. Ct. at 2047–48. Once we determine whether the district court has abused its discretion in departing from the Guidelines, we review the departure for reasonableness. 18 U.S.C. § 3742(e)(3); *United States v. White*, 893 F.2d 276, 278 (10th Cir. 1990); *cf. Williams v. United States*, 503 U.S. 193, 204 (1992) (even if district court departs from the Guidelines based on an erroneous factor, appellate court may affirm the sentence if it is satisfied the district court would have made the same sentence without the erroneous factor, and the degree of departure is reasonable).

We now turn to the question whether the district court abused its discretion in departing from the Guidelines. The presentence report documented Mr. Shumway's extensive past illegal conduct of looting archaeological sites. Part of this evidence included Mr. Shumway's own statements at a trial related to his 1984 illegal acts at Horse Rock Ruin. Specifically, Mr. Shumway stated under oath he had been digging artifacts from public lands since a young age and had looted archaeological sites "thousands of times." Additionally, Mr. Shumway appeared in a videotaped documentary that focused on the looting of archaeological sites in San Juan County, Utah. In the documentary, Mr. Shumway discussed how low the chances were of an experienced looter being caught. The presentence report also summarized an article in which Mr. Shumway was quoted as saying: "If the government can come down here and say we don't have the right to dig in a place where we've lived all our lives, I'd just as soon go to prison. I'm not gonna bring my kid into a world where you can't go out and dig up an old ruin."

The district court considered this information set out in the presentence report and found Mr. Shumway had looted "at least 100 other times" than those which resulted in convictions, and had "made a way of life out of pot hunting down there on government lands and apparently thought or may still think that he has the right to do this." Additionally, the district court found "there's a strong likelihood he will commit other crimes." Based on these findings, the district court treated Mr. Shumway as if he had one additional felony, and added three criminal history points, which resulted in a criminal history category of IV.

We conclude the district court did not abuse its discretion in departing from the Guidelines. The court relied on U.S.SG § 4A1.3, p.s., which allows a court to use "reliable information" in determining whether to adjust the criminal history category. Specifically, U.S.SG § 4A1.3(e) lists "prior similar adult conduct not resulting in a criminal conviction" as reliable information. In determining Mr. Shumway's past criminal conduct was sufficiently unusual to warrant an upward departure from the guideline range, the district court relied on Mr. Shumway's own admissions of his repeated illegal looting of archaeological sites, and relied on the probability Mr. Shumway would commit similar crimes in the future based on his "pot hunting" way of life, and his apparent belief he had every right to engage in such conduct. The district court relied on factors specifically listed in U.S.SG § 4A1.3, and we remain unconvinced the district court abused its discretion in departing from the guideline range based on these factors.

Mr. Shumway's arguments the district court failed to articulate its reasons for departure, and that the district court may have applied factors already taken into account by the Guidelines do not convince us otherwise. The district court articulated the information it relied on in making its decision to depart; it is clear the district court did not rely on factors already taken into account by the Guidelines. Rather, the district court relied on U.S.SG § 4A1.3(e), p.s., which is an "encouraged factor" for departure. An "encouraged factor" is one "'the Commission has not been able to take into account fully in formulating the guidelines.'" *Koon*, ___ U.S. at ___, 116 S. Ct. at 2045 (quoting U.S.SG § 5K2.0). Indeed, U.S.SG § 4A1.3 comment. (backg'd.) states: "This policy statement recognizes that the criminal history score is unlikely to take into account all the variations in the seriousness of criminal history that may occur." Consequently, the district court did not erroneously rely on factors the Guidelines had already taken into account. The district court relied on information that was sufficiently unusual to take Mr. Shumway's case outside the Guidelines' heartland.

Mr. Shumway also argues the district court's departure was not reasonable. We disagree. In assessing whether the degree of departure was reasonable, we consider the district court's reasons for imposing the particular sentence together with factors such as: "the seriousness of the offense, the need for just punishment, deterrence, protection of the public, correctional treatment, the sentencing pattern of the Guidelines, the policy statements contained in the Guidelines, and the need to avoid unwarranted sentencing disparities." *White*, 893 F.2d at 278; 18 U.S.C. § 3742(e)(3); 18 U.S.C. § 3553(a); see also *Williams*, 503 U.S. at 203–04.

The district court added three points to Mr. Shumway's criminal history level after analogizing Mr. Shumway's history to a defendant with one additional felony conviction. Such analogies are specifically provided for in U.S.SG § 4A1.3, p.s.: In considering a departure under this provision, the Commission intends that the court use, as a reference, the guideline range for a defendant with a higher or lower criminal history category, as applicable. For example, if the court concludes that the defendant's criminal history category of III significantly under-represents the seriousness of the defendant's criminal history, and that the seriousness of the defendant's criminal history most closely resembles that of most defendants with Criminal History Category IV, the court should look to the guideline range specified for a defendant with Criminal History Category IV to guide its departure. The district court closely followed this provision by adding the same number of criminal history points as if Mr. Shumway had one additional prior felony conviction.

The district court may use any "'reasonable methodology hitched to the Sentencing Guidelines to justify the reasonableness of the departure,'" which includes using extrapolation from or analogy to the Guidelines. *United States v. Jackson*, 921 F.2d 985, 991 (10th Cir. 1990) [quoting *United States v. Harris*, 907 F.2d 121, 124 (10th Cir. 1990)]. Here, the district court was explicit in its method of departure. Additionally, the departure is consistent with the factors to be considered in imposing a sentence under 18 U.S.C. § 3553(a). We hold the district court's degree of departure from the Guidelines was reasonable.

Accordingly, the district court is AFFIRMED in part and REVERSED in part, and we REMAND to the district court for resentencing in accordance with this opinion.

Notes

1. In *Shumway,* the government argued for substantial prison time and requested that the court accept an upward departure from the basic sentence due to the amount of damage and the defendant's career of looting archeological sites. The defendant was the same individual who eluded conviction in an ARPA trial more than 15 years earlier, when the judge instructed the jury that a midden was not protected by ARPA.

2. ARPA does not discuss restitution to an agency or a victimized Indian tribe, although restitution as a part of a sentence is always available. Fines are sums paid to the United States Treasury as an enhancement of the penalty when incarceration alone is not sufficient, or when incarceration is not appropriate. Fines do not go to the agency that is responsible for maintenance of the resource. The court, however, at the request of the government, may sentence the defendant to pay restitution to the victim agency. In an ARPA prosecution, restitution is the agency's present and future out-of-pocket costs of restoration and repair of the injured resources. Note that the ARPA uniform regulations refer to the cost of reinterment of human remains, in accord with religious custom and tribal law, as a compensable cost of restoration and repair [16 U.S.C. § 7.14(c)(7) (1997)].

Damage Assessment

Penalties for violating ARPA depend in part on damages. Thus, an understanding of how damages are computed pursuant to the Act is required. The calculation of damages in an ARPA enforcement action requires a damage assessment, which should be completed by an archeologist expert. Damages may be based either on the commercial value of archeological items in question or the archeological value of the injured area. Either of these values plus the cost of restoration and repair of all the archeological resources affected by the violation equal the total damage amount [16 U.S.C. § 470ee(d) (1997)].

For the nonarcheologist, commercial value is the simplest damage consideration to comprehend. Commercial value is the fair-market value of a protected item. The actual sale price or offered price is a good indicator of commercial value, as are the catalog prices of comparable items. Fair-market value in an ARPA case, however, always is based on the previolation condition of the item [see 43 C.F.R. § 7.14(b) (1997)].

Archeological value is the value of the information associated with a site. Determining archeological value requires developing a hypothetical construct and applying standard costs associated with contract archeology. Archeologists usually do not put a value on information because to them an archeological site is a priceless piece of nonrenewable and nonreplaceable information. Nevertheless, the law requires a standard for evaluating site damage in order to differentiate between lesser and major offenses. Archeological value, therefore, is an objective determination of actual costs to carry out fieldwork under the given conditions, based on a subjective analysis of what each site might require ["This value shall be appraised in terms of the costs of the retrieval of the scientific information prior to the violation." See 43 C.F.R. § 7.14(a) (1997)]. It depends on the characteristics of a specific victimized area, and is not the product of a hypothetical, "reasonable cost of data recovery" per cubic foot at a "reasonable site," multiplied by the actual number of cubic feet disturbed. Archeological value is derived from the cost of recovering scientific data from a location adjacent to the injured area and of comparable volume. Since every site is different, not every site needs to be subjected to the full battery of tests known to science. Thus, the archeologist who completes the site damage assessment needs to possess knowledge of the considerations and current costs of archeological field data recovery, as well as an understanding of the type of site that was damaged and the potential information it would have provided had it remained intact.

The cost of restoration and repair "shall be the sum of the costs already incurred for emergency restoration or repair work, plus those costs projected to be necessary to complete restoration and repair" [see 43 C.F.R. § 7.14(c) (1997)]. These out-of-pocket costs may include restoration of the resource, site stabilization, ground or surface contouring and stabilization, research necessary to carry out stabilization work, placement of physical barriers to prevent further loss, scientific examination of items retrieved, and the costs of preparing reports. Where human remains are involved, the cost of restoration and repair also may include the cost of reinterment in accordance with state, local, or tribal law [see 43 C.F.R. § 7.14(c)(7) (1997)]. Also, the cost of curation, pursuant to the regulations governing federally owned and administered archeological collections [36 C.F.R. Part 79 (1997)], is a cost of restoration and repair.

Because there is no qualitative component to a site damage assessment, the "significance" of a site to science is irrelevant for purposes of calculating damages. The damage assessment, being the work product of an expert, discusses the "archeological interest" of the site in order to establish it as an "archeological resource" subject to protection, and explains the line items that comprise the commercial value or archeological value of the resource, and the costs of restoration and repair.

Civil Enforcement

Civil ARPA enforcement was not available as a resource protection tool until 1984, when uniform regulations were promulgated [43 C.F.R. Part 7; 36 C.F.R. Part 296; 18 C.F.R. Part 1312; 32 C.F.R. Part 229) (1997)]. For an agency to conduct an ARPA proceeding, it must have access to an Administrative Law Judge (ALJ). The Department of the Interior has an Office of Hearings and Appeals, but not every land managing agency is similarly staffed. Lack of ALJs has not impeded the Department of Agriculture and the Tennessee Valley Authority from enforcing ARPA civilly, however, because they have executed Memoranda of Agreement with the Department of the Interior to use their ALJs. In fact, the Forest Service was the first agency to conduct a civil ARPA proceeding, which was heard by an ALJ from the Department of the Interior [*Eel River Sawmills, Inc., et al. v. United States*, Nos. ARPA 90-1 and ARPA 90-2 (Dept. of Interior, Off. Hearings and App., Hearings Div., Salt Lake City August 10, 1992)].

The use of civil enforcement to deter resource destruction has several advantages over criminal enforcement. The burden of proof in a civil matter is by a preponderance of the evidence rather than the higher criminal standard of beyond a reasonable doubt. Also, in criminal prosecutions, some juries may have difficulty understanding the proof of the elements of the case, while others might not sympathize with the policy of fighting looting and preserving the archeological record in place. Administrative law courts, by contrast, have no juries, and attorneys are optional. In addition, civil prosecution may present the land manager, in whose discretion the mode of enforcement initially lies, with fewer costs and a greater recovery of damages than a criminal prosecution.

Depending on the facts of the case and the nature of the perpetrator, civil prosecution may be a more appropriate means of addressing injury to archeological resources. Where, for example, the act was not undertaken for personal gain but out of negligence, civil prosecution may provide a more appropriate remedy. In *Eel River Sawmills,* a subcontractor operating a backhoe damaged an archeological site while building a road for a government contractor. Clearly, the backhoe operator knew he was on federal land, and he knew he was moving massive amounts of dirt, but he claimed he didn't know he was in the area of an archeological site. The land manager believed that monetary damages alone, and without the element of retribution inherent in criminal justice, would be the appropriate remedy for this ARPA violation. Interestingly, in *Eel River Sawmills,* the subcontractor was held strictly liable, but the ALJ found that the contractor could not be held vicariously liable under ARPA. The government chose to settle with the subcontractor rather than appeal the ALJ's decision, perhaps partly because of the nature of the contested facts and partly because *Eel River Sawmills* was the first decision rendered in a civil ARPA case, and application of the law was still developing.

Elements of Civil Enforcement

The elements of a civil penalty case are similar to those in a criminal case. There must be jurisdiction arising from contact with federal or Indian lands, and injury to, or removal of, an archeological resource without a permit or other authority. For example, a government contractor operating outside the scope, or in breach, of a contract may be in violation of ARPA. Intent is not an issue, only whether the alleged violator is responsible for the damage. Thus, the violator might be acting negligently and still cause a violation.

In a civil case the maximum amount of the civil penalty is the damage assessment amount. For a second or subsequent ARPA offense the amount of the assessment is automatically doubled. Consequently, proof of damages is a key issue. The 1988 amendments to ARPA clarified that the calculation of damages in both civil penalty and criminal cases is identical. In civil penalty cases, however, the entire civil penalty goes to the land manager or affected Indian or Indian tribe. In criminal prosecutions, the court may determine that part of the damage award is restitution payable to the land managing agency, and part is a fine payable to the Department of the Treasury.

The Civil Process

The initial decision to pursue an ARPA matter either criminally or civilly rests with the federal land manager. In either case, investigation and preparation of the damage assessment are the same. Criminal cases are referred to the United States Attorney for prosecution, and thereafter case management rests within the Department of Justice. Civil cases remain within the control and authority of the agency bringing the action. Although the statute and the uniform regulations do not prevent the land manager from proceeding without the benefit of counsel, Department of the Interior supplemental regulations [43 C.F.R. § 7.37(d)(2) (1997)] and most agency policies require the assistance of counsel.

Notice of Violation

A civil action begins with a notice of violation, which is served on each alleged violator. A corporate violator is served through a statutory agent who is listed in each state with the registering authority. Service may be by a process server, although the uniform regulations allow for service by registered mail, return receipt requested [see 43 C.F.R. § 7.15(b) (1997)]. Successful civil prosecution is predicated on an ability to show effective service. The notice of violation includes a short statement of the facts alleging a violation, the time and place of the violation, and a statement that forms the basis to find that the person served has committed or is responsible for the violation [see 43 C.F.R. § 7.15(b)(1) (1997)]. The notice also addresses the issue of permission—that is, the violator was acting without the benefit of a permit or outside the scope of the permit or government contract—and includes a demand for payment of the damage amount. A copy of the site damage assessment may accompany the notice, although the regulations do not mandate its enclosure.

The notice must advise the alleged violator of the available recourse, which is: (1) to discuss the matter informally with the land manager and negotiate a resolution; (2) to file a petition for relief and set the matter on the docket of the ALJ; and (3) to take no action, and await receipt of a final notice of assessment [see 43 C.F.R. § 7.15(b)(4) (1997)]. The notice also must advise the purported violator of the option to conclude the matter by making payment in full to the agency, and the right to seek judicial review of either the land manager's determination, the ALJ's administrative order, or both.

Prompt notice of a violation might be necessary in order to cause the violator to cease damaging the resource, even though completion of a site damage assessment might take several weeks. If the site damage assessment is not complete by the time the first notice of violation is served, an amended notice may be sent which provides the basis for, and the amount of, damage claimed to have occurred as a result of the violator's actions. A purported violator has 45 days from the time of service to respond to a notice containing the damage amount.

Response to the Notice of Violation

The alleged violator, now the respondent in the civil action, has 45 days to take action or be served with a final notice of assessment. The respondent may schedule a meeting with the land manager, request a formal hearing before an ALJ, or send full payment to satisfy the demand.

If requested, the land manager is obliged to meet with the respondent and discuss a resolution. This requirement is consistent with the Civil Justice

Reform order of 1991, which directs that no formal litigation be instigated without first attempting to resolve the matter informally [56 Fed. Reg. 55,195 (1991)]. This informal meeting, in the nature of a settlement negotiation, provides an opportunity for the respondent to convince the land manager that he or she was not responsible for the violation, or that the assessed damages are too high. Should the government and the respondent reach a compromise, they may enter into an agreement executed by, and enforceable against, all parties.

If the land manager determines that no violation has occurred, or that the respondent is not the responsible party, a written notice of no assessment is issued by the land manager [see 43 C.F.R. § 7.15(e)(3) (1997)]. Alternatively, if, after discussion, the land manager determines that there is cause for additional investigation, an amended notice of violation subsequently will issue, and the time periods will begin anew. Nothing in the regulations prohibits a second informal meeting after receipt of an amended notice, and a second meeting would be appropriate if so requested by the respondent.

Petition for Relief

The petition for relief is a written exception to the notice of violation that sets forth the facts upon which the respondent will rely to prove he or she is not the responsible party, or that the damage assessment is too high. It must be received by the land manager within 45 days of service of the notice of assessment. The petition for relief may request either a formal hearing with the land manager [see 43 C.F.R. § 7.15(d) (1997)] or an informal consideration without a hearing. If the parties undertake informal negotiations following the notice of violation, the time for filing the petition for relief could expire unless the parties agree in writing to an extension of time; the regulations do not address this issue.

Final Notice of Assessment

Following the informal or formal meetings and the 45 days for response (with or without input from the respondent), the land manager issues a final notice of assessment indicating the bases for the damage amount demanded and the conclusion that the respondent is responsible for the violation [see 43 C.F.R. § 7.15(f)(1) (1997)]. If there have been discussions with the respondent, those discussions are to be considered when drafting the final notice of assessment [see 43 C.F.R. § 7.15(e)(2) (1997)]. The notice must advise the respondent of the right to an administrative hearing, and provide the addresses of the ALJ and, if required, the agency counsel. It also must advise the respondent that ALJ determinations and orders are reviewable in federal district court [see 43 C.F.R. §§ 7.15(f)(2) and (3) (1997)]. Finally, the notice should advise the respondent that failure to request a hearing in writing within 45 days will result in waiver of the right to a hearing.

The land manager may issue a final notice of assessment that is less than the amount in the notice of violation. Reduction of the amount may be based on additional investigation, discussions with the respondent, or the consideration of any number of mitigating factors, but the reasons for any reduction must be expressly stated in the final notice of assessment. Mitigating factors include:

1.   agreement by the alleged violator to return archeological resources taken from federal or Indian lands, which may include items previously taken and not subject to the notice of violation;

2.   agreement by the respondent to assist in preservation, protection, and study of archeological resources on public and Indian lands, should the land manager devise a suitable program;

3.   agreement by the respondent to give information concerning other violations of ARPA which will assist law enforcement agents to detect, deter, and/or prosecute resource violations;

4.   for first-time offenders, a demonstrated inability to pay the assessment;

5.   absence of willfulness to commit the violation, where the violator acts out of negligence, or with a general intent to violate the law but without the specific intent of a knowing and purposeful violator;

6.   the possibility that the proposed penalty would be excessive and in violation of the Eighth Amendment to the Constitution;

7.   the possibility that the proposed penalty would be fundamentally unfair.
      [See 43 C.F.R. § 7.16(b)(1)(i)–(vii) (1997)].

Administrative Hearings

A hearing will be scheduled before an ALJ if a request in writing is made within the 45 days. The request may be sent by registered mail or delivered in person, but in either case the respondent should be able to show that the response was timely. The respondent need not appear with counsel before the ALJ, but most agencies prefer counsel to appear for the agency, especially when the respondent is represented by counsel.

The administrative law process is a function of the Executive Branch. Not every agency has an administrative law system, but an agency may bear the cost of using the administrative courts of another agency through a memorandum of agreement. All administrative law courts are governed by the Rules of Procedure for Administrative Hearings [5 U.S.C. §§ 554–557 (1997)].

During the hearing, each side presents evidence to the court. There is no jury, and the judge's findings form the basis of the ruling. The ALJ is not limited to the compromise penalty amount that the agency may have offered the respondent after the informal or formal meeting. Instead, the ALJ may find a damage amount that is consistent with the evidence, and it may be higher or lower than the figure in the final notice of assessment [see 43 C.F.R. § 7.15(g)(3) (1997)]. Thus, ARPA clearly encourages settlement without a hearing.

Final Orders and Appeal

The decision of the ALJ becomes final 30 calendar days after the written ruling is sent to the parties, unless either the respondent or the land manager files a notice of appeal during that time [Department of the Interior supplemental regulations, 43 C.F.R. § 7.37(e)(3) (1997)]. A notice of appeal is a brief statement of an intent to appeal, directed to the address provided in the regulation, with copies mailed to the other party and the judge who rendered the decision [Department of the Interior supplemental regulations, 43 C.F.R. § 7.37(f) (1997)]. An appeal is not a *de novo* review of the first hearing [see 43 C.F.R. § 4.1(b)(4) (1997)]. The review panel will decide the matter on the record and issue a final decision, constituting the final administrative determination of the matter [Department of the Interior supplemental regulations, 43 C.F.R. § 7.37(h) (1997)]. An appellate order is subject to review on appeal to the appropriate federal district court, and any administrative order that is not appealed is final and collectible.

Payment of the Penalty Amount

Payment of the penalty amount is due when:

1. the respondent receives a notice of violation and opts to pay the amount in full [see 43 C.F.R. § 7.15(c)(4) (1997)];

2. no hearing is requested, and 45 days have run from the final notice of assessment [see 43 C.F.R. § 7.15(c)(3) (1997)];

3. a notice of appeal is not filed within 30 days of the decision of the ALJ [Department of the Interior supplemental regulations, 43 C.F.R. § 7.37(e)(3) (1997)];

4. the Appeals Board renders a decision and no appeal to Federal District Court is filed within 45 days [Department of the Interior supplemental regulations, 43 C.F.R. § 7.37(f) (1997)];

5. the federal district court issues an order affirming the final administrative decision [16 U.S.C. § 470ff(b) (1997)].

Penalty amounts are paid to the agency bringing the action, with penalties collected from actions occurring on Indian lands being remitted to the appropriate Indian group [16 U.S.C. § 470gg(c) (1997)]. Once an order is final, it may be submitted to the United States Attorney in the applicable district for a collection action. Also, nothing precludes the agency from employing any of the creditor's rights available in the state in which the matter arose.

Forfeiture

Items may be retrieved from an ARPA violator in three ways.

(1) Stolen items of government or tribal property may be recovered.
(2) Items such as shoes or weapons may be retained as evidence.
(3) As specified in the law, items may be forfeited to the government or the tribe.

The law specifies that all archeological resources taken in violation of the law and "all vehicles and equipment of any person which were used in connection with such violation" may be forfeited to the agency bringing the action, or the appropriate tribe if the violation occurred on tribal lands [16 U.S.C. § 470gg(b) (1997)].

Forfeiture may be accomplished within the scope of a civil or criminal proceeding, or an action may be brought against the item *in rem*. If the government proceeds criminally, the indictment contains an additional paragraph that both describes the item to be forfeited and indicates that it was used in the commission of an act prohibited by ARPA. The jury then has the responsibility, when deciding guilt or innocence, to determine whether the item was used in the commission of the offense. If the answer is affirmative, the forfeiture is complete. In a civil proceeding, a complaint may be drafted to include a request for relief that includes forfeiture of specific items. The ALJ then determines whether the respondent is responsible for the injury to the resource, and whether the listed item was used in the commission of the violation. The final judgment will include the order for forfeiture of the item. If an item is found at an injured site, and it is not tied to a person, the government may proceed against the thing. This *in rem* action may be brought in federal district court or before an ALJ [16 U.S.C. § 470gg(b)(3)) (1997)]. The judge need not determine whether anyone in particular is responsible for the violation, only that the facts indicate that the item was used to violate the law. Service of process will have been accomplished by publication in a local newspaper to give the owner an opportunity to claim the item, but such a claim will not forestall forfeiture.

Items that may have been seized when government agents discovered a violation or executed a search warrant might be held pending completion of a site damage assessment and instigation of a civil or criminal prosecution.

A suspect could attempt to preempt government action, however, by demanding prompt release of the property. For a discussion of issues raised by forfeiture, see the section entitled "Issues In Enforcement."

Note

The defenses to forfeiture that apply generally also are available in ARPA forfeitures. Query how the "innocent owner" defense may apply in a forfeiture pursuant to ARPA. Even if the owner of the property did not personally violate ARPA, the property may be seized if he or she had knowledge of the use of the property. The owner has the burden of proving lawful ownership and lack of knowledge that the property would be used to commit the prohibited act.

Rewards

Bestowing rewards on members of the public who give information to assist in the protection of archeological resources is a positive way to deter the destruction of these heritage resources. Private entities can set up accounts to provide funds to the land manager to give rewards, but ARPA institutionalizes the process by including a reward provision. Under ARPA, the land manager may request that the Secretary of the Treasury pay a reward to persons who gave the government information leading to the successful conclusion of an ARPA case [16 U.S.C. § 470gg(a) (1997)]. Although the statute provides for rewards from both criminal and civil prosecutions, this provision in fact would appear to apply only in criminal prosecutions because all ARPA rewards are funded by fines paid by the violator into the Treasury of the United States, and these fines only occur as a result of criminal prosecution.

Several persons may share in a reward, which may not exceed $500 and not more than one-half of the fine collected. All federal employees and any other government agents who gave information in the performance of their official duties are ineligible to receive ARPA rewards.

3.   Native American Graves Protection and Repatriation Act

The treatment of heritage resources sensitive to Native Americans presents unique and complex legal issues that are discussed more fully in the chapter entitled "Native American Heritage Resources." Examination of the federal laws specifically prohibiting damage to cultural resources reveals that Native American cultural items and burials traditionally did not receive adequate protection. Both the Antiquities Act and ARPA, for example, emphasize protection for the benefit of science; and in any case, ARPA could not protect items of importance to Indians if they were less than 100 years old. Also, ARPA requires that a dollar value be placed on items in order to determine the seriousness of the offense—and it considers reburial merely in terms of a potential cost of restoration and repair—to be included in a damage assessment. These considerations, as well as reference to human remains and cultural or sacred items as "archeological resources," are offensive to many American Indians, Alaska Natives, and Native Hawaiians. Moreover, joint and communal ownership are not addressed in these laws. The Native American Graves Protection Act of 1990 (NAGPRA) sought to rectify these legal shortcomings [Pub. L. No. 101-601, 104 Stat. 3048 (1990), codified at 25 U.S.C. §§ 3001–3013 (1997)].

NAGPRA adopted two avenues for enforcement. First, a criminal law was created to punish persons who traffic in Native American human remains and other specified categories of cultural items. Second, a civil penalty section in the law sanctions museums receiving federal funds and holding Native American cultural items that do not comply with the law.

Illegal Trafficking in Native American Human Remains and Cultural Items

NAGPRA amends the federal Criminal Code by creating a new criminal law that directly responds to ARPA's inability to protect human remains that cannot be tied to federal or tribal lands [18 U.S.C. § 1170 (1997)]. The legislative history of this criminal law demonstrates that Congress intended to protect the remains of Native Americans wherever they are found and regardless of age. Other specified cultural items also are included in the law, but unlike human remains, they are not strictly protected.

(a) Whoever knowingly sells, purchases, uses for profit, or transports for sale or profit, the human remains of a Native American without the right of possession to those remains as provided in the Native American Graves Protection and Repatriation Act shall be fined in accordance with this title, or imprisoned not more than 12 months, or both, and the case of a second or subsequent violation, be fined in accordance with this title, or imprisoned not more than 5 years, or both.

(b) Whoever knowingly sells, purchases, uses for profit, or transports for sale or profit any Native American cultural items obtained in violation of the Native American Grave (sic) Protection and Repatriation Act shall be fined in accordance with this title, imprisoned not more than one year, or both, and in the case of a second or subsequent violation, be fined in accordance with this title, imprisoned not more than 5 years, or both.

[18 U.S.C. § 1170(a) (b) (1997)].

Jurisdiction

NAGPRA applies to federal lands, those lands owned or controlled by the United States, and to tribal lands [25 U.S.C. § 3001(5) (1997)]. It does not apply to sovereign territories which are not the lands of tribes listed as federally recognized by the Bureau of Indian Affairs. [ARPA, by contrast, protects sites on lands of the United States, including the fifty states, the District of Columbia, Puerto Rico, Guam, and the Virgin Islands (16 U.S.C. § 470bb(7) (1997)]. NAGPRA also confers federal jurisdiction over Native American human remains wherever they are found, and is not limited to human remains located or removed from federal or tribal lands. In recognition of the unique fiduciary responsibility of the federal government to Native Americans, the remains of their ancestors receive federal protection whenever they are subjected to a prohibited act by any person "without the right of possession." Only persons who have the right to determine the disposition of the human remains, such as lineal descendants, have the right of possession.

For purposes of jurisdiction, the criminal law treats cultural items differently than human remains. Liability for a crime under subsection (b) requires that an act associated with a protected cultural item be in violation of NAGPRA.

As NAGPRA has two components, there are two ways to violate the Act. One component of NAGPRA governs repatriation of items in museum collections to Indian tribes and Native Hawaiian organizations regardless of whether it can be proven that they originated on federal or tribal lands. Presuming that some items have been in museum collections so long that their provenance is long forgotten, this repatriation component requires that federal agencies and museums complete summaries of cultural items in their collections, and do item-by-item inventories of human remains and associated funerary items. Failure to comply with this process and to disclose the completed lists to interested groups who have standing under the law are violations of NAGPRA, as is the failure to proceed with repatriation as set forth in the Act. Consequently, noncompliance coupled with a prohibited activity will invoke federal criminal jurisdiction.

A second component of NAGPRA provides a means to determine ownership of cultural items discovered on federal or tribal lands after November 16, 1990 (the effective date of the Act). When cultural items belonging to one of the NAGPRA categories are found on federal or tribal lands they no longer will be government property, but instead will be turned over to the Native American owner, following a procedure for disposition. Thus, federal criminal jurisdiction exists when NAGPRA items discovered on federal or tribal lands are not turned over to their Native American owners, and are used in a prohibited activity. Like ARPA, this component of NAGPRA provides a land-based nexus for federal jurisdiction, but unlike ARPA, the items do not require a minimum age in order to be protected.

Protected Items

NAGPRA protects Native American human remains and specified categories of cultural items. "Native American human remains" means remains of, or related to, a tribe, people, or culture that is indigenous to the United States [25 U.S.C. § 3001(9) (1997)], and it includes American Indian, Alaska Native, and Native Hawaiian remains.

There are four other categories of protected cultural items [25 U.S.C. § 3001(3) (1997)]:

(1) **associated funerary objects** which shall mean objects that, as a part of the death rite or ceremony of a culture, are reasonably believed to have been placed with individual human remains either at the time of death or later, and both the human remains and associated funerary objects are presently in the possession or control of a Federal agency or museum, except that other items exclusively made for burial purposes or to contain human remains shall be considered as associated funerary objects;

(2) **unassociated funerary objects** which shall mean objects that, as part of the death rite or ceremony of a culture, are reasonably believed to have been placed with individual human remains either at the time of death or later, where the remains are not in the possession or control of the Federal agency or museum and the objects can be identified by a preponderance of the evidence as related to specific individuals or families of to known human remains or, by a preponderance of the evidence, as having been removed from a specific burial site of an individual culturally affiliated with a particular Indian tribe;

(3) **sacred objects** which shall mean specific ceremonial objects which are needed by traditional Native American religious leaders for the practice of traditional Native American religions by their present day adherents;

(4) **cultural patrimony** which shall mean an object having ongoing historical, traditional, or cultural importance central to the Native American group or culture itself, rather than property owned by an individual Native American, and which, therefore, cannot be alienated, appropriated, or conveyed by any individual regardless of whether or not the individual is a member of the Indian tribe or Native Hawaiian organization and such object shall have been considered inalienable by such Native American group at the time the object was separated from such group.

The distinction between associated and unassociated funerary items is of concern only to museums and agencies when they compile an inventory or a summary of protected items. Unassociated funerary items are considered in the summary of heritage resources, while associated funerary items belong on the itemized inventory. This distinction, however, is not relevant for criminal enforcement purposes. Thus, "funerary items" means items that were made exclusively for burial of an individual, or were placed in a burial at the time of death or later, regardless of whether the individual and the remains are housed together, or whether certain funerary items can be identified as belonging to a specific individual, as long as the funerary items are from a burial site that is culturally affiliated with American Indians, Alaska Natives, or Native Hawaiians.

NAGPRA defines sacred objects perhaps more narrowly than would Native Americans themselves. Also, the definition is silent with regard to whether these items may be owned individually or communally, even though sacred objects are not subject to repatriation if they have been alienated lawfully [25 U.S.C. § 3001(13) (1997); see the chapter entitled "Native American Heritage Resources" for a discussion of right of possession]. Items may retain the status of sacred objects even though they, or like objects, have not been used in ceremonies for many years. After all, some ceremonies might have been suspended or discontinued when the object was separated from the group, and their resumption might require the return of the item. Generally, traditional religious leaders who require the item in question for use in traditional religious ceremonies are the best providers of evidence that the item is a sacred object.

In some cases, an item might have fallen out of use in traditional Native American religion, but is still so fundamental to the definition of the group as to be culturally indispensable. This quality indicates objects of cultural patrimony. A key attribute of cultural patrimony is inalienability from the group, as determined at the time the item was separated from the group. If an item was regarded by the group as alienable at the time it was given away or sold, it would not be an object of cultural patrimony for purposes of NAGPRA, even if today the group considers the item to be cultural patrimony. The present owner would have the right of possession, and as the true owner, would hold the item as private property. The Native American group might purchase the item, but the transaction between the parties would fall outside the scope of NAGPRA.

Right of Possession

NAGPRA was enacted to address wrongs perpetrated as a result of the historical view that the right of ownership lay with the possessor of Native American heritage resources. The law does not demand that property be taken from its rightful owner, rather it seeks to be a vehicle for placing protected items in the possession of rightful owners, including previously disenfranchised native peoples. Thus, cultural items separated from Native

Americans without permission, or under an assumption of government ownership, are now reviewed for appropriate disposition. In the case of human remains or burial objects, the lineal descendants have authority to grant a right of possession if they can be identified. If not identifiable, that authority reverts to the Indian tribe or Native Hawaiian organization [25 U.S.C. § 3001(13) (1997)]. Permission to possess and own sacred objects and objects of cultural patrimony must have been obtained from one who had the right to alienate the item from the tribe at the time of alienation.

Cultural items in the possession of federal agencies and museums receiving federal funds must be handled in accordance with the law; there are no exclusions or exemptions for noncompliance. If, however, the museum obtained the item "with the voluntary consent of an individual or group that had authority of alienation," then the NAGPRA requirement for repatriation does not apply to that item [25 U.S.C. § 3001(13) (1997)] because the museum has the right of possession and, as the lawful owner, it controls the disposition of the item.

As in criminal theft, NAGPRA requires proof of lack of permission to possess the item in question. Specified activities involving Native American human remains that are undertaken without right of possession violate NAGPRA. The right of possession of human remains is conferred on lineal descendants, and lineal descendancy is difficult to show, as it requires an unbroken chain of descendance [43 C.F.R. § 10.2(b)(1) (1997)].

Prohibited Acts

The purpose of NAGPRA's criminal provisions is to stem the trade in certain cultural items, and thereby protect Native American burial sites and cultural heritage from looting in order to supply that trade [S. Rep. No. 473, 101st Cong., 2d Sess. 11 (1990)]. Thus, the criminal law focuses on financially motivated acts by prohibiting the sale, purchase, use for profit, or transportation for sale or profit of Native American human remains and cultural items. By requiring some financial incident attendant to the violation, the final legislation served to allay the fear of the scientific community that transporting items across state lines for the purposes of study and curation could be a crime.

NAGPRA is violated when a person financially benefits from Native American human remains for which he or she does not have the right of possession, or financially benefits from protected Native American cultural items either by obtaining them from federal or tribal lands, or by evading the repatriation process. As in traditional theft cases, the gravamen of a NAGPRA criminal case is the conversion of another's property to one's benefit without proper authority. Thus, private individuals may return protected items to an Indian tribe or Native Hawaiian organization, or donate them to a museum, without concern for prosecution under NAGPRA, but donating these items in order to take a tax benefit would result in a financial incident, and render the person liable under the criminal law.

Elements of the Offense

The elements of Illegal Trafficking in Native American Human Remains and Cultural Items [18 U.S.C. § 1170 (1997)] are:

(a)   1. financial incident (sale, purchase, use for profit), and

        2. Native American human remains, and

        3. without the right of possession (lineal descendant)[25 U.S.C. § 3001(13) (1997)].

(b)   1. financial incident (sale, purchase, use for profit), and

        2. Native American cultural items (burial, sacred, patrimony), and

        3. in violation of the Act, being either:

            i. removed from federal or tribal land without authority, as determined by Section 3 of the law [25 U.S.C. § 3002) (1997)], or

            ii. transferred without adherence to the repatriation process in Section 7 of the law [25 U.S.C. § 3005 (1997)].

Criminal Intent

NAGPRA is a general intent offense instrument. In other words, the accused must intend the financial result, but need not know that the items were protected. Anyone who deals in Native American cultural items without authority thus assumes the risk that an item belongs to one of the protected categories. It is not a defense to the law that the intended profit was not realized, only that the person *intended* to buy, sell, use for profit, or transport for sale or profit a protected item.

Criminal Penalties

The first conviction for a NAGPRA violation is punishable as a misdemeanor. A second or subsequent violation is a felony punishable by up to five years in prison and/or a fine [18 U.S.C. § 1170(a) (b); 18 U.S.C. § 3571 (1997)]. The law does not address, and therefore does not prohibit, the assessment of restitution to the Indian tribe or Native Hawaiian organization for purposes of reburial or curation.

UNITED STATES v. CORROW

119 F.3d 796 (10th Cir. 1997)

JOHN C. PORFILIO, Circuit Judge:

This appeal raises issues of first impression in this Circuit under the Native American Graves Protection and Repatriation Act, 25 U.S.C. §§ 3001–3013 (NAGPRA); and the Migratory Bird Treaty Act, 16 U.S.C. §§ 701–712 (MBTA). Richard Nelson Corrow challenges the constitutionality of 25 U.S.C. § 3001(3)(D) of NAGPRA which defines "cultural patrimony," the basis for his conviction of trafficking in protected Native American cultural items in violation of 18 U.S.C. § 1170(b). First, he contends the definition is unconstitutionally vague, an argument the district court rejected in denying his motion to dismiss that count of the indictment and to reverse his conviction. *United States v. Corrow*, 941 F. Supp. 1553, 1562 (D. N.M. 1996). Second, he invites us to read a scienter requirement into § 703 of the MBTA to vitiate the government's proof he possessed protected bird feathers. Failing these propositions, he attacks the sufficiency of the evidence supporting his two counts of conviction. We affirm.

I. BACKGROUND

Until his death in 1991, Ray Winnie was a hataali, a Navajo religious singer. For more than twenty-five years Mr. Winnie chanted the Nightway and other Navajo ceremonies wearing Yei B'Chei originally owned by Hosteen Hataali Walker. Yei B'Chei or Yei B'Chei jish are ceremonial adornments, Native American artifacts whose English label, "masks," fails to connote the Navajo perception these cultural items embody living gods. Traditionally, a hataali passes the Yei B'Chei to a family or clan member who has studied the ceremonies or loans the Yei B'Chei to another Navajo clan, Mr. Winnie having acquired his Yei B'Chei from a different clan during his hataali apprenticeship. When Mr. Winnie died, he left no provision for the disposition of his Yei B'Chei, and no family or clan member requested them.

Richard Corrow, the owner of Artifacts Display Stands in Scottsdale, Arizona, is an aficionado of Navajo culture and religion, having, on occasion, participated in Navajo religious ceremonies. Some time after Mr. Winnie's death, Mr. Corrow traveled to Lukachukai, Arizona, to visit Mrs. Fannie Winnie, Mr. Winnie's 81-year-old widow, chatting with her; her granddaughter, Rose Bia; and other family members: a great granddaughter, Harriette Keyonnie; and a son-in-law. During one visit, Mrs. Winnie displayed some Navajo screens and robes, and Mr. Corrow inquired about the Yei B'Chei. By his third visit in August 1993, the Winnie family revealed the Yei B'Chei, twenty-two ceremonial masks, and permitted Mr. Corrow to photograph them. Mr. Corrow told Mrs. Winnie he wanted to buy them, suggesting he planned to deliver the Yei B'Chei to a young Navajo chanter in Utah to keep them sacred. Although Mr. Corrow initially offered $5,000, he readily agreed to the family's price of $10,000 for the Yei B'Chei, five headdresses, and other artifacts. Mr. Corrow drafted a receipt,[1] and Mrs. Winnie, who spoke no English, placed her thumbprint on the document after Ms. Bia read it to her in Navajo.

In November 1994, the owners of the East-West Trading Company in Santa Fe, New Mexico, contacted Mr. Corrow telling him that a wealthy Chicago surgeon was interested in purchasing a set of Yei B'Chei. In fact, the purported buyer was James Tanner, a National Park Service ranger operating undercover on information he had received about questionable trade at East-West. When Agent Tanner visited the business, its owners showed him photographs of seventeen of the twenty-two Yei B'Chei that Mr. Corrow purchased from Mrs. Winnie. In the photos, he noticed eagle and owl feathers in several of the large headdresses and ceremonial sticks bundled with small eagle feathers. After negotiations, Agent Tanner agreed to a purchase price of $70,000 for the Yei B'Chei, $50,000 for Mr. Corrow and a $20,000 commission to East-West's co-owners.

On December 9, 1994, Mr. Corrow arrived at the Albuquerque airport en route to Santa Fe carrying one large suitcase, one small suitcase, and a cardboard box. Yet once he was in Santa Fe, F.B.I. agents became worried East-West's owners had been alerted and abandoned their script for the planned buy, instead directly executing the search warrant. Agents found the two suitcases Mr. Corrow had carried to East-West, one holding Navajo religious objects, small bundles, herbs, mini prayer sticks, and other artifacts adorned with eagle feathers. Another suitcase contained eagle feathers rolled inside several cloth bundles, Yei B'Chei dance aprons, and five headdress pieces made of eagle and owl feathers. In the cardboard box was the set of twenty-two Yei B'Chei.

The government subsequently charged Mr. Corrow in a two-count indictment, Count one for trafficking in Native American cultural items in violation of 18 U.S.C. § 1170, 25 U.S.C. §§ 3001(3)(D), 3002(c), and 18 U.S.C. § 2; and Count two for selling Golden Eagle, Great Horned Owl, and Buteoine Hawk feathers protected by the MBTA in violation of 16 U.S.C. § 703, 16 U.S.C. § 707(b)(2), and 18 U.S.C. § 2. The court rejected Mr. Corrow's pretrial motion to dismiss Count one based on its purported unconstitutional vagueness, and the trial proceeded comprised predominantly of the testimony of expert witnesses clashing over whether the Yei B'Chei constitute "cultural patrimony" protected by NAGPRA. Having concluded they do, the jury convicted Mr. Corrow of illegal trafficking in cultural items, Count one, but acquitted him of Count two, selling protected feathers, instead finding him guilty of committing the lesser included offense, possession of protected feathers. Post-trial, Mr. Corrow attacked his conviction renewing his challenge to the constitutionality of §§ 3001(3)(D) and 3002(c) of NAGPRA and to the sufficiency of the evidence underlying his conviction. *Corrow*, 941 F. Supp. at 1553. The district court denied the motion and sentenced him to two concurrent five-year probationary terms and one hundred hours of community service.

In this renewed challenge, Mr. Corrow asserts the court erred in failing to dismiss Count one on the ground the NAGPRA definition of cultural patrimony is unconstitutionally vague,

---

[1][*Orig. fn.*] The receipt stated: Sold to Richard N. Corrow on this date for cash paid in full, all of the medicine bundles for yei be chai [sic] and fire dance including masks owned by Hosteen Ray Winnie of Lukachucki [sic], AZ. Selling these medicine bundles or jish is the wife of the late Mr. Winnie, Fanny [sic], and his granddaughter Rose, and his great granddaughter, Harriet, whose signatures are below. The selling price is in cash of $10,000. Received by below this date.

trapping the unwary in its multitude of meanings and creating easy prey for the untrammeled discretion of law enforcement.[2] Were NAGPRA's definitional bounds nevertheless discernible, Mr. Corrow then urges the evidence was insufficient to support his conviction on either count. Mr. Corrow acknowledges our de novo review of the legal question he raises, *United States v. Murphy*, 977 F.2d 503, 504 (10th Cir. 1992); and our task of deciding whether substantial evidence, both direct and circumstantial taken together, underpins the conviction to confirm a reasonable jury could find defendant guilty beyond a reasonable doubt. *United States v. Garcia-Emanuel*, 14 F.3d 1469, 1472 (10th Cir. 1994).

II. NAGPRA

Congress enacted NAGPRA in 1990 to achieve two principle objectives: to protect Native American human remains, funerary objects, sacred objects, and objects of cultural patrimony presently on Federal or tribal lands; and to repatriate Native American human remains, associated funerary objects, sacred objects, and objects of cultural patrimony currently held or controlled by Federal agencies and museums. H.R. Rep. No. 101-877, 101st Cong., 2d Sess. 1990, reprinted in 1990 U.S.C.C.A.N. 4367, 4368. The legislation and subsequent regulations, 43 C.F.R. §§ 10.1–10.17, provide a methodology for identifying objects; determining the rights of lineal descendants, Indian tribes and Native Hawaiian organizations; and retrieving and repatriating that property to Native American owners. NAGPRA's reach in protecting against further desecration of burial sites and restoring countless ancestral remains and cultural and sacred items to their tribal homes warrants its aspirational characterization as "human rights legislation." Jack F. Trope & Walter R. Echo-Hawk, *The Native American Graves Protection and Repatriation Act: Background and Legislative History*, 24 Ariz. St. L.J. 35, 37 (1992). Indeed, a Panel of National Dialogue on Museum-Native American Relations, which was convened to address the divergent interests of the museum and Native American communities, reported to Congress that "[r]espect for Native human rights is the paramount principle that should govern resolution of the issue when a claim is made." 1990 U.S.C.C.A.N. 4369–70.

Nonetheless to give teeth to this statutory mission, 18 U.S.C. § 1170 penalizes trafficking in Native American human remains and cultural items and creates a felony offense for a second or subsequent violation. Subsection 1170(b), the basis for prosecution here, states: Whoever knowingly sells, purchases, uses for profit, or transports for sale or profit any Native American cultural items obtained in violation of the Native American Grave Protection and Repatriation Act shall be fined in accordance with this title, imprisoned not more than one year, or both, and in the case of a second or subsequent violation, be fined in accordance with this title, imprisoned not more than 5 years, or both. One must look to NAGPRA, 25 U.S.C. § 3001, for the definition of "cultural item." Section 3001(3) states:

---

[2][*Orig. fn.*] Mr. Corrow does not specifically address 25 U.S.C. § 3002(c) which prohibits the intentional removal of Native American cultural items unless done with (1) a permit; (2) after consultation with or consent of the Indian tribe; and (3) proof of tribal consultation or consent. Our disposition of section 3001(3)(D) subsumes without directly addressing the issue.

"cultural items" means human remains and... (D) "cultural patrimony" which shall mean an object having ongoing historical, traditional, or cultural importance central to the Native American group or culture itself, rather than property owned by an individual Native American, and which, therefore, cannot be alienated, appropriated, or conveyed by any individual regardless of whether or not the individual is a member of the Indian tribe or Native Hawaiian organization and such object shall have been considered inalienable by such Native American group at the time the object was separated from such group.[3]

Thus, to be judged "cultural patrimony"[4] the object must have (1) ongoing historical, cultural, or traditional importance; and (2) be considered inalienable by the tribe by virtue of the object's centrality in tribal culture. That is, the cultural item's essential function within the life and history of the tribe engenders its inalienability such that the property cannot constitute the personal property of an individual tribal member. "The key aspect of this definition is whether the property was of such central importance to the tribe or group that it was owned communally." Francis P. McManamon & Larry V. Nordby, *Implementing the Native American Graves Protection and Repatriation Act*, 24 Ariz. St. L.J. 217, 233–34 (1992). The regulations mirror this definition and incorporate the Senate Report for its version of the bill which did not pass, S. Rep. No. 473, 101st Cong., 2d Sess. 1 (1990). 43 C.F.R. § 10.2(d)(4).[5]

In this prosecution, then, the definition of cultural patrimony divided into its three component parts required the government prove Mr. Corrow trafficked in an object that (1) was not owned by an individual Native American; (2) that could not be alienated, appropriated, or conveyed by an individual; and (3) had an ongoing historical, traditional, or cultural importance central to the Native American group. Mr. Corrow contends the first and second

---

[3][*Orig. fn.*] There are three other components of "cultural items" included in section 3001(3): (A) "associated funerary objects"; (B) "unassociated funerary objects"; and (C) "sacred objects." The government alleged the Yei B'Chei are "cultural patrimony" and has not argued they constitute "sacred objects," defined as "specific ceremonial objects which are needed by traditional Native American religious leaders for the practice of traditional Native American religions by their present day adherents." 16 U.S.C. § 3001(3)(C).

[4][*Orig. fn.*] Webster's Third New International Dictionary defines "patrimony" as "anything derived from one's father or ancestors: HERITAGE; an inheritance from the past; an estate or property held by ancient right."

[5][*Orig. fn.*] 43 C.F.R. § 10.2(d)(4) states: Objects of cultural patrimony means items having ongoing historical, traditional, or cultural importance central to the Indian tribe or Native Hawaiian organization itself, rather than property owned by an individual tribal or organization member. These objects are of such central importance that they may not be alienated, appropriated, or conveyed by any individual tribal or organization member. Such objects must have been considered inalienable by the culturally affiliated Indian tribe or Native Hawaiian organization at the time the object was separated from the group. Objects of cultural patrimony include items such as Zuni War Gods, the Confederacy Wampum Belts of the Iroquois, and other objects of similar character and significance to the Indian tribe or Native Hawaiian organization as a whole.

elements are unintelligible.[6] Thus, he argues, relying upon *United States v. Agnew*, 931 F.2d 1397, 1403 (10th Cir. 1991), the definition does not comport with the due process clause of the Fourteenth Amendment because it fails to give ordinary people fair notice about what conduct is prohibited in such a manner that discourages arbitrary and discriminatory law enforcement.

In support, Mr. Corrow arrays the conflicting expert testimony, characterized by the amicus curiae[7] as a conflict between orthodox and moderate Navajo religious views. For the government, Alfred Yazzie, an ordained hataali and Navajo Nation Historic Preservation representative, testified the Yei B'Chei must remain within the four sacred mountains of the Navajo for they represented the "heartbeat" of the Navajo people.[8] Also for the government, Harry Walters, a Navajo anthropologist, stated there is "no such thing as ownership of medicine bundles and that these are viewed as living entities." He equated ownership with use, knowing the rituals, but acknowledged often cultural items are sold because of economic pressures. For Mr. Corrow, Jackson Gillis, a medicine man from Monument Valley, testified that if no claim is made by a clan relative or other singer, the jish pass to the widow who must care for them. If the widow feels uncomfortable keeping the jish, Mr. Gillis stated she has the right to sell them. Harrison Begay, another of Mr. Corrow's expert witnesses, agreed, explaining that because the masks themselves are "alive," a widow, uneasy about their remaining unused, may sell them. Billy Yellow, another hataali testifying for Mr. Corrow, reiterated the traditional disposition of a hataali's Yei B'Chei to a spouse, the children, and grandchildren, although he stated nobody really owns the jish because they are living gods.

Given these conflicting views on the alienability of the Yei B'Chei, Mr. Corrow asks how an individual, even one educated in Navajo culture, indeed, one accepting the responsibility of inquiring further about the status of the item as the district court deduced from its reading of NAGPRA, can "ascertain ownership when the group itself cannot agree on that point?" The shadow cast by this question, he insists, sufficiently clouds the meaning of "cultural patrimony" to render it unconstitutional. Mr. Corrow's invocation of void-for-vagueness review, however, obfuscates both its doctrinal reach and its application to the facts of this case.

---

[6][*Orig. fn.*] Before the district court, Mr. Corrow challenged the third element as well contending there was nothing unique about these Yei B'Chei. On appeal, he targets only the question of alienability.

[7][*Orig. fn.*] The Antique Tribal Art Dealers Association, a trade organization promoting authenticity and ethical dealing in the sale of Native American artifacts, filed an amicus brief contending the government in this case "exploited a controversy between orthodox and moderate Navajo religious perspectives."

[8][*Orig. fn.*] He stated, "This is my heartbeat, this is my life, this is my teaching. This causes me to behave right. It allows me to teach my children to behave. So it's a God-given gift to the Navajos and it has everything to do with the welfare and the health and wisdom." He explained the hataali is responsible for caring for the jish, restoring them in the event of exposure to the wrong people or places: "when they do come back we would have to use what we call a diagnosis to see what can be done and how we can treat them and bring them back to the respect that they should have." He explained the Navajo tradition of compensating a person who gives his Yei B'Chei to another chanter.

"[T]he void-for-vagueness doctrine requires that a penal statute define the criminal offense with sufficient definiteness that ordinary people can understand what conduct is prohibited and in a manner that does not encourage arbitrary and discriminatory enforcement." *Kolender v. Lawson*, 461 U.S. 352, 357 (1983). Although *Kolender* acknowledged a judicial shift from concern over deciding whether the statute provides actual notice to "the more important aspect of the vagueness doctrine... the requirement that a legislature establish minimal guidelines to govern law enforcement," id. at 358, the legality principle, no crime or punishment without law, is the essence of a Fifth Amendment due process challenge. See 1 W. LaFave & A. Scott, Substantive Criminal Law § 3.1, at 271 (1986). That is, given the limitations of language and syntax, a statute must convey to those individuals within its purview what it purports to prohibit and how it will punish an infraction. While the Court equates that requirement roughly with a notion of "fairness," it swathes it with the constitutional guarantees of the Fifth Amendment.[9]

A couple of applications of these principles are instructive to our review. *In Palmer v. City of Euclid*, 402 U.S. 544 (1971), the Court held a suspicious person municipal ordinance was "so vague and lacking in ascertainable standards of guilt that, as applied to Palmer, it failed to give 'a person of ordinary intelligence fair notice that his contemplated conduct is forbidden.'" Id. at 545 [quoting *United States v. Harriss*, 347 U.S. 612, 617 (1954)]. The city ordinance defined a "suspicious person" as one wandering about the streets at late or unusual hours without visible or lawful business and a satisfactory explanation for his presence. The police had charged James Palmer with violating this ordinance after he had dropped a woman off late at night and then pulled onto the street, parked with his headlights on, and used a two-way radio. Mr. Palmer's imprecise explanation for his behavior coupled with the conduct itself, the police decided, violated the ordinance. The Court held, however, "in our view the ordinance gave insufficient notice to the average person that discharging a friend at an apartment house and then talking on a car radio while parked on the street was enough to show him to be 'without any visible or lawful business.'" Id. at 545–46.

In *Kolender*, the Court invalidated a California criminal statute which required persons loitering or wandering on the streets to provide "credible and reliable" identification. 461 U.S. at 353. Because the statute failed to describe with sufficient particularity "what a suspect must do to satisfy the statute," that is, what constitutes "credible and reliable" identification, the Court found it unconstitutional on its face "because it encourages arbitrary enforcement." Id. at 361. Hence, while *Kolender's* focus is the potential for unrestrained police discretion, that concern remains rooted in the Court's predicate finding the statutory requirement of "credible and reliable" identification is unfair. In void-for-vagueness review "[t]he same facets of a statute usually raise concerns of both fair notice and adequate enforcement standards." *United States v. Gaudreau*, 860 F.2d 357, 359 (10th Cir. 1988). Consequently, under *Kolender's* guidance, we "treat each as an element to be analyzed separately." Id. at 359–60.[10]

---

[9][*Orig. fn.*] When a federal statute is involved, the due process clause of the Fifth Amendment is implicated. However, a void-for-vagueness challenge to a state statute involves the Fourteenth Amendment's due process clause.

[10][*Orig. fn.*] Gaudreau delineates the differences in void-for-vagueness review when a criminal rather than a civil statute is involved. *United States v. Gaudreau*, 860 F.2d 357, 360 (10th Cir. 1988).

However, the Court has made equally clear our analysis is not global. "[V]agueness challenges to statutes which do not involve First Amendment freedoms must be examined in the light of the facts of the case at hand." *United States v. Mazurie*, 419 U.S. 544, 550 (1975). Thus, to succeed, the proponent "who engages in some conduct that is clearly proscribed [by the challenged statute] cannot complain of the vagueness of the law as applied to the conduct of others." *Village of Hoffman Estates v. Flipside, Hoffman Estates, Inc.*, 455 U.S. 489, 495 (1982); *United States v. Austin*, 902 F.2d 743, 745 (9th Cir. 1990). Further, in a facial challenge raising no First Amendment or other claim that the act reaches constitutionally protected conduct, the complainant "must demonstrate that the law is impermissibly vague in all of its applications." Id. at 497.

Mr. Corrow cannot meet that burden. First, deciding whether the statute gave him fair notice, the district court found, after reviewing all of the expert testimony, Mr. Corrow is knowledgeable about Navajo traditions and culture and "would have been aware that various tribal members viewed ownership of property differently." 941 F. Supp. at 1560. The court cited the testimony of Ms. Charlotte Frisbie, author of *Navajo Medicine Bundles or Jish: Acquisition, Transmission and Disposition in the Past and Present* (1987). Ms. Frisbie related several calls from Mr. Corrow inquiring about the prices of certain Navajo artifacts. Id. at 1562 n. 13. Although she stated he did not specifically ask her about these Yei B'Chei, she expressed her objection to dealers and commercial handlers selling Native American cultural objects in the open market. Id. Ms. Frisbie also reminded him both of the Navajo Nation's implementing procedures to return cultural items and of the enactment of NAGPRA. Id. Most damning, Ms. Bia, Mrs. Winnie's granddaughter, recounted Mr. Corrow's representation that he wanted to buy the Yei B'Chei to pass on to another young chanter in Utah. Reasonably, a jury could infer from that representation that Mr. Corrow appreciated some dimension of the Yei B'Chei's inherent inalienability in Navajo culture. Although Mrs. Winnie stated she believed the Yei B'Chei belonged to her, she testified, "[t]here was another man that knew the ways and he had asked of [the Yei B'Chei] but I was the one that was stalling and ended up selling it." Id. at 1565. Although this man trained with her husband, he had not offered her any money. This is not a case of an unsuspecting tourist happening upon Mrs. Winnie's hogan and innocently purchasing the set of Yei B'Chei. Nor is it even close to *Palmer* or *Kolender* where the unwary had no means or ability to discern their conduct violated the acts in question.

Surely, this evidence establishes Mr. Corrow had some notice the Yei B'Chei he purchased were powerfully connected to Navajo religion and culture. While it may be true that even the experts in that culture differed in their views on alienability, no expert testified it was acceptable to sell Yei B'Chei to non-Navajos who planned to resell them for a profit, the very conduct § 1170(b) penalizes. All experts testified the Yei B'Chei resided within the Four Corners of the Navajo people and acknowledged the ritual cleansing and restoration required were the Yei B'Chei to be defiled in any way. Thus, while the parameters of the designation "cultural patrimony" might be unclear in some of its applications and at its edges, there is no doubt, in this case as applied to Mr. Corrow, the Yei B'Chei were cultural items which could not be purchased for a quick $40,000 turn of profit. Indeed, the Court observed in *Hoffman Estates*, 455 U.S. at 494 n. 6, that "ambiguous meanings cause citizens to 'steer far wider of the unlawful zone'...than if the boundaries of the forbidden areas were clearly marked.'" *Baggett v. Bullitt*, 377 U.S. 360, 372 (1964) [quoting *Speiser v. Randall*, 357 U.S. 513, 526 (1958)] (internal quotation marks omitted). Consequently, even if the term cultural patrimony "might reflect some uncertainty as applied to extreme situations, the conduct for which [defendant] was prosecuted and convicted falls squarely within the core of the [Act]." *United States v. Amer*, 110 F.3d 873, 878 (2d Cir. 1997) [challenge to International Parental Kidnapping Crime Act attacking such terms as "lawful exercise of parental rights" as unconstitutionally vague failed where defendant's retention of three children in Egypt when at least two of the children were born in New York and other child had stayed in New York for eight years was clearly proscribed by IPKCA].

Consequently, we believe Mr. Corrow had fair notice—if not of the precise words of NAGPRA—of their meaning that Native American objects "having ongoing historical, traditional, or cultural importance central to the Native American group... rather than property owned by an individual Native American" could not be bought and sold absent criminal consequences. Moreover, contrary to Mr. Corrow's assertion, § 3001(3)(D) is not infirm because it fails to list examples of cultural items. "In short, due process does not require that citizens be provided actual notice of all criminal rules and their meanings. The Constitution is satisfied if the necessary information is reasonably obtainable by the public." *United States v. Vasarajs*, 908 F.2d 443, 449 (9th Cir. 1990) (citations to LaFave & Scott omitted) (statute barring reentry onto military base was not unconstitutionally vague because it failed to inform individuals of the precise boundaries of the base).

While not dispositive, we would add § 1170(b) includes scienter as an element of the offense ("Whoever knowingly sells, purchases, uses for profit..."). "A statutory requirement that an act must be willful or purposeful may not render certain, for all purposes, a statutory definition of the crime which is in some respects uncertain. But it does relieve the statute of the objection that it punishes without warning an offense of which the accused was unaware." *Screws v. United States*, 325 U.S. 91, 101–02 (1945) (Douglas, J., concurring). Here, the government was required to prove Mr. Corrow knowingly used the Yei B'Chei for profit assuring his understanding of the prohibited zone of conduct.[11] "[A] scienter requirement may mitigate a criminal law's vagueness by ensuring that it punishes only those who are aware their conduct is unlawful." *Gaudreau*, 860 F.2d at 360.

Our analysis of the fairness issue infuses our disposition of the second vagueness concern, the potential for arbitrary and discriminatory enforcement. Unlike the police in *Kolender* who had complete discretion to judge what "reliable and credible" identification might be, in this case, as the district court found, the statute as applied caused law enforcement offic-

---

[11][*Orig. fn.*] We do not say that a scienter requirement alone will rescue an otherwise vague statute, recognizing "it is possible willfully to bring about certain results and yet be without fair warning that such conduct is proscribed." 1 W. LaFave & A. Scott, Jr., Substantive Criminal Law § 2.3, at 131 (1986). We would add in Sherry Hutt, *Illegal Trafficking in Native American Human Remains and Cultural Items: A New Protection Tool*, 24 Ariz. St. L.J. 135, 146 (1992), the author states as a general-intent crime, "the prosecution must prove that the defendant knew he was engaging in a financial activity, but need not prove that the defendant knew that the item was protected. One who deals in Native American cultural items does so at the risk that an item may be protected by NAGPRA. Failure to realize an intended profit is not a defense to a section 4 violation. If the defendant bought, sold, used for profit, or transported for intended sale or profit a protected item, the law is violated, regardless of the actual beneficial outcome of the transaction." The discussion, of course, presumes the constitutionality of NAGPRA and its penalty provision.

ers to inquire of tribal officials to determine whether the cultural item in question constituted cultural patrimony. 941 F. Supp. at 1564. Here, the Department of the Interior National Park Service officer, Mr. Young, examined a photograph of the Yei B'Chei and discussed their significance with other knowledgeable Park Service officers and representatives of the Navajo Nation before deciding the items constituted cultural patrimony. Mr. Young testified he participated in other NAGPRA investigations and was aware that law enforcement officers must first consult with tribal representatives to determine whether an item has ongoing historical, cultural, or traditional importance. We conclude, therefore, as applied to Mr. Corrow, § 1170(b) provides sufficient guidance to law enforcement to dispel the fear of subjective enforcement.[12] We affirm the district court's denial of Mr. Corrow's motion to dismiss Count One.

Having failed in his constitutional challenge, Mr. Corrow urges we examine the same evidence which defeated the legal claim to support his contention the government failed to prove Mrs. Winnie was not the rightful owner of the Yei B'Chei. The evidence we detailed infra the expert and family members' testimony as well as that of Forest Service agents—viewed in the government's favor—satisfies us that a rational jury could find beyond a reasonable doubt the Yei B'Chei are cultural patrimony which Mr. Corrow could not resell for profit. We therefore affirm the district court's denial of the motion for judgment of acquittal on Count One.

* * *

Note

In *Corrow,* both sides utilized the testimony of expert witnesses as to tribal custom and tradition. That opinions may differ affects only the weight the trier of fact may give to the evidence, and not the admissibility of such evidence. Corrow claimed that he had no notice that the item was cultural pat-

---

[12][*Orig. fn.*] We would note there have been similar challenges to federal statutes protecting items deemed antiquities under the Antiquities Act of 1906, 16 U.S.C. § 431–433 (1988), and the Archeological Resources Protection Act (ARPA), 16 U.S.C. §§ 470aa–470mm. Although the Ninth Circuit invalidated the Antiquities Act, sustaining a challenge to its penalizing appropriating "objects of antiquity situated on lands owned and controlled by the Government of the United States," as applied to taking three- or four-year-old face masks from a cave, *United States v. Diaz*, 499 F.2d 113 (9th Cir. 1974), we upheld the same act in *United States v. Smyer*, 596 F.2d 939 (10th Cir. 1979), where defendants excavated a prehistoric Mimbres ruin at an archeological site, removing objects of antiquity. We held in light of defendants' conduct, the Antiquities Act was not unconstitutionally vague. Later, the Ninth Circuit upheld the Antiquities' Act's successor, ARPA, in *United States v. Austin*, 902 F.2d 743 (9th Cir. 1990). Defendant there unsuccessfully argued the terms, "weapons" and "tools" were unconstitutionally vague, the court's having found regarding defendant "there can be no doubt nor lack of fair notice that the scrapers and arrow points for which he was convicted are indeed weapons and tools." Id. at 745. These predecessors were instructive to the district court's analysis.

rimony. The court applied a reasonableness standard that relied on the reasonable knowledge of the perpetrator, rather than a reasonable person. This standard does not imply a specific intent requirement, it merely clarifies the test for knowledge, or lack thereof, when it is asserted as a defense.

Civil Enforcement of NAGPRA

NAGPRA includes a penalty section that applies to a museum that fails to comply with the requirements of the Act [25 U.S.C. § 3007 (1997)]. The drafters of the law wished to make it clear that compliance was not an option or an eventual occurrence, and directed that penalties be assessed after due process, taking into account the value of the item and the damages to the aggrieved party [25 U.S.C. § 3007(b) (1997)]. The civil assessment process is detailed in the NAGPRA regulations [Civil Penalties Interim Rule, 62 Fed. Reg. 1,820 (1997); final rule to be codified at 43 C.F.R. § 10.12].

The NAGPRA civil penalty process mirrors that of ARPA. A notice of failure to comply is issued to the museum by the designee of the Secretary of Interior, who is the Director of the National Park Service. The notice must state the provisions of the law believed to have been violated and the penalty. The museum also must be advised of the right to seek a hearing and judicial review, or to pay the penalty amount.

If a hearing is requested by the museum, the petition for relief must state whether they contest the penalty or the amount, and it must be filed with the Secretary of the Interior within 45 days of service of the notice of failure to comply. If no petition for relief is filed, the Director of the National Park Service issues a notice of assessment, which becomes a judgment that can be submitted to the United States Attorney's office for a collection action if payment is not received within 45 days. If a hearing is requested, it is held before a Department of the Interior ALJ, whose findings are appealable to the United States district court.

4. National Marine Sanctuaries Act

Full treatment of this statute and its implementing regulations is found in the chapter entitled "Heritage Resources Law in the Marine Environment." The National Marine Sanctuaries Act (NMSA) provides a mandate for integrated management and protection of natural and heritage resources in specified, federally protected areas of the marine environment. Study of the evolving case law, in which the enforcement provisions of the NMSA are applied to looting and other recovery of heritage resources within these marine areas, reveals how the courts are addressing issues in submerged heritage resources law that traditionally were the domain of the admiralty law of salvage and the law of finds. In addition, comparing the effectiveness of the civil penalty provisions of the NMSA with the criminal and civil sanctions that may be available under other laws might be useful.

5. Heritage Resources Regulations of Land Managing Agencies

Each land managing agency has limited enforcement authority through rules published in the Code of Federal Regulations. Most of the specific regulations pertaining to protection of cultural resources were modeled on the Antiquities Act. After the criminal enforcement provision of the Antiquities Act was found unconstitutional by the Ninth Circuit Court of Appeals in *Diaz*, the cultural resources protection regulations were rewritten and modeled after ARPA. Regulatory enforcement is effectuated by an enforcement agent for the land managing agency issuing a citation to the violator. The defendant then is entitled to a hearing before a federal magistrate, or may elect to pay the fine.

6. Future Legislation

As protection for archeological resources has heightened, the theft of paleontological resources from public and Indian lands has grown. Congress attempted numerous times to draft specific legislation to protect fossils— which are not protected by ARPA or the Antiquities Act—but without success. These resources, however, remain government or Indian property if they are on public or Indian lands, and subject to laws prohibiting theft and injury to property [see also Note, *Bones of Contention: The Regulation of Paleontological Resources on the Federal Public Lands*, 69 Ind. L.J. 601 (1994) (authored by David Lazerwitz)].

BLACK HILLS INSTITUTE OF GEOLOGICAL RESEARCH, INC. v. WILLIAMS

88 F.3d 614 (8th Cir. 1996)

MAGILL, Circuit Judge:

The Black Hills Institute of Geological Research, Inc. (the Institute) appeals the district court's (footnote omitted) holding that it was not entitled to a $209,000 lien against a tyrannosaurus rex fossil for work performed in excavating and preparing the fossil. We affirm.

I.

The facts surrounding the discovery, excavation, and preparation of the fossil are discussed at length *in Black Hills Inst. of Geological Research v. South Dakota Sch. of Mines & Tech.*, 12 F.3d 737 (8th Cir. 1993) (Black Hills III), *cert. denied*, ___ U.S. ___, 115 S. Ct. 61 (1994). We will discuss herein only those facts necessary for this appeal.

In August 1990, employees of the Institute discovered a tyrannosaurus rex fossil on Maurice Williams's land. The Institute excavated the fossil and gave $5,000 to Williams, allegedly in exchange for title to the fossil. Over the course of the next few years, the Institute spent approximately $209,000 in excavating and preparing the fossil.

Williams's land, however, is located within the Cheyenne River Sioux Indian Reservation of South Dakota, which is held in trust for Williams by the United States. On December 15, 1993, this Court concluded that the fossil was held in trust by the United States for Williams and, as such, it was not alienable by Williams absent approval by the Department of the Interior (DOI). See id. at 742–44 (applying 25 U.S.C. §§ 464 and 483). Because the fossil was removed from the land without the knowledge or consent of the United States, the attempted sale was void and the Institute had no legal right, title, or interest in the fossil as severed from the land.

On February 8, 1994, the Institute filed a lien statement under South Dakota law, asserting a $209,000 lien against the fossil. The Institute then filed a complaint in South Dakota state court seeking either a statutory or common law lien on the fossil for the work performed in excavating and preparing it.

The case was removed to the federal district court for the District of South Dakota. The district court granted summary judgment in favor of the defendants. The court noted that the Institute did not meet the requirements for a statutory lien, and the court refused to impose an equitable lien on the grounds that the Institute acted with willful blindness to statutes which clearly precluded the Institute from gaining rights to the fossil absent government permission. The Institute now appeals.

II.

The law of this case is that the fossil, even after severance from the land, is held in trust by the United States for Williams and is not alienable by Williams absent DOI approval. See id. The Institute conceded this at oral argument, but nevertheless contends that because it spent a considerable amount of money in excavating the fossil while under a mistaken belief that the fossil was alienable, it is entitled to an equitable or statutory lien. We disagree.

A.

An equitable lien "is implied and declared by a court of equity out of general considerations of right and justice as applied to the relations of the parties and the circumstances of their dealings." In re *Doyen*, 56 B.R. 632, 633 (Bankr. D.S.D. 1986) [citing *Farmers & Merchants Bank v. Commissioner of Internal Revenue*, 175 F.2d 846, 849 (8th Cir. 1949)]; see also *Dorman v. Crooks State Bank*, 55 SD 209, 225 NW 661, 664 (1929) (describing equitable lien). While equity will impose a lien in favor of a bona fide purchaser who improves the purchased item in the mistaken belief that he is the true owner, equity will not impose a lien in favor of one who makes improvements knowing that title is in another. See 41 Am. Jur. 2d, Improvements s 11 (1995).

In the present case, the district court concluded that the Institute did not act in good faith in excavating the fossil, noting that [The Institute] was willfully blind to the existing statutes and regulations governing Indian trust land. Had [the institute] spent the time necessary to research the law, the only inescapable conclusion would have been that [the Institute] had no right to the fossil without the government's permission. Mem. Op. at 8 (D. S.D. Aug. 11, 1995). Because the conclusion that the Institute acted in bad faith is a factual determination, we review only for clear error. See *Garwood v. American Motorists Ins. Co.*, 775 F.2d 228, 231 (8th Cir. 1985).

This Court has already noted that the Institute could have taken any number of steps to protect itself and that the fact "that the fossil was embedded in land located within the boundaries of the Cheyenne River Sioux Indian Reservation should have alerted Black Hills to the possibility that the federal government had some interest in [the fossil]." *Black Hills III*, 12 F.3d at 744. It is a long settled rule that a party who has knowledge of facts that would cast doubt upon the transferability of title has a duty to investigate that title, and that a lack of caution and diligence in such situations amounts to bad faith. See State ex rel. *Dept. of Revenue v. Karras*, 515 NW2d 248, 251 (SD 1994) ("notice of facts which would put a prudent person upon inquiry[ ] impeaches the good faith of the subsequent purchaser") [quoting *Betts v. Letcher*, 1 SD 182, 46 NW 193, 196 (1890)]; see also *Moelle v. Sherwood*, 148 U.S. 21, 30 (1893) (bona fide nature of transaction depends in part on reasonable diligence in ascertaining whether transfer is a "mere speculative chance in the property"); *Brush v. Ware*, 40 U.S. (15 Pet) 93, 111 (1841) (having failed to diligently investigate known facts which cast doubt upon validity of title, the purchaser cannot prejudice the rights of innocent persons through his negligence). Given the Institute's failure to diligently investigate whether the fossil could be alienated absent government approval, it cannot be considered a good faith, bona fide purchaser. It is therefore not entitled to an equitable lien in its favor.

B.

The Institute also contends that a statutory lien may be imposed in its favor. Under South Dakota law, the lien ceases 120 days after any work, skill, services, or material was furnished to the fossil, unless a statement of lien is filed within this period. S.D.C.L. § 44-9-15 (1983). The last day any work was performed on the fossil—the day it was seized by federal authorities—was May 14, 1992. The lien statement was not filed until February 8, 1994, well after the expiration of the filing period. Because the statute is quite clear that the 120-day clock begins to run upon the completion of the work, and not upon the date when the parties' interests in the item are finally adjudicated, the Institute does not meet the requirements for a statutory lien.

III.

The Institute is not entitled to either an equitable lien or a statutory lien. Therefore, the decision of the district court is affirmed.

SECTION C.   GENERAL FEDERAL ENFORCEMENT STATUTES AND REGULATIONS THAT MAY BE APPLIED TO HERITAGE RESOURCES

1.   Federal Criminal Statutes

As a result of *Diaz* and the attenuation of the Antiquities Act penalty provision, federal prosecutors looked to laws in the federal Criminal Code to deter heritage resources destruction. These statutes remain viable tools for enforcement.

Theft of, and Injury to, Government Property

Cultural resources on federal lands are government property, and the appropriation of government property without permission constitutes theft, in violation of 18 U.S.C. § 641 (1997). Government property also is protected against vandalism, destruction, or other injury [18 U.S.C. § 1361 (1997)]. Consequently, excavation of heritage resources on public lands and the removal of these resources without a permit are violations of federal criminal law.

UNITED STATES v. JONES

607 F.2d 269 (9th Cir. 1979)

TANG, Circuit Judge:

On December 22, 1977 Forest Service officers and archaeologists allegedly observed the defendants, Kyle Jones, Thayde Jones, and Robert Gevara, digging in Indian ruins located on federal government land in the Brooklyn Basin of the Cave Creek Range District of the Tonto National Forest. The officers arrested the defendants, and a grand jury returned a two count indictment. Count I of the indictment charged that the defendants wilfully and knowingly stole Indian artifacts consisting of clay pots, bone awls, stone metates and human skeletal remains, of a value in excess of $100, in violation of 18 U.S.C. §§ 641 and 2. Count II charged that the defendants, by means of a pick and shovel, injured the Indian ruins located in the Brooklyn Basin of the Cave Creek Range District of the Tonto National Forest, causing damage to the property in excess of $100, in violation of 18 U.S.C. §§ 1361 and 2.

The defendants moved to dismiss the indictments, and in a published opinion, *United States v. Jones*, 449 F. Supp. 42 (D. Ariz. 1978), the district court granted the motion. After reviewing the legislative history of the Antiquities Act, 16 U.S.C. § 433, and the theft and malicious mischief statutes, 18 U.S.C. §§ 641 and 1361, the district court concluded that

Congress intended that the Antiquities Act be the exclusive means of prosecuting the conduct alleged in the indictment. Because this court had previously held that the penal provision of the Antiquities Act was unconstitutionally vague, *United States v. Diaz*, 499 F.2d 113 (9th Cir. 1974),[1] the Government's inability under the ruling to proceed under 18 U.S.C. § 641 or § 1361 meant that there was no statute under which the defendants could be prosecuted. The Government appeals the dismissal of the indictments. We reverse.

Initially, we set forth the statutes in question. The penal provision of the Antiquities Act, 16 U.S.C. § 433, provides that: Any person who shall appropriate, excavate, injure, or destroy any historic or prehistoric ruin or monument, or any object of antiquity, situate on lands owned or controlled by the Government of the United States, without the permission of the Secretary of the Department of the Government having jurisdiction over the lands on which said antiquities are situated, shall, upon conviction, be fined in a sum of not more than $500 or be imprisoned for a period of not more than ninety days, or shall suffer both fine and imprisonment, in the discretion of the court. Under 18 U.S.C. § 641: Whoever embezzles, steals, purloins, or knowingly converts to his use or the use of another, or without authority, sells, conveys or disposes of any record, voucher, money, or thing of value of the United States or of any department or agency thereof, or any property made or being made under contract for the United States or any department or agency thereof; or Whoever receives, conceals, or retains the same with intent to convert it to his use or gain, knowing it to have been embezzled, stolen, purloined or converted shall be fined not more than $10,000 or imprisoned not more than ten years, or both; but if the value of such property does not exceed the sum of $100, he shall be fined not more than $1,000 or imprisoned not more than one year, or both. The word "value" means face, par, or market value, or cost price, either wholesale or retail, whichever is greater. Under 18 U.S.C. § 1361: Whoever willfully injures or commits any depredation against any property of the United States, or of any department or agency thereof, or any property which has been or is being manufactured or constructed for the United States, or any department or agency thereof, shall be punished as follows: If the damage to such property exceeds the sum of $100, by a fine of not more than $10,000 or imprisonment for not more than ten years, or both; if the damage to such property does not exceed the sum of $100, by a fine of not more than $1,000 or by imprisonment for not more than one year, or both.

We have encountered a number of situations where certain conduct is proscribed by more than one statute. The rule we apply is straightforward: "where an act violates more than one statute, the Government may elect to prosecute under either unless the congressional history indicates that Congress intended to disallow the use of the more general statute." *United States v. Castillo-Felix*, 539 F.2d 9, 14 (9th Cir. 1976). See *United States v. Batchelder*, ___ U.S. ___, ___, 99 S. Ct. 2198 (1979); *United States v. Gomez-Tostado*, 597 F.2d 170 (9th Cir. 1979); *United States v. Burnett*, 505 F.2d 815 (9th Cir. 1974), *cert. denied*, 420 U.S. 966 (1975); *United States v. Brown*, 482 F.2d 1359 (9th Cir. 1973). Repeals by implication are not favored, and effect should be given to overlapping statutes where possible. *Burnett*, 505 F.2d at 816. See *United States v. Georgia-Pacific Co.*, 421 F.2d 92, 102 (9th Cir. 1970).

---

[1][*Orig. fn.*] In *United States v. Smyer*, 596 F.2d 939 (10th Cir. 1979), the Tenth Circuit disagreed with our conclusion, and held that the penal provision of the Antiquities Act was not unconstitutionally vague.

The district court acknowledged this rule, *Jones*, 449 F. Supp. at 43, but held that our analysis in *Kniess v. United States*, 413 F.2d 752 (9th Cir. 1969), was controlling. In *Kniess*, a defendant who was charged with passing counterfeit postal money orders pleaded guilty to violations of both 18 U.S.C. § 472 (passing counterfeit securities) and 18 U.S.C. § 500 (passing forged postal money orders). After reviewing the congressional history of § 500, and observing that Congress had consistently designated a more lenient punishment for § 500 than § 472 each time it reenacted § 500, we concluded that Congress intended that § 500 be the exclusive means of prosecuting the conduct in question, and vacated Kniess's sentence under § 472.

In light of *Kniess*, the district court undertook a review of the historical development of both the Antiquities Act and 18 U.S.C. §§ 641 and 1361. Because the Antiquities Act, in addition to proscribing destruction of ruins penally, also authorized the President to declare National Monuments by proclamation and provided for the issuance of permits for the examination and excavation of ruins, the court concluded that the act set out a "comprehensive method" for protecting remains that are still in the public domain or on Indian reservations. *Jones*, 449 F. Supp. at 44 [citing H.R. Rep. No. 2224, 59 Cong., 1st Sess. (1906)].

The court then turned to the history of the present theft and malicious mischief statutes. It found that §§ 641 and 1361 originated in § 47 of the Act of March 4, 1909, ch. 321, § 48, 35 Stat. 1095, 1096–98, which prohibited theft of government property.[2] Because § 47 differed little from the theft statute in existence when the Antiquities Act was passed,[3] the court concluded that Congress, in passing the Antiquities Act either assumed that Indian ruins and artifacts were not "property" within the meaning of the theft statutes, or that five years imprisonment was too harsh a punishment for this type of conduct. Although injury to government property was not prohibited until § 35 of the Act of March 4, 1909 was amended in 1937, the court concluded that § 35 was amended to prevent injury to the same property protected by the theft statute and therefore § 35, like § 47, did not apply to Indian artifacts and ruins regulated by the Antiquities Act.

We compliment the district court's thoughtful consideration of this issue, but we are compelled to disagree with its conclusion. We begin our analysis by stressing that the alleged conduct of the defendants is prohibited by the express language of §§ 641 and 1361. There can be little doubt that the ruins located in the Tonto National Forest and the relics found on the ruins are the property of the United States government. The issue, then, is whether the passage of the Antiquities Act makes inapplicable the plain language of the §§ 641 and 1361.[4]

---

[2][*Orig. fn.*] Section 47 provided that Whoever shall embezzle, steal, or purloin any money, property, record, voucher, or valuable thing whatever, of the moneys, goods, chattels, records, or property of the United States, shall be fined not more than five thousand dollars, or imprisoned not more than five years, or both.

[3][*Orig. fn.*] The Act of March 3, 1875, 18 Stat. 479 provided that any person who shall embezzle, steal, or purloin any money, property, record, voucher, or valuable thing whatever, of the moneys, goods, chattels, records, or property of the United States, shall be deemed guilty of felony.

[4][*Orig. fn.*] In general, we are reluctant to look beyond the express language of the statute where the statute is unambiguous. See *Intern. Tel. & Tel. Corp. v. General Tel. & Elec. Corp.*, 518 F.2d 913, 917–18 (9th Cir. 1975).

We restate the rule: where statutory coverage overlaps, the Government may elect to prosecute under either statute "unless the congressional history indicates that Congress intended to disallow the use of the more general statute." *Castillo-Felix*, 539 F.2d at 14. We think that the district court gave too much weight and accorded too much significance to the sparse legislative history[5] of the statutes in question. From our examination of this history, we find no indication that Congress, in passing the Antiquities Act, meant to limit the applicability of the general theft statutes; nor do we find that Congress in passing the general statutes, intended that they would not apply to conduct covered by the Antiquities Act. The history of each statute is simply silent on the effect it would have on the other statute. Given this silence, we cannot find that Congress intended to disallow use of the more general statute. See id.

The district court labeled the Antiquities Act a "comprehensive" method for protecting Indian remains and inferred from this that it was designed as the sole means of prosecuting the conduct it proscribes. We do not think, however, that even if the Antiquities Act was "comprehensive" that, without more, we can infer that Congress intended that it be the exclusive means of dealing with this conduct. Otherwise, we would be required to ascribe to Congress an intent to limit the punishment of theft and depredation on Indian ruins by means of a $500 fine, no matter how great the theft or depredation. This we cannot do. Where the statute applies to the conduct in question and there is no affirmative evidence that Congress intended to limit the application of the more general statute, the prosecutor is free to elect to prosecute under either. We cannot ignore the plain meaning and application of a statute unless Congress affirmatively indicates that it intends that the statute should not apply. In the absence of such evidence, we must assume that Congress meant what it said.

We are also unpersuaded by the district court's analysis of the historical development of the general theft and depredation statutes. We are willing to assume that, when Congress enacted the general statutes it did not specifically contemplate whether they would apply to theft and depredation on Indian lands. Where the words and purpose of a statute plainly apply to a particular situation, however, the fact that the specific application of the statute never occurred to Congress does not bar us from holding that the situation falls within the statute's coverage. See *Patagonia Corp. v. Board of Governors of the Federal Reserve System*, 517 F.2d 803, 811 (9th Cir. 1975); *Eastern Airlines v. Civil Aeronautics Board*, 122 U.S. App. D.C. 375, 354 F.2d 507, 510–11 (D.C. Cir. 1965).

Kniess is distinguishable. In *Kniess*, by tracing the history of several enactments of the narrow statute, we found that Congress intended that the narrow statute should preclude application of the more general statute. Such was not the case here. Other than the mere passage of the Antiquities Act and the scant history surrounding its enactment, there was nothing from which we can infer that Congress intended to preclude resort to the general theft and depredation statutes. Unlike *Kniess*, there has been here only congressional silence since the passage of the narrow statute.

---

[5][*Orig. fn.*] The Senate report accompanying the Antiquities Act, S. Rep. No. 3937, 59th Cong., 1st Sess. (1906) is only one page long; the House report, H.R. Rep. No. 2224, 59th Cong., 1st Sess. (1906), is only eight pages in length, six pages of which merely described the ruins that would be covered under the Act.

There is another meaningful distinction between this case and *Kniess*. In *Kniess*, where the narrow statute required proof of guilty knowledge and the general statute did not, we minimized the significance of the difference in language contained in the statutes. *Kniess*, 413 F.2d at 754. Because the narrow statute also carried a lesser penalty, we found it implausible that Congress would adopt a statutory scheme in which the more specific a person's guilty knowledge the less severe was his penalty. The present case is different. The Government must prove specific intent as an element of the proof of a violation of §§ 641 or 1361, see *Ailsworth v. United States*, 448 F.2d 439 (9th Cir. 1971), but specific intent is not an element of 16 U.S.C. § 433. On the other hand, §§ 641 and 1361 provide greater penalties than § 433. Thus, there exists a rational statutory framework in which the degree of punishment corresponds to the presence of specific intent. In contrast to the situation in *Kniess*, our interpretation of the overlapping statutes is compatible with a rational congressional policy.

Reversed and remanded.

Note

The case against the defendants was reinstated, but before trial, ARPA became law. Rather than risk conviction of felonies carrying sentences of 10 years, the defendants preferred to enter into a plea agreement calling for dismissal of the original charges and the filing of an ARPA complaint. The defendants then pled guilty to ARPA felony counts and became the first persons convicted under ARPA. One of the defendants received a sentence of 18 months incarceration, which for 10 years stood as the longest prison sentence for an ARPA violation.

Embezzlement from Indian Tribes

Because Indian tribes themselves do not have jurisdiction to prosecute felonies in tribal court, theft from tribal organizations is subject to federal prosecution [18 U.S.C. § 1163 (1997)]. Evidence of the particular tribal law determines whether the item alleged to have been taken was removed without permission, as tribal law or custom is controlling with regard to ownership and the ability to dispose of property. Tribal organizations may own property communally, or may have inalienable property that is in the custody and care of a tribal member.

Archeological resources on Indian lands are the property of the Indian landowner, regardless of anthropological association. Native American cultural items on tribal lands are property of the Indian tribe or Native Hawaiian organization, subject only to the rights of lineal descendants to human remains of their ancestors. Tribal landowners do not have a fiduciary responsibility to protect heritage resources located on their lands but associated with other groups, but they do have the rights of a property owner, and may seek federal prosecution of anyone who violates those rights.

Theft of Major Artwork

It is a federal felony offense to steal "objects of cultural heritage" from an American museum if the object is "(A) over 100 years old and worth in excess of $5,000, or (B) worth at least $100,000." [18 U.S.C. § 668 (1996)]. This statute also prohibits receiving, concealing, exhibiting, or disposing of items known to have been stolen.

National Stolen Property Act

The first section of the National Stolen Property Act prohibits the transportation in interstate or foreign commerce of any goods that are stolen and have a value of $5,000 or more [18 U.S.C. § 2314 (1997)]. The Act also punishes anyone who receives, conceals, stores, barters, sells, or disposes of any goods that are stolen, have a value of over $5,000, and are moved in interstate or foreign commerce [18 U.S.C. § 2315 (1997)]. It has been invoked to reclaim property belonging to other governments that was brought into this country illegally. The National Stolen Property Act also may be used to prosecute individuals who steal property within the boundaries of the United States and move the items interstate, and who export or import stolen property. Violations of the Act may be punished by a fine of up to $10,000 and/or incarceration of up to 10 years. The National Stolen Property Act does not preclude the government from requesting restitution to pay for curation or restoration of the item. Of course, in addition to the penalties, the stolen item is confiscated and returned to the victim.

The National Stolen Property Act is a general intent offense instrument. The government must prove the defendants knew they were transporting stolen property and did not have title to it, but it need not prove that the defendants specifically knew the property laws of the country from which the items were taken. Also, it is sufficient for the government to indicate in the pleadings that property was stolen under federal, state, or foreign law without stating the content of the law. A trial for violation of the Act is, in effect, a trial within a trial. First, the underlying theft is proved, and then the prosecution proves that the items were transported in interstate or foreign commerce after the theft.

The value of the item stolen must be determined in order to establish that the action qualifies for enforcement under the Act, and it may be established in several ways. The standard test for value is the fair-market value, or what a willing buyer will pay to a willing seller. While in transit or hiding, the stolen item may have a value to the defendant that is substantially higher than a similar item that is lawfully held, and the law allows the higher value to be utilized to meet the legal threshold.

UNITED STATES v. HOLLINSHEAD

495 F.2d 1154 (9th Cir. 1974)

DUNIWAY, Circuit Judge:

These are consolidated appeals from judgments of conviction of conspiracy to transport stolen property in interstate commerce and of causing the transportation of stolen property in interstate commerce in violation of 18 U.S.C. § 2314. Between them, Fell and Hollinshead raise nine claims of error. However only one of them is sufficiently colorable to warrant serious consideration.

In barest outline, the salient facts are these. Hollinshead, a dealer in pre-Columbian artifacts, arranged with one Alamilla, a co-conspirator, to procure such artifacts in Central America, and to finance Alamilla in doing so. Although there were other such artifacts handled by the conspirators, the evidence centered primarily on one of them. This is a pre-Columbian stele known as Machaquila Stele 2, a rare and choice item worth many thousands of dollars. It was found in a Mayan ruin in the jungle of Guatemala, cut into pieces, and brought to Fell's fish packing plant in Belize, British Honduras. There the pieces were packed in boxes and marked 'personal effects' and addressed to Hollinshead at Santa Fe Springs, California. This was done in the presence of Hollinshead and Fell as well as other conspirators. Also present were some Guatemalan officers, who departed after receiving bribes. The stele was shipped to Miami, Florida, where Fell and another conspirator, Dwyer, picked it up. They attempted, without success, to sell it to various collectors and museums in this country, traveling with it to Decatur, Georgia, to New York City, to Wisconsin and to Raleigh, North Carolina. Ultimately it wound up in Hollinshead's possession in California, and he, too, attempted to sell it.

Eight of the claims raised by appellants relate to the sufficiency of the evidence or to the admission or exclusion of particular evidence at the trial. We have reviewed each of these claims and find none of them meritorious. There was ample independent evidence of the conspiracy to support the admission of evidence of co-conspirator's declarations and acts against each defendant. There was certainly enough evidence of the existence of a single conspiracy to submit the issue to the jury. The trial judge properly exercised his discretion when he permitted certain cross-examination of Hollinshead to which objection was made and when he disallowed the improper cross-examination of witnesses Feeney and Dwyer; *United States v. Brown*, 455 F.2d 1201, 1204 (9th Cir. 1972); *United States v. Haili*, 443 F.2d 1295, 1299 (9th Cir. 1971). The admission of witnesses Lujan's expert testimony was also proper.

Appellants' one arguable contention is that the court erroneously instructed the jury that there is a presumption that every person knows what the law forbids. *Devitt & Blackmar*, § 13.04, pages 274–5. They point to the fact that it is the law of Guatemala that characterizes the stele as stolen property, and that there is no presumption that they knew Guatemalan law. Essentially their claim is that the instruction was overbroad and that it should have been supplemented with or limited by an instruction requested by appellants which made it clear that there is no such presumption as to knowledge of foreign law.

The court had received expert testimony as to the law of Guatemala regarding artifacts such as Machaquila Stele 2. Under that law, all such artifacts are the property of the Republic, and may not be removed without permission of the government. There was also overwhelming evidence that the defendants knew that it was contrary to Guatemalan law to remove the stele, and that the stele was stolen. Both their conduct and admissions that they made to investigators and others almost compel such a conclusion. It would have been astonishing if the jury had found that they did not know that the stele was stolen.

Early in his instructions, in defining the offenses charged, the judge defined the word 'stolen' as used in 18 U.S.C. § 2314:

> 'Stolen' means acquired, or possessed, as a result of some wrongful or dishonest act or taking, whereby a person willfully obtains or retains possession of property which belongs to another, without or beyond any permission given, and with the intent to deprive the owner of the benefit of ownership.

There was no objection to this instruction.

Later in his instructions, the judge gave the instruction to which appellants objected and now object. He did so because the law under which the appellants were charged was the law of the United States, and also, because, while the government was required to prove that appellants knew that the stele was stolen, *McAbee v. United States*, 434 F.2d 361, 362 (9th Cir. 1970), it was not required to prove that appellants knew where it was stolen, *cf. Pugliano v. United States*, 348 F.2d 902, 903 (1st Cir. 1965). It follows that it was not necessary for the government to prove that appellants knew the law of the place of the theft. Appellants' knowledge of Guatemalan law is relevant only to the extent that it bears upon the issue of their knowledge that the stele was stolen. The judge specifically instructed the jury that it must find beyond a reasonable doubt that appellants knew that the stele had been stolen. Thus, the judge's failure to clarify the issue of the proof of knowledge of the law of Guatemala, while it may have been error, was not, in our opinion, prejudicial. Viewing the instructions as a whole, we think it most unlikely that the jury thought that the questioned instruction referred to the law of Guatemala. *Cf. Cohen v. United States*, 378 F.2d 751, 752 (9th Cir. 1967).

Affirmed.

UNITED STATES V. PRE-COLUMBIAN ARTIFACTS

845 F. Supp. 544 (N.D. Ill. 1993)

HART, District Judge:

The United States filed this interpleader action to determine who is entitled to certain pre-Columbian artifacts seized from interpleader defendants Louis Krauss, Jerome Grunes, and Barbara Grunes (the "Grunes defendants") in November 1990. The artifacts are alleged to have been exported from Guatemala in violation of Guatemalan law. The Grunes defendants claim a lawful interest in the property (footnote omitted). The Republic of Guatemala claims that the artifacts were illegally exported and/or stolen and should be returned to the Republic. Presently pending is the Grunes defendants' motion to strike the Republic's claim of possession or, alternatively, for judgment on the pleadings.

The parties do not address the question of the appropriate legal standard. Under certain circumstances, conflicting claims with respect to an interpleader res can be resolved on the pleadings. See C.A. Wright, A. Miller, & M.K. Kane, Federal Practice & Procedure § 1715 at 588–89 (2d ed. 1986). "The usual rules of good pleading are applicable in an interpleader action." Id. at 587. It will be assumed, as the parties apparently do, that the Republic must state a claim for entitlement to the artifacts that would withstand a motion to dismiss under Rule 12(b)(6). One of the disputes, however, depends upon the construction of Guatemalan law. While any determination as to foreign law is a legal question, any relevant material or source, including testimony, may be considered in establishing foreign law. See Fed. R. Civ. P. 44.1; *Republic of Turkey v. OKS Partners*, 146 FRD 24, 27 (D. Mass. 1993). Commonly, oral or written expert testimony accompanied by foreign legal materials is provided. See id.; C.A. Wright & A. Miller, Federal Practice & Procedure s 2444 at 406 (1971). There is no requirement that foreign law and its supporting material be pleaded; "other reasonable written notice" will also suffice. Fed. R. Civ. P. 44.1; Wright & Miller, § 2443 at 402. Therefore, alleging in a pleading that property is stolen under a foreign law is a sufficient pleading without providing the specifics of the foreign law. See *Republic of Turkey v. OKS Partners*, 797 F. Supp. 64, 66 (D. Mass. 1992) (allegations that ancient coins belonged to Turkey under Turkish law and therefore were held by defendants in violation of the National Stolen Property Act could not be dismissed on the pleadings).

The Republic of Guatemala does not argue that the legal issue raised by the Grunes defendants cannot be considered on the pleadings. On the Grunes defendants' motion, however, the Republic's contentions as to provisions of Guatemalan law will be taken as true; no attempt will presently be made to parse the specific language of the Guatemalan legislation. For purposes of resolving the present motion, it is also assumed that the artifacts were illegally exported from Guatemala.

As stated by the Republic in its brief: For the purposes of this motion, it is accepted that the law of Guatemala provides that upon export without authorization, the artifacts are confiscated in favor of the Republic of Guatemala, and become the property of Guatemala. Article 21 of Guatemala's "Congressional Law for the Protection and Maintenance of the Monuments, Archeological, Historical, Artistic Objects and Handicrafts" provides for "confiscation in favor of the State" upon illicit export.

The Republic contends that this law therefore makes the Grunes defendants' possession of the allegedly illegally exported property the possession of stolen property in violation of the National Stolen Property Act ("NSPA"), 18 U.S.C. §§ 2314–15. It is undisputed that stolen property possessed in violation of the NSPA is subject to being seized. The Grunes defendants, however, argue that, even assuming unlawful exportation, the artifacts must have belonged to the Republic prior to exportation in order for the artifacts to be considered stolen property under the NSPA. Since the Republic only contends that Guatemalan law makes the artifacts its property upon illegal exportation, the legal issue raised by the Grunes defendants can be resolved on the pleadings.

The NSPA is designed to discourage both the receiving and the taking of stolen property. *United States v. O'Connor*, 874 F.2d 483, 488 (7th Cir. 1989); *United States v. Gardner*, 516

F.2d 334, 349 (7th Cir.), *cert. denied*, 423 U.S. 861 (1975); *United States v. McClain*, 545 F.2d 988, 994 ("McClain I"), *rehearing denied*, 551 F.2d 52 (5th Cir. 1977). "Stolen," as used in the NSPA, is not a term of art and instead is broad in scope with a "wide-ranging meaning." *McClain I*, 545 F.2d at 995. Accord *United States v. Darrell*, 828 F.2d 644, 649–50 (10th Cir. 1987). The NSPA applies to stolen goods transported in either interstate or foreign commerce. The Grunes defendants do not dispute that foreign ownership laws and thefts in foreign countries can be the basis for finding goods to be stolen. See *United States v. Rabin*, 316 F.2d 564, 566 (7th Cir.), *cert. denied*, 375 U.S. 815 (1963); *McClain I*, 545 F.2d at 994; *United States v. McClain*, 593 F.2d 658, 664 (5th Cir.), *cert. denied*, 444 U.S. 918 (1979) ("McClain III"); *United States v. Hollinshead*, 495 F.2d 1154 (9th Cir. 1974).

Mere violation of export restrictions does not make possession of the illegally exported property a violation of the NSPA. *McClain I*, 545 F.2d at 996, 1002; *Government of Peru v. Johnson*, 720 F. Supp. 810, 814 (CD Cal 1989), *aff'd by unpublished order*, 933 F.2d 1013 (9th Cir. 1991). For the property to be stolen, it must belong to someone else. See *McClain I*, 545 F.2d at 995, 1002; *Peru*, 720 F. Supp. at 814. Here, there is no allegation that the artifacts were stolen from any Guatemalan individual. The only allegation is that the artifacts belong to the Republic. The NSPA "protects ownership derived from foreign legislative pronouncements, even though the owned objects have never been reduced to possession by the foreign government." *McClain III*, 593 F.2d at 664. Guatemalan law (as assumed for purposes of the present motion) provides that, upon illegal export, the artifacts became the property of the Republic. Therefore, the moment the artifacts left Guatemala they became the property of the Republic. Thus, while traveling in foreign commerce, the artifacts were stolen in that they belonged to the Republic, not the person who unlawfully possessed the artifacts. The Republic has alleged facts under which the artifacts would be subject to being seized as being stolen property possessed in violation of the NSPA. The Grunes defendants' motion will be denied.

* * *

GOVERNMENT OF PERU v. JOHNSON

720 F. Supp. 810 (C.D. Cal. 1989)

GRAY, District Judge:

The Government of Peru, plaintiff in this action, contends that it is the legal owner of eighty-nine artifacts that have been seized by the United States Customs Service from defendant Benjamin Johnson. The plaintiff charges the defendant with conversion of these articles and seeks an order for their return. Judgment will be rendered for the defendant.

Irrespective of the decision in this matter, the court has considerable sympathy for Peru with respect to the problems that it confronts as manifested by this litigation. It is evident that many priceless and beautiful Pre-Columbian artifacts excavated from historical monuments in that country have been and are being smuggled abroad and sold to museums and other collectors of art. Such conduct is destructive of a major segment of the cultural heritage of Peru, and the plaintiff is entitled to the support of the courts of the United States in its determination to prevent further looting of its patrimony.

However, there is substantial evidence that Mr. Johnson purchased the subject items in good faith over the years, and the plaintiff must overcome legal and factual burdens that are heavy indeed before the court can justly order the subject items to be removed from the defendant's possession and turned over to the plaintiff. The trial of this action has shown that the plaintiff simply cannot meet these burdens.

1. THE PLAINTIFF CANNOT ESTABLISH THAT THE SUBJECT ARTIFACTS WERE EXCAVATED IN MODERN DAY PERU.

The plaintiff has no direct evidence that any of the subject items came from Peru. It alleges, on information and belief, that they were taken from Peru or excavated from archeological sites in that country. The plaintiff's principal witness was Dr. Francisco Iriarte, who, according to the plaintiff's counsel, is Peru's foremost archeologist in Pre-Columbian artifacts. Dr. Iriarte examined each of the eighty-nine artifacts and in almost every instance asserted that he recognized it as an item of Peruvian style and culture, and he usually asserted the belief that it came from a particular excavation site or specific area in Peru. I have no doubt that Dr. Iriarte has seen artifacts taken from those respective locations that are very similar to the items that he was examining in court. However, Dr. Iriarte admitted that Peruvian Pre-Columbian culture spanned not only modern day Peru, but also areas that now are within the borders of Bolivia and Ecuador, and many of the population centers that were part of the Peruvian Pre-Columbian civilization, and from which artifacts have been taken, are within those countries. The fact that the subject items are identifiable with excavation sites in modern Peru does not exclude the possibility that they are equally similar to artifacts found in archeological monuments in Bolivia and Ecuador. Indeed, the evidence shows that at least one of the subject items is very similar to a figure depicted in a photograph that appears in an article concerning the cultural anthropology of Ecuador.

Moreover, Columbia also borders Peru, and customs documents that appear to pertain to some of the subject items assert Columbia to be the country of origin. Such an assertion is, of course, hearsay and, even though the documents may be business records kept in ordinary course, they should not be given great weight. However, they do further point up the difficulty that the court has in concluding that any specific one of the items concerned in this action originated within the present boundaries of Peru.

I was impressed by Dr. Iriarte's testimony. He doubtless is knowledgeable in his field and honest in his beliefs. He also has a genuine interest in helping his country recover artifacts that are such an important part of its patrimony, and this desire necessarily plays a part in his conclusions as to the origins of the objects at issue. In some instances, he admitted that an item may have come from Ecuador or Columbia or Mexico or even Polynesia, but nonetheless retained the opinion that it had been found in a particular area of Peru, due to its similarity to other objects taken from that site. Because of the many other possibilities, this court cannot base a finding of ownership upon such subjective conclusions. We are far from certain as to the country of origin of any of the artifacts here concerned. This unfortunate circumstance precludes an adjudication that they came from Peru.

2. THE PLAINTIFF CANNOT ESTABLISH ITS OWNERSHIP AT THE TIME OF EXPORTATION.

Even if it were to be assumed that the artifacts came from Peru, in order for the plaintiff to recover them, it must prove that the Government of Peru was the legal owner at the time of their removal from that country. Such ownership depends upon the laws of Peru, which are far from precise and have changed several times over the years.

(a) 1822–1929. The plaintiff, in its Second Post Trial Brief, submitted for the first time copies of the statutes upon which it relies to establish that, from 1822 to the present time, Peru owned the artifacts located in that country. However, in its pleadings, its responses to discovery requests, and its pretrial memoranda, the plaintiff identified Law No. 6634 of June 13, 1929, as the earliest enactment that formed the legal basis for its ownership claims. Federal Rule of Civil Procedure 44.1 provides that "[a] party who intends to raise an issue concerning the law of a foreign country shall give notice by pleadings or other reasonable written notice." I find that initial presentation of these purported pre-1929 enactments after the case has been tried cannot constitute "reasonable notice," and I decline to consider them in rendering this decision.

In any event, the plaintiff's present reliance upon pre-1929 law is substantially undercut by the trial testimony of its expert witness on Peruvian law, Roberto MacLean, a former Chief Justice of the Supreme Court of that country. In response to a question regarding Peru's statutes concerning government ownership of Pre-Columbian artifacts, he said: "even though there are several rules which have some academic importance but for all practical purposes the first law is from 1929; if I recall correctly from 13 of June of 1929."

The defendant's expert, Professor Alan Sawyer, whose qualifications concerning artifacts are comparable to those of Dr. Iriarte, testified that it is impossible to determine from examination of the items here concerned when they were excavated or left the country of origin, and that many Peruvian artifacts were brought into the United States before 1929. It follows that if any of the subject items left Peru before 1929, the plaintiff cannot claim ownership of them.

(b) 1929–1985. A written opinion by Professor MacLean asserts that what Law No. 6634 means "is that if a person found an archeological object before June of 1929 this object belongs to him; but if that person found the object after June 1929 it belongs to the State." Article 11 of Law No. 6634 provides that privately owned Pre-Columbian artifacts must be registered in a special book "which shall be opened at the National Museum of History", and that any "[o]bjects which, after one year beginning on the day the book is opened, have not been registered, shall be considered the property of the State."

From the record at the trial, I cannot determine when the "special book" called for by Article 11 was opened or whether it ever has been opened. Interrogatory No. 9, propounded to the plaintiff by the defendant, asks for the date or approximate date upon which the special book was "opened"; the response was that "[t]his date is unknown." The plaintiff submitted a supplemental answer which said that the "so called 'book' is a card registry" that has been "adequately ordered since 1969 to date." The response further states that "[u]p to the year 1972 the books are found at the National Museum of Anthropology and Archeology, since 1972 to date, the books are found at the 'Museum of the Nation.'" The record does not show whether either of these named institutions is the same as the National Museum of History, where the special book was to be opened.

On January 5, 1985, Law No. 6634 was repealed and replaced by Law No. 24047. According to Professor MacLean's written opinion, "[a]fter that date there is also the obligation for private persons to register their archeological objects and if they do not comply with this obligation that could mean that the objects belong to the State."

In undertaking to evaluate Peru's ownership claims in this confusing situation, I am assuming that none of the artifacts have been duly registered. However, I do not know whether the repeal of Law No. 6634 nullifies the registration requirement therein contained. If it does, a private owner could have retained an unregistered item through January 1985 without losing his title. In any event, if the private owner caused his unregistered artifact to be removed from Peru within one year following the opening of the "special book" (whenever that may have occurred), title would not have been transferred from such person to the plaintiff.

(c) From January 1985 To The Present. As is mentioned above, on January 5, 1985, the 1929 law was repealed and replaced by Law No. 24047. Professor MacLean's written opinion states that under the latter statute "if a person finds after 5th January of 1985 an archeological object it can belong to him." The next relevant official document is a Supreme Decree of the President of Peru, dated February 27, 1985, which proclaims that Pre-Hispanic artistic objects "belonging to the nation's cultural wealth are untouchable," and that their removal from the country is categorically forbidden. This Decree does not clearly establish state ownership of any such art objects. However, on June 22, 1985, a new statute provided specifically that all archeological sites belong to the state. "So if a private person digs a site and excavates its objects [he] is taking somebody else's property," according to Professor MacLean's written opinion. Thus, it would appear that if any artifacts here concerned were privately excavated between January 5 and June 22, 1985, they would constitute private property, rather than being owned by Peru.

3. MICHAEL KELLY'S TESTIMONY DOES NOT ESTABLISH PERU'S OWNERSHIP.

Mr. Michael Kelly testified that in August 1987 he brought to Mr. Johnson's home in California certain artifacts that he believed to have come from Peru. But all of his information as to the country of origin of these items was strictly hearsay. I am also skeptical of Mr. Kelly's ability to identify any of the specific objects here concerned as having been part of the 1987 shipment. Some of the subject items doubtless were in Mr. Johnson's home when Mr. Kelly was present, and he well may have seen them. However, Mr. Johnson submitted documents that quite clearly established his having purchased many of them in the United States well before 1987.

Despite Mr. Kelly's testimony, which was designed to show that Mr. Johnson was implicated in, or at least was aware of, the smuggling activities of Mr. Kelly and Mr. Swetnam, I am not satisfied that Mr. Johnson received any of the items here concerned with the knowledge that they were illegally removed from Peru.

4.   THE UNCERTAINTY OF THE DOMESTIC APPLICATION OF PERU'S OWNERSHIP LAWS.

Official documents of Peru long have asserted, in one way or another, the interest of the state in preserving its artistic objects as "part of the national cultural wealth," that they are "untouchable, inalienable and inprescriptable," and that their removal from the country is "categorically forbidden." See, *e.g.*, Supreme Decree of February 27, 1985. Such declarations are concerned with protection and do not imply ownership. However, the law of June 13, 1929, does proclaim that artifacts in historical monuments are "the property of the State" and that unregistered artifacts "shall be considered to be the property of the State." Nonetheless, the domestic effect of such a pronouncement appears to be extremely limited. Possession of the artifacts is allowed to remain in private hands, and such objects may be transferred by gift or bequest or intestate succession. There is no indication in the record that Peru ever has sought to exercise its ownership rights in such property, so long as there is no removal from that country. The laws of Peru concerning its artifacts could reasonably be considered to have no more effect than export restrictions, and, as was pointed out in *United States v. McClain*, 545 F.2d 988, 1002 (5th Cir. 1977), export restrictions constitute an exercise of the police power of a state; "[t]hey do not create 'ownership' in the state. The state comes to own property only when it acquires such property in the general manner by which private persons come to own property, or when it declares itself the owner."

The second time that the case of *United States v. McClain* came before the Fifth Circuit, the opinion stated: "It may well be, as testified so emphatically by most of the Mexican witnesses, that Mexico has considered itself the owner of all pre-Columbian artifacts for almost 100 years. If so, however, it has not expressed that view with sufficient clarity to survive translation into terms understandable by and binding upon American citizens." 593 F.2d 658, 670 (5th Cir. 1979). Under all of the above discussed circumstances, I find the same comment to be applicable here.

5.   CONCLUSION.

Peru may not prevail in this action to recover the artifacts here concerned because:

(a) We do not know in what country they were found and from which they were exported.
(b) If they were found in Peru, we do not know when.
(c) We do not know if they were in private possession in Peru more than one year after the official registry book was opened.
(d) The extent of Peru's claim of ownership as part of its domestic law is uncertain.

UNITED STATES v. McCLAIN

593 F.2d 658 (5th Cir. 1979)

GEE, Circuit Judge:

Again before us come Patty McClain, Mike Bradshaw, Ada Simpson and William Simpson, challenging their second round of convictions for having received, concealed and/or sold stolen goods in interstate or foreign commerce and also for conspiracy to do the same, violations of 18 U.S.C. §§ 371, 2314 and 2315. The goods in which they dealt are pre-Columbian artifacts, and in neither this nor the prior trial was there evidence that the appellants or anyone else had taken the items from the personal possession of another. The legal theory under which the case was tried was that the artifacts were "stolen" only in the sense that Mexico generally has declared itself owner of all pre-Columbian artifacts found within its borders. Thus, anyone who digs up or finds such an item and deals in it without governmental permission has unlawfully converted the item from its proper owner.[1]

By various formulations, appellants and the amicus curiae, the American Association of Dealers in Ancient, Oriental & Primitive Art, raise basically three issues in this appeal. They challenge: (1) the propriety of the application of the National Stolen Property Act (N.S.P.A.), 18 U.S.C. §§ 2314, 2315, to dealings in pre-Columbian artifacts; (2) the correctness and sufficiency of the jury instructions regarding the Mexican law of pre-Columbian artifacts; and (3) the sufficiency of the evidence to support the convictions as measured under their view of the Mexican law. Though in raising these issues the appellants did not distinguish between their convictions on the substantive count and their convictions on the conspiracy count, we find that their arguments regarding jury instructions compel reversal of the substantive count only. On the conspiracy charges, we find the shortcomings below merely harmless error and thus affirm the convictions on that count for the reasons expressed below. This mixed disposition requires a more detailed account of the facts than is present in the earlier opinion. We first review, therefore, the evidence adduced at trial, cast in the light most favorable to the government's verdict.

---

[1][*Orig. fn.*] See generally *United States v. McClain*, 545 F.2d 988 (5th Cir.), *rehearing denied*, 551 F.2d 52 (5th Cir. 1977). Only one other reported conviction has resulted from application of the National Stolen Property Act to dealings in pre-Columbian artifacts. In *United States v. Hollinshead*, 495 F.2d 1154 (9th Cir. 1974), Clive Hollinshead of Los Angeles, California, was successfully prosecuted for transporting into the United States a known and cataloged Guatemalan stela. Hollinshead was on probation for this offense during the events leading to the instant prosecution. At least appellants Simpson and Bradshaw knew Hollinshead and were aware of his conviction and probation. Hollinshead was to have supplied several of the artifacts that appellants were selling when they were arrested.

I. THE APPELLANTS' DEALINGS IN PRE-COLUMBIAN ARTIFACTS.

In May 1973, Joseph Rodriguez, a resident of Calexico, California, arrived at a Dallas motel with a collection of pre-Columbian artifacts for display and sale.[2] He sold pieces at least to a local art dealer and to a law professor who was staying in the same motel. He thereafter moved his wares to a San Antonio motel, apparently as a result of his dealings with the professor, who taught in San Antonio. From the new location Rodriguez contacted prospective buyers, including Alberto Mejangos, who unbeknownst to Rodriguez was director of the Mexican Cultural Institute, an educational outpost of the Mexican government located in San Antonio. Suspecting Rodriguez of illicit dealings, Mejangos and Adalina Diaz-Zambrano, the librarian at the institute, visited Rodriguez to see the collection, without identifying themselves as officials of the Mexican government. Rodriguez showed them a large collection of fine artifacts, many of which were caked with mud and straw. When he was asked how it was possible that he had all these ancient artifacts, Rodriguez said that he had five squads working in various Mexican archaeological zones and that the objects were passed, a few at a time "by contraband" to his Calexico store, which served as a front for his operation. When he amassed enough objects, he said, he would sell them in different localities. He priced the items he showed Mr. Mejangos and Ms. Diaz-Zambrano at figures ranging between $5,000 and $20,000, explaining that the prices had gone up as a result of the February 1972 presidential agreement between the United States and Mexico. He said he now had to give more money to the people who were passing the objects to him.

At some time after these meetings in San Antonio, Rodriguez returned to Calexico, leaving the collection behind with appellants William and Ada Simpson who were authorized to sell the items. The next known transaction regarding the Rodriguez artifacts occurred in early December 1973. Simpson and appellant Mike Bradshaw contacted William Maloof of Cleveland, Ohio, a college friend of Bradshaw, in an effort to raise money for an oil importation venture. They offered Maloof several of the artifacts as collateral for the loan Maloof considered making. Simpson, Bradshaw, and a third man whom Maloof spoke with only by phone,[3] told Maloof that the items had been "stolen" or "smuggled" out of Mexico. They said that a man named Rodriguez was "chief of the Mexican Secret Service" and had gotten the artifacts from "a vault" in Mexico. Patty McClain was mentioned as an appraiser who knew the value of the artifacts. Simpson and Bradshaw told Maloof that they planned to take most of the objects to Europe, "auction" them off, and then return them to the United States. This process would yield bills of sale from European art dealers, which would facilitate later resale. Maloof, suspecting he was being swindled, contacted the FBI and showed the objects to them. After being alerted by the Cleveland office, the Houston office of the FBI delegated Special Agent John McGauley, to determine whether stolen pre-Columbian artifacts were being sold by the group. To assist in the covert investigation, McGauley brought in Travis Benkendorfer, who had proven to be a reliable informant on other occasions.

---

[2][*Orig. fn.*] Rodriguez, a codefendant at the original trial, was not retried with the others because he was found mentally incompetent in the interim.

[3][*Orig. fn.*] The man identified himself as Harry McClain, who is appellant Patty McClain's husband.

In February 1974, after failing to contact Harry McClain, Benkendorfer succeeded in reaching the Simpson residence by telephone. Identifying himself as a Mr. Benks, Benkendorfer told Mrs. Simpson a cover story that he was interested in acquiring stolen treasury bills, stocks, bonds, or other stolen or illegal merchandise for resale. He said that he represented an international combine with Mafia or other underworld connections and that any stolen merchandise they purchased would immediately be flown out of the country by private plane. Mrs. Simpson replied that her husband and his partner Patty McClain were then in California, waiting for a shipment of pre-Columbian artifacts to cross the border. She said that she would have her husband and Mrs. McClain contact Benkendorfer. When Simpson called Benkendorfer the next morning, Benkendorfer repeated his story. He explained that he had gotten Simpson's name through a Long Island man with Mafia connections and had been instructed to discover for his principal whether Simpson had any artifacts for sale. Simpson replied that he had approximately 150 pieces already in San Antonio and was in Calexico awaiting a new shipment from the diggings. He described a "conduit" by which the items were taken from the diggings to the archaeological institute in Mexico, where documents or permits were forged or backdated. The items were then trucked in disguise to the border at Calexico before distribution to various cities in the United States, particularly San Antonio. Simpson stated that what they were doing "is illegal, but really not illegal, because if the Mexican authorities knew basically what we were doing, they would take them away from us, because the Mexicans really claim all of the items belong to them." Simpson explained further that the backdating of the papers was due to a new "presidential law" that had gone into effect in Mexico, prohibiting private ownership of artifacts after its effective date. He said that the group had planned to ship the items to Europe for sale but that they could save shipping and breakage costs if Benkendorfer and his principal bought the new shipment right at the border. Simpson said that Rodriguez and Patty McClain each had collections that also would be available. Benkendorfer said he would discuss the offer with his principal. He later relayed the message through Mrs. Simpson that he would prefer to have all the items shipped to San Antonio for a single viewing and purchase decision. Simpson agreed to this proposal, emphasizing that all of them would have to be extremely discreet. He said they would get into a lot of problems if the United States government caught them since what they were doing was against the law. He repeated that the Mexicans claimed ownership of the items. Simpson also mentioned during the conversation that his associate Mike Bradshaw was flying from Alabama to Calexico with money to pay for the items that were coming across the border.

Several days later, Benkendorfer received word from Mrs. Simpson that trouble had developed in the conduit or channel. Patty McClain confirmed this when she later contacted Benkendorfer to discuss terms for the sale of her collection. She said that the driveshaft of the truck carrying the artifacts had broken south of the border and that Simpson was sending a new truck to the interior to bring in the goods. In terms highly similar to Simpson's she also described the "channel" from the diggings and the system for getting backdated permits and trucking the items to Calexico developed by Joe and "staff." She said that she and Simpson were responsible for distributing the goods to various points away from Calexico, especially if they were bound for the European market. When Benkendorfer repeated his cover story, McClain gave him some of her artifacts to show to his principal, Mr. Dooley (Agent McGauley). McClain made Benkendorfer promise not to show the items to an art dealer or museum because a recent similar showing had caused the FBI to investigate. McClain agreed that Benkendorfer and McGauley might bring their own appraiser to the

San Antonio showing, though she was anxious that the appraiser not come from Mexico City. She explained that she was afraid he might return and report their doings to the authorities because "what we are basically doing is against the law." A final topic during this meeting involved a mild expression of interest by Benkendorfer in purchasing Mexican gold. When Benkendorfer next spoke with Simpson, in addition to repeating the story of the broken driveshaft, Simpson offered to sell Benkendorfer some gold bars that were coming out of Mexico via the same conduit as the artifacts. Simpson then put "his partner" Joe Rodriguez on the phone to explain the gold deal, which Benkendorfer rejected after hearing the details.

During his next phone conversation with Simpson, who was still in Calexico, Benkendorfer spoke with appellant Mike Bradshaw for the first time. Bradshaw's comments evidenced his knowledge of the conduit and the planned sale, and he stressed the need for discretion due to the danger.

Following this round of contacts the defendants seemed to grow even more cautious. Simpson interrogated Benkendorfer about where he had learned Simpson's name; McClain expressed concern about the amount of information Simpson and Bradshaw had conveyed to Benkendorfer by phone; several of the appellants sought to assure themselves that Benkendorfer was not with the FBI. McClain even tried to renegotiate the timetable of the showing and sale so that the new shipment would not be sold until after the in-country items had been successfully conveyed. Such a split timetable was ultimately agreed upon after Benkendorfer told Simpson that his New York connection had authorized the purchase of artifacts currently held by Simpson, Rodriguez, and McClain and that a decision whether to buy the next shipment would come later.[4]

On the appointed date, March 4, 1974, Agent McGauley and Benkendorfer arrived at the San Antonio Holiday Inn, chosen by Simpson because it had a meeting room with an outside entrance that would be "discreet." Over supper with the four appellants and Mike Bradshaw's fiance, they discussed various aspects of the deal. McGauley repeated the cover story, adding that his New York syndicate was trying to corner the market on pre-Columbian artifacts. The defendants again voiced concern that McGauley's appraiser was coming from Mexico and might return to inform the Mexican government. McGauley assured them that the expert had been adequately paid and that he had methods of ensuring the man's silence. The defendants mentioned that the items were coming from a dig that the Mexican authorities did not know about. Simpson commented that if the FBI knew the artifacts were at the hotel they would seize them. McGauley assured them that he was not an FBI agent.

At supper the defendants further suggested that McGauley also go to the west coast to buy some very valuable stelae and large figurines accumulated there by Clive Hollinshead. Because McGauley had obtained only a single certified bank draft for the "purchase," the parties worked out an escrow agreement to handle the need to inspect the items at separate

---

[4][*Orig. fn.*] During one of the conversations to perfect details of the San Antonio meeting, Simpson asked whether Benkendorfer and McGauley would be interested in purchasing a three-ton stela from the Mexican interior. Simpson was contemplating a burro trip down to the monument so the buyers could inspect it before it was cut into three pieces for transportation out of the country. Benkendorfer declined the offer when he learned that the object was still in place.

locations. After supper, Benkendorfer and McGauley briefly viewed the artifacts in the locked meeting room and retired for the night.

The next morning the "appraiser," Dr. Eduardo Montes Moctezuma of the Mexican Department of Archaeology, arrived with his "interpreter," another undercover FBI agent. While these two men, Agent McGauley, William Simpson and Patty McClain examined the artifacts one by one, Benkendorfer, Bradshaw and Mrs. Simpson stayed in the coffee shop. During the wait, Bradshaw informed Benkendorfer that he had invested a great deal of time and money to make Rodriguez' conduit secure, that he had been to the diggings and followed the conduit all the way up through Calexico, California. Bradshaw confirmed earlier Simpson comments that the Indians who were stealing the artifacts had no idea of their worth and were paid only a small sum to get the artifacts from the diggings, to "rob the graves." He also stated that Rodriguez had paid off several customs inspectors along the border to pass the items across.

During the appraisal in the meeting room, McClain and Simpson confirmed that, in addition to the artifacts still located in California, Rodriguez was bringing more across the border and that they would be available to McGauley. These had not crossed yet because of the truck breakdown. McGauley arranged to purchase the goods he had just inspected, contingent upon inspection of the items available in California.

Over lunch McGauley negotiated the sale terms with appellants agreeing on a price of $115,000 for the San Antonio lot, including McClain's items. Bradshaw and Simpson then arranged to meet McGauley, the "appraiser" and the "interpreter" in Los Angeles the next day to view the Hollinshead artifacts. McClain and Mrs. Simpson agreed to remain behind and rewrap and store the items. The next day, March 6, 1974, Simpson and Bradshaw were arrested in Los Angeles during the course of negotiations to purchase the Hollinshead artifacts for $850,000. McClain and Mrs. Simpson were arrested in San Antonio the same day.

There was evidence at trial that none of the items "purchased" by Agent McGauley bore the indicia of registration with the Archaeological Registry maintained by the Mexican government since 1934 a permanent, coded number placed with indelible ink on an inconspicuous area of the piece. Nor were any documents of registration for these pieces in the names of either Rodriguez or any of the appellants found in the registry. Additionally, no export permits had been obtained for the items. In fact, since 1897 the Mexican government has issued only temporary export permits, and those are issued exclusively to cultural institutions or universities. Permits have never been issued to private individuals or for commercial purposes.

II. APPLICATION OF N.S.P.A. TO DEALINGS IN PRE-COLUMBIAN ARTIFACTS.

Appellants attack the application of the N.S.P.A. to their conduct under two different theories. They first argue that Congress never intended the N.S.P.A. to reach items deemed "stolen" only by reason of a country's declaration of ownership. In any event, they claim, the N.S.P.A. was superseded by the 1972 Law on Importation of Pre-Columbian Monumental or Architectural Sculpture or Murals, 19 U.S.C. §§ 2091–95, which provides only the civil penalty of forfeiture[5] for importation of certain types of pre-Columbian artifacts.[6] Second, they and their amicus argue that due process is violated by imposing criminal penalties through reference to Mexican laws that are vague and inaccessible except to a handful of experts who work for the Mexican government.

We view appellants' first argument as foreclosed by our doctrine of law of the case. Under that doctrine it is our practice to apply a rule of law enunciated by the court to the same issues in subsequent proceedings and appeals in the same case. Unlike the rule of res judicata, the doctrine applies only to issues that were decided in the former proceeding but not to questions that might have been decided but were not. *Carpa, Inc. v. Ward Foods, Inc.*, 567 F.2d 1316, 1320 (5th Cir. 1978). Though appellants articulated their theories in a slightly different manner in the first appeal, they provoked a square holding that, in addition to the rights of ownership as understood by the common law, the N.S.P.A. also protects ownership derived from foreign legislative pronouncements, even though the owned objects have never been reduced to possession by the foreign government. *United States v. McClain*, 545 F.2d 988, 994–97 (5th Cir. 1977). Moreover, the earlier panel had considered evidence of the 1972 statute, its legislative history and UNESCO negotiations, holding nevertheless that neither statute nor treaty nor our historical policy of encouraging the importation of art more than 100 years old had the effect of narrowing the N.S.P.A. so as to make it inapplicable to artifacts declared to be the property of another country and illegally imported into this country. 545 F.2d at 996–97. Appellants' attempt to raise these points again on appeal is therefore foreclosed *unless* "(1) the evidence on a subsequent trial was substantially different, (2) controlling authority has since made a contrary decision of the law applicable to such issues, or (3) the decision was clearly erroneous and would work manifest injustice." *Morrow v. Dillard*, 580 F.2d 1284, 1290 (5th Cir. 1978), quoting *White v. Murtha*, 377 F.2d 428, 431–32 (5th Cir. 1967).

Of these customary heads of exception, only the third is even a colorable issue. Appellants attempt to identify clear error in the panel's decision largely by pointing to the legislative history of the 1972 statute. From stray congressional remarks, such as that of Representative Byrnes of Wisconsin that the legislation deals with "items stolen in the country

---

[5][*Orig. fn.*] 19 U.S.C. § 2093 details the only penalties contained in the 1972 Importation Act. It provides that any object imported in violation of the Act shall be seized and subject to forfeiture under the customs laws.

[6][*Orig. fn.*] This statute prohibits importation into the United States, unless the country of origin has certified exportation, of "stone carvings and wall art which are pre-Columbian monumental or architectural sculpture or murals." The latter term is defined in § 2095(3) as any stone carving or wall art (or fragment or part thereof) that (1) is the product of pre-Columbian Indian culture of Mexico, Central America, South America, or the Caribbean Islands; (2) was an immobile monument or architectural structure or was a part of, or affixed to, any such monument or structure; and (3) is subject to export control by the country of origin. Though some of the artifacts seized in San Antonio and Los Angeles seem to come within this definition, the majority of the pieces are movable items such as ceramic dishes, pots, or figurines that may not have been part of or affixed to monuments or walls within the apparent meaning of the statute.

of origin, and we are saying that if it is stolen it cannot be brought in,"[7] coupled with the statute's noncoverage of movable artifacts such as ceramic pots or figurines and provision of civil forfeiture as the only penalty, appellants seek to establish a very specific legislative understanding and intent. They argue (1) that Congress believed that pre-Columbian artifacts were not forfeitable under preexisting laws such as the N.S.P.A.; (2) that Congress must have intended to allow importation of movable items like most of those in the Rodriguez/Simpson/McClain collections; and (3) that Congress intended that illegal importation of immovables be punished by forfeiture of the item and not by imprisonment or fine under the criminal laws.

Our study of the statute and its scant legislative history persuades us that appellants' reading of it is not correct. Both the Report by the House Ways and Means Committee and the Report by the Senate Finance Committee explicitly refer to the presence of other unspecified sanctions: "While legal remedies for the return of such objects are available in U.S. courts in some cases, these procedures can be extremely expensive and time consuming and do not provide a meaningful deterrent to the pillage of pre-Columbian sites now taking place."[8] Moreover, the Act covers objects imported from all the countries of Latin America. These countries may have acted quite differently to protect their cultural heritages, some by declaring national ownership and others merely by enacting stringent export restrictions. Since it covers artifacts from such a large number of countries, the Act is better seen not as an indication that other available penalties were thereby precluded, but rather as a recognition that additional deterrents were needed. We cannot see in this congressional intent any desire to prevent application of criminal sanctions for dealing in items classified as stolen because a particular country has enacted national ownership of its patrimony.[9]

---

[7][*Orig. fn.*] 118 Cong. Rec. 37,098 (1972).

[8][*Orig. fn.*] H.R. Rep. No. 92-824, 92d Cong., 2d sess. 3 (1972); S. Rep. No. 92-1221, 92d Cong., 2d sess. 2 (1972).

[9][*Orig. fn.*] During the congressional debates, Rep. Byrnes also stated: The situation is that a narrow class of very valuable archaeological objects from the pre-Columbian period in South America are being taken out of that country (sic) illegally, and being brought into this country. There is no prohibition in this country about bringing in these articles, the prohibition is against taking these articles out of the country in which they are found, and this is an attempt to cooperate with these countries to avoid this exploitation that is taking place. 118 Cong. Rec. 37,097 (1972). Instead of reading into these remarks the specific and technical meaning attributed to them by appellants, we understand the congressman to be referring to the general state of American law regarding the importation of items illegally exported from another country. As the earlier panel observed, the fundamental rule, absent modification as by the 1972 statute, is that it is not a violation of law to import an item of art or anything else simply because it has been illegally exported from another country. 545 F.2d at 996. But that generalized principle does not preclude federal criminal liability for concealing, selling, or transporting across state or international borders items that are not only illegally exported from a country such as Mexico, but are also incapable of being privately owned or conveyed. Dealing in such items is dealing in stolen goods and may be punished accordingly, irrespective of import regulations.

Appellants' second challenge is not so easily resolved. It is elementary that criminal statutes must give notice of the acts they prohibit before valid penalties may be imposed thereunder. In their first appeal, appellants argued broadly that a reference to any foreign law for the purpose of determining what is or is not "stolen" would "inject an unacceptable degree of uncertainty into the administration" of the N.S.P.A. This argument also drew a firm holding a ruling that application of the N.S.P.A. to foreign exportation did not render that statute void for vagueness. 545 F.2d at 1001, 1002 n.30. The court reasoned that the statute's specific scienter requirement eliminates the possibility that a defendant is convicted for an offense he could not have understood to exist. In support, the court cited *Boyce Motor Lines v. United States*, 342 U.S. 337, 340 (1952), for the proposition that it is not "unfair to require that one who deliberately goes perilously close to an area of proscribed conduct shall take the risk that he may cross the line." The court finally noted that it would have been impossible for the statute to have explicitly described every type of theft that might fall within its broad purview. Id.

In assessing whether the law of the case doctrine precludes further challenge under a void-for-vagueness theory, we first observe that the panel's holding was in response to a challenge about reference to foreign law Generally and not to a challenge about the specific Mexican statutes. Moreover, we think it very significant that the panel's response was made in the context of its independent review of the relevant Mexican statutes. Its study of those statutes led the court to conclude that Mexico had not Unequivocally declared national ownership of All artifacts until 1972. 545 F.2d at 997–1000. Entailed in the proposition that criminal penalties on the basis of the 1972 declaration of ownership are proper, is the probable corollary that criminal penalties on the basis of, for instance, the 1897 Mexican statute alone would have been improper because that statute did not declare the nation's ownership of movables with sufficient clarity.[10] The panel's opinion is consistent with the view that, had there been no subsequent enactments that declared ownership with enough specificity to be accessible to and understandable by our citizenry, criminal penalties may well have violated our fundamental standards of due process. We are therefore convinced that, insofar as criminal liability in the second trial may possibly have been predicated on a conclusion that the 1897 Act declared Mexican ownership of all artifacts, appellants' precise due process challenge was not decided before and therefore survives. Because the due process challenge is so closely linked with the issue of the proper view of Mexican law, further discussion of this issue will be postponed until we have described and assessed the record on that point.

---

[10][*Orig. fn.*] Article 1 of the Law on Archaeological Monuments, May 11, 1897 [Diaro Oficial de 11 de Mayo de 1897, See XIV Annario de Legislacion y Jurisprudencia (1897)], declared "archaeological monuments" to be the "property" ("propriedad") of the nation, but "archaeological monuments" were defined in article 2 as "ruins of cities, Big Houses (Casas Grandes), troglodytic dwellings, fortifications, palaces, temples, pyramids, sculpted rocks or those with inscriptions, and in general all the edifices that in any aspect may be interesting for the study of civilization and history of the ancient settlers of Mexico." There was no corresponding declaration of ownership of movable artifacts such as codices, idols, amulets, though exportation of such items was forbidden unless legally authorized. Art. 6.

III. JURY INSTRUCTIONS REGARDING MEXICAN LAW, SUFFICIENCY OF EVIDENCE.

At appellants' first trial a deputy Attorney General of Mexico testified as an expert witness, and the trial court subsequently instructed the jury that Mexico had, since 1897, vested itself with ownership of all pre-Columbian artifacts found in that country. As mentioned above, its independent review of translations of the various Mexican statutes convinced the earlier panel that Mexico had not unequivocally claimed ownership of All such artifacts until 1972. The earlier Mexican statutes seemed only to have claimed national ownership of immovable monuments and such movable artifacts as were found on, and possibly in, the immovable objects.[11] Movable objects not in the above classes seemed capable of being privately owned and conveyed, though the Mexican government required that such objects be registered and retained the right to acquire items of great cultural or archaeological value by purchase at a fair price. Certain other provisions referred to in the petition for rehearing seem to have established a presumption against private ownership of any movable not registered within the applicable time limits.[12] In view of the complicated and gradual nature of Mexico's apparent declarations of ownership, the earlier panel ruled that the defendants were entitled to a new trial because of the prejudice that may have resulted from the erroneous instruction that Mexico owned all artifacts as early as 1897. Its analysis of the changes in Mexican law convinced the panel that the jury should have been told to determine when the artifacts had been exported from Mexico and to "apply the applicable Mexican law to that exportation." 545 F.2d at 1003.

When the additional complication of the statutory presumptions was raised in the petition for rehearing, the court explained that its earlier discussion of Mexican law had not been "an exegesis of every relevant statutory clause or a holding on every issue that was or might have been raised." Rather, the court contemplated that on remand "objective testimony" on the meaning of the relevant Mexican enactments would be introduced, so as to lighten the burden both of the district court and reviewing court. The court reiterated that the earlier instructions had been "clearly in error" as to Mexican law but added that at any

---

[11][*Orig. fn.*] For instance, the Law for the Protection and Preservation of Archaeological and Historical Monuments, Typical Towns and Places of Scenic Beauty, January 19, 1934 (82 Diario Oficial 152, 19 de enero de 1934), broadened the definition of "monuments" to include "all vestiges of the aboriginal civilizations dating from before the completion of the Conquest." Art. 3. But art. 4 clearly declared national ownership of artifacts in more limited categories "immovable archaeological monuments" and "objects which are found (in or on) immovable archaeological monuments." See 545 F.2d at 998–99, including n.20 that explains the dispute over movable items found in immobile monuments.

[12][*Orig. fn.*] Art. 9 of the 1934 statute, supra note 11, created a Register of Private Archaeological Property ("Propriedad") with which private individuals were to register movable monuments in their "control" or "ownership." (Translation of any terms suggestive of private ownership was hotly disputed at trial.) Art. 12 of that statute prescribed that objects not registered within the period stipulated in the Act's transitory articles "shall be presumed to come from archaeological monuments which are real property." Because the Act had earlier declared national ownership of all immovable monuments, Supra note 11, the force of this presumption seems to nationalize all movable artifacts not registered by the end of the transitory period. There is a similar presumption in the statute that superseded the 1934 Act, the Federal Law Concerning Cultural Patrimony of the Nation, December 16, 1970 (303 Diario Oficial 8, 16 de diciembre de 1970). See art. 55 thereof, which provides that movable objects not registered within the allowed time limits are presumed "the property of the nation" ("propriedad").

subsequent trial "experts will have an opportunity to correct any misconstruction of which this Court may have been guilty in venturing forth in the arcane field of the Mexican law of pre-Columbian artifacts." *United States v. McClain*, on petition for rehearing, 551 F.2d 52, 54 (5th Cir. 1977).

Pursuant to these instructions, at the second trial the judge admitted testimony from several government and defense witnesses about the relevant Mexican law. Only two of the witnesses were accepted by the court as experts specifically on the Mexican law of archaeological monuments. The first, Javier Andres Oropeza-Secura, is the Director of the Judicial Branch of the National Institute of Anthropology and History of Mexico, the office in charge of the official registry for ancient artifacts. The second was Ricardo de los Rios, an attorney who currently works at the Ministry of Labor and who formerly worked in the Attorney General's office, where he prosecuted about 150 cases under the Mexican laws regulating artifacts. Since each of these men is an employee of the Mexican government and was challenged by defendants as possibly biased, the government introduced other witnesses to corroborate their testimony. Carlos Schon, an attorney in Mexico City with a general practice and a heavily American clientele, was allowed to testify as a licensed practitioner of the general laws of Mexico from whom one may seek legal opinions. His testimony on archaeological law was based on his review of the various statutes and the Mexican Constitution. Though the testimony of these witnesses varied on a specific point here and there, the weight of their testimony as a whole indicated a general opinion that the Mexican government owned all pre-Columbian artifacts at least as early as 1897.[13] Rights of private indi-

---

[13][*Orig. fn.*] The witnesses, though very emphatic in affirming their understanding of longstanding national ownership of all artifacts, were unable to identify specific passages (apart from the 1934 and 1970 presumptions) in the 1897, 1930, 1934, or 1970 statutes that claimed outright ownership of the sort of movables largely involved in this case. By contrast, those statutes contain several explicit declarations of ownership of immovables and smaller movable items found on, and possibly in, the immovable monuments. Supra, notes 10 and 11. On cross-examination, appellants tried to lead the government witnesses to admit that the specific pronouncements of ownership of some objects indicated an obvious legislative intent to leave undisturbed private ownership of other objects, especially since various provisions seem clearly to contemplate private ownership. For instance, art. 26 of the 1930 statute provides that "(i)n order to determine the ownership ('propriedad') of movable things of artistic, archaeological or historical value that are discovered in a casual manner and not as a result of archaeological excavation or exploration, the provisions of the Civil Code of the Federal District and Federal Territories related to treasures will apply, but the Federal Government may acquire the discovered objects for their fair price, when it deems this appropriate." The witnesses stood their ground, however, arguing that the expressions of limited ownership did not preclude general ownership of all artifacts. Without succeeding in rationalizing the statutory provisions with his categorical view of government ownership, Carlos Schon at least attempted to identify an arguable source of national ownership by reference to art. 27 of the Mexican Constitution of 1917. That provision, as explained by Schon, provides that the property of the land and the water within the limits of the national territory belongs originally to the nation, which has the power to transmit them to private individuals as private property. He interpreted art. 27 as extending to manmade items buried in the land, in addition to the natural deposits of minerals and ores found therein. Under his view, unless the legislature acts to grant to individuals derived ownership rights regarding any of these things, national ownership is retained. The testimony of Ricardo de los Rios also touched on art. 27, and there are indications he may have held similar views of its meaning. The questions he was asked did not cause him to focus on the issue with sufficient precision for us to determine his position, however.

viduals were limited to the right of possession, but only if the particular artifact had been properly registered, and the mere right to possess does not confer the right to sell an item or to give it as security for a loan.

These views were further corroborated by two civilian witnesses, one Mexican and one American. Ms. Diaz-Zambrano testified that she had learned in elementary school that the Mexican people own all vestiges of pre-Hispanic civilizations found in the country. Dr. Richard E. W. Adams, Professor of Anthropology and Dean of Humanities and Social Science at The University of Texas in San Antonio, testified that he had participated in several archaeological excavations in Mexico. He stated that in 1953 at a class he attended at the School of Anthropology and History in Mexico City, he was told that all archaeological items are the property of the nation and cannot be exported. He also testified that, insofar as it affected his work and the difficulty of exporting legitimately excavated objects from Mexico, the Mexican law had not changed in the last twenty years.

Against this massive record, appellants offered, in addition to their own views of Mexican law, the testimony of Ignacio Gomez Palacio, an attorney in Mexico who engages in legal research, writing, and a general practice. Like Mr. de los Rios, his opinion was based on independent review of the Mexican Constitution and relevant statutes, rather than on any long-held expertise on the particular subject of pre-Columbian artifacts. His testimony was similar to the conclusions reached earlier by the Fifth Circuit panel, and he seems to be the only witness to explain persuasively several passages in the statutes that are anomalous under the categorical views advanced by the government witnesses.[14]

On this new record the trial judge faced a dilemma. The Fifth Circuit had ruled him in error for having concluded that Mexico had claimed ownership as early as 1897, and the panel had re-emphasized its ruling even while instructing him to allow experts to correct any error in the appellate opinion. Yet the great weight of the government's new expert testimony indicated that his earlier conclusion might still be the proper view of Mexican law at least as interpreted by some of the few Mexican nationals qualified to express an authoritative opinion. Perhaps in view of this dilemma about the paths open to him and because none of the parties urged that it was his function to decide the question of applicable foreign law, the trial judge gave the jury the task of deciding whether and when Mexico

---

[14][*Orig. fn.*] As observed in note 13, supra, it was difficult for the government witnesses to account for the statutory declarations of ownership of Some items if the government supposedly owned All types of artifacts already. The declaratory passages made much more sense under Gomez' view that the government only gradually expanded its ownership claims. Contrary to Schon's analysis, Gomez read art. 27 of the 1917 Constitution as restricted to land, subsoil, and materials naturally occurring therein, such as minerals, precious stones, ores, oil. He classified manmade items that were found in the soil as "treasure trove" and noted that ownership claims to such items were regulated by provisions of the Civil Code of the Federal District. He analyzed art. 26 of the 1930 statute, set out in note 13, supra, as incorporating by reference the treasure trove statutes and as further evidence of the ability of private persons to own at least some artifacts under the earlier statutes.

Validly enacted national ownership of the artifacts involved.[15] In addition to now urging for the first time that the court erred in failing to make the determination of foreign law, the appellants argue that certain aspects of the instructions were erroneous and that the court erred in refusing to give the instructions they had offered.[16]

---

[15][*Orig. fn.*] The judge instructed the jury as follows: "Now, in order to find any one or more of the defendants guilty on one or more of the counts in the indictment, the government must prove three essential elements of the offense charged in this case beyond a reasonable doubt as follows: 1. That the Republic of Mexico was the owner of the alleged artifacts, if any, at the time such artifacts were exported if and only if you so find, from the Republic of Mexico into the United States of America; 2. That such artifacts, if any, were in fact exported from Mexico and thus imported into the United States of America from the Republic of Mexico; and 3. That such alleged artifacts were produced before the Spanish Conquest of Mexico and the government of the Republic of Mexico had not issued or granted a permit or license allowing and authorizing the defendants or any other person, firm, corporation, governmental agency or others to export such artifacts, if any, from Mexico to the United States of America or to any other country or place; and such artifacts, if any, had not been registered under Mexican law. As I have said, all three and each and every one of the essential elements that I have just given you must be proved and established to your satisfaction beyond a reasonable doubt before you can find the defendants guilty in this particular case. Now, there is absolutely no presumption that the defendants or any one of them knew the Mexican law. On the other hand, the United States of America is under no obligation to prove that the defendants knew the place from which the artifacts were allegedly stolen, if it is shown beyond a reasonable doubt that they were in fact stolen. What the United States must prove to your satisfaction beyond a reasonable doubt is that the defendants knew that the artifacts were in fact stolen under the laws of Mexico regardless of where they came or from where they were stolen and that the Mexican government had in fact effectively adopted valid laws acquiring ownership of such artifacts, if any, which were in existence at the time of such theft, if any, and that the defendants knew and understood such laws and that such laws had been violated."

[16][*Orig. fn.*] On numerous occasions during the trial the judge had clearly indicated his intent to give this issue to the jury. Beyond one tentative expression of doubt by an assistant prosecutor, none of the parties objected to putting this burden on the jury. The judge had also requested assistance from the parties in formulating the instructions on Mexican law, but none responded until the last moment, when they proffered handwritten requests in part tracking the earlier panel opinion. The judge thought his own set of instructions carefully followed the panel opinion because the jury was being told, in effect, to apply the applicable Mexican law to the defendants' behavior. In objecting to the charge, defendants' only points were that their proffered instructions were more precise renditions of the panel's legal conclusions than were the trial judge's. When, during the bench conference after the instructions had been given, the judge commented, "I put quite a burden on (the jury to find whether the Mexican laws were valid enactments)," appellants' attorneys failed to comment on the procedure.

Rule 26.1 of the Federal Rules of Criminal Procedure provides in part that "(t)he court, in determining foreign law, may consider any relevant material or source, including testimony, whether or not submitted by a party or admissible under (Rule 26). The court's determination shall be treated as a ruling on a question of law." Despite appellants' fond hopes, Rule 26.1 does not itself mandate that the judge rather than the jury decide all questions of foreign law. Rather, it provides that any determination a judge Does make shall be treated as a ruling on a question of law. This "functional approach," carefully sidestepping the issue of who is to decide the question, was deliberate on the part of the draftsmen.[17]

Our pre-Rule cases make clear that the proper procedure is for the judge rather than the jury to determine questions of foreign law. *Daniel Lumber Co. v. Empresas Hondurenas*, SA, 215 F.2d 465 (5th Cir. 1954), *cert. denied*, 348 U.S. 927 (1955); *Liechti v. Roche*, 198 F.2d 174 (5th Cir. 1952). To close the gap left in the Federal Rules of Criminal Procedure, we reaffirm that division of functions now, as we have done in the corresponding civil context. *First National City Bank v. Compania de Aquaceros*, SA, 398 F.2d 779, 782 (5th Cir. 1968). But it does not necessarily follow that putting the matter to the jury is reversible error. There is no automatic prejudice to the substantial rights of a defendant inherent in letting the jury decide the question on the basis of expert testimony. Indeed, the question whether the right to a jury trial in criminal matters requires submission of a question of foreign law to the jury, because it can be found as a matter of fact, has never been definitively laid to rest.[18] In the absence of compelling evidence of prejudice, we would be loath to reverse a conviction such as this where the evidence of guilt and of intent to violate both foreign and domestic law is near overwhelming. We believe, nevertheless, that reversal of at least the substantive count is required here because the most likely jury construction of Mexican law upon the evidence at trial is that Mexico declared itself owner of all artifacts at least as early as 1897. And under this view of Mexican law, we believe the defendants may have suffered the prejudice of being convicted pursuant to laws that were too vague to be a predicate for criminal liability under our jurisprudential standards.

It may well be, as testified so emphatically by most of the Mexican witnesses, that Mexico has considered itself the owner of all pre-Columbian artifacts for almost 100 years. If so, however, it has not expressed that view with sufficient clarity to survive translation into

---

[17][*Orig. fn.*] The Advisory Committee Notes on the Fed. R. Civ. P. 44.1 to which we are referred by the draftsmen of the Rules of Criminal Procedure observe that Rule 44.1, to which Rule 26.1 is substantially identical, does not address itself to this problem because the rules generally refrain from allocating functions between judge and jury. The committee adds, "It has long been thought, however, that the jury is not the appropriate body to determine issues of foreign law," citing, among other authorities, our pre- Federal Rules cases, *Daniel Lumber Co. v. Empresas Hondurenas*, SA, 215 F.2d 465 (5th Cir. 1954), *cert. denied*, 348 U.S. 927 (1955), *and Liechti v. Roche*, 198 F.2d 174 (5th Cir. 1952). Advisory Committee Note to Rule 44.1, Fed R Civ P, Title 28, U.S.C.A.

[18][*Orig. fn.*] See, *e.g.*, Kaplan, "Continuing Work of the Civil Committee: 1966 Amendments of the Federal Rules of Civil Procedure (II)," 81 Harv. L. Rev. 591, 617 (1968). Because no one argues the point here, we express no opinion on the issue.

terms understandable by and binding upon American citizens.[19] Neither the early statutes nor the Constitution of 1917 clearly declare national ownership of the sort of pre-Columbian movable artifacts in which appellants dealt. One of the government experts testified that a literal translation of the Mexican statutes into English would mislead those not familiar with Mexican law into thinking that such movables had been capable of being privately owned.[20] Another admitted that there were "confusions" in the 1934 statute caused by the lack of technical language and that subsequent statutes had been designed to clarify the legal situation.[21]

The 1972 statute, on the other hand, is clear and unequivocal in claiming ownership of all artifacts.[22] Deferring to this legitimate act of another sovereign, we agree with the earlier panel that it is proper to punish through the National Stolen Property Act encroachments upon legitimate and clear Mexican ownership, even though the goods may never have been physically possessed by agents of that nation. Nor does the infirmity of vagueness attach to the 1970 and possibly the 1934 statute insofar as they established presumptions that unregistered movables belong to the sovereign. Had these theories alone (either post-1972 exportation or post-1934 appropriation, coupled with failure to register) been presented to the

---

[19][*Orig. fn.*] Because of our disposition of the claims in this appeal largely on the ground of unconstitutional vagueness and harmless error, we need not now undertake the delicate task of deciding the meaning of the Mexican statutes and the manner in which the various provisions interact. We leave that task to subsequent courts should the government prosecute others by reference to pre-1972 Mexican statutes, either directly or as incorporated by art. 4 of the 1972 Transitory. See note 22 infra.

[20][*Orig. fn.*] Carlos Schon took issue with the translations offered in evidence by the defendants the translations used by the earlier panel in assessing the Mexican statutes. He especially objected to translating the word "propriedad" as "ownership" or "property," though he conceded that that rendering was proper in some of the statutory passages. He said that only one familiar with the Mexican law could decide when to translate the word as "ownership" because in many instances regarding artifacts the law limits "propriedad" to connoting mere possessory rights. Translation of "propriedad" as "property" might incorrectly lead those unfamiliar with Mexican law to believe some artifacts could be "outright property." Mr. Schon further testified that "translacion de dominion" could be translated as "acts of conveyance," provided the latter term was not understood to include "transfer of property or outright ownership." The literal translation, "transfer of dominion," would also be misleading, since the correct meaning of the law does not go beyond allowing "transfer of possession."

[21][*Orig. fn.*] As an instance of such "confusion" in the 1934 statute, Mr. Oropeza identified art. 10, which can be translated as requiring registration of private "transfers of ownership." In the original it reads: "Los proprietarios de objetos inscritos deberan dar conocimiento de las traslaciones de propriedad, para que se haga la anotacion correspondiente."

[22][*Orig. fn.*] The 1972 statute also contains a grandfather clause under which rights gained under previous statutes are preserved. Transitory, Article Fourth. Thus, if private persons were allowed ownership as opposed to mere possessory rights under the earlier laws, those rights would be retained provided the owner complied with the requirements of those laws.

jury, our appellate task would have been much simpler.[23] There is no doubt that the evidence is sufficient to have sustained convictions under either theory, and there would have been little prejudice involved in letting the jury decide the appropriate Mexican law to apply. But the expert testimony in the main allowed the jury to conclude that Mexico had long owned all these items outright. There was thus little need for the jury to consider legal and factual technicalities such as the probable date of exportation or the effect of the presumptions upon appellants' unregistered items. Unfortunately, under this broad view of Mexican law, our basic standards of due process and notice preclude us from characterizing the artifacts as "stolen." Though the National Stolen Property Act is not void for vagueness because the general class of offenses to which it is directed is plainly within its terms, it cannot properly be applied to items deemed stolen only on the basis of unclear pronouncements by a foreign legislature. The principle from Boyce Motor Lines, employed in the earlier appeal, cannot be used to deflect the vagueness charges directed at the early Mexican statutes. The basic premise of Boyce the existence of an area of conduct that is proscribed in reasonably certain terms is absent. *Boyce Motor Lines v. United States*, 342 U.S. at 340. The 1897 statute, the 1930 statute, and even the 1934 and 1970 statutes, unless there is specific focus on the presumption mechanism, do not clearly announce any line that appellants' willfulness can have led them to cross. As the Supreme Court observed in *Screws v. United States*, 325 U.S. 91, 105 (1945), "willful conduct cannot make definite that which is undefined." We therefore conclude that the convictions pursuant to the substantive count must be reversed.

By contrast, the requisite degree of prejudice for reversal is lacking as to the conspiracy count. The evidence presented to the jury amply showed that appellants' conspiracy was much broader than an intent to deal in the single collection already in the United States for an unspecified length of time. It is abundantly clear that they conspired to bring in at least one other load, and most likely a continuing stream of articles that, owing to a broken drive shaft and appellants' subsequent arrest, never arrived. Their plans regarding those loads and the conduit itself were clearly illegal under any view of Mexican law, including that presented by their own witnesses. The evidence is massive that appellants knew and deliberately ignored Mexico's post-1972 ownership claims. In addition, the continuing nature of their enterprise was highlighted in the closing arguments to the jury by the government and

---

[23][*Orig. fn.*] We express no opinion regarding the claim, made by amicus in its brief in the earlier appeal, that predicating criminal liability on a presumption contained in a foreign statute would also infringe due process.

the defendants alike.[24] Moreover, the instructions regarding the conspiracy count were separated from the instructions regarding the substantive count and, in outlining the required elements of the offense, the judge made no reference back to the jury's role regarding Mexican law. He correctly charged that the defendants need never have completed the illegal object of their conspiracy to be found guilty and also correctly instructed that none of the overt acts need themselves be illegal. The phone calls and meetings with McGauley and Benkendorfer and indeed the sale of the Rodriguez/Hollinshead/McClain collection can each be seen as overt acts in stringing along the "Mafia" buyers until the channel for regular importation of newly dug items was fully operational, as the buyers had requested.

Given the strength of this evidence regarding the continuing illegal purpose of appellants which, if effectuated, would necessarily entail dealing in "stolen" property under Any view of Mexican law, we hold that the dubious shifting of the determination of Mexican law constituted harmless error as to the conspiracy count.[25]

Accordingly, appellants' convictions on the conspiracy count are AFFIRMED, and the convictions on the substantive court are REVERSED.

---

[24][*Orig. fn.*] During closing arguments, William Simpson, who was defending himself, referred to the testimony about the continuing conspiracy and sought to turn it to his own advantage: "Mr. Rodriguez, according to Mrs. Zambrano's testimony, …told her that there were five groups of Mexicans, peons, farmers, people trying to make money apparently digging in Mexico and supplying him with great quantities of artifacts. The same thing holds true with that story. It can't possibly be true. Mrs. Zambrano under my examination, cross examine (sic) stated emphatically that that was happening at the present time, that that was a continuing operation; yet we have an inventory and it has been established that these pieces are the same pieces that Mr. Rodriguez left with me at that time, May of 1973. If Mrs. Zambrano's testimony was accurate, and I'm not saying it wasn't told to her, I don't believe it was, but if it was accurate, by necessity, being a conspiracy as we are charged here today, that inventory would have increased considerably. Five groups of Mexicans in a conduit as represented by Mrs. Zambrano channeling it into San Antonio, my goodness gracious, it would have filled up my house. We would not only have had the bedroom and the living room filled, it would have been added to and added to in great quantities."

[25][*Orig. fn.*] For these and additional reasons, we reject appellants' other challenges to the jury instructions. We can detect no affirmative errors in the statements about Mexican law made by the court. Nor did the judge err in refusing to give the instructions offered by appellants. The proffered summaries of Mexican law were fatally flawed in their treatment of the presumptions in the 1934 and 1970 statutes. Those presumptions, as part of statutes repealed by enactment of subsequent statutes, no longer have independent legal force. But they were not thereby rendered totally nugatory. The character of items excavated and held without registration for the statutory period may have been irrevocably impressed with a presumption of government ownership. In any event, no legal ownership of such items seems possible after the effective date of the 1972 statute. All items not legally owned by individuals were then nationalized, and it became impossible legally to own items without complying with the requirements of the earlier statutes. Transitory, Art. Fourth.

2. General Enforcement Regulations of
Land Managing Agencies

In addition to the sections of the Code of Federal Regulations that specifically protect heritage resources, there are general prohibitions that land managing agencies may use alone or in conjunction with other laws for protection purposes. For example, it is illegal to possess an archeological resource or a metal detector in any National Park, or to be in some parks after closing, or to park off-road of a Bureau of Land Management roadway. Also, most agencies have regulations prohibiting the destruction of plant material within a resource area, and they may be invoked when vegetation is damaged incidentally during the illegal excavation of an archeological site or is used to conceal the injured area. The C.F.R. violations may be cited individually for appearance in federal magistrate court, or they may be combined with felony counts in a criminal indictment or information.

SECTION D.   STATE ENFORCEMENT LAWS

Each state has heritage resource protection laws either as part of the burial protection legislation in its health and safety code, or as part of the criminal code. These laws apply on state and private lands [see C. Carnett, *A Survey of State Statutes Protecting Archeological Resources* (Dept. of the Interior, National Park Service, Off. of the Departmental Consulting Archeologist, Archeological Assistance Study No. 3, and National Trust for Historic Preservation, Preservation Law Reporter, Special Report, August 1995)].

SECTION E.   ISSUES IN ENFORCEMENT

With the rise of litigation in heritage resources enforcement, a number of legal issues have arisen and many remain unresolved. This section lists a few of these issues and offers some analysis to prompt further discussion.

1.   Double Jeopardy

Double jeopardy may arise as an issue in two areas. The first area of concern is when an agency law enforcement officer issues a citation for a heritage resource violation, and a criminal indictment or information follows for an activity arising from the same set of facts. If an individual is cited with a C.F.R. citation for injuring archeological resources, and the defendant appears and enters a plea or pays a fine in the magistrate court, then the government is precluded from charging the individual with an ARPA violation. The government, however, need not abandon any claim in forfeiture for items that can be seized under the forfeiture provision of ARPA, such as the tools or vehicles used in the commission of the offense.

Double jeopardy does not occur when different sovereigns take action. Thus, conviction in a state court for grave desecration on private land does not create double jeopardy for an individual later charged under ARPA for selling archeological resources from the grave in a second state. Also, violation of a state or local law is a predicate act for conviction under ARPA's interstate trafficking provision [16 U.S.C. § 470ee (1997)], but does not require that the conviction in state or local court be finalized.

Double jeopardy may also arise when, following a forfeiture proceeding for vehicles or tools used in the commission of an offense, there is a prosecution for an ARPA offense. Seizure of vehicles or tools used in the commission of an ARPA offense will occur almost immediately on discovery in order to avoid dissipation of the asset. However, because of the time involved in the preparation of a damage assessment, it usually takes several weeks or months thereafter to obtain an ARPA indictment. If the suspect forces the government to move ahead with forfeiture proceedings or release the items, the question may be asked whether the forfeiture proceeding constitutes double punishment for the offense. ARPA provides that forfeiture may be a separate proceeding that will not preclude criminal or civil prosecution for the actions of the underlying offense. Items such as vehicles and tools may be seized and forfeited under ARPA in an *in rem* proceeding, where they are not identified with an individual perpetrator.

2. Eighth Amendment

In *Austin v. United States*, 509 U.S. 602 (1993), the United States Supreme Court discussed whether forfeiture may constitute an excessive fine in violation of the Eighth Amendment. The forfeiture occurred in the context of a drug case, but the issue nonetheless is relevant. In *Austin,* the Court, acknowledging that forfeiture could serve the dual purposes of punishment and removal of the instrumentality of the crime, held that a close connection was required between the property seized and the underlying offense.

An ARPA forfeiture is not likely to violate the Eighth Amendment because ARPA provides a narrower scope of forfeiture than do drug forfeiture laws. Houses and vehicles in which stolen archeological resources merely are found are not automatically subject to seizure. Instead, the vehicle or tool must be used in connection with the actual offense in order to subject it to seizure. Moreover, the Supreme Court in *Austin* indicated that society may be compensated through forfeiture for harm done by the illegal activity. The Court's analysis is particularly applicable to ARPA forfeitures, when the archeological resources are irreplaceable pieces of the public's heritage, and when the financial ability of the defendant even to compensate for the cost of restoration and repair of the resource is inadequate. Thus, the application of the Eighth Amendment to vacate an ARPA forfeiture is unlikely.

3.   Treasure Trove

Although the public has a general fascination with finding hidden, mislaid, lost, or abandoned objects (with some people even adhering to a folkloric belief in their right to find them), the mining of heritage resources on public or private lands without permission is a crime. Furthermore, burials, National Historic Sites, National Monuments, National Battlefields, and National Parks are not treasure trove sites, and are not open for gratuitous discovery.

CHARRIER v. BELL

496 So.2d 601 (La. App. 1986)

PONDER, Judge (retired):

Plaintiff appealed the trial court's judgment denying both his claim as owner of Indian artifacts and his request for compensation for his excavation work in uncovering those artifacts under the theory of unjust enrichment. We affirm.

Plaintiff is a former Corrections Officer at the Louisiana State Penitentiary in Angola, Louisiana, who describes himself as an "amateur archeologist." After researching colonial maps, records and texts, he concluded that Trudeau Plantation,[1] near Angola, was the possible site of an ancient village of the Tunica Indians. He alleges that in 1967 he obtained the permission of Mr. Frank Hoshman, Sr., who he believed was the owner of Trudeau Plantation, to survey the property with a metal detector for possible burial locations. After locating and excavating approximately 30 to 40 burial plots, lying in a circular pattern, plaintiff notified Mr. Hoshman that he had located the Tunica village. Although the evidence is contradictory, plaintiff contends that it was at that time that Mr. Hoshman first advised that he was the caretaker, not the owner, of the property.

Plaintiff continued to excavate the area for the next three years until he had located and excavated approximately 150 burial sites, containing beads, European ceramics, stoneware,

---

[1][*Orig. fn.*] Trudeau Plantation consists of approximately 150 acres located on a bluff in the southeast quadrant of the meeting of the Mississippi River and Tunica Bayou. Angola is on the other side of the bayou.

glass bottles; iron kettles, vessels and skillets; knives, muskets, gunflints, balls and shots; crucifixes, rings and bracelets; and native pottery. The excavated artifacts are estimated to weigh two to twoand one-half tons.

In search of a buyer for the collection, plaintiff talked to Dr. Robert S. Neitzel of Louisiana State University, who, in turn, informed Dr. Jeffrey D. Brain of Harvard University. Dr. Brain, who was involved in a survey of archeology along the lower Mississippi River, viewed the artifacts and began discussions of their sale to the Peabody Museum of Harvard University. The discussions resulted in the lease of the artifacts to the Museum, where they were inventoried, catalogued and displayed.

Plaintiff initially informed Dr. Neitzel and Dr. Brain that he had found the artifacts in a cave in Mississippi, so as to conceal their source; later he did disclose the actual site of the find to Dr. Brain, who had expressed his concern over the title of the artifacts. Dr. Brain then obtained permission from the landowners to do further site testing and confirmed that it was the true source of the artifacts.

Confronted with the inability to sell the collection because he could not prove ownership, plaintiff filed suit against the six nonresident landowners of Trudeau Plantation, requesting declaratory relief confirming that he was the owner of the artifacts. Alternatively, plaintiff requested that he be awarded compensation under the theory of unjust enrichment for his time and expenses.

The State of Louisiana intervened in the proceeding on numerous grounds, including its duty to protect its citizens in the absence of the lawful heirs of the artifacts. In 1978, the State purchased Trudeau Plantation and the artifacts from the six landowners and agreed to defend, indemnify and hold the prior owners harmless from any and all actions.[2]

In 1981 the Tunica and Biloxi Indians were recognized as an American Indian Tribe by the Bureau of Indian Affairs of the Department of the Interior. The Tunica-Biloxi Indians of Louisiana, Inc. intervened in the instant suit seeking title to the artifacts and the site of the burial ground. At the same time, the tribe removed the action to federal district court, where they also filed a parallel action seeking title to the artifacts. The federal district court, on September 8, 1982, remanded the matter to state court and stayed the parallel action. *Charrier v. Bell*, 547 F. Supp. 580 (M.D. La. 1982). The Tunicas then withdrew, without prejudice, their claim to the property where the artifacts were located and the State subordinated its claim of title or trust status over the artifacts in favor of the Tunicas.

The trial judge held that the Tunica-Biloxi Tribe is the lawful owner of the artifacts, finding that plaintiff was not entitled to the artifacts under La. Civ. Code art. 3423 as it read prior to amendment by Act No. 187 of 1982, which required discovery "by chance." The judge also found that plaintiff had no claim to the artifacts on the basis of abandonment under La. Civ. Code art. 3421, as it read prior to the amendment by Act No. 187 of 1982, because the legal concept of abandonment does not extend to burial goods.

The trial court also denied relief under the theory of unjust enrichment, finding that any impoverishment claimed by plaintiff was a result of his attempts "for his own gain" and that his presence and actions on the property of a third party placed him in a "precarious position, if not in legal bad faith."

---

[2][*Orig. fn.*] Plaintiff filed a motion for litigious redemption which was granted by the trial court, but rejected by this court. The matter was remanded for trial. *Charrier v. Bell*, 380 So.2d 155 (La. App. 1979).

The issues before this court are the adequacy of proof that the Tunica-Biloxi Indians are descendants of the inhabitants of Trudeau, the ownership of the artifacts, and the applicability of the theory of unjust enrichment.

Plaintiff first argues that the evidence that the members of the Tunica-Biloxi Indians of Louisiana, Inc., are legal descendants of the inhabitants of Trudeau Plantation was insufficient to entitle them to the artifacts. He asserts that federal recognition of the tribe "merely proves that the Tribe is the best representative of the Tunica Indians for purposes of receiving federal benefits," and points to evidence of intermixing by the Tunica tribe with other tribes.

The fact that members of other tribes are intermixed with the Tunicas does not negate or diminish the Tunicas' relationship to the historical tribe. Despite the fact that the Tunicas have not produced a perfect "chain of title" back to those buried at Trudeau Plantation, the tribe is an accumulation of the descendants of former Tunica Indians and has adequately satisfied the proof of descent. This is evident from the "Final Determination for Federal Acknowledgment of the Tunica-Biloxi Indian Tribe of Louisiana," 46 Fed. Reg. 38,411 (July 27, 1981), which specifically found that the "contemporary Tunica-Biloxi Indian Tribe is the successor of the historical Tunica, Ofa and Avoyel tribes, and part of the Biloxi tribe." The evidence supports the finding that at least some portion of the Tunica tribe resided at Trudeau Plantation from 1731–1764. No contrary evidence, other than that suggesting intermixing, was presented at the trial of this case. Plaintiff's argument is without merit.

Plaintiff next argues that the Indians abandoned the artifacts when they moved from Trudeau Plantation, and the artifacts became res nullius until found and reduced to possession by plaintiff who then became the owner.

Plaintiff contends that he has obtained ownership of the property through occupancy, which is a "mode of acquiring property by which a thing which belongs to nobody, becomes the property of the person who took possession of it, with the intention of acquiring a right of ownership upon it." La. Civ. Code art. 3412, prior to amendment by Act No. 187 of 1982.[3]

One of the five methods of acquiring property by occupancy is "By finding (that is, by discovering precious stones on the sea shore, or things abandoned, or a treasure.)" La. Civ. Code art. 3414, prior to amendment by Act No. 187 of 1982. Plaintiff contends that the artifacts were abandoned by the Tunicas and that by finding them he became the owner.

---

[3][*Orig. fn.*] La. Civ. Code art. 3412, 3414 and 3421 cited herein were repealed by Acts 1982, No. 187, § 1, effective January 1, 1984. The provisions replacing those articles reproduce their substance. Although the language has changed, they do not change the law. See specifically La. Civ. Code art. 3412 and 3418, as adopted by Acts 1982, No. 187, § 1 and the comments. The articles previously read as follow: La. Civ. Code art. 3412 : Occupancy is a mode of acquiring property by which a thing which belongs to nobody, becomes the property of the person who took possession of it, with the intention of acquiring a right of ownership upon it. La. Civ. Code art. 3414: There are five ways of acquiring property by occupancy, to wit: By hunting. By fowling. By fishing. By finding (that is, by discovering precious stones on the sea shore, or things abandoned, or a treasure.) La. Civ. Code 3421: He who finds a thing which is abandoned, that is, which its owner has let [left] with the intention not to keep it any longer, becomes master of it in the same manner as if it had never belonged to any body.

Both sides presented extensive expert testimony on the history of the Tunica Indians, the French, English and Spanish occupation of the surrounding territory and the presence or absence of duress causing the Tunicas to abandon the Trudeau site.

However, the fact that the descendants or fellow tribesmen of the deceased Tunica Indians resolved, for some customary, religious or spiritual belief, to bury certain items along with the bodies of the deceased, does not result in a conclusion that the goods were abandoned. While the relinquishment of immediate possession may have been proved, an objective viewing of the circumstances and intent of the relinquishment does not result in a finding of abandonment. Objects may be buried with a decedent for any number of reasons. The relinquishment of possession normally serves some spiritual, moral, or religious purpose of the descendant/owner, but is not intended as a means of relinquishing ownership to a stranger. Plaintiff's argument carried to its logical conclusion would render a grave subject to despoliation either immediately after interment or definitely after removal of the descendants of the deceased from the neighborhood of the cemetery.

Although plaintiff has referred to the artifacts as res nullius, under French law, the source of Louisiana's occupancy law, that term refers specifically to such things as wild game and fish, which are originally without an owner. The term *res derelictae* refers to "things voluntarily abandoned by their owner with the intention to have them go to the first person taking possession." P. Esmein, Aubry & Rau Droit Civil Francais, Vol. II, §168, p. 46 (7th Ed. 1966). Some examples of res derelictae given by Aubry and Rau include things left on public ways, in the cities or to be removed by garbage collectors.

The artifacts fall into the category of res derelictae, if subject to abandonment. The intent to abandon res derelictae must include the intent to let the first person who comes along acquire them. Obviously, such is not the case with burial goods.

French sources have generally held that human remains and burial goods located in cemeteries or burial grounds are not "treasure" under article 716 of the French Civil Code and thereby not subject to occupancy upon discovery. *Blancherot v. Couilhy*, Bordeaux, 6 Aug. 1806, 38 Dalloz Jurisprudence Generale, § 186 n. (1), p. 230 (1857). The reasoning has been that any contrary decision would lead to and promote commercial speculation and despoilment of burial grounds. The French commentator Demolombe noted the special treatment that should be given to burial goods, stating that such objects "have not been placed underground with the same intention which informs the deposit of what is called treasure, which in the latter case is, for a temporary period... Rather, they are an emplacement for a perpetual residence therein..." 13 C. Demolombe, Cours de Code Napoleon § 37, pp. 45–46 (2c ed. 1862).

The same reasoning that the French have used to treat burial goods applies in determining if such items can be abandoned. The intent in interring objects with the deceased is that they will remain there perpetually, and not that they are available for someone to recover and possess as owner.

For these reasons, we do not uphold the transfer of ownership to some unrelated third party who uncovers burial goods. The trial court concluded that La. Civ. Code art. 3421, as it read prior to passage of Act No. 187 of 1982, was not intended to require that objects buried with the dead were abandoned or that objects could be acquired by obtaining possession over the objections of the descendants. We agree with this conclusion.

The cases cited by plaintiff are distinguishable.

In *Touro Synagogue v. Goodwill Industries of New Orleans Area, Inc.*, 233 La. 26, 96 So2d 29 (1957), the court found that a cemetery had been abandoned for burial purposes and the owner had the right to sell the property; however, the court conditioned the sale on the disinterment and reinterment (in another cemetery) of the remains of the deceased.

In *Ternant v. Boudreau*, 6 Rob. 488 (1844), jewelry interred with the decedent was stolen and recovered. The plaintiff claimed the ownership of all such goods on the basis that he purchased the decedent's succession from defendant who was the heir. The court found that the plaintiff was the lawful owner of the jewelry since there had been a valid sale from the descendant. The sale evidenced an express intent by the descendant not to retain ownership of the burial goods.

The court in *McEnery v. Pargoud*, 10 La. Ann. 497 (1855) found that the temporary use of land as a cemetery, from 1794 to 1800, did not exclude it from commerce. There was no mention of the abandonment of the remains of the dead or the burial goods and there is no inconsistency in that decision and the opinion stated herein.

Humphreys v. Bennett Oil Corporation, 195 La. 531, 197 So 222 (1940) merely acknowledges that descendants have a cause of action against a person who disturbs a cemetery.

Plaintiff strongly argues that a finding that Indians did not abandon the artifacts will necessarily require the federal court to conclude that the Tunicas did not abandon the real property at Trudeau Plantation and could work havoc with the stability of Louisiana land titles. However, the question of the abandonment of the real property was excluded from the case. This opinion should not be interpreted as making any expression thereon.

Plaintiff next argues that he is entitled to recover a sum of money to compensate his services and expenses on the basis of an actio de in rem verso.

The five criteria of such a claim de in rem verso are: (1) there must be an enrichment, (2) there must be an impoverishment, (3) there must be a connection between the enrichment and resulting impoverishment, (4) there must be an absence of justification or cause for the enrichment and impoverishment, and (5) there must be no other remedy at law available to plaintiff. *Creely v. Leisure Living, Inc.* 437 So2d 816 (La 1983*); Edmonston v. A-Second Mortgage Company of Slidell Inc.*, 289 So2d 116 (La 1974).

We first question whether there has been an enrichment. While the nonresident landowners were "enriched" by the sale of the property to the state, the ultimate owners of the artifacts presented substantial evidence that the excavation caused substantial upset over the ruin of "ancestrial burial grounds," rather than any enrichment.

Even if the Indians have been enriched, plaintiff has failed to prove that he has sustained the type impoverishment for which de in rem verso, may be used. His alleged loss resulted from the hours he spent excavating the artifacts, the greater portion of which activity was done at a time when plaintiff knew he was on property without the consent of the landowner. While contradictory testimony was presented regarding whether plaintiff initially had permission to go on the property, and whether that permission was adequate, by his own admission, plaintiff was informed by Hoshman that he did not own the property before the cessation of the excavating. Plaintiff's knowledge is further evidenced by his attempts to keep the location of his work secret; he did not identify Trudeau Plantation as the location of the find for almost five years after his discovery and he failed to seek out the landowners of the property until it was required for sale negotiations, although he removed two and one half tons of artifacts from their property. Plaintiff further acknowledges that he knew that the Tunica Indians might object to his excavations.

The actio de in rem verso, explained by the Louisiana Supreme Court in *Minyard v. Curtis Products, Inc.*, 251 La. 624, 205 So2d 422 (1967) and derived from the similar French action, is influenced greatly by French Civil Code articles from which our own are copied. *Minyard*, 205 So2d 432. The impoverishment element in French law is met only when the factual circumstances show that it was not a result of the plaintiff's own fault or negligence or was not undertaken at his own risk. Comment, Actio De In Rem Verso in Louisiana: *Minyard v. Curtis Products, Inc.*, 43 Tul. L. Rev. 263, 286 (1969); *Brignac v. Boisdore*, 288 So2d 31, 35 n. 2 (La. 1973). Obviously the intent is to avoid awarding one who has helped another through his own negligence or fault or through action taken at his own risk. Plaintiff was acting possibly out of his own negligence, but more probably knowingly and at his own risk. Under these circumstances, plaintiff has not proven the type of impoverishment necessary for a claim of unjust enrichment.

Additionally, plaintiff has failed to show that any enrichment was unjustified, entitling him to an action to recover from the enriched party. An enrichment will be unjustified "only if no legal justification for it exists by reason of a contract or provision of law intended to permit the enrichment or the impoverishment or to bar attack upon the enrichment." Justice A. Tate, *The Louisiana Action for Unjustified Enrichment*, 50 Tul. L. Rev. 883, 904 (1976). Any enrichment received by the Tribe was justified. *Humphreys v. Bennett Oil Corp.*, 195 La. 531, 197 So 222 (1940); *Choppin v. LaBranche*, 48 La. Ann. 1217, 20 So. 681 (1896). In *Humphreys*, the court recognized a right of action to recover damages for mental anguish and pain and suffering for desecration of a cemetery, while *Choppin* allowed injunctive relief against a tomb owner threatening to remove remains of the dead. Thus, descendants have a right to enjoin the disinterment of their deceased relatives, as well as to receive damages for the desecration involved. Such a right would be subverted if descendants were obliged to reimburse for the expenses of the excavation. See *V & S Planting Company v. Red River Waterway Commission*, 472 So2d 331 (La. App. 1985), *writ denied*, 475 So2d 1106 (1985); *G. Woodward Jackson Co., Inc. v. Crispens*, 414 So2d 855 (La. App. 1982). There is a legal justification for any enrichment received by the Tribe and plaintiff is not entitled to invoke the equitable theory.

For these reasons the judgment of the trial court is affirmed at appellant's costs.
AFFIRMED.

Note

The Court in *Charrier* clearly held that burials were not abandoned property subject to random finds, and that it was not unjust enrichment to return to tribal people their own property. The claimant had no right of ownership and, therefore, no claim to the items. Further, he had no right to expect compensation for his efforts. Also, the court's comment about the right of tribal people to seek tort damages from persons who desecrate the burials of their dead is noteworthy.

CHAPTER FOUR

NATIVE AMERICAN HERITAGE RESOURCES

In my native language, Tewa, the word **nung** translates into English as both "earth" and "us." We and the earth are one and the same. Every stone, every mountain, every tree, every animal, even the clay we use to make our pottery, is a living thing. We share the life of the world, and are a part of it. For us, respect for the sacredness of the earth is as essential as respect for the sacredness of life itself.

Our approach to the world in which we live has been very different from that of European-Americans. We thanked the earth for giving us clay for pottery, and through the process of making the pot we would speak with it and ask for its help to make a beautiful vessel. When a man killed a deer to feed his family, he would thank the deer for giving its life for the family. When the corn first was brought in during harvest it would be greeted and welcomed into the village.

Our world view extends to our view of "cultural property." While the Euro-centric legal system understands a "site" as being a place that shows clear evidence of human occupation, our definition also would include everything in and around the "site" that contributed to its occupation. A site is not a confined space where an isolated event occurred as much as it is the combination of everything that contributed to it being where it is. Thus, in the Pueblo world the physical pueblo structure is only a part of what makes up the village. The whole village really is made up of the surrounding mountains, the agricultural fields, and the sacred places, near and far, that are all part of a complete life.

It is encouraging to see that the American legal system is attempting to accommo-date and incorporate Native American world views as rights to which we are entitled. Because the world views of native peoples and this legal system are, on many levels, alien to each other, the process always will be complex. Each tribe has its own history and unique way of structuring its world; each one will value different places and events in different ways. The best hope I have for the future is that, with training, American lawyers and land management professionals will have a clearer understand-ing of how the law affects, and has been affected by, the concerns of native peoples for their cultural patrimony.

Tessie Naranjo, member, Santa Clara Pueblo; chair, Native American Graves Protection and Repatriation Act (NAGPRA) Review Committee, 1993–; board member, Keepers of the Treasures.

SECTION A.   AN OVERVIEW AND BRIEF HISTORY

Like the other resources discussed in this book, Native American heritage resources may be prehistoric or historic, terrestrial or maritime. They are unique, however, in that they often are subject to the fiduciary management of the federal government, but nevertheless are defined and controlled by separate sovereigns within the national borders. Thus, the United States government may enact laws and promulgate regulations to protect Native American heritage resources, but Native Americans determine whether the items in question are defined resources falling within the scope of those laws and regulations.

Because identification of heritage resources varies among Native American groups, this text does not survey American Indian tribal law on property. Instead, it focuses on federal and state heritage resources law that take traditional American concepts of property law and applies them to Native American property. Respecting the civil rights of indigenous peoples does not create new law, but, rather, existing legal theory is applied to a previously disenfranchised group.

In the past, both Congress and the courts distinguished Native American and non-Native American property rights. Applying European concepts of individual property and Christian concepts of burial practice to Native American heritage resources, they repeatedly treated Native American heritage resources as a discrete property category. Thus, in *Onondaga Nation v. Thacher* [29 Misc. 428, 61 N.Y.S. 1027 (1899), *aff'd*, 53 A.D. 561, 65 N.Y.S. 1014 (1900), *aff'd*, 169 N.Y. 584, 62 N.E. 1098 (1901), *reargument denied*, 169 N.Y. 596, 62 N.E. 1098 (1902), *error dismissed*, 189 U.S. 306 (1903)], the Onondaga did not have standing to assert a property right to Wampum belts (although more than 80 years after the case was filed, the Wampum belts were returned in an out-of-court settlement). Also, the state courts historically declined to protect Native American burial places, either because Indian burials were not marked in the manner of Christian cemeteries or because all old skeletons were held to be so disintegrated as to no longer merit protection [*Wana the Bear v. Community Construction, Inc.*, 128 Cal. App. 3d 536, 180 Cal. Rptr. 423 (1982)]. In addition, the courts historically have declined to protect Native American religious practices on the grounds that to do so would violate the Establishment Clause of the Constitution. As a result, Navajo gods could be drowned by Lake Powell, and Cherokee sacred sites could be flooded by the Tellico Dam.

STATE v. GLASS

27 Ohio App. 2d 214, 273 N.E.2d 893 (1971)

Syllabus by the Court

1. An excavation ceases to be a 'grave' under R.C. 2923.07 when the human remains originally placed therein have decomposed to such a degree that they no longer meet the definition of a 'corpse' or 'dead body.'
2. The reenactment of a statute creates a presumption of legislative adoption of a previous judicial construction of such statute.

GRAY, Judge:

This cause is in this court on an appeal on questions of law from a judgment of the Court of Common Pleas of Brown County. Defendant was convicted by a three judge court of what is commonly know as 'grave robbing,' an offense denounced by R.C. § 2923.07 and also of the offense denounced by R.C. § 155.03 in that defendant without lawful authority did remove certain monuments, gravestones and grave markers from a cemetery.

Defendant, feeling aggrieved by this result of her trial, filed her notice of appeal and assigned the following errors:

First Assignment of Error—The court erred in permitting the State to amend the indictment and the bill of particulars to allow the state to obtain a conviction on proof that the offenses charged in the indictment had occurred two years before the dates set forth in the indictment and in the bill of particulars.

Second Assignment of Error—A delay of over two years in the initiation of prosecution operated to deny appellant a fair trial and to deprive her of rights guaranteed by due process of law.

Third Assignment of Error—The court erred in excluding testimony which tended to demonstrate that appellant had not acted willfully in committing the acts charged in the indictment-testimony which was relevant to the question of guilt or innocence.

Fourth Assignment of Error—The court erred in admitting hearsay testimony, over the objection of counsel for appellant, to the prejudice of appellant.

Fifth Assignment of Error—The court erred in denying appellant's motion for judgment of acquittal at the conclusion of the state's case where the state had failed to offer any probative evidence tending to establish that appellant had acted willfully and unlawfully as charged in the indictment.

Sixth Assignment of Error—By repeatedly reciting facts outside of the record, facts designed to demonstrate the prosecutor's personal knowledge of relevant information, the prosecutor acted in a manner to deny appellant a fair trial.

Seventh Assignment of Error—The court erred in predicating conviction solely upon a finding that appellant had transferred bodies from one grave to another without fully complying with all applicable statutes where the court admitted and the evidence demonstrated that appellant had not acted willfully in violation of the law.

Defendant is a real estate developer who had purchased a tract of approximately 60 acres of land in Huntington Township, Brown County. In developing the land, she ordered bulldozers to level land upon which a cemetery was located. The cemetery contained 21.6 poles of land and four graves. This land was excepted from the operation of her deed. There were three headstones and an 'ordinary big rock' that served as a headstone for one grave. It was determined that Alexander and Isabel Raines were buried there along with their cousin, Eleanor, who had an engraved headstone also.

It could not be determined which grave the 'ordinary big rock' marked. Defendant secured a health permit to remove the bodies. She employed a licensed undertaker to move the bodies to another cemetery and also paid for moving the stones.

She attempted to secure approval of the Huntington Township Trustees, but the township records do not disclose any action of approval of the project. Several heated sessions and confrontations occurred which no doubt were the moving forces that caused the matters to be taken before the grand jury.

The first count of the indictment was based upon the language of R.C. § 2923.07. The offense stated in that section is commonly known as 'grave robbing.'

A 'grave robber' is defined in Webster's Third New International Dictionary as 'one that breaks open a grave to obtain interred valuables or to remove the body (as for illicit dissection): a body snatcher: Ghoul.'

The caption of R.C. § 2923.07 (effective October 1, 1953) is 'Grave Robbing.'

Consideration of the title is especially proper where, as in Ohio, the title is prefixed by a solemn vote of the legislature passing the law, and there is a constitutional provision that no bill shall contain more than one subject, which shall be clearly expressed in the title.

The title of an act may be utilized for determining the purpose which induced the enactment of the law, which purpose may be considered in arriving at a correct interpretation of its terms.

In the interpretation of statutes, the titles thereof have been declared to be persuasive and entitled to great weight when one is determining their meaning.

Applying the law to the facts of this case, we are of the opinion that there is no evidence tending to prove the defendant is guilty of the offense of 'grave robbing.'

Ethel Raines Davis testified for the prosecution. Her testimony revealed that she was then 79 years old and that Alexander and Isabel Raines were her grandparents. These grandparents would have had to have been buried many years ago. Considering the state of the art of embalming at that time, the type of caskets and burial equipment then in use, and an elapse of time of approximately 125 years, the bodies would be entirely decomposed.

25A C.J.S. Dead Bodies § 1, p. 488, states in part as follows:

The term 'dead body' is synonymous with the word 'corpse,' and as used in a legal sense means the body of a human being deprived of life. When the word 'body' is used to denote human remains it suggests a corporeal or tangible entity, and thus the terms 'body' and 'dead body' do not include the remains of a human body which has long since decomposed. (Citing *Carter v. Zanesville*, 59 Ohio St 170, 52 NE 126.)

In 1880, when the statute in question (R.S. § 7034, 77 Ohio Laws 85) was first enacted in present form, the caption of the section read: 'Penalty for grave robbing.'

When this statute became part of the General Code (Section 13391) the caption read 'Grave Robbing.'

Thus, we see that for over 90 years and after two major revisions of our code, the legislature acquiesced in the title and synopsis of the contents of this section. The meaning of the words 'corpse' and 'body' was interpreted by the Supreme Court in the case of *Carter v. Zanesville*, 59 Ohio St. 170, 52 N.E. 126 (1898). It construed a related section of the code (R.S. § 3764) which read in part as follows:

> Any person, association or company, having unlawful possession of the body of any deceased person shall be jointly and severally liable with any and all other persons, associations and companies, that had or have had unlawful possession of such corpse...

The court at page 178, 52 N.E. at page 127 of the opinion said:

> This statute is directed against such persons, et cetera, as have unlawful possession of a 'body' of a deceased person. The section further refers to the 'body' as such 'corpse.' The terms 'body' and 'corpse' found in this statute do not include the remains of persons long buried and decomposed.

Where a word or phrase has previously received a judicial construction in a related section of the code and there have been major revisions of the code by the General Assembly since that time, it will be presumed that the General Assembly had the intention to adopt the construction placed upon the word or phrase by the courts. *Cf. Goehring v. Dillard*, 145 Ohio St. 41, 60 N.E.2d 704.

As an aid in the construction of a statute, it is to be assumed or presumed that the legislature was acquainted with, and had in mind, the judicial construction of former statutes on the subject.

Accordingly, where words used in a statute have acquired a settled meaning through judicial interpretation and the same terms are used in a subsequent statute upon the same or an analogous subject, they are generally interpreted in the latter as in the former, where the object to which the words are applied, or the connection in which it stands, does not require it to be differently understood in the two statutes, or where a contrary intention of the legislature is not made clear by other qualifying or explanatory terms.

Since it may be presumed that the legislature knew the construction, long acquiesced in, which had been given by the courts to statute reenacted by the legislature, it may equally be presumed that the legislature intended to adopt the construction as well as the language of the prior enactment. It is, accordingly, a settled rule of statutory construction that when a statute or a clause or provision thereof has been construed by a court of last resort, and the same is substantially reenacted, the legislature may be regarded as adopting such construction. This rule has been generally held to be persuasive and in some cases is even regarded as binding upon the courts.

The purpose of the General Assembly is a dominant factor in determining the meaning of any statutory legislation. There is no better key to a difficult problem of statutory construction than the law from which the challenged statute emerged. Remedial laws are to be interpreted in the light of previous experience and prior enactment. *United States v. Congress of Industrial Organizations*, 335 U.S. 106, 112, 113.

Reenactment of a statute creates a presumption of legislative adoption of previous judicial construction. A statute susceptible of either of two opposing interpretations must be read in the manner which effectuates, rather than frustrates, the major purpose of the legislative draftsman. *Shapiro v. United States*, 335 U.S. 1, 2.

It is also a well established rule of statutory construction that all the provisions of a code bearing upon a single subject matter should be construed harmoniously.

The record shows that this plot of ground was grown up with brambles, briars, weeds and was abandoned for all intents and purposes.

The undertaker testified that he had to use probes to determine where the graves had originally been located. The relative softness of the ground revealed where the ground had once been disturbed.

We are of the view that these former places of excavation ceased to be graves when no 'body' or 'corpse' remained and that R.C. § 2923.07 does not relate to the remains of persons long buried or decomposed. *Carter v. Zanesville*, supra.

We are also of the view that this section of the law applies only to 'grave robbers,' ghouls and the like, ones who have nefarious purpose in disturbing the excavations.

It is interesting to note that neither the undertaker, the gravedigger who allegedly disinterred the bodies, nor the bulldozer operator who levelled the ground were charged with any offense. From the record, we learn that this defendant was ordered to Lima State Hospital for 60 days for a sanity examination upon the bald statement in a journal entry that:

> It appearing to the Court that the defendant herein was found guilty of the offense of opening a grave under such Section 2923.07 of the Revised Code of Ohio;
>
> And, it further appearing to the Court that the said defendant may be mentally ill, a mentally deficient offender, or a psychopathic offender...

The record does not show that there was any medical evidence adduced that would warrant such action on the part of the trial court. After her examination at Lima for 60 days, she was found to be sane.

She did everything required by the law, but failed in the end to get the necessary permit.

These mortal remains must have been buried for at least 125 years and under the definition given in *Carter v. Zanesville*, supra, they were no longer 'bodies' or 'corpse(s).' A grave has been defined as an excavation in the earth in which a dead body is or is buried.

Since there was no corpse in this excavation, there was no grave in the sense intended by the various General Assemblies in motivating them to enact R.C. § 2923.07 and previous related sections.

The offense denounced by this section is classed as a felony and hence serious consequences flow from a conviction thereunder. There is no evidence that anything of value was found in this plot of land.

A cadaver is not an everlasting thing. After undergoing an undefined degree of decomposition, it ceases to be a dead body in the eyes of the law. Disinterment of anything not remotely identifiable as a human corpse, though carried out with no good intent, could not amount to 'grave robbing.'

In a famous English ecclesiastical case, *Gilbert v. Buzzard*, 161 Eng. Rep. 761 (1820), in an opinion written by Sir William Scott (later Lord Stowell), the court held that the right of burial extends in time no farther than the period needed for complete dissolution.

The prosecution failed to convict defendant by the requisite degree of proof and she is therefore discharged on the first count.

R.C. § 155.03 in pertinent part states as follows:

> No person shall, without lawful authority, remove... a gravestone, gravemarker, or other marker erected to perpetuate the memory or (sic)... other person...

Under the facts of this case as developed in the record, defendant did not have any lawful authority to remove the gravestone, therefore, she is guilty of the offense charged in the second count of the indictment.

Judgment accordingly.

ABELE, P. J., concurs.

STEPHENSON, Judge (dissenting):

The indictment upon which the defendant was prosecuted provided in its material part that:

> ... one B. F. Glass, did unlawfully and willfully open a grave where a corpse had been deposited, contrary to Section 2923.07 of the Revised Code of Ohio.

R.C. § 2923.07 is captioned 'grave robbing' and reads as follows:

> No person shall willfully and unlawfully open a grave or tomb where a corpse has been deposited, or remove a corpse from its sepulchre, or knowingly deliver a corpse so removed to another for medical or surgical study, or receive, conceal, or secrete a corpse, knowing it to have been so removed or delivered.
>
> Whoever violates this section shall be imprisoned not less than one nor more than five years.

The above section had its inception in 44 Ohio Laws 77, 1846, wherein an act was published which stated the purpose in the title- 'To secure the inviolability of places of human sepulchre.' Section 1 of the act provided:

> That if any person shall open the grave of any deceased person, or the tomb where the body of any deceased person has been deposited, or shall remove the body or remains of any deceased person from its grave or other place of sepulchre, for the purpose of dissection or any surgical or anatomical experiments, or for any other purpose, without the consent of the near relatives of the deceased, if there are any, otherwise without the consent of the trustees of the township in which such body has been deposited, or, if within any incorporated city, town or borough, without the consent of the municipal authorities thereof, or shall, in any way, aid, assist or procure the same to be done, or shall receive, conceal or secrete any such body, or shall aid or assist in any

surgical or anatomical experiments or demonstrations therewith, or dissection thereof, knowing said body to have been so taken or removed from the place of its sepulchre, every such person, upon conviction thereof, shall be fined in any sum not exceeding one thousand dollars, or imprisoned not more than six months, or both, at the discretion of the court.

The section was embodied in the Revised Statutes of 1880 as Section 7034. In 77 Ohio Laws 85, the section was amended to read:

Whoever, without lawful authority, willfully opens the grave or tomb where any corpse has been deposited, or removes any corpse from its place of sepulchre, or knowingly delivers any corpse so unlawfully removed to another for medical or surgical study, and whoever receives, conceals, or secretes any corpse so removed or delivered, knowing it to have been so removed or delivered, shall, upon conviction removed be imprisoned in the penitentiary not more than five years nor less than one year; and whoever assists in any surgical or anatomical experiment or demonstration upon any corpse unlawfully obtained, knowing it to have been so unlawfully obtained, shall be fined not more than one thousand dollars nor less than one hundred dollars, or imprisoned not more than one year nor less than six months or both.

In 1883, in *Schneider v. State*, 40 Ohio St. 336, the Ohio Supreme Court stated, with respect to R.S. § 7034, concerning an alleged offense which occurred in 1879:

The statute, section 7034 Rev. Stats., under which the indictment is framed, defines several distinct offenses. It is directed against any person who without lawful authority opens a grave, or removes the corpse from its place of sepulcher, or delivers it to another for surgical study, or who receives, conceals or secretes the same so removed, or assists in any surgical demonstration, knowing it to have been so removed or delivered.

R.S. § 7034 was enacted into the General Code as Section 13391. It was captioned 'grave robbing' and provided:

Whoever, willfully and unlawfully opens a grave or tomb where a corpse has been deposited, or removes a corpse has been sepulchre, or knowingly delivers a corpse so unlawfully removed to a person for medical or surgical study, or receives, conceals or secretes a corpse, knowing it to have been so removed or delivered, shall be imprisoned in the penitentiary not less than one year nor more than five years.

Where I differ initially from my colleagues in this case is that I am not persuaded the offense charged in this case is that of 'grave robbing.' Admittedly, R.C. § 2923.07, under which the indictment is drawn bears that title. However, by the provisions of R.C. § 1.01, the title, chapter and section headings do not constitute any part of the law as contained in the Revised Code. The decision of the Supreme Court in *Schneider v. State*, supra, in construing R.S. § 7034, is clear authority that several offenses are embraced in R.C. § 2923.07, one of which is the willful and unlawful opening of a grave in which a corpse has been deposited. It is that latter offense, and solely that, laid in the indictment herein.

I find I must differ, also, from the majority opinion in the conclusions that the conduct proscribed; *i.e.*, the wilful or unlawful opening of a grave is lawful or unlawful depending upon the state of preservation of the corpse.

The legal distinction pointed out in the majority opinion between what is meant by 'body' and that which remains after the body decomposes has long been recognized. By the same token, the legal distinction between the body of the deceased and the grave itself has also been recognized. In 21 ALR2d 476 at 477, the following is stated:

> In considering the law of dead bodies, two concepts are to be borne in mind: (1) In legal contemplation a grave and the body interred within it are separate entities. (2) A cadaver is not an everlasting thing; after undergoing an undefined degree of decomposition it ceases to be a dead body in the eyes of the law.
>
> A grave is nothing more than a place where a body (or the ashes of a cremated body) is buried. It continues to be a grave as long as it is recognized or is recognizable as such. This may extend over centuries, long after the interred body and its trappings have merged with the soil and have become altogether undiscernible.

In carefully considering R.C. § 2923.07 and the predecessor enactments, it would appear anomalous that the legislature intended a criminal sanction in unlawfully opening a grave where a body is preserved and intended no sanction if decomposition has occurred and only skeleton remnants remain. Particularly is this so in light of the original enactment that it is an offense 'if any person shall open the grave of any deceased person, or the tomb where the body of any deceased person has been deposited.'

The reason is well stated in 21 ALR2d 476, as follows:

> The normal treatment of a corpse, once it is decently buried, is to let it lie. This idea is so deeply woven into our legal and cultural fabric that it is commonplace to hear it spoken of as a 'right' of the dead and a charge on the quick. Neither the ecclesiastical, common, nor civil system of jurisprudence permits exhumation for less than what are considered weighty, and sometimes compelling, reasons. Securing 'unbroken final repose' has been the object of both civil and criminal legislation.

The gist of the violation here charged is violation of the grave and not the body. Thus, the decision of the Ohio Supreme Court in *Carter v. Zanesville*, 59 Ohio St. 170, 52 N.E. 126, where the gist of the civil action under R.S. § 3764 was the possession of a 'body,' is not inconsistent with the view here adopted.

Assuming, without conceding its correctness, the view of the majority that a 'body' must be in the opened grave for a violation to occur, the record is such that the trier of fact could fairly and reasonably conclude that bodies were moved. The funeral director testified that he was hired to remove the 'remains' from the graves and then stated that he removed four 'bodies.' The exact date these persons were buried is not discernible from the record. The paucity of the record as to the state of the bodies results from the fact that no attempt was made to defend in the trial court or here upon the basis that the bodies were decomposed. I am not persuaded that this court may, with propriety, assume the bodies to have been completely decomposed because of embalming practices, type of caskets and burial equipment with respect to such deceased persons, when the record is silent in such matters.

Under the facts of this case, there could be no question that defendant acted willfully. It is also an element of the offense that the opening of the grave be unlawful. R.C. § 517.21 regulates the removal of bodies from abandoned cemeteries by township trustees and R.C. § 517.23 regulates the removal by township trustees upon application of the next of kin. The record reflects that defendant knew of such statutes and knew further that the township trustees refused to act upon her request to move the bodies. She had secured a permit from the health department as contemplated by R.C. § 517.23. She could not herself apply under R.C. § 517.23 to remove the bodies as she was not a next of kin. Even had such next of kin made application, removal would still be unlawful without action by the trustees.

I have considered the errors assigned and do not believe them well taken. The case was fairly tried, in my view, and the record supports the finding of guilt, and, therefore, I would affirm the judgment below.

Note

The dissent held that opening a grave is unlawful, and that the character of the activity does not depend on the status of the deceased. How likely is it that the dissent would prevail if the matter were decided today? Does a grave protection statute fail for lack of specificity if the age of the corpse is not expressly stated? The case discusses statutory interpretation in detail. Is the result consistent with the discussion?

NEWMAN v. STATE

174 So.2d 479 (Fla. Dist. Ct. App. 1965)

KANNER, Judge (Ret.):

The skull of a Seminole Indian, John Osceola, about two years deceased at the time, was taken from a box or coffin situated on the ground in a sawgrass island of Big Cypress Swamp in the Florida Everglades, Collier County, by defendant-petitioner, Arnold Clifford Newman, a fourth year student at the University of Miami. He was charged by the State with wantonly and maliciously disturbing the contents of a tomb or grave. Jury trial was waived; Newman was tried before the county judge, found guilty, and was sentenced to six months imprisonment in the county jail. Appeal was taken to the circuit court which, without opinion, affirmed the judgment and sentence.

Newman seeks through petition for writ of certiorari to quash the circuit court's judgment of affirmance, urging in effect that the State failed to establish that he had committed the criminal offense as denounced by the statute[1] under which he was tried and convicted and that, because of this, there was a departure from the essential requirements of law. Primarily, the State's position is that petitioner presents nothing warranting the issuance of writ of certiorari because there was no flagrant departure from the essential requirements of law and that this petition, rather, is an attempt to gain a second appeal.

Under the circumstances reflected by the record, petitioner is entitled to have his case reviewed. As announced in *Haile v. Bullock*, 83 Fla. 538, 91 So. 683, 684 (1922), questions of the weight and probative force of conflicting testimony ordinarily may not be considered; and mere errors of procedure that do not obviously prejudice fundamental rights, to the material injury of complaining parties, may not cause a judgment to be quashed on certiorari; but serious irregularities or material fundamental errors in applying the law, or the entire absence of essential evidence with resulting material injury may be ground for quashing a judgment on certiorari. Thus, as to the facts in review on certiorari, the rule articulated in *State Beverage Department v. Willis*, 159 Fla. 698, 32 So.2d 580, 583 (1947), is that 'on certiorari the court will not ordinarily review conflicting testimony, but only such absence of evidence as results in injury sufficient to amount to a departure from the essential requirements of law.' As more recently phrased by the supreme court in *Cohen v. State*, 99 So.2d 563, 565 (Fla 1957), 'A judgment that has no competent substantial evidence to support it cannot and should not stand; and an affirmance of that judgment is such a departure from the essential requirements of law as to require this court, in the exercise of its ancient power to issue the common-law writ of certiorari, to quash the order of affirmance.'

In taking cognizance of the petition for the writ under the above pronouncements, we have examined the record and find that there is no competent substantial evidence to support the judgment of conviction.

The State produced as witnesses two Seminole Indians and a deputy sheriff, calling to testify for it additionally a young lady who had come with petitioner as his witness. The import of the testimony of all three witnesses other than the one last mentioned was mainly to identify the burial place of John Osceola, to describe the scene, and to explain the burial customs of the tribe or clan.

The witness, William McKinley Osceola II, in his identification testimony, stated that he was present at the burial of John Osceola. He explained that the Indians never asked permission from any official or from the county, that they bury their dead any place they want to, chosen by the Indians themselves. He did not know who owned the land. He stated that the kin of the dead cannot go back except four moons, or two months, after a body is buried; in all his life he never saw an Indian go back to a grave. After the fourth moon they forget about the body altogether, unless there is some reason to go back. To mark the grave, four

---

[1][*Orig. fn.*] 872.02 Disfiguring tomb. Whoever willfully destroys, mutilates, defaces, injures or removes any tomb, monument, gravestone or other structure or thing placed or designed for a memorial of the dead, or any fence, railing, curb or other thing intended for the protection or ornamentation of any tomb, monument, gravestone or other structure before mentioned, or for any enclosure for the burial of the dead, or willfully destroys, mutilates, removes, cuts, breaks or injures any tree, shrub or plant placed or being within any such enclosure, or wantonly and maliciously disturbs the contents of a tomb or grave, shall be punished by imprisonment not exceeding one year, or by fine not exceeding five hundred dollars.

sticks are placed across a box and after that everything just rots down to the ground, that's all. The burial place, he said, is kept secret. The other Indian witness, Ruby Osceola, gave further identification testimony.

The deputy sheriff's testimony indicated that he went to the scene the day before the arrest and took pictures. He had never been there before; he could not say whether this was John Osceola or someone else; and of his own knowledge he did not know who took the skull. As an officer dealing with the Indians, he knew this was an Indian burial ground. The land was not part of an Indian reservation, and he did not know who owned it nor whether the Indians had any permission to use that particular land. The witness stated that the box or casket containing the remains was in the thick of a long sawgrass and cypress swamp on high ground; there was no fence, no signs or anything of that type; it was just a swamp. Pictures taken by him and introduced into evidence, by the officer's description in response to questioning, showed a casket, a decomposed body with the head missing, numerous boards lying around, and the lower jaw of a head lying beside the coffin. From his knowledge of the Indians, the usual custom is to put their dead with their personal belongings on the ground open to the elements.

The only eye witness was a young lady above mentioned, who at the time was and had been for three years a student at the University of Miami, a psychology major. She accompanied petitioner into the Everglades and saw him take the skull. The two of them went to the site to take pictures; she herself took a few pictures. As she described the place at various points in her testimony, there was no fence nor anything to show that this was a burial ground; they walked through the sawgrass and there ahead were trees and that's where it was. The top of the box was off and it was just sitting there; she saw it was mutilated, with clothes torn up. After taking the photographs, petitioner took the skull; it was already detached, and he did no poking around and didn't break anything open to get at it; it was just a question of seeing it there, and you just don't know what to make of it. Petitioner made no attempt to hide the skull but told everybody about it and took it in broad daylight. She characterized petitioner as one interested in things naturalistic, a very serious minded student who liked to go hunting and who collected animal and alligator skulls.

At the conclusion of the State's case, as above summarized, petitioner moved for a verdict of acquittal, which the court denied.

Among the defense witnesses, several college students, acquaintances of petitioner, testified essentially that, unaccompanied by petitioner, they had made a trip into the Everglades prior to the incident in question and had come upon the coffin. Aside from the Indians themselves, these were the first witnesses to have seen it. The gist of their testimony was that the skull was then lying on the ground a few feet away from the coffin, which was already open. Wishing to take pictures one of the boys picked up the skull and positioned it in the coffin. All described petitioner as a serious minded boy with an interest in zoology and things of nature.

Petitioner, by his testimony, indicated that he had seen the pictures taken by the other boys and knew the location. He had just purchased a polaroid camera, and he, along with the young lady mentioned, had gone into the Everglades swamp for the purpose of taking pictures also. He found two alligator skulls which he took back. As to the spot in question, there was nothing visible as an indication that it was a burial ground, but there was just an open box that was disintegrated by weather and time. He thought it was abandoned out there in the Everglades; it was so isolated; all he knew of Indian graves was the Indian mounds he had seen on trips into the Everglades. He had taken zoology and other science electives and had done some work for the zoology department at the university, a field which he had been pursuing outside of school; he had been employed the preceding summer at the Miami serpentarium. He stated that there was no intent to do anybody wrong or an injustice or commit a moral wrong; if he could make amends, he would appreciate the opportunity to do so. On cross-examination, the State inquired if he wished at that time to make an apology to the Seminole Indian Nation or if that were what he stated on direct examination; petitioner replied, 'That is absolutely correct.'

Two University of Miami assistant professors who were also assistant deans gave character testimony for petitioner, representing the university through sanction or suggestion of their dean. The testimony of the first disclosed that petitioner was a fourth year student and was to graduate in August of that year, that he had a definitely clean record of moral and general deportment, that he had taken the basic courses in zoology and geology, that he had earned four B's and an A during the past semester, that he liked to tramp through the woods and go snake hunting, and that he was a serious minded boy. That assistant dean explained, upon questioning, that he wouldn't be there representing the University of Miami officially if there were any blotch on petitioner's character and stated that he wished the students were all like petitioner. The case had been assigned for investigation by the university to the second of these professors, assistant to the dean of men; a thorough investigation was conducted, with results satisfactory to the university.

At the close of all the evidence, petitioner renewed his motion for a directed verdict; it was again denied.

The offense charged may be considered broadly as falling within the classification of malicious mischief. Statutes are found in many states defining malicious mischief, prescribing its punishment, and sometimes expressly enumerating what acts must be proved to constitute it. 3 Underhill's Criminal Evidence, 5th edition, chapter 45, Malicious Mischief, section 620, pages 1486, 1487. Generally, malice has been held to be an essential ingredient of the offense of malicious mischief, although in some states the statutes are worded so as not to require the injury to be committed maliciously. In that case, it has been held that the crime is in the nature of a trespass. Chapter 24, Malicious Mischief, section 657, page 455 of 2 Wharton's Criminal Law and Procedure by Ronald A. Anderson, based on Wharton's Criminal Law, 12th edition and Wharton's Criminal Procedure, 10th edition.

It is significant that, in the statute under which the present charge is laid, the word 'willfully' is the ingredient which attaches to the doing of the specified acts of destruction, mutilation, and the like as these apply to the things denoted throughout the body of the statute, on down to that point where disturbing the contents of a tomb or grave is condemned; there, the single qualifying adverb is changed, and the words, 'wantonly and maliciously,' are chosen. Hence, the gravamen of the offense is the proscription against a wrongful act which has been wantonly and maliciously perpetrated. The language of the statute connotes a particular intent which fastens to and is a part of the crime prescribed. If an act is criminal only when done with a particular intent, the presence of the designated intent must be proved. The rule as to proof of malicious intent has been thus stated, 'Usually, proof of the injury alone is not enough, and this is always the case where a statute requires that it shall be proved to have been wantonly or maliciously inflicted.' 2 Underhill's Criminal Evidence, supra, sections 624 and 621, pages 1493 and 1487. The important and essential element here, therefore, is that the wrongful act must have been done wantonly and maliciously in order to establish the crime by reason of the statutory prescription. So more is required than the mere doing of the deed.

Statutes penal in character must be strictly construed. State ex rel. *Cooper v. Coleman*, 138 Fla. 520, 189 So. 691 (1939). An accused must be plainly and unmistakably within the criminal statute to justify a conviction. *Watson v. Stone*, 148 Fla. 516, 4 So.2d 700 (1941).

We have here an unusual situation which concerns unfamiliar and secret tribal burial customs involving as the setting a scene of disarray in a wild sawgrass and cypress swamp. Aside from the testimony of petitioner himself and his companion at the time, the only witnesses to the act complained of, the evidence yields nothing which could even connect petitioner with that act. The responses of these two were in accord and the narrative which emerged through their testimony consistent. This evidence shows that there was no attempt at the trial to deny the taking of the skull and no attempt to conceal the act at any time. The object of the trip into the Everglades expressly was that of taking pictures as the other boys had previously done. Both petitioner and his companion did take pictures.

We have found no Florida case that has been decided as to the statutory offense charged, and we have found no case in any jurisdiction involving circumstances like those here presented. The sanctity of the final resting place of the Indian peoples or any other peoples should be recognized and should be accorded highest respect. However, as we have indicated, in order to constitute the offense under the statute, the wrongful act must have been done wantonly and maliciously; or, otherwise stated, the petitioner must be plainly and unmistakably within the statute in order to justify a conviction. We must conclude that, under the proof required by the statute, there is no competent substantial evidence to support the judgment of conviction. For that reason, the judgment of affirmance is a departure from the essential requirements of law and is accordingly hereby quashed.

It is so ordered.

WHITE, Acting C. J., and DOWNEY, James C., Associate Judge, concur.

BADONI v. HIGGINSON

638 F.2d 172 (10th Cir. 1980)

LOGAN, Circuit Judge:

This is an appeal from an order granting summary judgment, which effectively denied relief to Indian plaintiffs making constitutional and statutory claims against federal officials. We are asked to determine whether the religion clauses of the First Amendment apply to the government's management of the Rainbow Bridge National Monument and the Glen Canyon Dam and Reservoir, and whether an environmental impact statement concerning operation of the Glen Canyon Dam and Reservoir is required under the National Environmental Policy Act, 42 U.S.C. § 4321 *et seq.* The trial court's order and opinion is reported at 455 F. Supp. 641 (D. Utah 1977).

The Rainbow Bridge National Monument is a 160-acre tract of land in southern Utah, set aside by executive order for scientific and historical purposes. 36 Stat. 2703 (1910).

Within this parcel is Rainbow Bridge, a great sandstone arch 309 feet high with a span of 278 feet. The Monument, which is surrounded by the Navajo reservation, is administered by the National Park Service. Glen Canyon Dam, located on the Colorado River fifty-eight miles below the Monument, is a 710-foot high structure built pursuant to Congressional authorization.[1] See 43 U.S.C. § 620. Glen Canyon Reservoir, known as Lake Powell, formed behind the dam after its completion in 1963. By 1970 the lake had entered the 160-acre tract of the Monument and by 1977 the water had a peak depth of 20.9 feet directly under the Bridge. If the lake fills to its maximum capacity, the water apparently will be 46 feet deep under the Bridge.

Glen Canyon Dam and Lake Powell are operated by the Bureau of Reclamation under the direction of the Secretary of the Interior. 43 U.S.C. § 620. The federal lands adjacent to Lake Powell, other than the Monument, comprise the Glen Canyon National Recreation Area, see 16 U.S.C. § 460dd, and are administered by the National Park Service. See id. §§ 1, 460dd–3.

Prior to the creation of Lake Powell, Rainbow Bridge National Monument was isolated and was visited by few tourists. The lake now provides convenient access to the Monument. Boats licensed by the Commissioner of the Bureau of Reclamation and the Director of the National Park Service bring tourists to the Monument. Docking facilities have been constructed near the Bridge to serve tour boats and private boats.[2] Visitors to the Monument are subject to the regulation and control of the National Park Service. See 16 U.S.C. § 1 *et seq.*

The individual plaintiffs are Indians residing in the general area of Rainbow Bridge National Monument in southern Utah and are enrolled members of the Navajo Tribe. Three of these plaintiffs are recognized among their people as medicine men, "religious leaders of considerable stature among the Navajo, learned in Navajo history, mythology and culture, and practitioners of traditional rites and ceremonies of ancient origin." 455 F. Supp. at 642. Three plaintiffs are Navajo chapters, which are local organizations of the Navajo Nation, each consisting of the adult members of its respective community.

In 1974 plaintiffs commenced this action for declaratory and injunctive relief against the Secretary of the Interior, the Commissioner of the Bureau of Reclamation and the Director of the National Park Service.[3] In their amended complaint plaintiffs asserted two claims for relief relevant to this appeal: First, that defendants' operation of Glen Canyon Dam and Reservoir and management of Rainbow Bridge National Monument violated plaintiffs' rights under the Free Exercise Clause of the First Amendment; second, that defendants are re-

---

[1][*Orig. fn.*] For a comprehensive description of the statutory scheme governing Glen Canyon Dam and Reservoir, see *Friends of the Earth v. Armstrong*, 485 F.2d 1 (10th Cir. 1973), *cert. denied*, 414 U.S. 1171 (1974).

[2][*Orig. fn.*] The Park Service also permitted operation of a floating marina near the Bridge. The government states, however, that the marina has been moved to a different canyon. Appellee's Br. 20 n.6.

[3][*Orig. fn.*] The court also granted motions of the Colorado River Water Conservation District, the Southwestern Water Conservation District, the State of Colorado, the State of Utah, and the Central Utah Water Conservancy District to intervene. The interests of these intervenors concern only the operation of Glen Canyon Dam and Reservoir. In this appeal, their arguments are substantially the same as those presented by the government.

quired by 42 U.S.C. § 4332(2)(C) to provide an environmental impact statement concerning the operation of Glen Canyon Dam and Reservoir and that the continuing operation of the Dam and Reservoir without such a statement violates 42 U.S.C. §§ 4331–35. After consideration of the pleadings, affidavits and discovery documents in the record, the trial court granted defendants' motions for summary judgment, from which this appeal was taken.

I

In essence, plaintiffs' free exercise claim is that government action has infringed the practice of their religion in two respects: (1) by impounding water to form Lake Powell, the government has drowned some of plaintiffs' gods and denied plaintiffs access to a prayer spot sacred to them; and (2) by allowing tourists to visit Rainbow Bridge, the government has permitted desecration of the sacred nature of the site and has denied plaintiffs' right to conduct religious ceremonies at the prayer spot.

The trial court gave two reasons for granting summary judgment against plaintiffs. First, the court ruled that plaintiffs do not have a cognizable free exercise claim because they have no property interest in the Monument. 455 F. Supp. at 644–45. In the alternative, it held that the federal government's interests in the Glen Canyon Dam and Reservoir as a major water and power project outweigh plaintiffs' religious interests in the Monument. 455 F. Supp. at 645–47. While we affirm the summary judgment in defendants' favor, our reasoning differs somewhat from that of the trial court.

At the outset, we reject the conclusion that plaintiffs' lack of property rights in the Monument is determinative. The government must manage its property in a manner that does not offend the Constitution. See *Sequoyah v. TVA*, 620 F.2d 1159, 1164 (6th Cir. 1980) (lack of property interest not conclusive, but is a factor in weighing free exercise and competing interests). We must look to the nature of the government action and the quality of plaintiffs' positions to determine whether they have stated a free exercise claim. See *Wisconsin v. Yoder*, 406 U.S. 205, 215 (1972).

Analysis of a free exercise claim involves a two-step process. We first determine whether government action creates a burden on the exercise of plaintiffs' religion. "(I)t is necessary in a free exercise case to show the coercive effect of the enactment as it operates against…the practice of (their) religion." *School Dist. of Abington v. Schempp*, 374 U.S. 203, 223 (1963). The practice allegedly infringed upon must be based on a system of belief that is religious, see, *e.g.*, *Wisconsin v. Yoder*, 406 U.S. at 215–16; *Kennedy v. Meacham*, 540 F.2d 1057, 1060–61 (10th Cir. 1976), and sincerely held by the person asserting the infringement, see, *e.g., United States v. Ballard*, 322 U.S. 78, (1944). If such a burden is found, the action is violative of the Free Exercise Clause, unless the government establishes an interest of "sufficient magnitude to override the interest claiming protection under the Free Exercise Clause." *Wisconsin v. Yoder*, 406 U.S. at 214. "(O)nly those interests of the highest order and those not otherwise served can overbalance legitimate claims to the free exercise of religion." Id. at 215.

In reviewing a summary judgment, we view the facts and reasonable inferences drawn therefrom in the light most favorable to plaintiffs. The pertinent facts in this case are as follows. Rainbow Bridge and a nearby spring, prayer spot and cave have held positions of central importance in the religion of some Navajo people living in that area for at least 100 years. These shrines are regarded as the incarnate forms of Navajo gods, which provide protection and rain-giving functions. For generations Navajo singers have performed ceremonies near the Bridge and water from the spring has been used for other ceremonies. Plaintiffs believe that if humans alter the earth in the area of the Bridge, plaintiffs' prayers will not be heard by the gods and their ceremonies will be ineffective to prevent evil and disease. Because of the operation of the Dam and Lake Powell, the springs and prayer spot are under water. Tourists visiting the sacred area have desecrated it by noise, litter and defacement of the Bridge itself. Because of the flooding and the presence of tourists, plaintiffs no longer hold ceremonies in the area of the Bridge.

A

With respect to the government action of impounding water in Lake Powell the stated infringement is the drowning of the Navajo gods, the increased tourist presence attributable to the level at which the lake is kept, and the denial of access to the prayer spot now under water. We agree with the trial court that the government's interest in maintaining the capacity of Lake Powell at a level that intrudes into the Monument outweighs plaintiffs' religious interest. This Court has previously considered the importance of the Glen Canyon Dam and Reservoir as a crucial part of a multi-state water storage and power generation project. *See Friends of the Earth v. Armstrong*, 485 F.2d 1 (10th Cir. 1973), *cert. denied*, 414 U.S. 1171 (1974). In the instant case unrebutted evidence, by affidavit, shows that the storage capacity of the lake would be cut in half if the surface level were dropped to an elevation necessary to alleviate the complained of infringements. The required reduction would significantly reduce the water available to the Upper Basin States of Colorado, New Mexico, Utah and Wyoming from the Colorado River. Such a reduction of use in each of the above Upper Colorado River Basin States would among other things limit and reduce the development of water supplies within these States on either a permanent basis or on a limited long-term basis for irrigation purposes, for development of mineral and other natural resources, and for municipal and industrial water supplies. Aff. of David L. Crandall, Regional Director of the Upper Colorado Region of the Bureau of Reclamation. Moreover, it is reasonable to conclude that no action other than reducing the water level would avoid the alleged infringement of plaintiffs' beliefs and practices. In these circumstances we believe the government has shown an interest of a magnitude sufficient to justify the alleged infringements.[4]

B

The second basis for plaintiffs' free exercise claims concerns management of the Monument by the National Park Service. Specifically, plaintiffs assert that tourists visiting the Monument desecrate the area by noisy conduct, littering and defacement of the Bridge and that the presence of tourists prevents plaintiffs from holding ceremonies near the Bridge.

---

[4][*Orig. fn.*] Because we agree with the trial court that the government's interest in maintaining the level of Lake Powell is compelling, we do not reach the question whether the government action involved infringes plaintiffs' free exercise of religion.

The gravamen of plaintiffs' claim is that by permitting public access and the operation of commercial tour boats the government has burdened the practice of plaintiffs' religion. In their complaint plaintiffs seek an order requiring the government officials "to take appropriate steps to operate Glen Canyon Dam and Reservoir in such a manner that the important religious and cultural interests of Plaintiffs will not be harmed or degraded," and "to issue rules and regulations to take adequate measures preventing further desecration and destruction of the Rainbow Bridge area by tourists, and otherwise to take adequate measures to preclude impairment of the Rainbow Bridge National Monument." (R. 543) In their brief-in-chief, plaintiffs state they "seek only some measured accommodation to their religious interest, not a wholesale bar to use of Rainbow Bridge by all others." (Appellants' Br. 8.) They suggest some specific types of relief, such as prohibiting consumption of beer at the Monument and closing the Monument on reasonable notice when religious ceremonies are to be held there. (Appellants' Br. 25.) In their reply brief, plaintiffs summarize their claim as follows: "The main thrust of appellants' claim seeks to eliminate government actions which encourage destructive visitor use of the Bridge, and to permit, on infrequent occasions, appellants or other Navajos to conduct religious ceremonies there in private." (Appellants' Reply Br. 3.)

Free exercise claims generally challenge government dictates which compel citizens to violate tenets of their religion; see *Wisconsin v. Yoder*, 406 U.S. 205 (1972) (Wisconsin's compulsory education law violated Amish free exercise of religion); *Wooley v. Maynard*, 430 U.S. 705 (1977) (statute requiring all motor vehicles of New Hampshire to bear the motto "Live Free or Die" violated Jehovah's Witness followers' First Amendment rights), or government action which conditions a benefit or right on renunciation of a religious practice. See *McDaniel v. Paty*, 435 U.S. 618, 633–34 (1978) (Tennessee provisions barring ministers from serving as delegates or legislators violated the First Amendment); *Sherbert v. Verner*, 374 U.S. 398 (1963) (disqualification of appellant from unemployment compensation because of refusal to work on Saturday contrary to religious beliefs violated Free Exercise Clause).

The government here has not prohibited plaintiffs' religious exercises in the area of Rainbow Bridge; plaintiffs may enter the Monument on the same basis as other people. It is the presence of tourists at the Monument and their actions while there that give rise to plaintiffs' complaint of interference with the exercise of their religion. We are mindful of the difficulties facing plaintiffs in performing solemn religious ceremonies in an area frequented by tourists. But what plaintiffs seek in the name of the Free Exercise Clause is affirmative action by the government which implicates the Establishment Clause of the First Amendment. They seek government action to exclude others from the Monument, at least for short periods, and to control tourist behavior.

Unquestionably the government has a strong interest in assuring public access to this natural wonder. Congress has charged the Park Service with the duty to provide "for the enjoyment of (parks and monuments)... by such means as will leave them unimpaired for the enjoyment of future of the generations." 16 U.S.C. § 1. Toward this end, the Secretary of the Interior is empowered to grant privileges, leases, and permits for the use of land for the accommodation of visitors in the various parks, monuments, or other reservations provided for under section 2 of this title, but for periods not exceeding thirty years; and no natural curiosities, wonders, or objects of interest shall be leased, rented, or granted to anyone on such terms as to interfere with free access to them by the public... 16 U.S.C. § 3. The Park Service's action of allowing public access to the Monument in accordance with this legislative grant provides the legal basis for plaintiffs' presence as well as the presence of the tourists.

Issuance of regulations to exclude tourists completely from the Monument for the avowed purpose of aiding plaintiffs' conduct of religious ceremonies would seem a clear violation of the Establishment Clause. The test may be stated as follows: what are the purpose and the primary effect of the enactment? If either is the advancement or inhibition of religion then the enactment exceeds the scope of legislative power as circumscribed by the Constitution. That is to say that to withstand the strictures of the Establishment Clause there must be a secular legislative purpose and a primary effect that neither advances nor inhibits religion. *School Dist. of Abington v. Schempp*, 374 U.S. at 222. Exercise of First Amendment freedoms may not be asserted to deprive the public of its normal use of an area. *Shuttlesworth v. Birmingham*, 394 U.S. 147, 152 (1969); *Amalgamated Food Employees Union v. Logan Valley Plaza, Inc.*, 391 U.S. 308, 320 (1968); *Cox v. Louisiana*, 379 U.S. 536, 554–55 (1965); *Niemotko v. Maryland*, 340 U.S. 268, 271 (1951). Government action has frequently been invalidated when it has denied the exercise of First Amendment rights compatible with public use. Wherever the title of streets and parks may rest, they have immemorially been held in trust for the use of the public and, time out of mind, have been used for purposes of assembly, communicating thoughts between citizens, and discussing public questions. Such use of the streets and public places has, from ancient times, been a part of the privileges, immunities, rights, and liberties of citizens. The privilege of a citizen of the United States to use the streets and parks for communication of views on national questions may be regulated in the interest of all; it is not absolute, but relative, and must be exercised in subordination to the general comfort and convenience, and in consonance with peace and good order; but it must not, in the guise of regulation, be abridged or denied. *Hague v. CIO*, 307 U.S. 496, 515–16 (1939). We find no basis in the law for ordering the government to exclude the public from public areas to insure privacy during the exercise of First Amendment rights.

We must also deny relief insofar as plaintiffs seek to have the government police the actions of tourists lawfully visiting the Monument. Although Congress has authorized the Park Service to regulate the conduct of tourists in order to promote and preserve the Monument, see 16 U.S.C. §§ 1, 3, we do not believe plaintiffs have a constitutional right to have tourists visiting the Bridge act "in a respectful and appreciative manner." (Appellants' Reply Br. 4.) The First Amendment protects one against action by the government, though even then, not in all circumstances; but it gives no one the right to insist that in the pursuit of their own interests others must conform their conduct to his own religious necessities... We must accommodate our idiosyncracies, religious as well as secular, to the compromises necessary in communal life. *Otten v. Baltimore & O. R. Co.*, 205 F.2d 58, 61 (2d Cir. 1953) (Learned Hand, J.) (footnote omitted). Were it otherwise, the Monument would become a government-managed religious shrine.

The Park Service already has issued regulations applicable to the Monument prohibiting disorderly conduct, 36 C.F.R. § 2.7 (1979), intoxication and possession of alcoholic beverages by minors, id. § 2.16, defacement, id. § 2.20, littering, id. § 2.24, and tampering with personal property, id. § 2.29. These regulations no doubt would be justified as authorized under its charge to conserve and protect the scenery, natural and historic objects for the enjoyment of the public. See 16 U.S.C. § 1. These regulations also provide the relief plaintiffs request as to control of tourist behavior, except perhaps for a total ban on beer drinking.

What of the request stated in the appellant's reply brief for access "on infrequent occasions" to conduct religious ceremonies in private? The government asserts that plaintiffs, in common with other members of the public, may apply for a public assembly permit to hold religious ceremonies at the Bridge.[5] No one suggests such a permit could not be used to permit access after normal visiting hours when privacy might be assured. The courts have held permit requirements unconstitutional when they have been used to restrain First Amendment rights without narrow, objective standards. *E.g., Shuttlesworth v. Birmingham*, 394 U.S. 147 (1969). *Cf. Chess v. Widmar*, 635 F.2d 1310 (8th Cir. 1980) (use of university facilities). Our problem is that there is no allegation that any such permit was requested and denied. The pleadings, affidavits and interrogatories suggest no specific time or schedule for religious ceremonies. Indeed, plaintiffs' answers to interrogatories and the proffered affidavit of their expert Karl Luckert indicate the ceremonies are infrequent and scheduled at the request of individual Navajos when a need seems to exist.

Plaintiffs cite the Park Service's proposed guidelines for use of Grand Canyon National Park, which prohibit entry on certain sacred Indian religious sites. They also cite the American Indian Religious Freedom Act, 42 U.S.C. § 1996, which states a public policy to permit Indians access to sacred sites for worship, and perhaps to protect them from intrusion. See H.R. Rep. No. 1308, 95th Cong., 2d Sess. (1978), reprinted in (1978) U.S. Code Cong. & Ad. News, pp. 1262, 1264. But we do not have before us the constitutionality of those laws or regulations or of any action taken by defendants in alleged violation of them. The pleadings, even as supplemented by the expanded requests in the brief and supported by the proffered evidence, afford no basis for relief...

AFFIRMED.

SEQUOYAH v. TENNESSEE VALLEY AUTHORITY

480 F. Supp. 608 (E.D. Tenn. 1979)

ROBERT L. TAYLOR, District Judge:

This is an action seeking injunctive relief against impoundment of the Tellico Reservoir on the Little Tennessee River. The ground for such relief is that the flooding of the Little Tennessee will violate plaintiffs' constitutional and statutory rights to freely exercise their religion. Before the Court are plaintiffs' motion for a preliminary injunction and defendant's motion to dismiss the complaint for failure to state a claim upon which relief can be granted, Fed. R. Civ. P. 12(b)(6). Both motions have been exhaustively briefed and argued orally before this Court.

---

[5][*Orig. fn.*] 36 C.F.R. § 2.21 provides in pertinent part: (a) Public meetings, assemblies, gatherings, demonstrations, parades and other public expressions of views are permitted within park areas on lands which are open to the general public provided a permit therefor has been issued by the Superintendent. "Park area" is defined in the regulations as "all federally owned or controlled areas administered by the National Park Service." 36 C.F.R. § 1.2(f).

I. FACTS

In 1966, Congress appropriated the first construction funds for the Tellico Dam and Reservoir project. Since then over $111,000,000 have been spent on the project which is now near completion. A fruitful source of litigation, the dam has been the subject of at least nine lawsuits on the district court level alone. This, the latest one, was filed on the eve of its completion, even though the plaintiffs have known about the project and its attendant First Amendment issues since 1965. Although enjoined twice by the courts, the project has been free from any injunction for at least nine of the last fourteen years. It is difficult to understand why plaintiffs have waited until now to raise their constitutional arguments in court.

In 1967, the Tennessee Valley Authority began acquiring privately owned property along the Little Tennessee River as the initial step in its project to impound a reservoir there. The latest lawsuit against the dam, before this one, resulted in a permanent injunction against impoundment of the reservoir based on the Endangered Species Act, 16 U.S.C. Chapter 35, Sec. 1531 *et seq.* See *TVA v. Hill*, 437 U.S. 153 (1978). On September 24, 1979, the President signed into law the Energy and Water Development Appropriation Bill, providing, in relevant part, as follows: (N)otwithstanding provisions of 16 U.S.C., Chapter 35 or any other law, the Corporation is authorized and directed to complete construction, operate, and maintain the Tellico Dam and Reservoir Project for navigation, flood control, electric power generation, and other purposes, including the maintenance of a normal summer reservoir pool of 813 feet above sea level.

Since that time, TVA has been working toward completion of the dam and impoundment of the reservoir. Although no specific date has yet been set for closing the gates of the dam to begin impoundment, such action is imminent, to occur sometime after November 9, 1979.

The plaintiffs in this lawsuit are two bands of the Cherokee Indian nation and three individual Cherokee Indians. Plaintiffs claim that the land along the Little Tennessee River which will be flooded by the Tellico Reservoir is sacred to the Cherokee religion and a vital part of the Cherokee religious practices. The land includes several old Cherokee settlements and burial grounds with religious significance to the Cherokee people.

The plaintiffs contend that impoundment of the reservoir will violate their constitutional right to free exercise of their religion, in addition to their claimed statutory rights of access to lands of religious and historical significance. These statutory claims are based on the American Indian Religious Freedom Act, 42 U.S.C. § 1996; the National Historic Preservation Act, 16 U.S.C. §§ 470 *et seq.*; and the Tennessee cemetery statutes, Tenn.Code Ann. Sec. 46-401 *et seq.* TVA contends that impoundment will infringe none of the plaintiffs' legal rights.

II. PLAINTIFFS' CLAIMED STATUTORY RIGHTS

The Congress and the President have authorized and directed TVA to impound the Tellico Reservoir "notwithstanding provisions of 16 U.S.C., Chapter 35 or any other law." There is no question here that Congress has the power to make exceptions to rights either it or state legislatures have created by statute, as long as such exceptions are not invidiously discriminatory. Rather, plaintiffs contend that Congress has not exercised its power to exempt the Tellico project from the American Indian Religious Freedom Act, the National Historic

Preservation Act, and the Tennessee cemetery statutes. Plaintiffs cite the law disfavoring implied repeal stated *in TVA v. Hill*, 437 U.S. 153, 189–190 (1978). However, this is not a case, like Hill, in which a general appropriations measure with no repeal or exception language of any kind is presented to the Court as an implied repeal of a specific statute. Instead, there is an expressed Congressional mandate to impound the Tellico Reservoir "notwithstanding... any other law." There is nothing implied or ambiguous about this language and the law of implied repeal stated in *Hill* is inapposite.

Plaintiffs also cite, *D. C. Federation of Civic Associations, Inc. v. Volpe*, 140 U.S. App. D.C. 162, 434 F.2d 436 (D.C. Cir. 1970). In that case, the D.C. Circuit interpreted a Congressional mandate to complete construction of a highway project to be consistent with the procedural requirements of Title 23 of the United States Code. In so interpreting the Congressional language, the Court was merely trying to avoid the Constitutional issues presented by that case. Unfortunately, such a recourse is not available to this Court. The language exempting the Tellico Dam project from "any other law" is clear and explicit. The creation of a reservoir will necessarily prevent access to many of plaintiffs' sacred sites. If the statutes cited by plaintiffs do guarantee access to these sites, as argued by plaintiffs, they are unavoidably repugnant to Congress' order to complete the dam. Congress has clearly and expressly exempted the Tellico Reservoir from any law repugnant to its completion.

III. CONSTITUTIONAL CLAIMS

Plaintiffs base their constitutional challenge to the Tellico Reservoir on the First, Fifth, and Ninth Amendments to the Constitution. The First Amendment guarantees the right to freely exercise one's religion. The Fifth Amendment, through the due process clause, guarantees equal protection of the law by the federal government. See, *e.g.*, *Schlesinger v. Ballard*, 419 U.S. 498 (1974). The Ninth Amendment simply provides that the specification of certain rights in the Constitution shall not be construed to deny or disparage other rights retained by the people. Of course, Congress cannot exempt the Tellico project from any of these constitutional provisions. The Court assumes that the land to be flooded is considered sacred to the Cherokee religion and that active practitioners of that religion would want to make pilgrimages to this land as a precept of their religion.

Since the Ninth Amendment grants no substantive rights to plaintiffs, *see Tanner v. Armco Steel Corp.*, 340 F. Supp. 532 (S.D. Texas 1972), the complaint fails to state a cause of action under that amendment.

The real substantive issue in this lawsuit is whether the impounding of the Tellico Reservoir would infringe the free exercise clause of the First Amendment. An essential element to a claim under the free exercise clause is some form of governmental coercion of actions which are contrary to religious belief. *Wooley v. Maynard*, 430 U.S. 705 (1977); *Wisconsin v. Yoder*, 406 U.S. 205 (1972); *Board of Education v. Allen*, 392 U.S. 236, 248–249 (1968); *Sherbert v. Verner*, 374 U.S. 398 (1963); *Abington School District v. Schempp*, 374 U.S. 203, 223 (1963*); Torcaso v. Watkins*, 367 U.S. 488 (1961); *Braunfeld v. Brown*, 366 U.S. 599 (1961). This governmental coercion may take the form of pressuring or forcing individuals not to participate in religious practices. See, *e.g. McDaniel v. Paty*, 435 U.S. 618 (1978). Other than preventing access to certain land, however, the impound of the Tellico Reservoir has no coercive effect on plaintiffs' religious beliefs or practices. The question thus becomes whether the denial of access to government-owned land considered sacred and necessary to plaintiffs' religious beliefs infringes the free exercise clause. The federal government uses the land it owns for a wide variety of purposes, many of which require limiting or denying public access to the property. See, *e.g.*, *Downing v. Kunzig*, 454 F.2d 1230 (6th Cir. 1972). The Court has been cited to no case that engrains the free exercise clause with property rights. The free exercise clause is not a license in itself to enter property, government-owned or otherwise, to which religious practitioners have no other legal right of access. Since plaintiffs claim no other legal property interest in the land in question, aside from the statutory claims previously discussed, a free exercise claim is not stated here.

This leaves only plaintiffs' equal protection argument. There is certainly nothing invidiously discriminatory about impoundment of a reservoir in itself. To state a colorable equal protection claim the plaintiffs must allege that a denial of a right or benefit be invidiously discriminatory. *Ferguson v. Skrupa*, 372 U.S. 726 (1963). This is not present here. As discussed previously, neither plaintiffs nor the general public have a right or interest in access to land merely because it is owned by the federal government. The flooding of the Little Tennessee will prevent everyone, not just plaintiffs, from having access to the land in question.

Defendant also raises defenses based on estoppel and laches. In light of the Court's disposition of the issues raised by plaintiffs, the Court need not decide these questions.

For the foregoing reasons, it is ORDERED that plaintiffs' motion for a preliminary injunction be, and the same hereby is, denied. It is further ORDERED that defendant's motion to dismiss be, and the same hereby is, granted.

Order Accordingly.

Prior to 1989, Native American human remains, as well as objects considered by Native Americans to be sacred group property or cultural patrimony, were regarded as objects of antiquity (by the Antiquities Act) or as archeological resources (by the Archaeological Resources Protection Act). Also, all Native American human remains and cultural items located on federal lands were presumed to be federal property subject to treatment, study, and curation by the Smithsonian Institution or by other government agencies at university or agency repositories. Consequently, Native American human remains could be housed in storage boxes long after the reburial of non-Native Americans whose remains might have been exhumed during archeological field study. No legal mechanism existed to deaccession these human remains and other cultural items. The Archaeological Resources Protection Act (ARPA) peripherally addressed the return of human remains to tribes for reburial as a cost item in the calculation of a damage assessment [43 C.F.R. § 7.14 (c)(7) (1994)], but no statute provided a means to determine how human remains could be returned, or to whom they should be released. ARPA also made several references to the responsibility of the federal land manager to consult with tribes when cultural or religious sites located on federal lands would be impacted by a permitted activity, but tribal permission to impact the area was required only if the sites were located on tribal land [43 C.F.R. § 7.7 (1994)]. Thus, before 1989, heritage resources laws favored the interests of science at the expense of giving Native Americans a voice in the management of their cultural heritage.

SECTION B.   FEDERAL LAWS THAT APPLY TO NATIVE AMERICAN HERITAGE RESOURCES

During the 1990s, American property law assimilated some previously un-recognized Native American interests and rights in heritage resources. Two key pieces of legislation, the National Museum of the American Indian Act and the Native American Graves Protection and Repatriation Act, addressed Native American decision-making in heritage resources management in the United States, and although they did not exclude input from the science and museum communities, these laws constructively embodied a public policy for Native American rights in cultural heritage that could not be subordi-nated to scientific inquiry.

1.   National Museum of the American Indian Act of 1989

The National Museum of the American Indian Act [Pub. L. No. 101-185, 103 Stat. 1345 (1989), 20 U.S.C. § 80q (1994)] was written to give the Smithsonian Institution the ability to repatriate the 18,000 Native American human remains stored at this national repository for government property [20 U.S.C. § 80q-9 (1994)]. It also provided the enabling legislation for the creation of a new museum, the National Museum of the American Indian, to be situated on the Mall in Washington, D.C. [20 U.S.C. §§ 80q-1–80q-7 (1994)].

Initially, the National Museum of the American Indian Act (NMAI Act) applied only to Native American human remains and funerary objects in the possession of the Smithsonian Institution. It defined "funerary object" as "an object that, as part of a death rite or ceremony of a culture, is intention-ally placed with individual human remains, either at the time of burial or later" [20 U.S.C. § 80q-14(4) (1994)]. Standing to make a claim was given to Indian tribes recognized by the United States [25 U.S.C. § 450b(e) (1994)] and to Native Hawaiians, who are the aboriginal people occupying and exer-cising sovereignty in Hawaii prior to 1778, and their descendants [20 U.S.C. §§ 80q-14(7), (8), (10), (11) (1994)].

Under the NMAI Act the Secretary of the Smithsonian Institution must:

a.   inventory the human remains and funerary objects in the control of the
     Smithsonian Institution in consultation and cooperation with Indian religious

leaders and Native Hawaiian organizations having expertise in Native Hawaiian affairs, and, using the best scientific and historical documentation, identify the origins of the remains and objects;

b.   notify the affected Indian tribe or Native Hawaiian organization when the remains and objects have been identified by "a preponderance of the evidence";

c.   return to a descendant, or an Indian tribe, or a Native Hawaiian organization making a request the culturally affiliated remains along with any associated funerary objects; and

d.   return expeditiously to a requesting Indian tribe or Native Hawaiian organization funerary objects not associated with an individual, but having come from a specific burial site that is culturally affiliated with that tribe.

20 U.S.C. §§ 80q-9–80q-14 (1994).

Native American human remains and funerary objects in the control of the Smithsonian Institution must be returned expeditiously. The law does not limit the ability of the Smithsonian Institution to repatriate the human remains, and nothing in the law limits the ability of descendants, tribes, and Native Hawaiian organizations to assert their rights under any other law or cause of action. Thus, this law recognizes that Indian tribes and Native Hawaiian organizations have standing to assert property and possessory rights in their heritage resources.

To assist the Smithsonian Institution in facilitating return of Indian human remains and funerary objects, a five-member committee was established, to be appointed by the Secretary of the Smithsonian Institution, with three of the members to be chosen from nominations submitted by Indian tribes and organizations [20 U.S.C. § 80q-10 (1994)]. In 1996, this committee was expanded to seven members, four of whom must be nominated by tribes and organizations, with two of those four being traditional Indian religious leaders. The committee assures a fair assessment of the identification of remains and objects, reviews requests for repatriation, and resolves any disputes that may arise in the process. It reports to the Secretary of the Smithsonian Institution, and is not subject to the Federal Advisory Committee Act [5 U.S.C. App. (1994)].

Immediately after the NMAI Act was passed in 1989, there were few requests for the return of remains or funerary objects, perhaps due to the fact that the law included a grant provision to assist tribes, which only became effective in the 1991 fiscal year [20 U.S.C. § 80q-12 (1994); the appropriation for 1991 was $1,000,000 (20 U.S.C. § 80q-9(f) (1994)]. More likely, however, the infrequent responses from tribes derived from the absence of both a process whereby the tribes would have access to the contents of the collection, and a procedure for reviewing and identifying the remains or objects of concern to a tribe. Also, the key term "consultation" was not defined or further described in the law. These shortcomings to a well-intentioned law provided the Smithsonian Institution with an opportunity to promulgate regulations in order to facilitate inventory, identification, and return of the heritage resources in question, but to date, they have declined to do so. The NMAI Act, however, was amended in 1996 to specify a time limit for completion of an "inventory," to be no later than June 1, 1998 [Pub. L. No. 104-278, 110 Stat. 3355 (1996), 20 U.S.C. § 80q-9(a)(2) (1997)]. The purpose of the inventory is to provide potential claimants with notice of the contents of the collection. An inventory is:

> a simple itemized list that, to the extent practicable, identifies, based upon available information held by the Smithsonian Institution, the geographic and cultural affiliation of the remains and objects...
>   20 U.S.C. § 80q-9(a)(3) (1997).

The NMAI Act, which was passed over a year before the more comprehensive Native American Graves Protection and Repatriation Act (NAGPRA), did not require the Smithsonian Institution to follow the same compliance procedures that NAGPRA later imposed on museums. Nevertheless, because NAGPRA's structured process ultimately was useful for museum compliance, the 1996 NMAI Act amendments adopted most of NAGPRA's procedural requirements [20 U.S.C. § 80q-9a (1997)]. The NMAI Act amendments also expanded the categories of items subject to repatriation to include sacred objects and objects of cultural patrimony (in addition to human remains and funerary items). Summaries of these object categories were to be completed by December 31, 1996. Thus, both the NMAI Act and NAGPRA operate in a similar fashion to return individual human remains and cultural items to their owners and lawful custodians. Since the current NMAI Act expressly adopts NAGPRA's definitions and procedural requirements, these provisions are discussed in the section on NAGPRA.

2.   Native American Graves Protection and Repatriation Act

The Native American Graves Protection and Repatriation Act [NAGPRA; Pub. L. No. 101-601, 104 Stat. 3048 (1990), 25 U.S.C. §§ 3000–3013 (1994)] statutorily recognizes the property rights of Native Americans in certain cultural items, and close examination of its provisions reveals its expansive scope. As with any civil rights legislation, the substantive provisions of NAGPRA are construed literally, but the purpose of the law may be interpreted liberally.

Brief Legislative History

In 1986, a Native American Claims Commission was proposed in Congress to provide a process for repatriating skeletal remains and cultural items held by the United States government, but it failed to gain support from the Smithsonian Institution and the scientific community. An ongoing dialogue on Native American-museum relations ensued over the next two years under the auspices of the Heard Museum, an art and ethnographic museum of Indian culture in Phoenix, Arizona. These meetings produced a consensus on four categories of Native American culture—human remains, funerary objects, sacred objects, and cultural patrimony—that would be the basis for defining the scope of NAGPRA generally, and the categories of protected Native American cultural heritage in particular.

In 1989, Senator McCain proposed a bill [S. 1021, 101st Cong., 1st Sess. (1989)] that would require federal agencies to inventory the human remains in their collections and give notice to tribes, and would provide authority for federal agencies and museums receiving federal funds to repatriate human remains under their control. The McCain bill also included criminal penalties for illegal trafficking in Native American cultural property. Another bill, proposed by Senator Inouye [S. 1980, 101st Cong., 1st Sess. (1989)], expanded on the McCain draft by also requiring museums receiving federal funds to complete an inventory of their collections. The Inouye bill also added a review committee for the purpose of resolving disputes. In addition, Senator Inouye proposed that all Indian and Native Hawaiian human remains and defined cultural items no longer be classified as archeological resources, and thus no longer be available for excavation subject to an archeological resources permit. That provision was deleted in the final version of the law, but Native Hawaiians (as they are defined in the NMAI Act) were given standing under the law to assert repatriation claims along with Indians and Alaska Natives.

NAGPRA became effective immediately upon passage (November 16, 1990), although implementing regulations were not promulgated for another five years (January 3, 1996). In establishing a framework for Native Americans to exercise their civil rights to human remains and defined cultural property, NAGPRA sought to reflect the relationship between the government of the United States and Indian tribes and Native Hawaiian organizations. Most notably, it virtually required an ongoing dialogue between custodians of repositories containing Native American human remains and cultural items and Indian, Alaska Native, and Native Hawaiian potential claimants.

Below is a comparison of NAGPRA with other heritage resource legislation affecting land use.

Date	Law	Statute	Controlling Party	Basis
1906	Antiquities Act	16 U.S.C. § 431	Government	land (ownership/control)
1966	NHPA	16 U.S.C. § 470a	Government/private parties	federal/federally assisted undertakings
1979	ARPA	16 U.S.C. § 470aa	Government	land; trafficking in violation of state/local law
1990	NAGPRA	25 U.S.C. § 3001 18 U.S.C. § 1170	Native American	Native American property rights

Scope of the Law

NAGPRA requires compliance by federal agencies and museums receiving federal funds with respect to their collections of Native American human remains and defined cultural property, including associated funerary objects, unassociated funerary objects, sacred objects, and cultural patrimony. Indian tribes and Native Hawaiian organizations have no obligations under the law; instead, standing is conferred upon Native Americans to enforce their property rights in cultural items by bringing claims for repatriation. By definition, Native Americans include

> any tribe, band, nation, or other organized or community of Indians, including any Alaska Native village (as defined in or established pursuant to, the Alaska Native Claims Settlement Act), which is recognized as eligible for the programs and services provided by the United States to Indians because of their status as Indians,

and

> any individual who is a descendant of the aboriginal people who, prior to 1778, occupied and exercised sovereignty in the area that now constitutes the State of Hawaii.
> 25 U.S.C. §§ 3001(7), (10) (1994).

To comply with the law federal agencies and museums receiving federal funds must compile information on their collections into "summaries" and "inventories," and disseminate that information broadly among geographically and culturally affiliated tribes and Native Hawaiian organizations. In addition, NAGPRA overrules the historic assumption that all items on federal land are federal property. Thus, in cases where protected items are discovered on federal or tribal lands after the effective date of the Act, a process exists to determine ownership in the first instance. Guiding the process of repatriation is a review committee that also may arbitrate disputes.

Summaries of Native American Cultural Items

Each federal agency and museum receiving federal funds must complete a summary of the scope of their Native American collection as it existed on November 16, 1990 [25 U.S.C. § 3004 (1994)]. A summary is a general description of the kinds of objects in the collection, the geographical area represented in the collection, the date and circumstances of acquisition, and when known, the cultural affiliation of the items. In giving Indian tribes and Native Hawaiian organizations an insight into a collection, the summary serves as the means to begin a dialogue between the museum or agency and the tribes or Native Hawaiian organizations.

A summary is not an itemized list (although the agency or museum could opt to compile an item-by-item list). It is a general categorization of items that could possibly constitute unassociated funerary items, sacred objects, or cultural patrimony. The purpose of the law is to bring Native Americans into a dialogue with repositories in possession or control in order to obtain a more complete identification of items, so NAGPRA does not require museums or agencies to know if their possessions fit one of the NAGPRA protected categories. Thus, an all-inclusive summary meets both the letter and spirit of NAGPRA.

The federal agency or museum summary only refers to items in the collection and in the repository's control. For purposes of NAGPRA, control exists in the entity that historically exerted authority over an item. Items in a repository that are on loan from federal agencies or other museums are not the responsibility of that repository because it does not control them [43 C.F.R. § 10.2(a)(3)(i) (1996)].

NAGPRA requires that agencies and museums rely on available information when compiling their summaries and inventories. It does not require additional investigation or scientific inquiry. Since the Act anticipated that repositories would share information with Indian tribes and Native Hawaiian organizations by making available to them the largest set of data possible, it neither requires nor condones the performance of scientific testing.

Summaries must be mailed to all Indian tribes and Native Hawaiian organizations who might be affiliated with any item referenced in the summary. The purpose of the summary is to initiate discussion. Therefore, inclusion of an item in the summary is not a commitment to repatriate the item, and does not even constitute a determination by the agency or museum that the item necessarily fits one of the protected categories. Also, receipt of a summary by an Indian tribe or a Native Hawaiian organization is not a determination by the agency or museum that the groups of items in the summary are culturally affiliated with the recipient of the summary.

The law does not require the museum or agency to copy and send all the information in their possession to every possible tribe which could have an interest in items, only that they afford reasonable access to that information [25 U.S.C. § 3004(b)(2) (1994)]. The reasonableness of a repository's action rests on whether complete summaries were distributed broadly to all Indian tribes and Native Hawaiian organizations that might have an interest in items, and on whether inquiring Native American groups were given access to records, catalogues and available studies.

The consultation process may begin prior to the completion of a summary. Both the museum or agency and the Indian tribe or Native Hawaiian organization stand to benefit from consultation, with the Native American group being able to locate its cultural property and the repository in control being able to close gaps in the body of scientific knowledge. Depending on information known to the Native American group, consultation could result in the deletion of some objects from consideration as NAGPRA-defined cultural items, or it might assist in identifying sacred objects or cultural patrimony.

Summaries were due three years from the day NAGPRA became law, and the Act did not provide for an extension of time for completion. The failure of a museum to complete a summary by November 16, 1993, exposed it to liability for a civil penalty [25 U.S.C. § 3007 (1994); only museums are subject to penalties for non-compliance]. Penalties could not be assessed, however, until a procedure was established through regulation, so a grace period—from November, 1993 to January, 1996—existed for museums to complete their summaries.

The issue arises as to whether museums not receiving federal funds in 1990 (when NAGPRA became law) must comply with the repatriation process if they subsequently receive federal funding. Another question is whether museums or federal agencies coming into possession of NAGPRA-protected items after the date of the Act have a duty to amend their summaries. The ongoing requirement of disclosure and consultation is an issue to be addressed in regulations, but including newly acquired items within the scope of NAGPRA and requiring museums to comply with the law whenever they receive federal funds might be a logical extension of the Act.

Inventories

All federal agencies and museums receiving federal funds were to have completed item-by-item inventories of Native American human remains and associated funerary objects in their collections (as constituted on November 16, 1990) within five years from the enactment of NAGPRA. These inventories would include sufficient information, briefly stated, to identify individuals [25 U.S.C. § 3003 (1994)]. Unlike a summary, identification of an individual in an inventory is a determination of cultural affiliation by the issuing agency or museum based on information already known to them and obtained through consultation. Notice was to be sent to the lineal descendants and the tribes or Native Hawaiian organizations culturally affiliated with the identified individuals [43 C.F.R. §§ 10.9(e)(1), (3) (1996)] within six months of inventory completion. The Departmental Consulting Archeologist (Department of the Interior) was responsible for publishing all notices of inventory completion in the Federal Register [25 U.S.C. § 3003(d)(3) (1996)].

An inventory must contain:

a.   the identity of each Native American for whom remains or funerary objects can be identified, and information concerning acquisition;

b.   a list of all human remains and associated funerary objects for which tribal affiliation can be determined; and

c.   a list of human remains and associated funerary objects which, given the totality of the circumstances, are Native American, but whose cultural affiliation cannot be determined.

This information may result in further consultation and identification of individuals. Any individuals whose cultural identity cannot be determined eventually will be removed to a final resting place to be recommended by the NAGPRA Review Committee, and their disposition will be subject to future regulation.

The five-year period for completing an inventory could be extended upon request to the Secretary of the Interior and a showing of a good faith attempt to complete the inventory in a timely fashion [25 U.S.C. § 3003(c) (1994)]. The request also would require submission of a written plan and a timetable to carry inventory process to completion. In order to ensure completion, subsequent implementing regulations required that requests for an extension of time also furnish the title of the person responsible for the inventory, as well as evidence to demonstrate the existence of a schedule and funding. Extensions are available to museums (which are subject to a penalty for noncompliance), but not federal agencies.

Scientific Investigation and Study

One of the factors motivating the passage of NAGPRA was the disparate treatment afforded Native Americans, whose remains still could be found in storage boxes awaiting scientific study long after non-Native American remains had been turned over to religious leaders for reinterment. The Act expressly precludes the claim by a federal agency or museum that they need to retain possession or control of Native American human remains and certain cultural items for future scientific study, and thus that they must prolong repatriation. Although NAGPRA does allow a narrow exception for scientific study, "the outcome of which would be of major benefit to the United States" [25 U.S.C. § 3005(c) (1994)], the museum first must obtain an extension from the Secretary of Interior by providing a basis for the request and a timetable for completion. Repatriation then must proceed within 90 days of completion of the study.

Human remains or cultural items remain in control of the federal agency or museum until actual repatriation, resolution of a dispute among claimants, or the completion of an approved scientific study. NAGPRA is silent about whether scientific study may occur during the period of summary and inventory completion (to the extent that the timing of repatriation is unaffected). That the law put no affirmative requirement or prohibition on scientific investigation was not an oversight. On the one hand, the legislative history of NAGPRA reveals that some Native American groups were opposed to any study whatsoever, while others had no objection to studies conducted in a respectful manner. On the other hand, research institutions feared that if they were required to undertake scientific analyses in order to obtain cultural identifications prior to repatriation, whole budgets would be consumed given the size of some collections. Eventually, Native Americans, museums and federal agencies, and Congress agreed that identification and repatriation could be accomplished using the existing body of scientific knowledge together with information obtained during consultation. Nevertheless, pending summary and inventory completion, the repository in control would appear to have authority to conduct scientific investigations. NAGPRA, however, may not be used to justify such study.

NA IWI O NA KUPUNA O MOKAPU v. DALTON

894 F. Supp. 1397 (D. Haw. 1995)

DAVID ALAN EZRA, District Judge:

After hearing argument and reviewing the motions and the supporting and opposing memoranda, the court GRANTS the Federal Defendant's Motions for Summary Judgment, and DENIES Plaintiff Hui Malama's Cross-Motion for Partial Summary Judgment regarding Count II of the Complaint.

BACKGROUND

Congress enacted the Native American Graves Protection and Repatriation Act ("NAGPRA") on November 16, 1990. On March 25, 1992, the Federal Defendant awarded a contract to the Bishop Museum to prepare an inventory of the human remains disinterred from the Mokapu Peninsula (hereinafter "the Mokapu remains" or "the Na Iwi") in compliance with NAGPRA Section 3003. This was the first Department of Defense project falling under NAGPRA.

At the time the contract was awarded, there were no federal regulations or guidelines for preparing an inventory under NAGPRA. The proposed implementing regulations relating to NAGPRA were not issued until May 28, 1993, and as of this date are still not finalized. The Department of the Interior did not provide inventory guidelines and examples until March 1995.

The Mokapu remains represented the largest single group of Native Hawaiian remains housed at the Bishop Museum at the time of the inventory. The general objective of the Mokapu inventory was to provide an accurate list of the human remains and funerary objects from the Mokapu Peninsula, and to establish a minimum number of individuals represented by the remains. The enumeration of individuals was effectively to be a census, with morphometric and macroscopic assessments of sex, age, and distinguishing characteristics noted as aids to compare with the limited information contained in the previously prepared Osteology Catalog.[1]

Because several different research scholars, curators, and other staff listed the remains, the descriptions in the Osteology Catalog relating to sex, age, distinguishing physical attributes and pathological observations varied. Review of such data revealed a significant number of discrepancies between the accessions described as one individual and the remains actually present.[2]

The lack of a systematic curatorial program left the Mokapu collection in some disarray. At the commencement of the inventory, there was some confusion of skeletal parts within the collection of remains. The actual minimum number of individuals represented was not determinable based on the existing data. In addition, there was extensive commingling of remains within accessions. That is, though an accession listed only one individual, more than one individual was in fact often present.

As a result of the commingling and discrepancies between the remains and the records relating to them, the data contained in the Osteology Catalog could not be used to conduct a proper inventory. It became necessary to examine the Mokapu remains using standard physical anthropology techniques. The inventory report indicates that Bishop Museum employed such techniques. The museum performed no DNA analyses, nor did the museum conduct extensive metric or nonmetric analyses of the remains.[3]

During the inventory process, pursuant to Section 3003(b)(1)(A) of NAGPRA, consultations were held with, inter alia, Hui Malama. Formal meetings were held on March

---

[1][*Orig. fn.*] The Osteology Catalog is a book that contains information regarding the human remains.

[2][*Orig. fn.*] Accession documents contain information on the method of acquisition, the date the items were received, the date they were collected, the locality from which they were collected, the donor name and address, and other pertinent information.

[3][*Orig. fn.*] Only in the case of four sets of remains did Bishop Museum perform more extensive metric and nonmetric analyses. This was allegedly done only because, on preliminary examination, there was a definite question as to cultural affiliation/ethnicity of the remains.

25, 1992, January 13, 1993, and February 27, 1993. Telephone consultations also occurred periodically.

Among the issues specifically discussed during these consultations were the difficulties encountered by Bishop Museum. Bishop Museum advised Hui Malama that it intended to use current anthropological methods of determining age and sex to obtain a more accurate enumeration of individuals.

At the January 13, 1993 meeting, representatives of the Federal Defendant made presentations regarding the methodologies Bishop Museum was using in conducting the inventory and the status of the project. The Federal Defendant's representatives reported the preliminary results of the physical anthropological examinations relating to age, sex, skeletal completeness and recorded pathologies.

At the next meeting on February 27, 1993, the parties specifically discussed the discrepancies discovered in the curatorial records versus the actual remains and the problems associated with separation and commingling of the remains. Topics discussed included skeletal completeness, skeletal alteration, determinations of ethnicity, sex, and age, pathologies, and metric determinations.

Bishop Museum finalized the inventory, consisting of the narrative report and appendices, in January 1994. The Secretary of the Interior published the notice of completion in the Federal Register in accordance with NAGPRA. See 25 U.S.C. § 3003(d)(3). Potential claimants received copies of the inventory upon request. Distribution of the inventory to date has been limited primarily to: (1) claimants; (2) persons involved in this litigation; (3) Navy personnel; (4) the Review Committee and National Park Service Consulting Archaeologist pursuant to NAGPRA requirements; and (5) requestors under the Freedom of Information Act, 5 U.S.C. § 552. The inventory has not yet been published.

On June 14, 1994, Hui Malama brought suit against the Federal Defendant and the Bishop Museum for declaratory and injunctive relief.[4] The complaint alleged: (Count I)—that the Federal Defendant failed to return expeditiously the Mokapu remains in violation of NAGPRA Sections 3005 and 3010; and (Count II)—that the Federal Defendant conducted additional scientific research on the Mokapu remains in derogation of alleged agreements between the Federal Defendant and Hui Malama and in violation of NAGPRA Sections 3003 and 3010. Complaint at 6-9.

Hui Malama's original Complaint prayed that the court: (1) declare that the Federal Defendant violated NAGPRA Section 3005 by failing to return expeditiously the Mokapu remains; (2) declare that the Federal Defendant violated NAGPRA Section 3003 by undertaking additional research on the Mokapu remains; (3) order that the results of the additional research be deleted from all published inventory reports; (4) order that the research information be placed under seal, subject to disclosure only upon the express written approval of Hui Malama; (5) order the expeditious return of the Mokapu remains to Hui Malama; and (6) grant Hui Malama its costs and attorney fees. Id. at 9-10.

---

[4]Pursuant to Rule 41(a)(1) of the Federal Rules of Civil Procedure, the parties stipulated on January 27, 1995, to dismiss with prejudice Defendant Bishop Museum from the present action, as a result of Bishop Museum transferring all drafts and final copies of the subject inventory to the Federal Defendant and deleting any and all drafts of the inventory from its computers. For the purpose of the present disposition, reference to "the Federal Defendant" will hereinafter incorporate actions taken by Bishop Museum as well as the Federal Defendant.

The Federal Defendant filed its first Motion for Summary Judgment on January 27, 1995 (hereinafter "Federal Defendant's January Motion for Summary Judgment") regarding both Counts I and II of Hui Malama's Complaint. Hui Malama subsequently withdrew Count I regarding the request for immediate repatriation to Hui Malama. See discussion infra part I. Following settlement negotiations during Spring 1995, the Federal Defendant filed a second Motion for Summary Judgment on May 11, 1995 (hereinafter "Federal Defendant's May Motion for Summary Judgment"), addressing only the additional scientific research issue contained in Count II. Hui Malama also filed a Cross-Motion for Partial Summary Judgment on May 11, 1995, seeking summary judgment on Count II.

STANDARD OF REVIEW

Summary judgment is appropriate when there is no genuine issue as to any material fact and the moving party is entitled to judgment as a matter of law. Fed. R. Civ. P. 56(c). The moving party has the initial burden of "identifying for the court those portions of the materials on file in the case that it believes demonstrate the absence of any genuine issue of material fact." *T.W. Elec. Serv., Inc. v. Pacific Elec. Contractors Ass'n*, 809 F.2d 626, 630 (9th Cir. 1987) (citing *Celotex Corp. v. Catrett*, 477 U.S. 317, 323 (1986)). In a motion for summary judgment, the court must view the facts in the light most favorable to the nonmoving party. *State Farm Fire & Casualty Co. v. Martin*, 872 F.2d 319, 320 (9th Cir. 1989).

Once the moving party has met its burden of demonstrating the absence of any genuine issue of material fact, the nonmoving party must set forth specific facts showing that there is a genuine issue for trial. *T.W. Elec.*, 809 F.2d at 630; Fed. R. Civ. P. 56(e). The opposing party may not defeat a motion for summary judgment in the absence of any significant probative evidence tending to support its legal theory. *Intel Corp. v. Hartford Accident & Indemnity Co.*, 952 F.2d 1551, 1558 (9th Cir. 1991). The nonmoving party cannot stand on its pleadings, nor can it simply assert that it will be able to discredit the movant's evidence at trial. *T.W. Elec.*, 809 F.2d at 630; *Blue Ocean Preservation Soc. v. Watkins*, 754 F. Supp. 1450, 1455 (D. Haw. 1991); Fed. R. Civ. P. 56(e). If the nonmoving party fails to assert specific facts, beyond the mere allegations or denials in its response, summary judgment, if appropriate, shall be entered. *Lujan v. National Wildlife Fed'n*, 497 U.S. 871, 884 (1990); *T.W. Elec.*, 809 F.2d at 630; Fed. R. Civ. P. 56(e). There is no genuine issue of fact if the opposing party fails to offer evidence sufficient to establish the existence of an element essential to that party's case. *Celotex*, 477 U.S. at 322; *Citadel Holding Corp. v. Roven*, 26 F.3d 960, 964 (9th Cir. 1994); *Blue Ocean*, 754 F. Supp. at 1455.

In considering a motion for summary judgment, "the court's ultimate inquiry is to determine whether the 'specific facts' set forth by the nonmoving party, coupled with undisputed background or contextual facts, are such that a rational or reasonable jury might return a verdict in its favor based on that evidence." *T.W. Elec.*, 809 F.2d at 631 (*citing Anderson v. Liberty Lobby*, 477 U.S. 242, 248 (1986)). Inferences must be drawn in favor of the nonmoving party. *T.W. Elec.*, 809 F.2d at 631. However, when the opposing party offers no direct evidence of a material fact, inferences may be drawn only if they are reasonable in light of the other undisputed background or contextual facts and if they are permissible under the governing substantive law. Id. at 631–32. If the factual context makes the opposing party's claim implausible, that party must come forward with more persuasive evidence than otherwise necessary to show there is a genuine issue for trial. *Bator v. State of Hawaii*, 39 F.3d 1021,

1026 (9th Cir. 1994) (citing *California Architectural Bldg. Prods., Inc. v. Franciscan Ceramics*, 818 F.2d 1466, 1468 (9th Cir. 1987), *cert. denied*, 484 U.S. 1006 (1988)).

DISCUSSION

I. Federal Defendant's January Motion for Summary Judgment on Count I: Failure to Return Mokapu Remains to Hui Malama

Hui Malama's original Complaint alleged that the Federal Defendant violated NAGPRA Section 3005 by failing to return expeditiously the Mokapu remains to Hui Malama once cultural affiliation was known. Complaint at 6-8. At the time Hui Malama filed the Complaint the organization believed itself to be the only group requesting repatriation of the remains. Hui Malama withdrew Count I after learning that fourteen other groups also made claims to the remains. Hui Malama thus concedes that it is no longer seeking adjudication of its repatriation claim pending the Federal Defendant's decision regarding which group is entitled to receive the Mokapu remains. Hui Malama's concession effectively renders Count I of the Complaint and the issues relating to it moot. However, Hui Malama has not formally withdrawn Count I as set forth in the original Complaint. Because the Federal Defendant has moved this court for summary judgment on Count I and Hui Malama has responded to the motion, and because this issue is likely to arise again, the court here addresses the questions relating to repatriation.

Hui Malama contends that in the context of a repatriation dispute, the Federal Defendant would adequately represent the interests of any claimant to the remains not joined with Hui Malama. This argument fails. In no way can the Federal Defendant be considered an adequate representative of other claimants' interests in this context. The myriad differences in the parties' respective motivations and concerns with respect to the issues in this case makes consideration of the Federal Defendant and Native Hawaiian groups as parties with common interests untenable. The other claimants are indispensable parties who must be joined before a repatriation claim may proceed.

Regarding the Federal Defendant's exhaustion and ripeness arguments, Hui Malama suggests that if a repatriation claim was still at issue, exhaustion of administrative remedies would not be required for the claim to be ripe. According to Hui Malama, the fact that NAGPRA contains a savings clause and an enforcement provision giving district courts jurisdiction of suits brought under NAGPRA indicates that there is no exhaustion requirement. See 25 U.S.C. §§ 3009, 3013. However, NAGPRA clearly provides for an administrative process under which the agency will decide to whom remains should be repatriated. See 25 U.S.C. § 3005. To date, the Federal Defendant has not made a decision on repatriation of the Mokapu remains. Until the Federal Defendant repatriates the Mokapu remains in accordance with NAGPRA provisions, there is no final agency action to challenge.[5] Judi-

---

[5]If a party were to make a colorable claim that a federal agency or museum was not properly following NAGPRA repatriation procedures and was thereby causing undue delay, judicial intervention might be warranted in the absence of final agency action. However, there is no present objection by Hui Malama that the current repatriation process violates NAGPRA procedural mandates.

cial intervention prior to the agency's decision would disrupt the agency process and result in a waste of judicial resources. This is precisely the type of administrative decision to which exhaustion requirements and the ripeness doctrine are intended to apply. Hui Malama's challenge to the repatriation process as contained in Count I of the Complaint is therefore not appropriately before this court.

For these reasons, the court GRANTS the Federal Defendant's January Motion for Summary Judgment on Count I of the Complaint alleging failure to return the Mokapu remains to Hui Malama in violation of NAGPRA Section 3005.[6]

II.   Standing Issues

A.   Standing; Human Remains

The Complaint filed on June 14, 1994 lists the Na Iwi, or the Mokapu remains, as Plaintiffs. The Na Iwi purportedly brought this action by and through their alleged guardian, the Native Hawaiian organization Hui Malama. Consistent reference to "Plaintiffs Na Iwi" in the Complaint as well as Hui Malama's Memorandum in Opposition to Defendant's January Motion for Summary Judgment make it clear that the Mokapu remains were intended as Plaintiffs in their own right. Hui Malama asserts that according to Hawaiian custom, human remains are spiritual beings that possess all of the traits of a living person. The Federal Defendant's physical examination of the remains was, they contend, a violation and desecration of the remains. As a result, the remains have allegedly suffered an injury to their spiritual well-being and have standing to bring suit.

However, as the Federal Defendant correctly contends, neither the provisions of NAGPRA nor the common law afford standing to the Mokapu remains. Human remains are explicitly classified as "cultural items" under NAGPRA. See 25 U.S.C. § 3001(3). NAGPRA simultaneously fails to list human remains as legally recognized "persons" or as an entity with a legally protected interest under the statute. See 25 U.S.C. §§ 3001–3013; 43 C.F.R. § 7.3 (1993). Because Congress omitted human remains from all NAGPRA provisions concerning statutory participants and their rights, fundamental tenets of statutory construction dic-

---

[6]Count I contained two additional allegations: (1) that the Bishop Museum failed to repatriate the Mokapu remains in good faith in derogation of NAGPRA Section 3005(f); and (2) that the Federal Defendant violated an alleged fiduciary obligation to Hui Malama in derogation of NAGPRA Section 3010. See Complaint at 8. Hui Malama formally withdrew its lack of good faith allegation against the Bishop Museum when it stipulated to dismiss the Bishop Museum from the suit, thereby eliminating the need for this court's determination of that issue. See supra note 4. However Hui Malama only informally withdrew the violation of fiduciary duty allegation against the Federal Defendant in the repatriation context. The court's present disposition of the Federal Defendant's January Motion for Summary Judgment regarding Count I therefore formally disposes of the violation of fiduciary duty allegation. The court more thoroughly addresses the Federal Defendant's obligations under NAGPRA Section 3010 in its discussion of Count II. See infra note 12.

tate that the court assume Congress did not consider human remains as having a legally protected interest under the Act. See *West Coast Truck Lines, Inc. v. Arcata Community Recycling Center, Inc.*, 846 F.2d 1239, 1244 (9th Cir), *cert. denied*, 488 U.S. 856 (1988). The provisions of NAGPRA do not grant the Mokapu remains standing to sue under the Act.

No court has addressed the issue of whether human remains have legal standing at common law. Hui Malama cites several cases where federal courts have apparently permitted non-human entities, such as animals and natural habitats, to bring suit, and attempts to draw an analogy with the human remains.[7] None of the cases Hui Malama cites, however, contains any indication that the parties or the court challenged the standing of the non-human plaintiffs. This court has previously denied standing to a non-human plaintiff where the opposing party timely objected. See *Hawaiian Crow v. Manuel Lujan, Jr.*, Civ. No. 91-00191 (D. Hawaii Sept. 13, 1991). Furthermore, all of the cases cited by Hui Malama involved more than one named plaintiff, supporting the inference that at least one of the other named plaintiffs had proper legal standing. These cases leave the legal status of non-human entities for standing purposes in doubt.

The court finds no sound legal basis for granting standing to human remains. Even the cases cited by Hui Malama refer to living organisms or dynamic ecosystems that are generally recognized as capable of suffering real injury in terms of physical or demonstrable detriment. Objects or entities without any attributes of life in the observable or provable sense are generally not afforded a legally protected interest for standing purposes.

The court notes that inanimate entities such as ships and corporations are accorded standing in their own right, but these forms of standing are legal fictions created for the benefit of living members of society. Allowing these entities to act as parties to lawsuits facilitates business and commerce, which in turn furthers societal interests and benefits individual persons. Hui Malama has not shown that a comparable identifiable benefit to living members of society would result from affording human remains standing. Even Justice Douglas' dissenting opinion in *Sierra Club v. Morton*, 405 U.S. 727 (1972), one of the most creative treatments of the subject, supports only the idea that inanimate entities should be granted legal status for standing when they act as surrogates for the interests of living things: The river, for example, is the living symbol of all the life it sustains or nourishes—fish, aquatic insects, water ouzels, otter, fisher, deer, elk, bear, and all other animals, including man, who are dependant on it or who enjoy it for its sight, its sound, or its life. The river as plaintiff speaks for the ecological unit of life that is part of it. *Sierra Club*, 405 U.S. at 743 (Douglas, J. dissenting). In sum, it is unclear whether this court could even reach the issue of the remains' eligibility for legal standing.

The court need not further consider the remains' eligibility for standing, however, because the court finds that the Mokapu remains have not met common law standing requirements. A plaintiff must meet three requirements to have standing: (1) the plaintiff must have

---

[7]See, *e.g.*, *Palila v. Hawaii DLNR*, 852 F.2d 1106, 1107 (9th Cir. 1988) (acknowledging that the endangered palila bird "has legal status and wings its way into federal court as a plaintiff in its own right"); *Mount Graham Red Squirrel v. Yeutter*, 930 F.2d 703 (9th Cir. 1991) (recognizing a squirrel's status as plaintiff); *Sun Enterprises, Ltd. v. Train*, 532 F.2d 280 (2d Cir. 1976) (recognizing an ecosystem's plaintiff status).

suffered an "injury in fact"—an invasion of a legally protected interest; (2) there must be a causal connection between the injury and the conduct complained of—the injury must be fairly traceable to the challenged action of the defendant; and (3) it must be likely that the injury will be redressed by a favorable decision. See *Lujan v. Defenders of Wildlife*, 504 U.S. 555, 559–61 (1992); *Valley Forge College v. Americans United*, 454 U.S. 464, 472 (1982).

There is no evidence that the remains have suffered an "injury in fact."[8] NAGPRA's designation of human remains as "items" and not as persons with legally protected rights or as an entity with a legal personality precludes this court from contravening Congress' obvious intent to deny human remains an interest susceptible to injury in the legal sense. Even if this court could ignore the clear legislative mandate and permit a showing that the remains have suffered some injury, Hui Malama's unsubstantiated assertions would not suffice to show that the remains did in fact suffer an injury. The Mokapu remains have not suffered a legally cognizable injury.

Further, even if the court recognized the Mokapu remains as having suffered some legally cognizable injury, Hui Malama has shown no causal connection between any injury and actions taken by the Federal Defendant. The record demonstrates that the Federal Defendant has attempted to conform its actions to its perceived obligations under NAGPRA regarding proper treatment and repatriation of the human remains in its care. Hui Malama has presented no evidence showing that the Federal Defendant either intentionally or incidentally caused any harm to the well-being of the Mokapu remains. Hui Malama's failure to demonstrate any traceable relationship between the Federal Defendant's actions and any alleged injury suffered by the Mokapu remains precludes the court from granting standing to the Mokapu remains.

A practical concern further cautions this court against granting standing to the Mokapu remains. Granting standing would necessitate a guardian to accomplish the tasks involved with litigation. NAGPRA does not contemplate any kind of guardianship regarding the disposition of claims or disputes concerning human remains. Although NAGPRA does mention Hui Malama in its definitional section as an organization providing guidance and expertise in decisions regarding Native Hawaiian cultural issues, see 25 U.S.C. § 3001(6), Congress did not clearly confer guardian status upon Hui Malama by this reference.

Hui Malama argues that, under Hawaiian law, the government is obligated to protect all rights "customarily and traditionally exercised" by Native Hawaiians, and therefore this court should recognize the Hawaiian concept of spiritual guardianship. The underlying argument is not entirely without merit. See *Pele Defense Fund v. Paty*, 73 Haw. 578, 837 P.2d 1247, 1271 (1992), *cert. denied*, 507 U.S. 918 (1993); H.R.S. § 1-1. However, as the court does not recognize the Mokapu remains' standing to bring suit, discussion about any kind of guardianship—legal, spiritual, or otherwise—is moot. Moreover, even if the court granted standing to the remains, nowhere does Hawaiian law acknowledge Hui Malama as the sole

---

[8]The court notes its discomfort with applying the conventional concept of "injury" in an area of such deeply-held belief. However, the fact that a specific statutory scheme now exists for the protection of the interests at issue here makes the decision whether to expand the concept of "injury" to represent more diverse perspectives unnecessary in this case.

guardian for all Native Hawaiian human remains. Where claims among several Native Hawaiian groups may conflict, equity would require that all the groups serve jointly as guardian of the human remains for the purpose of negotiating or litigating on the remains behalf prior to proper repatriation.

According to the foregoing analysis, Congress did not confer statutory standing upon human remains under NAGPRA, and the Mokapu remains do not satisfy common law standing requirements. The court finds that the Mokapu remains do not have standing to sue and are not plaintiffs in this action. Further, even were the remains to have standing, neither NAGPRA nor Hawaiian law legally confers guardian status solely upon Hui Malama. Hui Malama's participation in that capacity for any reason would be improper without joining as co-guardians all other parties whose rights and interests may be affected.

B. Standing; Hui Malama

As the Mokapu remains do not have standing to bring suit, Hui Malama must satisfy standing requirements in its own right for the suit to survive. Although the Federal Defendant concedes that Hui Malama has proper standing relating to Count II of the Complaint, this court must satisfy itself that Hui Malama has legal standing before it can properly recognize Hui Malama as Plaintiff.

Hui Malama contends that NAGPRA itself grants Hui Malama standing under two provisions. First, Hui Malama asserts that its inclusion in the definitional section of the statute effectively grants the organization standing. See 25 U.S.C. § 3001(6). While NAGPRA recognizes Hui Malama as a party with an interest in Native Hawaiian matters generally, the court does not construe this recognition as conferring standing. Absent an express provision granting standing to Hui Malama, the court cannot infer that Congress intended to do so. The conspicuous absence in the legislative history of any indication that Congress intended to grant standing to Hui Malama under the statute furthers the inference that there was no such intention. The court construes Congress' mention of Hui Malama in the definitional section as providing an intended source of information that parties working under the provisions of NAGPRA may consult in order to better facilitate the statute's goal, namely proper repatriation of Native Hawaiian cultural items. The words of the statute convey nothing more.

Hui Malama also contends that NAGPRA provides it standing under Section 3013. Section 3013 reads in pertinent part: "The United States district courts shall have jurisdiction over any action brought by *any person* alleging a violation of this chapter..." 25 U.S.C. § 3013 (emphasis added). Hui Malama argues that as a corporation it qualifies as a "person" and may sue on behalf of its injured members. See, *e.g., Hunt v. Washington Apple Advertising Comm'n*, 432 U.S. 333, 343 (1977). The court agrees with this construction. If Hui Malama satisfies settled constitutional organizational standing requirements, Hui Malama may qualify as a "person" entitled to sue under NAGPRA.

For an association or organization to have standing to bring suit on behalf of its members, three requirements must be met: (1) the association's members must otherwise have standing to sue in their own right; (2) the interests the members would seek to protect must be germane to the association's purpose; and (3) the claims asserted or the relief requested must require the participation of individual association members in the lawsuit. *Hunt*, 432 U.S. at 343. Hui Malama satisfies all three requirements.

First, as conceded by the Federal Defendant, members of Hui Malama have allegedly been personally injured by the Federal Defendant's actions in a sense sufficient to satisfy standing requirements. Through declarations of its members, Hui Malama has alleged actual injury to particular members of the organization, which the Federal Defendant allegedly caused and which this court has the power to redress.[9] As such Hui Malama members have demonstrated sufficient injury in fact to confer individual standing and satisfy the first part of the Hunt test.

Second, efforts by Hui Malama members to expunge the results of the physical examination are consistent with Hui Malama's purpose. According to Hui Malama members, the organization's function is to care for and protect Native Hawaiian remains. See Declarations of Edward Halealoha Ayau at 3–4, Kunani Nihipali at 4, and Pualani Kanahele at 2–3. NAGPRA states that Hui Malama's main function is to provide guidance and expertise in decisions dealing with Native Hawaiian cultural issues, particularly burial issues. See 25 U.S.C. § 3001(6). Hui Malama members view the interest they currently seek to protect as consistent with both the self-styled and statutorily defined purposes of Hui Malama. In the context of this case, the court agrees. The organization's central function as described in the declarations does not deviate significantly from the one enumerated in NAGPRA. The declarations therefore provide sufficient evidence that the interest in expunging the information contained in the inventory report is germane to Hui Malama's purpose.

Finally, members of Hui Malama who have allegedly suffered emotional, spiritual, and physical harm as a result of the inventory report's publication must participate in the litigation to satisfactorily adjudicate the issue. Through submission of declarations to help the court understand the issues and abate any perceived harm, the participation of individual Hui Malama members is indispensable.

As all three requirements of *Hunt* are satisfied, the court finds that Hui Malama has standing to act as Plaintiff in this suit. Rule 17(a) provides that "[n]o action shall be dismissed... until a reasonable time has been allowed after objection for ratification of commencement of the action by, or joinder or substitution of, the real party in interest." Fed. R. Civ. P. 17(a). For the purposes of this disposition, the court hereby substitutes Hui Malama as Plaintiff sua sponte.[10]

---

[9]Hui Malama members Edward Halealoha Ayau, Kunani Nihipali, and Pualani Kanahele describe the alleged harm suffered by Hui Malama members in their declarations. They allege both physical and spiritual harm. By accepting a sacred covenant under Hawaiian tradition and custom to care for the disinterred remains, harm will allegedly befall members who fail to protect and care for or who permit the desecration of the remains. Members allege they also suffer emotional trauma as a result of publication of the inventory report, and fear for the physical and spiritual safety of themselves and their families. The court respects these personal beliefs.

[10]Hui Malama argues that because it seeks only to expunge inventory information and does not seek repatriation, its claims do not affect the rights of the other claimants. It therefore contends that joinder of the other claimants as co-plaintiffs is not required. This argument misses the mark. Hui Malama has not shown unanimity on the inventory issue among the fifteen claimants. To allow Hui Malama to unilaterally litigate the issue of inventory disclosure would deny equal weight to the rights and potentially divergent interests of the other Native Hawaiian groups involved. Absent the present disposition of the case, the court would require joinder of the other claimants.

III.   Count II: Additional Scientific Research in Violation of NAGPRA Sections 3003 and 3010

Count II of the Complaint alleges that the Federal Defendant, without informing Hui Malama and in derogation of agreements by Defendant in consultation with Hui Malama,[11] undertook additional scientific research on the Mokapu remains, and prepared a report concerning the results of the research, in violation of NAGPRA Sections 3003 and 3010.[12] Complaint at 8–9.

As set forth below, the Freedom of Information Act ("FOIA") controls the resolution of Count II.[13] In accordance with FOIA, and consistent with NAGPRA, the court DENIES Hui Malama's requests to: (1) delete and place under seal certain information contained in the

---

[11]The federal government consulted with Hui MalaUa pursuant to NAGPRA Section 3003(b)(1)(A) several times throughout the inventory process. However, Hui Malama presented no evidence indicating the existence of an explicit agreement between Hui Malama and the Federal Defendant regarding the inventory or repatriation of the Mokapu remains. Any agreement concerning the Mokapu remains entered into prior to completion of the inventory between these two parties would nonetheless be invalid. NAGPRA does not restrict federal agencies or museums from entering into agreements as to the disposition of cultural items with the consent of the culturally affiliated tribe or organization. See 25 U.S.C. § 3009(1)(B). However, no such affiliation could have been appropriately determined prior to conducting the inventory and reviewing the claims of all interested parties. See 25 U.S.C. §§ 3003, 3005. The court will therefore review Count II in the statutory context only.

[12]NAGPRA Section 3010 provides: § 3010. Special Relationship between Federal Government and Indian Tribes. This chapter [NAGPRA] reflects the unique relationship between the Federal Government and Indian tribes and Native Hawaiian organizations and should not be construed to establish a precedent with respect to any other individual, organization or foreign government. 25 U.S.C. § 3010. The court disagrees with Hui Malama's assertion that Section 3010 establishes a trust or fiduciary relationship between the government and Hui Malama. If Congress had intended to establish such a relationship, it could have used explicit language. It is not permissible for the court "to construe a statute on the basis of a mere surmise as to what the Legislature intended and to assume that it was only by inadvertence that it failed to state something other than what it plainly stated." *Doski v. M. Goldseker Co.*, 539 F.2d 1326, 1332 (4th Cir. 1976) (*citing United States v. Deluxe Cleaners and Laundry, Inc.*, 511 F.2d 926, 929 (4th Cir. 1975)). This court has previously found that the federal government has no trust responsibility to Native Hawaiians where the relevant statutory language does not explicitly indicate a trust duty. *Han v. Department of Justice*, 824 F. Supp. 1480, 1486 (D Hawaii 1993), *aff'd* 45 F.3d 333 (9th Cir. 1995). Here, the court views NAGPRA Section 3010 as a disclaimer intended to ward off tangential repatriation claims from groups other than Native Americans or Native Hawaiians rather than as establishing a fiduciary obligation on the federal government. Accordingly, the court finds there is no violation of NAGPRA Section 3010, and will address Count II in light of Section 3003 only.

[13]FOIA is codified at 5 U.S.C. § 552.

Mokapu inventory; (2) declare that the Federal Defendant violated NAGPRA Section 3003 by its examination of the Mokapu remains; and (3) grant Hui Malama its attorney fees and costs.

A.   FOIA Mandates Disclosure of Complete Inventory

The Freedom of Information Act mandates the disclosure of information controlled by the federal government. FOIA "reflect[s] 'a general philosophy of full agency disclosure unless information is exempted under clearly delineated statutory language.'" *John Doe Agency v. John Doe Corp.*, 493 U.S. 146, 152 (1989) (citing *Department of Air Force v. Rose*, 425 U.S. 352, 360–61 (1976) (quoting S. Rep. No. 813, 89th Cong., 1st Sess. 3 (1965)). "The basic purpose of FOIA is to ensure an informed citizenry, vital to the functioning of a democratic society, needed to check against corruption and to hold the governors accountable to the governed." *NLRB v. Robbins Tire & Rubber Co.*, 437 U.S. 214, 242 (1978).

1.   The Inventory is Subject to FOIA

FOIA provides that "every agency shall, upon request for identifiable records..., make such records promptly available to any person." 5 U.S.C. § 552(a)(4)(A). Although the Act does not specifically define what constitutes an "agency record," the United States Supreme Court has proffered two standards which materials must meet to qualify as "agency records" under FOIA. First, the agency must "either create or obtain" the requested materials. Second, "the agency must be in control of the requested materials at the time the FOIA claim is made." *United States Dep't of Justice v. Tax Analysts*, 492 U.S. 136, 145 (1989); see *also Kissinger v. Reporters Comm. for Freedom of the Press*, 445 U.S. 136, 150–52 (1980).

The Mokapu inventory qualifies as an agency record under these standards. The Federal Defendant contracted for and obtained the inventory. In addition, the inventory is in the Federal Defendant's control now and for the foreseeable future.[14] As such, the inventory constitutes an agency record for FOIA purposes and is subject to the Act's disclosure requirement, unless one of FOIA's enumerated exemptions applies.

2.   No FOIA Exemptions Apply to the Inventory

FOIA contains specific exemptions that allow non-disclosure in certain narrow circumstances. The exemptions do not, however, obscure the clear underlying policy of full disclosure where the exemptions do not directly apply. See *John Doe Agency*, 493 U.S. at 152; *Rose*, 425 U.S. at 361. The exemptions are to be narrowly construed so that the underlying policy of full disclosure is furthered to the greatest extent possible. *See Department of State v. Ray*, 502 U.S. 164, 180 (1991) ("[W]e have repeatedly held that FOIA's exemptions 'must be narrowly construed.'") (citing *John Doe Agency*, 493 U.S. at 152).

---

[14][*Orig. fn.*] Hui Malama argues that the FOIA defense is not ripe because there is no present request for disclosure. Hui Malama cannot argue the issue of ripeness regarding a defense it caused the Federal Defendant to raise through its own Complaint.

The Congressional message behind FOIA is unequivocal. The government must make available documents it possesses to anyone who requests disclosure. Congress explicitly listed the only possible exemptions in the Act. See 5 U.S.C. § 552(b)(1)–(9). The spirit and purpose of FOIA mandate a strong presumption in favor of disclosure. See *Ray*, 502 U.S. at 173.

As an agency record, the Federal Defendant can only withhold the Mokapu inventory if it falls under one of the nine FOIA exemptions. Both parties agree that only two of the nine exemptions potentially apply to the inventory, 5 U.S.C. § 552(b)(3) ("Exemption Three") and 5 U.S.C. § 552(b)(6) ("Exemption Six").

Exemption Three excludes materials specifically exempted by so-called "withholding" statutes. 5 U.S.C. § 552(b)(3). Exemption Six excludes materials such as personnel and medical files which, if released, would constitute a "clearly unwarranted invasion of personal privacy." 5 U.S.C. § 552(b)(6). The court finds that neither Exemption Three nor Exemption Six applies to the Mokapu inventory.

a. NAGPRA Is Not a Withholding Statute Under FOIA Exemption Three

FOIA Exemption Three provides that the Act's general disclosure requirement does not apply to matters that are: specifically exempted from disclosure by statute... provided that such statute (A) requires that the matters be withheld from the public in such a manner as to leave no discretion on the issue, or (B) establishes particular criteria for withholding or refers to particular types of matters to be withheld. 5 U.S.C. § 552(b)(3). For NAGPRA to qualify as a withholding statute for FOIA purposes, it must fit within Subsection A or B of Exemption Three.

"When interpreting a statute, the court's objective is to ascertain the intent of Congress and to give effect to legislative will." *Meyerhoff v. EPA*, 958 F.2d 1498, 1501 (9th Cir. 1992) (citing *Moorhead v. United States*, 774 F.2d 936, 941 (9th Cir. 1985)). "It is assumed that the legislative purpose is expressed by the ordinary meaning of the words used, and absent a clearly expressed legislative intention to the contrary, the language must ordinarily be regarded as conclusive." Id.

Courts have consistently held that a statute is a withholding statute for FOIA purposes only when it explicitly states in unambiguous terms that information gathered under the statute is not to be released to the public or is to be kept confidential. See, *e.g.*, *Baldrige v. Shapiro*, 455 U.S. 345, 359 (1982) (holding Census Act is a withholding statute as it explicitly provides for nondisclosure); *Association of Retired R.R. Workers v. Railroad Retirement Bd.*, 830 F.2d 331, 334 (D.C. Cir. 1987) (finding Railroad Unemployment Insurance Act, which requires specific types of information to be kept confidential, to be a withholding statute).

FOIA became law in 1966. Congress passed NAGPRA in 1990, and did not make NAGPRA a withholding statute. The NAGPRA section dealing with inventories, Section 3003, does not explicitly exempt any information contained in inventories from disclosure. Nowhere does it contain any indication that inventory results are to be confidential or privileged in any respect. NAGPRA does not require that an agency withhold any matters from the public, much less grant the government any discretion on the issue, see 5 U.S.C. § 552(b)(3)(A), nor does NAGPRA establish any criteria for withholding or refer to particular types of matters to be withheld, see 5 U.S.C. § 552(b)(3)(B). According to the plain language standard set forth in *Meyerhoff*, NAGPRA does not satisfy either Subsection A or Subsection B of FOIA Exemption Three.

Hui Malama argues that the language in NAGPRA which defines an inventory as a "simple itemized list" impliedly prohibits the inclusion of any further information. See 25 U.S.C. § 3003(e). According to Hui Malama NAGPRA thus mandates the withholding of any such additional information, thereby qualifying as an Exemption Three withholding statute. The court does not agree. The legislative history is replete with indications that the primary reason Congress included the simplified inventory definition in the statute was to alleviate the initial burden placed on agencies and museums in meeting the inventory compilation requirements under NAGPRA. See generally, H.R. Rep. No. 877, 101st Cong., 2d Sess. (1990). Contrary to any secretive intent, the legislative history actually suggests that where information exists, it should be made available generally where no undue burden on the government will ensue. See H.R. Rep. No. 473, 101st Cong., 2d Sess. (1990); see also infra part III.B.

According to its express language, its legislative history, and its spirit and purpose, NAGPRA does not qualify as a withholding statute under FOIA Exemption Three.

b. Exemption Six Protecting Individuals from Invasions of Privacy Does Not Apply

Exemption Six provides for the withholding of "personnel and medical files and similar files the disclosure of which would constitute a clearly unwarranted invasion of personal privacy." 5 U.S.C. § 552(b)(6). This exemption aims to protect individuals from public scrutiny regarding personal affairs. In determining what constitutes a "clearly unwarranted invasion of personal privacy," the court must balance the privacy interests that would be harmed by disclosure against the public interest in the open dissemination of information in the government's control. *Ray*, 502 U.S. at 175; *Department of Justice v. Reporters Comm. for Freedom of the Press*, 489 U.S. 749, 762 (1989); *Painting Industry of Hawaii v. Department of Air Force*, 26 F.3d 1479, 1482 (9th Cir. 1994). "[U]nless the invasion of privacy is 'clearly unwarranted,' the public interest in disclosure must prevail." *Ray*, 502 U.S. at 177.

The court need not reach this balancing approach, however, because the information contained in the inventory falls outside Exemption Six altogether. Exemption Six is intended to protect information regarding particular living persons. *See Department of State v. Washington Post Co.*, 456 U.S. 595, 602 (1982). The cases addressing this exemption have uniformly dealt with revealing personal information about particular individuals, such as identity, wage information, home address, or religious affiliation. See *Department of Defense v. FLRA*, 510 U.S. 487, ___, 114 S. Ct. 1006, 1013 (1994) (home address); *Painting Industry of Hawaii*, 26 F.3d 1479 (wage information); *Church of Scientology v. Department of Army*, 611 F.2d 738, 747 (9th Cir. 1979) (religious affiliation). Congress' evident intent to protect the privacy of living members of contemporary society does not encompass the Mokapu remains. *Cf.* supra part II.A.

Even if Congress did intend to protect the privacy of individual human remains, information pertaining to a large group of individuals is not covered under FOIA Exemption Six. The main thrust of Exemption Six is to avoid identification of particular individuals. Where such a danger is absent or unlikely, Exemption Six is inapplicable. See *Arieff v. Department of the Navy*, 712 F.2d 1462, 1467–68 (D.C. Cir. 1983) (holding that merely being one of a group of 600 persons who may be identified by the release of information relating to the entire group is not sufficient to trigger Exemption Six protection). As there is no real danger here that any particular individuals will be identified by disclosure of the inventory, the concern of Exemption Six is avoided.

Furthermore, according to the text of the statute, its legislative history, and the Supreme Court's interpretation of the exemption, Exemption Six "does not apply to an invasion of privacy produced as a secondary effect of the release." *Arieff*, 712 F.2d at 1468 (emphasis in original). To trigger Exemption Six protection, the actual production of the documents must constitute a clearly unwarranted invasion of "personal" privacy. Id. "Obviously, that can only occur when the documents disclose information [directly] attributable to an individual." Id.; see also *Rose*, 425 U.S. at 378–82 (holding mere speculation as to which particular individual may be affected by disclosure of government documents insufficient to invoke protection of Exemption Six); accord H.R. Rep. No. 1497, 89th Cong., 2d Sess. 11 (1966) ("The exemption [5 U.S.C. § 552(b)(6)] is... intended to cover detailed Government records on an individual which can be identified as applying to that individual..."). Because there is no reasonable fear that any individual with a legally cognizable privacy interest will be affected by disclosure of the inventory, Hui Malama's invocation of Exemption Six fails on this basis as well.

In sum, this court will not create a new kind of privacy interest by expanding this limited statutory FOIA exemption while interpreting FOIA in connection with another statute, NAGPRA, which fails to provide for such an interest.

For the foregoing reasons, Exemption Six does not apply to the Mokapu inventory.

3.   *FOIA Precludes Exercise of Equity Power*

Hui Malama also requests that, FOIA notwithstanding, this court use its equity power to prevent the release of inventory information. In enacting FOIA, Congress performed the balancing test normally performed by courts in determining whether to invoke equitable remedies in situations involving disclosure of government information. Congress found that, with the exception of materials that fall squarely within one of FOIA's nine enumerated exemptions, the equities mandated disclosure. "The Act's broad provisions favoring disclosure, coupled with the specific exemptions, reveal and present the 'balance' Congress has struck" between the public's right to have access to government-controlled information and the government's need to keep certain information confidential. *John Doe Agency*, 493 U.S. at 152–53. Congress intended to preempt the courts' discretion regarding disclosure of agency records. See *Weinberger v. Catholic Action of Hawaii*, 454 U.S. 139, 144–45 (1981); *Federal Open Market Comm. v. Merrill*, 443 U.S. 340, 351–52 (1979).

A court's equity decision must "comport to and remain compatible with the prevailing legislative intent." *Seguros Banvenez, S.A. v. S/S Oliver Drescher*, 761 F.2d 855, 863 (2nd Cir. 1985), quoting In re *Bell*, 700 F.2d 1053, 1057 (6th Cir. 1983), *cert. denied*, 104 S. Ct. 342, 343 (1983). Additionally, "a court's equity powers may not be exercised in such a manner as to deprive a person of constitutionally or statutorily protected rights." Id.; see also *Carter v. Gallagher*, 452 F.2d 315, 324 (8th Cir. 1971), *cert. denied*, 406 U.S. 950 (1972).

The Ninth Circuit specifically addressed the scope of courts' equity powers in the FOIA context in *Weber Aircraft Corp. v. United States*, 688 F.2d 638 (9th Cir. 1982), *rev'd on other grounds*, 465 U.S. 792 (1984). Weber held that courts may use their equity power to authorize nondisclosure of information under FOIA "only in 'extreme' or 'exceptional' circumstances." Id. at 646; see also *Theriault v. United States*, 503 F.2d 390, 392 (9th Cir. 1974) (district courts may authorize nondisclosure using their equity powers only when "dire adverse potentialities" would result); accord *Halperin v. Department of State*, 565 F.2d 699, 706 (D.C. Cir. 1977) (district courts have "some discretion in extreme circumstances" to use their equity powers to avoid disclosing government information which would "do grave damage to the national security"). In the instant case, Hui Malama has failed to legally substantiate its claim that dire results will ensure [sic] from permitting the disclosure of the inventory information. The information contained in the inventory does not compromise national security. No extreme or exceptional circumstances exist which would justify this court in preventing the disclosure of the information contained in the Mokapu inventory in compliance with FOIA. This court must adhere to Congress' clear intent, recognized by the Ninth Circuit and other circuit courts, to ensure disclosure of government information where no narrowly drawn statutory exemption applies. Accordingly, the court has no appropriate basis upon which to exercise its equity power to prevent disclosure of the Mokapu inventory.

B. NAGPRA Does Not Limit Disclosure of the Inventory

The plain language of NAGPRA indicates that Congress did not intend to limit the disclosure of inventory information. It is fundamental that "the starting point for interpreting a statute is the language of the statute itself. Absent a clearly expressed legislative intention to the contrary, that language must ordinarily be regarded as conclusive." *Consumer Prod. Safety Comm'n v. GTE Sylvania*, 447 U.S. 102, 108 (1980); see also *Burlington N. R.R. v. Oklahoma Tax Comm'n*, 481 U.S. 454, 461 (1987). As discussed below, NAGPRA contains no language evincing a legislative intent to keep any inventory information confidential. This court cannot hold otherwise.

Hui Malama first contends that NAGPRA's definition of an inventory as a "simple itemized list" evinces Congress' alleged intent to prohibit the disclosure of information regarding sex, age, and pathology. 25 U.S.C. § 3003(e). Accordingly, Hui Malama asserts that such information in the Mokapu inventory must be deleted. Contrary to Hui Malama's contention, the legislative history actually elucidates Congress' intent to provide for the disclosure of as much information as possible. Congress did not insert the language in NAGPRA defining an inventory as a "simple itemized list" as a stifling mechanism but rather as a minimum standard to avoid placing undue time and cost burdens on museums and federal agencies. See *Protection of Native American Graves and the Repatriation of Human Remains and Sacred Objects: Hearing on H.R. 1381, H.R. 1646, and H.R. 5237 Before the House Committee on Interior and Insular Affairs*, 101st Cong., 2d Sess. 166–67 (1990) (statement of Dr. Richard H. Thompson, Director, Arizona State Museum; alerting Congress to the immense amounts of time and money which mandatory compliance with NAGPRA preliminary draft H.R. 5237's more detailed inventory requirements would entail). Congress intended not only to permit but to favor inventories containing more than a simple list to provide for more definite cultural affiliation and ethnicity determinations, which would in turn better satisfy NAGPRA's ultimate goal, accurate and efficient repatriation. See H.R. Rep. No. 877, 101st Cong., 2d Sess. 31 (1990). Drafters expressly anticipated occasional additional research during the inventory process to facilitate proper repatriation of human remains and other cultural items: The cost of preparing an accurate inventory of the origin and tribal affiliation of human remains can vary considerably depending on the information already available, the amount of research needed to accurately determine tribal affiliation and the contentiousness surrounding individual pieces. [Financial estimates for total repatriation include] research to determine origin... [E]xtensive studies costing up to $500–$600 per remain may be necessary to determine the origin of some of the remains; however, such studies generally are not required by [NAGPRA]. S. Rep. No. 473, 101st Cong., 2d Sess. 19 (1990). Not only did Congress consider that further research during the inventory process would often be necessary for proper repatriation, it impliedly approved it.

NAGPRA Section 3003(e) contains no language which proscribes the kind of examination conducted by the Federal Defendant in the course of compiling an original inventory. Examinations done for the purpose of accurately identifying cultural affiliation or ethnicity are permissible because they further the overall purpose of NAGPRA, proper repatriation of remains and other cultural items. As discussed above, the legislative history bears out this intention. Commentators have also uniformly interpreted Section 3003(e) as permitting, though not requiring, further examination to facilitate proper repatriation. See, *e.g.*, Francis P. McManamon and Larry V. Nordby, *Implementing the Native American Graves Protection and Repatriation Act*, 24 Ariz. St. L.J. 217, 247 (1992) ("Although additional identification studies are not prohibited, the initiation of studies to acquire new scientific information is not required as part of the inventory. Optional studies might include ethnographic research to help identify sacred objects, burial practices, or physical anthropological studies to document or confirm ethnicity.") Because NAGPRA contains no language demonstrating an intent by Congress to prevent museums or federal agencies from conducting the kind of examination that the Federal Defendant performed on the Mokapu remains during the inventory process, the results may be disclosed under NAGPRA.

The legislative history also emphasizes the importance of ensuring access to available information on Native Hawaiian and Native American remains because of the "need to learn for the future from the past." H.R. Rep. No. 877, 101st Cong., 2d Sess. 13 (1990). At Congressional hearings Native American witnesses did not object to scientific studies as long as they had a specific purpose and definite time period. The only objection was to the indefinite retention of remains by museums for alleged "continuing" studies. See S. Rep. No. 473, 101st Cong., 2d Sess. 4–5 (1990). There is no indication that the Federal Defendant intended to delay or actually delayed repatriation of the remains by performing its cursory examination. According to the record, the information that the Federal Defendant gathered and included in the inventory was necessary for an accurate enumeration of the individuals represented by the Mokapu remains. No federal guidelines relating to NAGPRA inventory compilation existed at the time the Federal Defendant compiled the Mokapu inventory.[15] Based on a careful review of the record the court finds that the Federal Defendant conducted the Mokapu inventory according to a good faith, reasonable reading of the statute. It obtained and included in the inventory information which it believed was necessary to accurately describe the remains in its possession. The Federal Defendant's interpretation of recently enacted legislation, an interpretation with which this court cannot disagree, is reasonable. The information provided furthered the identification of the cultural affiliation and ethnicity of individual skeletons,[16] and thus served NAGPRA goals. According to the letter and spirit of NAGPRA Section 3003(e), the inventory was proper.

Hui Malama's alternative argument that NAGPRA Section 3003(b)(2) restricts the scope of inventories to exclude the information reported by the Federal Defendant is also unavail-

---

[15][*Orig. fn.*] The National Park Service issued guidelines for NAGPRA inventories and provided generic examples of proper inventories on March 3, 1995. Although the Federal Defendant did not have access to these guidelines, the examples promulgated therein provided for identification of age and sex and a description of the state of the remains. The Federal Defendant's examination resulted in the accurate determination of just such information. As the National Park Service is the agency charged with NAGPRA's implementation, this court affords substantial deference to that agency's interpretation of NAGPRA's inventory requirement. *See Chevron, U.S.A., Inc. v. Natural Resources Defense Council, Inc.*, 467 U.S. 837, 843–45 (1984) (holding an agency's interpretation of a statute is entitled to particularly substantial deference where the agency is charged with administering the statute); see also *Rembold v. Pacific First Federal Sav. Bank*, 798 F.2d 1307, 1311 (9th Cir. 1986), *cert. denied*, 482 U.S. 905 (1987) (holding courts must defer to an agency's construction of a statute which Congress mandates that it implement, absent a showing that Congress would not have sanctioned such a construction).

[16][*Orig. fn.*] Hui Malama contends that the Federal Defendant acknowledged that the cultural affiliation of the remains was "Native Hawaiian from the Mokapu Peninsula" in the contract authorizing the inventory even before the inventory began, and therefore any further examination of the remains was unwarranted. See Plaintiff's Supplemental Submission in Support of Plaintiff's Reply to Federal Defendant's Memorandum in Response to Plaintiff's Cross-Motion for Summary Judgment. This argument does not take into consideration the fact that the Federal Defendant discovered the inconsistencies in the available records only after it initiated the NAGPRA inventory. Some cursory examination became necessary to correct the mistakes and discrepancies contained in the Osteology Catalog and thereby compile an accurate inventory. In the course of the examination, the actual cultural affiliation of at least four sets of remains appeared ambiguous, and required more exacting scrutiny. Had the Federal Defendant blindly relied on the information available before the inventory process, some remains may have been repatriated to an incorrect party. Such a result is obviously not intended by NAGPRA and was probably avoided by the Federal Defendant's concern for accuracy.

ing.[17] Hui Malama misconstrues Section 3003(b)(2)'s language as prohibiting any and all examination of human remains in a museum or federal agency's possession. The organization contends that a museum or federal agency may only rely on the available written record in determining cultural or geographical affiliation. This is not the law.

NAGPRA Section 3003(b)(2) merely prevents federal agencies and museums from conducting additional research after completion of the initial inventory. Section 3003(b)(2) is wholly inapposite to examinations conducted at the inventory compilation stage. The section's restrictive language only applies "[u]pon request by an Indian tribe or Native Hawaiian organization which receives or should have received notice [of the completed inventory,... for] additional available documentation to supplement the [inventory] information required by subsection (a) of [Section 3003]." 25 U.S.C. § 3003(b)(2). Because the Federal Defendant did not conduct its examination in response to a request for information, Section 3003(b)(2) is of no consequence.

In light of the Congressional concerns which led to the enactment of NAGPRA itself, the reason for the distinction between inventory and post-inventory examinations is apparent. Congress intended for museums and federal agencies to conduct proper and complete inventories. Congress also wanted Native American and Native Hawaiian groups to have access to any existing information which museums or agencies possessed but did not include in the inventories, so that competing claimants could more fully assess their respective claims. However, Congress was very aware of museums and agencies which in the past had conducted protracted studies on Native American and Native Hawaiian remains without concern for timely repatriation of the remains to legitimate parties. Through NAGPRA Congress intended to correct this trend to the greatest practical extent. It therefore included

---

[17][*Orig. fn.*] Section 3003 provides in pertinent part:

§ 3003. Inventory for human remains and associated funerary objects

(a) In general

   Each Federal agency and each museum which has possession or control over holdings or collections of Native American human remains and associated funerary objects shall compile an inventory of such items and, to the extent possible based on information possessed by such museum or Federal agency, identify the geographical and cultural affiliation of such item.

(b) Requirements

   (2) Upon request by an Indian tribe or Native Hawaiian organization which receives or should have received notice, a museum or Federal agency shall supply additional available documentation to supplement the information required by subsection (a) of this section. The term "documentation" means a summary of existing museum or Federal agency records, including inventories or catalogues, relevant studies, or other pertinent data for the limited purpose of determining the geographical origin, cultural affiliation, and basic facts surrounding acquisition and accession of Native American human remains and associated funerary objects subject to this section. Such term does not mean, and this chapter shall not be construed to be an authorization for, the initiation of new scientific studies of such remains and associated funerary objects or other means of acquiring or preserving additional scientific information from such remains and objects. 25 U.S.C. § 3003.

Section 3003(b)(2)'s restrictive language to prevent agencies and museums from using a request for additional documentation as an excuse to initiate new studies and further delay the repatriation process. Section 3003(b)(2) targets additional studies unrelated to the initial inventory. "[NAGPRA Section] 3003(b)(2) does not preclude further scientific study" necessary to conduct the inventory itself in an accurate fashion. Jack F. Trope and Walter R. Echo-Hawk, *The Native American Graves Protection and Repatriation Act: Background and Legislative History*, 24 Ariz. St. L.J. 35, 62 (1992). Congress would not require accurate inventories under NAGPRA and then deny museums and federal agencies the necessary tools to comply effectively with that specific requirement.

By its own terms, then, Section 3003(b)(2) does not apply unless an Indian tribe or Native Hawaiian organization requests additional available documentation after the inventory is completed to supplement the inventory information. As no claimant requested additional information, Section 3003(b)(2) is irrelevant to the issue of whether the examinations were permissible.

The court finds that the Federal Defendant properly conducted its examination of the Mokapu remains under NAGPRA. Accordingly, the examination results are subject to disclosure.

C. NAGPRA Does Not Override FOIA

Even if the court found that the Federal Defendant had violated NAGPRA, such a violation would not allow the court to grant the relief Hui Malama requests. As discussed above, NAGPRA does not contain any indication that Congress intended that it repeal or escape the disclosure requirements of FOIA. Where a statute equivocally repeals or avoids the operation of a prior act, the statute is strictly construed to effectuate a consistent operation with the previous legislation. See *Preston v. Heckler*, 734 F.2d 1359, 1368 (9th Cir. 1984); see also *1A Sutherland Statutory Construction*, § 23.10, at 353 (5th ed. 1992) ("Where the repealing effect of a statute is doubtful, the statute is strictly construed to effectuate its consistent operation with previous legislation.").

There is no language in NAGPRA demonstrating an intent to avoid or repeal FOIA. Furthermore, the plain language of NAGPRA and the lack of concern over secrecy in the legislative history demonstrate that Congress affirmatively intended disclosure versus withholding of information under NAGPRA provisions. See supra part III.B. Any potential violation of NAGPRA would not compel a subsequent violation of FOIA.

CONCLUSION

For the foregoing reasons, the court GRANTS the Federal Defendant's Motions for Summary Judgment on Counts I and II, and DENIES Hui Malama's Cross-Motion for Summary Judgment on Count II along with Hui Malama's requested relief.

IT IS SO ORDERED.

Repatriation

At any point during consultation, anyone with standing may request return of a protected item from the museum or federal agency controlling it. Also, once cultural affiliation has been established, the process of repatriation may be carried to completion [25 U.S.C. § 3005 (1994)].

Standing to Make a Claim

Lineal descendants have standing to claim human remains of ancestors with whom they can show an unbroken chain of lineage [43 C.F.R. § 10.14 (1996)]. They also may claim the funerary objects associated with the deceased. Lineal descendants do not have to establish cultural affiliation in order to validate a claim.

The culturally affiliated Indian tribe or Native Hawaiian organization has standing to request the return of human remains, funerary objects, and sacred objects [25 U.S.C. § 3005 (a)(5)(C) (1994)] if there is no claim by a lineal descendant. Cultural patrimony, which by definition is central to the ongoing well-being of the group and cannot be alienated by an individual, may only be repatriated to the culturally affiliated group. Whether sacred objects can be owned by an individual or are exclusively group property is a matter of law or custom for each Native American group.

If it wishes to use NAGPRA, a culturally affiliated Native American group not recognized by the United States government as having standing to request the return or repatriation of a protected item must have another culturally affiliated group with standing claim and obtain the item, and then transfer it to the true owner. Employing NAGPRA in this manner may be appropriate, for example, when political boundaries, such as the United States-Canada border, divide Indian tribes, or when the most closely associated group presently is not recognized as a matter of law.

Determination of Cultural Affiliation

Cultural attribution of human remains and associated funerary items on an inventory is sufficient to establish a claim of affiliation. If, however, affiliation was generally noted on a summary, or was determined during consultation, the requesting group has the burden of establishing cultural affiliation. The group with standing must make a claim that is not contested to establish cultural affiliation (when cultural affiliation is questioned, NAGPRA's dispute resolution process is triggered). Under NAGPRA, any defined Native American group desiring the return or repatriation of an item, and believing it can show cultural affiliation, may make a claim. The federal agency or museum then must determine that the item in question belongs to one of the

NAGPRA categories, and that the claimant with standing has demonstrated cultural affiliation with the item.

Process of Repatriation

Once a group with standing makes a claim for a protected item, and absent a dispute, repatriation will occur within 90 days. During that period, the museum or federal agency must publish a "Notice of Intent to Repatriate" in the Federal Register [43 C.F.R. § 10.10(a)(3) (1996)]. If no competing claims arise, repatriation is to occur not less than 30 days following publication of the notice.

The method and manner of repatriation is determined by the repository in consultation with the Native American group or lineal descendent. Any costs arising from a repatriation ceremony or interment may be borne by either party, although NAGPRA does provide for grants, distributed yearly, to assist in repatriation. The repository must advise the recipient as to whether the item has been treated with any substance representing a potential hazard to the items themselves or persons handling them [43 C.F.R. § 10.10 (1996)]. Also, at the request of the recipient, the repository must protect information of a particularly sensitive nature from public disclosure [43 C.F.R. § 10.10(f)(2) (1996)]. Each museum and federal agency, however, is required to keep internal documentation of the content and recipient of every repatriation.

Ownership

Items in collections as of the date NAGPRA was enacted are subject to "repatriation" [25 U.S.C. § 3005 (1994)], while items located on federal or tribal lands after that date are subject to "disposition" pursuant to the section of the Act entitled "Ownership" [25 U.S.C. § 3002 (1994)]. A determination of ownership and disposition of newly discovered human remains and defined cultural heritage presumes that these items have not been acquired or possessed as government property. Instead, ownership is determined in the first instance, using a process that varies, depending on whether the discovery was intentional or inadvertent.

Intentional Excavation

A permit must be obtained pursuant to the Archaeological Resources Protection Act [ARPA; 16 U.S.C. § 470bb (1994)] when an intentional excavation is undertaken on federal land or within the exterior boundary of a tribal reservation. The ARPA permitting process requires consultation with any affected Indian tribe when the excavation will affect nonreservation land of importance to the tribe, and it includes devising a method for disposition of Native American human remains and defined cultural items to their owners. Excavation on tribal lands pursuant to an ARPA permit also requires permission from the affected Indian tribe or Native Hawaiian organization.

NAGPRA has left unresolved several issues concerning intentional excavation. First, pursuant to the definition of "tribal land" [25 U.S.C. § 3001 (15) (1994)], landowners within the exterior boundaries of an Indian reservation are required to obtain ARPA permits, to be administered by the Bureau of Indian Affairs [43 C.F.R. § 10.3(b)(1) (1996)], even though ARPA permits do not require permission of Indian tribes for excavations otherwise occurring on private land. Second, giving defined cultural items from private land to a tribe (pursuant to the NAGPRA section on ownership) likely would result in a taking prohibited by the Fifth Amendment to the United States Constitution. Some takings issues may be averted by operation of common law or state law on private lands to exempt burials from ownership by private landowners.

Inadvertent Discovery

Lawful excavation undertaken by a government contractor or government employee on federal land not pursuant to an ARPA permit, or work performed on tribal lands by authority of the tribe must, nevertheless, meet the requirements of NAGPRA. If, in the course of a legal activity not requiring an ARPA permit, Native American human remains or cultural items are discovered on federal or tribal lands after the date of the Act, the actor must immediately advise the land manager in writing [25 U.S.C. § 3002(d) (1994)]. If the discovery occurred during an activity such as mining, logging, agriculture, or construction, that activity must cease for 30 days in order to allow for notice to, and consultation with, affected Native American groups. The actor also must use reasonable efforts to protect the inadvertently discovered items. Work stoppages may be avoided, however, by prior agreement between potentially affected Native American groups and the actor.

Unlawful excavation on federal or tribal lands may produce inadvertent discoveries of protected items, which may be held as evidence for trial. Disposition of the items thereafter reasonably will follow the NAGPRA disposition process.

Priority of Ownership

Ownership of cultural items discovered on federal and tribal lands after November 16, 1990, is determined in the following order:

1. Lineal descendants have the priority right to human remains and associated funerary objects of their ancestors, regardless of whether they are located on federal or tribal lands.

2. In deference to tribal sovereignty, on tribal lands the tribal landowner has priority over all others, except a lineal descendant.

3. On federal land, if no lineal descendant is identified, priority is in the closest culturally affiliated tribe with standing that makes a claim.

4. On federal land, if the closest culturally affiliated tribe cannot be determined, priority is in the recognized tribe which was the aboriginal occupant of the area, unless:

   a. another tribe can show a stronger cultural affiliation than the aboriginal occupant of the area of discovery, and that tribe makes a claim and provides adequate evidence of affiliation; or

   b. human remains are identified as Native American and there are no claimants, or cultural affiliation cannot be determined. These human remains form a class of "unclaimed" cultural items whose disposition, along with "unidentified" human remains already in collections, awaits guidance from the NAGPRA Review Committee and future regulation.

The following table compares the ownership and repatriation components of NAGPRA. The priority of control or disposition is different in the two sections of the law. Culturally affiliated tribes have priority over all others except lineal descendants for repatriation of collections; tribal landowners have priority over all claimants except lineal descendants for ownership of discoveries on tribal lands.

Transfer Method:	Ownership/Disposition	Repatriation
Application:	future discovery on federal or tribal lands	past federal agency and museum collections
Effective Date:	after November 16, 1990	as of November 16, 1990
Priority of Control:	1. lineal descendant 2. tribal landowner 3. culturally affiliated tribe 4. aboriginal occupant 5. other tribe with cultural relationship 6. unclaimed	1. lineal descendant 2. culturally affiliated tribe 3. unidentifiable
Authority:	25 U.S.C. § 3002 (1994) 43 C.F.R. §§ 10.3–.7 (1996)	25 U.S.C. §§ 3003-3005 (1994) 43 C.F.R. §§ 10.8–.13 (1996)

Dispute Resolution

NAGPRA explicitly allocates the burden of proof in a claim for return or repatriation, and specifies the kind of evidence that may be used to support a claim [25 U.S.C. § 3005 (a)(4) (1994)]. It also safeguards against unconstitutional takings of private property [25 U.S.C. §§ 3001(13), 3005 (c) (1994)]. In addition, the Act provides penalties for museum noncompliance [25 U.S.C. § 3007 (1994)], as well as protection from liability for repatriations that otherwise comply with the law [62 Fed. Reg. 1,820 (1997), 25 U.S.C. § 3005 (f) (1994)]. Parties are encouraged to resolve disputes through informal negotiations.

A dispute does not become ripe until after a museum or federal agency decides the cultural affiliation of an item. NAGPRA provides a method for facilitating dispute resolution through the creation of a federal review committee [25 U.S.C. § 3006 (1994)]. When requested by an affected party, the Committee reviews the matter and makes findings, and decides whether to convene the parties. Appearance before the NAGPRA Review Committee is not mandatory, and its findings are not binding, but the Committee's records and findings are persuasive authority for parties seeking to resolve issues of Native American cultural heritage. After the Committee has presented its findings, the parties may decide to settle the matter or proceed to federal district court. Review Committee findings (as well as the agenda for each Committee meeting) are published in the Federal Register.

Review Committee

The Review Committee is comprised of seven members, three of whom are nominated by Indian tribes, Native Hawaiian organizations, and traditional Native American leaders, and three of whom are nominated by the museum and scientific communities [25 U.S.C. § 3006 (b) (1994)]. Two of the tribal nominees must be traditional religious leaders. These six Review Committee members meet and, by consensus, develop a list of nominees for a seventh position, to be selected by the Secretary of the Interior. None of the Review Committee members may be federal officers or employees. The Review Committee is responsible for:

1. designating a chairperson;

2. monitoring the inventory and identification process to assure consideration of all relevant information and evidence;

3. upon request, making findings as to cultural affiliation and identity, and the return of items;

4. facilitating resolution of disputes among parties concerning the return of items;

5. compiling an inventory of culturally unidentifiable human remains in the possession of federal agencies and museums, and making recommendations for their ultimate disposition;

6.   consulting with tribes and museums on matters within the scope of work of the committee, and affecting such tribes or organizations;

7.   consulting with the Secretary of the Interior on regulations;

8.   performing other functions assigned to the committee by the Secretary of the Interior; and

9.   making recommendations on the future care of repatriated items.

25 U.S.C. § 3006 (c) (1994).

Initially, the Review Committee predominantly facilitated consultation between Native Americans and repositories, and advised the Secretary of Interior on regulations. During the first five years following passage of NAGPRA, the Committee heard very few disputes, but after regulations were promulgated and the deadline for summaries and inventories passed, it became increasingly likely that the Committee would divide its time between hearing disputes and facilitating consultation. The 1996 regulations, however, did not contain procedures for assessing civil penalties against museums failing to comply with NAGPRA, and did not provide for the disposition of unidentified or unclaimed human remains. Thus, prior to 1997 when interim regulations governing civil penalties were published (62 Fed. Reg. 1,820), few disputes came before the Review Committee.

As a forum for alternative dispute resolution, the Review Committee accepts a dispute for hearing when the parties have been unable to resolve the matter informally and in good faith [43 C.F.R. § 10.17 (1996)]. Although the findings and records of the NAGPRA Review Committee are not binding on the parties to the dispute, they function as an aid to settlement prior to litigation. Parties are not required to exhaust this administrative remedy, and United States district courts have jurisdiction to hear actions arising under the Act regardless of whether the parties previously appeared before the Review Committee [25 U.S.C. § 3013 (1994)]. Nonetheless, and despite the fact that it is not bound by the Administrative Procedure Act, the Review Committee's records and findings may be admissible in any action brought in court that alleges a violation of NAGPRA [25 U.S.C. § 3006 (d) (1994)]. NAGPRA Review Committee input may be accorded great weight in a case before the United States district court. The Review Committee does not hear disputes concerning determination of ownership of new discoveries on federal and Indian land.

Burden of Proof

As the following chart shows, there may be three levels of proof for demonstrating the right to repatriation of cultural items pursuant to NAGPRA.

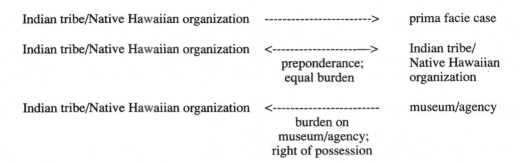

Initially, an Indian tribe or Native Hawaiian organization must make a *prima facie* showing of cultural affiliation. Any competing claims are then resolved by weighing the preponderance of the evidence. Where a presumption of cultural affiliation exists, a museum would have to show right of ownership by a preponderance of the evidence in order to overcome the presumption of rights in the Native American group making the claim.

A group with standing under NAGPRA need only provide a *prima facie* showing of cultural affiliation in order to make a claim for cultural items [25 U.S.C. § 3005 (c) (1994)]. *Prima facie* evidence of cultural affiliation exists when the inventory prepared by a museum or federal agency identifies individual human remains and associated funerary objects with a particular Native American group [25 U.S.C. § 3005 (a)(4) (1994)]; the claimant needs no further proof [25 U.S.C. § 3005 (a)(1) (1994)]. Information from a summary also may be used to assert a *prima facie* claim for an item, but a summary is not a final decision, and as it may include items that ultimately are not defined as cultural items, it does not constitute a commitment from the repository to repatriate items merely listed by general category.

When two or more groups with standing assert a *prima facie* case for cultural affiliation, or when other groups disagree with the attribution of the cultural affiliation by the museum or federal agency in the inventory, competing claims arise. The group proving its claim by a preponderance of the evidence will prevail. Before the Review Committee or a federal district court hears the dispute, however, the federal land manager or museum official first must make an initial determination of cultural affiliation. This decision is not binding on the parties, and it does not place a burden of proof on the nonprevailing party. No group is presumed by law to have a right of ownership; therefore, all groups with standing approach the court on an equal footing, and until the dispute is resolved the museum or federal agency retains the item in dispute [25 U.S.C. § 3005 (e) (1994)].

NAGPRA was enacted in order to address past nonrecognition of Native American property rights. It does not establish new property rights, and does not countermand an otherwise valid ownership right in property. If a group with standing has shown it is culturally affiliated with an item protected by

NAGPRA, the museum or federal agency must return the item, unless it is able to overcome the presumption of Native American ownership by demonstrating its own right of possession. The burden of proof, however, lies with the museum or federal agency to prove its claim by a preponderance of the evidence [25 U.S.C. § 3005 (c) (1994)].

Although they arise under different circumstances, the burden of proof for ownership claims under NAGPRA is consistent with the burden of proof for repatriation claims. The law establishes a priority for disposition of items found to be culturally affiliated with a Native American group (25 U.S.C. § 3002 (1994)). However, because the determination of ownership is contingent on future discoveries on federal land, and because the federal government will not claim ownership of protected items, there exist no federal agency claims to rebut. Consequently, potential disputes exist only when two or more groups with standing to make a claim believe they have the stronger cultural relationship to a cultural item [25 U.S.C. § 3002 (a)(2)(C)(2) (1994)]. Groups with identical priority stand equally before the court to show the weight of their respective claims by a preponderance of the evidence.

Evidence

NAGPRA provides that traditional Native American knowledge may be used as evidence to make a claim for cultural items. Under the Act cultural affiliation may be shown by evidence of:

1. geographical location
2. kinship
3. biology
4. archeology
5. anthropology
6. linguistics
7. folklore
8. oral tradition
9. history
10. other relevant evidence or expert opinion

   25 U.S.C. § 3005 (a)(4) (1994).

Although NAGPRA does not excuse any of this evidence from the requirements of relevancy and credibility, it nevertheless responds to a concern that the word of a Native American religious leader might not be admitted in court like the testimony of a scientist. The weight given to any evidence is for the trier of fact, but the foundation for the evidence in a NAGPRA claim is rooted in law. The impact of this provision outside the context of NAGPRA remains to be seen, but as in all human rights legislation, a broad impact might be expected.

Good Faith

NAGPRA would have been merely a well-intentioned, but ineffective, law had it not provided a good faith defense to causes of action arising out of repatriation. The "good faith" defense gives museums an incentive to comply with the Act, and to do so expeditiously. NAGPRA provides that:

> Any museum which repatriates any item in good faith pursuant to this Act shall not be liable for claims by an aggrieved party or for claims of breach of fiduciary duty, public trust, or violations of state law that are inconsistent with the provisions of this Act.
> 25 U.S.C. § 3006 (f) (1994).

Congress intended that within five years and six months from the date of the Act notices of intent to repatriate would be posted in the Federal Register, and that the return of property would be accomplished. They included the common law protection of good faith in the statute to underscore this intent [25 U.S.C. § 3003 (b)(1)(B), (c)(1) (1994)].

Return of objects after a determination of cultural affiliation must be expeditious; there is no impediment to prompt repatriation [25 U.S.C. § 3005 (a)(4) (1994)]. NAGPRA does not require that cultural affiliation be determined beyond a reasonable doubt, or that return of items wait until all possible claimants assert claims. If future information comes to light that might possibly have changed the disposition of an item, the recipient and new claimant may resolve the matter between themselves.

Penalties

To induce expeditious repatriation, NAGPRA provided that museums failing to comply with the law could be assessed a civil penalty [25 U.S.C. § 3007 (1994)]. The Secretary of the Interior, who is responsible for promulgating regulations governing civil penalties, determines the penalty amount, and can recover the penalty through a civil collection action in federal district court. Until interim regulations were published [62 Fed. Reg. 1,820 (1997)] museums effectively had a grace period during which penalties could not be assessed (although the absence of penalty regulations did not excuse noncompliance with the Act).

Pursuant to interim regulations, a "failure to comply" with the law occurs when:

(1) protected items are sold after November 16, 1990, and prior to compliance with the law; or

(2) summaries are not completed by November 16, 1993; or

(3) inventories are not completed by November 16, 1995, and an extension has not been obtained; or

(4) Indian tribes and Native Hawaiian organizations are not notified within 6 months of inventory completion; or

(5) an obligation to repatriate is ignored; or

(6) repatriation occurs prior to 30 days after publication of a "Notice of Intent to Repatriate" in the Federal Register.

62 Fed. Reg. at 1821–1822 (1997), to be codified at 43 C.F.R. § 10.12(b).

Factors to be considered in assessing a penalty include:

(1) the archeological, historical, or commercial value of the item in question;

(2) the economic and non-economic damages suffered by an aggrieved party; and

(3) the number of violations that have occurred.

25 U.S.C. § 3007 (b) (1994).

Penalties are based on .25% of the museum's annual budget or $5000, whichever is less, plus an additional $100 per day for every day the violation continues after the initial order [62 Fed. Reg. at 1,822 (1997), to be codified at 43 C.F.R. § 10.12(d)]. Penalties may be reduced in the discretion of the Secretary of the Interior if the violation is not willful, there are other agreements to pay restitution or otherwise mitigate the harm, or the penalty would create a hardship or constitute excessive punishment. The interim regulations also provide a detailed process for notice of violation, and an opportunity to discuss the assessment.

Disputes concerning penalty assessments are heard by Administrative Law Judges for the Office of Hearings and Appeals at the Department of the Interior. Any final administrative decision assessing a civil penalty is appealable to federal district court.

The Attorney General of the United States may institute a collection action in the United States district court for the district where the museum is located if there is no objection to the penalty assessment, and the assessment is part of a judgment by the Administrative Law Judge. Absent a provision to the contrary, all penalties are remitted to the general fund of the United States Treasury.

Note

Query whether, in an action for damages on behalf of an aggrieved party, the United States has a fiduciary responsibility to remit damage awards to the aggrieved party. What impact would a penalty assessment have on the private right of action of the aggrieved party to independently pursue damages?

Fifth Amendment Takings and the Right of Possession

NAGPRA essentially operates to remedy possible violations of the Fifth Amendment to the United States Constitution by seeking to afford Indian tribes, Native Hawaiian organizations, and museums the guarantee that they will not be separated from their property without just compensation. It does not, however, change the law of property. A museum may overcome a Native American claim for return or repatriation of defined cultural items if it can show a right of possession; otherwise requiring return or repatriation would constitute a taking of private property in violation of the Fifth Amendment. The Fifth Amendment's prohibition against takings is not violated by requiring an entity to give up property which it does not lawfully possess.

The proponent of the right of possession has the burden of proving lawful possession. "Right of possession" means possession obtained with the voluntary consent of an individual or group that had authority of alienation, with authority of alienation being determined at the time the item was separated from the group [25 U.S.C. § 3001(13) (1994)]. Thus, if an individual Native American had the ability to gift or sell an item at the time they gave it or sold it to another person, the right of possession in the eventual owner would not be diminished by the fact that today, the Indian tribe or Native Hawaiian organization considers the item cultural patrimony, and therefore inalienable. Conversely, the good faith purchase by a museum of a defined cultural item for fair-market value would not create a right of possession if, at the time it first was separated from the group, the item was stolen or sold in violation of tribal custom or law.

ABENAKI NATION OF MISSISSQUOI v. HUGHES

805 F. Supp. 234 (D. Vt. 1992), *aff'd*, 990 F.2d 729 (2nd Cir. 1993)

PARKER, Chief Judge:

I. INTRODUCTION

Plaintiffs moved for a temporary restraining order and preliminary injunction to enjoin defendants from all actions associated with raising the spillway elevation of the Orman Croft Generating Station, a hydroelectric facility in Highgate, Vermont. The parties agreed to a hearing on the merits and plaintiffs withdrew their temporary restraining order in early

September, 1992. The parties understood and agreed that a decision on the merits would obviate the need for a preliminary injunction.

The litigation stems from the authorization granted to the Village of Swanton (hereafter "the Village") to raise the spillway elevation of the Orman Croft Generating Station (hereafter "the Project") by the Army Corps of Engineers (hereafter "the Corps") on July 15, 1992. Pursuant to Section 404 of the Federal Water Pollution Control Act, 33 U.S.C. § 1344(e), this authorization was granted under a general permit, General Permit 38, first issued by the Corps in 1982 and reissued in 1987.

Plaintiffs claim that General Permit 38 (hereafter "GP 38") is invalid because of procedural violations. Even if valid, plaintiffs claim that the Project is not eligible for authorization under GP 38. Plaintiffs also allege that the authorization granted by the Corps under GP 38 violates a variety of federal statutes, specifically (1) The National Environmental Policy Act, 42 U.S.C. §§ 4321–4347 (1992) (hereafter "NEPA"); (2) the Federal Water Pollution Control Act, 33 U.S.C. §§ 1251–1387 (1992) (popularly known as the Clean Water Act) (hereafter "CWA"); (3) the National Historic Preservation Act, 16 U.S.C. § 470 *et seq.* (1992) (hereafter "NHPA"); and (4) the Native American Graves Protection and Repatriation Act, 25 U.S.C. §§ 3001–3013 (1992) (hereafter "NAGPRA"). For these reasons plaintiffs claim that the authorization by the Corps is void and that until the Project is properly permitted all activity connected with it must cease.

II. BACKGROUND

The Village has operated a hydroelectric facility at Highgate Falls since 1928. It has upgraded the facility twice before, in 1930 and 1954, and in 1979 decided to upgrade it again.[1]

In order to proceed with this proposed Project, the Village was required to apply for a license from the Federal Energy Regulatory Commission (hereafter "FERC") pursuant to the Federal Power Act, 16 U.S.C. §§ 791a–828 (1992). It also needed a permit from the Corps for the discharge of dredged or fill material[2] into the Mississquoi River pursuant to the Corps' responsibilities under the CWA, 33 U.S.C. § 1344.

Before issuing a license, the FERC must consider not only the power and development issues involved with a project but also issues related to the project's impact on environmental quality.[3] For its part, the Corps may issue individual permits on a project by project basis

---

[1][*Orig. fn.*] To increase the output of electric energy, the Village initially sought to install a fourth turbine generator in the powerhouse and raise the dam to an elevation of 200 feet. The Village's final proposal seeks to raise the level of the dam to 190 feet.

[2][*Orig. fn.*] The "discharge" in this case consists of the placement of concrete to raise the concrete spill of the dam from an elevation of 167.5 feet to 175 feet with an inflatable spillway rubber gate installed atop the new crest for a total height of 190 feet.

[3][*Orig. fn.*] Specifically, the Federal Power Act requires that [T]he [FERC], in addition to the power and development purposes for which licenses are issued, shall give equal consideration to the purposes of energy conservation, the protection, mitigation of damage to, and enhancement of, fish and wildlife (including related spawning grounds and habitat), the protection of recreational opportunities, and the preservation of other aspects of environmental quality. 16 U.S.C. § 797(e).

(otherwise known as individual s 404 permits) or general permits, if activities involved "will cause only minimal adverse environmental effects when performed separately and will have only minimal cumulative adverse effects on the environment," on a State, regional or nationwide basis. 33 U.S.C. § 1344(e)(1).[4]

On October 22, 1982 the Corps issued GP 38 (administrative record (AR) 170) for certain hydroelectric development activities in the New England region.[5] The public notice of the proposed GP 38 declared that

> [T]o avoid duplicating the regulatory control exercised by the Federal Energy Regulatory Commission (FERC) for hydropower development or expansion projects which cause minimal or no adverse environmental effects, the New England Division of the U.S. Army Corps of Engineers proposes to issue a general permit that, subject to certain conditions, would eliminate the need for Corps of Engineers approval of fills associated with such work at existing dams or at new or existing run-of-river projects throughout New England.
> (AR 146).

GP 38 was subject to six Special Conditions ("SC") and 24 General Conditions. (AR 189). The second SC states that the "activity which includes the discharge must be licensed or formally exempted by the [FERC]. No discharge is allowed unless and until the [FERC] license or formal exemption, as well as all other required local, State and Federal licenses and permits have been obtained." (AR 189).

In short, GP 38 provided for FERC to be the lead agency in regulating hydroelectric projects in the New England Region and ensuring that they complied with applicable regulations, including NEPA and NHPA. While the Corps was still responsible for ensuring compliance with the dictates of the CWA, GP 38 called for the Corps to utilize the information gathered by the FERC and issue authorization if the discharge "cause[d] minimal or no

---

[4][*Orig. fn.*] The distinction between nationwide permits and regional permits (both of which are general permits) is an important one in light of some last minute argument submitted by plaintiffs. A nationwide permit is just that--a permit issued by the Office of the Chief of Engineers that provides a nationwide permit for the discharge of dredged or fill material into navigable waters such as the Mississquoi. Projects meeting the conditions set out in the permit itself and in the regulations promulgated by the Corps in accordance with section 404 of the CWA, 33 C.F.R. § 330 (1992), are eligible under these nationwide permits and can thereby avoid the individual § 404 permitting process. Regional permits are issued on a regional basis by the division or district engineer. Regional permits may either modify a nationwide permit for a particular region, 33 C.F.R. § 330.1(d), or be issued unrelated to any nationwide permit and authorizing other discharges which meet the conditions set forth in the regional permit and in the regulations governing it, 33 C.F.R. § 325. Thus a regional permit can be directly related to a nationwide permit or distinctly independent.

[5][*Orig. fn.*] GP 38 implemented a Memorandum of Understanding ("MoU") entered into by FERC and the Secretary of the Army for the purpose of minimizing duplication of Federal review in regard to hydroelectric projects in the New England region. (AR 104).

adverse environmental effects." If FERC concluded that there would be more than minimal adverse effects, or if the Corps determined on its own that a proposed action was outside the realm of GP 38, permit applicants would not be eligible for authorization under GP 38 and would have to proceed with an individual s 404 permit application.

Some time after the Corps issued GP 38 the Village commenced efforts to obtain the necessary permits for the envisioned improvements to the Highgate facility. Pursuant to the FPA and NEPA, the FERC conducted an Environmental Assessment ("EA") of the Project and made a Finding of No Significant Impact ("FONSI"). (AR 105). Specifically it found that the project would result in only "short-term minor [environmental] impacts" and concluded that "issuance of a license, as conditioned herein, for the project will not constitute a major Federal action significantly affecting the quality of the human environment." (AR 105 at p. 8).[6]

Prior to issuance of the FERC license, the Corps determined that the project was eligible under GP 38 and issued the authorization to proceed on January 24, 1984. The Corps based its determination on the Village's application for a permit, its FERC license application and the EA conducted by FERC. (AR 143). On May 24, 1984 FERC issued a license for the Project. (AR 105).

In 1987 GP 38 was reissued for another five years with several changes and amendments after public notice was given (AR 178) and a supplement to the 1982 Statement of Findings was made.[7] (AR 188). In the meantime, work on the Project remained in the initial stages. On January 22, 1990, the Village filed a request with FERC for the amendment of its license, proposing to reduce the overall height of the project.[8] In considering this request, FERC found that the amended project would "reduce the adverse effects of the project, most significantly those impacts on cultural resources and wetlands." (AR 106 at p. 2). On March 14, 1991, FERC issued an order amending the original license to conform with the Village's proposed changes. (AR 106).

On September 5, 1991, the Village submitted a request to the Corps for authorization under GP 38 for the reduced Project. The Village initially believed that the authorization

---

[6][*Orig. fn.*] FERC's finding that the Project did not constitute a major Federal action was based on its EA and on the conditions imposed on the Village by the License. These conditions included a mitigation plan to compensate for the loss of any wetlands caused by the Project and for the Village to fund a cultural resource management plan for "previously unrecorded archaeological or historical sites" discovered during the construction. (AR 105, article 44). FERC's finding meant that the threshold for triggering a more detailed environmental impact statement ("EIS") under NEPA was not crossed. Plaintiff does not contest the license issued by FERC.

[7][*Orig. fn.*] GP 38 was reissued in almost its original form save for three new permit conditions, added as a result of comments received by the Corps and the withdrawal of Rhode Island and Massachusetts from its scope. The new conditions made GP 38 a reporting general permit, and implemented further reporting and authorization recommendations from the states of Vermont and Connecticut.

[8][*Orig. fn.*] The Village sought to reduce the proposed increased elevation of the dam from 200 feet to 190 feet.

granted by the Corps in 1984 was suitable ground to grant authorization in 1991. (AR 5). In informal meetings and discussions as early as mid-September 1991 (AR 4) and as late as February, 1992, (AR 44) Corps personnel from the New England Division informed the Village that the Project was not eligible for authorization under GP 38 and that an individual § 404 permit would be necessary. This conclusion was based upon an expressed concern regarding the adverse impact of the Project on wetlands and the inadequacy of proposed mitigation plans.

Corps Headquarters agreed with the New England Division that an individual § 404 permit would be required if mitigation plans were not adequate but also stated that a conditioned general permit assuring adequate mitigation would allow authorization under GP 38. (AR 84). It advised the New England Division that adequate mitigation could be considered to remain below the minimal impact threshold for the general permit just as under NEPA it can be considered to reach a finding of no significant impact. (AR 103).

After consultation with the Vermont state archeologist concerning historical resources at the mitigation sites (AR 87, 94), the Village (AR 92), and Corps Headquarters (AR 101, 103), the Corps issued a conditioned authorization under GP 38 on July 15, 1992. (AR 132). This conditioned authorization imposed 23 Special Conditions ("SC") which the Corps believes ensures that the Project will cause minimal or no adverse impact making it eligible for authorization under GP 38.[9] It is this authorization to which plaintiffs object.

---

[9][*Orig. fn.*] The twenty-three Special Conditions ("SC") attached to the Village's permit establish an intensely detailed plan for achieving the mitigation goal of replacing lost wetland functions and values, and protecting cultural and historic resources threatened, as a result of the Project. The plan requires a two year monitoring period to determine if manipulation is necessary to create the compensatory wetlands and detailed instructions for the manner of conducting such monitoring. (SC 4, 5, 6). If manipulation or flooding is necessary to create the wetlands, the Village must develop and submit a site design for review and approval by the Corps. (SC 5, 10). SC 7 and 18 provide specific steps to be taken in order to protect any cultural or historic resources located at the mitigation sites in the event that manipulation or flooding is necessary and for the location of staging areas. These steps include conducting a Phase I and if necessary, a Phase II archaeological study, mitigation in the way of avoidance or data recovery, hand excavating any monitoring wells which may be necessary by the Village's consulting archaeologist, joint supervision of the site by the Corps, the Advisory Council on Historic Preservation and the Vermont State Historic Preservation Office, and a prohibition on work at the site until written approval has been received from the Corps. Following the completion of the mitigation areas, a five year period of monitoring to determine the mitigation sites' degree of success will be required of the Village with detailed, semiannual reports to be submitted to the Corps for review and approval. (SC 12) If after the five year monitoring period the Corps determines that the mitigation sites have failed to provide 30 acres of compensatory wetlands, a supplementary mitigation site and proposal must be prepared by the Village and reviewed and approved by the Corps. This supplementary proposal, upon Corps approval, will be added as a Special Condition to the permit. (SC 17). There is also provision for riverbank stabilization, (SC 21) and an erosion control plan. (SC 22). The Special Conditions are mandatory and failure to comply with them would violate the permit and subject the Village to the Corps' enforcement provisions. (AR 132).

III. DISCUSSION

A. Basis of Review

1. Jurisdiction

Plaintiffs allege violations of the Administrative Procedure Act, 5 U.S.C. §§ 500–590 (1992) (hereafter "APA"), NEPA, CWA, NHPA and NAGPRA. The court has jurisdiction under 28 U.S.C. § 1331 to hear these claims.

2. Standard of Review

Courts traditionally afford the decisions of administrative agencies due deference in reviewing agency action. See, *Citizens to Preserve Overton Park v. Volpe*, 401 U.S. 402, 415 (1971).

The Second Circuit has stated the appropriate standard of review when reviewing actions and decisions by the Corps to issue permits. "In reviewing the validity of a decision by the Corps to issue a permit under the [CWA], a court should, as provided by the [APA], uphold the decision unless it is 'arbitrary, capricious, an abuse of discretion, or otherwise not in accordance with law.'" *Sierra Club v. United States Army Corps of Eng.*, 701 F.2d 1011, 1032 (2d Cir. 1983) (quoting 5 U.S.C. § 706(2)(A). In defining arbitrary and capricious, the Second Circuit has stated that [A]n agency's decision is held to be arbitrary and capricious when it relies on factors Congress did not want considered, or utterly fails to analyze an important aspect of the problem, or offers an explanation contrary to the evidence before it, or its explanation... is so implausible that it cannot be ascribed to differing views or agency expertise. *Sierra Club v. United States Army Corps of Eng.*, 772 F.2d 1043, 1051 (2d Cir. 1985).

Accordingly, any review of the decision by the Corps to authorize the Project under GP 38 is limited to the arbitrary and capricious standard as established by statute and defined by relevant case law.

B. Plaintiffs' Claims

* * *

6. Claim VI—NAGPRA violation

Plaintiffs' final claim is made under NAGPRA, 25 U.S.C. § 3005(a)(4).[23] Plaintiffs claim that because the mitigation plan leaves the fate of the remains and artifacts which may be unearthed in the hands of the Corps, the State and the Village, it violates NAGPRA and is unlawful. Prior to reaching the merits of plaintiffs' claim, several definitional hurdles must be cleared.

---

[23][*Orig. fn.*] Where cultural affiliation of Native American human remains and funerary objects has not been established in an inventory prepared pursuant to section 3003 of this title or the summary pursuant to section 3004 of this title, or where Native American human remains and funerary objects are not included upon any such inventory, then, upon request and pursuant to subsections (b) and (e) of this section and, in the case of unassociated funerary objects, subsection (c) of this section, such native American human remains and funerary objects shall be expeditiously returned where the requesting Indian tribe or native Hawaiian organization can show cultural affiliation by a preponderance of the evidence based upon geographical, kinship, biological, archaeological, linguistic, folkloric, oral traditional historical, or other relevant information or expert opinion."

NAGPRA defines Indian tribe as follows: "Indian tribe" means any tribe, band, nation, or other organized group or community of Indians, including any Alaska Native village... which is recognized as eligible for the special programs and services by the United States to Indians because of their status as Indians. 25 U.S.C. § 3001(7). As discussed earlier, it is undisputed that the Abenaki Nation of Mississquoi is not an "Indian tribe" recognized by the Secretary of the Interior. Nonetheless, that plaintiff contends that for purposes of NAGPRA it does constitute an Indian tribe, citing its receipt of federal funds and a recent decision by the Vermont Supreme Court.[24]

Plaintiff's argument that it does indeed constitute an Indian tribe may have practical merit as to the receipt of federal funds but appears to be stretching the Elliot decision rather thin. In any event, the merits of those arguments need not be addressed here because the language of NAGPRA includes "organized group or community of Indians... eligible for the special programs and services provided by the United States to Indians because of their status as Indians." The regulation which sets out the procedures for establishing that an American Indian group exists as an Indian tribe, 25 C.F.R. § 83 (1992), defines Indian group or group to mean "any Indian aggregation within the continental United States that the Secretary of the Interior does not acknowledge to be an Indian tribe." The Abenaki Nation of Mississquoi falls squarely within this definition and the fact that it receives funds and assistance from the United States because of its members status as Indians includes it within the class protected by NAGPRA.

NAGPRA applies to the disposition of Native American cultural items that are "excavated or discovered on federal or tribal lands." 25 U.S.C. § 3002(a). Federal lands are defined in relevant part as "land other than tribal lands which are controlled or owned by the United States." § 3001(5). Plaintiffs urge a broad construction of "control" to include the Corps' regulatory powers under the CWA and its involvement in devising and supervising the mitigation plan.

Such a broad reading is not consistent with the statute, which exhibits no intent to apply the Act to situations where federal involvement is limited as it is here to the issuance of a permit.[25] To adopt such a broad reading of the Act would invoke its provisions whenever the government issued permits or provided federal funding pursuant to statutory obligations.

As yet there have been no cultural or funerary items discovered at the mitigation site, though the possibility of their existence is extremely high. However, NAGPRA applies to cultural and funerary objects already possessed or under the control of a Federal agency or museum, § 3003 and § 3004, or those already discovered or excavated, § 3002. As to plaintiffs' claim, the court must hold that even if NAGPRA were to apply, which it does not, the claim is premature.[26]

---

[24][*Orig. fn.*] *State of Vermont v. Raleigh Elliott et al.*, 159 Vt. 102, 616 A.2d 210 (1992).

[25][*Orig. fn.*] The legislative history of the statute repeatedly uses the language "federal lands." See 1990 *U.S. Code Cong. & Admin. News* at 4367–4392.

[26][*Orig. fn.*] Plaintiffs' claim based on common law and property rights appears to be subsumed by the NAGPRA claim. Its violation of fiduciary duty claim is extremely nebulous and rehashes arguments that have been previously addressed. It is enough to note that though a general fiduciary duty may be owed to the plaintiffs by the government, "a general fiduciary relationship does not mean that any and every claim by [an Indian] necessarily states a proper claim for breach of the trust...." *Pawnee v. U.S.A.*, 830 F.2d 187, 191 (Fed Cir. 1987), *cert. denied*, 486 U.S. 1032 (1988).

IV. CONCLUSION

On the basis of the foregoing discussion the court holds that the Plaintiffs have failed to sustain any of the claims pled and accordingly the Defendants are entitled to judgement as a matter of law. The July 15, 1992 conditioned authorization of the Corps of Engineers to the Village of Swanton to raise the spillway of the Orman Croft Generating Station is affirmed.

Note

Did the Court properly determine standing? Were there defined cultural items protected by NAGPRA at issue? Was there a violation of NAGPRA? Was it the same violation as the one argued before the Court?

SECTION C. INDIAN SACRED SITES

Indian tribes have long sought to protect sacred sites located on federal land, but to date they have been unsuccessful in persuading the courts that the First Amendment to the United States Constitution either grants them the right to practice their religion in a traditional manner and at their traditional places [e.g., *Lyng v. Northwest Indian Cemetery Protective Association*, 485 U.S. 439 (1988)], or requires places such as Rainbow Bridge National Monument to exclude tourists in order to protect the sanctity of the site [e.g., *Badoni v. Higginson*, 638 F.2d 172 (10th Cir. 1980), *cert. denied*, 452 U.S. 954 (1981)]. As a result, Native American groups have taken their cause to the president and Congress. On May 24, 1996, President Clinton issued an executive order (No. 13,007, 61 Fed. Reg. 20,771) setting forth the position of the Executive Branch on Indian sacred sites. It requires federal agencies to allow tribes access to sacred sites for ceremonial use, and to avoid adversely affecting those sites. A sacred site is:

> any specific, discrete, narrowly delineated location on Federal land that is identified by an Indian tribe, or Indian individual determined to be an appropriately authoritative representative of an Indian religion, as sacred by virtue of its established religious significance to, or ceremonial use by, an Indian religion: provided that the tribe or appropriately authoritative representative of an Indian religion has informed the agency of the existence of such a site.
>
> Executive Order (No. 13,007, 61 Fed. Reg. 20, 771)

The executive order requires each agency to develop implementing regulations within one year to specify the process by which Indian tribes provide notice to the government of sacred sites to be protected, and the government provides tribes with notice when an impact to a sacred site occurs. Accommodation must be made for vested property rights to avoid a taking of property. Whether the Establishment Clause would permit the government to exclude non-Indians from these sites in order to allow Indian religious practices is an issue that likely will be visited by the courts.[*]

SECTION D.   INDIAN ARTS AND CRAFTS

In 1935, pursuant to the Indian Arts and Crafts Act [25 U.S.C. §§ 305-305e (1994)], Congress created the Indian Arts and Crafts Board in the Department of the Interior "to promote the economic welfare of the Indian tribes and Indian individuals through the development of Indian arts and crafts and expansion of the market for the products of Indian art and craftsmanship" [25 U.S.C. § 305a (1994)]. The Board acts as a chamber of commerce for Indian art and artists, and it has the authority to do market research, give assistance to artists, and promote economic opportunity. It also administers a loan program for the production and sale of Indian products. Amendments to the Indian Arts and Crafts Act, in 1990, broadened the authority of the Board to register and assign to an individual Indian or Indian tribe, and without charge, trademarks of genuineness and quality, to set standards for the use of trademarks, and to charge for licenses to use these trademarks [25 U.S.C. § 305a (1994)]. By bringing Indian arts and crafts under federal regulation, the Act precludes state control and taxation of Indian arts and crafts produced within Indian country.

The Indian Arts and Crafts Act protects the work of Indian artisans by providing a cause of action against any person who wrongfully represents that a product is Indian-produced. Both civil and criminal sanctions are available for violations of the law—

> against a person who offers or displays for sale or sells a good, with or without a Government trademark, in a manner that falsely suggests it is Indian produced, an Indian product, or the product of a particular Indian or Indian tribe or Indian arts and crafts organization, resident within the United States...
> 25 U.S.C. § 305e (a), 18 U.S.C. § 1159 (a) (1994).

---

[*]See *Bear Lodge Multiple Use Ass'n v. Babbitt*, No. 96-CV-063-D, 1998 U.S. Dist. LEXIS 5751 (D. Wy. Apr. 2, 1998), upholding the constitutionality of a "voluntary climbing ban" on Devil's Tower during the month of June to respect tribal religious practices, after earlier holding that an actual ban on commercial climbing violated the Establishment Clause.

For purposes of the Act, "Indian tribe" means a group with either federal or state recognition [18 U.S.C. § 1159 (c)(3) (1994)], and "Indian arts and crafts organization" means a legally established organization composed of members of Indian tribes [18 U.S.C. § 1159 (c)(4) (1994)].

A civil action may be brought in federal district court by a tribe, a tribal member, an Indian arts and crafts organization, or the Department of Justice [on behalf of the Indian(s)]. Persons who initiate a civil action may seek:

1. injunctive relief, and

2. the greater of treble damages or $1000 per day for each day the display or sale continues, and

3. punitive damages with attorney fees.

25 U.S.C. § 305(e) (1994).

Criminal prosecution for misrepresentation of Indian-produced goods and products is brought by the Department of Justice, and the Arts and Crafts Board may refer a matter directly to the Federal Bureau of Investigation. Because the unlawful actions that comprise a criminal or civil offense are identical, whether to proceed civilly or criminally is a matter of prosecutorial discretion predicated on the totality of the circumstances of each case. Failure to ascertain the nature of goods sold in a retail outlet, for example, might subject the store owner to a civil action based on negligent conduct, while persons who profit by fraud might be prosecuted criminally.

Criminal penalties fall under the Federal Sentencing Guidelines, but by statute [18 U.S.C. § 1159(b) (1994)] they include: for a first offense, up to five years and/or $250,000 for an individual, and a fine of up to $1,000,000 for a person other than an individual; and for a subsequent offense, up to fifteen years and/or $1,000,000 for an individual, and a fine of up to $5,000,000 for a person other than an individual.

Counterfeiting an Indian Arts and Crafts Board trademark is a specific intent crime. It is unlawful to knowingly, willfully, or corruptly reproduce the trademark on products to be used for sale, or to make false statements in order to obtain a valid trademark [18 U.S.C. § 1158 (1994)]. Penalties for violating the law are identical to the penalties for misrepresenting Indian-produced goods and products.

SECTION E.   AMERICAN INDIAN RELIGIOUS FREEDOM ACT

The American Indian Religious Freedom Act [AIRFA; 42 U.S.C. § 1996 (1994)] was passed in 1978 to ensure to Native Americans the First Amendment rights of the religion clauses. AIRFA does not protect traditional religions of Native Americans beyond the First Amendment guarantees, and it contains no affirmative relief provisions. It merely requires that laws enacted subsequent to AIRFA take Native American religious practice into consideration. AIRFA simply states:

> On and after August 11, 1978, it shall be the policy of the United States to protect and preserve for American Indians their inherent right of freedom to believe, express, and exercise the traditional religions of the American Indian, Eskimo, Aleut, and Native Hawaiians, including but not limited to access to sites, use and possession of sacred objects, and the freedom to worship through ceremonies and traditional rites.
> 42 U.S.C. § 1996

As a result of this law, all federal land managers are required to include consultation with traditional Native American religious leaders in their management plans. For example, ARPA, which was passed a year after AIRFA, provides that if an ARPA permit might result in harm to a tribal religious or cultural site, the federal land manager must notify any tribe that might consider the site as having religious or cultural importance prior to issuing the permit [16 U.S.C. § 470cc (c) (1994)]. ARPA, however, does not require land managers to abide by Native American opinion, or obtain consent for an action occurring on federal land. AIRFA was used to reroute road and railroad construction around Indian sacred sites [*Northwest Indian Cemetery Protective Ass'n v. Peterson*, 552 F. Supp. 951 (N.D. Cal. 1982); *New Mexico Navajo Ranchers Ass'n v. I.C.C.*, 850 F.2d 729 (D.C. Cir. 1988)], but it did not prevent the expansion of a ski area onto sacred mountains located in one national forest [*Wilson v. Block*, 708 F.2d 735 (D.C. Cir. 1983), *cert. denied*, 464 U.S. 956 (1983), *cert. denied*, 464 U.S. 1056 (1984)], or mining activities in sacred areas within another national forest [*Havasupai Tribe v. U.S.*, 752 F. Supp. 1471 (D. Ariz. 1990), *aff'd*, 943 F.2d 32 (9th Cir. 1991), *cert. denied*, 503 U.S. 959 (1992)].

SECTION F.   OTHER LAWS THAT PROTECT NATIVE AMERICAN HERITAGE RESOURCES

1.   Federal Law

In addition to federal laws that specifically protect Native American cultural heritage, general property laws also apply to these resources. If a non-Indian

takes, injures, or destroys heritage resources within Indian country that belong to an Indian, federal statute provides that the offender shall pay an
amount equal to twice the just value of the property [18 U.S.C. § 1160 (1994)].
If the defendant is unable to pay damages at least equal to the fair value of
the injured property, the victim is to be compensated out of the Treasury of
the United States. This archaically drafted law is pled as a relief claim within
an overlying cause of action. Although it indemnifies Indians for actions by
judgment-proof vandals, as written, this law is more a limitation on causes
of action by Indians than a protection from theft or vandalism. Despite its
place in the criminal code, this statute really amounts to the codification of a
common lawsuit in tort, with the only remedy for a violation being monetary
damages. The courts have held it to be an enhancement of "the sentence of
one who has engaged in conduct proscribed by other criminal statutes," and
not an independent claim in negligence [*Coosewoon v. Meridian Oil Co.*, 25
F.3d 920 (10th Cir. 1994)]. By invoking this statute, restitution for some
ARPA and NAGPRA violations occurring on Indian lands could be doubled,
even for a first offense. This statute may also be used in conjunction with a
charge under Embezzlement and Theft from Indian Tribal Organizations (18
U.S.C. § 1163 (1994).

2.   State Law

Each state has laws protecting burials situated on state and private lands [see
C. Carnett, "A Survey of State Statutes Protecting Archeological Resources"
(Dept. of the Interior, National Park Service, Off. of the Departmental Consulting Archeologist, Archeological Assistance Study No. 3, and National
Trust for Historic Preservation, Preservation Law Reporter, Special Report,
August 1995)]. These laws are codified either as criminal statutes or health
and safety statutes. Few states had laws that were interpreted to protect unmarked or prehistoric burials prior to 1988; where these laws did exist they
often were classified as minor offenses. In the wake of NAGPRA and the
national attention given to heritage resources protection, most states amended
their laws to provide criminal sanctions for damage to any burial, regardless
of its age or whether it is marked. In some states extreme conduct or repeated violations may constitute a felony offense. Also, since 1990, several
states have enacted repatriation provisions, and have extended state protection to funerary objects recovered from private land.

WHITACRE v. STATE

619 N.E.2d 605 (Ind. App. 1993)

BARTEAU, Judge:

Robert W. Whitacre appeals the trial court's judgment in favor of the Indiana Department of Natural Resources (IDNR) on Whitacre's petition for declaratory judgment. The sole issue on appeal is whether Indiana Code 14-3–3.4, the Indiana Historic Preservation and Archeology Act (the "Act"), is applicable to privately owned property. We conclude that it is and affirm the trial court.

FACTS

The facts are straightforward. Whitacre and his wife are amateur archeologists. In 1982, they discovered a Hopewell Indian site with artifacts dating to circa 150 A.D. on a 40-acre farm in Dearborn County, Indiana. With permission from the property owner, they began excavating areas of the site and removing artifacts. In 1987, the Whitacres purchased the farm and continued excavating and conducting investigations. In July, 1989, after hearing that a new law had been passed, Whitacre inquired of an archeologist at IDNR about the necessity of a permit for conducting investigations on his own property. Whitacre was informed that he would need a permit. After investigating the law on his own, Whitacre determined that he did not need a permit and filed this declaratory judgment action.

The trial court concluded that Ind. Code 14-3–3.4 was applicable to private property and not just property owned or leased by the State of Indiana.

DISCUSSION

The thrust of this appeal is whether a person needs to have an archeological plan approved by the Indiana Department of Natural Resources before that person may disturb private property for the purpose of discovering artifacts or burial objects.

The Historic Preservation and Archeology Act, I.C. 14-3–3.4, established the division of historic preservation and archeology within the IDNR to administer and develop the programs and policies of the Act. I.C. 14-3–3.4-2. As gleaned from the Act, the policies to be furthered by the Division include encouraging the continuous maintenance and integrity of historic sites and structures and coordinating the activities of local historical associations, commissions and private individuals and organizations interested in the historic culture of Indiana. It has been stated that protecting our national and state heritage through the preservation of archeological sites is included in the broad spectrum of legitimate interests of government. *Indiana Dept. of Natural Resources v. Indiana Coal Council, Inc.*, 542 NE2d 1000, 1005 (Ind. 1989). "The information in these sites expands our knowledge of human history and prehistory and thus enriches us as a state, nation and as human beings." Id.

When construing a statute, this court is guided by several rules of statutory construction. First, it must be noted that when a statute is clear and unambiguous on its face, the court need not, and indeed may not, interpret the statute. *Economy Oil Corp. v. Indiana Dept. of State Revenue* 162 Ind. App. 658, 321 N.E.2d 215, 218 (1974). When a statute is ambiguous, the court must ascertain the intent of the legislature and interpret the statute to effectuate that intent. Id. When so doing, we read the statutes of an act as a whole and attempt to give effect to all provisions. Id. A statutory amendment changing a prior statute indicates a legislative intention that the meaning of the prior statute has been changed. *Wright v. Fowler*, 459 NE2d 386 (Ind. App. 1984). Another consideration in construing a statute is to give effect to the purpose of the statute. *State v. Adams*, 583 N.E.2d 799 (Ind. App. 1992), *trans. denied*.

With these guidelines in mind, we conclude that private property is included within the scope of I.C. 14-3–3.4 as amended. Unless the legislature intended to give the state the power to oversee and regulate the treatment of historical and archeological findings on private property, section 15 of the amended act is virtually meaningless, as a review of the old and new statutes shows. Prior to 1989, I.C. 14-3–3.4 restricted activities that affected historic sites or structures only within the boundaries of property owned or leased by the state. Indiana Code 14-3–3.4-7 provided: A person who knowingly, without a permit, conducts a field investigation or alters historic property within the boundaries of property owned or leased by the state commits a Class B misdemeanor. Thus, prior to 1989, Whitacre was not required to have an archeological plan approved by the state in order to conduct archeological investigations and excavations on his own property.

In 1989, the legislature amended I.C. 14-3–3.4. Specifically, I.C. 14-3–3.4-7 was amended to provide: Except as provided in sections 14 through 16 [I.C. 14-3–3.4-14—14-3–3.4-16] of this chapter, a person who knowingly, without a permit, conducts a field investigation or alters historic property within the boundaries of property owned or leased by the state commits a Class A misdemeanor. Sections 14 through 16 are new sections that provide for (1) the adoption of rules establishing standards for plans, I.C. 14-3–3.4-14, (2) the necessity of a plan, I.C. 14-3–3.4-15, and (3) steps to take when buried human remains are disturbed, I.C. 14-3–3.4-16. Of particular relevance to this appeal is section 15, which provides: (a) A person who disturbs the ground for the purpose of discovering artifacts or burial objects must do so in accordance with a plan approved by the department under section 14 [I.C. 14-3–3.4-14] of this chapter. (b) A person who recklessly, knowingly, or intentionally violates this section commits a Class A misdemeanor. I.C. 14-3–3.4-15. "Plan" is defined as "an archeological plan for the systematic recovery, analysis, and disposition by scientific methods of material evidence and information about the life and culture in past ages." I.C. 14-3–3.4-1.

Nothing in chapter 3.4 explicitly states that the chapter applies only to property owned or leased by the state or that it applies to private property. However, section 13 does provide that the requirement of a plan when disturbing ground does not apply to (1) surface coal mining regulated under I.C. 13–4.1, (2) cemeteries and human remains subject to I.C. 23-14, (3) disturbing the earth for an agricultural purpose, and (4) collecting any object (other than human remains) that is visible on the surface of the ground. These activities are typically conducted on private property, not state owned or leased property; thus, section 13 is superfluous if the chapter applies only to state owned or leased property.

Further, prior to the amendments, I.C. 14-3–3.4-7 prohibited conducting field investigations or altering historic property within the bounds of property owned or leased by the state without a permit. "Historic property" is defined as "any historic site or structure," I.C. 14-3–3.4-1, and "historic site" or "historic structure" is any site or structure important to the "general, archeological, agricultural, economic, social, political, architectural, industrial, or cultural history of Indiana." Id. Thus, in effect, I.C. 14-3–3.4-7 already prohibited disturbing the ground of state owned or leased property without a permit if anything of historic significance was on the property. The new section 15 adds nothing to the chapter unless it is interpreted as expanding the scope of coverage by prohibiting the disturbance of any "ground" for purposes of discovering artifacts or burial objects without an approved plan. I.C. 14-3–3.4-15. The legislature specifically did not restrict this section to only "the ground" of state owned or leased property as it did in section 7. Thus, we conclude that the legislature intended to mean any ground within the State of Indiana, whether owned by the state or privately owned.

This construction of the statute effectuates the policies of the Act. The purpose of the Historical Preservation and Archeology Act is to further our understanding of the state's heritage and historical culture by preserving and studying what has been left behind. Obviously, not all sites of historical or archeological significance are located on property owned or leased by the state. Consequently, prior to the 1989 amendments, the state did not have the means to prevent the destruction, inadvertent or intentional, or share in the knowledge of possibly significant sites located on private property. The legislature, through the 1989 amendments, expanded the scope of the Act to include not only "historic sites" and "historic structures," as defined in I.C. 14-3–3.4-1, and located on state owned or leased property, but also to include any property where a person discovers or tries to discover "artifacts" or "burial objects," as defined in I.C. 14-3–3.4-1. Through the amendments, the state may regulate activities on private property that affect our historical and archeological culture; thus, the state is better able to discover and preserve more of our heritage. This is the purpose of the Act and is best effectuated by construing the Act to include private, as well as state owned, property.

We also find support for interpreting the statute to protect private as well as state owned property in a recent opinion from the Seventh Circuit Court of Appeals. In *United States of America v. Gerber*, 999 F.2d 1112 (7th Cir. 1993), the Seventh Circuit had to decide if a conviction pursuant to the federal Archaeological Resources Protection Act of 1979 was valid where the Indian artifacts had come from privately owned land in Indiana. The Court interpreted the Act as applying to artifacts found on privately owned property as well as property owned by the federal government or by Indian tribes, even though the Act explicitly refers only to property owned by the federal government or by Indian tribes. The Court concluded that such an interpretation best furthered the purposes of the Act "to secure, for the present and future benefit of the American people, the protection of archaeological resources and sites…" *Gerber*, 999 F.2d at 1114. It is also interesting to note that the Court assumed the amended Indiana statute at issue in our case applied to privately owned land. 999 F.2d at 1116 ("Granted, all fifty states have laws expressly protecting their archaeological sites; and in 1989, too late for this case, Indiana amended its law to forbid—redundantly—what Gerber had done [which was to disturb artifacts on private property].") Consistent with the interpretation of the federal Act, we interpret the Indiana Act as applying to privately owned property.

The trial court's judgment is affirmed.

SHARPNACK, C.J., and CONOVER, J., concur.

3. Tribal Code

When a tribal code includes a section on the protection of heritage resources belonging to either the tribe or an individual member, it controls misdemeanor criminal and civil actions against members, and civil actions against nonmembers, which are brought in tribal court. In addition, a tribal code might specify the appropriate treatment of human remains and cultural items falling within the NAGPRA categories of sacred objects or cultural patrimony. In the absence of tribal code, other evidence for traditional treatment of these items might be required in a court proceeding. Tribal court judgments against nonmembers must be domesticated in the state in which the violator holds property or lives, so that the judgment may be enforced in state court. Although tribal court jurisdiction is a developing and unsettled area of the law, the United States Supreme Court has acknowledged that tribal courts have subject matter jurisdiction over nonmember conduct on a reservation which threatens or harms the welfare of tribal members [*Strate v. A-1 Contractors*, 520 U.S. 438 (1997)].

SECTION G. ISSUES FOR DISCUSSION

1. Tort Claims

Tort actions may be brought in state court for conduct arising on state or private land within the state, or in tribal court for actions occurring on tribal lands and affecting members of the tribe, to recover damages for pain, suffering, and other harms caused by negligent conduct toward heritage resources [see *Charrier v. Bell*, 496 So.2d 601 (La. App. 1986), *writ denied*, 498 So.2d 753 (La. 1986)]. The desecration of a burial, for example, could expose the offender to an action in tort by lineal descendants or other tribal members.

ALDERMAN v. FORD

146 Kan. 698, 72 P2d 981 (1937)

Syllabus by the Court

1. The widow of a deceased man has a right to possession of the dead body of her husband in the same condition in which it was when he died.
2. An autopsy unauthorized by his widow, or some other person having authority to so authorize, on the dead body of a man, is an invasion of the right of the widow to possession of the body, as described in the above paragraph of the syllabus.

3. A widow may maintain an action for mental pain and suffering, the direct result of the unauthorized autopsy on the body of her husband, even though she suffered no physical injury.
4. An action such as described in the foregoing of the syllabus is one for injury to the rights of another and may be commenced within two years from the time when the cause of action arose.

SMITH, Justice:

This was an action for money. Judgment was for defendants sustaining a demurrer to the petition on the ground that it did not state facts sufficient to constitute a cause of action. Plaintiff appeals.

The petition alleged that one Alderman had been the husband of the plaintiff and that he died December 20, 1935; that one of the defendants, who was a surgeon, and the other defendant, who was not a surgeon, "did cut open and cut into the dead body of Arthur Alderman, and did then and there cut into and probe into, and look into and inspect and study the body and parts of the dead body of Arthur Alderman, all on the 20th day of December, 1935, and at and within Montgomery County, Kansas, and all without the knowledge, presence or consent of plaintiff." The petition then alleged that plaintiff had the right to dispose of the corpse of her dead husband and had the exclusive right of sepulcher and had the exclusive right to the possession of the dead body of Alderman in the same condition it was when the breath of life left it; that plaintiff at the instance of defendants was denied a view of the body of Alderman until it was clothed and in its coffin; that after the body of Alderman had been interred one of the defendants told her that he had the body cut open in order to see whether he would be liable for his death. The petition then stated that plaintiff "suffered great mental suffering, and great injury to her feelings, and was in mental anguish, on account of the wrongful and tortious acts of the defendants herein in mutilating the corpse." The petition then alleged that plaintiff had been damaged on account of these violated rights by defendants.

Defendant Ford demurred to this petition on the grounds: First, that the petition did not state facts sufficient to constitute a cause of action; second, that the petition showed on its face that it was barred by the statute of limitations, the action not having commenced within one year from the date of the cause of action, if any arose.

Defendant Hudiburg demurred on the first ground stated above.

These demurrers were sustained generally and plaintiff was given 20 days in which to amend. Plaintiff stood upon the allegations in the petition. Hence this appeal.

The question argued in this court by both parties is whether the petition stated facts sufficient to constitute a cause of action. It will be noted that the petitioner did not allege any physical injury. She alleged mental pain and suffering only.

Defendants argue that on this account she cannot recover in this action. They rely on the rule that in this state one cannot recover for mental anguish and injury to feelings unless in connection therewith there is a physical injury or there is malice or wantonness shown. See *City of Salina v. Tropser*, 27 Kan. 544.

At the outset it may be stated that this is not a case where recovery depends on negligence. The right of plaintiff, the invasion of which she claims enables her to recover here, is the right to receive the dead body of her late husband in the condition it was when he died so that she could give it decent burial. This right has been recognized by statute in this state. It is provided that the unclaimed dead body of any criminal or other person may be delivered to a medical college for purposes of study, but not if the deceased during his last sickness requested to be buried, and not if any relative or friend asked to have the body buried, and the body may never be turned over to a school until the person in charge of deceased at the time of his death shall have made diligent search for relatives and friends of deceased and no response has been received. See G. S. 1935, 65-901 to 65-905. This statute does not apply to this case because the dead body here was not that of a criminal or unclaimed person. It indicates, however, that the Legislature recognized the right of the next of kin to bury the dead body of a relative. There is a statute that makes it a crime to remove a dead body from the place of interment for the purpose of selling it or for mere wantonness or mischief. There is an exception to this statute where the disinterment is done with the consent of the "near relations" of deceased. See G. S. 1935, 21-911 to 21-914. This statute does not cover a case of unauthorized autopsy such as we have here. It is referred to here mainly because it is indexed in our statutes under the head of "Crimes Against Public Morals and Decency." We do not consider that it would add anything to this opinion to discuss the question of whether the right the next of kin have in a corpse is a property right. Others have spoken on this subject in a more fitting language than is ours to command. See Jackson on The Law of Cadavers, page 170, which says: "Questions which relate to the custody and disposal of the remains of the dead do not depend upon the principles which regulate the possession and ownership of property, but upon the considerations arising partly out of the domestic relations, the duties and obligations which spring from family relationship and the ties of blood; partly out of the sentiment so universal among all civilized nations, ancient and modern, that the dead should repose in some spot where they will be secure from profanation; partly out of what is demanded by society for the preservation of the public health, morality and decency, and partly out of what is required by proper respect for and observance of the wishes of the departed themselves."

See, also, *Fox v. Gordon*, 16 Phila. (Pa.) 185.

The question of the right of the next of kin of a deceased person to recover for an unauthorized autopsy on the body of deceased was considered in *Woods v. Graham*, 140 Minn. 16, 167 NW 113. There the action was brought by a mother to recover damages for an autopsy on the body of her daughter without the mother's consent. The answer of the defendant admitted the performance of the autopsy without the consent of the mother but alleged that the autopsy was made in good faith for the purpose of ascertaining the cause of death and alleged that the autopsy was in a decent manner and no incisions were made that were not necessary in order to ascertain the cause of death. The plaintiff demurred to this answer and the trial court sustained the demurrer and the defendant appealed. The defendant raised the question we have here. The court affirmed the judgment on the authority of *Larson v. Chase*, 47 Minn. 307, 50 N.W. 238. That was an action for damages for the unlawful mutilation of the body of plaintiff's deceased husband. The only damages alleged were mental suffering and nervous shock. In support of his demurrer, which was overruled by the trial court, the defendant argued that a dead body was not property and that mental anguish and injury to the feelings, independent of any actual tangible injury to person or property, constituted no ground of action. The court first dealt briefly with the history of the development of the law from the time when the ecclesiastical courts had jurisdiction of the custody of dead bodies and kindred matters up until the time when the American colonies repudiated the ecclesiastical law and left the temporal courts the sole protector of the dead and the rights of the living in the dead. The court then said: "This has been accomplished by a process of gradual development, and all courts now concur in holding that the right to the possession of a dead body for the purposes of decent burial belongs to those most intimately and closely connected with the deceased by domestic ties, and that this is a right which the law will recognize and protect."

The court then said: "We have no doubt, therefore, that the plaintiff had the legal right to the custody of the body of her husband for the purposes of preservation, preparation, and burial, and can maintain this action if maintainable at all."

We choose to follow the above rule, both because it is based on the tenets and practice of a Christian people, and for the further reason that it accords with what our Legislature has undoubtedly thought was the desire of our people when it enacted the statutes mentioned.

The court in considering further the rights of the wife said: "But whatever may have been the rule in England under the ecclesiastical law, and while it may be true still that a dead body is not property in the common commercial sense of that term, yet in this country it is, so far as we know, universally held that those who are entitled to the possession and custody of it for purposes of decent burial have certain legal rights to and in it."

The court further said: "The important fact is that the custodian of it has a legal right to its possession for the purposes of preservation and burial, and that any interference with that right by mutilating or otherwise disturbing the body, is an actionable wrong. And we think it may be safely laid down as a general rule that an injury to any right recognized and protected by the common law will, if the direct and proximate consequence of an actionable wrong, be a subject for compensation… Wherever the act complained of constitutes a violation of some legal right of the plaintiff, which always, in contemplation of law, causes injury, he is entitled to recover all damages which are the proximate and natural consequence of the wrongful act. That mental suffering and injury to the feelings would be ordinarily the natural and proximate result of knowledge that the remains of a deceased husband had been mutilated, is too plain to admit of argument."

The above case drew an analogy between cases of the sort we are considering and cases of assault without physical violence, cases of false imprisonment, and actions for seduction. This court has considered such cases. In the case of *Anthony v. Norton*, 60 Kan. 341, 56 P. 529, this court held that a mother could recover damages for the seduction of her 25 year old daughter even though no loss of services was shown. The basis of recovery was placed altogether on the mental anguish of the parent over the fall of the daughter from virtue. In *Lonergan v. Small & Co.*, 81 Kan. 48, 105 P. 27, the plaintiff sued a storekeeper for assault. It appeared that plaintiff was in the store of defendant and that defendant snatched a box from under the arm of plaintiff under such circumstances as to constitute an assault and at the same time held plaintiff out to the bystanders as a shoplifter and thief. The jury awarded the plaintiff damages. In answer to special questions the jury found that plaintiff did not suffer any bodily injuries from the assault and that any mental suffering she might have endured was not occasioned by physical injury. No damages were allowed for slander. It will thus be seen that the judgment of the trial court rested entirely upon the mental suffering endured by plaintiff. The defendant made the same argument in that case that is made here, that is, that the plaintiff could not recover for mental suffering alone when there had been no physical injury. This court held that the assault was the invasion of a right of plaintiff to personal security, to be free from such things, to be let alone, and that the mental suffering was a consequence of such invasion. So in this case the plaintiff had a right to the body of her dead husband, in the condition in which it was when he died. She alone could give authority for an autopsy on that body, except in case where death might occur under such circumstances as to warrant the coroner in conducting an autopsy, a circumstance we do not have here. The unauthorized cutting into the body of plaintiff's husband was an invasion of that right. The mental suffering she alleges she endured was a direct consequence of that invasion.

This conclusion is borne out by the holding in *Coty v. Baughman*, 50 S.D. 372, 210 N.W. 348; *Burney v. Children's Hospital*, 169 Mass. 57, 47 N.E. 401; *Louisville & N. Railroad Co. v. Blackmon*, 3 Ga. App. 80, 59 S.E. 341; *Darcy v. Presbyterian Hospital*, 202 N.Y. 259, 95 N.E. 695. See, also, *Hill v. Travelers' Ins. Co.*, 154 Tenn. 295, 294 S.W. 1097. This case is also reported in 52 ALR 1442, where the subject is annotated at length. It appears from the note to which reference was just made that the universal holding of the courts is as outlined already in this opinion.

Defendant makes the further point that the petition does not state a cause of action because there is no allegation of the amount or extent of damage or injury caused by the allegedly unlawful acts of defendants. The first sentence of the petition is as follows: "Plaintiff, Bertha Alderman, a citizen and resident of Dearing, Kansas, sues Sherman Ford and W. S. Hudiburg for five thousand dollars damages, for this..."

Then follows a detailed statement of the acts of defendants. The last paragraph of the petition before the prayer is as follows: "That plaintiff has been damaged on account of the violated rights of hers by the defendants as previously mentioned, and damaged by the mental anguish and depression of spirits, and insult to her feelings all caused by the wrongful and tortious acts and misconduct of these defendants."

Then follows the prayer. This petition is not in the usual form for petitions but as against a general demurrer it complies with G. S. 1935, 60-704.

Defendant Ford included in his demurrer the ground that the petition showed on its face that it was barred by the statute of limitations since it shows that it was not brought within one year of the date when the cause of action arose. As will be noted, we have concluded that this action is for an injury to the rights of another and could be maintained within two years of the time when the action arose. See G. S. 1935, 60-306, third. See, also, *Hill v. Travelers' Ins. Co.*, supra.

The judgment of the trial court is reversed, with directions to proceed with the trial of the cause in accordance with the views expressed herein.

Note

The way in which a society respects its dead defines the group [see M. Bowman, *The Reburial of Native American Skeletal Remains: Approaches to the Resolution of a Conflict*, 13 Harv. Envtl. L. Rev. 167 (1989)]. Arguably, if the cultural tradition of a Native American group holds that the deceased must be revered in a particular manner, courts, invoking public policy as embodied in NAGPRA, might recognize claims for damages arising from the adverse treatment of graves or other sacred sites.

---

2. Fifth Amendment Takings and Rights of Ownership

Legal traditions concerning property rights in the United States can be traced back to such theorists as John Locke, who believed that men unite and place themselves under government rule in part to protect their property from invasion by others. These notions of property, in turn, were embedded in the Fifth Amendment to the United States Constitution, which provides that private property shall not be taken for public use without just compensation. Government may regulate the use of property for the public benefit without being required to compensate the owner, but only to the extent that regulation of private use does not result in a "taking" under the Fifth Amendment [*Penn Central Transportation Co. v. City of New York*, 438 U.S. 104 (1978); *Pennsylvania Coal Co. v. Mahon*, 260 U.S. 393 (1922)]. Property rights may exist in land or in tangible items, and different considerations may apply to each type of property.

Regulation to control property use has evolved together with the law of property. For example, noncompensable, government-imposed limits on an owner's use of land include: the doctrine of nuisance to restrict the use of land in a manner that may cause harm to another; the police power to zone land in order to organize its use and preserve its value; social regulation and the assessment of costs for the public good; the doctrine of pubic trust to impose a fiduciary burden on government to preserve unallocated resources such as air, water, and biological diversity; and the natural use doctrine to preserve the natural or traditional use of land [see McElfish, Warburg, and Pendergrass, *Property: Past, Present, and Future*, Sept./Oct. The Envtl. Forum 20 (1996)].

A compensable taking occurs when the property owner loses the "bundle of sticks," or the totality of the attributes of property rights [*Lucas v. South Carolina Coastal Council*, 505 U.S. 1003 (1992)]. These rights include the right to exclude others, to occupy, to sell or devise, and to use. Use of the land includes historic or reasonable uses, but not all possible or speculative uses.

 Objects embedded in the land belonged to the landowner under common law. Ownership has since evolved to delineate between surface and subsurface rights to things such as minerals and water. Rights to burials, however, have remained unchanged from the English common law. Thus, descendants retain property rights in their ancestors' remains and burial items. NAGPRA statutorily acknowledged this right on federal and Indian lands, and states have affirmed it on state and private lands. Consequently, landowners do not have the authority to alter burials on their land absent the property right to do so.

HUNZIKER v. STATE

519 N.W.2d 367 (Iowa 1994)

LAVORATO, Justice:

The issue in this case is whether the district court properly concluded as a matter of law that the plaintiffs were not entitled to compensation on a regulatory taking theory for land they own. We think the district court was correct and we affirm.

The plaintiffs—Erben A. Hunziker, Donald M. Furman, R. Friedrich and Sons, Inc., and Buck Construction Company, Inc.—are land developers. In May 1988 they purchased a fifty-nine acre tract of farm land to develop. The plaintiffs platted the tract as the Second Addition, Northridge Parkway Subdivision.

In May 1990 the plaintiffs sold lot 15 in the addition for $50,000. The buyer—Dr. Jon Fleming—planned to build a home on the lot.

In April 1991 the state archaeologist learned that lot 15 has a Native American burial mound on it. The state archaeologist probed lot 15 and found some human bones. Studies indicated that the burial mound on lot 15 was made between 1000 and 2500 years ago by Native Americans of the Woodland Period.

Pursuant to Iowa Code section 305A.9 (1991), the state archaeologist prohibited disinterment of the burial mound and required a buffer zone around the mound to ensure its protection. Given the size of lot 15, the location of the mound near the center of the lot, and the need for the buffer zone, construction of a house on lot 15 was not feasible. Because of (1) the state archaeologist's determination, (2) the prohibition against disinterment, and (3) the buffer zone requirement, the city refused to issue a building permit for lot 15.

The plaintiffs refunded the purchase price to Dr. Fleming and took the lot back. The plaintiffs then brought this mandamus action, alleging the State's action amounted to a regulatory taking without compensation. The plaintiffs asked the court to enter a writ of mandamus commanding the State to condemn lot 15 and provide them just compensation for it.

Both parties moved for summary judgment. The district court granted the State's motion and denied the plaintiffs' motion. The court also overruled the plaintiffs' subsequent motions. The plaintiffs appealed.

I. SCOPE OF REVIEW.

Because mandamus is an equitable action, our review is de novo. *Fitzgarrald v. City of Iowa City*, 492 N.W.2d 659, 663 (Iowa 1992). Mandamus is a procedural device to compel condemnation when there has been a taking of private property for public use without just compensation. *Phelps v. Board of Supervisors*, 211 N.W.2d 274, 276 (Iowa 1973). Mandamus is limited to determining whether a factual issue exists that would permit a condemnation commission or a jury on appeal of an award to find an intrusion that produced a measurable decrease in the property's market value. The mandamus court may find the evidence insufficient as a matter of law to compel the summoning of a condemnation commission, but that court is simply not called upon to rule as a matter of law that a taking has occurred. To do so would create an undesirable issue preclusion problem in a later trial of a condemnation proceeding. It is for the condemnation commission or trial jury to fix the loss of value, if any, suffered by the property owner. *Fitzgarrald*, 492 N.W.2d at 663–64. So our task here is to determine whether the district court correctly determined there was no factual issue that would permit a finding of a compensable intrusion. This, of course, is the same question posed by a motion for summary judgment. *Hasbrouck v. St. Paul Fire & Marine Ins. Co.*, 511 N.W.2d 364, 366 (Iowa 1993).

II. WHETHER THERE WAS A FACTUAL ISSUE THAT WOULD PERMIT A FINDING OF A COMPENSABLE INTRUSION.

In its summary judgment motion, the State urged, among other things, that the plaintiffs never had a vested property right under statutory or common law to build a house on an ancient burial mound. For this reason, the State argued, no regulatory taking occurred. The district court agreed and entered summary judgment in favor of the State.

A. Applicable law. The Fifth Amendment to the federal Constitution provides that "private property [shall not] be taken for public use, without just compensation." U.S. Const. amend. V. This provision of the Fifth Amendment is made binding on the states through the Fourteenth Amendment to the federal Constitution. *Webb's Fabulous Pharmacies, Inc. v. Beckwith*, 449 U.S. 155, 160 (1980). An Iowa Constitutional provision similarly provides that "[p]rivate property shall not be taken for public use without just compensation first being made…" Iowa Const. art. I, § 18.

"Taking," for purposes of the federal and Iowa constitutional right of just compensation, does not necessarily mean the appropriation of the fee. It may be anything which substantially deprives one of the use and enjoyment of his property or a portion thereof. *Phelps*, 211 NW2d at 276.

Here the plaintiffs' claim for compensation is based on what has been referred to as inverse condemnation. Inverse condemnation is a shorthand description of the manner in which a landowner recovers just compensation for a taking of his property when condemnation proceedings have not been instituted. *United States v. Clarke*, 445 U.S. 253, 257 (1980).

Land-use regulation does not effect a taking requiring compensation if it substantially advances a legitimate state interest. *Lucas v. South Carolina Coastal Council*, 505 U.S. ___, ___, 112 S. Ct. 2886, 2897 (1992). There are two exceptions. When the regulation (1) involves a permanent physical invasion of the property or (2) denies the owner all economically beneficial or productive use of the land, the State must pay just compensation. Id. at ___, 112 S. Ct. at 2900; *Iowa Coal Mining Co. v. Monroe County*, 494 N.W.2d 664, 670 (Iowa 1993).

When the regulation denies the owner all economically beneficial or productive use of the land, the State—under limited circumstances—may resist payment of compensation. The limited circumstances include those instances where it can be shown that the property owner's "bundle of rights" never included the right to use the land in the way the regulation forbids. *Lucas*, 505 U.S. at ___, 112 S. Ct. at 2899; *Iowa Coal Mining Co.*, 494 N.W.2d at 670. Whether or not the property owner's "bundle of rights" included the right to use the land in the way the regulation forbids is to be determined under state nuisance and property law. *Lucas*, 505 U.S. at 112 S. Ct. at 2900.

B. Analysis. The Iowa legislature passed Iowa Code § 305A.7 in 1976. In 1978, the Iowa legislature passed Iowa Code §§ 305A.9 and 716.5. Section 305A.7 provides in part: The state archaeologist shall have the primary responsibility for investigating, preserving and reinterring discoveries of ancient human remains. For the purposes of [this section] ancient human remains shall be those remains found within the state which are more than one hundred fifty years old... 1976 Iowa Acts ch. 1158, § 7 [renumbered as Iowa Code section 263B.7 (1993)].

Section 305A.9 provides: The state archaeologist shall have the authority to deny permission to disinter human remains that the state archaeologist determines have state and national significance from an historical or scientific standpoint for the inspiration and benefit of the people of the United States. 1978 Iowa Acts ch. 1029, § 26 [renumbered as Iowa Code section 263B.9 (1993)].

Section 716.5(2) provides that a person commits criminal mischief in the third degree when the person [i]ntentionally disinters human remains that have state and national significance from an historical or scientific standpoint for the inspiration and benefit of the United States without the permission of the state archaeologist. 1978 Iowa Acts ch. 1029, § 50.

The plaintiffs do not challenge the findings of the state archaeologist that he made a significant find. Nor do they challenge the authority of the state archaeologist to designate an area as a significant find and to preserve that area pursuant to sections 305A.7 and 305A.9.

The plaintiffs, however, contend that if, in so preserving the find, the state archaeologist deprives the landowner of all beneficial use of the land—as in the case of lot 15—there has been a regulatory taking for which the owner is entitled to compensation. The plaintiffs interpret *Lucas* as requiring the State to show that even without sections 305A.7, 305A.9, and 716.5(2), the plaintiffs would not—under Iowa property law—have been able to construct a family residence on lot 15. The plaintiffs argue that because the State cannot make such a showing there has been a taking for which they should be compensated.

In addition, the plaintiffs believe that here a "taking" did not occur until the state archaeologist (1) made a significant find and (2) took action denying permission to disinter the human remains on lot 15. Because this did not happen until after the plaintiffs purchased the land, the plaintiffs argue there was a "taking" at that time. In support of their argument, the plaintiffs rely on language in *Lucas* that regulatory takings can happen from a law or decree and that such regulatory action may well have the effect of eliminating the land's only economically productive use.

Apparently, then, the plaintiffs concede the sections in question and the state archaeologist's determination with respect to lot 15 advance a legitimate state interest. Whether there has been a taking in the *Lucas* sense depends on two things. The first is whether the plaintiffs are correct that the State must show that, without sections 305A.7, 305A.9, and 716.5(2), the plaintiffs would not under Iowa property law have been able to construct a family residence on lot 15. The second is whether the taking occurred when the plaintiffs claimed it did.

We do not interpret Lucas as restrictively as the plaintiffs do. Section 305A.7 was in existence and therefore part of Iowa's property law some twelve years before the plaintiffs purchased the land in question. Sections 305A.9 and 715.5(2) were in existence and therefore part of Iowa's property law some ten years before the plaintiffs purchased the land in question. So the "bundle of rights" the plaintiffs acquired by their fee simple title did not include the right to use the land contrary to the provisions of those three Iowa Code sections. Any prohibited use of lot 15 is directly attributable to the provisions of these three Code sections. The plaintiffs took title to the land in question subject to the provisions of these sections. These sections and their resulting prohibitions concerning the use of land ran—so to speak—with the land.

In addition, in Lucas, the regulation in question was passed after the plaintiffs acquired title. In contrast, here the statutes—sections 305A.7, 305A.9, and 715.5(2)—were in existence at least a decade before the plaintiffs acquired title. This is an important distinction.

More important, implicit in the Supreme Court's "bundle of rights" analysis is that the right to use the land in the way contemplated is what controls. Here, when the plaintiffs acquired title, there was no right to disinter the human remains and build in the area where the remains were located. For that reason, there was no taking when the state archaeologist made the significant find and took action denying permission to disinter the human remains. We find support for this conclusion in the following passage from Lucas:

> Where "permanent physical occupation" of land is concerned, we have refused to allow the government to decree it anew (without compensation), no matter how weighty the asserted "public interests" involved... though we assuredly *would* permit the government to assert a permanent easement that was a preexisting limitation upon the landowner's title.... We believe similar treatment must be accorded confiscatory regulations, i.e., regulations that prohibit all economically beneficial use of land: *Any limitation so severe cannot be newly legislated or decreed (without compensation), but must inhere in the title itself, in the restrictions that background principles of the State's law of property and nuisance already place upon land ownership.* A law or decree with such an effect must, in other words, do no more than duplicate the result that could have been achieved in the courts—by adjacent landowners (or other uniquely affected persons) under the State's law of private nuisance, or by the State under its complimentary power to abate nuisances that affect the public generally, or otherwise.

Lucas, 505 U.S. at ___, 112 S. Ct. at 2900 (citations omitted). Here, at the time the plaintiffs acquired title, the State, under existing state law, could have prevented disinterment. This limitation or restriction on the use of the land inhered in the plaintiffs' title.

For all these reasons, there was—as a matter of law—no taking requiring payment of compensation. Because there was no fact issue on the issue of taking, the district court correctly sustained the State's motion for summary judgment.

AFFIRMED.

All Justices concur except SNELL, J., who dissents.

SNELL, Justice (dissenting):

I respectfully dissent.

This case is about whether the State of Iowa has the right to take a person's land and not pay for it. The majority opinion establishes the principle that the state can do that whenever it finds human bones over 150 years old buried on land that the state archaeologist declares has historical significance. I believe this is not the law of Iowa nor should it be.

The Fifth Amendment through the Fourteenth Amendment of the United States Constitution provides that the government shall not take private property for public use without just compensation. *Agins v. City of Tiburon*, 447 U.S. 255, 260 (1980); *Bakken v. City of Council Bluffs*, 470 N.W.2d 34, 36 (Iowa 1991).

Iowa law has recognized the principle of inverse condemnation, when the government does not actually condemn property but its action amounts to the same thing. *Scott v. City of Sioux City*, 432 N.W.2d 144, 145 n. 1 (Iowa 1988). By establishing that an inverse condemnation has occurred, a property owner may recover just compensation. *United States v. Clarke*, 445 U.S. 253, 257 (1980). In this mandamus action plaintiffs do not seek to prevent the state from preserving the burial mound site for historical or scientific benefit. They claim only that they are entitled to compensation for the economic loss that befalls them from the state taking their property. I find their claim to be just and supported by law.

The trial court granted the State's motion for summary judgment and the majority affirms on the ground that plaintiffs cannot prevail as a matter of law. I believe this result occurs from a misapplication of the statutory and common law. I would reverse the decision granting the State's summary judgment and remand for entry of an order sustaining plaintiffs' summary judgment motion.

We have recognized the inevitable danger to private property that exists if the "just compensation" requirements of the Fifth Amendment to the federal Constitution and article I, section 18 of the Iowa Constitution could be circumvented through the guise of police power regulation. *Business Ventures, Inc. v. Iowa City*, 234 N.W.2d 376, 381–82 (Iowa 1975). Although not every police power regulation that restricts some beneficial use of property creates a compensable taking the frustration of investment-backed expectations may constitute a taking for which compensation is due. *Fitzgarrald v. City of Iowa City*, 492 NW2d 659, 665 (Iowa 1992) (citing numerous cases).

Lot 15, the burial mound area, is part of an investment-backed expectation of plaintiffs in developing a 59-acre tract for homes. It had been sold for $50,000 and is now worth $100 because nothing can be built on it. The State argues that the plaintiffs caused their own loss by buying property without recognizing a burial mound was on it that they could not use for home development. The State also promotes the idea that plaintiffs are undeserving of compensation because they made so much money selling other lots in the 59-acre tract that their loss of Lot 15 is but a fraction of their investment and therefore "de minimus." This patronizing view of entrepreneurship is unfounded in law and economic reality.

The majority result is premised on the law quoted from *Lucas v. South Carolina Coastal Council*, 505 U.S. ___, ___, 112 S. Ct. 2886, 2899 (1992), and our state statutes. The language of the *Lucas* case relied upon is dictum expressing an undefined exception to the general rule that compensation must be paid for a taking. The holding of the *Lucas* case sustained the landowner's claim that a taking had occurred and rejected the State's argument that it owed no compensation because it was for the public benefit. The law established by *Lucas* actually supports the claim of plaintiffs in the case at bar. The Supreme Court in Lucas said: In general (at least with regard to permanent invasions), no matter how minute the intrusion, and no matter how weighty the public purpose behind it, we have required compensation. *Id.* at ___, 112 S. Ct. at 2893. We think, in short, that there are good reasons for our frequently expressed belief that when the owner of real property has been called upon to sacrifice all economically beneficial uses in the name of the common good, that is, to leave his property economically idle, he has suffered a taking. *Id.* at 112 S. Ct. at 2895. In the case of land, however, we think the notion pressed by the Council that title is somehow held subject to the "implied limitation" that the State may subsequently eliminate all economically valuable use is inconsistent with the historical compact recorded in the Takings Clause that has become a part of our constitutional culture. *Id.* at ___, 112 S. Ct. at 2900. As we have said, a "State, by ipse dixit, may not transform private property into public property without compensation..." *Id.* at ___, 112 S. Ct. at 2901 (quoting *Webb's Fabulous Pharmacies, Inc. v. Beckwith*, 449 U.S. 155, 164 (1980)).

The prohibition by the State of Iowa from using the burial mound in the instant case is a complete taking because there is no practical use of it left to the plaintiffs. It is more insidious than zoning laws that we have held to effect a taking when they deny the economically viable use of the land. See *Agins*, 447 U.S. at 260; *Osborn v. City of Cedar Rapids*, 324 N.W.2d 471, 474 (Iowa 1982); *Woodbury County Soil Conservation Dist. v. Ortner*, 279 N.W.2d 276, 278 (Iowa 1979). It is pernicious because there is virtually no notice to a landowner of the State's claim and no opportunity to review the government action or appeal to the courts.

The Iowa statutes cited as preventing full ownership of land containing a burial mound give no notice of the State's inchoate claim of authority to deny compensation while prohibiting use. See Iowa Code §§ 263B.7, 263B.9, and 716.5(2) (1993). Nor do they state or even imply that land with a burial mound bears a perpetual cloud on the title removable only by authority of the state archaeologist. Section 305A.9, giving the state archaeologist authority to deny permission to disinter human remains, is not a self-executing statute creating a covenant running with the land. By its own terms the statute is activated only by an application for permission to disinter. Moreover, there is no indication from the language of these statutes that the legislature intended to take property for historical or scientific inspiration without paying for it.

In this case, a dead bones doctrine has risen from the soil, like a phoenix, to consume the live marrow of land ownership. The history surrounding these ancient bones should be preserved by granting compensation for its resurrection.

Note

If the restrictive covenant had not predated the purchase of the land, would the burial still receive protection under the common law, or would there have been a taking? If the site in question had been a sacred site rather than a burial, would there have been a different result?

THOMPSON v. CITY OF RED WING

455 N.W.2d 512 (Minn. App. 1990)

DAVID R. LESLIE, Judge:

Appellant State of Minnesota ("State") seeks review of the trial court's judgment compelling it to commence condemnation proceedings against a 19.7-acre portion of respondents' land. The State also appeals the trial court's award to respondents of attorney fees. We reverse.

FACTS

The land involved has been in the Thompson family for many years. Respondent Leslie Thompson (father of the other three respondents, all of whom are collectively referred to herein as the "Thompsons") has lived on the property for many years and has consistently farmed and grazed animals on the land. The parcel is transected by Highway 61 and contains about 73.37 acres, most of which lies north of Highway 61.

Although the topography of the entire parcel can be characterized as rolling, the northern-most quarter consists of a peninsula-shaped bluff surrounded on the north, east and south sides by a wooded ravine. The top of the bluff has always been farmed by the Thompsons, while the ravine areas have been used for animal grazing and gathering wood for fuel. The ravine on the north edge of the peninsula continues past the northern boundary of the Thompson land to the Cannon River, a few hundred feet beyond. This topography continues westerly through an adjoining property. A large, unique Indian burial mound formation stretches along the top of the peninsula.

In January of 1983, the Thompsons were approached by a road construction subcontractor, which sought to extract gravel from the Thompson land for an improvement project planned for Highway 61. The Thompsons entered into an agreement permitting gravel extraction from the peninsula. Throughout this period the land was zoned R-1 for single family residential.

As part of the gravel agreement, the subcontractor agreed to re-grade the land, filling in the ravine with soil removed from the bluff. The re-grading plan would flatten the bluff overlooking the river and grade the land to descend from the peninsula area west of the Thompson parcel's borders. The State, MNDOT and the City of Red Wing ("City") soon learned of these plans. In the city attorney's opinion, the plans involved mining, not land reclamation, and mining was not a permitted use of land zoned R-1. The Thompsons also sought to have their land rezoned I-1, light industrial, and the city attorney pointed out that mining is also not a permitted use of land zoned I-1. The Thompsons also sought a conditional use permit for mining. The city's planning director recommended that these requests be denied.

The State Trunk Highway Archaeologist, who works with MNDOT to manage the impact of road construction on archaeological sites, apparently notified several agencies of the potential impact on the burial site. Soon the State Archaeologist, Christie A.H. Caine

("Caine"), learned of the Thompsons' plans to excavate the bluff. She wrote Leslie Thompson, informing him of the presence of the statutorily protected human burial remains. The Thompsons' attorney responded, challenging the existence of remains. Caine provided specific verification and offered to assist the Thompsons in locating and marking the sites, and in developing plans which would maximize land use potential consistent with the burial remains. She also offered her assistance with possible removal and relocation of burials. The Thompsons never responded to Caine's offers.

After public hearings, the City Council voted to deny the rezoning and conditional use permit requests. Construction of Highway 61 ultimately used other gravel, but the Thompsons suffered no penalty for not providing gravel under their agreement. The Thompsons took no further action until filing this complaint against the City, State, and Caine. Among other claims, they alleged they were deprived of all reasonable uses of a 19.7-acre portion of their land. That 19.7 acres, never previously identified as a separate parcel, was designated as the peninsula and surrounding ravines. The mounds themselves are scattered over no more than four or five acres on top of the peninsula.

At trial, the only surviving claim against the State was that Minn. Stat. § 307.08 (1988), which protects human burial remains, effected an inverse condemnation of the 19.7-acre portion of the Thompsons' land. On January 13, 1989, the City settled with the Thompsons. That settlement granted the Thompsons a retroactive rezoning of their property from R-1 to I-1, effective June 13, 1983, and also granted a conditional use permit for a period of 30 months, retroactive to June 13, 1983. The claims against the City were dismissed with prejudice.

After trial, the court found that the statute effected an inverse condemnation against the Thompsons' property. The trial court ordered the State to commence condemnation proceedings within 30 days and to compensate the Thompsons, under Minn.Stat. § 117.045 (1988), for a portion of their attorney fees, excluding those expenses incurred in bringing claims against the City. The State was ordered to pay more than $24,000 in attorney fees to the Thompsons. The findings and conclusions were amended and the amended final judgment was entered on June 26, 1989. The State appeals.

ISSUES

1. Were the Thompsons' claims ripe for adjudication?
2. Did the trial court err in compelling the State to commence condemnation proceedings against the Thompsons' land?
3. Did the trial court err in ordering the State to reimburse the Thompsons' attorney fees?

ANALYSIS

Because of technical errors in the original judgment, the State moved for amendments. The amended judgment was entered on July 26, 1989. Because the State did not move for a new trial, the scope of review on appeal is limited to determining whether the evidence sustains the amended findings and whether the amended findings sustain the amended conclusions of law and amended judgment. *Gruenhagen v. Larson*, 310 Minn. 454, 458, 246 N.W.2d 565, 569 (1976).

I.

The State repeatedly challenged the Thompsons' claims as not ripe for adjudication. Although the trial court never directly addressed this challenge, the State correctly argues that by hearing the claims on the merits, the trial court implicitly ruled that the Thompsons' claims were ripe for review.

Where a land owner has not yet obtained a final decision regarding application of a land regulation to the particular property in question, the claim is not ripe for review. *Williamson County Regional Planning Commission v. Hamilton Bank*, 473 U.S. 172, 186 (1985). The Thompsons asked the City to grant rezoning of their land and to issue a conditional use permit for a gravel mining operation. This request was denied for a variety of reasons.

A challenge to the application of a regulation is not ripe when the landowners have not submitted a development plan. *Agins v. City of Tiburon*, 447 U.S. 255, 260 (1980). The Thompsons never submitted any development plans or proposals to demonstrate proposed uses for the land. A takings claim also is not ripe where only one plan is rejected and no other plan is proposed. *Penn Central Transportation Co. v. City of New York*, 438 U.S. 104, 136–37 (1978). The only plan the Thompsons ever submitted was for gravel extraction and re-grading.

The Thompsons concede that they never responded to offers by the State and Caine to assist in locating the mounds, in seeking relocation if necessary, and developing alternate uses consistent with the applicable statute. After learning of the possible conflict between the gravel extraction plans and the existing burial mounds on their property, the Thompsons did nothing for almost a year and a half and then sued the State seeking to compel condemnation. It is not clear what impact the statute had on the City's decision to deny the Thompsons' requests. However, there has been no final determination by any State agency with regard to application of the statute to the parcel in question.

Economic impact and interference with expectation interests cannot be evaluated until after a final application of the regulations to the land in question. *MacDonald Sommer & Frates v. Yolo County*, 477 U.S. 340, 349 (1986); *Williamson*, 473 U.S. at 191 (citing *Penn Central*, 438 U.S. at 124). Here, there has been no final State application of the statute to the Thompsons' property. Therefore, the takings claims should have been dismissed as premature. However, because the trial court considered the merits of this case, we will review its decision. *Hay v. City of Andover*, 436 N.W.2d 800, 805 (Minn. App1989).

II.

Whether a taking has occurred is a question of law which this court may review de novo. *Alevizos v. Metropolitan Airports Commission*, 298 Minn. 471, 484, 216 N.W.2d 651, 660–61 (1974). The trial court's finding that the protected human burial ground deprives the plaintiffs of all reasonable uses of 19.7 acres of their 73.37 acre parcel is not supported by the record and is in reality a conclusion of law.

The right to use property as one wishes is subject to, and limited by, the proper exercise of police power in the regulation of land use. Such regulation does not constitute a compensable taking unless it deprives the property of all reasonable use. *Hubbard Broadcasting, Inc. v. City of Afton*, 323 N.W.2d 757, 761 (Minn. 1982) (citation omitted). Where a property can be used for agricultural and residential purposes, as is the Thompson parcel, the parties are not deprived of all reasonable use. Id. at 766. The burial mounds qualify as a rare and unique portion of the property which can be used to meet open space requirements, with construction arranged around the portion prohibited from being destroyed. Id. Where only one functional use has been denied, such as gravel mining, it is purely speculative to conclude that all reasonable use is denied. Id. The Thompsons had been reasonably using the land for agricultural and residential purposes and were never threatened with deprivation of this use. Therefore, they failed to establish that this statute effects an inverse condemnation.

The trial court also found as fact that the statute contains both arbitration and enterprise elements, which caused a substantial diminution in the market value of the 19.7 acres and deprived the Thompsons of all reasonable use of their land. These findings constitute conclusions of law.

The arbitration/enterprise analysis was adopted by the United States Supreme Court in *Penn Central*, 438 U.S. 104. The Minnesota Supreme Court applied the analysis in *McShane v. City of Faribault*, 292 N.W.2d 253 (Minn. 1980) (zoning regulation, which burdened private land underneath flyway of municipal airport, adopted to benefit governmental enterprise; therefore, standard employed was whether substantial diminution in market value occurred). The enterprise test is applied where a regulation burdens land owned by a few individuals, to benefit a specific government enterprise which serves the public. Id. at 258–59.

Where no specific government enterprise benefits from the regulation, its purpose involves government arbitration between competing land uses. The standard employed is whether a deprivation of all reasonable use has resulted. The arbitration test applies where comprehensive regulations create reciprocal benefits and burdens for citizens in general. *McShane*, 292 N.W.2d at 257–58. Regulations for the purpose of historic preservation do not constitute enterprise functions. Id. at 259 n. 4 (citing *Penn Central*, 438 U.S. 104). McShane establishes that in Minnesota, enterprise function analysis is triggered only where a specific governmental enterprise takes an effective easement, causing a substantial diminution in market value. In the absence of such an enterprise, the arbitration function analysis, with its deprivation of reasonable use standard, is applied.

The Thompsons alleged that an energy park planned by the City was the specific government enterprise benefited by restrictions the statute imposed on the Thompsons' property. The City apparently had planned an energy park but was forced to change its plans significantly when the burial mounds were brought to its attention. This chain of burial mounds extends from the Thompson property to the property the City had planned to buy. The alleged taking challenged by the Thompsons involves a state statute, which did not benefit the City's energy park plans at the Thompsons' expense. Rather, the City was similarly forced to cope with the presence of protected remains. The purposes of the statute bear no relationship to any government enterprise.

Regulation of land use does not constitute a compensable taking unless it deprives the property of all reasonable use. *Larson v. County of Washington*, 387 N.W.2d 902, 907 (Minn. App. 1986), *pet. for rev. denied* (Minn. Aug. 20, 1986) (quoting *McShane*, 292 N.W.2d at 257). The burden is on the landowner to show deprivation of all reasonable use. *Larson*, 387 N.W.2d at 907. Where "secondary uses" remain, no taking has been established. Id. at 908. Here, the trial court found that the State's regulation deprived plaintiffs of all reasonable use of 19.7 acres. This amended finding of fact contradicts the evidence. Furthermore, this statutory interpretation by the trial court is properly a matter of law to which this court need give no deference. *Hibbing Education Association v. Public Employment Relations Board*, 369 N.W.2d 527, 529 (Minn. 1985).

The record establishes that the Thompsons have consistently farmed and grazed the entire property. This activity is not prohibited, even atop the actual mounds. The statute prohibits destruction, mutilation, injury or removal of human burials. Minn. Stat. § 307.08, subd. 2. It is not shown whether the extensive plowing performed by the Thompsons has caused damage, however, the State has never interfered with the Thompsons' longstanding agricultural activities, nor have the Thompsons accepted the State's offer of assistance in evaluating the compatibility of these or other land use plans.

The Thompsons also contend that their agricultural and grazing activities are forbidden because the statute prohibits removal of any tree, shrub or plant from a burial site. Minn. Stat. §307.08, subd. 2. As the State points out, lawn mowing and gardening at cemeteries are clearly not prohibited. In referring to the removal of any tree, shrub or plant from any public or private cemetery or unmarked human burial ground, the statute protects trees, shrubs and ornamental plants from uprooting or destruction. We disagree that all agricultural and grazing activities are therefore categorically prohibited. In any event, the only activity that the Thompsons have been prohibited from conducting is the gravel mining operation, which was frustrated by a combination of conditions, many of which are unrelated to Minn. Stat. § 307.08.

Not every regulation challenged as effecting a taking can give rise to an action for inverse condemnation. Only where the taking or damage is irreversible will such an action lie. *McShane*, 292 N.W.2d at 259. The Thompsons have failed to demonstrate an enterprise function for which the substantial diminution in market value standard is applicable, and have failed to establish that the statute deprived them of any reasonable use of that portion of their land. As a matter of law, the requisite elements of a compensable taking are absent here.

III.

The trial court ordered the State to reimburse the Thompsons for that portion of their attorney fees deemed to have arisen from their case against the State, an amount in excess of $24,000. The trial court concluded that pursuant to Minn. Stat. § 117.045, the Thompsons were entitled to their attorney fees. That statute entitles landowners to petition for reimbursement of attorney fees upon successfully compelling eminent domain proceedings against real property omitted from any current or completed eminent domain proceeding. That language has been held to include compelling condemnation proceedings where no current or completed eminent domain proceeding was brought. *Spaeth v. City of Plymouth*, 344 N.W.2d 815, 823 (Minn. 1984).

In *Spaeth*, the supreme court held that whenever a landowner successfully brings an action to compel eminent domain with respect to land which was omitted from a proceeding which should have been commenced, Minn. Stat. § 117.045 applies. *Spaeth* at 823. Unlike Spaeth, the Thompsons failed to establish facts sufficient to support the conclusion that a taking occurred. Thus, in view of our disposition of their takings claim, the Thompsons are not entitled to attorney fees under the eminent domain statute.

DECISION

The Thompsons' claims were not ripe for adjudication because no final State action had been taken with respect to the land in question. Minn. Stat. § 307.08 does not serve an enterprise function. The trial court erred in deciding that the State, through Minn. Stat. § 307.08, effected a taking of the Thompsons' property, and in ordering the State to commence condemnation proceedings against a portion of the land. The trial court's decision awarding attorney fees is also reversed.

Reversed.

Note

If the traditional use of the land for farming also had caused damage, and assuming the state enacted a burial protection measure that made illegal all impacts to burials, would a taking have resulted?

DEPARTMENT OF NATURAL RESOURCES v. INDIANA COAL COUNCIL, INC.

542 N.E.2d 1000 (Ind. 1989)

DeBRULER, Justice:

This is an appeal from the Dubois Circuit Court and the determination there that certain provisions of Indiana's version of the Surface Mining Control and Reclamation Act ("SMCRA"), I.C. 13-4.1-1-1, *et seq.*, and regulations promulgated thereunder, 310 I.A.C. 12-2-1, *et seq.*, as applied by the Indiana Department of Natural Resources to land owned by Huntingburg Machinery & Equipment Rental, Inc. ("HUMER") amounted to an unconstitutional taking under the Fifth Amendment to the Constitution of the United States. Under Appellate Rule 4(A)(8), this Court has exclusive jurisdiction to hear cases in which a statute has been declared unconstitutional, and because of the important constitutional issues involved, transfer is granted.

The land at issue, owned by HUMER, is currently being farmed but sits atop three seams containing approximately 1.537 million tons of mineable coal. In a small, 6.57 acre portion of the land, sitting on top of approximately 55,200 tons of coal, lies what has become known as the Beehunter Site, an archaeologically significant area, rich in cultural deposits with substantial historic and scientific value. The Beehunter Site's importance stems from the fact that below the plow zone it contains a substantially intact "midden," with artifacts from four distinct cultural periods of occupation, which would allow anthropologists to make cross-cultural comparisons of different adaptations to the same environmental niche. The site was nominated and found eligible for listing on the National Register of Historic Places. 51 Fed. Reg. 6677 (1986).

The Wabash Valley Archaeological Society, Inc. ("Wabash Valley") petitioned the Department of Natural Resources ("DNR") to have the site designated as an area unsuitable for surface coal mining under I.C. 13-4.1–14-2. The director of DNR may declare an area unsuitable for surface coal mining if the coal mining operation will "affect fragile and historic lands in which the operation could result in significant damage to important historic, cultural, scientific, and esthetic values and natural systems." I.C. 13-4.1–14-4. A public hearing was held and on November 19, 1985, pursuant to this provision and Wabash Valley's petition, the director made an initial determination that Beehunter was an area unsuitable for surface coal mining. By this time the Indiana Coal Council ("Coal Council") and the Council for the Conservation of Indiana Archaeology ("CCIA") had entered the proceedings. The Coal Council and HUMER filed timely objections and a hearing was held on December 19, 1985, pursuant to I.C. 4-22-1-12 (repealed 1986). A final order was issued by the director of the DNR on January 3, 1986 designating the Beehunter Site unsuitable for surface coal mining.

As part of his final order, the director included a mitigation plan which provided a means by which the designation of "area unsuitable" could be removed. It calls for a program of site testing and data recovery conducted by an archaeological contractor approved by DNR. The plan does not require HUMER to carry out the plan, to expend any money, or to convey any property or property right to the State. It affects no existing contractual rights. In fact, the designation does not prevent HUMER from continuing to farm the land, nor from mining virtually all of the coal under its farmland, so long as the coal that lies underneath the 6.57 acre Beehunter Site is extracted by means other than strip mining, a process which would destroy the archaeological information contained in the site. For these reasons, and those delineated below, we hold that the director's order, designating the Beehunter Site as an area unsuitable for surface coal mining and providing a mitigation plan by which the designation may be removed, does not amount to an unconstitutional taking of property.

The Fifth Amendment provides that "[no] private property [shall] be taken for public use, without just compensation," and, of course, applies to the states through the Fourteenth Amendment. This seemingly simple mandate has become increasingly difficult to apply as the complexities of modern life have necessitated a wide variety of land use regulations. More than sixty years ago, Justice Holmes recognized that "[g]overnment hardly could go on if to some extent values incident to property could not be diminished without paying for every such change in the general law," *Pennsylvania Coal Co. v. Mahon*, 260 U.S. 393, 413 (1922), but also noted that "while property may be regulated to a certain extent, if regulation goes too far it will be recognized as a taking," id., 260 U.S. at 415. The difficulty has been in devising rules that establish a line between regulation that is permissible and that which "goes too far." Consequently, the determination often rests on "ad hoc factual inquiries" involving the facts and circumstances of each particular case. *Keystone Bituminous Coal Ass'n v. DeBenedictis*, 480 U.S. 470, 508 (1987) (Rehnquist, C.J., dissenting), citing *Penn Central Transp. Co. v. City of New York*, 438 U.S. 104, 124 (1978).

However, we are not without guidance in this area. Recent United States Supreme Court cases have provided a two-prong test as an aid in making the determination. Under this rule, when applied to a particular piece of property, a land use regulation will not effect a taking if it substantially advances a legitimate state interest and does not deprive an owner of economically viable use of his property. *Nollan v. California Coastal Comm'n*, 483 U.S. 825, 834 (1987). Until recently, the inquiry generally focused on the second of the two prongs, attempting to determine the economic impact of the regulation on the land. See *Keystone*, 480 U.S. 470; *Penn Central*, 438 U.S. 104. In *Nollan*, however, the Court emphasized the first prong in striking down a condition placed upon the granting of a zoning variance, finding that the condition did not substantially advance the interests sought to be achieved by the regulation. The two prongs are indicative of the various guises that a constitutional attack on a land use regulation may take.

The essence of the first prong of the test is whether government had the right to exercise its police power in the manner it did, regardless of the burden to the property. Or, in other words, it asks the question: has government regulated where it should not have done so? If the regulation does not bear a substantial relation to the legitimate ends sought to be achieved, either through a failure of the statute as a whole to serve those ends or as applied to a particular piece of property, then the exercise of the police power is deemed to be unreasonable. A variation of this type of challenge would exist where the ends themselves were not legitimate. The state could not, for example, regulate property simply because it does not agree with the religious or political views of the land owner. See *Williamson Co. Regional Planning Comm'n v. Hamilton Bank*, 473 U.S. 172, 202 n. 1 (1985) (Stevens, J., concurring).

The economic inquiry of the second prong of the test has its roots in Justice Holmes's decision in *Pennsylvania Coal*, 260 U.S. 393, which is generally regarded as the seed from which all modern regulatory taking cases have grown. In that case, a Pennsylvania statute requiring that a certain amount of coal be left unmined so as to prevent subsidence to the surface estate was struck down as unconstitutional because it interfered with the distinct investment-backed expectations of the owners of the mineral estate and did not provide compensation for the coal that was "taken." This consideration for distinct investment-backed expectations remains essential today. See, *Kaiser Aetna v. United States*, 444 U.S. 164, 175 (1979); *Penn Central*, 438 U.S. 104, 124. It is also necessary to examine the economic impact of the regulation on the claimant in terms of the diminution in value of the land, id., and the extent of any interference with the present use of the land, *Penn Central*, 438 U.S. at 136. In determining the degree of diminution in value, the particular segment that is affected is not considered alone, but the claimant's property as a whole is compared to that portion which is encumbered. *Keystone*, 480 U.S. at 497. Of course, the nature and character of the interference is also relevant, and where a regulation results in permanent physical occupation of property, a taking will almost invariably be found. Id., 480 U.S. at 488–489 n. 18; *Loretto v. Teleprompter Manhattan CATV Corp.*, 458 U.S. 419 (1982).

All of the economic inquiries deal with the degree to which a property has been encumbered by a regulation. In that sense, the essence of the second prong of the test is whether government has regulated to a greater extent than it should have so that a land owner has been effectively deprived of productive use of his property.

We turn now to the claims of HUMER and the Coal Council that the director's order here declaring the Beehunter Site as an area unsuitable for surface mining of coal is an unconstitutional taking. We note at the outset that HUMER and the Coal Council have challenged the director's order as invalid under the Fifth Amendment and that the burden on a party attempting to show that a regulatory taking has occurred is a heavy one. See *Keystone*, 480 U.S. at 499. Turning to the second prong of the analysis, it is clear that the economic impact on HUMER here is comparatively slight and no showing to the contrary was made in any of the proceedings below. The record indicates that HUMER or its predecessors have held the land upon which the Beehunter Site is located since the mid-1940s. It has been farmed since that time and there is no indication that it was acquired with the intent to mine coal. In fact, the seams of coal were apparently discovered rather recently. It cannot be said, therefore, that the designation of Beehunter has interfered with HUMER's distinct and reasonable investment-backed expectations since there was no expectation of coal mining at the time investment in the property was made. Furthermore, the designation obviously does not interfere with HUMER's present use of the property. It has been farming the land and presumably will continue to do so.

More importantly, the overall effect on the value of the land is minute here. The Beehunter Site represents approximately 6.57 acres of a 305 acre farm, or just slightly over two percent of the whole. In terms of mineable coal, the designation affects only 6.5 percent of the total coal resources on the land and, if alternative methods of mining were used, such as auguring, that figure could be reduced to less than three percent. This Court has previously upheld much more "intrusive" restrictions upon land in the context of zoning. In *Young v. City of Franklin* (1986), Ind, 494 NE2d 316, it was noted that a land owner is not entitled to the highest and best use of his land and a taking results under the economic impact inquiry only when all reasonable use of the land is prevented by the land use regulation. Id. at 318, citing *City of Anderson v. Associated Furniture & Appliances, Inc.* (1981), Ind., 423 N.E.2d 293; *Foreman v. State ex rel. Department of Natural Resources* (1979), 180 Ind. App. 94, 387 NE2d 455. This position is in harmony with decisions of other courts that have sustained land use regulations despite their having the effect of severely reducing or holding down the land value from that of its desired use. *Penn Central*, 438 U.S. 104; *Euclid v. Ambler Realty Co.*, 272 U.S. 365 (1926); *Pompa Construction Corp. v. Saratoga Springs*, 706 F.2d 418 (2d Cir. 1983); *Rogin v. Bensalem Township*, 616 F.2d 680 (3d Cir. 1980), *cert. denied sub nom. Mark-Garner Associates, Inc. v. Bensalem Township*, 450 U.S. 1029 (1981); *William C. Haas & Co. v. City and County of San Francisco*, 605 F.2d 1117 (9th Cir. 1979), *cert. denied*, 445 U.S. 928 (1980).

Thus, because HUMER's investment-backed expectations and present use of the land have not been interfered with and because there has been no significant diminution of the land's value, it is clear that from an economic standpoint, the extent of government's intrusion into HUMER's property is comparatively small and, in and of itself, does not rise to the level of a taking of property. However, HUMER and the Coal Council rely, for the most part, on the first prong of the takings inquiry in their attack on the constitutionality of the designation, arguing the director's order and accompanying mitigation plan do not substantially advance legitimate state interests. In so doing, they challenge the constitutionality of the statute and regulation not as a whole, but as applied to HUMER's property.

There is no set rule to apply in making the determination of what constitutes a legitimate state interest but it is generally accepted that government has the power to enact laws and regulations to promote order, safety, health, morals and the general welfare of society. The decisions of this Court and the Courts of Appeals have not dwelled on this aspect of the takings inquiry. However those decisions implicitly make clear that a broad range of government interests satisfy the legitimacy requirement. *Young*, 494 N.E.2d 316 (upholding refusal to rezone land to residential class); *Alanel Corp. v. Indianapolis Redevelopment Comm'n* (1958), 239 Ind. 35, 154 N.E.2d 515 (upholding redevelopment acts dealing with acquisition of blighted urban areas); *Foreman*, 180 Ind. App. 94, 387 N.E.2d 455 (upholding flood control act). Federal decisions have reached similar conclusions. *Agins v. Tiburon*,

447 U.S. 255 (1980) (scenic zoning); *Penn Central*, 438 U.S. 104 (landmark preservation); *Barrick Realty, Inc. v. City of Gary*, 491 F.2d 161 (7th Cir. 1974) (maintaining stable integrated neighborhoods).

Protecting our national and state heritage through the preservation of archaeological sites must be included in this broad spectrum of legitimate interests of government. The information in these sites expands our knowledge of human history and prehistory and thus enriches us as a state, nation and as human beings. The general welfare of the public is greatly enhanced by such knowledge. We note that our Court of Appeals implicitly recognized this in *State Highway Comm'n v. Ziliak*, 428 N.E.2d 275 (Ind. App. 1981), declaring that highway construction projects must adhere to the Indiana Environmental Policy Act which requires that all practicable means be used to coordinate resources to "preserve important historic, cultural, and natural aspects of our national heritage." Id. at 281; I.C. 13-1-10-2. We recognize it explicitly here.

In examining the nexus between the land use regulation and the state interest, we have relied on the phrasing of earlier Supreme Court cases, and have required that there be a "substantial relationship" between the two. *Young*, 494 N.E.2d at 318; see *Nectow v. City of Cambridge*, 277 U.S. 183 (1928); *Ambler Realty*, 272 U.S. 365. However, there is authority that suggests that a land use regulation need only be "reasonably related" to the legitimate state interests to be valid, *Penn Central*, 438 U.S. 104, 131; *Foreman*, 387 N.E.2d 455, 461, or that it be "reasonably necessary to the effectuation of a substantial public purpose," *Penn Central*, 438 U.S. at 127, or that it "substantially advance" a legitimate state interest, *Agins*, 447 U.S. 255, 260. The Supreme Court has, as yet, been unable to settle on an exact standard for assessing the connection between the regulation and the state interest, *Nollan*, 483 U.S. at 834, and we see no reason to depart from the standard as stated in Young that there be a "substantial relation" between the two. The basis for the inquiry is to assure that the state does not effect a collateral purpose or end under the guise of a legitimate purpose or end, regulating where it has no right to do so. Such assurance is obtained when the effect of the regulation is substantially consistent with the legitimate ends of the state.

Here the legitimate ends of protecting cultural resources from the threat of strip mining are served by both the designation of the Beehunter Site as an area unsuitable for surface mining of coal and by the mitigation plan which allows a means for removal of the designation once the information in the site is scientifically recovered. The order is completely consistent with legitimate state ends.

Be that as it may, HUMER and the Coal Council direct this Court's attention to *Nollan v. California Coastal Commission*, 483 U.S. 825, and argue that case has imposed an entirely new analytical framework on takings inquiries where the state places a condition on the removal of a land use restriction. They maintain that, in such an instance, the condition must serve the same legitimate police power interest as the land use restriction to be valid and that where the condition requires a conveyance to the state or would otherwise amount to a taking, a heightened level of scrutiny should be employed in examining the state action.

The Nollan Court relied on the rule from Agins that the regulation "substantially advance" a legitimate state interest and did hold that a condition to removal of a land use restriction must similarly advance that end. Id., 483 U.S. at 834. However, it did not adopt any particular level of scrutiny to be applied across the board to all takings inquiries: We are inclined to be particularly careful about the adjective ["substantial"] where the actual conveyance of property is made a condition of the lifting of a land use restriction, since in that context there is a heightened risk that the purpose is avoidance of the compensation requirement rather than the stated police power objective. Id., 483 U.S. at 841. If this amounts to a heightened scrutiny, it clearly extends only to situations where government requires an actual conveyance of property as a condition to removal of a land use restriction. Furthermore, the stated test used by this Court, that there be a "substantial relation" between the regulation or the condition and the legitimate state interest, is essentially the same standard.

In their reliance on *Nollan*, HUMER and the Coal Council attempt to cast the director's inclusion of a mitigation plan with his order as amounting to a condition requiring an intrusion tantamount to an actual conveyance of property. The order and mitigation plan require nothing of the sort. HUMER is required to do nothing and it is free to continue the present use of farming the land in question. The extent of the intrusion here does not rise to the level of that in *Ziliak* where the State made an outright demand for access to the owner's land to conduct an archaeological dig by state-employed archaeologists. *Ziliak*, 428 N.E.2d 275. Here, the State is not seeking to physically occupy the land nor requiring any conveyance, it is only attempting to preserve the information at Beehunter until any qualified archaeologist can recover it. As noted above, the intrusion here is minimal from an economic standpoint and amounts to mere regulation.

Furthermore, such conditions to the removal of land use restrictions are wholly within the perimeters of *Nollan*: [T]he Commission's assumed power to forbid construction of the house in order to protect the public's view of the beach must surely include the power to condition construction upon some concession by the owner, even a concession of property rights, that serves the same end. If a prohibition designed to accomplish that purpose would be a legitimate exercise of the police power rather than a taking, it would be strange to conclude that providing the owner an alternative to that prohibition which accomplishes the same purpose is not. *Nollan*, 483 U.S. at 836. We have already noted that the purpose of the alternative to the prohibition here, the mitigation plan, is consistent with the legitimate government interest served by the prohibition itself: preservation of areas culturally significant to our heritage. Even if we accept the appellees' characterization of DNR's mitigation plan as conditioning the removal of the area unsuitable designation upon HUMER's "conveying" archaeological information to the State for public use without compensation, it is clear that under *Nollan* such a condition would be a constitutionally valid exercise of the police power, since the removal of a restriction may be conditioned even on "a concession of property rights." Id. It would be not only strange, but against all reason to conclude that the State's prohibition of surface mining of the Beehunter Site was a legitimate exercise of the police power but that providing HUMER with an alternative to the prohibition which, like the prohibition itself, also helped to preserve our cultural heritage was not a legitimate exercise of that power. Id.

HUMER and the Coal Council argue that the director's order and mitigation plan do not substantially advance the legitimate state interest of preservation of our cultural heritage because they protect Beehunter only against destruction from surface coal mining. They suggest that because the site could be destroyed by any number of other means that have not been protected against by the State, including malicious destruction by the owner, the government's legitimate interest is not substantially advanced by the designation alone. However, we do not read the cases delineating takings jurisprudence to require that a regulation be successful in accomplishing substantially all possible ends that further the legitimate state interest, only that it substantially achieve those ends the legislature, in furtherance of legitimate state interests, deems necessary to address. The nature of the political process dictates that "[l]egislatures may implement their program step by step... in such economic areas, adopting regulations that only partially ameliorate a perceived evil and deferring complete elimination of the evil to future regulations." *City of New Orleans v. Dukes*, 427 U.S. 297, 303 (1976).

Here the state interest sought to be protected is our cultural heritage by prohibiting the destruction of cultural data from strip mining. That the legislature has not, as yet, chosen to address other threats to these archaeologically significant areas does not automatically transpose their action into a taking or an unconstitutional exercise of the State's police power. The regulations as applied to HUMER's property through the director's order and mitigation plan bear a substantial relation to the legitimate state interest of preserving our cultural heritage by protecting culturally significant data from strip mining. They are, thus, a legitimate exercise of the State's police power and since the economic impact of the regulations is slight, they do not amount to an unconstitutional taking of HUMER's property.

Finally, HUMER and the Coal Council argue that the director's order was arbitrary and capricious and an abuse of discretion. The rule as to administrative actions has been well stated by our Court of Appeals, and we adopt it here, that an administrative act is arbitrary and capricious only where it is willful and unreasonable, without consideration and in disregard of the facts or circumstances in the case, or without some basis which would lead a reasonable and honest person to the same conclusion. *Metropolitan School District*, 451 N.E.2d 349 (Ind. App. 1983). Moreover our decisions have stated that courts may not substitute their own judgment or opinion for that of the administrative body acting in discretionary matters within its jurisdiction. *Mann v. City of Terre Haute*, 240 Ind. 245, 163 N.E.2d 577 (1960). HUMER and the Coal Council maintain that the director should have accepted a mitigation plan proposed by HUMER in place of the plan that was made a part of the order; and, by not doing so, the intent of the statute was not carried out because HUMER is forced to bear the cost of an archaeological dig and is given an incentive to destroy the site by other means. These issues have been addressed above. They look no better cloaked in a challenge based on arbitrariness, capriciousness or abuse of discretion than they do in a constitutional guise. The mitigation plan proposed by the director requires nothing of HUMER except to refrain from strip mining coal in a small portion of its property until important cultural information can be recovered. HUMER introduced no evidence at any of the administrative hearings that its plan was superior to that proposed by the director, or even that it was minimally adequate to accomplish that end. As to any incentive HUMER may have to maliciously destroy Beehunter, it is entirely plausible for the director to have concluded that the low regard in which any such action would be held by the DNR at subsequent hearings for removal of the "area unsuitable" designation was a sufficient deterrent to such unethical behavior.

In short, the director's order is entirely reasonable and there is a sufficient basis in the record which would lead a reasonable and honest man to the same conclusion. The director fulfilled his statutory obligation to prepare a detailed statement on the potential coal resources of the area, the demand for coal, and the impact of the designation on the economy, the environment and the coal supply. I.C. 13-4.1–14-3. The record shows that Wabash Valley and CCIA introduced expert witnesses whose testimony tended to support the director's decision and HUMER and the Coal Council produced no experts whatsoever. The order is neither arbitrary, capricious nor an abuse of discretion.

The request for oral argument is denied. The decision of the Dubois Circuit Court setting aside the order of the director of the Department of Natural Resources is vacated and the cause is remanded to that court to enter a decree denying relief from that order.

SHEPARD, C.J., and GIVAN, PIVARNIK and DICKSON, J.J., concur.

Note

Can an argument be made for a temporary taking? If there was a cost to the coal company for the removal of the archeological remains, would there have been a taking, or merely a permissible exercise of the police power?

---

3. Other Issues

Adverse Possession

Property rights exist in tangible personal property and intellectual property, in addition to real property. Personal property rights may originate from the creation of an item, receipt as a gift from a willing donor, purchase, or a contract. All of these rights assume that the property owner had authority to retain the item conferred by a party having authority to alienate it. Absent ownership by adverse possession, wrongful appropriation of property is not legitimized by the passage of time, even if the eventual recipient pays fair-market value or receives the property from a willing possessor. NAGPRA places the burden of proof on museums to overcome a *prima facie* showing of a property right in defined cultural items by a tribe or Native Hawaiian organization for this reason.

Adverse possession is a remedy in equity that operates to confer ownership in the possessor where open and notorious possession has existed for a defined number of years. A museum in possession of an item for a long period, and in reliance on the belief that it owns the item, might claim ownership by adverse possession. If the item is a defined Native American cultural item, however, the period for reckoning adverse possession cannot begin until the museum provides notice, through a NAGPRA-mandated summary or inventory, that it controls the item as part of its collection. The time period for adverse possession is tolled so long as a Native American group effectively is disenfranchised and unable to bring a claim.

Battlefield Plunder, Prizes, and Pickup

Items retrieved from a battlefield during, or immediately after, battle and subsequently placed in commerce could be subject to ownership disputes. In any case, removal of items from any historical battlefield located on federal, state, or private lands without permission from the landowner does not confer lawful ownership on the finder.

CHAPTER FIVE

HERITAGE RESOURCES LAW IN THE MARINE ENVIRONMENT

SECTION A.   AN OVERVIEW

Heritage resources law in the marine environment often involves considerations that do not arise in a terrestrial setting because this area of the law involves a distinct environment, range of resources, and group of stakeholders against a unique backdrop of law and policy. For example, the interplay between federal, state, and international law—including admiralty and maritime law—is important to the unique way that the law treats submerged heritage resources. The international Law of the Sea marine zone in which a heritage resource lies (for example, the Territorial Sea, Contiguous Zone, Exclusive Economic Zone, High Seas, Continental Shelf, or "the Area") is also a primary factor in determining ownership of or control over the resource.

This chapter begins by identifying the heritage resources in question and the different stakeholders who have an interest in them, and follows with a section on the treatment of these resources by federal courts in admiralty, both prior to and after passage of the Abandoned Shipwreck Act of 1987. The remainder of the chapter discusses the heritage resource statutes, policies, case law, and diverse public interests underlying resource management in the marine environment. Various subthemes, such as resource protection, public access, multiple use management, user conflicts, and enforcement mechanisms, are also identified.

International law is an important component of heritage resources law in the marine environment. Consequently, this chapter presents an overview of the sources of international law, such as custom, treaties, conventions, and other agreements, followed by a discussion of the background considerations, purpose, and provisions of the United Nations Convention on the Law of the Sea (LOS), and the specific LOS provisions regarding heritage resources. The World Cultural Heritage Convention and the Salvage Convention of 1989 are also included in this discussion. While large gaps in the law threaten *in situ* preservation of heritage resources in the marine environment, solutions to counter these threats are currently being explored in international forums.

SECTION B.   HISTORICAL BACKGROUND

1.   The Resources

The diverse range of submerged heritage resources provides an interesting expression of human experience, particularly through maritime history, the most obvious heritage resource in the marine environment being shipwrecks and their cargo. Until the 1950s, these material remains of past human existence were left undisturbed in the marine environment, preserved as discrete time capsules, largely because they were inaccessible. With the continuing advances in scuba and other technology, however, they have become increasingly more vulnerable to disturbance and destruction. It is helpful in understanding heritage resources law in the marine environment and its evolution to recognize what and where these heritage resources are, who is interested in them, and what values are at stake.

Shipwrecks

Sunken vessels and their cargo (shipwrecks) are a record of our maritime heritage. They also encapsulate a moment frozen in time, namely the date on which they were wrecked. A shipwreck can yield information on economic and technological history, and historical events. Shipwrecks might also hold gold, silver, jewels, and other intrinsically valuable items that, in the past, piqued the interest of sovereigns and pirates, and continue today to attract the attention of sovereigns, treasure hunters, insurance companies, and others.

The most widely recognized heritage resource in the worldwide marine environment is the RMS *Titanic*, the most famous shipwreck of the twentieth century. Since its sinking in 1912, the *Titanic* has been the subject of numerous movies, books, and articles. Although for many years historians believed that the *Titanic* sank as the result of large gashes in the hull, recent nonintrusive research indicates that numerous small gashes in the hull actually caused it to sink.

One of the best known shipwrecks in the United States is the USS *Monitor*, a Civil War-era ironclad that became famous following a battle with the Confederate ironclad CSS *Virginia* (formerly the USS *Merrimac*). The *Monitor* was lost when it sank off the coast of North Carolina in the "Graveyard of the Atlantic" in 1862. Its discovery in 1973 was accompanied by both excitement and concern lest it be destroyed through looting or unwanted salvage. To ensure its on-site protection and preservation, the USS *Monitor* was designated a national historic landmark pursuant to the National Historic Preservation Act, and in 1975, became the first National Marine Sanctuary.

Another category of shipwrecks, Spanish galleons, holds valuable information about the European Colonial period, as well as the cultural record of native peoples of Central and South America. Spanish galleons have been the most popular targets for treasure salvors because of the treasure cargoes they purportedly carried. The most treacherous part of the journey for a convoy of merchant ships and armed escorts traveling from the New World to Spain lay from Havana, Cuba, along the Florida Straits and the coastal area within the Gulf Stream, to just past the Bahamas. Spanish treasure fleets ran aground and sank off the coast of Florida in 1622, 1715, and 1733. In the 1960s, the discovery of the 1715 silver plate fleet off Vero Beach, Florida, started a rush of treasure hunters to Florida. After many years of searching, Melvin Fisher found the *Atocha*, whose cargo, he alleges, is valued at $400 million.

Shipwrecks such as the *Central America* and the *Brother Jonathan*, which are associated with the gold rushes of both California and Alaska, have been the recent focus of treasure hunters. The *Central America* sank during a hurricane in 1857, in 8,000 feet of water approximately 160 miles east of Charleston, South Carolina. It carried gold coins and bars with an estimated present-day value of $1 billion. The *Brother Jonathan,* which sank approximately four and a half miles west of Crescent City, California, on state submerged lands, may also have carried a cargo that included gold.

Aircraft Wrecks

Certain aircraft wrecks are also heritage resources because they are associated with historically significant events. For example, if the airplane Amelia Earhart flew at the time of her disappearance were discovered under water, it would be a heritage resource because of her importance in the history of aviation. Some efforts have been undertaken to locate this wreck, as well as other aircraft associated with historically significant persons, such as the one flown and wrecked during World War II by former President George Bush. Another example belonging to this category of heritage resources is the USS *Macon*, a World War I-era dirigible that crashed off the coast of California in 1937. It now rests on the seabed in the Monterey Bay National Marine Sanctuary.

The management of shipwrecks, aircraft wrecks, and other heritage resources in the marine environment requires the additional consideration of whether human remains are present. If such remains are present, these sites are entitled to respect as graves, and must not be disturbed without the explicit permission of the sovereign [J. Ashley Roach, *Sunken Warships and Military Aircraft*, 20/4 Marine Policy 351-54 (1996)]. Former terrestrial sites that are now inundated are also worthy of respect, as they, too, may contain the remains of early native peoples.

Native American Resources

People have fished, boated, and established temporary and permanent settlements along the coasts for thousands of years. During the most recent Ice Age (10,000–20,000 years before present), the sea level was approximately 300–400 feet lower than it is today. Subsequently, as a result of glacial melting, some terrestrial sites became submerged. Scientists believe that evidence of past human existence may lie as far as the Outer Continental Shelf. In fact, heritage resources have been found in Grey's Reef National Marine Sanctuary, 17.5 miles off the present-day coast of Georgia; items culturally identified with the Chumash Indians have been recovered from the seabed in Channel Islands National Marine Sanctuary; and the skeletal remains of a mastodon were reportedly recovered from the seabed of Stellwagen Bank, more than three miles off the present-day coast of Massachusetts [see B. Terrell, *Fathoming Our Past: Historical Contexts of the National Marine Sanctuaries* (National Oceanic and Atmospheric Administration, 1994)].

Other Resources

Wharves, lighthouses, and other structures are also of archeological or historical value for the information they provide about maritime cultural heritage. Even isolated debris fields might contain information about fishing, maritime transport and trade, and naval history.

2.   Stakeholders and Values

The diverse resources found in the marine environment capture the interest of many different people and groups. As indicated in the legislative history of the Abandoned Shipwreck Act of 1987 (ASA), three primary groups interested in historic shipwrecks have been identified: archeologists/historians, treasure salvors, and recreational divers [H.R. Rep. No. 887, 98th Cong., 2d Sess. Part 1 (1984)]. Museums and the general public also have an interest in underwater heritage.

Archeologists and Historians

Submerged heritage resources contain information about past human experience of interest to archeologists and historians. This scientific information reveals how people interacted with the marine environment, and it might support or rebut theories concerning historical events and processes. Estimating their number in the United States to be several thousand, Congress identified archeologists and historians in the legislative history of the Abandoned Shipwreck Act as the second largest group interested in historic shipwrecks [H.R. Rep. 887, 98th Cong., 2d Sess. Part 1 (1984)]. This group differs most from the treasure salvors regarding the disposition of submerged cultural heritage in that it prefers to preserve these submerged resources where they lie in the maritime environment. Treasure salvors, in contrast, argue that these resources are in "peril" and need to be "rescued" from the marine environment.

Treasure Salvors

The removal by "treasure salvors" of historic shipwrecks from the marine environment did not really begin in earnest until the post-World War II commercial development of the self-contained underwater breathing apparatus (scuba). Historic shipwrecks were being discovered by scuba divers in the clear and shallow waters of Florida by the 1950s. These discoveries and recoveries were aided by technologies such as the propeller-wash deflector, or "mailbox," which has the power to create a hole in the seabed that is 15 feet deep, 30 feet in diameter at the top, and 15 feet in diameter at the bottom.[1] Remote-controlled submarines equipped with video recorders, cameras, robotic arms, and remote sensors have recently been used to identify and recover resources from shipwrecks such as the RMS *Titanic* and the SS *Central America* in deep water. Treasure salvage, however, is more commonly associated with less sophisticated efforts at recovering Spanish galleons.

Approximately 19–22 Spanish galleons wrecked off the coast of southern Florida. They comprise the 1622 fleet, the 1715 silver plate fleet, and the 1733 fleet, as well as other, individual galleon wrecks. Throughout the 1950s and 1960s—and even into the 1970s—treasure hunters salvaged the 1733 fleet. By the 1980s, little remained to salvage from this fleet, and the cost of salvage approached or exceeded the return brought from the sale of the recovered resources. Consequently, in the late 1960s, treasure hunters began shifting their activity to the 1715 fleet, located near Fort Pierce, on the At-

---

[1]Mailboxing has been likened to strip mining [Throckmorton, *The World's Worst Investment: The Economics of Treasure Hunting with Real Life Comparisons*, Underwater Archaeology Proceedings from the Society for Historical Archaeology Conference, page 6 (T. Carrel ed. 1990), analyzing 16 Caribbean expeditions of which the author had personal knowledge]. A National Geographic video described the site of the *Atocha* as a battleground filled with moon-like craters [*Atocha: Quest for Treasure* (1986)]. In *U.S. v. Fisher*, 977 F. Supp. 1193, 1197 (S.D. Fla. 1997), experts for the United States testified that the destruction to the seabed and seagrass caused by the respondent was comparable to the destruction inadvertently caused by Navy bombs off the coast of Puerto Rico.

lantic shoreline. In contrast to the Florida Keys dive season, the Atlantic shoreline season was short, the dive sites were characterized by turbulence, and the wrecks were dispersed, making discovery and recovery of the 1715 fleet more difficult than that of the 1733 fleet. Also in the 1960s, Melvin Fisher started looking for the *Atocha*, one of the vessels in the 1622 fleet. The shipwreck he located in 1971, approximately 40 nautical miles from Key West and 11 miles from the Marquesses Key, was positively identified as the *Atocha* in 1973, when serial numbers on silver bars that were recorded in the *Atocha*'s manifest appeared on bars recovered from the wreck. Fisher continues to salvage the *Atocha* and other sites today.

Estimates vary for the number of full-time commercial treasure hunters. A 1991 report stated that at the time, there were approximately 100 active treasure hunters compared to about half a dozen in 1968 [Arnold, *Treasure Hunting Becoming a Growth Industry*, Boston Globe, October 21, 1991, at 27, col. 1]. Another study reported that worldwide, about 25 treasure hunting companies start up every year, with half that number collectively able to raise $100 million to finance their operations [Throckmorton, *The World's Worst Investment: The Economics of Treasure Hunting with Real Life Comparisons*, Underwater Archaeology Proceedings from the Society for Historical Archaeology Conference 6 (T. Carrel ed. 1990)]. By yet another estimation, during the 1970s, there could have been as many as 1,000 salvage divers regularly recovering artifacts from shipwrecks located throughout United States waters, most of them recreational wreck divers operating in California, New England, New Jersey, North and South Carolina, and Florida [Memorandum from Duncan Mathewson, salvor and archeologist, to Ole Varmer, Office of the General Counsel, National Oceanic and Atmospheric Administration (November 10, 1993)].

Recreational Divers

Underwater heritage resources are enjoyed by divers and snorkelers, boaters, and fishermen. In the legislative history of the Abandoned Shipwreck Act, Congress identified the sport diving community (estimated at two million people in 1984) as the largest group interested in historic shipwrecks [H.R. Rep. No. 887, 98th Cong., 2d Sess. Part 1 (1984)]. A decade later, the Forest Service estimated that 7.24% of the population 16 years or older (14.5 million people) engaged in snorkeling and/or scuba diving in the United States [Outdoor Recreation and Wilderness Assessment Group, Forest Service, U.S. Dept. of Agric., National Survey on Recreation and the Environment (1994-95)]. This group will likely continue to grow.

In Florida, one of the more popular domestic diving destinations, submerged heritage resources have been found to contribute to the totality of the recreational diving experience [F.W. Bell, The 1990 Florida Recreational

Survey (1993)], and studies conducted by the National Oceanic and Atmospheric Administration (NOAA) found that they also are an important component of the regional economy. According to NOAA estimates, from June 1995 to May 1996, scuba divers and snorkelers in the Florida Keys (visitors and residents) represented a user value of $170,590,000. During that time, an estimated 831,019 snorkelers and scuba divers used the Florida Keys a total of 3,053,100 user days, of whom 39,310 (18%) participated in wreck diving amounting to 130,200 user days. Each diver had a daily recreational user value of $77, and the total user value for all wreck divers was $7.4 million [B. Leeworthy & P. Wiley, Visitor Profiles: Florida Keys/Key West, National Oceanic and Atmospheric Administration Report, 1996; B. Leeworthy & P. Wiley, A Socioeconomic Analysis of the Recreation Activities of Monroe County Residents in the Florida Keys/Key West, National Oceanic and Atmospheric Administration Report, 1997]. Divers appreciate wrecks that are preserved in place. In a study that evaluated the recreational use benefits of a marine park with historic shipwrecks, a respondent, on average, was willing to pay $13.50 for a hypothetical daily use permit to dive in a Great Lakes aquatic park [Kaoru & Hoagland, The Value of Historic Shipwrecks: Conflicts and Management, Vol. 22, No. 2 *Coastal Management* 204 (April-June 1994)]. Other people, however, wish to enjoy underwater cultural heritage without diving.

Museums and Museum Patrons

Museums conserve, display, and interpret heritage resources, and make them available for use by researchers, educators, students, and the general interested public. In fact, the Abandoned Shipwreck Act guidelines suggest that museums might be sources of funding for archeological programs [55 Fed. Reg. 50,128 (1990)]. A large part of the general public, however, enjoys and appreciates the value of heritage resources even if it does not directly use, touch, or see them.

General Public

Researchers have found that the public values the existence of heritage resources even if there is no physical encounter with them in the marine environment or in a museum. Perhaps the general public has come to appreciate the underwater cultural heritage through educational programs, books, oral histories, or other media.

Mitchell and Carson conducted research on the economic valuation of resources and identified four types of "existence value" that fall into two main categories: "vicarious consumption" and "stewardship." First, in the case of vicarious consumption values, the researchers found that utility is gained from knowing about the consumption of others. The "others" may be generalized, or they may be particular individuals known to the respondent. Second, Mitchell and Carson distinguished two types of stewardship values: bequest values and inherent values. Bequest values exist when an individual enjoys knowing that the current provisions of an amenity will make it available for others—family or future generations—to enjoy in the future. Inherent values stem from the respondent's satisfaction that an amenity itself—a wilderness area, for example—is preserved regardless of use by anyone [R. Mitchell & R.T. Carson, *Using Surveys to Value Public Goods: The Contingent Valuation Method*, Resources of the Future 463 (1989)].

Kaoru and Hoagland also conducted research, and suggested that theories of nonmarket valuation be applied to the management of submerged heritage resources. They identified three types of nonuse values: existence, option, and bequest. Option value is the premium over expected future benefits from historic shipwreck resources that individuals are willing to pay in order to preserve future access. Individuals may be uncertain about the future availability or importance of one or more particular shipwrecks, and the "option value" concept is a method of characterizing this value. Bequest value is an individual's willingness to pay for the satisfaction of preserving particular historic shipwrecks for future generations [Kaoru & Hoagland, The Value of Historic Shipwrecks: Conflicts and Management, Vol. 22, No. 2 *Coastal Management* 203 (April-June 1994)].

3.   Evolution of the Laws that Specifically Protect Heritage Resources in the Marine Environment

Historically, the impetus for enacting most environmental laws has been a disaster or other action that threatened the environment in general, or a particular resource, and thereby served to focus the public's attention and the will of the public's representatives in Congress on redressing the problem. For example, environmental disasters in the late 1960s, such as the dumping of radioactive wastes in the marine environment and an oil spill along the coast off Santa Barbara, California, motivated the passage of the Marine Protection, Research, and Sanctuaries Act of 1972.

The primary impetus for the laws protecting heritage resources in the marine environment has been the actual and threatened removal of these resources for private benefit pursuant to the maritime law of salvage and the common law of finds. The application of maritime law by the courts to historic shipwrecks has proved to be a legal basis for taking heritage resources that has no parallel in the terrestrial environment. Prior to enactment of the Abandoned Shipwreck Act of 1987, coastal states relied on the Submerged

Lands Act of 1953 (SLA) as authority for implementing state historic preservation laws to protect heritage resources abandoned in and on their submerged lands. However, in many federal court cases, where the states invoked the SLA to assert ownership of these resources, the courts, sitting in admiralty, upheld the application of the maritime law of salvage and the common law of finds over the SLA. This line of decisions caused the states and heritage resource professionals concern over the loss of these resources. In particular, the 1985 legal victory of treasure hunter Melvin Fisher in *Cobb Coin* was a significant catalyst for Florida, Texas, and other coastal states to petition Congress for a law that specifically would protect abandoned shipwrecks located within state waters. That law, the Abandoned Shipwreck Act, was passed in 1987, and became effective in 1988.

The laws of salvage and finds likely will still apply, and have been applied, well beyond any territorial jurisdiction. For example, a federal court allowed an admiralty action seeking salvage to the RMS *Titanic,* located on the Canadian continental shelf. Unless a shipwreck is protected by one of the statutes identified in Section D, the law of salvage will probably continue to provide the legal authority to conduct treasure hunting.

SECTION C. ADMIRALTY AND MARITIME LAW, AND SUBMERGED HERITAGE RESOURCES

Federal heritage resources laws that apply specifically to the marine environment must be viewed against the backdrop of admiralty and maritime law, for not only is this body of law relevant to the evolution of heritage resources laws in the marine environment, it still remains quite relevant to the disposition of the resources themselves. It is important to consider why treatment of submerged heritage resources is different from that of terrestrial heritage resources—simply because the resources are located underwater—even if they were once located on land. (As discussed in chapter three, unpermitted excavation of heritage resources on publicly owned or controlled land would be considered looting.) Traditionally, admiralty and maritime law had been applied to recent casualties, and not to shipwrecks that met their demise hundreds of years ago. Nevertheless, treasure salvors have been successful in convincing federal courts sitting in admiralty to apply this body of law to submerged heritage resources.

1. Jurisdiction

Treasure salvors have typically sought legal rights to the shipwrecks that they salvage by means of filing *in rem* actions against the subject shipwrecked vessel and its cargo in federal district courts sitting in admiralty pursuant to 28 U.S.C. § 1333. Jurisdiction over shipwrecks is created through a legal fiction, by "arresting" a piece of the shipwreck or its cargo and thereby bringing it into the territorial jurisdiction of the admiralty court. Under this exercise of quasi-*in rem* jursidiction, the shipwreck could theoretically be located anywhere in the world, but if a piece of it is physically brought into admiralty court, the court can exercise jurisdiction over the entire shipwreck and its cargo. [See, *e.g., R.M.S. Titanic, Inc. v. Wrecked and Abandoned Vessel*, 924 F. Supp. 714 (E.D. Va. 1996) (district court exercised jursidiction over the *Titanic*, located beyond the Exclusive Economic Zone of the United States at a depth of 2.5 miles below the surface, on Canada's continental shelf).]

The rule of bringing a piece of the shipwreck, or the *res*, into court "is predicated upon admiralty's fiction of convenience that a ship is a person against whom suits can be filed and judgments entered." [*Treasure Salvors, Inc. v. The Unidentified, Wrecked and Abandoned Sailing Vessel*, 569 F.2d 330, 333–34 (1978).] As a practical matter, however, it may be impossible to bring the entire shipwreck and her cargo within the territorial jurisdiction of the federal court. Courts, though, are not disturbed by this practical constraint, as "there is little danger that the res, against which any claims might be satisfied, will escape an in rem decree against it." [*Treasure Salvors* at 335.] In these circumstances, an exception is made, and the court exercises quasi-*in rem* jurisdiction over those portions of the shipwreck that rest outside of the court's territorial jurisdiction. [*Moyer v. The Wrecked and Abandoned Vessel, Known as the Andrea Doria*, 836 F. Supp. 1099, 1104 (D.N.J. 1993).] The policy behind the exercise of quasi-*in rem* jurisdiction is based on an assumption made by the courts that there is a "'reasonable likelihood' that the salvage operation will result in other portions of the shipwreck being brought into the territorial—and, thus, *in rem*—jurisdiction of the court." [*Andrea Doria* at 1104, citing *Treasure Salvors, Inc. v. The Unidentified , Wrecked and Abandoned Sailing Vessel, "Nuestra Senora De Atocha,"* 546 F. Supp. 919, 929 (S.D. Fla. 1981) (remand).]

In personam jurisdiction also plays a role in actions to obtain title to, or a salvage award for recovery of, a shipwrecked vessel and her cargo. Although *in rem* or quasi-*in rem* jurisdiction is exercised over the shipwreck and her cargo, courts also exercise *in personam* jurisdiction over the plaintiff. *In personam* jurisdiction is also exercised over any claimant who may intervene in the action. [*Andrea Doria* at 1103.]

2. The Common Law of Finds

Treasure salvors have, in the past, sought title to abandoned historic shipwrecks by asserting the common law of finds. Under this common law doctrine, title vests in the person who first reduces the shipwreck in question to his or her possession with the intention of becoming the owner thereof. [See *Hener v. United States*, 525 F. Supp. 350, 354–55 (S.D.N.Y. 1981).] The main prerequisite for asserting the application of the law of finds, though, is that the subject shipwreck be abandoned.

The law of finds generally assigns ownership of or title to the abandoned property without regard to where the property is found. Two exceptions to this rule are recognized: 1) if the abandoned property is *embedded* in the submerged lands, the owner of the submerged lands also owns the abandoned property; and 2) if the owner of the submerged lands on which the property is found (whether located on or embedded in the seabed) has *constructive possession* of the property such that it cannot be deemed to be "lost," the owner of the submerged lands also owns the property. [See *Klein v. Unidentified, Wrecked and Abandoned Sailing Vessel*, 758 F.2d 1511 (11th Cir. 1985).]

The issue of whether shipwrecks are abandoned has been the subject of much litigation. Some courts have inferred abandonment by the mere passage of time and the failure of the owner to assert an ownership claim. [See, *e.g., Andrea Doria* at 1105.] Other courts have adopted a "totality of the circumstances" test to determine whether a shipwreck is indeed abandoned. [See *Commonwealth v. Maritime Underwater Surveys, Inc.*, 531 NE2d 549, 552 (Mass. 1988).] Recently, courts have looked to whether technological advances existed to rescue a shipwreck in order to determine if that shipwreck is abandoned. [See, *e.g., Columbus-America Discovery Group v. Atlantic Mutual Insurance Company*, 974 F.2d 450 (4th Cir. 1992).][2] It should be noted, however, that the United States and other nations take the position that their sovereign shipwrecked vessels, no matter where in the world they are located, are *not* abandoned, absent an express renunciation of ownership by the proper authority. [See, *e.g., United States v. Steinmetz*, 973 F.2d 212 (3rd Cir. 1992).]

---

[2]For a further discussion of the term "abandonment" as used in admiralty/maritime cases, see Section D. 1. of this chapter.

TREASURE SALVORS, INC. v. THE UNIDENTIFIED, WRECKED AND ABANDONED SAILING VESSEL

569 F.2d 330 (5th Cir. 1978)

GEWIN, Circuit Judge:

Treasure Salvors, Inc., and Armada Research Corp., Florida corporations, sued for possession of and confirmation of title to an unidentified wrecked and abandoned vessel thought to be the Nuestra Senora de Atocha. The Atocha sank in the sea off the Marquesas Keys in 1622 while en route to Spain. The United States intervened, answered, and counterclaimed, asserting title to the vessel. Summary judgment was entered for the plaintiffs, 408 F. Supp. 907 (S.D. Fla. 1976), and the government appealed. We modify the district court's judgment, and affirm.

This action evokes all the romance and danger of the buccaneering days in the West Indies. It is rooted in an ancient tragedy of imperial Spain, and embraces a modern tragedy as well. The case also presents the story of a triumph, a story in which the daring and determination of the colonial settlers are mirrored by contemporary treasure seekers.

In late summer of 1622 a fleet of Spanish galleons, heavily laden with bullion exploited from the mines of the New World, set sail for Spain. Spain, at this period in her history, was embroiled in the vicious religious conflicts of the Thirty Years' War and desperately needed American bullion to finance her costly military adventures. As the fleet entered the Straits of Florida, seeking the strongest current of the Gulf Stream, it was met by a hurricane which drove it into the reef-laced waters off the Florida Keys. A number of vessels went down, including the richest galleon in the fleet, Nuestra Senora de Atocha. Five hundred fifty persons perished, and cargo with a contemporary value of perhaps $250 million was lost. A later hurricane shattered the Atocha and buried her beneath the sands.

For well over three centuries the wreck of the Atocha lay undisturbed beneath the wide shoal west of the Marquesas Keys, islets named after the reef where the Marquis of Cadereita camped while supervising unsuccessful salvage operations. Then, in 1971, after an arduous search aided by survivors' accounts of the 1622 wrecks, and an expenditure of more than $2 million, plaintiffs located the Atocha.[1] Plaintiffs have retrieved gold, silver, artifacts, and armament valued at $6 million. Their costs have included four lives, among them the son and daughter-in-law of Melvin Fisher, plaintiffs' president and leader of the expedition.[2]

---

[1][*Orig. fn.*] Plaintiffs began their salvage operation pursuant to a contract with the state of Florida. Under the contract, the state was entitled to 25% Of the finds. The decision in *United States v. Florida*, 420 U.S. 531, 95 S. Ct. 1162, 43 L. Ed.2d 375 (1975), refuted Florida's claim to the wreck site, and the contract was cancelled. *See also United States v. Florida*, 425 U.S. 791, 96 S. Ct. 1840, 48 L. Ed.2d 388 (1976). It is undisputed that the wreck lies on the continental shelf, outside the territorial waters of the United States. (A. 68).

[2][*Orig. fn.*] Our brief historical summary is based in part on Lyon, The Trouble with Treasure, 149 National Geographic 787 (June 1976).

JURISDICTION

The district court did not specify its basis of jurisdiction. With respect to the controversy presented by the parties, it was clearly within the court's power to declare title to those objects within its territorial jurisdiction. The government, however, contends that the court lacked in rem jurisdiction to determine the rights of the parties to that portion of the res situated beyond the territorial jurisdiction of the court.

In rem actions in admiralty generally require, as a prerequisite to a court's jurisdiction, the presence of the vessel or other res within the territorial confines of the court. *American Bank of Wage Claims v. Registry of District Court of Guam*, 431 F.2d 1215, 1218 (9th Cir. 1970); 7A Moore's Federal Practice P E.05, at E-202 (1977). This rule is predicated upon admiralty's fiction of convenience that a ship is a person against whom suits can be filed and judgments entered. *Continental Grain Co. v. Barge FBL-585*, 364 U.S. 19, 22-23, 80 S. Ct. 1470, 1472-1473, 4 L. Ed.2d 1540, 1543 (1960). Personification of the ship allows actions to be brought against the vessel when her owner can not be reached. *Id.* In these circumstances the fiction may perform a useful and salutary function. But when a legal fiction which exists solely to effectuate the adjudication of disputes is invoked for the opposite purpose, we have no hesitation in declining to employ it.[3]

Other courts faced with similar challenges to their jurisdiction have refused to myopically apply this fiction where its application was inappropriate to the situation before them. In *Booth Steamship Co. v. Tug Dalzell No. 2*, 1966 A.M.C. 2615 (S.D.N.Y. 1966), the claimant to the res contested the court's in rem jurisdiction on the grounds that the res was not within the territorial jurisdiction of the court. In its pleadings the plaintiff had alleged, as in the case before us, that the res was within or during the pendency of the proceedings would be within the court's jurisdiction. The claimant's answer admitted this allegation. After reviewing the decisions on this question the court held:

> (T)he mandate of Admiralty Rule 22 requiring that in an in rem action, the libel allege the presence of the res in the district, does not relate to subject matter jurisdiction, and therefore actual local seizure or a tangible substitute thereof, such as the posting of a bond, is not a prerequisite to the maintenance of an in rem action. The claimants-petitioners, by admitting the presence of the res within the district, by filing a claim to the tug Dalzell # 2 and by filing and serving a general appearance, have submitted that vessel to the jurisdiction of this court.
>
> *Id.* at 2618.

The Third Circuit reached a similar conclusion in *Reed v. Steamship Yaka*, 307 F.2d 203 (3d Cir. 1962), *rev'd on other gds.*, 373 U.S. 410, 83 S. Ct. 1349, 10 L. Ed.2d 448 (1963). There, the res was also outside the court's territorial jurisdiction, but the claimant voluntarily appeared and answered the complaint "to avoid attachment and delay of the vessel if it should subsequently be present" within the court's jurisdiction. The court held that by this act the claimant had waived the requirement that the res be arrested by the court and had consented to the court's jurisdiction over its interest in the vessel. *Id.* at 204-05.

---

[3]*[Orig. fn.]* The fiction of a ship's personality is criticized in G. Gilmore & C. Black, *The Law of Admiralty*, 615-22 (2d ed. 1975).

Finally, the Supreme Court, in *Continental Grain Co. v. Barge FBL-585*, 364 U.S. 19, 80 S. Ct. 1470, 4 L. Ed.2d 1540 (1960), *aff'g*, 268 F.2d 240 (5th Cir. 1959), permitted the transfer under 28 U.S.C. § 1404(a), with the claimant's consent, of an in rem action in admiralty to a district in which the res was not present. The Court based its decision upon the fact that this transfer would prevent "unnecessary inconvenience and expense to parties, witnesses, and the public." *Id.* at 21, 80 S. Ct. at 1472, 4 L. Ed.2d at 1542. It is true, as Justice Whittaker stated in his dissent in Continental Grain, that the Court did not decide the question of whether the owner's consent can confer in rem jurisdiction in an action where the res is not within the territorial jurisdiction of the court. However, as commentators have noted, the Supreme Court appears to favor the position that the presence of the res within the district is not an absolute prerequisite to the court's jurisdiction.[4]

These decisions evidence the common concern of the courts with finding the most practical and efficacious means of resolving the disputes before them. An interest in rendering justice rather than an automatistic reliance upon rigid legalisms characterizes each of them. It is with these examples before us that we turn to an examination of the merits of the government's jurisdictional challenge.

Initially we note that for all practical purposes it was impossible to bring the entire remains of the vessel and her cargo within the territorial jurisdiction of the court. Thousands of items retrieved from the wreck site were brought into the district, but the bulk of the wreck lies buried under tons of sand in international waters. The district court did everything within its power to have the marshal arrest the vessel and bring it within the custody of the court.[5] Thus, there is little danger that the res, against which any claims might be satisfied, will escape an in rem decree against it.

---

[4][*Orig. fn.*] *See* 7A Moore's Federal Practice P E.05 at E203-E206 (1977); The Law of Admiralty, *supra* n.3, at 616 n. 75a. See also 2 E. Benedict, *The Law of American Admiralty* s 242 (1940).

[5][*Orig. fn.*] Plaintiffs strenuously argue that in addition to the artifacts seized and brought within the jurisdiction of the court, the vessel itself was in custodia legis pursuant to an order of the court. The record lends some support to this contention. On February 26, 1976, the United States moved the court "for an order commanding the United States Marshal for the Southern District of Florida, to arrest and take into custody the defendant vessel, her tackle, apparel, cargo and armament, and to retain the same in his custody until further order of this Court," and, in the alternative, "for an order continuing its order of October 28, 1976 (sic), appointing plaintiffs custodians of the defendant vessel." (A. 88). On October 28, 1975, the court had ordered "that TREASURE SALVORS, INC., and ARMADA RESEARCH CORP. be, and are hereby appointed the custodian of said vessel to retain the same in his (sic) custody for possession and safekeeping for the aforementioned compensation until further order of this court," and had further ordered that "all Marshal's costs be paid prior to the release of said vessel and all further constructive costs be borne by Plaintiffs." (A. 51). The Marshal's return filed November 11, 1975, certifies service of a warrant in rem upon "The unidentified Wrecked and Abandoned Sailing Vessel . . . Located within 2500 yards of a point at coordinate 24o 31.5' North Latitude and 82o 20' West Longitude, said sailing vessel is believed to be the 'Nuestra Senora de Atocha'." (A. 28).

In this case, as in the three cases we have discussed, the court had in personam jurisdiction over the claimants,[6] thus rendering the vessel's arrest nonessential to the resolution of the action. The United States intervened in plaintiffs' in rem action as a party defendant and filed a counterclaim asserting a property right in the res. The government, by intervening in this action and by stipulating to the court's admiralty jurisdiction (A. 67), waived the usual requirement that the res be present within the territorial jurisdiction of the court and consented to the court's jurisdiction to determine its interest in the extraterritorial portion of the vessel.

Alternatively, we note that assuming a lack of in rem jurisdiction of that part of the wreck lying outside the territorial waters of the United States, the district court is not deprived of jurisdiction over the government's counterclaim if that claim rests upon an independent basis of jurisdiction. *Sachs v. Sachs*, 265 F.2d 31 (3d Cir. 1959); *Haberman v. Equitable Life Assurance Soc'y of United States*, 224 F.2d 401, 409 (5th Cir. 1955); *Isenberg v. Biddle*, 75 U.S. App. D.C. 100, 102, 125 F.2d 741, 743 (1944). In its counterclaim the government requested that "a declaratory judgment be issued affirming the property right of the United States in the Atocha, her tackle, armament, apparel and cargo." (A. 10). While no basis of jurisdiction was stated in the counterclaim regarding the extraterritorial portion of the wreck, the record reveals that the government based its claim to rights in the sunken vessel on the Antiquities Act, 16 U.S.C. § 431 *et seq.*, and the Abandoned Property Act, 40 U.S.C. § 310.[7] The district court thus had jurisdiction under 28 U.S.C. § 1331 to determine the applicability of these statutes to that portion of the vessel situated in international waters.

To summarize, the district court properly adjudicated title to all those objects within its territorial jurisdiction and to those objects without its territory as between plaintiffs and the United States.[8] In affirming the district court, we do not approve that portion of its order

---

[6][*Orig. fn.*] In *The Fairisle*, 76 F. Supp. 27, 34 (D. Maryland), the court held that owners who appeared in an in rem action to contest the plaintiffs' claim "may equitably be treated as if they had been brought into court by personal process," citing The Dictator, L.R. Probate Division 304 (1892). This view was adopted by the Ninth Circuit in *Mosher v. Tate*, 182 F.2d 475, 479-80 (1950). *See* The Law of Admiralty, *supra* n.3, at 802-05.

[7][*Orig. fn.*] The government invoked these statutes in its claim of ownership filed in the district court pursuant to admiralty rule 6(c). (A. 6-7).

[8][*Orig. fn.*] On February 19, 1976, the district court entered the following order of final judgment:

Pursuant to this Court's opinion Order of Summary Judgment of February 2, 1976, it is

ORDERED and ADJUDGED that judgment be and the same hereby is entered in favor of plaintiffs and against the United States of America and all other claimants. The Counterclaim of the United States of America is hereby dismissed with prejudice.

It is further ORDERED that plaintiffs, Treasure Salvors, Inc. and Armada Research Corporation, are confirmed in their sole title to, and right to immediate and sole possession of, the vessel identified in this matter as "Nuestra Senora de Atocha" together with all her tackle, armament, apparel and cargo, wherever the same may be found.

It is further ORDERED and ADJUDGED that no person, organization or governmental agency shall interfere with the plaintiffs in the lawful exercise of their right to possession or of their salvage rights in the vessel, tackle, armament, apparel and cargo.

Jurisdiction of this matter is hereby retained for the purpose of enforcement of this Order.

(A. 86-87).

which may be construed as a holding that plaintiffs have exclusive title to, and the right to immediate and sole possession of, the vessel and cargo as to other claimants, if any there be, who are not parties or privies to this litigation.

One further procedural matter must detain us. The government asserts that summary judgment was improper in light of two material issues of fact left unresolved by the district court. The first issue, whether the United States has established procedures for the protection and recovery of objects on the outer continental shelf, concerns administrative or legislative action which is subject to judicial notice. *See* Wright and Miller, Fed. Practice and Procedure 2410. The government was obliged, under Fed.R.Civ.P. 56(e), to set forth any procedures or controlling statutes not already brought to the attention of the court. The government cannot claim to be a party unable, under Fed.R.Civ.P. 56(f), to gather and present material showing the existence of such procedures or statutes.

The second issue, whether plaintiffs were in possession of the Atocha and that portion of her tackle, armament, apparel, and cargo which had not been found, cannot be said to be in dispute as a matter of fact. The government adopted plaintiffs' description of the vessel in its claim of ownership (A. 6). It is uncontested that other artifacts exist in the vicinity of plaintiffs' salvage operation. The government offered no affidavits or other evidence contesting plaintiffs' protection and control of the wreck site. Absent evidence disputing plaintiffs' affidavits, the district court appropriately considered the facts settled on motion for summary judgment.

SALVAGE

The government argues that one of the elements of a salvage action the existence of a marine peril is absent from this controversy, and that the district court erred in applying the law of salvage. We believe the government misconstrues both the nature of the law applied by the district court and the law of salvage itself.

The Atocha is indisputedly an abandoned vessel.[9] Whether salvage law or the adjunct law of finds should be applied to property abandoned at sea is a matter of some dispute.[10] Martin J. Norris, in his treatise on salvage law, states that under salvage law the abandonment of property at sea does not divest the owner of title. M. Norris, The Law of Salvage, § 150 (1958). Courts, however, have rejected the theory that title to such property can never be lost and have applied the law of finds. *Wiggins v. 1100 Tons, More or Less, of Italian Marble*, 186 F. Supp. 452, 456-57 (E.D. Va. 1960). *See Nippon Shosen Kaisha, K.K. v. United States*, 238 F. Supp. 55, 59 (N.D. Cal. 1964); *Rickard v. Pringle*, 293 F. Supp. 981, 984 (E.D. N.Y. 1968). Under this theory, title to abandoned property vests in the person who reduces that property to his or her possession. In Rickard, for example, the court held that title to a propeller recovered from a vessel abandoned on the ocean floor for sixty years

---

[9][*Orig. fn.*] The parties stipulated that "the wreck believed to be the Nuestra Senora de Atocha, her tackle, armament, apparel and cargo has been abandoned by its original owners." (A. 69)

[10][*Orig. fn.*] *See* Eleazer, The Recovery of Vessels, Aircraft, and Treasure In International Water 34-35, in Some Current Sea Law Problems, (S. Wurfel ed. 1975) (University of North Carolina Sea Grant Publication No. U.N.C.-SG-75- 06).

vested in "the first finder lawfully and fairly appropriating it and reducing it to possession, with the intention to become its owner." *Id.* at 984, citing *Wiggins, supra, sub nom. The Clythia.*

The court below correctly applied the law of finds.[11] Disposition of a wrecked vessel whose very location has been lost for centuries as though its owner were still in existence stretches a fiction to absurd lengths. The law of salvage does not contemplate a different result. Salvage awards may include the entire derelict property.[12]

The government's argument that no marine peril existed ignores the reality of the situation. Marine peril includes more than the threat of storm, fire, or piracy to a vessel in navigation.[13] In *Thompson v. One Anchor and Two Chains,* 221 F. 770, 773 (W.D. Wis. 1915), "(t)he 'marine peril' consisted in the fact that the anchors and chains were actually lost. If they had been resting on a reef, where they could be seen, they would undoubtedly have been in 'peril' of being lost, and the 'marine peril' certainly was not diminished or extinguished by the fact that they were actually lost." There is no dispute that the Atocha was lost. Even after discovery of the vessel's location it is still in peril of being lost through the actions of the elements. Thus, under either theory plaintiffs are entitled to award of the property if the government does not prevail in this action.

On this appeal the United States claims the treasure chiefly upon two grounds: (1) Application of the Antiquities Act, 16 U.S.C. §§ 431-433, to objects located on the outer continental shelf of the United States; and (2) The right of the United States, as heir to the sovereign prerogative asserted by the Crown of England, to goods abandoned at sea and found by its citizens. In support of the second contention the government relies not only upon English common law but also upon the Antiquities Act, *supra,* the Abandoned Property Act, 40 U.S.C. § 310, and other generalized statutes and regulations.

THE ANTIQUITIES ACT

The Antiquities Act authorizes executive designation of historic landmarks, historic and prehistoric structures, and objects of historic or scientific interest situated upon lands owned

---

[11][*Orig. fn.*] Norris raises the spectre of violent clashes between competing finders in international waters if abandoned property is held to be a find. Norris, *supra* at s 158 (Supp.1974). We fail to see how salvage law, which gives the right of possession to first salvors, Norris, supra at s 152, would provide a more effective deterrent to such clashes. Under either doctrine the property or an award for the value of the salvage efforts goes to the one who is first able to seize possession. The primary difference between the two doctrines is that under salvage law the claim of the finder of abandoned property is satisfied by proceeds from the sale of the property paid into court. *See* Norris, *supra* at s 156.

[12][*Orig. fn.*] *See Brady v. S.S. African Queen,* 179 F. Supp 321, 324 (E.D. Va. 1960).

[13][*Orig. fn.*] According to Norris, The Law of Salvage s 185 (1958), "(t)he peril required in a salvage service need not necessarily be one of imminent and absolute danger. The property must be in danger, either presently or reasonably to be apprehended." *See Fort Myers Shell & Dredging Co. v. Barge NBC512,* 404 F.2d 137, 139 (5th Cir. 1968).

or controlled by the United States as National Monuments. Permission to examine ruins, excavate archaeological sites, and gather objects of antiquity must be sought from the secretary of the department exercising jurisdiction over such lands. As the district court noted, the Antiquities Act applies by its terms only to lands owned or controlled by the Government of the United States. The wreck of the Atocha rests on the continental shelf, outside the territorial waters of the United States.[14]

The government asserts that the Outer Continental Shelf Lands Act (OCSLA), 43 U.S.C. § 1331 *et seq.*, demonstrates Congressional intent to extend the jurisdiction and control of the United States to the outer continental shelf. OCSLA was passed, along with the Submerged Lands Act, 43 U.S.C. § 1301 *et seq.*, to clarify the respective interests of coastal states and the United States in the natural resources of the subsoil and seabed of the continental shelf. A look at the background and interpretation of OCSLA is necessary to determine its scope.

The Truman proclamation of September 28, 1945,[15] spurred national and international interest in exploitation of the mineral wealth of the oceans. The proclamation asserted the jurisdiction and control of the United States over the mineral resources of the continental shelf, but was not intended to abridge the right of free and unimpeded navigation of waters above the shelf, nor to extend the limits of American territorial waters. *See* 13 Dep't State Bull. 485 (Sept. 30, 1945). The Convention on the Continental Shelf,[16] written thirteen years later, assured to each coastal nation the exclusive right to explore and exploit the

---

[14][*Orig. fn.*] The continental shelf is defined as the seabed and subsoil of the submarine areas adjacent to the coast but outside the area of the territorial sea, to a depth of 200 meters or, beyond that limit, to where the depth of the superjacent waters admits of the exploitation of the natural resources of the said areas. This is a legal, not a geological, definition. The territorial sea of the United States includes those waters lying not more than three miles (or three marine leagues in the Gulf of Mexico in the case of certain Gulf states) from the baseline (the artificial coast line). All parts of the sea not included in the territorial or internal waters of a nation constitute high seas. Nations maintain limited jurisdiction over waters lying not more than twelve miles from the baseline, in order to prevent or punish infringement of customs, fiscal, immigration or sanitary regulations within their territory or territorial sea. This belt of limited control is the contiguous zone. See generally Convention on the Continental Shelf, done April 29, 1958, (1964) 15 U.S.T. 471, T.I.A.S. No. 5578, in force June 10, 1964; Convention on the Territorial Sea and the Contiguous Zone, done April 29, 1958, (1964) 15 U.S.T. 1606, T.I.A.S. No. 5639, in force Sept. 10, 1964; Convention on the High Seas, done April 29, 1958, (1962) 13 U.S.T. 2312, T.I.A.S. No. 5200, in force Sept. 30, 1962; Report of Albert B. Maris, Special Master, *United States v. Maine* 65-68 (No.35 Original, August 27, 1974) (hereinafter Master's Report); Note, Marine Archaeology and International Law: Background and Some Suggestions, 9 San Diego L.Rev. 668, 673-77 (1972) (hereinafter Note, Marine Archaeology).

[15][*Orig. fn.*] Pres. Proc. No. 2667, 10 Fed. Reg. 12303, 59 Stat. 884

[16][*Orig. fn.*] Convention on the Continental Shelf, done April 29, 1958, (1964) 15 U.S.T. 471, T.I.A.S. No. 5578, in force June 10, 1964.

resources of the seabed and subsoil, not only of its territorial sea, but also of the adjacent continental shelf beyond the territorial sea. *See* Master's Report, *supra* n.14, at 69.

During the years following the Truman proclamation, intense interest in exploiting ocean resources resulted in disputes between the United States and coastal states asserting jurisdiction over territorial waters. In *United States v. California*, 332 U.S. 19, 67 S. Ct. 1658, 91 L. Ed. 1889 (1947), and its progeny,[17] the United States was held to have rights in the offshore seabed superior to and exclusive of the states. The political reaction to these decisions led to passage of the Submerged Lands Act in May 1953 and the Outer Continental Shelf Lands Act a few months later. *See* 15 Va. J.Int'l. L. 1009, 1011 (1975). By enactment of the Submerged Lands Act, Congress recognized the coastal states' title to and ownership of the lands and natural resources beneath navigable waters within the territorial sea. *See United States v. Maine*, 420 U.S. 515, 525, 95 S. Ct. 1155, 1160, 43 L. Ed.2d 363, 370-71 (1975). In the Outer Continental Shelf Lands Act, "Congress emphatically implemented its view that the United States has paramount rights to the seabed beyond the three-mile limit." *Id.* at 526, 95 S. Ct. at 1161, 43 L. Ed.2d at 371.

The superiority of the federal claim to resources on the outer continental shelf to the claims of the states was clearly established in 1975 in *United States v. Maine, supra*. The United States asserted in its complaint in Maine only "…sovereign rights over the seabed and subsoil underlying the Atlantic Ocean, lying more than three geographic miles seaward from the coastline to the outer edge of the continental shelf for the purpose of exploring the area and exploiting its natural resources…" Master's Report, *supra* n.14, at 3. The special master found the "basic question involved" in the litigation to be "whether the right to explore and exploit the natural resources of the seabed and subsoil of that portion of the continental shelf … belongs to the United States or to the defendant States or any of them." *Id.* at 1. After Maine, the primacy of federal over state interests in the natural resources of the outer continental shelf cannot be doubted. But the decision in Maine did not address the extent of control by the United States of the shelf in all circumstances.

43 U.S.C. § 1332(a) declares the policy of the United States to be "that the subsoil and seabed of the outer Continental Shelf appertain to the United States and are subject to its jurisdiction, control, and power of disposition as provided in this subchapter." Certain language in the Conference Committee report on the bill supports the view that Congress intended to extend the jurisdiction and control of the United States to both the seabed and subsoil.[18] However, this language must be taken in the context of the bill's stated purpose "… to amend the Submerged Lands Act in order that the area in the outer Continental Shelf beyond boundaries of the States may be leased and developed by the Federal Government…"[19]

---

[17][*Orig. fn.*] *United States v. Louisiana*, 339 U.S. 699, 70 S. Ct. 914, 94 L. Ed. 1216 (1950); *United States v. Texas*, 339 U.S. 707, 70 S. Ct. 918, 94 L. Ed. 1221 (1950)

[18][*Orig. fn.*] "… the jurisdiction and control of the United States is extended to the seabed and subsoil of the entire outer Continental Shelf adjacent to the shores of the United States instead of merely to the natural resources of the subsoil and seabed as in the original House version . . . ." Conf.Rep. No. 1031, 83rd Cong., 1st Sess. (1953), reported at 2 U.S. Code Cong. & Admin. News 1953, p. 2184.

[19][*Orig. fn.*] House Report No. 413, 83rd Cong., 1st Sess. (1953), reported at 2 U.S. Code Cong. & Admin. News 1953, p. 2177.

This court held in *Guess v. Read*, 290 F.2d 622, 625 (1961), *cert. denied*, 386 U.S. 957, 82 S. Ct. 394, 7 L. Ed.2d 388 (1962), that "(t)he Continental Shelf Act was enacted for the purpose, primarily, of asserting ownership of and jurisdiction over the minerals in and under the Continental Shelf." The structure of the Act itself, which is basically a guide to the administration and leasing of offshore mineral-producing properties, reinforces this conclusion. The Act consists almost exclusively of specific measures to facilitate exploitation of natural resources on the continental shelf. In addition, 43 U.S.C. § 1332(b) provides that the Act "shall be construed in such manner that the character as high seas of the waters above the outer Continental Shelf and the right to navigation and fishing therein shall not be affected." As the court below noted, an extension of jurisdiction for purposes of controlling the exploitation of the natural resources of the continental shelf is not necessarily an extension of sovereignty.

We believe that a limited construction of the Act comports with the primary purpose of resolving competing claims to ownership of the natural resources of the offshore seabed and subsoil. So read, the Act is consistent with Article 2 of the Convention on the Continental Shelf:

1. The coastal state (nation) exercises over the continental shelf sovereign rights for the purpose of exploring it and exploiting its natural resources.[20]

The Convention on the Continental Shelf was a product of the United Nations Conference on the Law of the Sea convened at Geneva in 1958. It was the result of eight years' work by the International Law Commission. *See generally* Neblett, The 1958 Conference on the Law of the Sea: What was Accomplished, in The Law of the Sea (L. Alexander ed. 1967). The Convention on the Continental Shelf became effective as law in the United States eleven years after passage of the Outer Continental Shelf Lands Act and superseded any incompatible terminology in the domestic statute. *United States v. Ray*, 423 F.2d 16, 21 (5th Cir. 1970). *See Cook v. United States*, 288 U.S. 102, 118-19, 53 S. Ct. 305, 311, 77 L. Ed. 641, 649-50 (1932).

Interpretations of the Convention and the Act by legal scholars have, with remarkable accord, reached the same conclusion regarding the nature of control of the United States over the continental shelf.[21] The most compelling explication of the Convention regarding national control over non-resource-related material in the shelf area is contained in the comments of the International Law Commission:

It is clearly understood that the rights in question do not cover objects such as wrecked ships and their cargoes (including bullion) lying on the seabed or covered by the sand of the subsoil.[22]

---

[20][*Orig. fn.*] Natural resources are defined in Article 2 as "the mineral and other non-living resources of the seabed and subsoil together with living organisms belonging to sedentary species...."

[21][*Orig. fn.*] *See* Perry, "Sovereign Rights in Sunken Treasures," 7 *Land and Natural Resources Division Journal* 89, 111-12 (1969); H. Miller, *International Law and Marine Archaeology* 22, 25-26 (1971) (monograph by Counsel to Subcommittee on Oceans and Atmosphere, Committee on Commerce, United States Senate, published by Academy of Applied Science); Note, Marine Archaeology, 9 San Diego L.Rev. 668, 675, 686, 697 (1972).

[22][*Orig. fn.*] 11 U.S. GAOR, Supp. 9 at 42, U.N. Doc. A/3159 (1956).

This comment is consistent with the Commission's general perception of national jurisdiction over the continental shelf:

> (The Commission) was unwilling to accept the sovereignty of the coastal State over the seabed and subsoil of the continental shelf... the text as now adopted leaves no doubt that the rights conferred upon the coastal state cover all rights necessary for and connected with the exploration and exploitation of the natural resources of the continental shelf.[23]

We have demonstrated the limited scope of American control over the wreck site. We conclude that the remains of the Atocha are not situated on lands owned or controlled by the United States under the provisions of the Antiquities Act.[24]

SOVEREIGN PREROGATIVE

The United States also claims the treasure as successor to the prerogative rights of the king of England. At first glance the English prerogative would seem irrelevant to the wreck of a Spanish vessel discovered by American citizens off the coast of Florida. The government contends, however, that the English common law rule granting the Crown title to aban-

---

[23][*Orig. fn.*] *Id.* In the same vein:

> The Commission accepted the idea that the coastal State may exercise control and jurisdiction over the continental shelf, with the proviso that such control and jurisdiction shall be exercised solely for the purpose of exploiting its resources; and it rejected any claim to sovereignty or jurisdiction over the superjacent waters.

> *Id.* at 40.

[24][*Orig. fn.*] We note that even were we to find that the Antiquities Act did cover this salvage operation, its enforcement provision, 16 U.S.C. § 433, has been held unconstitutionally vague. *United States v. Diaz*, 499 F.2d 113 (9th Cir. 1974).

doned property found at sea and reduced to possession by British subjects[25] is incorporated into American law, and that Congress has specifically asserted jurisdiction over the res in this dispute.

While it may be within the constitutional power of Congress to take control of wrecked and abandoned property brought to shore by American citizens (or the proceeds derived from its sale), legislation to that effect has never been enacted. The Antiquities Act, which was intended to facilitate preservation of objects of historical importance, could hardly be read to subrogate the United States to the prerogative rights of the Crown. The Abandoned Property Act, 40 U.S.C. § 310, authorizes the administrator of General Services to protect the interests of the government in wrecked, abandoned, or derelict property "being within the jurisdiction of the United States, and which ought to come to the United States." But the Abandoned Property Act has limited application.

In *Russell v. Proceeds of Forty Bales Cotton*, 21 Fed.Cas. No. 12,154, p. 42 (S.D. Fla. 1872), the United States intervened and claimed, as its prerogative, the residue of proceeds after a salvage award from the sale of goods found derelict at sea. The government relied upon the predecessor of 40 U.S.C. § 310[26] as statutory authority for its claim. In a thorough

---

[25][*Orig. fn.*] The decision in *The Aquila*, 1 C. Rob. 36, 41-42, 165 Eng.Rep. 87, 89 (1798), is often referred to:

> It is certainly very true that property may be so acquired (by finding and possession): but the question is, to whom is it acquired? By the law of nature, to the individual finder or occupant: But in a state of civil society, although property may be acquired by occupancy, it is not necessarily acquired to the occupant himself; for the positive regulations of the State may have made alterations on the subject; and may, for reasons of public peace and policy, have appropriated it to other persons, as, for instance, to the State itself, or to its grantees.
>
> It will depend, therefore, on the law of each country to determine, whether property so acquired by occupancy, shall accrue to the individual finder, or to the sovereign and his representatives? and I consider it to be the general rule of civilized countries, that what is found derelict on the seas, is acquired beneficially for the sovereign, if no owner shall appear. Selden (De Don. Maris, lib. i, c. 24) lays it down as a right annexed to sovereignty, and acknowledged amongst all nations ancient and modern. Loccenius (Lib. i, c. 7, 10) mentions it as an incontestable right of sovereignty in the north of Europe. Valin (Lib. iv, tit. 9, art. 26) ascribes the same right to the crown of France . . .. In England this right is as firmly established as any one prerogative of the crown. . . .

[26][*Orig. fn.*] 6 Stat. 380 (1870). The statute originally authorized the Secretary of the Treasury "to make such contracts and provisions as he may deem most advantageous for the interests of the government, for the preservation, sale, or collection, of any property, or the proceeds thereof which may have been wrecked, abandoned, or become derelict, being within the jurisdiction of the United States, and which ought to come to the United States, (and any moneys, dues, and other interests, lately in the possession of or due to the so called Confederate States, or their agents, and now belonging to the United States, which are now held or retained by any person, corporation or municipality whatever, and which ought to have come into the possession and custody of, or been collected or received by, the United States.") The bracketed clause was omitted as obsolete when the statute was codified.

and scholarly opinion, the district court determined that the Act applied only to property which should belong to the United States as a result of its participation in the War between the States.[27] The judgment was affirmed on appeal without opinion, 21 Fed.Cas. p. 50. The court in *United States v. Tyndale*, 116 F. 820 (1st Cir. 1902) presented with the same question,[28] held "(t)he resolution of June 21, 1870 (16 Stat. 380), now section 3755 of the Revised Statutes, relates, apparently, to property which ought equitably to go to the United States, and not to wreckage of any kind." 116 F. at 822.

We accord great weight to the decision in Russell, especially since the court was construing legislation then only two years old. However, we believe the less narrow construction accorded the Act in Tyndale is more appropriate in light of continued, through infrequent, use of the Abandoned Property Act by the government to regulate salvage of property abandoned on its lands, *Corbino v. United States,* 488 F.2d 1008, 203 Ct. Cl. 278 (1973), or property in which it has an equitable claim to ownership, 23 Op. Atty. Gen. 76, 77 (1900) (concerning Spanish vessels lying on Cuban coast, wrecked by naval vessels of United States during Spanish-American War). In any event, the Abandoned Property Act is not a legislative enactment of the sovereign prerogative.[29] Since the United States has no claim of equitable ownership in a Spanish vessel wrecked more than a century before the American Revolution, and the wreck is not "within the jurisdiction of the United States," the Abandoned Property Act has no application to the present controversy. We have considered other statutes and regulations cited by the United States and find no support for the government's position in them.

The government insists that a legislative assertion of the sovereign prerogative is not a necessary prerequisite to the exercise of that jurisdiction by courts of the United States. A number of the royal colonies having asserted certain prerogative rights to abandoned prop-

---

[27][*Orig. fn.*] "The naval and military operations, both of the United States and the so-called Confederate States during the late war, had strewn the harbors of the entire coast with numerous wrecks, and also many portions of the country with abandoned or derelict property, that rightfully 'should come to the United States,' either from being originally the property of the United States, or the property of the public enemy, or from having been engaged in violating the blockade. The continuation of the resolution points more plainly at the fact that in the mind of the legislator the property, dues, and claims 'that ought to come to the United States' through the late war were intended, and no others." 21 Fed.Cas. at p. 43.

[28][*Orig. fn.*] The government intervened in an action by the salvors for the residue of money recovered from a body found at sea. The court had retained the money remaining after payment of a liberal salvage award in its registry for two years. The action in the district court is reported as *Gardner v. Ninety-Nine Gold Coins*, 111 F. 552 (D. Mass. 1901).

[29][*Orig. fn.*] See Perry, Sovereign Rights in Sunken Treasure, 7 Land and Natural Resources Division Journal 89, 97-104 (1969), for a description of the aforementioned cases. He also cites unpublished Treasury Department memorandum opinions, *e.g.*, Treasury File Op. No. 195, Oct. 16, 1936, construing 40 U.S.C. § 310 to give the United States no authority to claim derelict property in which the United States has no property interest. *Id.* at 102.

erty found within their jurisdiction,[30] the sovereign prerogative is said to have become a part of American maritime law and practice before the Revolution. After the Revolution, according to Kent, "if found at sea, they (wrecks) are supposed to belong now to the United States, as succeeding in this respect, to the prerogative of the English crown."[31]

In spite of the arguments advanced by Chancellor Kent, the notion of sovereign prerogative never took root in America. One early decision, *Peabody v. Proceeds of Twenty-Eight Bags of Cotton*, 19 Fed.Cas. No. 10,869, p. 39 (D. Mass. 1829), a veritable treatise on the disposition of derelict property found at sea, concluded that sovereign prerogative had become a part of American maritime law.[32] Peabody did not control the decision in *Gardner v. Ninety-Nine Gold Coins*, 111 F. 552 (D. Mass. 1901), and it was overruled in *United States v. Tyndale*, 116 F. 820, 822-23 (1st Cir. 1902). The reasoning of that court is impeccable:

> Notwithstanding these propositions, the United States rely on the very learned opinion of Judge Davis in Peabody v. Proceeds of 28 Bags of Cotton... The difficulties which we meet were not considered by Judge Davis, the whole force of whose reasoning only leads up to the proposition, which we admit, that it is within the constitutional powers of congress to take control of this fund, and of others like it. The conclusions which he draws from what was said by Mr. Dane and Chancellor Kent are hardly supported by the text of those learned writers.

* * *

> it is enough to say that, whatever was the title of the king at common law, it was based on the royal prerogative, was appurtenant to the crown, and was, for the most part, classified among the royal revenues. This is fully explained at various points by Blackstone, and by Lord Chief Justice Hale in "De Jure Maris." It is clearly summed up by Hall on the Seashore (2d ed.) 80, as follows:

> "In like manner, wreck (when no owner can be found) is part of the king's ordinary revenue, in right of his royal prerogative, and is a flower of the crown. So, also, flotsam, jetsam, and ligan are prerequisites of the crown."

---

[30][*Orig. fn.*] *See* 2 Kent, Commentaries on American Law 359-60 (5th ed. 1844). Cf. *Thompson v. The Catharina*, 23 Fed.Cas. No. 13,949, pp. 1028, 1030 (D. Pa. 1795) ["(T)he change in the form of our government has not abrogated all the laws, customs and principles of jurisprudence, we inherited from our ancestors, and possessed at the period of our becoming an independent nation."]

[31][*Orig. fn.*] 2 Kent at 359.

[32][*Orig. fn.*] However, the court was reluctant to adopt the strict English practice of vesting property absolutely in the sovereign if unclaimed within a year and a day from the decree of salvage. He preferred "to consider the sovereign authority as holding such property in trust, to be surrendered to reasonable claims which may be presented." 19 Fed.Cas. at p. 48.

All of these could be granted by the king without authority of parliament. A singular instance of this is given by Dane (volume 3, 137) in reference to the grant of the province of Maine from the King to Sir Ferdinando Gorges. While there can be no question that the sovereign peoples in Anglo-Saxon America, whether the various states or the United States, did, in some way, succeed to all the rights of the English king and of the English people, yet, until some recognized line of procedure or some action of congress intervenes, it is not within the province of the courts to determine that the treasury of the United States represents any particular royal prerogative.

Other American cases are in accord with *Tyndale*. *See Russell v. Proceeds of Forty Bales Cotton*, 21 Fed.Cas. No. 12,154, pp. 42, 45-50 (S.D. Fla. 1872), *aff'd*, 21 Fed.Cas. p. 50; *In re Moneys in Registry*, 170 F. 470, 475 (E.D. Pa. 1909); *Thompson v. United States*, 62 Ct. Cl. 516, 524 (1926). Although at least one state court has invoked English common law to award ownership of a sunken vessel to the sovereign,[33] the "American rule" vesting title in the finder has been widely recognized by courts and writers. *See* Kenny and Hrussoff, The Ownership of the Treasures of the Sea, 9 Wm. & Mary L.Rev. 383, 392-98 (1967).[34] *See also* H. Miller, *International Law and Marine Archaeology* 18 (1971). We accept the "American rule" as it has been uniformly pronounced in the courts of this nation for over a century.[35]

Finally, the United States asserts a generalized power to control the activities of its citizens and corporations beyond the limits of territorial jurisdiction. While this power no doubt exists,[36] we can find no authority in law or in reason to countenance interference with plaintiffs' activities simply because they are American citizens, or because they chose to incorporate in Florida rather than in some other country.

The judgment is modified and as modified is AFFIRMED.

---

[33][*Orig. fn.*] *Ervin v. Massachusetts Co.*, 95 So.2d 902 (Fla. 1956), *cert. denied*, 355 U.S. 881, 78 S. Ct. 147, 2 L. Ed.2d 112 (1957).

[34][*Orig. fn.*] " . . . (I)t is somewhat difficult to assess the place of *State ex rel. Ervin v. Massachusetts Co.* in American law. In any event, in the federal courts it remains the settled rule that, after the original owner, the finder's claim is preferred to the sovereign's." *Id.* at 398.

[35][*Orig. fn.*] Eleazer, supra n. 10, at 34, reaches the following conclusion concerning the applicable rules: The nations of the world fall into two groups, generally speaking, as regards the ownership of recovered treasure. For the sake of clarity, the first group will be said to adhere to the English Rule recovered treasure belongs to the sovereign. The second group adheres to the American Rule recovered treasure belongs to the finder. The crucial characteristic to note is that the title to recovered treasure vests in either the sovereign or the finder.

[36][*Orig. fn.*] We are cited to the controls over American fishermen on the high seas, including the North Pacific Fisheries Act, 16 U.S.C. § 1021 *et seq.*, the Northwest Atlantic Fisheries Act, 16 U.S.C. § 981 *et seq.*, and the Tuna Conventions Act, 16 U.S.C. § 951 *et seq.*

KLEIN v. UNIDENTIFIED, WRECKED AND ABANDONED SAILING VESSEL

758 F.2d 1511 (11th Cir. 1985)

HANCOCK, District Judge:

While sport diving in the Biscayne National Park in 1978, Gerald Klein spotted a likely target for his spear. As he pursued his prey, it darted behind an object. One can only imagine his surprise when he discovered that the object in question was a cannon affixed to the remains of an 18th century English vessel. Equally surprising must have been the array of cutlasses, onion bottles[1] and other objects lying about in the area. In October of 1979, Mr. Klein brought the articles he removed from the wreck to the attention and custody of the district court. Klein thus began an action to declare himself rightful owner of the shipwreck, or alternatively to recover a salvage award for his efforts in removing the articles from the shipwreck. Following a bench trial, the district court, Judge C. Clyde Atkins presiding, found that plaintiff[2] was not entitled to either ownership of the shipwreck or to a salvage award. We affirm.

The factual background is summarized in the following findings of fact made by Judge Atkins:

1. Gerald Klein found the defendant wreck in the summer of 1978 while sport diving with some friends.

2. Gerald Klein first brought artifacts removed from the wreck to the attention and custody of this Court on October 4, 1979.

3. The remains of the vessel claimed by the plaintiff in this action lie entirely within the confines of Biscayne National Park and entirely within the submerged lands of the territorial sea of the United States.

4. The remains of the vessel claimed by plaintiff lie entirely in lands owned and administered by the United States as part of the National Park system.

5. All of the artifacts removed from the remains of the vessel claimed by plaintiff, which are listed on an inventory of custodianship dated October 26, 1979, were removed from within the confines of Biscayne National Park and were found by Gerald Klein within the territorial sea of the United States.

6. The United States owns in fee simple the land in which the remains of the vessel claimed by plaintiff lie.

7. The United States has known of the existence and approximate location of the subject 18th century shipwreck located within Legare Achorage in the Biscayne National Park since at least 1975 and probably as early as 1970.

---

[1][*Orig. fn.*] Onion bottles are bottles peculiarly designed for use on board ships. The bottles are wide at the bottom with a narrow neck in order to avoid spilling.

[2][*Orig. fn.*] Gerald Klein was originally the party plaintiff. Upon his death during the pendency of the action, Joan Klein, his widow and the personal representative of his estate, was substituted.

8. Although the government was aware of the existence of the defendant wreck and had documented its approximate location as early as February, 1975, it did not physically locate the wreck until July 4, 1980.

9. The remains of the vessel claimed by plaintiff are objects of antiquity being over 200 years old.

10. The remains of the vessel claimed by plaintiff are historic ruins revealing the remains of past human life and activities which are of archeological interest.

11. Before the filing of this action the United States did not know that Gerald Klein had removed artifacts from the wreck.

12. It is in the public interest that if artifacts are to be removed from the wreck the removal be conducted with scrupulous care.

13. The historic value of each artifact is enhanced by careful monitoring of archeological provenience, the exact location at which each item is found in terms of horizontal and vertical coordinates, the extent of burial, water depth and its spatial relationship to other items found.

14. Archeological provenience is not only important for the historical information that it provides, but it also adds to the value of the artifacts for donation or sale to interested buyers.

15. Gerald Klein neither applied for nor received a permit from the federal government or the State of Florida to excavate or remove artifacts or objects from the defendant wreck.

16. Before the filing of this action Gerald Klein did not notify the United States that he had removed artifacts from the wrecksite nor did he return those artifacts to the United States or its agents.

17. The United States had never initiated salvage activities on the defendant vessel before the initiation of this action.

18. The United States removed artifacts from the wreck after it was appointed custodian.

19. The State of Florida has voluntarily withdrawn from this action and has no right or title in the submerged lands in which the defendant wreck lies.

20. The artifacts removed from the wreck site by the United States are presently stored at the Southeast Archeological Survey Offices in Tallahassee, Florida.

Two issues are presented on this appeal. First, we review the district court's determination that the United States is the owner of the shipwreck. Second, we review the district court's determination that appellant is not entitled to a salvage award for the work done in removing articles from the shipwreck.

1.   OWNERSHIP OF THE VESSEL.

Appellant argues that the subject shipwreck is rightfully hers under the maritime law which holds that one who discovers an abandoned wreck and reduces it to possession is entitled to it. The district court rejected the applicability of maritime law and applied the common law of finds, ruling that the United States was the owner of the shipwreck based on either of two exceptions to the law of finds. Appellant further argues that even if the law of finds applies, the district court incorrectly applied it. We disagree.

The Fifth Circuit was faced with a question of ownership similar to that presented by the case at bar in *Treasure Salvors, Inc. v. Unidentified, Wrecked and Abandoned Sailing Ves-*

sel, 569 F.2d 330 (5th Cir. 1978).[3] In order to determine the ownership of a shipwreck on the outer continental shelf—outside the territorial waters of the United States—the Fifth Circuit relied on the law of finds instead of the maritime salvage law. The court reasoned that because application of maritime salvage law was predicated on the fiction that the owner of the wrecked vessel was still in existence, it would be absurd to apply maritime salvage law to a vessel whose very location has been lost for centuries. *Id.* at 337. Instead, the court held that title to abandoned property vests in the person who reduces that property to his or her possession. *Id. See also Treasure Salvors, Inc. v. Unidentified, Wrecked and Abandoned Sailing Vessel*, 640 F.2d 560 (5th Cir. 1981); *Wiggins v. 1100 Tons, More or Less, of Italian Marble*, 186 F. Supp. 452, 456-57 (E.D. Va. 1960). The common law of finds is the appropriate law to examine to determine the ownership of the shipwreck.

The common law of finds generally assigns ownership of the abandoned property without regard to where the property is found. Two exceptions to that rule are recognized: First, when the abandoned property is embedded in the soil, it belongs to the owner of the soil; Second, when the owner of the land where the property is found (whether on or embedded in the soil) has constructive possession of the property such that the property is not "lost," it belongs to the owner of the land. *See Bishop v. Ellsworth*, 91 Ill. App. 2d 386, 234 N.E.2d 49 (1968); *Allred v. Biegel*, 240 Mo. App. 818, 219 S.W.2d 665 (1949); *Flax v. Monticello Realty Co.*, 185 Va. 474, 39 S.E.2d 308 (1946); *Schley v. Couch*, 155 Tex. 195, 284 S.W.2d 333 (1955). *See also Elwes v. Briggs Gas Company*, 33 Ch. 562. Both exceptions operate to give the United States ownership in this case.

The ship is buried in the soil. The soil belongs to the United States as part of its National Park system. In 1973, the land was transferred to the United States by the State of Florida for the purpose of allowing the United States to establish a National Park area partially because of the historical value of the many shipwreck sites to be found in the area. When the United States acquired title to the land from Florida in 1973, it also acquired title to the shipwrecks embedded in that soil.

Since 1975 the United States has had constructive possession of the wreck by virtue of a Preliminary Archeological Assessment of Biscayne National Monument prepared for the Park Service. This assessment noted the presence of an 18th century shipwreck in the area of the wreck. Furthermore, the United States has had the power[4] and the intention[5] to exercise dominion and control over the subject shipwreck. Thus the United States has never

---

[3][*Orig. fn.*] The Eleventh Circuit, in the en banc decision *Bonner v. City of Pritchard*, 661 F.2d 1206, 1209 (11th Cir. 1981), adopted as precedent decisions of the former Fifth Circuit rendered prior to October 1, 1981.

[4][*Orig. fn.*] The Eleventh Circuit, in the en banc decision *Bonner v. City of Pritchard*, 661 F.2d 1206, 1209 (11th Cir.1981), adopted as precedent decisions of the former Fifth Circuit rendered prior to October 1, 1981.

[5][*Orig. fn.*] One stated purpose of the National Park Act is the conservation of historic objects for the enjoyment of future generations. A vast matrix of statutes and regulations have been established toward that goal. *See e.g., the Antiquities Act of 1906*, 16 U.S.C. § 431; The National Park Service Act, 16 U.S.C. § 1; Archeological Resources Protection Act of 1979, 16 U.S.C. § 470aa; 36 C.F.R. §§ 1.11(a), 2.20(a)(1).

legally lost the subject shipwreck and, as the owner of the land on and/or in which the shipwreck is located, it owns the shipwreck.

Congress has broad powers over all public lands pursuant to the Property Clause of the United States Constitution. *See Kleppe v. New Mexico*, 426 U.S. 529, 96 S. Ct. 2285, 49 L. Ed.2d 34 (1976).

2. SALVAGE AWARD.

Failing in her efforts to acquire title to the shipwreck, appellant urges that she should be given a salvage award for the cost of recovering the articles from the wreck. A claim for a salvage award requires that three elements be shown:

(1) A maritime peril from which the ship or other property could not have been rescued without the salvor's assistance.

(2) A voluntary act by the salvor—that is, he must be under no official or legal duty to render the assistance.

(3) Success in saving, or in helping to save at least part of the property at risk.

G. Gilmore & C. Black, Jr., The Law of Admiralty 534-35 (1975); *See also Cobb Coin Co. v. Unidentified Wrecked and Abandoned Sailing Vessel*, 549 F. Supp. 540, 547 (S.D. Fla. 1982).

Plaintiff's salvage efforts were directed toward a vessel that was not lost or suffering any marine peril. Indeed, the owner of the property may not even have desired for the property to be "rescued." When and if the United States determined it to be in the best interest of the administration of Biscayne National Park to remove the shipwreck, it was certainly capable of "rescuing" the property at that time without plaintiff's assistance. Furthermore, plaintiff's salvage efforts were not successful. The articles removed from the shipwreck site were not marked or identified so as to preserve their archeological provenience. As the district court points out "the plaintiff's unauthorized disturbance of one of the oldest shipwrecks in the Park and his unscientific removal of the artifacts did more to create a marine peril than to prevent one." The lower court correctly denied plaintiff's prayer for a salvage award. A contrary result would encourage persons to enter Biscayne National Park and to continue the unauthorized removal of articles from the various shipwrecks there located which were sought to be protected by the creation of that park.

Because we can find no error whatsoever in the conclusions or analysis of the district court, we affirm.

KRAVITCH, Circuit Judge, specially concurring in part and dissenting in part:

I agree with the majority's conclusion that the United States is the rightful owner of the shipwreck. In my view, however, such a conclusion is compelled not by the "embedded in the soil" and "constructive possession" exceptions to the common law of finds, which are of dubious relevance in the context of a sunken ship,[6] but rather by the Antiquities Act of 1906, 16 U.S.C. § 433. The Antiquities Act provides:

> Any person who shall appropriate, excavate, injure, or destroy any historic or prehistoric ruin or monument, or any object of antiquity, situate on lands owned or controlled by the Government of the United States, without the permission of the Secretary of the Department of the Government having jurisdiction over the lands on which said antiquities are situated, shall upon conviction, be fined in a sum of not more than $500 or be imprisoned for a period of not more than ninety days, or shall suffer both fine and imprisonment, in the discretion of the court.
>
> *Id.*

In the instant case, the shipwreck was found on submerged lands belonging in fee simple to the United States, and the vessel undoubtedly is an "antiquity."[7] Therefore, the Antiquities Act's prohibition of "[appropriat[ion]]" and "[excavat[ion]]" supersedes the principles of maritime law on which plaintiff relies, and defeats plaintiff's claim of ownership of the vessel.

At the same time, I respectfully dissent from that portion of the majority opinion holding that plaintiff is not entitled to a salvage award. The majority accepts the government's argument that the vessel "was not lost or suffering any marine peril." Yet it is undisputed that the government's 1975 survey of shipwrecks located in the Biscayne National Park misidentified the vessel in question and listed only its "approximate" location. In fact, the government was unable precisely to locate the vessel until July 4, 1980, some two years after plaintiff discovered it and a full nine months after plaintiff's discovery came to the government's attention.[8]

---

[6][*Orig. fn.*] In fact, both in its brief and at oral argument, the government eschewed reliance on these land-based exceptions to the common law of finds. The government argued instead that the district court's conclusion, that the shipwreck belongs to the United States, should be affirmed on the basis of various federal statutes.

[7][*Orig. fn.*] The vessel is believed to be more than 240 years old. *United States v. Diaz*, 499 F.2d 113 (9th Cir. 1974), in which the Ninth Circuit found the penal provisions of the Antiquities Act unconstitutionally vague, is thus distinguishable. In *Diaz*, the "antiquities" in question were only three or four years old. The instant case is much more similar to *United States v. Smyer*, 596 F.2d 939 (10th Cir.), *cert. denied*, 444 U.S. 843, 100 S. Ct. 84, 62 L. Ed.2d 55 (1979), in which the Tenth Circuit rejected a constitutional challenge to the Antiquities Act as applied to objects between 800 and 900 years old.

[8][*Orig. fn.*] The vessel is believed to be more than 240 years old. *United States v. Diaz*, 499 F.2d 113 (9th Cir. 1974), in which the Ninth Circuit found the penal provisions of the Antiquities Act unconstitutionally vague, is thus distinguishable. In Diaz, the "antiquities" in question were only three or four years old. The instant case is much more similar to United States v. Smyer, 596 F.2d 939 (10th Cir.), cert. denied, 444 U.S. 843, 100 S. Ct. 84, 62 L. Ed.2d 55 (1979), in which the Tenth Circuit rejected a constitutional challenge to the Antiquities Act as applied to objects between 800 and 900 years old.

The record shows that, in early 1980, the government even went to court in an attempt to force plaintiff to divulge the exact location of the shipwreck. I find it hard to believe that the vessel was not "lost," when the government obviously had such difficulty finding it.

As to the existence of a "marine peril," in my view the majority opinion conflicts with *Treasure Salvors, Inc. v. Wrecked and Abandoned Sailing Vessel*, 569 F.2d 330 (5th Cir. 1978), *aff'd in part and rev'd in part*, on other grounds, *sub nom. Florida Department of State v. Treasure Salvors, Inc.*, 458 U.S. 670, 102 S. Ct. 3304, 73 L. Ed.2d 1057 (1982), in which this court's predecessor explained:

> The government's argument that no marine peril existed ignores the reality of the situation.

> Marine peril includes more than the threat of storm, fire, or piracy to a vessel in navigation... There is no dispute that the [shipwreck] was lost. Even after discovery of the vessel's location it is still in peril of being lost through the actions of the elements.
> *Id.* at 337 (emphasis added; footnotes and citations omitted).

The *Treasure Salvors* rule applies even when the sunken vessel is "impervious to weather conditions above the surface of the sea," with "sand prevent[ing] deterioration underwater." *See Platoro Limited, Inc. v. Unidentified Remains of a Vessel*, 614 F.2d 1051, 1055 & n. 8 (5th Cir. 1980); *see also Cobb Coin Co., Inc. v. Unidentified, Wrecked and Abandoned Sailing Vessel*, 549 F. Supp. 540, 557 (S.D. Fla. 1982) ("It is established in this Circuit that a marine peril exists in an ancient, abandoned shipwreck for purposes of meeting the requirements of a valid salvage action.").[9]

Finally, I disagree with the majority's conclusion that plaintiff is not entitled to a salvage award because plaintiff's salvage efforts were "unsuccessful." Plaintiff performed a highly valuable service simply by locating the shipwreck, and should be compensated accordingly. The fact that plaintiff failed to employ proper archeological techniques in removing artifacts from the shipwreck may reduce the amount of any salvage award, but should not altogether deprive plaintiff of such an award. I therefore would remand this case to the district court for the purpose of calculating a salvage award based on the value of plaintiff's services in locating the vessel, reduced by any damage caused by plaintiff's unauthorized removal of artifacts from the vessel.

---

[9][*Orig. fn.*] The Fifth Circuit recently has interpreted Treasure Salvors as holding that "marine peril existed as a matter of law where the ship's location was unknown." Platoro Limited, Inc. v. Unidentified Remains of a Vessel, 695 F.2d 893, 901 (5th Cir.) (emphasis added), cert. denied, ___ U.S. ___, 104 S. Ct. 77, 78 L. Ed.2d 89 (1983). The Fifth Circuit also rejected the government's argument that, for a salvage award to be justified, a vessel must still be in peril after its location is discovered. See *id.* at 901 n. 9. While this Fifth Circuit decision is not binding on our court, I find it persuasive, especially since it, like the instant case, involves the interpretation of former Fifth Circuit precedent.

3.   The Law of Salvage

As an alternative to seeking title to shipwrecks, treasure salvors often assert that they should be given liberal salvage awards for rescuing ships and their cargo from "marine peril" and returning them back to the stream of commerce. The purpose behind the maritime law of salvage traditionally has been to encourage efforts to save property from destruction by providing the rescuer a right to compensation from the owner. The law of salvage is also intended to provide an incentive system under admiralty law that discourages embezzlement by salvors.

Under the law of salvage, the property at issue is not abandoned. Rather, the owner of the property retains title to the goods "saved from peril" by a salvor, and the salvor is entitled to a reward for "rescuing" the property. In conferring a salvage award, the court may issue an award which may include all or a portion of the goods recovered.

Salvors must prove that they have met the following elements to establish a successful claim under the law of salvage:

1.   the property is in marine peril, placing it at risk of loss, destruction or deterioration;

2.   salvage services must be rendered *voluntarily* and not be required by contract or duty; and

3.   the salvage efforts must be successful in either whole or part.

[*The Blackwell,* 77 U.S. (10 Wall.) 1 (1869); and *The Sabine,* 101 U.S. 384 (1879).] It should be noted that, although the law of salvage permits salvage without the consent of the owner, the owner of the shipwreck can *refuse* salvage. [See T.J. Schoenbaum, *Admiralty and Maritime Law* 504 (West, 1987).]

Further, salvors, in order to obtain exclusive possession and protection from rival salvors, must exercise due diligence over the wreck site. In other words, "[o]ne who discovers but does not assiduously undertake to rescue abandoned property may lose his right to uninterrupted salvage operations. Notorious possession is a prerequisite to the creation and maintenance of a salvor's privilege." [*MDM Salvage,* 631 F. Supp. at 312 (citing *Cobb Coin v. Unidentified, Wrecked, and Abandoned Sailing Vessel,* 525 F. Supp. 186, 204–205 (S.D. Fla. 1981))]. In this regard, "the law of finds and salvage merge to give the first finder/salvor sole possession of the property." [*MDM Salvage,* 631 F. Supp. at 311–12 (citations omitted).]

Some admiralty courts have also imposed an "archaeological duty of care" on salvors recovering property from historic shipwrecks. This duty of care is imposed under both the maritime law of salvage and the common law of finds. [See *Marex International, Inc. v. The Unidentified, Wrecked and Aban-*

doned Vessel, 952 F. Supp. 825, 829 (S.D. Ga. 1997).] Specifically, it "requires that the finder or salvor document to the court's satisfaction the shipwreck's archaeological 'provenance data.' Documentation of 'provenance data' is accomplished by mapping or recording the location, depth and proximity of each artifact recovered in relation to the other artifacts." [*Marex,* 952 F. Supp. at 829.] (footnote omitted). [See also *Cobb Coin Company, Inc. v. The Unidentified, Wrecked and Abandoned Sailing Vessel,* 525 F. Supp. 186 (S.D. Fla. 1981).]

Salvors who are successful in establishing a claim under the law of salvage are entitled to an award. The amount of the award has traditionally been determined by applying the six different factors set forth in the matter of *The Blackwell,* 77 U.S. (10 Wall) 1, 13–14 (1869), as follows:

1. The labor expended by the salvors in rendering the salvage service;

2. The promptitude, skill and energy displayed in rescuing the property;

3. The value of the property employed by the salvors in rendering the service, and the danger to which such property was exposed;

4. The risk incurred by the salvors in securing the property from impending peril;

5. The value of the property salvaged; and

6. The degree of danger from which the property was rescued.

[*Columbus-America Discovery Group v. Atlantic Mutual Insurance Company,* 56 F.3d 556, 569 fn 17 (4th Cir. 1995) (citing *The Blackwall,* 77 U.S. (10 Wall) at 13–14).] In addition to the six factors listed above, the Fourth Circuit, in the *Columbus-America Discovery Group* case, recognized two more factors: (1) the salvor's preservation of the historical and archaeological value of the wreck and cargo; and (2) other considerations, (which, in the *Columbus-America Discovery Group* case, included consideration of the high-risk nature of the investment to engage in the salvage of the *Central America* shipwreck in order "to provide an inducement for potential salvors [in the future] to seek and recover property lost at sea." [*Columbus-America Discovery Group,* 56 F.3d at 573–74.]

COLUMBUS-AMERICA DISCOVERY GROUP v. ATLANTIC MUTUAL INSURANCE CO.

56 F.3d 556 (4th Cir. 1995)

K.K. HALL, Circuit Judge:

INTRODUCTION

In September 1988, a long and difficult search ended for Columbus-America Discovery Group soon after the crew aboard the recovery vessel ARCTIC DISCOVERER had lowered NEMO, Columbus-America's aptly named undersea robot, almost one and one-half miles into the depths of the Atlantic Ocean. As NEMO's camera scanned wood, coal, and other debris along the ocean floor, it suddenly revealed the distinctive sidewheels of the S.S. CENTRAL AMERICA, a nineteenth-century passenger ship. A mighty hurricane had sunk the CENTRAL AMERICA about 160 miles east of Charleston, South Carolina, on September 12, 1857, nearly four years before the first shots were fired on Fort Sumter. The doomed ship had taken with her more than 400 lives and over $1 million worth of California gold—an astounding sum in those days.

Columbus-America commenced an in rem proceeding in the district court to establish its rights regarding the CENTRAL AMERICA, and, in 1989, moved the court to declare that it owned the gold and other artifacts aboard the ship. British and American insurers and their successors-in-interest opposed the motion, each asserting that it had underwritten the risk of loss of a portion of the gold and had paid claims filed in the aftermath of the disaster.[1] The district court scheduled a trial of the matter to begin on April 3, 1990.

On the very eve of trial, the district court permitted Columbia University, Jack F. Grimm, and Harry G. John to intervene as of right.[2] In 1983-84, these three had cooperated in an effort to locate the CENTRAL AMERICA. During the search, sonar aboard the research vessel CONRAD imaged a target very near to where Columbus-America ultimately found the CENTRAL AMERICA. The intervenors asserted a proprietary interest in the information generated as a result of the CONRAD expedition, and they alleged that Columbus-America improperly obtained and relied on that information to make its discovery.

At the trial's conclusion, the district court ruled that the underwriters had abandoned any interest in the gold, and Columbus-America was therefore entitled to keep it all. The court also found that there was no evidence to support the intervenors' claim. The underwriters and the intervenors appealed, and a divided panel of this court held that the district court erred in applying the law of finds, rather than the law of salvage, to determine the parties' respective rights in the gold. *Columbus-America Discovery Group v. Atlantic Mut. Ins. Co.*, 974 F.2d 450, 468 (4th Cir. 1992), *cert. denied*, 507 U.S. 1000, 113 S. Ct. 1625, 123 L. Ed.2d 183 (1993) (*CADG I*).[3] We held further that the court had abused its discretion by refusing the intervenors an opportunity for discovery prior to trial. *Id.* at 470. We remanded the case to the district court to apply the law of salvage and determine an appropriate award for Columbus-America. We also instructed the court to conduct a new trial on the intervenors' misappropriation claim, after allowing them a reasonable time for discovery.

On remand, the district court determined that Columbus-America was entitled to a salvage award of ninety percent. By separate order, the district court denied the underwriters' request to divide the gold in specie so that each party could market its own share; the court instead assigned to Columbus-America the task of selling all of the gold, with the proceeds

---

[1][*Orig. fn.*] We will refer to the claimant insurers and their successors collectively as the "underwriters."

[2][*Orig. fn.*] *See Fed.R.Civ.P.* 24(a).

[3][*Orig. fn.*] The circumstances surrounding the last voyage of the CENTRAL AMERICA, along with extensive background information concerning the parties to this litigation, are detailed in *CADG I*, 974 F.2d at 454-59, and are not, except where necessary, repeated here.

to be thereafter divided among it and the underwriters. The district court, apparently uncertain of the scope of our remand, declined to make specific findings as to whether any or all of the underwriters had sufficiently proved what, if any, portion of the gold aboard the CENTRAL AMERICA each had paid claims on and thereby owned as subrogees. As for the intervenors'[4] claim, the district court again held the proof insufficient to establish that Columbus-America had availed itself of any of the data gathered during the CONRAD expedition. The underwriters and the intervenors again appeal (Nos. 94-1105 and 94-1200).

In light of the district court's decision to defer, pending this appeal, an examination of the validity of each underwriter's ownership claim, Columbus-America cross-appeals (No. 94-1106), urging us to direct the court to put the underwriters to their proof. Because various matters respecting the continuing rights and responsibilities of the parties remain to be decided in the district court, jurisdiction over these appeals lies in this court under 28 U.S.C. § 1292(a)(3).[5]

We now affirm the district court's judgment in nearly all respects. We hold that sufficient evidence supports the court's finding that Columbus-America did not misappropriate the CONRAD data. We also agree with the district court that, in return for recovering the gold aboard the CENTRAL AMERICA, Columbus-America deserves a ninety percent salvage award. We hold further that the court correctly decided that the gold should be marketed as a whole, with Columbus-America designated as the marketing authority. However, that Columbus-America is entitled to a ninety percent salvage award does not automatically mean that the underwriters may, merely by virtue of bringing suit, walk out the courthouse door with the remaining ten percent. We therefore instruct the district court, on remand, to consider the evidence and decide whether each underwriter actually owns the portion of the gold that it claims.

II.   THE INTERVENORS' CLAIM

A.   A Tripartite Alliance

On September 16, 1983, Thomas G. Thompson of Columbus, Ohio, flew to Milwaukee at the behest of Harry G. John to discuss locating and salvaging the CENTRAL AMERICA.

---

[4][*Orig. fn.*] Only Grimm and Joanne Lampe Charlton, representing John's estate, remain as intervenors. Columbia settled with Columbus-America on June 29, 1993—the day retrial began.

[5][*Orig. fn.*] Section 1292(a)(3) confers jurisdiction on the courts of appeals over "[i]nterlocutory decrees of ... district courts or the judges thereof determining the rights and liabilities of the parties to admiralty cases in which appeals from final decrees are allowed." Decrees that "determin[e] the rights and liabilities of the parties" are those that determine substantive rights and liabilities, and not those that merely resolve procedural, tactical, or adjectival matters. *E.g., Martha's Vineyard Scuba HQ, Inc. v. Unidentified, Wrecked and Abandoned Steam Vessel*, 833 F.2d 1059, 1063 (1st Cir.1987); *Miskiewicz v. Goodman*, 341 F.2d 828, 830-31 (4th Cir.1965); *see also 9 James W. Moore et al., Moore's Federal Practice* ¶ 110.19[3] (2d ed.1995). The orders on appeal before us amply qualify.

Thompson, a research scientist and engineer for the Battelle Memorial Institute's laboratories in Columbus, became interested in the CENTRAL AMERICA in the 1970s. John knew of Thompson's interest and that Thompson had researched the shipwreck's potential location. Thompson, for his part, wanted to organize a search for the CENTRAL AMERICA and knew that John had money to invest.

As a result of their meeting, John, on behalf of his company, Santa Fe Communications, Inc., commissioned Thompson to conduct further research on the CENTRAL AMERICA and submit the names of persons who might be equipped to look for it. In late 1983, John and Thompson flew to Seattle to meet with Michael Williamson, an expert in sonar surveys whose skills Thompson hoped to employ in the search. Together, the three traveled to International Submarine Technology in nearby Redmond to inspect its manufacturing facilities and discuss the technical aspects of a new generation of side-looking sonars, known as the SeaMARCs,[6] that IST had developed.

Thompson had provided John with alternative contacts, including Columbia University's Lamont-Doherty Geological Observatory, home to one of the three largest institutions for oceanographics in the United States. In 1980, Lamont-Doherty, in collaboration with IST, built the first SeaMARC. The SeaMARC I allowed Columbia's oceanographers to obtain high resolution sonar imaging of the ocean floor and objects on it in a swath some ten times wider than the preexisting technology had permitted. Lamont-Doherty frequently accepted research grants to map areas of the ocean floor, but the demand for SeaMARC I's services meant that prospective clients were ordinarily forced to endure at least a two-year wait.

The wait was two years, that is, unless the client was Texas oilman Jack F. Grimm. In 1980, Grimm, who was then searching for the TITANIC, had given Lamont-Doherty approximately one-third of a million dollars to purchase the SeaMARC I and other equipment; in return, Grimm received the right to use the sonar for five years. John learned of this arrangement and contacted Grimm, who consented to help John negotiate with Columbia's trustees for a better place in line. These negotiations were a success; John, on behalf of Santa Fe, agreed to fund a $300,000 grant to have Lamont-Doherty survey 400 square miles of ocean floor with the SeaMARC I aboard the research vessel ROBERT D. CONRAD.

B.   Ryan's search

The CONRAD expedition, under the direction of Dr. William Ryan, a Senior Research Scientist at Lamont-Doherty, set out from Norfolk, Virginia, on February 26, 1984, and docked in Bermuda two weeks later. During the trip, the SeaMARC I imaged seven targets on the ocean floor within the survey area. Ryan interpreted the data gathered by the SeaMARC, and, by letter dated April 27, 1984, informed John of the results. Ryan concluded that, of the seven targets, "[o]nly one, target # 4, is a candidate feature that correlates with the expected distribution of wreckage of the S.S. CENTRAL AMERICA... Target # 4 at 2180 m (7200 feet) water depth is 250 to 300 feet long and of very high reflectivity." Ryan noted that the size estimate was consistent with the CENTRAL AMERICA's 280-foot length. He wrote:

---

[6][*Orig. fn.*] SeaMARC is an acronym for "Sea Mapping and Remote Characterization."

[T]his target is almost certainly the scattered debris of a shipwreck... I would speculate that the cluster of debris upwind from target # 4 could be the materials cut loose
from the decks, spars, etc. of the S.S. CENTRAL AMERICA in the attempt to try to
fuel the boilers... In my opinion, you and Mr. Jack Grimm have a likely candidate for
further exploration. As you know, we were unable to undertake any photography...
after completing the sonar operations due to gale force winds and seas. Target # 4 is
sufficiently well located (to plus or minus one nautical mile) to make it sensible and
cost-effective to next use... submersibles for the subsequent stage of target development.

The "subsequent stage" was never reached. A scant eight months later, Santa Fe deeded
"all its right, title, and interest to any and all claims arising out of its interests in undersea
salvage operations, including... its partnership interest in Central America Limited Partnership and... research performed by Columbia University incident thereto" to Catholic monks
of the Capuchin Order at St. Benedict Friary in Milwaukee.[7]

C. The Columbus-America Effort

Meanwhile, Thompson's interest in the CENTRAL AMERICA had not diminished, though
he and John had parted ways soon after their 1983 encounter. Thompson continued to research historical accounts of the disaster, but also began to compile information from more
contemporary sources. He gave particular attention to how hurricanes affected navigational
accuracy at sea, as well as the effect of such storms on drift variables, such as prevailing
currents and wind direction, that might determine the path of a swamped vessel whose crew
was far less concerned about steering than just staying afloat.

Thompson was still determined to mount his own search for the shipwreck, and, when
his proposal to John for financing fell through, he solicited venture capital from private
investors who lived, for the most part, in and around Columbus. In May 1985, Thompson
and some of his investors formed Recovery Limited Partnership, with Thompson as the
general partner. RLP's assets derived solely from its ongoing sale of interests in the partnership; these funds were used to finance Thompson's company, Columbus-America Discovery Group, Inc., in its continuing efforts to locate and salvage the CENTRAL AMERICA.

Thompson was aware that John had contracted with Lamont-Doherty to conduct a survey in early 1984. He also knew, just one day after the CONRAD's arrival in Bermuda, that

---

[7][*Orig. fn.*] The Capuchins never realized any benefit from the gift until they gave it back to
John in exchange for ten dollars on March 22, 1990, less than two weeks prior to the first
trial in the district court. As we noted in *CADG I*, "John did nothing to enlighten [the
Capuchins] on the discovery of the ship or the upcoming trial.... [T]he monks must have
protested, for on April 10 both John and Grimm signed an agreement with the Capuchins
giving the Order one-third of any judgment they... would recover." 974 F.2d at 459.

the survey had failed to positively identify the CENTRAL AMERICA.[8] Thompson contacted Ryan at Lamont-Doherty soon thereafter to discuss sonar in general and the SeaMARC in particular, and how the data from the SeaMARC was analyzed to enable the user to recognize and define anomalies, or targets, on the ocean floor. Between 1984 and 1986, Thompson and Ryan had numerous conversations concerning various sonar searches that Lamont-Doherty had conducted using the SeaMARC I, culminating in Thompson's February 12, 1986, request for copies of the sonar record and contour map data from the 1984 CONRAD survey.

Ryan passed on Thompson's request to his Division Administrator, who, on March 19, 1986, wrote a letter to Thompson at Battelle granting the request on the condition that the data would be for Thompson's sole use and not reproduced for others, because "the data... is not in the public domain." The letter also stated that Columbia would not relinquish its exclusive right to publish the data until its graduate students who were working with the data had published their dissertations. Thompson agreed to Columbia's terms and received the data, which, in addition to the sonar photographs and the contour chart, included the CONRAD's ship track lines, indicating the vessel's path within the survey boundaries.[9]

Columbus-America hired Williamson's company to perform a survey, using the SeaMARC IA, during June and July 1986. Thompson and the other project directors worked with Dr. Lawrence D. Stone, a search theorist, to create a "probability map" from which an efficient search plan could be devised. The map divided almost 1500 square miles of ocean into two-mile by two-mile cells and assigned each cell a probability. The numbers in the cells reflected a mosaic of sorts—an amalgam derived from the three major eyewitness accounts of the disaster, with each scenario accorded a greater or lesser weight depending on a subjective determination of its likely accuracy. The calculations were then refined by introducing the drift variables that Thompson had earlier researched.

The search plan was designed to survey all of the high- and medium-probability cells, and as many low-probability cells as possible. During the survey, however, Williamson had difficulty adhering exactly to the course dictated by the plan. Like a gardener who has overestimated the cutting width of his lawnmower, Williamson was forced to make addi-

---

[8][*Orig. fn.*] Employees of Lamont-Doherty and IST had worked together closely to develop the SeaMARC I. Dale Chayes, who had been aboard the CONRAD, told John Shaw, IST's General Manager, about the survey. Shaw, in turn, told Williamson, who passed the information on to Thompson.

Thompson then telephoned Chayes. Thompson's recollection of the conversation was hazy, but he testified that he called Chayes "probably... to see if the [CONRAD] data was going to become available." Chayes referred Thompson to Ryan. Chayes testified that he told Ryan that he "had gotten a call from this guy who was at Battelle, ...he was asking about shipwrecks."

[9][*Orig. fn.*] Thompson violated, at least technically, Columbia's conditions for disclosing the CONRAD data by copying the materials for inclusion in a Columbus-America file. That file was in Thompson's possession aboard Williamson's vessel during the 1986 survey, detailed infra. By sharing the data with Williamson and Robert D. Evans, one of Columbus-America's project directors, Thompson may have committed further violations.

tional sonar runs between the planned track lines to ensure that there were no "holidays," or gaps, in the survey. It was near the terminus of one of these extra runs, very close to the southwest extreme of the probability map and in a cell with an assigned probability of less than one in one thousand, that the sonar recorded an image of what turned out to be the CENTRAL AMERICA. Of course, because a sonar image has appreciably less resolution than a conventional photograph, positive identification of any of the targets discovered during the survey had to wait until cameras could be lowered into the depths. The following summer, Thompson's group went to sea aboard the ARCTIC DISCOVERER. The group, however, did not immediately proceed to the "correct" target; they instead traveled to a similar target in a more promising, high-probability cell over thirty miles to the northeast. After recovering several lumps of coal, along with some pottery and other artifacts from the site, Columbus-America received an injunction from the district court granting them the exclusive right to operate in the immediate area.

Columbus-America explored the site throughout the summer of 1987, but was unable to obtain any proof of the wreck's identity. That winter, the group reexamined the survey data and noticed similarities between the target they had been exploring and the target thirty miles to the southwest. When, during the summer of 1988, Columbus-America lowered NEMO to the ocean floor near this new target, the robot's almost immediate revelation of the ship's sidewheels provoked an exuberant uproar in the ARCTIC DISCOVERER's control room. Not long thereafter, the group found the proof that it had been seeking—the bell of the CENTRAL AMERICA.

D. From the Control Room to the Courtroom

Unfortunately for Columbus-America, the CENTRAL AMERICA turned out to be located very near to where the CONRAD had, in 1984, imaged Target # 4 along the eastern edge of the Lamont-Doherty survey. The intervenors assert that Columbus-America improperly used the materials that Ryan sent Thompson in 1986 to locate the shipwreck. Upon remanding this case for a new trial, we advised that "[s]hould it be found that Columbus-America used the intervenors' information and such use contributed to the discovery of the CENTRAL AMERICA, a salvage award [for the intervenors] could be proper." *CADG I* at 470.

On retrial, the district court concluded that Columbus-America did not rely on the CONRAD data to find the CENTRAL AMERICA. In weighing the evidence, the court was acting pursuant to its role as factfinder, and we may set aside the court's finding only if it is clearly erroneous. Fed.R.Civ.P. 52(a); *see McAllister v. United States*, 348 U.S. 19, 20, 75 S. Ct. 6, 7-8, 99 L. Ed. 20 (1954) ("No greater scope of review is exercised by the appellate tribunals in admiralty cases than they exercise under Rule 52(a)..."). A finding is clearly erroneous when, "although there is evidence to support it, the reviewing court on the entire evidence is left with a definite and firm conviction that a mistake has been committed." *Id.* (citations omitted); *see also Concrete Pipe & Prod. of Calif., Inc. v. Constr. Laborers Pension Trust*, 508 U.S. 602, 113 S. Ct. 2264, 2279, 124 L. Ed.2d 539 (1993).

To prove that Columbus-America misappropriated the CONRAD data, logic dictates that the intervenors had to demonstrate (1) that Columbus-America obtained the data, (2) that the intervenors had a proprietary interest in the data, and (3) that Columbus-America, without authority, actually used the data in a manner inconsistent with the intervenors' proprietary interest. Further, we are of the opinion that, as a prerequisite to receiving a salvage award, the intervenors were required to show also that the data materially assisted Columbus-America in finding the CENTRAL AMERICA.

Columbus-America readily admits that it received, through Thompson, the sonar photographs, contour charts, and track lines from the CONRAD expedition; thus, the first part of the test is satisfied. The district court determined, however, that the CONRAD information, contrary to the assertions made by Lamont-Doherty's Division Administrator in her March 1986 letter, *see* Section II-C, *supra*, was in the public domain, and, therefore, the intervenors could claim no proprietary interest in it. The court also found that Columbus-America made no use of the data; that the data were of no material assistance is, of course, a corollary to that finding.[10]

The district court's ultimate finding that Columbus-America did not misappropriate the CONRAD data can be clear error only if all three of the finding's factual underpinnings are likewise clearly erroneous. To the contrary, we believe that the court's findings are sound.

1. The Intervenors' Proprietary Interest in the CONRAD Data

Lamont-Doherty had not published the CONRAD data and, indeed, had clearly reserved its exclusive right to initial publication. Though Ryan testified that, pursuant to a preexisting agreement between Columbia and the government, he probably submitted a report of the survey to the Office of Naval Research, the evidence indicated that the report would not, for national security reasons, have been susceptible to disclosure under the Freedom of Information Act. Because there is no evidence that, as of March 1986, the CONRAD data were otherwise freely available, it is unlikely that the information was actually in the public domain.[11]

It does not necessarily follow, however, that the intervenors had a proprietary interest in the data; in fact, we shall see that they did not. As the district court pointed out, Article VII of the survey agreement between Columbia's trustees and John and Grimm provided that "[i]t is agreed that Columbia will be free to publish the results of this research without

---

[10][*Orig. fn.*] The court nevertheless specifically stated that "there is a lack of evidence, factual or circumstantial, to show... that the Columbia data assisted [Columbus-America] in locating the CENTRAL AMERICA.... [Such a conclusion] would be pure speculation or conjecture...."

[11][*Orig. fn.*] The intervenors contend that "[t]he District Court did not decide whether the [CONRAD data were] in the public domain...." Intervenors' Opening and Answering Brief at 30. The court's statement in its opinion that it "need not decide this question on whether the information was in the public domain" appears, at first blush, to support the intervenors' contention. However, we believe that the unequivocal pronouncements of the court, e.g., "[Lamont-Doherty's] statement that the information was not in the public domain was not true," and that the Observatory's assertion to the contrary "was a misstatement," as well as its comprehensive analysis of the issue, make clear that "this question" to which the district court referred was the larger question of Columbus-America's alleged misappropriation, and that, had the court instead resolved the public domain issue in the intervenors' favor, such a resolution would not have been determinative of their claim.

restriction, but not less than one year after termination of contract." The one-year restriction was added to the agreement by John and Grimm, and both initialed the entire provision. The agreement terminated, according to its terms, on September 30, 1984, and, as previously detailed, *see* Section II-C, *supra*, Thompson did not request the CONRAD data until February 1986, well after the one-year restriction had expired.

Had Columbia decided to publish the CONRAD data at that time, John and Grimm, according to the agreement's unambiguous terms, would have had no say in the matter, and thus could not have been heard to complain had Thompson gone to his local library and availed himself of the information. That Columbia instead "published" the data directly to Thompson does not alter the inescapable conclusion that, if any party had a proprietary interest in the use of the CONRAD data, it was Columbia—and Columbia has already settled its claim. *See* note 5, *supra*. The intervenors' resultant lack of a proprietary interest in the data provides an independent ground for our affirmance of the district court's judgment.

2. Columbus-America's Alleged Misuse of the Data

The district court considered the testimony of Thompson and nine of his associates involved in searching for the CENTRAL AMERICA. Although Thompson, Williamson, and Evans each testified that he had seen the CONRAD data before or during the 1986 survey, *see* note 10, *supra*, all denied making any use of the data; the other seven, each an important member of the search team, all denied having seen the data prior to 1990. As all, or nearly all, of the Columbus-America witnesses testified in person before the court at one time or another, it was afforded an ample opportunity to evaluate their comportment and demeanor, and, despite some inconsistencies in Thompson's testimony,[12] the district court expressly found Columbus-America's witnesses to be credible in the main.

Absent extraordinary circumstances, we will not disturb a factfinder's credibility determinations. Fed.R.Civ.P. 52(a) ("due regard shall be given to the opportunity of the trial court to judge... the credibility of the witnesses."); *see United States v. Saunders*, 886 F.2d 56, 60 (4th Cir. 1989); *see also Concrete Pipe & Products, supra*: [I]n the usual case, the factfinder is in a better position to make judgments about the reliability of some forms of evidence than a reviewing body acting solely on the basis of a written record of that evidence. Evaluation of the credibility of a live witness is the most obvious example. 508 U.S. at ___, 113 S. Ct. at 2280.

---

[12][*Orig. fn.*] Thompson testified during the first trial that he did not discuss the CONRAD data with Williamson or his associates, and that he was unsure that the data were even aboard Williamson's vessel, the PINE RIVER, during the 1986 survey. On retrial, Thompson testified during cross-examination that he had shown the sonar records (but not the contour chart or the ship track lines) to Williamson aboard the PINE RIVER, and that the two had briefly discussed some general characteristics of the records and the imagery contained on some of the photographs, including particular targets. The matter was fully before the district court, which also had to consider certain inconsistencies in the testimony of the intervenors' witnesses. For instance, Ryan admitted during the first trial that he had made an inaccurate statement in an earlier affidavit, and Grimm himself offered testimony of dubious credibility concerning his purported efforts in 1987 to follow up on the 1984 CONRAD survey.

Against the uniform denials of the Columbus-America witnesses, the intervenors offered a theory of the case that hinged on what could charitably be called circumstantial evidence. The intervenors asked the district court to believe, in essence, that Thompson contacted Ryan in early 1984 with an eye toward gaining the latter's confidence so that, a full two years later, Thompson could casually request data that would definitively reveal the location of the CENTRAL AMERICA—though the intervenors themselves had not acted on this "definitive" information,[13] and had, in fact, felt so little stirred by it that they gave all their rights in it to a midwestern monastery.

The intervenors further suggested that, in a master stroke of deception, Columbus-America spent millions of dollars to devise an enormously intricate—but nevertheless pretextual—search plan and conduct a bogus sonar survey for several weeks during the summer of 1986; of course, it was relatively easy to manufacture an excuse for not precisely following the recorded plan. According to the intervenors, Thompson and his cohorts then intentionally searched thirty miles away from the CENTRAL AMERICA's actual location for several months in 1987. Finally, the piece de resistance: Columbus-America, despite having fought off other would-be salvors who attempted to violate their court-protected search area, waited over a year to return so that the shipwreck could appear to have been "accidentally" found somewhere outside the search area.[14]

While we would not foreclose all possibility that persons with the demonstrated intelligence, initiative, resourcefulness, and determination of those associated with Columbus-America could be capable of such Machiavellian deceit, we are far from being left with "a definite and firm conviction" that the district court made a mistake by finding to

---

[13][*Orig. fn.*] Actually, the district court found that CONRAD Target # 4, despite its apparent similarity in size and admitted proximity to the proven location of the CENTRAL AMERICA, was not in fact the shipwreck. Because we affirm the court's denial of the intervenors' claim on sufficient alternative grounds, we need not review this particular finding.

[14][*Orig. fn.*] One possible motive for this alleged ruse, detailed in Section III-A, infra, is that Columbus-America needed time to develop NEMO, its undersea robot.

the contrary. We therefore affirm the court's judgment in favor of Columbus-America on the intervenors' claims.[15]

III.   THE SALVAGE AWARD

We remanded this case so that the district court could, through the exercise of its equitable powers, "determine the proper salvage award for Columbus-America." *CADG I* at 468. We suggested that the award might be expressed as a percentage of the total recovery, and we instructed the court that it could adjust the award upward or downward to account for the merit of the salvor's services in relation to the property salvaged. *See id.* at 468-69. We neither interposed a floor nor erected a ceiling to limit the district court's discretion to set an award, except to opine that "we are hazarding but little to say that Columbus-America should, and will, receive by far the largest share of the treasure," and, later, "[f]rom a distance, it appears that... considerations militate towards awarding Columbus-America a sig-

---

[15][*Orig. fn.*] The intervenors contend that they were forced to rely on circumstantial evidence because the district court erred by failing to direct Columbus-America to produce certain navigational records, diving logs, and various other materials, and by allowing Columbus-America to redact some of the discovery that it did produce. The intervenors also complain that they were denied inquiry into the last-minute settlement agreement between Columbia and Columbus-America, see note 5, *supra*, which, they assert, was designed in part to keep Ryan from testifying at retrial and thereby obstruct the truth-finding process.

The scope and conduct of discovery are within the sound discretion of the district court. *Erdmann v. Preferred Research, Inc.,* 852 F.2d 788, 792 (4th Cir.1988). As to the navigational and related records, the court was well aware that Columbus-America had been forced to actively defend its injunction area, graphically demonstrating the need to keep the precise location of its ongoing salvage efforts a secret. The court might have nevertheless compelled additional discovery if it expected that relevant evidence might be produced; however, in light of the rather fantastic theory relied on by the intervenors, the court did not abuse its discretion by striking the balance in Columbus-America's favor. Likewise, denying inquiry into the settlement agreement was hardly an abuse of discretion, inasmuch as Ryan's deposition and trial testimony from the previous proceeding were already in the record.

A final matter concerning the intervenors' appeal remains to be addressed. One of the trial exhibits that Columbus-America designated for inclusion in the Joint Appendix was a color copy of a slide taken from a computer monitor, showing the CENTRAL AMERICA as imaged by Williamson's radar. When the Joint Appendix was compiled, the exhibit was apparently recopied using ordinary, non-color xerographic methods, resulting in an unsatisfactory reproduction. The intervenors objected and filed a motion asking that Columbus-America be directed to submit the original exhibit. While the motion was pending, Columbus-America represented to the Court that it could not find the original and instead submitted a duplicate. The intervenors have not objected to this submission; hence, we consider the matter closed.

nificant portion of the recovered gold." *Id.* at 468. We nevertheless made it quite clear that it was the district court's job to take the evidence and make an appropriate decision.

To inform the court's analysis, we described the six factors, announced by the Supreme Court in *THE BLACKWALL*, 77 U.S. (10 Wall.) 1, 13-14, 19 L. Ed. 870 (1869), that have been traditionally applied by admiralty courts to determine salvage awards.[16] In light of the shipwreck's age, we directed the district court to consider a seventh factor: the degree to which the salvors have worked to protect the historical and archaeological value of the wreck and items salvaged.

On remand, the district court considered the *BLACKWALL* factors and concluded that Columbus-America's reward for salvaging the underwriters' property should be ninety percent of the value of that property. Our review of that decision is limited, as salvage awards are left to the district court's wide discretion. *Waterman S.S. Corp. v. Dean*, 171 F.2d 408, 411 (4th Cir. 1948), *cert. denied*, 337 U.S. 924, 69 S. Ct. 1168, 1171, 93 L. Ed. 1732 (1949). The amount "is primarily a matter of judgment to be exercised by the trial court[,] and[,] beyond a careful examination of the facts[,] little remains for the appellate court except to determine whether the judgment has been exercised in accordance with the general principles respecting salvage..." *Id.*

In the face of this extremely deferential standard of review, the underwriters nevertheless appeal what they believe to be an excessive award. We will examine the district court's findings, but we must first briefly address two arguments posed by the underwriters that, if correct, would have circumscribed the court's discretion from the outset.

A.   The Doctrine of Unclean Hands

"The salvor who seeks a reward for his services in rescuing property on navigable waters[ ] must act in entire good faith and with honesty of purpose. He must come into court with clean hands." *3A Martin J. Norris, Benedict on Admiralty* 99 (7th ed. 1993) [hereinafter *Benedict*]. The underwriters maintain that the salvage award—regardless of the amount finally approved—should be reduced, because, they allege, Columbus-America (1) deceitfully obtained and used the CONRAD data, *see* Section II, *supra*, and (2) misrepresented to the district court that it had found the CENTRAL AMERICA within the original injunction box in 1987 so that it could retain its exclusive right to search the area, thereby purchasing the additional year it needed to finish building NEMO.

1.   The CONRAD Data Revisited

To decide whether Columbus-America acted in good faith regarding the CONRAD data, we employ an analytical framework much like the one we used to decide the intervenors'

---

[16][*Orig. fn.*] These factors are (1) the labor expended by the salvors in rendering the salvage service; (2) the promptitude, skill, and energy displayed in rendering the service and saving the property; (3) the value of the property employed by the salvors in rendering the service, and the danger to which such property was exposed; (4) the risk incurred by the salvors in securing the property from the impending peril; (5) the value of the property salvaged; and (6) the degree of danger from which the property was rescued.

misappropriation claim, see Section II-D, *supra*. The difference is that we focus more closely on the question of whether Columbus-America culpably intended to use, and did use, the data in a manner inconsistent with any colorable proprietary interest that it perceived the intervenors to have, and far less closely on the intervenors' actual rights in the data and whether the information materially assisted Columbus-America's efforts.

Although the analytical framework may be somewhat different, we nevertheless reach the same conclusion. The district court's finding that Columbus-America made no use of the CONRAD data is based on what it reasonably perceived to be credible evidence and, hence, is not clearly erroneous.

2. Columbus-America's Disclosures to the District Court

The underwriters' second assertion that Columbus-America lacked "honesty of purpose" concerns the latter's alleged manipulation of the district court to keep other potential salvors from reaching the shipwreck first. Like the intervenors, the underwriters contend that Williamson's 1986 survey was a sham, intended only to obfuscate Columbus-America's true purpose—to use the CONRAD data to find Target # 4, then obtain a high-resolution sonar image to verify that it was the CENTRAL AMERICA.

During the winter of 1986-87, according to the underwriters, Columbus-America learned that other potential salvors were planning to survey the area. This potential competition was a problem, because, though Columbus-America had the ability to lower cameras into the deep water, it was not yet able to recover any objects from the ocean floor.

The solution, according to the underwriters, was for Columbus-America to conduct additional sham operations the following summer and, by informing the court that it had almost certainly found the CENTRAL AMERICA at a particular site—when the wreck was actually far distant—obtain exclusive rights to an injunction area. Any injunction area would suffice, because the appearance that the wreck had been found, lent credibility by the court's decree, would serve to dissuade potential competitors. Only in the summer of 1988, when NEMO had finally been constructed and tested, could Columbus-America risk traveling to the CENTRAL AMERICA's actual location to obtain the evidence of provenance necessary to secure a new injunction.

The district court rejected the underwriters' theory. It instead credited the testimony of the Columbus-America witnesses that several targets imaged during the 1986 survey were good candidates for further exploration. The court accepted that Thompson and the rest had sincerely believed that they had located the shipwreck in 1987, and that, until 1988, when the group reprocessed its sonar data using new software with improved image processing capabilities, what turned out to be the CENTRAL AMERICA had previously been thought to be a sonar image of a geological formation.

The district court's conclusion was based upon its belief that the witnesses for Columbus-America were credible and truthful. The record, viewed in its entirety, does not demonstrate that the court's belief was an unreasonable one. Its account of the evidence was plausible, and is thus beyond our power to reproach. *See Davis v. Food Lion*, 792 F.2d 1274, 1277 (4th Cir. 1986) ("[W]e can find no clear error if there are two permissible views of the evidence, and the district court as factfinder chooses one over the other.") [citing *Anderson v. City of Bessemer City, N.C.*, 470 U.S. 564, 573-74, 105 S. Ct. 1504, 1511-12, 84 L. Ed.2d 518 (1985)]. We therefore affirm the district court's rejection of the underwriters' "unclean hands" theory.

B.   The Moiety Rule

In a typical salvage case, a seaworthy vessel renders assistance to one that has become disabled, but has not yet sunk. Depending on the severity of the trouble, the salvor may tow the disabled vessel back to port, it may take possession of perishables or other cargo, or it may even rescue the crew and passengers from imminent peril.

Many years ago, when the cash value of a salvaged ship's cargo was difficult to ascertain, distributions in kind were more common, and courts consequently eschewed attempts to evaluate, on a case-by-case basis, the value of the services rendered by an individual salvor. *See Benedict*, 240. The moiety rule emerged. It awarded a successful salvor, as a matter of course, one-half of the imperiled goods salvaged from a derelict vessel.

Most courts found this rule unsatisfactory, because it failed to account for the particular salvor's skill, the labor expended, and the relative difficulty of the operation. *Id.* One authority has stated that the rule's abandonment is usually explained by the fact that, as steam replaced sail, the value of ships became so great that awards of a moiety would have been absurdly inflated... [T]he award will never be for more than half of the value of the property, so that the moiety has become a ceiling instead of a floor. In fact, except where the property saved is of trifling value, the award of anywhere near 50% would be exceptional. *Grant Gilmore & Charles L. Black, Jr., The Law of Admiralty*, 8-10 (2d ed. 1975) [hereinafter *Gilmore & Black*].

The underwriters urge that the moiety rule curbs the district court's discretion in this case to impose a salvage award of greater than fifty percent. We disagree. What the underwriters have failed to appreciate is that, even long after "steam replaced sail," the ability of salvors to rescue sunken cargo was severely limited by their inability to delve beyond only the most shallow reaches of the ocean. The vast majority of salvage operations were then conducted at sea level, and, even today, full-blown salvage of a shipwreck in even moderately deep water (let alone one and one-half miles) is a rare occurrence. *See Benedict*, App. D (documenting American salvage cases from the eighteenth century to the present); *Gilmore & Black*, 8-2 ("The prototypical act is rescuing a ship in peril at sea and towing her to a place of safety.").

While it may offend our sensibilities to allow a salvor who has provided but minimal towing services to receive one-half of a distressed ship's cargo, especially where that cargo is particularly valuable,[17] we are in no sense offended by the possibility that a salvor who has "boldly gone where no one has gone before"—indeed, where no one could have gone when the moiety rule unfolded—might be entitled to the lion's share of a long-lost treasure. We recognized almost fifty years ago that the moiety rule, in lieu of a reasoned analysis of the circumstances surrounding a particular case, cannot serve as a floor on a salvage award. *See* note 18, *supra*. Today we recognize that the rule is equally inapt as a ceiling.

C.   The *BLACKWALL* Analysis

We now begin our review of the district court's exercise of its equitable judgment in accordance with the general principles respecting salvage. *See* note 17, *supra*, and accompanying text.

---

[17][*Orig. fn.*] *See Waterman, supra*, at 412 (moiety of $450,000 urged by salvors who had floated a vessel that had run aground would be "absurdly excessive").

1. The Labor Expended by the Salvor

Addressing the first BLACKWALL factor, the district court found the following: In addition to surveying more than 1,400 [square] miles of ocean bottom, an area the size of Rhode Island, hundreds of runs were made to recheck objects and to photograph them. The salvors spent 487 days at sea working shifts of 12 hours each. Personnel of [Columbus-America] logged some 411,295 hours of labor from 1985 through 1992, at a cost for labor of $8,421,733.66. This figure does not record the fact that Thompson had been doing research since the early 1970 [ ]s and Evans for some period prior to 1985.

Our research has revealed only two other sunken property cases in which it was reported that the salvor's operations lasted longer than a month.[18] The vast majority of such cases involve operations lasting only a few hours or days. *See Benedict*, App. D 7. Even if a salvor had expended but a fraction of the labor detailed in the above account, that fraction alone would represent a huge investment. In the actual case, it is apparent that Columbus-America's effort was monumental.

2. The Salvor's Promptitude, Skill, and Energy

Regarding the second *BLACKWALL* factor, the district court had this to say: A considerable amount of equipment was specially designed, manufactured and assembled for the project. Selection of the personnel to assist was from those most highly qualified and experienced in the contemplated activities... From the inception of the project, [Columbus-America] had assembled experts in the various fields of science, archeology, history, maritime, marketing and publicity, to advise and assist in the use, care and preservation of the shipwreck site... It is sufficient to say they are the leaders in their field[s] of science and calling.

When we write an opinion, our tendency to emphasize those discrete facts necessary to our legal conclusions sometimes serves to distort the broader perspective. Were we to allow that to occur in this case, it would be a disservice to Columbus-America and the significance of its accomplishments. Hence, a brief review is in order.

Thompson, a man of modest means, became fascinated with the CENTRAL AMERICA and its history and resolved to find it. When he could not obtain financing from traditional sources, he made his pitch locally, stringing together a syndicate of small investors. Faced with searching in waters well over a mile deep, he hired a company with access to some of the best sonar equipment available. To find an exceedingly small needle in a dauntingly large haystack, he painstakingly researched the available information and consulted a leading expert in mathematical search theory. Upon discovering that no existing machine would allow an efficient recovery of items from the ocean bottom while simultaneously maintaining the integrity of even the smallest of those items, Thompson's response was, in effect, "No problem—we'll build one." Thompson and Columbus-America indeed "built one," and it worked.

---

[18][*Orig. fn.*] *See Treasure Salvors, Inc. v. Unidentified Wrecked and Abandoned Sailing Vessel*, 569 F.2d 330 (5th Cir. 1978) (several months spent salvaging the galleon NUESTRA SENORA DE LA ATOCHA); *Rickard v. Pringle*, 293 F. Supp. 981, 984 (E.D.N.Y. 1968) (recovery of ACARA's propeller over ten-month period).

In short, we cannot imagine anyone demonstrating more diligence, skill, and energy than Columbus-America has shown here. Its efforts provide a standard against which all others should be judged.

3. The Value of the Property Employed by the Salvors

The record evidence is that NEMO, the ARCTIC DISCOVERER, and the rest of Columbus-America's recovery equipment are worth in excess of $6 million. Columbus-America rented additional equipment and incurred related expenses of millions more. We once more refer to salvage cases involving sunken property, of which—we must again point out—there are relatively few, and note that no case reports a salvor to have employed property of a comparable value. *See Benedict*, App. D. 7.

4. The Risk Incurred by the Salvors

This factor is often important where a distressed vessel's immediate peril likewise imperiled its attempted savior. This scenario was not present here. Nevertheless, the crew of the ARCTIC DISCOVERER constantly dealt with heavy equipment—not the least of which was the six-ton NEMO—and the vessel's 160-mile distance from shore meant that treatment for the most severe injuries was hours away.

While many salvage operations have occurred at a considerable distance from shore, none appear to have been conducted for such an extended period. As the district court noted, "[a]nytime a ship goes to sea, there is danger to the ship and the persons aboard." Although the risk to the crew of the ARCTIC DISCOVERER at any particular time may not have been unusually great, the 487 days that it spent at sea multiplied the intrinsic risks accordingly.

5. The Value of the Property Saved

The testimony of the trial experts varied substantially as to the precise value of the CENTRAL AMERICA's cargo; however, it now appears that the treasure's value will not approach one billion dollars, as earlier speculated. *See, e.g., CADG I* at 454. It is nevertheless clear that, when the salvage is completed and all the treasure is eventually sold, the haul will be one of the largest in history. One commentator has suggested that "[t]he combination of high values and highly meritorious service should result in a high award." *Benedict*, 258. We entirely agree.

6. The Degree of Danger to the Salvaged Property

As we have pointed out, this is not the typical case where a rescuer chances upon a vessel in immediate peril. The gold and other cargo aboard the CENTRAL AMERICA came to rest about one-and-one-half miles beneath the ocean, and, because of the prevailing conditions, was found to be relatively free of accumulated sediment, notwithstanding that 131 years had passed. Whether property that is greatly endangered because it is about to sink becomes any less imperiled once it actually slips below the ocean's surface—with all possibility of an immediate recovery disappearing along with it—is an interesting question. The argument for an affirmative answer appears to be that property progresses from being endangered, as it is sinking, to some state of oblivion once it has sunk. The question of the degree of danger posed to the property would then be a matter of evaluating the conditions within the oblivion once the property is rediscovered.

We reject this argument. While it is true that the ocean itself presents no danger to the essential nature of gold and similar substances, it is also true that any value that our society attributes to gold depends entirely on the ability of someone to assert a property interest in it. Because property is far less certain of being recovered once it has sunk, especially when it has sunk in deep water, we perceive that its sinking sharply increases the degree of danger to its continued existence and utility as property. We have little doubt that, if the *BLACKWALL* Court were transported over 125 years into the future to decide this case, it would consider Columbus-America's salvage of the CENTRAL AMERICA to be the ultimate rescue from the ultimate peril.

7. The Salvor's Preservation of the Historical and Archaeological Value of the Wreck and Cargo

The district court was convinced that Columbus-America had taken extraordinary care in preserving the CENTRAL AMERICA, benefiting a range of sciences and disciplines:

> [Columbus-America's expert] witnesses described the care and means used to pre-serve the artifacts and objects recovered, how [Columbus-America] maintained moni-toring and schedules, and how [it] followed their advice and suggestions for handling and preserving the articles. They described the scientific value of such articles, the discovery of new species, and of the unparalleled opportunities while aboard the re-search vessel to see first-hand the operation and collection of objects…[,] species never before seen and artifacts.

The court continued:

> Video tapes of the operation of things recovered and the means used to care for such articles were shown and then introduced in evidence as exhibits. Likewise, samples of the articles and artifacts recovered were presented for inspection. They demon-strated the particular care exercised in recovering and handling delicate items such as jewelry, china, cloth, papers and so on. One of the items was a cigar, which appeared in perfect condition.[19]

The district court noted further that Columbus-America had published a book and pro-moted a television account of its endeavors, and had provided educational materials to schools interested in teaching their students about the CENTRAL AMERICA and its his-tory. The court found that "the efforts to preserve the site and the artifacts have not been equaled in any other case," and no evidence to the contrary is before us. (Footnote omitted)

* * *

---

[19][*Orig. fn.*] We were given the opportunity at oral argument to examine the very cigar of which the district court spoke.

It will not be often, if ever, that all of the principles governing salvage awards will so overwhelmingly militate in the salvor's favor. It will also be rare that a ship and cargo will have been imperiled for so long, and will be so difficult to objectively value, that a flat percentage award will be preferred to a sum certain. Nevertheless, this is that exceptional case, and though the district court's ninety percent award is a generous one, we cannot say that it is excessive.[20]

Other Considerations

"It is... the policy of the admiralty law to make salvage awards sufficiently liberal so as to encourage salvors to take the risks involved... It has been declared that the underlying theory of salvage is based on the encouragement of voluntary exertions for the saving of imperiled ships and cargoes." Benedict, 233-34 (citations and internal quotation marks omitted). It is undoubtedly sound public policy to set salvage awards high enough to provide an inducement for potential salvors to seek and recover property lost at sea.

To ensure that its award provided sufficient incentive for future endeavors of like kind, the district court, after obtaining a base figure by calculating the expenses incurred by Columbus-America, considered the opportunity cost of the venture capital provided by the RLP investors and the high-risk nature of the investment. We believe that the court's actions were entirely appropriate.

Neither a salvor's expenses nor its expected return on investment are factors to be taken into account in determining whether the salvage services rendered are meritorious. However, once the BLACKWALL and other relevant factors establish that the salvor merits an award, expenses plus a minimally sufficient inducement bonus may act to serve as a floor for that award. To say that a salvor's services may be so outstanding as to merit an amount above that deemed minimally sufficient is but to say that admiralty courts should provide an incentive for salvors to conduct their operations in a more than minimally sufficient manner.[21]

---

[20][*Orig. fn.*] As have the intervenors, *see* note 16, *supra*, the underwriters contend that the district court abused its discretion by allowing the curtailment or outright denial of discovery into various matters. The underwriters primarily object to the court permitting Columbus-America to produce only edited videotapes and selected photographs of the wreck site, and to the court's refusal to allow discovery into RLP's profits or the identity of its investors. *See* Section II-C, *supra*. Because it appears from the credible evidence that the requested videotapes and photographs would not have mandated a different conclusion as to the preservation issue, and because it appears unlikely that inquiry into RLP's profits or investors would have produced relevant evidence, the district court's discovery rulings were not an abuse of discretion.

[21][*Orig. fn.*] An answer to the question, "How large should an award be to serve as an inducement?" may be more easily determined if the owner has previously attempted to negotiate a contract for the salvage of his or her property. We noted in our previous opinion that one underwriter had attempted to negotiate a salvage of the CENTRAL AMERICA whereby the salvor would receive 98% of the treasure. *CADG I* at 467.

Two other matters require our attention at this juncture. The first concerns the underwriters' claim to some of the silver—in addition to the gold—aboard the CENTRAL AMERICA. The underwriters first brought this claim to the district court's attention late in the proceedings, more than three months after the retrial had concluded. The court ruled that the underwriters had essentially waived the claim, and that, in any event, the claim had no support in the evidence. We see no reason to disturb the court's ruling on either point. The second matter concerns the underwriters' motion on appeal to strike Columbus-America's reply brief, which, at forty-seven pages, is twenty-two pages too long on its face. *See Fed. R. App.* p. 28(g) ("Except by permission of the court... reply briefs must not exceed 25 pages..."). Columbus-America has conceded that it did not obtain the court's prior permission to exceed the maximum page limit. Accordingly, we strike and refuse to consider Pages 26-47 of Columbus-America's reply brief, thereby granting the underwriters' motion as modified.

IV. THE MARKETING RULING

On January 13, 1994, the district court entered an order that, inter alia, designated Columbus-America as the central marketing authority for all of the gold salvaged from the CENTRAL AMERICA. The underwriters contend that the district court was without jurisdiction to deprive them of the right, as owners, to possess their share, and they urge us to direct the court to divide the gold in specie, so that they may dispose of their property as they see fit.

Ordinarily, we might agree with the underwriters' position. The difficulty in this case, however, is that there is just too much gold involved to allow more than one party to market it. The loss of the gold aboard the CENTRAL AMERICA significantly affected the precious metal and financial markets in 1857, and there is evidence that the gold's recovery could, upon its re-entry into the market, have a significant effect today.

Our review of the expert testimony introduced at trial convinces us that a unified plan is necessary to ensure the maximum return from the sale of the gold. Where there can be but one plan, we think it eminently sensible to allow the party with by far the greatest interest in the plan's success to coordinate it; that party, of course, is Columbus-America.[22]

We do not share the underwriters' alleged concern, expressed at oral argument, that "their share" will be sold at bargain basement prices to straw parties in collusion with Columbus-America. To the contrary, to the extent that the marketing proposal accords the underwriters a "share" of anything, it is a share of the proceeds from the sale of the gold, and not the gold itself. If the gold must eventually be sold at a discount, it is Columbus-America that will suffer no less than ninety percent of the damage. We note also that, because of the ongoing nature of these admiralty proceedings, the district court will

---

[22][*Orig. fn.*] To the extent that Columbus-America's designation as the central marketing authority for all of the gold appears to unduly interfere with the underwriters' ownership rights, it must be remembered that separate marketing of the gold would be less efficient and inevitably result in a lower total return. Thus, Columbus-America would be left with nine-tenths of a smaller pie, to the detriment of their eventual ownership rights.

retain jurisdiction over the marketing of the gold. Any allegations of impropriety on the part of Columbus-America can be investigated and adjudicated there.[23]

V. EVIDENCE OF THE UNDERWRITERS' OWNERSHIP

The final matter concerns Columbus-America's cross-appeal. From the time that the underwriters filed their claim on September 29, 1989, the district court has never made findings concerning the amount of gold aboard the CENTRAL AMERICA that each underwriter—or its predecessor-in-interest—had insured and obtained by subrogation upon paying a claim of loss. The court was not dilatory; until *CADG I* was decided in 1992, the court believed that there was no need to determine the ownership interests of the individual underwriters because it had held that, under the law of finds, all of the underwriters had abandoned any interest they may have had.

On remand, Columbus-America asked the court to address the ownership issue. The court noted that it was reluctant to do so, because it believed that our opinion in *CADG I* could be construed to have decided that each underwriter had established the validity of its claim. For example, we stated in the earlier opinion that

> The lower court... found "prima facially" that the underwriters did insure the treasure and that they received ownership interests in the gold once the claims were paid... [W]e find that the district court did not err when it held that the underwriters who are now parties, or their predecessors in interest, paid off claims upon and become the owners of the commercial shipment of gold in 1857.

CADG I at 465. Earlier, we had said that "[S]hould more than $1,219,189 (1857 valuation) of gold be rescued, Columbus-America should be found the owner of any surplus." *Id.* at 465 n. 6.

The underwriters maintain that the above-quoted language demonstrates that we "found," in resolving the previous appeal, that they collectively owned the $1.2 million of insured gold that had been reported lost. They interpret our directive that "[o]n remand, the district court... must determine what percentage of the gold each underwriter insured," *CADG I* at 468, to mean that the court was required merely to divide the ownership interest in the gold among the individual underwriters to ensure that all $1.2 million was distributed and that each underwriter got something.[24]

It is a basic tenet of our legal system that, although appellate courts often review facts found by a judge or jury to ensure that they are not clearly erroneous, they do not make such

---

[23][*Orig. fn.*] With regard to the marketing and valuation issues, the underwriters have moved to supplement the record with documents obtained from the public record of unrelated judicial proceedings, involving a witness who testified before the district court in the present matter. We grant the motion.

[24][*Orig. fn.*] The underwriters have agreed among themselves on how to distribute the CENTRAL AMERICA proceeds, and have submitted their agreement to the district court.

findings in the first instance. *Maine v. Taylor*, 477 U.S. 131, 144-45, 106 S. Ct. 2440, 2450-51, 91 L. Ed.2d 110 (1986) ("Factfinding is the basic responsibility of district courts, rather than appellate courts"), quoting *Pullman-Standard v. Swint*, 456 U.S. 273, 291, 102 S. Ct. 1781, 1791-92, 72 L. Ed.2d 66 (1982) (internal citation omitted); *Minnesota Mining and Mfg. Co. v. Blume*, 684 F.2d 1166, 1170 (6th Cir. 1982), ("Fact-finding is entrusted to the district court..."), *cert. denied*, 460 U.S. 1047, 103 S. Ct. 1449, 75 L. Ed.2d 803 (1983) and 461 U.S. 939, 103 S. Ct. 2110, 77 L. Ed.2d 314 (1983).

Of course, it was necessary for the district court, when faced with claims from over thirty underwriters, to make an initial finding that the claimants had standing to pursue their claims. As the above-quoted language from our prior opinion indicates, the district court was satisfied that the underwriters who were parties to the appeal had made at least a prima facie showing of ownership, and we were satisfied that the district court had not clearly erred in thus finding. Indeed, the claims of several underwriters were dismissed prior to the first trial, presumably because they could not make a prima facie showing.

Our prior opinion should not be read, however, to hold that a prima facie showing is all that is required for the individual underwriters to prove their claims. A pair of excerpts from the opinion serve to clarify the matter:

> [T]he district court had bifurcated the trial, so that the first part would concern only whether Columbus-America was entitled to finder or salvor status... If the latter scenario were found to be true, a second phase of the trial would be necessary, wherein the Court would have to determine what each underwriter had insured...

and

> The Court had earlier bifurcated the trial so that the first phase only concerned whether the underwriters had abandoned the gold; should no abandonment be found, a second phase, examining what the underwriters actually insured... would also be necessary.

CADG I at 459 and 470. We suppose that we might have more clearly expressed ourselves, but it ought to be crystal clear that a claimant cannot prove his or her claim merely by filing a lawsuit.

The district court must, therefore, consider each underwriter's admissible evidence of the validity of its claim to a portion of the gold salvaged from the CENTRAL AMERICA. Columbus-America is entitled to introduce admissible evidence, if any, to rebut these claims. The district court must then weigh all of the evidence and decide whether each underwriter has proved all or any portion of its claim. If the total amount of gold proved owned by the underwriters constitutes less than one hundred percent of the gold salvaged—either because the proof of ownership fails with regard to one or more underwriters, or because a significant portion of uninsured gold is recovered, or for any other reason—Columbus-America may retain the excess.[25]

---

[25][*Orig. fn.*] *See CADG I* at 465 ("[A]n abandonment may be found, and Columbus-America may be declared the finder and sole owner, as to any recovered parts of the ship, all passenger possessions, and any cargo besides the insured shipments.").

VI.   CONCLUSION

What Thompson and Columbus-America have accomplished is, by any measure, extraordinary. We can say without hesitation that their story is a paradigm of American initiative, ingenuity, and determination. Almost as extraordinary, perhaps, have been the efforts of the district judge, who has intrepidly waded through the morass of records and filings, and who has consistently evidenced good humor, notwithstanding the occasional contentiousness among the parties. He is to be commended.

The judgment of the district court is affirmed, and the case is remanded for further proceedings consistent with this opinion.

AFFIRMED AND REMANDED.

Note

Query whether a shipwreck that has been embedded in the seabed for hundreds of years is in "marine peril." For a further discussion of this issue, see *Subaqueous Exploration & Archaeology, Ltd. v. The Unidentified, Wrecked and Abandoned Vessel*, 577 F. Supp. 597, 611 (D. Md. 1983).

---

4.   The Substantive Admiralty Law Can Be Altered, Qualified, or Supplemented

Courts have held that the substantive law of admiralty can be modified and/or supplemented. The *Lathrop* court (see chapter 2) also recognized this point: "Congress may constitutionally 'alter, qualify, or supplement the substantive admiralty law [presumed to be in existence at the writing of the Constitution].'" (*Lathrop*, 817 F. Supp. at 962 [quoting *Panama R.R. Co. v. Johnson*, 264 U.S. 375, 386 (1924) (alteration in original)].) This power to supplement or modify admiralty law, however, does have limits. The Supreme Court in *Panama R.R. Co.* discussed these limitations:

> One is that there are boundaries to the maritime law and admiralty jurisdiction which inhere in those subjects and cannot be altered by legislation, as by excluding a thing falling clearly within them or including a thing falling clearly without. Another is that the spirit and purpose of the constitutional provision require that these enactment[s]... shall be co-extensive with and operate uniformly in the whole of the United States.

[*Panama R.R. Co.* 265 U.S. at 386–87.] As the *Lathrop* court explained, "Congressional enactments restricting the manner in which a potential salvor excavates property located on federally owned or managed lands does not offend these sound constitutional limitations." [*Lathrop*, 817 F. Supp. at

962.] Accordingly, regulation concerning the methodology of salvage does not offend the substantive law of admiralty. Rather, it is an important legislative function of "Congress—through appropriate legislation—to substantively supplement admiralty law and determine the lawfulness of certain salvage activities." [*Lathrop*, 817 F. Supp. at 962.]

SECTION D.   FEDERAL LAWS THAT SPECIFICALLY APPLY TO HERITAGE RESOURCES IN THE MARINE ENVIRONMENT

1.   The Abandoned Shipwreck Act of 1987

For decades, state governments asserted ownership rights to submerged heritage resources pursuant to the Submerged Lands Act (SLA) and state historic preservation laws. In some cases, states successfully argued that the Eleventh Amendment to the United States Constitution, which recognizes a state's sovereign immunity from suit, bars a federal admiralty court from determining the state's interest in a shipwreck. In other cases, states waived their immunity and convinced the federal admiralty courts that they owned shipwrecks embedded in their sovereign state submerged lands. However, in many federal admiralty cases, treasure salvors prevailed in getting ownership rights to submerged heritage resources under the law of finds.

Congress passed the Abandoned Shipwreck Act (ASA)[3] in response to the need to protect certain submerged cultural heritage and address the confusion over ownership, the role of admiralty law, and other public interests. Congressional findings support the view that the states already had the authority to manage the submerged heritage resources pursuant to the SLA, and that the ASA merely codifies this line of admiralty cases.[4] However, confusion as to the scope of the ASA continues to cloud the ability of state governments to protect and manage heritage resources in the marine environment.

Asserting Ownership Over Abandoned Shipwrecks

In passing the ASA, Congress exercised its sovereign prerogative to protect certain submerged heritage resources by asserting title to abandoned shipwrecks embedded in state submerged lands and coralline formations, and to

---

[3]43 U.S.C. §§ 2101–106 (effective April 28, 1988).

[4]43 U.S.C. § 2101.

those that were located on state submerged lands and determined historic.[5] Under Section 6(c) of the Act, title to these shipwrecks simultaneously was transferred to the states.[6] Title to abandoned shipwrecks on certain public lands, such as National Parks and Indian lands, was reserved to the United States.[7] Although many people presumed that the ASA protected all historic shipwrecks in or on state submerged lands, subsequent litigation has shown the vulnerability of the Act. In some cases, salvors shift their strategy by arguing that the shipwrecks are not abandoned and, therefore, are not covered by the ASA. In turn, they demand liberal salvage awards or division of the recovered goods pursuant to salvage contracts with owners-insurers. The results are mixed, but they clearly bring into question the scope of protection afforded by the ASA.

Abandonment

The ASA protects "any abandoned shipwreck" that is "(1) embedded in the submerged lands of a State; (2) embedded in coralline formations protected by a State on submerged lands of a State; or (3) located on the submerged lands of a State and is included in or determined eligible for inclusion in the National Register."[8] The term "abandoned," however, is not expressly defined by the ASA[9] because Congress relied on cases including the *Treasure Salvors* case and its progeny, where the courts inferred abandonment of long lost shipwrecks based on the passage of time and the absence of a claim thereto.[10] Under admiralty law, the process for determining abandonment is

---

[5]43U.S.C. § 2105 (a) (A shipwreck is determined "historic" if it is included in, or determined eligible for inclusion in, the National Register of Historic Places).

[6]43 U.S.C. § 2105(c).

[7]43 U.S.C. §§ 2101, 2105. The ASA assertion of title and the transfer of that title to states with reservations for public lands is very similar to the transfer and reservations of title to submerged lands under the SLA.

[8]43 U.S.C. § 2105(a).

[9]"Shipwreck" is defined to mean "a vessel or wreck, its cargo, and other contents." [43 U.S.C. § 2102(d).] It should be further noted that shipwrecks entitled to sovereign immunity, such as warships or other sovereign non-commercial vessels, are generally not considered to be abandoned by the flag nation, regardless of their location. The U.S. Navy vessels are, likewise, not abandoned. [ASA Guidelines, 55 Fed. Reg. 50120 (Dec. 4, 1990).]

[10]"The Committee notes that... abandonment... may be implied... by an owner never asserting any control over or otherwise indicating his claim of possession of the shipwreck." [H.R. Rep. No. 100-514(I), at 2. See also *Moyer v. Wrecked & Abandoned Vessel, Known as the Andrea Doria*, 836 F. Supp. 1099, 1105 (D.N.J. 1993) (insurance company's failure to attempt salvage from 1956 to 1993 constituted abandonment).]

an inferential one, based on the totality of the circumstances.[11] With regard to long-lost historic shipwrecks, the inference of abandonment was tantamount to a presumption.[12] By not codifying this meaning of "abandonment," Congress left the National Park Service, which was charged with developing the ASA guidelines,[13] the several states, and ultimately, the federal admiralty courts, to define it. As a result, conflicting case law has subsequently developed over whether shipwrecks are abandoned, who has the burden of proving abandonment, and what evidence is needed to demonstrate abandonment.

Several issues raised by the ASA came to a head in *Deep Sea Research (DSR), Inc. v. The Brother Jonathan and California*.[14] Shortly after the *Brother Jonathan,* a double side-wheeled paddle steamer, sank off the coast of California in 1865, five San Francisco insurance companies paid claims on approximately one-third of the cargo. The remaining two-thirds of the cargo and the vessel itself were uninsured. The Ninth Circuit Court of Appeals held that California had not proved by a preponderance of the evidence that "the vessel is abandoned and embedded in the subsurface or coralline formations of the territorial waters of the State," or in the alternative, that the vessel "is abandoned" and "eligible for listing in the National Register." Even though there was no effort to salvage the vessel for well over 100

---

[11]*Russell v. Forty Bales of Cotton*, 21 F. Cas. 42, 46 (S.D. Fla. 1872)(abandonment inferred by "the absence of a claimant or the neglect to claim"); *Commonwealth v. Maritime Underwater Surveys, Inc.*, 531 N.E.2d 549, 552 (Mass. 1988)("[S]ince the Wydah has rested undisturbed and undiscovered beneath the sea for nearly three centuries, it is proper to consider the wreck abandoned."); T. Schoenbaum, *Admiralty and Maritime Law* §16-7, at 240 (2d ed. West 1994) ("In virtually all of the treasure salvage cases involving wrecks of great antiquity, the law of finds, not salvage is appropriate because '[d]isposition of a wrecked vessel whose very location has been lost for centuries as though its owner were still in existence stretches the fiction to absurd lengths.'") [quoting *Treasure Salvors*, 569 F.2d 330, 332(5th Cir. 1978)].

[12]Id.; *Martha's Vineyard Scuba Headquarters, Inc. v. Unidentified, Wrecked & Abandoned Steam Vessel*, 833 F.2d 1059, 1065 (1st Cir. 1983)(long lost shipwreck presumed abandoned).

[13]The definition of abandoned shipwreck in the ASA Guidelines follows the admiralty cases that presume abandonment by the passage of time and the absence of a claim therein. In addition, the definition adds that a shipwreck may be considered abandoned if an owner fails to either mark and subsequently remove the wrecked vessel and its cargo or to provide legal notice of abandonment to the U.S. Coast Guard and U.S. Army Corps of Engineers. [*See* Rivers and Harbors Act, 33 U.S.C. § 409.] Such shipwrecks ordinarily are treated as being abandoned after the expiration of 30 days from the sinking.

[14]102 F.3d 379 (9th Cir. 1996), *aff'd in part, vacated and remanded in part*, 118 S. Ct. 1464 (1998).

years, the Court held that this long-lost historic shipwreck was not abandoned and, consequently, not subject to the ASA; therefore, it could be salvaged under admiralty law. The Court reasoned that the *Brother Jonathan* was not an abandoned shipwreck because the technology to locate and recover the wreck had been developed only recently and because insurance claims were paid on one-third of the cargo. In effect, the Ninth Circuit applied the law of salvage and rejected both traditional admiralty law and the line of ASA cases, holding that abandonment is presumed by the mere passage of time and the absence of an ownership claim.

The Ninth Circuit's analysis of the issue of abandonment in the *Brother Jonathan* case[15] exposes the vulnerability of other submerged heritage resources. Despite the fact that no action to recover the wreck or its cargo had been undertaken since 1865, the Court refused to infer abandonment because the technology used to discover and recover the wreck had only recently been developed. Thus, on the basis of available technology, and a corresponding interest in recovery by a salvor-subrogee of an insurer of part of the cargo, an otherwise abandoned shipwreck falling within the scope of the ASA became subject to the law of salvage. Citing the ASA guidelines, the Court also reasoned that if a shipwreck is not considered abandoned when the full value of insurance is paid, then the fact that the insurers of one-third of the cargo assigned their title to Deep Sea Research ("DSR") and assured DSR that they had good title constituted evidence that the insurers had not abandoned the cargo. While acknowledging that the remaining two-thirds of the cargo, as well as the ship itself, were uninsured and therefore abandoned, the Court nevertheless ruled that, for purposes of judicial economy, the ship and its cargo should be treated as a unified *res*. It allowed salvage of the entire shipwreck, including the two-thirds that the court indicated were abandoned, reasoning that to apply the ASA to the abandoned portion of the shipwreck and salvage law to the nonabandoned portion would lead to separate legal proceedings in state and federal admiralty courts. In the Court's view, it was not likely that Congress had intended such a confusing and inefficient approach in adopting the ASA, so it ruled that salvage, and not the ASA, was the appropriate law of the case.

Although it criticized the analysis of the Fourth Circuit Court of Appeals in *Columbus-America Discovery Group v. Atlantic Mutual Insurance Company*,[16] in practice, the Ninth Circuit followed that case by rejecting the presumption of abandonment and favoring the law of salvage. When Congress enacted the ASA, however, it relied on the traditional admiralty analysis of

---

[15] 102 F.3d 379 (9th Cir. 1996).

[16] 974 F.2d 450 (4th Cir. 1992).

abandonment. That analysis is still followed by other circuits for determining whether a shipwreck is abandoned.[17]

Perhaps because of the confusion in the circuits regarding the roles of the Eleventh Amendment, admiralty law, and abandonment in ASA cases, as well as the scope of the ASA itself, the United States Supreme Court granted *certiorari* in the *Brother Jonathan* case on all three issues in the writ: 1) whether the Eleventh Amendment bars a federal court from deciding an *in rem* admiralty action where a state asserts title to the shipwreck under the ASA; 2) whether the lower court erred in ruling that the ASA preempts[18] state laws that regulate shipwrecks that are not abandoned; and 3) whether the lower court erred in finding that a long-lost historic shipwreck is not protected by the ASA because an insurance company may have paid a claim on a portion of the ship's cargo.

With regard to the issue of abandonment, the United States, California, and amici took issue with the Ninth Circuit's holding and analysis. The United States argued that the Ninth Circuit erred in its analysis of abandonment within the meaning of the ASA. Consistent with traditional admiralty case law and other ASA cases, the United States argued that the Ninth Circuit erred in rejecting the inference of abandonment when a long period of time has passed and the owner of the vessel has not attempted to salvage the vessel or establish a claim thereto. For the United States, the primary flaw in the Ninth Circuit's rationale was its refusal to infer abandonment because technology only recently had enabled the shipwreck to be salvaged. Not only had the Ninth Circuit departed from traditional admiralty case law, it effectively required an express renunciation of title. The United States also questioned the treatment of the *Brother Jonathan* as a unified *res*, and argued that the Court clearly erred in ruling that the vessel and two-thirds of the cargo, which admittedly was abandoned, nevertheless was subject to the maritime law of salvage.

The United States also explained to the Supreme Court how the Ninth Circuit had erred in finding that the savings provision of the ASA (Section 7) preempted California historic preservation law. It argued that the preemp-

---

[17]See *Zych v. Unidentified, Wrecked and Abandoned Vessel (Seabird)*, 941 F.2d 525 (7th Cir. 1991); *Sunken Treasure, Inc. v. Unidentified, Wrecked & Abandoned Vessel*, 857 F. Supp. 1129 (D.V.I. 1994). See also *Martha's Vineyard Scuba Headquarters, Inc. v. Unidentified, Wrecked & Abandoned Steam Vessel*, 833 F.2d 1059, 1065 (1st Cir. 1987) and *Treasure Salvors* (5th Cir. 1978).

[18]California also argued that its historic preservation statute precluded the application of salvage law to California's submerged cultural resources. The Ninth Circuit rejected that argument with little analysis, holding that the California statute was pre-empted by the ASA to the extent it protected shipwrecks that were not abandoned within the meaning of the ASA.

tion issue need not be reached if, on remand, the lower court finds that the *Brother Jonathan* is abandoned and subject to the ASA.

The primary argument of the United States focused on the Constitutional issue involving the Eleventh Amendment as applied to federal court *in rem* actions under admiralty law. The United States' position was that the Eleventh Amendment does not bar federal courts from determining whether the law of salvage or the ASA applies to a case, but it advocated that the Supreme Court remand the case to the lower court to reconsider the issue of abandonment and, if necessary, reach the issue of preemption.

Consistent with the suggestions of the Office of the Solicitor General of the United States, the Supreme Court vacated the Ninth Circuit's ruling that the law of salvage applied to the *Brother Jonathan*, and remanded the case for reconsideration on the issue of abandonment. The Court said that "the meaning of 'abandoned' under the ASA conforms with its meaning under admiralty law. The District Court's full consideration of the ASA's application on remand might negate the need to address the issue of whether the ASA pre-empts [the California historic preservation statute]."

By vacating the Ninth Circuit's ruling on abandonment, the abandonment analysis used by the Fourth Circuit also must be called into question. While the Fourth Circuit *Columbus-America* decision is a departure from the traditional admiralty law analysis of abandonment, the case itself clearly lies in admiralty. The Supreme Court thus could easily have affirmed the Ninth Circuit's ruling on abandonment or just let it stand. Instead, the court vacated and remanded this issue to the lower court, as the United States suggested.

A new trial in the United States District Court for the Northern District of California will determine whether the *Brother Jonathan* is an abandoned shipwreck subject to the ASA, or is not abandoned and subject to the maritime law of salvage. If the lower court adopts the argument of the United States, it should find that the shipwreck is abandoned and that the ASA applies to the case—not the law of salvage.

Law of Finds and Law of Salvage Do Not Apply: Constitutional Issues of Admiralty Court Jurisdiction Under Article III, and Sovereign Immunity of States Under the Eleventh Amendment

In addition to asserting and transferring title to abandoned shipwrecks, Congress expressly stated that the "law of salvage and finds shall not apply to abandoned shipwrecks...."[19] Congress sought to end the management of sub-

---

[19]43 U.S.C. § 2106.

merged heritage resources by federal admiralty courts, and instead intended to rely on state and national agencies to protect and manage this heritage when it enacted the ASA.[20] Treasure hunters, in turn, attempted to overcome Congress's asserted authority over their activities by arguing, albeit unsuccessfully, that any law preventing the application of the law of salvage to submerged resources violates Article III[21] of the United States Constitution because cases involving these resources clearly fall within admiralty, and therefore must be heard by federal admiralty courts and not state courts.

In *Zych v. Unidentified, Wrecked and Abandoned Vessel, Believed to Be the "Seabird,"*[22] the court stated that under the Constitution, a highly intricate interplay exists between the states and federal government. The court then went on to hold that Congress has the authority to revise, supplement, and even limit admiralty court jurisdiction. In limiting admiralty and maritime law, "Congress can neither exclude a thing that falls clearly within admiralty and maritime law, nor can it exclude a thing that clearly falls without." [*Zych*, 19 F.3d 1136, 1140 (7th Cir. 1994).] The court specifically held that the ASA does not interfere with Article III's purpose of ensuring national control over navigation, as well as interstate and foreign commerce. The court noted that this holding does not present an affront to the Constitution because an Article III court is determining whether to apply the maritime law of salvage or a codification of an exception to the common law of finds, the latter being a thing that clearly falls outside of admiralty and maritime law and, thus, within the authority of Congress to exclude. The court also noted that the result in this case was consistent with the result in maritime admiralty cases.[23] In addition, the *Zych* court held that, since the wreck at issue was abandoned and owned by the state under the ASA, the Eleventh Amendment precluded a federal admiralty court from hearing litigation con-

---

[20]"The purpose of [the ASA] is to give states title to certain abandoned shipwrecks that are buried in state lands or have historical significance and are on state lands, and to clarify the regulatory and management authority of states for these abandoned shipwrecks." H.R. Rep. No. 887, 98th Cong. 2d Sess. 2 (July 6, 1984).

[21]"[T]he judicial Power shall extend ... to all Cases of admiralty and maritime Jurisdiction." U.S. Const. art. III, § 2, cl. 1.

[22]746 F. Supp. 1334 (N.D. Ill. 1990), *rev'd*, 941 F.2d 525 (7th Cir. 1991), *on remand*, 811 F. Supp. 1300 (N.D. Ill. 1992), *aff'd*, 19 F.3d 1136 (7th Cir. 1994), *cert. denied*, 513 U.S. 961 (1994).

[23]*Zych*, 19 F.3d at 1141 citing, *Chance v. Certain Artifacts Found and Salvaged*, 606 F. Supp. 801, 804 (S.D. Ga. 1984) (pre-ASA case) and *Columbus-America Discovery Group* (post-ASA case).

cerning a state-owned shipwreck.[24] The court acknowledged that the intent of the ASA is to have states, not admiralty courts, protect and manage abandoned shipwrecks, and it rejected the salvors' arguments that admiralty courts should determine whether the ASA controls the case.

Since 1982, it generally has been accepted that because of state sovereign immunity under the Eleventh Amendment[25] of the United States Constitution, a federal court "did not have the power... to adjudicate the State's interest in the property without the State's consent."[26] However, the Supreme Court subsequently ruled that the Eleventh Amendment does not bar federal courts from deciding whether the law of salvage or the ASA applies to a case, unless the state is in "actual possession" of the shipwreck.[27] Citing decisions from the 1800s, the Court noted that the United States and foreign sovereigns are not immune from an *in rem* admiralty case unless the sovereign is in "actual possession" of the vessel.[28] It then reasoned that the sovereign immunity of the several states under the Eleventh Amendment should be the same as the standard for the United States and foreign sovereigns.[29] As a result, Justice Stevens admitted he made an error in his plurality decision in the 1982 Supreme Court *Treasure Salvors* case, and agreed that California may be bound by a federal court's *in rem* adjudication of rights to the *Brother Jonathan* and its cargo.[30]

The meaning of "actual possession" in the context of shipwrecks lying in and on state submerged lands likely will be litigated in the years to come. To trigger the Eleventh Amendment, states now will have to make a reasonable showing that the shipwreck is in their custody, that they have direct physical control over the shipwreck, or that they immediately occupy the shipwreck site. States likely will argue that they are in "actual possession" of shipwrecks embedded in their state submerged lands, and that these shipwrecks are controlled by state statutes and regulations over state natural and cultural

---

[24]*Zych v. Seabird*, 19 F.3d at 1136 (7th Cir. 1994); see also *Zych v. Unidentified, Wrecked & Abandoned Vessel ("Lady Elgin")*, 755 F. Supp. 213 (N.D. Ill. 1991), *rev'd*, 960 F.2d 665 (7th Cir. 1992); both citing *Florida Department of State v. Treasure Salvors, Inc.*, 458 U.S. 670 (1982).

[25]The Eleventh Amendment bars suits in federal court against states. States argue that disputes over their interests should be heard in the sovereign state courts and not federal court.

[26]*Florida Department of State v. Treasure Salvors, Inc.*, 458 U.S. 670, 682 (1982).

[27]*California v. Deep Sea Research, Inc. (the Brother Jonathan)*, ___ U.S. ___, 118 S. Ct. 1464 (1998).

[28]118 S. Ct. at 1468-470.

[29]118 S. Ct. at 1468-470.

[30]118 S. Ct. at 1470-474.

resources. To avoid federal admiralty court, states will now have to provide reasonable evidence that the ASA applies to the shipwreck in question, such as circumstantial evidence that the shipwreck is abandoned and embedded in state lands. States might argue that a historic shipwreck should be presumed to be abandoned if the owner did not attempt to salvage or otherwise claim it for a specified period of time. For example, in *Rickard v. Pringle*, 293 F. Supp. 981, 984 (E.D.N.Y. 1968), the court found that a ship's propeller, which had been lying on the ocean floor for 60 years, was presumed to be abandoned. If a state can show that the shipwreck is embedded in state submerged lands, the federal court should find that the shipwreck is abandoned and that the ASA applies. The state also should provide evidence of the historical significance of the shipwreck. If the shipwreck is not embedded, the state will need to show that the shipwreck is included in, or has been determined eligible for, the National Register of Historic Places.

Although the ASA is a viable law, the Supreme Court decision in the *Brother Jonathan* case ensures that treasure hunters will continue to challenge state—and other sovereign—ownership of historic shipwrecks by asking for salvage rights in federal admiralty courts. Ultimately, the ASA should prevail in protecting certain historic shipwrecks, but years of litigation might be necessary before the ASA and admiralty law are reconciled. In the meantime, the Supreme Court has raised questions about the protection and management of historic shipwrecks from unwanted salvage.

CALIFORNIA v. DEEP SEA RESEARCH, INC.

__ U.S. __, 118 S. Ct. 1464 (1998)

Justice O'CONNOR delivered the opinion of the Court.

This action, involving the adjudication of various claims to a historic shipwreck, requires us to address the interaction between the Eleventh Amendment and the in rem admiralty jurisdiction of the federal courts. Respondent Deep Sea Research, Inc. (DSR), located the ship, known as the S.S. Brother Jonathan, in California's territorial waters. When DSR turned to the federal courts for resolution of its claims to the vessel, California contended that the Eleventh Amendment precluded a federal court from considering DSR's claims in light of the State's asserted rights to the Brother Jonathan under federal and state law. We conclude that the Eleventh Amendment does not bar the jurisdiction of a federal court over an in rem admiralty action where the res is not within the State's possession.

I.

The dispute before us arises out of respondent DSR's assertion of rights to both the vessel and cargo of the Brother Jonathan, a 220-foot, wooden-hulled, double side-wheeled steamship that struck a submerged rock in July 1865 during a voyage between San Francisco and Vancouver. It took less than an hour for the Brother Jonathan to sink, and most of the ship's passengers and crew perished. The ship's cargo, also lost in the accident, included a shipment of up to $2 million in gold and a United States Army payroll that some estimates place at $250,000. *See* Nolte, "Shipwreck: Brother Jonathan Discovered," *San Francisco Chronicle*, Feb. 25, 1994, p. 1, reprinted in App. 127-131. One of few parts of the ship recovered was the wheel, which was later displayed in a saloon in Crescent City, California. R. Phelan, *The Gold Chain* 242 (1987).

Shortly after the disaster, five insurance companies paid claims totaling $48,490 for the loss of certain cargo. It is unclear whether the remaining cargo and the ship itself were insured. *See* "Wreck of the Steamship Brother Jonathan," *New York Times*, Aug. 26, 1865, reprinted in App. 140-147. Prior to DSR's location of the vessel, the only recovery of cargo from the shipwreck may have occurred in the 1930's, when a fisherman found 22 pounds of gold bars minted in 1865 and believed to have come from the Brother Jonathan. The fisherman died, however, without revealing the source of his treasure. Nolte, *supra*, App. 130. There appears to be no evidence that either the State of California or the insurance companies that paid claims have attempted to locate or recover the wreckage.

In 1991, DSR filed an action in the United States District Court for the Northern District of California seeking rights to the wreck of the Brother Jonathan and its cargo under that court's in rem admiralty jurisdiction. California intervened, asserting an interest in the Brother Jonathan based on the Abandoned Shipwreck Act of 1987 (ASA), 102 Stat. 432, 43 U.S.C. §§ 2101-2106, which provides that the Federal Government asserts and transfers title to a State of any "abandoned shipwreck" that either is embedded in submerged lands of a State or is on a State's submerged lands "and is included in or determined eligible for inclusion in the National Register," § 2105(a)(3). According to California, the ASA applies because the Brother Jonathan is abandoned and is both embedded on state land and eligible for inclusion in the National Register of Historic Places (National Register). California also laid claim to the Brother Jonathan under Cal. Pub. Res.Code Ann. § 6313 (West Supp.1998) (hereinafter § 6313), which vests title in the State "to all abandoned shipwrecks... on or in the tide and submerged lands of California."

The District Court initially dismissed DSR's action without prejudice at DSR's initiative. The case was reinstated in 1994 after DSR actually located the Brother Jonathan four and one-half miles off the coast of Crescent City, where it apparently rests upright on the sea floor under more than 200 feet of water. Based on its possession of several artifacts from the Brother Jonathan, including china, a full bottle of champagne, and a brass spike from the ship's hull, DSR sought either an award of title to the ship and its cargo or a salvage award for its efforts in recovering the ship. DSR also claimed a right of ownership based on its purchase of subrogation interests from some of the insurance companies that had paid claims on the ship's cargo.

In response, the State of California entered an appearance for the limited purpose of filing a motion to dismiss DSR's in rem complaint for lack of jurisdiction. According to the State, it possesses title to the Brother Jonathan under either the ASA or § 6313, and therefore, DSR's in rem action against the vessel is an action against the State in violation of the Eleventh Amendment. DSR disputed both of the State's statutory ownership claims, and argued that the ASA could not divest the federal courts of the exclusive admiralty and maritime jurisdiction conferred by Article III, § 2, of the United States Constitution. DSR also filed a motion requesting that the District Court issue a warrant for the arrest of the

Brother Jonathan and its cargo, as well as an order appointing DSR the exclusive salvor of the shipwreck.

The District Court held two hearings on the motions. The first focused on whether the wreck is located within California's territorial waters, and the second concerned the possible abandonment, embeddedness, and historical significance of the shipwreck, issues relevant to California's claims to the res. For purposes of the pending motions, DSR stipulated that the Brother Jonathan is located upon submerged lands belonging to California.

After the hearings, the District Court concluded that the State failed to demonstrate a "colorable claim" to the Brother Jonathan under federal law, reasoning that the State had not established by a preponderance of the evidence that the ship is abandoned, embedded in the sea floor, or eligible for listing in the National Register as is required to establish title under the ASA. 883 F. Supp. 1343, 1357 (N.D.Cal. 1995). As for California's state law claim, the court determined that the ASA pre-empts § 6313. Accordingly, the court issued a warrant for the arrest of the Brother Jonathan, appointed DSR custodian of the shipwreck subject to further order of the court, and ordered DSR to take possession of the shipwreck as its exclusive salvor pending the court's determination of "the manner in which the wreck and its cargo, or the proceeds therefrom, should be distributed." 883 F. Supp., at 1364.

The District Court stated that it was not deciding whether "any individual items of cargo or personal property have been abandoned," explaining that "[a]t this stage in the litigation, DSR is not asking the court to award it salvage fees from the res of the wreck, or to otherwise make any order regarding title to or distribution of the wreck or its contents." *Id.*, at 1354. The District Court thought that the most prudent course would be to adjudicate title after DSR completes the salvage operation. Following the District Court's ruling, the United States asserted a claim to any property on the Brother Jonathan belonging to the Federal Government.

The State appealed, arguing that its immunity from suit under the Eleventh Amendment does not hinge upon the demonstration by a preponderance of the evidence that the ASA applies to the Brother Jonathan. 102 F.3d 379, 383 (C.A.9 1996). According to the State, it had established sufficient claim to the shipwreck under state law by "assert[ing] that the Brother Jonathan is on its submerged lands and that... § 6313 vests title in the State to abandoned shipwrecks on its submerged lands." *Id.*, at 385. Underlying the State's argument was a challenge to the District Court's ruling that the ASA pre-empts the California statute. The State also maintained that it had a colorable claim to the Brother Jonathan under the ASA, arguing that it presented ample evidence of both abandonment and embeddedness, and that the District Court applied the wrong test by "requir[ing] that abandonment be shown by an affirmative act on the part of the original owner demonstrating intent to renounce ownership." *Ibid.*

The Court of Appeals for the Ninth Circuit affirmed the District Court's orders. The court first concluded that § 6313 is pre-empted by the ASA because the state statute "takes title to shipwrecks that do not meet the requirements of the ASA and which are therefore within the exclusive admiralty jurisdiction of the federal courts." *Id.*, at 384. With respect to the State's claim under the ASA, the court presumed that "a federal court has both the power and duty to determine whether a case falls within its subject matter jurisdiction," and concluded that "it was appropriate for the district court to require the State to present evidence that the ASA applied to the Brother Jonathan, i.e., that it was abandoned and either embedded or eligible for listing in the National Register, before dismissing the case." *Id.*, at 386. According to the court's reasoning, "in addressing the questions of abandonment, embeddedness, and historical significance of the wreck under the ASA, a federal court does not adjudicate the state's rights," because the ASA establishes the Federal Government's title to a qualifying shipwreck, which is then transferred to a State. *Id.*, at 387. Consequently, in the court's view, "a federal court may adjudicate the question of whether a wreck meets the requirements of the ASA without implicating the Eleventh Amendment." *Ibid.*

As to the specifics of the State's claim under the ASA, the court held that the District Court did not err in concluding that the State failed to prove that the Brother Jonathan is abandoned within the meaning of the statute. The court reasoned that, in the absence of a definition of abandonment in the ASA, "Congress presumably intended that courts apply the definition of abandonment that has evolved under maritime law." *Ibid.* In maritime law, the court explained, abandonment occurs either when title to a vessel has been affirmatively renounced or when circumstances give rise to an inference of abandonment. Here, the Court of Appeals concluded, the District Court's "failure to infer abandonment from the evidence presented by the State was not clearly erroneous," given the insurance companies' claims to the ship's insured cargo and undisputed evidence presented by DSR that the technology required to salvage the Brother Jonathan has been developed only recently. *Id.*, at 388. The court also rejected the State's bid to treat the uninsured portion of the wreck as abandoned, explaining that the District Court did not address the status of individual items of cargo or personal property, and that "divid[ing] the wreck of the Brother Jonathan into abandoned and unabandoned portions for the purposes of the ASA" would lead to both federal and state courts adjudicating the wreck's fate, which, in the court's view, would be "confusing and inefficient," and also "inconsistent with the general rule in maritime law of treating wrecks as a legally unified res." *Id.*, at 389.

Summarizing its reasoning, the court stated that, "[b]ecause the law is reluctant to find abandonment, and because a finding of partial abandonment would deprive those holding title to the unabandoned portion of the wreck access to the federal forum, we hold that the Brother Jonathan is not abandoned." *Ibid.* (internal citation omitted). The court reserved the question whether there might be some point at which the insured portion of a shipwreck "becomes so negligible" that the entire wreck would be abandoned under the ASA. *Ibid.* The court also declined to take judicial notice of evidence that, during pendency of the appeal, the Brother Jonathan was determined eligible for inclusion in the National Register.

By concluding that the State must prove its claim to the Brother Jonathan by a preponderance of the evidence in order to invoke the immunity afforded by the Eleventh Amendment, the Ninth Circuit diverged from other Courts of Appeals that have held that a State need only make a bare assertion to ownership of a res. *See Zych v. Wrecked Vessel Believed to Be the Lady Elgin*, 960 F.2d 665, 670 (C.A.7), *cert. denied*, 506 U.S. 985, 113 S. Ct. 491, 121 L. Ed.2d 430 (1992); *Maritime Underwater Surveys, Inc. v. The Unidentified, Wrecked and Abandoned Sailing Vessel*, 717 F.2d 6, 8 (C.A.1 1983). (footnote omitted) We granted certiorari to address whether a State's Eleventh Amendment immunity in an in rem admiralty action depends upon evidence of the State's ownership of the res, and to consider the related questions whether the Brother Jonathan is subject to the ASA and whether the ASA pre-empts § 6313. 520 U.S. ___, 117 S. Ct. 2430, 138 L. Ed.2d 192 (1997).

II.

The judicial power of federal courts extends "to all Cases of admiralty and maritime Jurisdiction." Art. III, § 2, cl. 1. The federal courts have had a unique role in admiralty cases since the birth of this Nation, because "[m]aritime commerce was... the jugular vein of the Thirteen States." F. Frankfurter & J. Landis, *The Business of the Supreme Court* 7 (1927). Accordingly, "[t]he need for a body of law applicable throughout the nation was recognized by every shade of opinion in the Constitutional Convention." *Ibid*. The constitutional provision was incorporated into the first Judiciary Act in 1789, and federal courts have retained "admiralty or maritime jurisdiction" since then. *See* 28 U.S.C. § 1333(1). That jurisdiction encompasses "maritime causes of action begun and carried on as proceedings in rem, that is, where a vessel or thing is itself treated as the offender and made the defendant by name or description in order to enforce a lien." *Madruga v. Superior Court of Cal., County of San Diego*, 346 U.S. 556, 560, 74 S. Ct. 298, 301, 98 L. Ed. 290 (1954).

The jurisdiction of the federal courts is constrained, however, by the Eleventh Amendment, under which "[t]he Judicial power of the United States shall not be construed to extend to any suit in law or equity, commenced or prosecuted against one of the United States by Citizens of another State, or by Citizens or Subjects of any Foreign State." Although the Amendment, by its terms, "would appear to restrict only the Article III diversity jurisdiction of the federal courts," *Seminole Tribe of Florida v. Florida*, 517 U.S. 44, 54, 116 S. Ct. 1114, 1122, 134 L. Ed.2d 252 (1996), the Court has interpreted the Amendment more broadly. *See*, e.g., *Blatchford v. Native Village of Noatak*, 501 U.S. 775, 779, 111 S. Ct. 2578, 2581, 115 L. Ed.2d 686 (1991). According to this Court's precedents, a State may not be sued in federal court by one of its own citizens, *see Hans v. Louisiana*, 134 U.S. 1, 10 S. Ct. 504, 33 L. Ed. 842 (1890), and a state official is immune from suit in federal court for actions taken in an official capacity, *see Smith v. Reeves*, 178 U.S. 436, 20 S. Ct. 919, 44 L. Ed. 1140 (1900).

The Court has not always charted a clear path in explaining the interaction between the Eleventh Amendment and the federal courts' in rem admiralty jurisdiction. Early cases involving the disposition of "prize" vessels captured during wartime appear to have assumed that federal courts could adjudicate the in rem disposition of the bounty even when state officials raised an objection. *See United States v. Peters*, 5 Cranch 115, 139-141, 3 L. Ed. 53 (1809). As Justice Story explained, in admiralty actions in rem,

"the jurisdiction of the [federal] court is founded upon the possession of the thing; and if the State should interpose a claim for the property, it does not act merely in the character of a defendant, but as an actor. Besides, the language of the [Eleventh] [A]mendment is, that 'the judicial power of the United States shall not be construed to extend to any suit in law or equity.' But a suit in the admiralty is not, correctly speaking, a suit in law or in equity; but is often spoken of in contradistinction to both."

2 J. Story, *Commentaries on the Constitution of the United States* § 1689, pp. 491-492 (5th ed. 1891).

Justice Washington, riding Circuit, expressed the same view in *United States v. Bright*, 24 F. Cas. 1232, 1236, No. 14,647 (CC Pa. 1809), where he reasoned:

"[I]n cases of admiralty and maritime jurisdiction the property in dispute is generally in the possession of the court, or of persons bound to produce it, or its equivalent, and the proceedings are in rem. The court decides in whom the right is, and distributes the proceeds accordingly. In such a case the court need not depend upon the good will of a state claiming an interest in the thing to enable it to execute its decree. All the world are parties to such a suit, and of course are bound by the sentence. The state may interpose her claim and have it decided. But she cannot lie by, and, after the decree is passed say that she was a party, and therefore not bound, for want of jurisdiction in the court."

Although those statements might suggest that the Eleventh Amendment has little application in in rem admiralty proceedings, subsequent decisions have altered that understanding of the federal courts' role. In *Ex parte New York*, 256 U.S. 490, 41 S. Ct. 588, 65 L. Ed. 1057 (1921) (New York I), the Court explained that admiralty and maritime jurisdiction is not wholly exempt from the operation of the Eleventh Amendment, thereby rejecting the views of Justices Story and Washington. *Id.*, at 497-498, 41 S. Ct., at 589-590. On the same day, in its opinion in *Ex parte New York*, 256 U.S. 503, 41 S. Ct. 592, 65 L. Ed. 1063 (1921) (New York II), the Court likewise concluded that the federal courts lacked jurisdiction over a wrongful death action brought in rem against a tugboat operated by the State of New York on the Erie Canal, although the Court did not specifically rely on the Eleventh Amendment in its holding.

The Court's most recent case involving an in rem admiralty action, *Florida Dept. of State v. Treasure Salvors, Inc.*, 458 U.S. 670, 102 S. Ct. 3304, 73 L. Ed.2d 1057 (1982), addressed whether the Eleventh Amendment "bars an in rem admiralty action seeking to recover property owned by a state." *Id.*, at 682, 102 S. Ct., at 3313 (internal quotation marks omitted). A plurality of the Court suggested that New York II could be distinguished on the ground that, in *Treasure Salvors*, the State's possession of maritime artifacts was unauthorized, and the State therefore could not invoke the Eleventh Amendment to block their arrest. *Id.*, at 695-699, 102 S. Ct., at 3320-3322 (citing *Ex parte Young*, 209 U.S. 123, 28 S. Ct. 441, 52 L. Ed. 714 (1908), and *Tindal v. Wesley*, 167 U.S. 204, 17 S. Ct. 770, 42 L. Ed. 137 (1897)). As the plurality explained, "since the state officials do not have a colorable claim to possession of the artifacts, they may not invoke the Eleventh Amendment to block execution of the warrant of arrest." 458 U.S., at 697, 102 S. Ct., at 3321.

That reference to a "colorable claim" is at the crux of this case. Both the District Court and the Ninth Circuit interpreted the "colorable claim" requirement as imposing a burden on the State to demonstrate by a preponderance of the evidence that the Brother Jonathan meets the criteria set forth in the ASA. *See* 102 F.3d, at 386, 883 F. Supp., at 1349. Other Courts of Appeals have concluded that a State need only make a bare assertion to ownership of a res in order to establish its sovereign immunity in an in rem admiralty action. *See*, e.g., *Zych*, 960 F.2d, at 670.

By our reasoning, however, either approach glosses over an important distinction present here. In this case, unlike in *Treasure Salvors*, DSR asserts rights to a res that is not in the possession of the State. The Eleventh Amendment's role in that type of dispute was not decided by the plurality opinion in *Treasure Salvors*, which decided "whether a federal court exercising admiralty in rem jurisdiction may seize property held by state officials under a claim that the property belongs to the State." 458 U.S., at 683, 102 S. Ct., at 3314; *see also id.*, at 697, 102 S. Ct., at 3321 ("In ruling that the Eleventh Amendment does not bar execution of the warrant, we need not decide the extent to which a federal district court exercising admiralty in rem jurisdiction over property before the court may adjudicate the rights of claimants to that property as against sovereigns that did not appear and voluntarily assert any claim that they had to the res.").

Nor did the opinions in New York I or New York II address a situation comparable to this case. The holding in New York I explained that, although the suit at issue was styled as an in rem libel action seeking recovery of damages against tugboats chartered by the State, the proceedings were actually "in the nature of an action in personam against [the Superintendent of Public Works of the State of New York], not individually, but in his [official] capacity." 256 U.S., at 501, 41 S. Ct., at 591. The action in New York II was an in rem suit against a vessel described as being "at all times mentioned in the libel and at present... the absolute property of the State of New York, in its possession and control, and employed in the public service of the State for governmental uses and purposes..." 256 U.S., at 508, 41 S. Ct., at 592. As Justice White explained in his opinion in *Treasure Salvors*:

> "The In re New York cases... reflect the special concern in admiralty that maritime property of the sovereign is not to be seized... [They] are but the most apposite examples of the line of cases concerning in rem actions brought against vessels in which an official of the State, the Federal Government, or a foreign government has asserted ownership of the res. The Court's consistent interpretation of the respective but related immunity doctrines pertaining to such vessels has been, upon proper presentation that the sovereign entity claims ownership of a res in its possession, to dismiss the suit or modify its judgment accordingly."
>
> 458 U.S., at 709-710, 102 S. Ct., at 3327 (opinion concurring in judgment in part and dissenting in part) (emphasis added).

It is true that statements in the fractured opinions in *Treasure Salvors* might be read to suggest that a federal court may not undertake in rem adjudication of the State's interest in property without the State's consent, regardless of the status of the res. *See*, e.g., *id.*, at 682, 102 S. Ct., at 3313 (plurality opinion) ("The court did not have power... to adjudicate the State's interest in the property without the State's consent"); *id.*, at 711, 102 S. Ct., at 3328 (White, J., concurring in judgment in part and dissenting in part) ("It is... beyond reasonable dispute that the Eleventh Amendment bars a federal court from deciding the rights and obligations of a State in a contract unless the State consents"). Those assertions, however, should not be divorced from the context of *Treasure Salvors* and reflexively applied to the very different circumstances presented by this case. In *Treasure Salvors*, the State had possession—albeit unlawfully—of the artifacts at issue. Also, the opinion addressed the District Court's authority to issue a warrant to arrest the artifacts, not the disposition of title to them. As the plurality explained, "[t]he proper resolution of [the Eleventh Amendment] issue... does not require—or permit—a determination of the State's ownership of the artifacts." *Id.*, at 699, 102 S. Ct., at 3322 (emphasis added); *see also id.*, at 700, 102 S. Ct., at 3322 (noting that while adjudication of the State's right to the artifacts "would be justified if the State voluntarily advanced a claim to [them], it may not be justified as part of the Eleventh Amendment analysis, the only issue before us"). Thus, any references in *Treasure Salvors* to what the lower courts could have done if they had solely adjudicated title to the artifacts, rather than issued a warrant to arrest the res, do not control the outcome of this case, particularly given that it comes before us in a very different posture, i.e., in an admiralty action in rem where the State makes no claim of actual possession of the res.

Nor does the fact that *Treasure Salvors* has been cited for the general proposition that federal courts cannot adjudicate a State's claim of title to property, *see*, e.g., *Idaho v. Coeur d'Alene Tribe of Idaho*, 521 U.S. ___, 117 S. Ct. 2028, 2043-2045, 138 L. Ed.2d 438 (1997) (O'CONNOR, J., concurring in part and concurring in judgment); *id.*, at ___, 117 S. Ct. at 2043-2045 (SOUTER, J., dissenting), prevent a more nuanced application of *Treasure Salvors* in the context of the federal courts' in rem admiralty jurisdiction. Although the Eleventh Amendment bars federal jurisdiction over general title disputes relating to State property interests, it does not necessarily follow that it applies to in rem admiralty actions, or that in such actions, federal courts may not exercise jurisdiction over property that the State does not actually possess.

In considering whether the Eleventh Amendment applies where the State asserts a claim in admiralty to a res not in its possession, this Court's decisions in cases involving the sovereign immunity of the Federal Government in in rem admiralty actions provide guidance, for this Court has recognized a correlation between sovereign immunity principles applicable to States and the Federal Government. *See Tindal v. Wesley*, 167 U.S., at 213, 17 S. Ct., at 773-774; *see also Treasure Salvors, supra*, at 710, 102 S. Ct., at 3327 (White, J., concurring in judgment in part and dissenting in part) (discussing analogy between immunity in "in rem actions brought against vessels in which an official of the State, the Federal Government, or a foreign government has asserted ownership of the res"). In one such case, *The Davis*, 10 Wall. 15, 19 L. Ed. 875 (1869), the Court explained that "proceedings in rem to enforce a lien against property of the United States are only forbidden in cases where, in order to sustain the proceeding, the possession of the United States must be invaded under process of the court." *Id.*, 77 U.S. at 20. The possession referred to was "an actual possession, and not that mere constructive possession which is very often implied by reason of ownership under circumstances favorable to such implication." *Id.*, at 21; *see also The Siren*, 7 Wall. 152, 159, 19 L. Ed. 129 (1868) (describing "exemption of the government from a direct proceeding in rem against the vessel whilst in its custody"). The Court's jurisprudence respecting the sovereign immunity of foreign governments has likewise turned on the sovereign's possession of the res at issue. *See*, e.g., *The Pesaro*, 255 U.S. 216, 219, 41 S. Ct. 308, 309, 65 L. Ed. 592 (1921) (federal court's in rem jurisdiction not barred by mere suggestion of foreign government's ownership of vessel).

While this Court's decision in *The Davis* was issued over a century ago, its fundamental premise remains valid in in rem admiralty actions, in light of the federal courts' constitutionally established jurisdiction in that area and the fact that a requirement that a State possess the disputed res in such cases is "consistent with the principle which exempts the [State] from suit and its possession from disturbance by virtue of judicial process." *The Davis, supra*, at 21. Based on longstanding precedent respecting the federal courts' assumption of in rem admiralty jurisdiction over vessels that are not in the possession of a sovereign, we conclude that the Eleventh Amendment does not bar federal jurisdiction over the Brother Jonathan and, therefore, that the District Court may adjudicate DSR's and the State's claims to the shipwreck. We have no occasion in this case to consider any other circumstances under which an in rem admiralty action might proceed in federal court despite the Eleventh Amendment.

III.

There remains the issue whether the courts below properly concluded that the Brother Jonathan was not abandoned for purposes of the ASA. That conclusion was necessarily influenced by the assumption that the Eleventh Amendment was relevant to the courts' inquiry. The Court of Appeals' determination that the wreck and its contents are not abandoned for purposes of the ASA was affected by concerns that if "the vessel had been partially abandoned, both the federal court and the state court would be adjudicating the fate of the Brother Jonathan." 102 F.3d, at 389. Moreover, the District Court's inquiry was a preliminary one, based on the concern that it was premature "for the court to find that any individual items of cargo or personal property have been abandoned." 883 F. Supp., at 1354. In light of our ruling that the Eleventh Amendment does not bar complete adjudication of the competing claims to the Brother Jonathan in federal court, the application of the ASA must be reevaluated. Because the record before this Court is limited to the preliminary issues before the District Court, we decline to resolve whether the Brother Jonathan is abandoned within the meaning of the ASA. We leave that issue for reconsideration on remand, with the clarification that the meaning of "abandoned" under the ASA conforms with its meaning under admiralty law.

Our grant of certiorari also encompassed the question whether the courts below properly concluded that the ASA pre-empts § 6313, which apparently operates to transfer title to abandoned shipwrecks not covered by the ASA to the State. Because the District Court's full consideration of the application of the ASA on remand might negate the need to address the pre-emption issue, we decline to undertake that analysis.

Accordingly, the judgment of the Court of Appeals assuming jurisdiction over this case is affirmed, its judgment in all other respects is vacated, and the case is remanded for further proceedings consistent with this opinion.

It is so ordered.

Justice STEVENS, concurring.

In *Florida Dept. of State v. Treasure Salvors, Inc.*, 458 U.S. 670, 102 S. Ct. 3304, 73 L. Ed.2d 1057 (1982), both the four Members of the plurality and the four dissenters agreed that the District Court "did not have power... to adjudicate the State's interest in the property without the State's consent." *Id.*, at 682, 102 S. Ct., at 3313; *see also id.*, at 699–700, 102 S. Ct., at 3322; *id.*, at 703, 102 S. Ct., at 3324, (White, J., concurring in judgment in part and dissenting in part). Our reasons for reaching that common conclusion were different, but I am now persuaded that all of us might well have reached a different conclusion if the position of Justices Story and Washington (that the Eleventh Amendment is no bar to any in rem admiralty action) had been brought to our attention. I believe that both opinions made the mistake of assuming that the Eleventh Amendment has the same application to an in rem admiralty action as to any other action seeking possession of property in the control of state officers.

My error, in writing for the plurality, was the assumption that the reasoning in *Tindal v. Wesley*, 167 U.S. 204, 17 S. Ct. 770, 42 L. Ed. 137 (1897), and *United States v. Lee*, 106 U.S. 196, 1 S. Ct. 240, 27 L. Ed. 171 (1882), which supported our holding that Treasure Salvors was entitled to possession of the artifacts, also precluded a binding determination of the State's interest in the property. Under the reasoning of those cases, the fact that the state officials were acting without lawful authority meant that a judgment against them would not bind the State. *See* 458 U.S., at 687–688, 102 S. Ct., at 3316 ("In holding that the action was not barred by the Eleventh Amendment, the Court in *Tindal* emphasized that any judgment awarding possession to the plaintiff would not subsequently bind the State"). That reasoning would have been sound if we were deciding an ejectment action in which the right to possession of a parcel of real estate was in dispute; moreover, it seemed appropriate in *Treasure Salvors* because we were focusing on the validity of the arrest warrant.

Having given further consideration to the special characteristics of in rem admiralty actions, and more particularly to the statements by Justice Story and Justice Washington quoted at pages 9 and 10 of the Court's opinion, I am now convinced that we should have affirmed the *Treasure Salvors* judgment in its entirety. Accordingly, I agree with the Court's holding that the State of California may be bound by a federal court's in rem adjudication of rights to the Brother Jonathan and its cargo.

Justice KENNEDY, with whom Justice GINSBURG and Justice BREYER join, concurring.

I join the opinion of the Court. In my view, the opinion's discussion of *Florida Dept. of State v. Treasure Salvors, Inc.*, 458 U.S. 670, 102 S. Ct. 3304, 73 L. Ed.2d 1057 (1982), does not embed in our law the distinction between a State's possession or nonpossession for purposes of Eleventh Amendment analysis in admiralty cases. In light of the subsisting doubts surrounding that case and Justice STEVENS' concurring opinion today, it ought to be evident that the issue is open to reconsideration.

Protection and Management of Abandoned Shipwrecks

The ASA directs states to protect abandoned shipwrecks, and defers to the states in determining how to manage them in a manner consistent with several broad provisions. States are to offer recreational and educational opportunities to interested groups, including divers and researchers.[31] The ASA presupposes that states will follow federal policy and establish multiple use management regimes for their shipwrecks that also incorporate the protection of natural resources.[32] This policy is consistent with other federal statutory management approaches such as an integrated coastal management under the Coastal Zone Management Act (CZMA),[33] and the multiple use manage-

---

[31]43 U.S.C. § 2103.

[32]43 U.S.C. § 2103.

[33]The ASA guidelines urge states to integrate their management of submerged heritage resources into their state Coastal Zone Management programs so that they can use CZMA's section 307(c) consistency provisions to protect historic wrecks and use CZMA grant money to fund research and management. [16 U.S.C. §§ 1451, 1456(c).]

ment approach mandated by the National Marine Sanctuaries Act. The ASA directed the National Park Service to develop guidelines for implementation of the ASA to assist states and national managers of submerged lands.[34]

The ASA guidelines[35] encourage states to assign their authority over abandoned shipwrecks to an appropriate and adequately staffed agency, and also advise states to use advisory boards when considering recommendations and advice of parties who use or have an interest in submerged heritage resources. The long-term management of heritage resources in the marine environment should reflect the broad, diverse, and often conflicting interests of stakeholders. The guidelines provide for the recovery by private parties of certain shipwrecks when the recovery is consistent with the ASA, for the public benefit, and subject to the oversight of the managing agency. They advise banning the use of destructive treasure hunting methods as unscientific and hazardous to natural resources as well as historical information.[36] There are also guidelines for the creation and management of underwater parks or preserves, as suggested by the ASA, to provide additional protection for historic shipwrecks.[37]

In addition to providing guidance to the states, the ASA guidelines contain provisions for national agency managers that supplement the other national historic preservation laws making up the federal government's archeology program. This program, and the ASA guidelines in particular, have been used to develop the National Marine Sanctuary management program for submerged heritage resources.

2. The National Marine Sanctuaries Act

Background

Congress enacted a series of environmental laws during 1972 that included the National Environmental Policy Act, the Clean Air Act, the Clean Water Act, the Coastal Zone Management Act, and the Marine Protection, Research,

---

[34]43 U.S.C. § 2104.

[35]The guidelines are advisory and therefore are non-binding upon the states and federal agencies. [55 Fed. Reg. 50116 (1990).]

[36]55 Fed. Reg. 50,132 (1990).

[37]43 U.S.C. § 2103(b)

and Sanctuaries Act of 1972 (MPRSA).[38] As reflected in the legislative history, the MPRSA arose out of public concern for ocean dumping, the development of the seabed for oil, gas, and minerals, and a desire to protect special areas of the marine environment for research, education, recreation, fishing, and other uses by present and future generations. It set out a plan for use of the marine environment by regulating dumping in certain areas (Title I) and setting aside significant areas as National Marine Sanctuaries for resources protection and other uses compatible with protection (Title III). Title I became known more commonly as the Ocean Dumping Act after amendment in 1988. The short title of Title III also became known as the National Marine Sanctuaries Act (NMSA) under the 1992 amendment to the MPRSA.

Legislation leading to the development of the National Marine Sanctuary Program can be traced to eleven bills introduced in the House of Representatives in 1968. These bills were a response to a public outcry from two major incidents that caused the degradation of popular, recreational marine areas—the dumping of nerve gas and oil wastes off the coast of Florida and an oil spill from a platform off the coast of Santa Barbara, California. The impetus for a sanctuary program was the perceived need for specially protected and managed areas of the marine environment, where no polluting activities would be permitted.[39] These bills were never reported by the House Merchant Marine and Fisheries Committee during the Ninetieth Congress because of opposition by the oil and gas industry to the bills' emphasis on preventing the exploration and development of oil, gas, and minerals in the proposed sanctuaries [Blumm & Blumstein, *The Marine Sanctuaries Pro-*

---

[38]Generally, Title I of the MPRSA (known as the Ocean Dumping Act) confers authority on the Environmental Protection Agency (EPA) to regulate ocean dumping, and empowers the Army Corps of Engineers (COE) to regulate dumping of dredged materials. Title II establishes a research and monitoring program under the authority of the Secretary of Commerce, through the National Oceanic and Atmospheric Administration (NOAA) and the EPA. Title III [16 U.S.C. § 1431, as amended (1994), known as the "National Marine Sanctuaries Act"] establishes the National Marine Sanctuary Program under the authority of the Secretary of Commerce. The Secretary's authority under the National Marine Sanctuaries Act is delegated to NOAA.

[39]The sanctuaries were envisioned as areas for studying natural systems unencumbered by pollution, and for preserving marine areas so that scenic beauty, ocean recreation, and fishing activities could be perpetuated. Virginia Institute of Marine Sciences, Report No. 70, *Marine and Estuarine Sanctuaries* 9 (1973).

gram: A Framework for Critical Areas Management in the Sea, 8 Envtl. L. Rep. (Envtl. L. Inst.) 50,016, 50,018 (1978)].

Public concern about the threat to the marine environment from ocean dumping caused the Council on Environmental Quality (CEQ) to study the issue. The council's 1970 report stated that marine pollution had seriously degraded the marine environment and endangered human health because of its effects on fisheries and recreational areas [U.S. Council on Envtl. Quality, Ocean Dumping: A National Policy 12–18 (1970); Bakalian, *Regulation and Control of United States Ocean Dumping: A Decade of Progress, an Appraisal for the Future*, 8 Harv. Envtl. L. Rev. 193–95, 207 (1984)]. The CEQ called for the development of strong domestic law and international cooperation. The following year, the Nixon administration submitted to the Senate a draft bill that would regulate ocean dumping [S. Rep. No. 451, 92d Cong., 1st Sess. 1 (1971), reprinted in 1972 U.S. Code Cong. & Admin. News 4234, 4253]. Also as a result of the CEQ report, the House of Representatives incorporated a marine sanctuaries provision into a bill, H.R. 9727, determining that Congress should address "the need to create a mechanism for protecting certain important areas of the coastal zone from intrusive activities by man" and that "the marine sanctuaries authorized by this bill would provide a means whereby important areas may be set aside for protection and may thus be insulated from the various types of 'development' which can destroy them" [H.R. Rep. No. 361, 92d Cong., 1st Sess. 15 (1971)].

Following passage by the House of Representatives in September 1971, H.R. 9727 was considered by the Senate Commerce Committee, which expressed doubts about whether federal jurisdiction existed to assert Title III over the super-adjacent water column outside the Territorial Sea and Contiguous Zone. The Senate Commerce Committee also noted that, under Title III, the Secretary of Commerce would have broader authority to protect these areas than would the Secretary of the Interior under the Outer Continental Shelf Lands Act (OCSLA). This is because the Secretary of the Interior's authority to withdraw certain lands in cases of proposed Outer Continental Shelf mineral lease sales does not extend to other development activities. Besides, it was argued, Title I and the OCSLA already provided sufficient authority to protect areas of the Outer Continental Shelf. (In fact, EPA authority to prevent dumping did not extend to threats of pollution from other sources.) Despite these objections to Title III, the Senate agreed with the concept of establishing marine sanctuaries which "set aside areas of the seabed and the super adjacent waters for scientific study, to preserve unique, rare, or characteristic features of the oceans, coastal, and other waters, and their total ecosystems" [S. Rep. No. 451, 92d Cong., 1st Sess. 15 (1971)]. After further objections, the Senate, in November 1971, agreed to pass a Conference Committee bill that included a modified version of Title III. H.R. 9727 was signed into law on October 23, 1972.

The Scope of the NMSA

The National Marine Sanctuaries Act (NMSA) authorizes the Secretary of Commerce, through the National Oceanic and Atmospheric Administration (NOAA), to set aside discrete areas of the marine environment having special national or international significance as National Marine Sanctuaries. [16 U.S.C. § 1431, *et seq.*] Marine sanctuaries are created to protect, conserve, and comprehensively manage these special areas for present and future generations by facilitating the multiple uses of the sanctuaries in a manner compatible with the primary objective of protecting resource or human use values. Resource values include natural ecosystems and assemblages of living resources, and historical and cultural features. Human use values include present and potential uses for research, education, recreation, subsistence, and commercial endeavors.[40] [16 U.S.C. § 1431(a)(2).] Generally, this objective is achieved by prohibiting incompatible uses, and by managing intrusive human activities through regulation and permitting.

Marine sanctuaries generally lie close to the shore because that is where significant natural resources exist, and where human activities, such as fishing, boating, and diving take place. Further, most of the submerged heritage resources are located near the shore because that is also where most of the human activities of previous cultures have traditionaly occurred. National Marine Sanctuaries, like the National Parks, are partially designed to protect heritage resources. However, whereas the National Park Service generally limits public access to heritage resources for archaeological research and nonintrusive viewing, NOAA, as manager of the National Marine Sanctuaries, has a multiple use management mandate that requires consideration of the entire range of socioeconomic uses of these special areas, including commercial purposes such as fishing, shipping, and tourism. [16 U.S.C. § 1431(b)(5) (1994).]

Interestingly, the first National Marine Sanctuary, designated in 1975, was created to protect and preserve in place the USS *Monitor*, one of the most significant historic shipwrecks in the United States [15 C.F.R. §§ 922.60–.62 (1997)], even though, at the time, historical, archeological, or cultural resources were not expressly included among the resources falling within

---

[40]The purpose of Title III, as stated in the 1972 version of the MPRSA, is to set aside sanctuaries "necessary for the purpose of preserving *or restoring* such areas for their conservation, recreational, ecological, or esthetic values." Also, any human activity permitted in marine sanctuaries would have to be "consistent with the purposes of this title." [33 U.S.C. § 1401 *et seq.*] In 1984, the law was amended and the words "or restoring" were deleted in order to avoid designating as sanctuaries areas that already are polluted and in need of clean-up actions. Also, these words were deleted to underscore the purpose of the NMSA in protecting and preserving significant and relatively pristine areas.

the purview of the NMSA.[41] The *Monitor* National Marine Sanctuary is the only National Marine Sanctuary designated solely to protect a heritage resource, and the only one where diving without a permit is prohibited. The sanctuary was proposed to be managed as an archeological site, where public access would be limited to research on the *Monitor* wreck, and then only if the potential benefits from such research outweighed the potential harm to the site arising from the research activities. Accordingly, the restrictions at the *Monitor* National Marine Sanctuary are the most stringent for any sanctuary, and they include prohibitions on diving, fishing, or even stopping in the sanctuary (an area approximately one square nautical mile). When, during the 1980s, diving at depths beyond the 130-foot safety standard became increasingly common, interest in diving on the *Monitor*, located at a depth of approximately 235 feet, increased. This interest eventually led to legal challenges and judicial scrutiny of the regulatory restrictions and underlying policies of the *Monitor* National Marine Sanctuary management plan regarding access to this public resource.[42]

Since the designation of the *Monitor* National Marine Sanctuary, eleven other sanctuaries have been established.[43] The most significant with regard to submerged heritage resources management is the Florida Keys National Marine Sanctuary. On November 16, 1990, Congress designated an area of the marine environment surrounding the Florida Keys as a National Marine Sanctuary in order to protect its unique, nationally significant natural resources, including seagrass meadows, mangrove islands, and coral reefs. In

---

[41]The original, 1972 version of the NMSA did not refer to historical or cultural resources. However, as a result of the USS *Monitor* being designated the first National Marine Sanctuary, Congress amended the NMSA to expressly include the protection and management of historic resources. [16 U.S.C. § 1431 *et seq.*]

[42]As the U.S.S. Monitor National Marine Sanctuary was designated to protect only one shipwreck, and is only about one square nautical mile, NOAA deemed a restrictive public access policy to be appropriate and not unduly burdensome on other uses of the marine environment, such as fishing and diving. Nevertheless, following the *Gentile* cases, NOAA changed its policy to permit non-intrusive public access to the *Monitor*, but only during certain times of the year, and only with a special use permit consistent with the NMSA. [16 U.S.C. § 1441 (1994)].

[43]The name of each National Marine Sanctuary can be found in 15 C.F.R. Part 922. NOAA also has proposed the Thunder Bay National Marine Sanctuary, in Lake Huron and off the eastern coast of Michigan, for the purpose of protecting a collection of approximately 160 shipwrecks and other submerged heritage resources. If designated, it would be the first sanctuary in the Great Lakes, and the first one located solely within state lands and waters. It also would be the first sanctuary designated to protect a collection of heritage resources of national and international significance, rather than a single heritage resource, as in the case of the Monitor National Marine Sanctuary.

the Florida Keys National Marine Sanctuary and Protection Act, Pub. L. 101-605, Congress directed the federal government and the state of Florida to jointly develop and implement a comprehensive program to reduce pollution in Florida's offshore waters, and to protect and restore the water quality, coral reefs, and other living marine resources there. The Act also protects sanctuary resources and prohibits particular types of vessels from entering an "area to be avoided." Leasing, exploration, development, and production of minerals or hydrocarbons are also prohibited in the sanctuary. [Pub. L. No. 101-605 §§ 3 and 6, 104 Stat. 3089 (codified as amended in scattered sections of 16 U.S.C.).] The Act also implicitly authorizes the restriction on activities having an adverse effect on sanctuary resources, property, qualities, values, or purposes (Section 3). The Act, using procedures set forth in the NMSA, directed the Secretary of Commerce to develop a comprehensive management plan and implement regulations in consultation with federal, state, and local authorities (Section 7). These procedures require, among other things, that NOAA identify the state authorities already regulating the resources in question, and that federal regulations be promulgated for the sanctuary that supplement existing state authorities. The Florida Keys Act also specifically states that resource protection may be achieved through the use of a zoning scheme (Section 7).

Although the Florida Keys were singled out for attention by Congress because of the existence of natural resources in the area, the presence of heritage resources was also recognized. Because the treasure salvage industry in the United States is largely concentrated in the Keys, the development of a final management plan to manage heritage resources in the Florida Keys National Marine Sanctuary was complicated and very controversial. Even before any implementing regulations for the sanctuary had been promulgated, the scope of sanctuary authority to regulate treasure hunters was the subject of litigation. That action was based on the statutory enforcement provisions of the NMSA in the area designated by Congress and was resolved in favor of the federal government.

Resource Protection and Management of Multiple Uses of National Marine Sanctuaries

There are several statutory and regulatory provisions designed to protect sanctuary resources as well as manage the various users of each National Marine Sanctuary and its resources. While sanctuary management facilitates multiple uses, resources protection is the beacon for applying the statute and regulations in day-to-day management decisions. The most important resource protection provisions are those that seek to preserve resources by preventing harmful or destructive activities.

While the statute provides broad authority to protect sanctuary resources and provide enforcement mechanisms to fulfill management objectives, the implementing regulations are generally more important for protecting sanctuary resources in day-to-day management. The regulations, in general, include a provision indicating that all activities (fishing, boating, diving, etc.) may be conducted in the sanctuaries unless prohibited or otherwise managed by individual sanctuary regulations. [15 C.F.R. § 922.42.]

The NMSA and its regulations follow the suite of federal statutes and regulations designed to protect heritage resources known as the federal archeology program to the maximum extent practicable with regard to management of submerged heritage resources. The regulations specifically state that:

> Program regulations, policies, standards, guidelines, and procedures under the Act [NMSA] concerning the identification, evaluation, registration, and treatment of historical resources shall be consistent, to the extent practicable, with the declared national policy for the protection and preservation of these resources as stated in the National Historic Preservation Act of 1966 (NHPA), 16 U.S.C. § 470 *et seq.*, the Archeological and Historical Preservation Act of 1974, 16 U.S.C. § 469 *et seq.*, and the Archaeological Resources Protection Act of 1979 (ARPA), 16 U.S.C. § 470aa *et seq.*
>
> 15 C.F.R. § 922.1(c)(4).

The Sanctuary Program Management of submerged heritage resources[44] by NOAA can be divided into three approaches. The first management approach is to prohibit physical public access to the resource, except for scientific research purposes. This approach was used in the *Monitor* Sanctuary from 1975 through 1991. The second approach, currently used by 13 sanctuaries, is to allow public access that is not harmful to natural or historic resources by strictly regulating intrusive archeological research through permits. This approach, however, does not allow any private recovery of historic sanctuary resources for profit. The third approach, used only in the Florida Keys National Marine Sanctuary, strictly regulates intrusive archeological research, but provides for the issuance of permits that allow for private recovery of historic sanctuary resources for profit, if recovery is determined to be in the public interest.[45]

---

[44]Under NOAA regulations, "historical" means a sanctuary resource possessing historical, cultural, archaeological, or paleontological significance, including sites, structures, districts, and objects significantly associated with or representative of earlier people, cultures, and human activities and events." [15 C.F.R. § 922.2(c).]

[45]NOAA, the state of Florida, and the Advisory Council on Historic Preservation have entered into a Programmatic Agreement under Section 106 of the NHPA to assure the preservation of the submerged heritage resources of the Florida Keys National Marine Sanctuary.

Prohibited Activities

With the policy of resources protection as a backdrop, the NMSA sets forth the types of activities that are prohibited:

> It is unlawful to
>
> (1)   destroy, cause the loss of, or injure any sanctuary resource managed under law or regulations for that sanctuary;
>
> (2)   possess, sell, deliver, carry, transport, or ship by any means any sanctuary resource taken in violation of this section;
>
> (3)   interfere with the enforcement of this chapter; or
>
> (4)   violate any provision of this chapter or any regulation or permit issued pursuant to this chapter.

[16 U.S.C. § 1436 (1994).]

In addition to the list of prohibited activities under the statute, nearly every sanctuary in the program also has regulations setting forth the types of activities that are prohibited, including: (1) the removal or injury of historic sanctuary resources and (2) any alteration of the seabed. While exceptions to the prohibition on alteration of the seabed exist, they are narrowly construed. (*See, infra, United States v. Craft.*)

Multiple Use Management

Resource protection is the primary objective of sanctuary designation and management. This objective is designed to ensure that people can continue to use and enjoy these special marine areas for future generations. Some members of the public, though, are concerned about how environmental protection will affect them. Specifically, they are concerned about whether designation and management of a marine sanctuary will interfere with their ability to earn a livelihood that depends on the use of marine sanctuaries and resources. (The primary example is fishermen, whose livelihood clearly depends on use of a sanctuary resource.) To assure the public (including fishermen) that sanctuaries will not preclude activities—provided that such activities do not destroy, cause the loss of, or injure sanctuary resources—Congress instituted a multiple use management concept. The purpose of this multiple use policy is set forth in the statute:

> (5) to facilitate to the extent compatible with the primary objective of resource protection, all public and private uses of the resources of these marine areas not prohibited pursuant to other authorities.
>
> 16 U.S.C. § 1431(b)(5).

Except for activities that harm, cause the loss of, or injure sanctuary resources, the statute provides no guidance on how the multiple use management policy is to be factored into the development of regulations, management plans, and subsequent management decisions, such as the decision to issue permits. However, a review of the legislative history of the NMSA does provide some guidance on the matter.

The original legislative intent behind the implementation of the NMSA was to provide for the conservation and preservation of resources in the marine environment.[46] However, debate in the House of Representatives included discussion of whether the NMSA was intended to prevent commercial uses of the sea, including development of the seabed. Representative Keith stated that Title III "provides for multiple use of the designated areas," meaning that the proposed law did not disturb fishing and other uses that were compatible with resource protection.[47] The original bill, though, did not expressly include this multiple use policy. Instead, the enunciated purpose of the 1972 version was to preserve and restore certain marine areas for their "conservation, recreational, ecological, or esthetic values."

Although the NMSA was silent on the subject, NOAA noted the reference to a multiple use management policy in the legislative history, and applied it to its management regime.[48] In the preamble to its first regulations implementing sanctuary management, NOAA stated that "the question of multiple use will need to be exercised on a case-by-case basis."[49]

Congress amended Title III in 1984, to expand and alter the purposes and policies of the marine sanctuary program, in response to confusion about whether the program's purpose and authority encompassed multiple use management. Consequently, the NMSA now expressly provides for a multiple use management mandate, and directs NOAA to manage sanctuaries in such a way that will "facilitate, to the extent compatible with the primary objective of resource protection, all public and private uses of the resources of these marine areas not prohibited by other authorities."[50] The sanctuary program continues to determine what activities are permitted and prohibited under a management plan on a case-by-case basis.

---

[46] The Marine Protection, Research, and Sanctuaries Act of 1972, Pub. L. No. 92-532, § 302(a), 86 Stat. 1052, 1061.

[47] Cong. Rec. H8190 (Sept. 8, 1971). See also Cong. Rec. H8232 (Sept. 9, 1971) (Cong. Pelly statement).

[48] See David A. Tarnas, "The U.S. National Marine Sanctuary Program: An Analysis of the Program's Implementation and Current Issues," 16 *Coastal Management* 275, 277 (1988).

[49] 15 C.F.R. § 922 (1974).

[50] 16 U.S.C. § 1431 (1984).

Special Use Permits

To further the objective of multiple use management, the NMSA provides for the issuance of special use permits to conduct activities that are compatible with the purposes for which a sanctuary is designated. Although "compatible" is not fully defined in the statute, other provisions of the law provide guidance on interpreting this term, such as 16 U.S.C. §§ 1436 and 1440, which state that research and educational activities are consistent with sanctuary goals and, thus, are clearly compatible with resource protection. Fishing is also defined as a compatible activity in the statute. [NMSA §§ 304 and 310; a special use permit is not required to engage in fishing activities within a sanctuary[51].] Clearly, however, the statute contemplates that compatible uses are those that are consistent with the primary policy of resource protection and do not cause injury to or the destruction of sanctuary resources:

> (a) Issuance of permits.—The Secretary may issue special use permits which authorize the conduct of specific activities in a National Marine Sanctuary if the Secretary determines such authorization is necessary—(1) to establish conditions of access to and use of any sanctuary resource; or (2) to promote public use and understanding of a sanctuary resource.

> (b) Permit Terms.—A permit issued under this section—(1) shall authorize the conduct of an activity only if that activity is compatible with the purposes for which the sanctuary is designated and with protection of sanctuary resources; ...(3) shall require that activities carried out under the permit be conducted in a manner that does not destroy, cause the loss of, or injure sanctuary resources...
>   [16 U.S.C. § 1441.]

Permits are not issued unless the proposed activities are determined to be compatible with resource protection and not to cause the destruction, loss, or injury of sanctuary resources. This policy is consistent with NMSA Sections 306 and 312, which clearly prohibit incompatible and harmful uses, and give rise to liability for damages arising therefrom.

One question that arises under the special use permit provisions of the statute is whether salvage of submerged heritage resources constitutes a "compatible use," and thus is a permissible activity in a National Marine Sanctuary. The legislative history for special use permits indicates that "salvage" is a compatible use:

---

[51]See 16 U.S.C. § 1441(f): "(f) Fishing.—Nothing in this section shall be considered to require a person to obtain a permit under this section for the conduct of any fishing activities in a National Marine Sanctuary."

Because not all activities can be adequately controlled under existing sanctuary regulations, such as those for research, education and salvaging, section 310 establishes a special use permitting system to complement those existing regulations.
[Congressional Record, July 26, 1988 H5820.]

Based on the language of the statute and the legislative history, research, education, fishing, and salvage of vessels all appear to be compatible uses, but ocean dumping and oil, gas, and mineral development are considered uses that generally are incompatible with resources protection. [Varmer & Santin, *Ocean Management under the Marine Protection, Research and Sanctuaries Act: Sanctuaries, Dumping and Development*, Coastal Zone 1990 (1993)].[52] Whether Congress, in referring to "salvaging," also meant to include recovery of historic sanctuary resources by treasure salvors is unclear. NOAA has taken the position that Congress did not intend to include these resources, because the term "salvage" has traditionally applied only to vessels subject to recent marine casualties. Little other guidance exists for determining what activities affecting submerged heritage resources constitute compatible uses.

Regardless of whether salvaging submerged heritage resources is a compatible use, there are situations in which it may be permitted. A NMSA provision may require permitting of activities that would otherwise be incompatible where the permittee has preexisting rights to conduct these activities. In this situation, issuance of a permit is authorized in order to avoid a Fifth Amendment takings problem:

Access and Valid Rights.—(1) Nothing in this title shall be construed as terminating or granting to the Secretary the right to terminate any valid lease, permit, license, or right of subsistence use or of access that is in existence on the date of designation of any National Marine Sanctuary. (2) The exercise of a lease, permit, license, or right is subject to regulation by the Secretary consistent with the purposes for which the sanctuary is designated.
[16 U.S.C. § 1434(c).]

---

[52]During consideration of H.R. 9727, there was repeated reference to the position that sanctuaries were to be areas isolated from ocean dumping. Representative Forsyth, in declaring his support for Title III, stated "the bill provides for establishment of ocean sanctuaries where no defilement by pollution will be permitted whatsoever." Similarly, Representative Frey stated that "the philosophy of establishing marine sanctuaries is that instead of designating areas where dumping may be conducted safely, we should determine which areas of our marine environment are most valuable and set them aside as sanctuaries." Representative Murphy recognized the need to save our water resources from the depredations of human beings, and suggested that the key to the effectiveness of H.R. 9727 was the "'no-dumping' marine sanctuary aspect of [the] legislation." [*See* Cong. Rec. H8192, 8193, 8249 (1971); *see also* H.R. Rep. No. 361, 92nd Cong., 1st Sess. 15 (1971).]

The courts have interpreted this provision narrowly. Preexisting rights generally require a lease, license, or permit from a federal or state agency. Treasure hunters, however, have tried to broaden the interpretation of this provision by attempting to include in this section on pre-existing rights the admiralty law of salvage and common law of finds. Their argument, though, has been uniformly rejected by the courts. (See discussion of *Craft v. National Park Service* and *United States v. Fisher,* below.)

Regulatory Permits

The NMSA regulations provide for the issuance of permits. No activity prohibited[53] by sanctuary regulations may be conducted except pursuant to a permit or other written authorization issued by NOAA. Other federal and/or state agencies continue to have jurisdiction and authority to prohibit, permit, and otherwise manage resources and human uses pursuant to their own regulations and underlying authorities (such as the Clean Water Act or the Submerged Lands Act). These permits are limited to their respective authorities, and do not constitute legal authority to conduct activities prohibited by sanctuary regulations. The sanctuary permit system seeks to avoid unnecessary duplication of regulatory authority and minimize regulatory oversight. Consequently, it often relies on existing management authorities, and provides exemptions to a prohibition if the activity is conducted pursuant to a federal or state permit. The sanctuary regulations may require that NOAA authorize or certify federal or state permits when there is no exemption. This process avoids duplicative permitting, while at the same time ensuring NOAA's ability to have its concerns about protecting sanctuary resources and uses addressed through the permitting process of other federal or state agencies. If the sanctuary's concerns cannot be addressed in an existing permit regime, then NOAA may issue a sanctuary permit.

NOAA's restrictive management of a submerged heritage resource was upheld in the *Gentile* case. Gentile, a diver, applied to NOAA for a permit to photograph the USS *Monitor*. The permit was denied because NOAA found that photography did not constitute a scientific research activity, and only scientific research activities are permitted in the *Monitor* Sanctuary.

---

[53]If an activity falls within a narrowly construed exception, it is not prohibited, and may be conducted in the sanctuary without a permit from NOAA.

IN THE MATTER OF: GARY GENTILE

6 Ocean Resources & Wildlife Rep. (O.R.W.) 285c (Dep't Comm. 1990)

Hugh J. Dolan, Administrative Law Judge

BACKGROUND

This Appeal and Recommended Decision represent another stage in a saga that has been ongoing for almost 6 years. Appellant, a scuba diver, underwater photographer and author, again seeks to dive on the wreck of the Monitor, the civil war "cheese box-on-a-raft" which sank off Cape Hatteras over a century ago. In 1974, it was designated as part of the Monitor Marine Sanctuary.[1] Under the Act, regulations and Management Plan, access to it is limited.

In 1989 after filing some 11 applications, two administrative appeals and a suit in Federal District Court Appellant received a permit which he and some 15 others thereafter utilized to dive on and take photographs of the Monitor within the Monitor National Marine Sanctuary.

Another application for a permit, dated July 12, 1990, was filed by Appellant. This was denied in a letter dated August 27, 1990.[2] This Appeal followed.

ISSUE

Does the Appellant's proposal to perform underwater photography constitute "research related to the Monitor" within the meaning of 15 C.F.R. § 924.5(a) and 16 U.S.C. § 1431(b).

STATUTE AND REGULATIONS

16 U.S.C. § 1431. Findings, purposes, and policies

(b)   Purposes and policies. The purposes and policies of this title are—

(1)   to identify areas of the marine environment of special national significance due to their resource or human-use values;

(2)   to provide authority for comprehensive and coordinated conservation and management of these marine areas that will complement existing regulatory authorities;

---

[1][*Orig. fn.*] A summary history of the Monitor and Sanctuary is set forth in the 17th annual report of the Council on Environmental Quality (1986 at pp 148-150).

[2][*Orig. fn.*] It is the July 12, 1990 application that is considered here not materials or references made after it was denied. Nor is the prior permit before me for review. All are reminded of the comment in the prior decision, "In neither case, has the requirement that the activity constitutes 'research' been addressed in any detail". It is here.

(3)   to support, promote, and coordinate scientific research on, and monitoring of, the resources of these marine areas;

(4)   to enhance public awareness, understanding, appreciation, and wise use of the marine environment; and

(5)   to facilitate, to the extent compatible with the primary objective of resource protection, all public and private uses of the resources of these marine areas not prohibited pursuant to other authorities. 15 C.F.R. § 924.5

Permitted activities

Any person or entity may conduct in the Sanctuary any activity listed in @ 924.3 of this part if:

(a)   Such activity is either:

(1)   For the purpose of research related to the Monitor....

WHAT CONSTITUTES SCIENTIFIC RESEARCH

Unlike pornography, scientific research is subject of some definition beyond knowing it when one sees it. *Jacobellis v. Ohio* 378 U.S. 184, 197 (1964). The definition of art is not for consideration here. The Fifth Circuit in two decisions has discussed the meaning of "research." To us "research" implies more than work. It involves the notion of lengthy, complex, technical investigation. *Hobbs v. U.S.* 376 F.2d 489, 496-497 (1967), 451 F.2d 849, 870 (1971). Inquiry into what the courts have defined as scientific research reveals numerous expostulations, in various contexts *e.g. Midwest Research Institute v. U.S.* 554 F. Supp. 1379 (1983); 95 *Yale Law Journal* 1857, (1965).

Scientific research is not undirected studies. It does not include activities of a type ordinarily carried on incident to commercial or business activities. It is not operating commercial enterprises, e.g. a Spaghetti Factory. *Midwest Research Activities v. U.S., supra.* Two examples come to mind that are particularly apropos here. Matthew Brady, the renowned Civil War era photographer, produced a historic record of that conflict that continues to promote graphic understanding of that carnage and era. That was his work. It was not scientific research. However, activities in perfecting the camera instrument, and the process for developing the photographic images would have constituted scientific research. The second example, involving truly memorable scientific research, is the activity of the Wright Brothers. Though perceived as untutored bicycle mechanics, in fact they spent years collecting the works and experiments of other researchers. Their own study, experimentation, and testing the work of others as well as the development of their theories, constituted scientific research. A parallel to those examples does not appear to fit here.

DISCUSSION

The appellant has said "...the real questions here are not scientific, but photogenic." (Appellant's Proposal dated July 12, 1990 at 7) and "The guiding incentive for photographic subjects is artistic rather than scientific,...". (Appellant's letter of April 1, 1990). Such appraisals hardly support the present contention that his underwater photography constitutes research under the Act and regulations.

Another principal thrust of Applicant's position is that he is "entitled" to visit, observe and photograph the remains of the Monitor. He is not. It is not an open public facility. It is a fragile, deteriorating fragment of the civil war era. The sanctuary designation preserves it from human interference. This was Appellant's own presentation here and in the hearing a year ago; my recent decision in the Channel Island[3] cases and the facts of life, demonstrate that public access would surely destroy any possibility of future meaningful archeological investigation (which constitutes scientific research). Disruption of the provenience of the site would impair future scientific inquiry. Protection of the resource is a primary objective of the statute. Public awareness may not be equated to public presence, particularly where it would compromise the resource.

Scientific research is not the donning of scuba gear and photographing a wreck on the sea bottom for recreational or commercial purposes, even if some added public awareness ultimately results. The terms of the regulations and Management Plan set forth standards and conditions for this particular sanctuary which are consistent with the Act. They bind the Agency and the Applicant.

FINDINGS

1. The Agency lacks the legislative authority to permit the proposed activity which is devoid of the statutorily required test of scientific research value. Nor does such activity constitute "research on the Monitor" within the framework of the implementing regulations.

2. The application does not meet the threshold test of describing scientific research.

3. The overall activity proposed by Appellant in his application does not constitute scientific research.

4. The Agency action of limiting access to the Monitor sanctuary area to rescue and research operations as outlined in the regulations and USS Monitor National Marine Sanctuary Management Plan constitutes a valid exercise of responsibility for the sanctuary.

5. Since the application failed to meet the qualifying activity requirement, evaluation of the five criteria was unnecessary.

CONCLUSION

The application and the stated purpose for the activity proposed fail to meet the research requirements of the statute and regulations. Therefore, the Appeal must be DENIED.

RECOMMENDATION

That the action denying the issuance of the permit be sustained and the Appeal be DENIED.

---

[3][*Orig. fn.*] Ocean Resource and Wildlife Reporter (NOAA October 17, 1990).

Note

After the *Gentile* court upheld NOAA's requirement that physical access to the USS Monitor be conditioned upon the permittee conducting scientific research, another challenge was brought against NOAA's permitting system. In *Peter E. Hess*, 6 O.R.W. 720a (1992), the administrative law judge went one step further, and upheld NOAA's requirement that a proposal to conduct scientific research must contain adequate detailed information, including a research objective, plan, design, and an explanation of the scientific methodology to be employed. [*Hess v. NOAA*, 6 O.R.W. 720a (1992); and *Hess v. NOAA*, 6 O.R.W. 720 (1992).]

Enforcement Provisions

The NMSA provides for enforcement mechanisms to ensure that resource protection is accomplished: "The Secretary [of Commerce] shall conduct such enforcement activities as are necessary and reasonable to carry out this chapter." [16 U.S.C. § 1437(a) (1994).] The NMSA enforcement provisions collectively provide perhaps the broadest and most comprehensive enforcement authority of any heritage resource management statute. The statute contains several specific enforcement mechanisms to carry out resource protection, and also describes the types of recoverable damages for injury to, or recovery of those resources.

Enforcement Authority

Enforcement of statutory and regulatory authority in the marine sanctuaries is primarily accomplished by officers in boats and, to a lesser extent, through surveillance from aircraft, satellites, and remote sensing equipment. The relevant provision concerning the powers of officers in carrying out their enforcement responsibilities is set forth in 16 U.S.C. § 1437(b), and clearly authorizes officers to employ a number of different tools to carry out their enforcement responsibilities:

> (b) Powers of Authorized Officers-Any person who is authorized to enforce this title may—(1) board, search, inspect, and seize any vessel suspected of being used to violate this title or any regulation or permit issued under this title and any equipment, stores, and cargo of such vessel; (2) seize wherever found any sanctuary resource taken or retained in violation of this title or any regulation or permit issued under this title; (3) seize any evidence of a violation of this title or of any regulation or permit issued under this title; (4) execute any warrant or other process issued by any court of competent jurisdiction; and (5) exercise any other lawful authority.
>
> [16 U.S.C. § 1437(b).]

Civil Penalties

While the major heritage resources statutes provide for criminal enforcement mechanisms, the NMSA uses civil remedies and authorizes civil penalties for violative activities in marine sanctuaries. Since federal and state criminal laws may also apply to these activities, the civil penalty enforcement tool provides resource managers and agency counsel with supplemental enforcement authority:

> (1) Civil penalty.—Any person subject to the jurisdiction of the United States who violates this title or any regulation or permit issued under this title shall be liable to the United States for a civil penalty of not more than $100,000 for each such violation, to be assessed by the Secretary. Each day of a continuing violation shall constitute a separate violation.
>   [16 U.S.C. § 1437(c).]

This section of the NMSA provides authority for civil enforcement penalty actions to be brought against violators of sanctuary regulations provided that the public has adequate notice that an activity is prohibited. In *Craft v. National Park Service*, Craft argued that he did not have notice that the sanctuary regulations applied to his activity of removing historic sanctuary resources and altering the seabed in the process. Craft's argument was rejected, and NOAA's regulations withstood the legal challenge to adequate notice. The Court explained that unless expressly exempted, the regulation is broadly worded to encompass all activities that alter the seabed and, thus, the public did have notice that the type of activity performed by Craft was prohibited.

The largest civil penalty assessed to date for a violation of regulations protecting historic resources in a marine sanctuary was assessed by Judge Hugh Dolan, a NOAA administrative law judge, in *Clifton B. Craft*, 6 O.R.W. 150 (1990). The seven respondents had been assessed penalties in the aggregate amount of $132,000, which Judge Dolan noted were inadequate. A larger penalty could not have been imposed, because of the statutory ceiling of $50,000 per violation, which was set forth in the original 1972 enactment. In 1992, the NMSA was amended and the ceiling was raised to $100,000. Moreover, under a more general authority, the ceiling is periodically updated to account for inflation. For example, in 1997, the ceiling on civil penalties was determined to be approximately $110,000. Applying Judge Dolan's formula to the current ceiling, the civil penalties could easily have reached $250,000.

CRAFT v. NATIONAL PARK SERVICE

34 F.3d 918 (9th Cir. 1994)

FLETCHER, Circuit Judge:

Clifton Craft, Jack Ferguson, and William Wilson ("appellants") appeal the district court's order affirming the assessment of civil penalties by the National Oceanic and Atmospheric Administration ("NOAA") for violations of the Marine Protection, Research, and Sanctuaries Act. NOAA assessed the penalties following a four week administrative trial, in which appellants were found to have violated NOAA regulations protecting the seabed and historic resources of the Channel Islands National Marine Sanctuary. We have jurisdiction and we affirm.

I

The Marine Protection, Research, and Sanctuaries Act, 16 U.S.C. §§ 1431-1445a, provides for the establishment of marine sanctuaries to protect important and sensitive marine areas and resources of national significance. *Id.* § 1431; S.Rep. No. 595, 100th Cong., 2d Sess. 1 (1988), reprinted in, 1988 U.S.C.C.A.N. 4387. Pursuant to this law, NOAA designated the Channel Islands National Marine Sanctuary ("CINMS") in 1980. The Channel Islands National Marine Sanctuary, 45 Fed. Reg. 65,198 (Oct. 2, 1980). The CINMS includes the marine waters surrounding several islands off the coast of California out to a distance of six nautical miles from the islands. 15 C.F.R. § 935.3.

To protect resources within the CINMS, NOAA has promulgated regulations which prohibit activities that might adversely affect sanctuary resources, including hydrocarbon operations, the discharge or deposit of substances, commercial vessel traffic, and the removal or damage of cultural or historical resources. 15 C.F.R. §§ 935.6 & 935.7. Activities that are not specifically prohibited are permitted. 15 C.F.R. § 935.5.

The regulations at issue in this appeal provide, in relevant part:

[T]he following activities are prohibited within the Sanctuary...

(2)   Alteration of, or construction on, the seabed. Except in connection with the laying of any pipeline as allowed by § 935.6, within 2 nautical miles of any Island, no person shall:

(i)   Construct any structure other than a navigation aid, or

(ii)   Drill through the seabed, or

(iii)   Dredge or otherwise alter the seabed in any way, other than

(A)   To anchor vessels, or

(B)   To bottom trawl from a commercial fishing vessel.

15 C.F.R. § 935.7(a)(2) (emphasis in original and added). The statute authorizes civil penalties for the violation of these regulations; criminal penalties are not authorized. 16 U.S.C. § 1437 (Supp. 1994).

Appellants are members of a diving club that took a trip on the boat "Vision" to the CINMS in October 1987. The club members participated in dives at four shipwrecks within the CINMS. Two National Park Service rangers were on board the Vision and witnessed violations of CINMS regulations by members of the diving club. Based on the rangers' testimony and other evidence, NOAA assessed civil penalties against appellants for violations of § 935.7(a)(2)(iii).[1]

Following a four week administrative trial, the ALJ concluded that appellants had violated § 935.7(a)(2)(iii) and recommended assessment of the penalties sought by NOAA. The ALJ specifically found that appellants removed artifacts from the shipwrecks and "excavated" the seabed with hammers and chisels. The ALJ found that both Craft and Wilson repeatedly hammered at the seabed and that Ferguson admitted that one site looked like a minefield due to the divers' activities. The ALJ also found that the alteration to the seabed was sufficiently extensive that the sites could be located days after the divers left the site. NOAA adopted the ALJ's findings and recommendations.

Appellants subsequently filed an action in district court, challenging NOAA's authority to impose the civil penalties on the grounds that the regulation in question is unconstitutionally overbroad and vague.[2] The district court rejected these contentions and granted the government's motion for summary judgment. Appellants timely appealed.

Because appellants raise a legal challenge involving the construction of a federal law and its application to undisputed facts, our review is de novo. *United States v. Doremus*, 888 F.2d 630, 631 (9th Cir. 1989), *cert. denied*, 498 U.S. 1046, 111 S. Ct. 751, 752, 112 L. Ed.2d 772 (1991).

II

Appellants first argue that the regulation is overbroad. The overbreadth doctrine requires that the enactment reach "a substantial amount of constitutionally protected conduct. If it does not, then the overbreadth challenge must fail." *United States v. Austin*, 902 F.2d 743, 744 (9th Cir.), *cert. denied*, 498 U.S. 874, 111 S. Ct. 200, 112 L. Ed.2d 161 (1990) (internal quotations omitted); *see also Hoffman Estates v. Flipside, Hoffman Estates*, 455 U.S. 489, 494, 102 S. Ct. 1186, 1191, 71 L. Ed.2d 362 (1982). Because appellants do not claim that any constitutional or fundamental right is prohibited by the regulation in question, their overbreadth challenge must fail. *See Austin*, 902 F.2d at 744-45 (no overbreadth challenge under Archaeological Resources Protection Act, which prohibits excavation of archaeological resources on public lands).

---

[1][*Orig. fn.*] Penalties were also assessed against appellants Ferguson and Wilson pursuant to 15 C.F.R. § 935.7(a)(5), which prohibits any person from "remov[ing] or damag[ing] any historical or cultural resource." Section 935.7(a)(5) also served as the sole basis for assessing penalties against plaintiff-appellants Michael King, Thomas Stocks, and Donald Jernigan. Appellants do not challenge the constitutionality of § 935.7(a)(5) on appeal to this court.

[2][*Orig. fn.*] Appellants also argued that they have a pre-existing right to perform salvage activities in the CINMS and that the regulations impermissibly restrict their rights under admiralty law principles to engage in the underlying activities. These claims were rejected by the district court.

III

Appellants also argue that 15 C.F.R. § 935.7(a)(2)(iii) is unconstitutionally vague as applied to their activities. Appellants do not raise a facial challenge.

"To pass constitutional muster against a vagueness attack, a statute must give a person of ordinary intelligence adequate notice of the conduct it proscribes." *United States v. 594,464 Pounds of Salmon*, 871 F.2d 824, 829 (9th Cir. 1989); *see also Austin*, 902 F.2d at 745. Thus, a statute's application might violate the constitutional mandate against vagueness if its terms are not sufficiently clear. *594,464 Pounds of Salmon*, 871 F.2d at 829.

We do not apply this standard mechanically, however. Instead, various factors affect our analysis. The degree of vagueness tolerated by the Constitution depends in part on the nature of the enactment: "[a] statute providing for civil sanctions is reviewed for vagueness with somewhat greater tolerance than one involving criminal penalties" because the consequences of imprecision are less severe. *Id.* (internal quotations omitted); *see also Hoffman Estates*, 455 U.S. at 498-99, 102 S. Ct. at 1193-94; *Big Bear Super Market No. 3 v. I.N.S.*, 913 F.2d 754, 757 (9th Cir. 1990). In addition, a scienter requirement may mitigate vagueness. Finally, "perhaps the most important factor affecting the clarity that the Constitution demands of a law is whether it threatens to inhibit the exercise of constitutionally protected rights," in which case a more stringent vagueness test applies. *Hoffman Estates*, 455 U.S. at 499, 102 S. Ct. at 1193-94; *Doremus*, 888 F.2d at 635.

In light of these principles, we conclude that 15 C.F.R. § 935.7(a)(2)(iii) is not unconstitutionally vague as applied to appellants' excavation activities. At the outset, we note that the regulation in question provides only for civil—and not criminal—penalties and does not inhibit the exercise of constitutionally protected conduct. Consequently, the Constitution tolerates a greater degree of vagueness in the regulation.

Even more significant, however, is our conclusion that the regulation by its terms clearly prohibits appellants' activities. With two exceptions, the regulation prohibits "dredg[ing] or otherwise alter[ing] the seabed in any way." 15 C.F.R. § 935.7(a)(2)(iii) (emphasis added). The word "alter" extends broadly to activities that "modify" the seabed, see Webster's II New Riverside Universal Dictionary, and the language "in any way" reinforces our understanding that the term "alter" applies to a broad range of conduct. There can be no question but that this language prohibits the excavation activities in which appellants were engaged.[3] *E.g., Austin*, 902 F.2d at 743-45 (criminal provision that prohibits "excavat[ing], remov[ing], damag[ing], or otherwise alter[ing] or defac[ing] any archaeological resource located on public lands or Indian lands" not unconstitutionally vague as applied to excavation of obsidian weapons and tools); *Doremus*, 888 F.2d at 635-36 (criminal provision that prohibits "[d]amaging any natural feature or other property of the United States" not unconstitutionally vague as applied to chopping down live trees on Forest Service land).

---

[3]*[Orig. fn.]* Appellants' attempts to characterize their activities as minimally harmful fanning of sediment and manual hammering are misleading. As noted above, the ALJ found that appellants' hammering and chiseling activities were "excavations" that resulted in identifiable scars on the seabed. These factual findings have not been challenged on appeal.

Appellants argue that "[w]here general words follow specific words in a statutory enumeration, the general words are construed to embrace only objects similar in nature to those objects enumerated by the preceding specific words." They suggest that because the term "altering" follows the terms "dredging," "construction," and "laying of pipeline," it must be read to proscribe only major industrial and commercial impacts on the seabed.

This principle of statutory construction is inapplicable, however, because § 935.7(a)(2)(iii) is not merely a general prohibition preceded by specific illustrative terms. Instead, the regulation includes two specific exceptions to the prohibition on "altering": (1) alterations that occur when anchoring vessels; and (2) bottom trawling from a commercial fishing vessel. 15 C.F.R. § 935.7(a)(2)(iii)(A) & (B). Moreover, contrary to appellants' contentions, the existence of listed exceptions to the prohibition on alterations further suggests that all alterations other than those that are specifically excepted are prohibited.

Appellants also rely on NOAA's Final Environmental Impact Statement ("FEIS") to argue that the regulations are unconstitutionally vague. They note that the FEIS discusses § 935.7(a)(2)(iii) only in the context of dredging, an activity that has a major effect on the seabed, and argue that the FEIS, as the only prior agency interpretation of the regulation in question, is entitled to substantial deference under *Chevron v. Natural Resources Defense Council*, 467 U.S. 837, 104 S. Ct. 2778, 81 L. Ed.2d 694 (1984).

Although appellants are correct that the FEIS discusses § 935.7(a)(2)(iii) only in the context of dredging, appellants' argument is unavailing. As we have previously noted, the regulatory language of § 935.7(a)(2)(iii) broadly prohibits alterations "of any kind." Even if NOAA did not originally consider whether this regulation would apply to activities such as hammering at the seabed, the regulatory language is sufficiently broad to provide fair warning to the public that such activities are prohibited. *See Hoffman Estates*, 455 U.S. at 498, 102 S. Ct. at 1193; *Doremus*, 888 F.2d at 635.

Moreover, the FEIS is not a definitive agency interpretation of the scope of the regulations in question. Instead, an FEIS is intended to be a detailed statement of the significant environmental effects of the regulation. *E.g., Sierra Club v. Clark*, 774 F.2d 1406, 1411 (9th Cir. 1985). Its purpose is to provide the agency with sufficiently detailed information to enable it to decide whether to proceed on a project in light of potential environmental consequences and to inform the public of the potential environmental impacts of the proposed enactment. *Id*. Because the FEIS is not intended to provide the public with a definitive statement of all activities that might fall within the regulation's prohibitions, its terms do not limit our construction of the regulation.

As a final matter, there can be no doubt that appellants were aware that their activities were prohibited. The ALJ found that Ferguson announced to the group of divers that the shipwrecks were located in a federal reserve and were protected. At one of the shipwrecks Ferguson announced that removing objects from the site was illegal and that an underwater alarm would alert the group if a National Park Service patrol approached. The ALJ concluded that appellants "set out with their picks, hammers... and other wreck raiding paraphernalia, fully intending to remove objects from these wrecks in the closed area within the Sanctuary, and that is what they did." Given these undisputed facts, appellants' claims that they lacked fair warning that their actions were prohibited ring hollow. *See United States v. Ellen*, 961 F.2d 462, 467 (4th Cir.), *cert. denied*, 506 U.S. 875, 113 S. Ct. 217, 121 L. Ed.2d 155 (1992); *United States v. Clinical Leasing Serv.*, 925 F.2d 120, 123 (5th Cir.), *cert. denied*, 502 U.S. 864, 112 S. Ct. 188, 116 L. Ed.2d 149 (1991).

IV

We hold that § 935.7(a)(2)(iii) is neither overbroad nor unconstitutionally vague as applied to appellants' conduct. The order of the district court is AFFIRMED.

Note

In *Craft*, criminal penalties were pursued by the state of California against the offenders at the same time that federal authorities pursued civil penalties under the NMSA. This dual-track enforcement authority is nearly nonexistent in other state and federal resource management regimes. To date, the civil penalties assessed in *Craft* remain the largest monetary sanction ever imposed for injury to, or destruction of, heritage resources.

Forfeiture

Because most of the users of marine sanctuaries depend on their marine craft to carry out their activities, the authority to confiscate vessels, equipment, and cargo pursuant to the NMSA's forfeiture provision is an effective protection tool when used in the appropriate situation. The provision provides:

> (1) In General.—Any vessel (including the vessel's equipment, stores, and cargo) and other item used, and any sanctuary resource taken or retained, in any manner, in connection with or as a result of any violation of this title or of any regulation or permit issued under this title shall be subject to forfeiture to the United States pursuant to a civil proceeding under this subsection. The proceeds from forfeiture actions under this subsection shall constitute a separate recovery in addition to any amounts recovered as civil penalties under this section or as civil damages under section 312. None of those proceeds shall be subject to set-off.
>   [16 U.S.C. § 1437(d).]

Actual forfeiture of vessels is a rare occurrence in NMSA enforcement actions. Usually, bonds are posted for the vessels in lieu of forfeiture to ensure the recovery of civil penalties under § 307 or damages under § 312. However, in some circumstances, particularly when an operator abandons a vessel, the forfeiture authority is used.

In a civil action brought against Melvin Fisher, his son, and Salvors, Inc., the forfeiture provision of the NMSA was invoked. The United States used this provision in two ways. First, NOAA invoked its authority to order the forfeiture of the vessels that were implicated in the violation. Second, NOAA actually used the forfeiture provision to seek the return of the submerged heritage resources that were illegally recovered from the Florida Keys National Marine Sanctuary. Ultimately, forfeiture of the vessels was not pursued, but the government did seek the return of the artifacts. Although not expressly stated in the opinion, the court granted the relief sought by NOAA when it invoked the forfeiture provision of the Act, and ordered the return of the artifacts to NOAA.

Injunctive Relief

Injunctive relief is an extremely important enforcement tool, because it can be used to prevent future destruction of sanctuary resources. Although such relief is an extraordinary remedy (see Chapter 2, "Federal Compliance Statutes," for a discussion on injunctive relief), if granted, it can be an effective enforcement tool. The NMSA provides the authority to seek this type of remedy:

> (I) Injunctive Relief.—If the Secretary determines that there is an imminent risk of destruction or loss of or injury to a sanctuary resource, or that there has been actual destruction or loss of, or injury to, a sanctuary resource which may give rise to liability under section 312, the Attorney General, upon request of the Secretary, shall seek to obtain such relief as may be necessary to abate such risk or actual destruction, loss, or injury, or to restore or replace the sanctuary resource, or both. The district courts of the United States shall have jurisdiction in such a case to order such relief as the public interest and the equities of the case may require.
> [16 U.S.C. § 1437(I).]

The authority to pursue injunctive relief may be used even when sanctuary-specific regulations addressing the destructive activities are not yet in place, as was the case in the action against destructive treasure hunting practices in the Florida Keys National Marine Sanctuary. In *United States v. Fisher*, treasure hunters were barred by a preliminary injunction from using their prop-wash deflectors in the sanctuary until a full hearing on the merits of the case could be held. After the trial, the treasure hunters were permanently enjoined from using such devices and removing heritage resources without a permit from NOAA.

UNITED STATES v. FISHER

22 F.3d 262 (11th Cir. 1994)

FRIEDMAN, Senior Circuit Judge:

This is an appeal from an order of the United States District Court for the Southern District of Florida preliminarily enjoining the appellants from violating the Marine Protection, Research, and Sanctuaries Act ("Sanctuaries Act"), 16 U.S.C. §§ 1431-45, and the Florida

Keys National Marine Sanctuary and Protection Act ("Florida Keys Act"), Pub.L. No. 101-605, 104 Stat. 3089 (1990), by conducting certain marine salvage operations. We hold that the district court did not abuse its discretion in granting the preliminary injunction and therefore affirm.

I

A.   The Statutory Scheme

Congress enacted the Sanctuaries Act in response to a "growing concern about the increasing degradation of marine habitats." S.Rep. No. 595, 100th Cong., 2d Sess. 1 (1988), reprinted in 1988 U.S.C.C.A.N. 4387. The Sanctuaries Act:

> provides for the protection of important and sensitive marine areas and resources of national significance through the establishment of marine sanctuaries. The purpose of these sanctuaries is to preserve or restore such areas for their conservation, recreational, ecological, or aesthetic value.
> *Id.*; *see also* 16 U.S.C. § 1431.

The statement of the "Purposes and policies" of the Act includes:

> (2)   to provide authority for comprehensive and coordinated conservation and management of these marine areas that will complement existing regulatory authorities;
>
> (5)   to facilitate, to the extent compatible with the primary objective of resource protection, all public and private uses of the resources of these marine areas not prohibited pursuant to other authorities.
> 16 U.S.C. § 1431(b).

The Sanctuaries Act gives the Secretary of Commerce ("Secretary") the authority to designate and manage marine sanctuaries and to specify in such designation the regulatory requirements for the particular sanctuary. 16 U.S.C. § 1433. The Secretary has delegated these responsibilities to the Department's National Oceanic and Atmospheric Administration ("Administration"). S.Rep. No. 595, 1988 U.S.C.C.A.N. at 4387-88.

The statute defines "sanctuary resource" broadly to mean

> any living or nonliving resource of a National Marine Sanctuary that contributes to the conservation, recreational, ecological, historical, research, educational, or aesthetic value of the sanctuary.
> 16 U.S.C. § 1432(8).

The Act specifies the procedures the Secretary must follow in designating a marine sanctuary. In "proposing to designate a National Marine Sanctuary," the Secretary must provide a management plan, an environmental impact statement, and other documents to accompany the notice of proposed designation. 16 U.S.C. § 1434(a)(1). The documentation is first provided in draft form for public comment by publication in the Federal Register and to the appropriate committees of both Houses of Congress. *Id.* Final documentation is published in the Federal Register and provided to Congress. 16 U.S.C. § 1434(b). The sanctuary designation "takes effect" forty-five days after the Secretary issues the final "notice of designation." The forty-five day period allows Congress the opportunity to disapprove "any of [the designation's] terms." *Id.*

The Secretary is authorized to "conduct such enforcement activities as are necessary and reasonable to carry out this [Sanctuaries Act]." 16 U.S.C. § 1437(a). Under 16 U.S.C. § 1443(a)(1),

[a]ny person who destroys, causes the loss of, or injures any sanctuary resource is liable to the United States for response costs and damages resulting from the destruction, loss, or injury.

The statute also provides for judicial equitable relief:

If the Secretary determines that there is an imminent risk of destruction or loss of or injury to a sanctuary resource, or that there has been actual destruction or loss of, or injury to, a sanctuary resource which may give rise to liability under section 1443 of this title, the Attorney General, upon request of the Secretary, shall seek to obtain such relief as may be necessary to abate such risk or actual destruction, loss or injury, or to restore or replace the sanctuary resource, or both. The district courts of the United States shall have jurisdiction in such a case to order such relief as the public interest and the equities of the case may require.
16 U.S.C. § 1437(I).

In addition to the designation of marine sanctuaries by the Secretary, Congress itself has designated sanctuaries. In the Florida Keys Act, Congress "designated as the Florida Keys National Marine Sanctuary under title III of the [Sanctuaries Act] [the area involved in this case]. The Sanctuary shall be managed and regulations enforced under all applicable provisions of such title III as if the Sanctuary had been designated under such title." Florida Keys Act § 5(a). The stated "purpose of this Act is to protect the resources of the [Florida Keys National Marine Sanctuary]." *Id.* § 3(b). Among the Congressional findings in the Act are that "spectacular, unique, and nationally significant marine environments, including seagrass meadows" are located adjacent to the "Florida Keys land mass" (*id.* § 2(2)) and that "[t]hese marine environments are subject to damage and loss of their ecological integrity from a variety of sources of disturbance." *Id.* § 2(5).

The Florida Keys Act requires a number of planning activities, coupled with public participation requirements, which parallel those in the Sanctuaries Act. For example, the Administration is directed to develop a comprehensive management plan for the sanctuary within 30 months to "facilitate all public and private uses of the Sanctuary consistent with the primary objective of Sanctuary protection." *Id.* § 7(a)(1). The Environmental Protection Agency is directed to prepare a comprehensive water quality protection program for the sanctuary. *Id.* § 8(a). The Administration is required to establish an intergovernmental advisory council to assist in the development and implementation of the management plan for the sanctuary. *Id.* § 9(a).

Both the Sanctuaries Act and the Florida Keys Act were later amended by the Oceans Act of 1992, which became effective after the injunction in this case. Pub. L. No. 102-587, 106 Stat. 5039 (1992). Among other provisions, the Oceans Act strengthens the liability and enforcement provisions of the Florida Keys Act; provides additional authority and resources to the Environmental Protection Agency to conduct monitoring programs in the sanctuary; and designates three additional national marine sanctuaries. *Id.*

B.   The Present Case

The appellants are maritime salvors. This case arises out of their conduct of salvaging operations involving the use of devices known as "prop wash deflectors," in an area known as Coffins Patch, which the Fishers stipulated "is entirely within the boundaries of the [Florida Keys Sanctuary]."

Prop wash deflectors, also known as "mailboxes," are used to direct propeller wash to remove seabed sediments and expose underlying materials. The Fishers stipulated that they used those deflectors in Coffins Patch "to remove overburden, sediments, and seagrass in which artifacts are contained," and had removed historic artifacts from Coffins Patch. The Fishers also stipulated that, while using prop wash deflectors in Coffins Patch, they had "created at least 100 depressions" in the seabed.

The United States filed a complaint against the appellants (the two Fishers, a corporation they own and control that "specializes in marine salvage and treasure hunting" [collectively, the Fishers] and three vessels used in their salvage operations). It sought damages and injunctive relief "arising out of defendants willfully destroying, causing the loss of, and injuring sanctuary resources, many of which are irreplaceable" in the Florida Keys sanctuary through their use of prop wash deflectors. It also sought forfeiture of the three vessels. The United States also sought a preliminary injunction to restrain the Fishers "from further dredging or salvage activities within the Florida Keys National Marine Sanctuary until trial or other disposition of the merits of this action." The Fishers cross-moved for an injunction to restrain the government from interfering with their activities.

The district court referred the motions to a magistrate judge. Extensive expert and other testimony describing the injury the Fishers' prop wash deflectors had inflicted on the sanctuary was introduced at a hearing before the magistrate judge.

The government presented expert testimony that the sanctuary had been irreparably injured. The testimony described the damage done to the seagrass and the coral reef ecosystem. The experts explained that the seagrasses were required to stabilize the sea bottom and preserve water quality. The testimony included a damage survey of at least 27 craters in Coffins Patch that were more than 30 feet across and more than 80 feet deep. The lack of algal growth established that these were recent excavations. The length of the grass blades and the rhizome system indicated that prop wash deflectors had been used. The experts also described the damage to fans, sponges, and historic artifacts unearthed by prop wash deflectors.

The experts described the destructive effects of prop wash deflector use, which included the following: (1) the sites would not reestablish themselves; (2) the displaced sediment buried seagrass to lethal depths; (3) the craters led to continuing erosion and destruction of the seagrass ledge; and (4) the absence of substrate and fill for craters precluded revegetation. These experts confirmed that the damage had been recent.

Eyewitnesses testified that all three of the Fishers' vessels in Coffins Patch were using prop wash deflectors. One eyewitness testified that several times a week he saw only the Fishers using those deflectors in the area of damage.

Some of the Fisher's own evidence was consistent with the government's. For example, one witness for the Fishers acknowledged the destructive potential of prop wash deflectors. Kane Fisher confirmed that only the Fishers had been using prop wash deflectors in Coffins Patch during the time when the damage was done to the sanctuary.

The magistrate judge filed a report recommending that the government's motion for a preliminary injunction be granted. The magistrate judge first held that the government was "substantially likely to prevail on its § 1443 claim against the defendants." He ruled that "[t]o prevail on its § 1443 claim, the government must show simply that the defendants have injured sanctuary resources." He stated that it was "undisputed" that the Fishers used prop wash deflectors in the sanctuary, that such use created at least 100 depressions in the area and that

> persuasive testimony by Dr. Joseph Zieman indicates that these depressions have injured and disrupted vital seagrass environments in the Sanctuary. (Transcript at 84-92.) This seagrass, anchored on the ocean's bottom, is an integral part of the coral reef ecosystem and serves as shelter, food, and habitat for myriad life forms present in the Sanctuary. Dr. Zieman testified that "regrowth of that grass is probably not going to occur within our life times."
> (*Id.* at 90.) (footnote omitted.)

The magistrate judge held that "the injured seagrass environments are clearly 'sanctuary resources' under the MPRSA. 16 U.S.C. § 1432(8). The Sanctuary Act expressly refers to the protection of 'seagrass meadows.' Sanctuary Act, 2(2), 2(3). There is little dispute that seagrass beds contribute to conservation, recreational, ecological, research, educational, and aesthetic values, as intended by the Sanctuary Act. *Id.* The magistrate judge rejected the Fishers' argument that under the Sanctuaries Act and the Florida Keys Act, the Florida Keys Sanctuaries had not yet been established and that the prohibitions of the Sanctuaries Act therefore were not operative there.

The magistrate judge held that irreparable injury would result if the Fishers' activities were not preliminarily enjoined and that a preliminary injunction would serve the public interest. The magistrate judge concluded, however, that "[t]he injunction sought by the government, barring the defendants from all salvage activities in the Sanctuary, is overbroad and unsupported by the evidence." Since the "government has only shown damage to the Sanctuary from the defendants' use of prop wash deflectors... an injunction barring the defendants from employing prop wash deflectors would be sufficient to ensure that the Sanctuary is not further damaged. This injunction should not bar the defendants from pursuing their livelihood by using other salvage techniques in the Sanctuary area."

The district court, "[b]ased upon the Magistrate's recommendation, and after independent review of the record," issued a preliminary injunction against the Fishers, and denied their motion.

II

A "preliminary injunction will be reversed only if the trial court clearly abused its discretion." *GSW, Inc. v. Long County, Georgia*, 999 F.2d 1508, 1518 (11th Cir. 1993). To obtain a preliminary injunction, the government must prove: (1) that it has a substantial likelihood of success on the merits; (2) that it will suffer irreparable harm if the injunction is denied; (3) that the injury to the government from denial of injunctive relief outweighs the damage to the other party if it is granted; and (4) that the injunction will not harm the public interest. *GSW, Inc.*, 999 F.2d at 1518.

The Fishers make no attempt to show that in granting a preliminary injunction, the district court misapplied these four factors. They argue only that the statutory provisions involved are not operative in the Florida Keys Sanctuary, and that, in any event, those provisions cannot be applied to them. Indeed, their briefs read like an appeal from a final judgment, not from a preliminary injunction.

These arguments presumably are directed to the magistrate judge's ruling on the first of the four relevant factors—that the government is substantially likely to prevail on the merits. The argument apparently is that since the statute does not apply to the Fishers' conduct, not only is the government not likely to prevail on the merits, but that it cannot possibly do so. As the Fishers have structured their argument, they have waived any challenge to the magistrate judge's ruling on the three other factors. Accordingly, we shall address only the merits of the government's positions.

A. The Fishers' principal contention is that the Florida Keys Sanctuary will not become an existing entity until the Secretary has promulgated a management plan for that sanctuary, which he has not done, and that the statutory provisions they are charged with violating are inoperative in the sanctuary and, therefore, cannot be applied to them.

The Fishers rely on § 1434(b) of the Sanctuaries Act, which provides that the Secretary's designation of a marine sanctuary "takes effect" 45 days after the Secretary has issued his final "notice of designation." They point out that the Florida Keys Act requires the Administration to promulgate a management plan for the Florida Keys Sanctuary within 30 months, and argue that the Congressional designation of the sanctuary, like the Secretary's designation of other sanctuaries, does not "take effect" until the management plan for it has been promulgated.

Unlike § 1434(b) of the Sanctuaries Act, however, there is nothing in the Florida Keys Act that states that Congressional designation of the Florida Keys Sanctuary does not "take effect" until the Administration has promulgated a management plan for that sanctuary. To the contrary, the language of the Florida Keys Act indicates that the Congressional designation of that sanctuary was effective on the effective date of the Act.

The caption of the Florida Keys Act describes it as an Act "[t]o establish" the Florida Keys National Marine Sanctuary. The Congressional findings include the statement that "[a]ction is necessary to provide comprehensive protection for these marine environments by establishing a Florida Keys National Marine Sanctuary..." Florida Keys Act § 2(7). Section 5(a) of the Act, captioned "DESIGNATION," provides that the described area "is designated as the Florida Keys National Marine Sanctuary... [and] shall be managed and regulations enforced under all applicable provisions [of the Sanctuaries Act] as if the Sanctuary had been designated under such title." Florida Keys Act § 5(a).

These provisions show that the Florida Keys Act itself established the Florida Keys Sanctuary and did not require any further action by the Administration for the sanctuary to come into existence. "It is well established that, absent a clear direction by Congress to the contrary, a law takes effect on the date of its enactment." *Gozlon-Peretz v. United States*, 498 U.S. 395, 404, 111 S. Ct. 840, 846, 112 L. Ed.2d 919 (1991). Here, as in *Gozlon-Peretz*, "[w]e find no such contrary directions in the language of [the statute] or in its evident purpose." *Id.*

There is a sound practical reason why, in the Florida Keys Act, Congress designated the Florida Keys Sanctuary effective immediately and did not delay the effectiveness of the designation for a stated period, as it did in sanctuaries designated by the Secretary under the Sanctuaries Act. In the latter situation, the 45-day delay of the taking effect of the Secretary's designation was designed to give Congress the opportunity to disapprove "any of [the designations] terms," [16 U.S.C. § 1434(b)] and the public the opportunity to make its views known. Where, however, Congress itself made the designation, there was no need or occasion for such delay. The public already has had the opportunity to comment upon the legislation while it was pending before Congress, and Congress fully considered the terms of the designation before the Act was enacted.

Although the Florida Keys Act requires the Secretary to develop, with public participation, a management plan for the Florida Keys Sanctuary, there was no reason for Congress itself to review that plan after the statute became effective, and no indication that Congress reserved that right. Indeed, in view of the Congressional concern over effectively protecting the Florida Keys Sanctuary that led Congress in the Florida Keys Act itself to create the sanctuary, it is difficult to believe that Congress would have delayed implementation of the sanctuary for the 30 months the Secretary had to promulgate a management plan. This 30-month period stands in sharp contrast to the 45 days that Congress has to review and possibly disapprove the Secretary's designation of a sanctuary under the Sanctuaries Act.

In the Florida Keys Act, Congress did not merely itself designate, in place of a "notice of designation" by the Secretary, a particular sanctuary. Instead, it provided that the sanctuary "is designated" and should be treated as if it "had been designated" under the Sanctuaries Act. Florida Keys Act § 5. Congress thus adopted a different procedure than it had provided for sanctuary designations by the Secretary.

The President so recognized when he signed the Florida Keys Act. In his accompanying statement, the President noted that Congress was "bypassing" the "usual process" of "designating after adherence to the comprehensive evaluation and designation procedures set forth in the [Sanctuaries Act]." *Statement by President George Bush Upon Signing H.R. 5909*, 26 Weekly Comp.Pres.Doc. 1829 (Nov. 19, 1990), reprinted in 1990 U.S.C.C.A.N. 4393-2. The President stated that Department of Commerce studies supported the designation, justifying this bypassing by Congress. *Id.* He concluded that this sanctuary designation would "augment" the federal government's efforts to protect the marine resources of the Florida Keys. *Id.*

B. The Fishers argue that 18 U.S.C. § 1434(a)(1) precludes the bringing of an enforcement action in the district court until the Secretary has promulgated a management plan for the sanctuary that includes enforcement activity. That section provides that "[i]n proposing to designate a National Marine Sanctuary, the Secretary," on the same day that the notice of the proposal is published in the Federal Register, shall submit to two specified House and

Senate committees "a prospectus on the proposal which shall contain," among other things, the "draft management plan detailing... enforcement, including surveillance activities for the area." Relying on the statement in the Florida Keys Act that the Florida Keys Sanctuary "shall be managed and regulations enforced under all applicable provisions" of the Sanctuaries Act "as if the Sanctuary had been designated under" that Act [Florida Keys Act, § 5(a)], the Fishers contend that the Secretary is required to submit a prospectus to Congress specifying his proposed enforcement actions for the Florida Keys Sanctuary before the government may maintain district court enforcement action.

The reference in § 1434(a)(1) to "enforcement, including surveillance activity in the area" refers to a marine sanctuary that the Secretary has proposed to designate, not to one that Congress itself has designated. The words "in the area" refer back to the previous section, which deals with designation of sanctuaries by the Secretary. Moreover, the "enforcement... activities" appear to be those administrative actions that the Secretary himself plans to conduct in the sanctuary he proposes to designate, pursuant to his authority under 16 U.S.C. § 1437(a), which states that "[t]he Secretary shall conduct such enforcement activities as are necessary and reasonable to carry out this chapter."

Nothing in these provisions requires that, before the government may file an enforcement action in the district court the Secretary must submit to Congress a prospectus specifying his enforcement plan. To the contrary, 16 U.S.C. § 1437(i) provides that, if the Secretary determines that there "is an imminent risk of destruction or loss of or injury to a sanctuary resource, or that there has been actual destruction or loss of, or injury to, a sanctuary resource which may give rise to liability under section 1443 of this title," the Attorney General, on request of the Secretary, shall seek in a district court relief "necessary to abate such risk or actual destruction, loss, or injury, or to restore or replace the sanctuary resource, or both."

The only requirements for the bringing of such an action thus are (1) the Secretary's determination of an imminent risk of destruction or loss of, or injury to, a sanctuary resource and (2) a request by the Secretary to the Attorney General to bring an enforcement action. Nothing in this section, pursuant to which the United States filed the present suit, even suggests, let alone requires, that prior thereto the Secretary must have informed Congress about his enforcement plans for the sanctuary.

C. The Fishers contend that before the United States may file an enforcement suit, the Secretary must have filed an environmental impact statement. They rely on 16 U.S.C. § 1434(a)(2), which requires the Secretary, in connection with a proposed designation of "a National Marine Sanctuary," to "prepare a draft environmental impact statement, as provided by the National Environmental Policy Act of 1969 (42 U.S.C. § 4321 *et seq.*), on the proposal that includes... maps depicting the boundaries of the proposed designated area..."

This provision, however, like other previously discussed provisions of the Sanctuaries Act upon which the Fishers rely, relates to a sanctuary designated by the Secretary, not to one designated by Congress. There is no requirement in the statute that before the Congressional establishment of a sanctuary becomes effective, the Secretary must first prepare an environmental impact statement for that sanctuary. If Congress had intended to impose that requirement for sanctuaries that it designated, presumably it would have said so explicitly—as it did with respect to sanctuaries that the Secretary designates.

The Fishers rely on the statement in the House Report on the Florida Keys Act that "the Committee expects that the Secretary will... prepare an environmental impact statement" for the Florida Keys Sanctuary. [H.R.Rep. No. 593, 101st Cong. 2d Sess., pt. 1 at 9 (1990)]. That comment, however, merely stated the Committee's expectation that the Secretary would prepare a statement. It did not provide that, until that statement had been prepared, the Congressional designation of the sanctuary would not be effective.

D. In holding that the government is substantially likely to prevail on the merits of its claim that the Fishers violated 16 U.S.C. § 1443, the magistrate judge noted that under that section, which makes liable to the United States "any person who destroys, causes the loss of, or injures any sanctuary resource," the government "must show simply that the defendants have injured sanctuary resources." He pointed out that in light of the stipulation, it was "undisputed" that the Fishers used prop wash deflectors in the Florida Keys Sanctuary and that such use created at least 100 openings in the seabed there. The magistrate judge stated that expert testimony indicated that "these depressions have injured and disrupted vital seagrass elements" there and he held that "the injured seagrass environments are clearly 'sanctuary resources' under the [Sanctuaries Act] 16 U.S.C. § 1432(8)." These facts and conclusions, which the Fishers do not here challenge, support the magistrate judge's conclusion that the government is substantially likely to prevail on the merits.

The district court also properly rejected the Fishers' purported defenses to the charges against them. Section 1434(c) in essence permits conduct in a sanctuary that was authorized by a permit in existence prior to the designation of the sanctuary. The Fishers stipulated, however, that they did not have a permit covering their use of prop wash deflectors in the Florida Keys Sanctuary. Although the Fishers assert that it would have been futile for them to have sought such a permit because the Administration had not adopted procedures for the issuance of permits and, in fact, was not issuing permits, the Fishers never applied for such a permit. We decline to speculate whether, if they had so applied, the Administration would have denied their application and, if it had done so, whether, on judicial review, the Fishers could have reversed that denial.

We discern no basis for the Fishers' contention that their history of prior salvage operations constitutes a defense to the violation of the Sanctuaries Act with which they are charged.

E. Considering all the circumstances, the district court justifiably concluded that the government had shown a substantial likelihood of success on the merits and did not abuse its discretion in granting the limited preliminary injunction, prohibiting only the use of prop wash deflectors. That injunction is AFFIRMED.

NMSA Enforceable Throughout the 200-Mile Exclusive Economic Zone Consistent with International Law

The NMSA provides clear authority to designate, protect, and manage sanctuaries not only within the 12-nautical-mile Territorial Sea but also to the outer extremities of the 200-nautical-mile Exclusive Economic Zone (EEZ). This authority is significant for protecting heritage resources in the marine environment. Clearly, the reach of the NMSA is much greater than that of any other heritage resources law:

(j) Area of Application and Enforceability.—The area of application and enforceability of this title includes the territorial sea of the United States, as described in Presidential Proclamation 5928 of December 27, 1988, which is subject to the sovereignty of the United States, and the United States exclusive economic zone, consistent with international law.
  [16 U.S.C. § 1437(I).]

The reach of the NMSA is of particular importance because the only other statute that expressly addresses the protection of historic shipwrecks, the Abandoned Shipwreck Act (ASA), only applies out to three miles from the shoreline. Heritage resources in national marine sanctuaries, however, are protected as public sanctuary resources from unregulated recovery occurring out to 200 nautical miles from shore. The NMSA also applies to the activities of foreign citizens and foreign flag vessels to the extent consistent with international law.[54] [The primary source of international law in the marine environment is the United Nations Convention on Law of the Sea (LOS).] Enforcement of the NMSA does not appear to conflict with the LOS. As discussed in the section entitled "Federal Laws that Generally Apply to Heritage Resources in the Marine Environment," NMSA enforcement could be considered consistent with the duties of coastal States to protect submerged heritage resources set forth in the LOS. Further, the practice of many nations seems to indicate a growing international consensus that the maritime law of salvage should not apply to submerged heritage resources. If international practice can be interpreted as constituting customary international law, it follows that using the enforcement provisions of the NMSA to protect submerged heritage resources is consistent with international law—even against foreign nationals out to the 200-mile EEZ—provided that no interference with LOS rights and duties (such as the freedom of navigation and overflights) occurs. Opponents of this position argue, however, that enforcement of the NMSA against foreign nationals is currently limited to the 12-mile Territorial Sea and the Contiguous Zone, which extends out to 24 miles from the Territorial Sea baseline. Nevertheless, the enforcement of the NMSA and other historic preservation laws largely depends on the maritime zone in which the offensive activity is conducted and the resources that are impacted.

---

[54]This title and the regulations issued under § 304 shall be applied in accordance with generally recognized principles of international law, and in accordance with the treaties, conventions, and other agreements to which the United States is a party. No regulation shall apply to or be enforced against a person who is not a citizen, national, or resident alien of the United States, unless in accordance with—"(1) generally recognized principles of international law; (2) an agreement between the United States and the foreign state of which the person is a citizen; or (3) an agreement between the United States and the flag state of a foreign vessel, if the person is a crew member of the vessel." [16 U.S.C. § 1435.]

Liability and Damages

The NMSA provides that offenders are strictly liable for violations. Accordingly, no proof of negligence is required. NOAA must only demonstrate that an offender caused the destruction of, or injury to, sanctuary resources:

> Any person who destroys, causes the loss of, or injures any sanctuary resource is liable to the United States for an amount equal to the sum of—(A) the amount of response costs and damages resulting from the destruction, loss, or injury; and (B) interests on that amount calculated in the manner described under section 1005 of the Oil Pollution Act of 1990. A person is not liable under this subsection if that person establishes that—(A) the destruction or loss of, or injury to, the sanctuary resource was caused solely by an act of God, an act of war, or an act or omission of a third party, and the person acted with due care; (B) the destruction, loss, or injury was caused by an activity authorized by Federal or State law; or (C) the destruction, loss, or injury was negligible.

[16 U.S.C. § 1443(a)(1).] This provision was modeled after other environmental laws providing for strict liability, such as § 311 of the Clean Water Act (CWA, 33 U.S.C. § 1321), and § 107(a) of the Comprehensive Environmental Response, Compensation, and Liability Act [CERCLA, 42 U.S.C. § 9607, and see H. R. Rep. No. 739, Part I, 100th Cong., 2d Sess. 22 (1988)].

If sanctuary resources are at imminent risk of destruction, loss, or injury, under § 312(b), NOAA is authorized to undertake all necessary response actions to prevent or minimize the harm. The cost of response actions can be passed on to the offender, in accordance with § 302(6). To recover these costs, as well as other damages recoverable under the NMSA, the Attorney General of the United States, at the request of NOAA, may commence a civil action in a United States district court in the appropriate district against any liable person or vessel. The Secretary of Commerce, acting as trustee for sanctuary resources for the United States, shall submit a request for a collection action to the Attorney General whenever a person may be liable for such costs or damages.

When an enforcement action is successful, § 312(d) dictates how the response costs and damages recovered will be retained and used:

> (1) Response Costs And Damage Assessments.—Twenty percent of amounts recovered under this section, up to a maximum balance of $750,000, shall be used to finance response actions and damage assessments by the Secretary. Amounts remaining after the operation of paragraph (1) shall be used, in order of priority—(A) to restore, replace, or acquire the equivalent of the sanctuary resources which were the subject of the action; (B) to manage and improve the National Marine Sanctuary within which are located the sanctuary resources which were the subject of the action; and (C) to manage and improve any other National Marine Sanctuary. Amounts recovered un-

der this section with respect to sanctuary resources lying within the jurisdiction of a State shall be used under paragraphs (2)(A) and (B) in accordance with the court decree or settlement agreement and an agreement entered into by the Secretary and the Governor of that State.

[16 U.S.C. § 1443(d).] Thus, NOAA is specifically authorized to use sums recovered under sanctuary damage cases to restore, replace, or acquire equivalent resources, as opposed the usual requirement that recovered sums be forwarded to the General Fund of the Treasury.

In *United States v. Fisher*, the defendants were held liable for damages under § 312. Although the United States was successful in obtaining an award of approximately $600,000 for damages to natural sanctuary resources (seagrass), it was unsuccessful in recovering monetary damages for the loss of contextual archeological information. The court acknowledged that contextual information is a sanctuary resource, but it held that the loss of such information was minimal in that case.[55]

UNITED STATES v. FISHER

977 F. Supp. 1193 (S.D. Fla. 1997)

EDWARD B. DAVIS, Chief Judge.

This action stems from Defendants' 1992 treasure-hunting activities in the Florida Keys National Marine Sanctuary (the Keys Sanctuary). In Case Number 92-10027-CIV-DAVIS, the United States alleges that the Defendants illegally destroyed seagrass in the Keys Sanctuary and removed artifacts. The government seeks damages and an injunction under the Marine Protection, Research and Sanctuaries Act (the Sanctuaries Act). In 1995, Motivation, Inc.,[1] filed a separate action, seeking title to the same artifacts and a salvage award. *See* Case Number 95-10051-CIV-DAVIS.

On May 9, 1997, the Court dismissed the three vessels, the *M/V Dauntless*, the *M/V Tropical Magic*, and the *M/V Bookmaker*, as Defendants in Case Number 92- 10027. The Court then tried this matter without a jury on May 12-13 and 19-21, 1997. At trial, the Court

---

[55]The United States also sought to recover curation costs for the artifacts that the defendants unlawfully took from the sanctuary. The court, however, was not convinced that such costs fell within the scope of recoverable damages under section 312, and, therefore, denied the requested relief.

[1][*Orig. fn.*] Salvors, Inc., and Motivation, Inc., are related treasure-hunting companies that Defendants Melvin and Kane Fisher operate.

dismissed Melvin A. Fisher as a Defendant in Case Number 92-10027, then dismissed Case Number 95-10051 entirely. Therefore, the only remaining Defendants are Kane Fisher and Salvors, Inc. (collectively referred to below as "the Defendants").

Based on the evidence adduced at trial and pursuant to Federal Rule of Civil Procedure 52(a), the court enters the following Findings of Fact and Conclusions of Law.

FINDINGS OF FACT[2]

A. Seagrass Damage

1. From January through March 1992, the *M/V Dauntless*, the *M/V Tropical Magic*, and *the M/V Bookmaker* conducted treasure-hunting operations in Atlantic Ocean waters off Grassy Key, Florida, known as Coffins Patch.

2. Coffins Patch is located within the boundaries of the Keys Sanctuary, a Congressionally designated National Marine Sanctuary. The Keys Sanctuary is comprised of 2,800 square nautical miles of coral reef, seagrass, mangrove fringe shoreline and hard-bottom habitats that Congress designated for special protection in passing the Florida Keys National Marine Sanctuary Act (the Keys Act) in 1990.

3. Kane Fisher, an employee of Salvors, Inc., was captain of the *M/V Dauntless* and directed its treasure-hunting activities in Coffins Patch from January through March 1992. Fisher also directed the activities of the *M/V Tropical Magic* and the *M/V Bookmaker* during those three months. All three boats were in some capacity working for Salvors, Inc.

4. The three vessels were equipped with prop wash deflectors, also known as mailboxes, while operating in Coffins Patch. The mailboxes assisted in treasure hunting.

5. Mailboxes consist of a pair of large, angular pipes mounted on the transom of a vessel. Once lowered from the transom, one end of each pipe fits directly over each of the vessel's propellers. The pipe turns at a ninety-degree angle and then aims straight down, directing the thrust of the ship's engines towards the sea bottom. The goal is to displace sediment and unearth buried items.

6. Mailboxes are powerful devices that can displace five feet of hard-packed mud in thirty-five feet of water. They also can excavate up to twenty-five feet of sand from the ocean bottom. They can make a hole in sand thirty feet across and three to four feet deep in fifteen seconds.

7. The water in Coffins Patch is very shallow, in many places only fifteen feet deep.

8. Using mailboxes, the Defendants made more than 600 holes in the Coffins Patch sea bottom during the first three months of 1992 while attempting to unearth artifacts. These holes are commonly referred to as blowholes. The mailboxes on the *M/V Dauntless* made 395 blowholes, and Kane Fisher personally ordered at least 300 of them to be dug.

9. The blowholes averaged twenty to thirty feet in diameter and three to five feet in depth, and extended along a line for more than a mile.

---

[2][*Orig. fn.*] To the extent that any Findings of Fact represent legal conclusions, they are adopted as Conclusions of Law.

10.   Bancroft Thorne is a Marathon dive boat operator who led ninety dive trips to Coffins Patch from 1987 through 1992. Thorne observed the *M/V Dauntless*, the *M/V Tropical Magic*, and *the M/V Bookmaker* using mailboxes in Coffins Patch on several occasions in January, February and March 1992. Neither he nor Kane Fisher saw any other boats salvaging in Coffins Patch during those three months.[3]

11.   The three vessels salvaged about 150 yards from where Thorne and his clients were diving. On several occasions, the mailboxes caused a large cloud of silt to wash over Thorne and his clients, reducing visibility to zero and forcing them to move dive locations.

12.   On at least one occasion after this happened, and after the three vessels had left, Thorne and other divers swam over to the area where the boats had been working. Thorne saw numerous blowholes that he had not previously seen.

13.   Kane Fisher placed spar buoys on the ocean surface to mark the site in Coffins Patch where he had salvaged for treasure. On March 23, 1992, Billy Causey, the Keys Sanctuary Superintendent, dove beneath one of the buoys in response to unconfirmed reports of damage to the ocean bottom. Causey counted nine blowholes on the sea bottom, all containing extensive seagrass damage.

14.   Causey returned to the area on March 29, 1992, with video camera. He documented twenty-five blowholes up to nine feet deep. Causey believed the blowholes were made in the middle of seagrass beds because (1) all had dead seagrass in them, and (2) he found long seagrass blades exposed at the edges of the blowholes—the type of blades normally found in the middle of seagrass beds. Causey believed the holes were made during the previous month because rubble in and around them was stark white—the normal color of freshly exposed rubble. There was no algae growth that he would have expected to see on older rubble.

15.   Harold Hudson, a Keys Sanctuary marine biologist, videotaped blowholes in Coffins Patch on April 4 and May 5-6, 1992. In May, Hudson and nine other divers video-taped seagrass damage in forty-one blowholes. Hudson documented large chunks of seagrass, some up to two feet thick, that had been ripped out and had fallen into the blowholes. He saw rubble and sediment on top of dead seagrass. Hudson believed the damage had occurred in the previous two months because fine sediment had settled on seagrass blades. If the damage had been older, that sediment would have washed off. Hudson described the seagrass damage as massive.

16.   On April 25, 1992, Curtis Kruer, an environmental biologist, photographed about twenty-five blowholes in Coffins Patch, some up to six feet deep. Kruer observed hay-bale-sized chunks of seagrass lying in the blowholes, and up to three feet of sediment on top of dead seagrass.

17.   Kruer believed the blowholes had been made no more than two months earlier because (1) sediment was still sitting on seagrass blades and (2) the coral rubble he observed was stark white. In addition, he believed the holes were man-made, rather than caused by tides and currents, because naturally caused craters are much shallower and not as steep as the blowholes he observed in Coffins Patch. There also had been no major storms in the

---

[3][*Orig. fn.*] Kane Fisher testified he observed several old blowholes in Coffins Patch when he first began digging there in January 1992, but saw no more than 10 on the first day and less than 100 during the entire time he salvaged there.

area that would have caused such severe natural erosion. The only similar damage that Kruer had seen was caused by bombs dropped from airplanes onto a bombing test range in waters near Puerto Rico.

18.   Dr. Joseph Zieman is an environmental science professor at the University of Virginia who has spent his career studying seagrass. Zieman visited Coffins Patch in May 1992. He observed blowholes up to forty feet wide and ten feet deep, many of which contained an "incredible amount" of dead seagrass. He also saw hay-bale-sized chunks of dead seagrass. In thirty years of working with seagrass, Zieman had never seen such extensive damage.

19.   Like other scientists, Zieman thought the holes had been made within the previous two months because the exposed coral rubble was still white. Like Kruer, he believed the holes were man-made, rather than natural, because of their symmetrical shape, depth, and steepness.

20.   The March 1993 "Storm of the Century" brought gale force winds to the Florida Keys for thirty-six hours. The storm moved substantial material on the ocean bottom and filled in the Coffins Patch blowholes. Neither of the defense experts who testified at trial, Harold Wanless and Anitra Thorhaug, saw the Coffins Patch blowholes before the storm filled them in.

21.   The blowholes that Defendants made damaged at least 1.63 acres of seagrass. This figure is based on Zieman's review of photographs taken of the damaged areas by McIntosh Marine in 1992, and a McIntosh Marine report calculating the damage based on (1) the number of holes and (2) the percentage of sand to seagrass throughout the area. Using the same photos, Zieman independently calculated the damage and came up with the same figure as McIntosh Marine. Zieman did other damage calculations based on different sets of photographs, and concluded that the damage could have been as high as 3.3 acres. However, he concluded that based on the quality of the McIntosh Marine photos, 1.63 acres was an accurate, albeit conservative, damage estimate.

B.   Restoration

22.   The Coffins Patch area is swept by high-energy waves that keep bare sand areas in motion. This inhibits or limits seagrass recolonization in the area.

23.   Natural recolonization in sandy areas of Coffins Patch is very slow. A full recovery of seagrass in the area where blowholes were made will take between 50 and 100 years.

24.   The National Oceanic and Atmospheric Administration (NOAA) conducted a pilot project to determine if it could restore seagrass in the Coffins Patch damage tract by transplanting it. However, none of NOAA's seagrass transplants survived. There have been no successful transplants in other areas with wave energy similar to that in Coffins Patch.

25.   The seagrass Defendants destroyed cannot be restored or replanted in the area of the blowholes.

26.   In December 1996, NOAA conducted a survey to identify potential seagrass restoration projects in the Keys Sanctuary that would be similar in scale and nature to the seagrass injuries in Coffins Patch. NOAA determined that the most viable off-site restoration project would be to transplant seagrass into boat-impacted areas which had later become no-motor zones (Prop Scar Restoration Project).

27.   NOAA selected boat-impacted areas because they 1) are among natural seagrass beds, 2) represent a human-induced injury, 3) can be found in hydrodynamically protected areas, 4) present large-scale scarring that is not recovering, 5) have been restored in this geographic area and elsewhere, 6) occur in sufficient acreage, and 7) constitute an injury not unlike that found in Coffins Patch.

28.   NOAA developed a restoration plan to implement the chosen project. The primary components of this plan include identifying methods of site marking, planting techniques, monitoring, and evaluating success.

29.   NOAA determined the appropriate scale of the compensatory seagrass restoration project using an assessment methodology known as the Habitat Equivalency Analysis (HEA). The HEA quantifies the total resource services lost due to an injury. The HEA determines the quantity of equivalent habitat necessary to be restored and/or created, so that total resource services gained through restoration equals total resource services lost due to the injury. "Services" refers to functions that a resource performs for other resources or humans.

30.   The HEA is appropriate to determine the scale of compensatory restoration projects when 1) the primary category of lost on-site services pertains to the ecological/biological function of an area; 2) feasible restoration projects are available that provide services of the same type, quality, and comparable value to those that were lost; and 3) sufficient data on the required HEA input parameters exist and are cost effective to collect.

31.   Since these three criteria were met in this case, the HFA is the most technically appropriate and cost-effective method to quantify the natural resource damage.

32.   Based on an estimated 1.63 acres of damaged seagrass in Coffins Patch, NOAA calculated the total services lost due to the seagrass injury, the total services provided by the Prop Scar Restoration Project, and the total acreage of compensatory habitat required, so that total resource services gained were equivalent to total resource services lost.

33.   An acre-year represents the total level of ecological services provided by one acre of seagrass over a single year. Using the HEA, NOAA calculated that 44.08 acre-years of services were lost due to the injury in Coffins Patch.

34.   NOAA also used the HEA to calculate the scale of compensatory habitat necessary to compensate for the 44.08 acre-years of lost seagrass services. NOAA determined that 1.55 acres of seagrass habitat must be restored under the Prop Scar Restoration Project to compensate for the lost seagrass services.

35.   NOAA has estimated the cost of implementing the 1.55-acre Prop Scar Restoration Project. The estimate includes the costs necessary to obtain aerial photographs of selected sites, perform on-site "groundtruthing," collect and install seagrass planting units, obtain necessary permits, and monitor the project. The estimate includes expected labor, materials, and travel costs for each of these steps.

36.   The total cost of implementing the Prop Scar Restoration Project is $351,648.

37.   NOAA has incurred certain costs to respond and assess damage to sanctuary resources in this case. Those costs total $211,130. As of January 1997, $26,533 in interest had accrued on these costs.[4]

---

[4][*Orig. fn.*] The parties have stipulated to the amount of response costs, damage assessment costs, and interest.

C. Artifacts

38.   Contextual information is the relationship between artifacts and materials in an archeological site that provides patterns through which archeologists may make inferences about the past.

39.   In widely scattered shallow water shipwrecks, a distinction may be drawn between primary cultural deposits, secondary scatter, and tertiary scatter.

40.   The primary cultural deposit is the location where the ship itself has sunk to the bottom of the sea. In this area, a homogenous assemblage of artifacts remain closely associated to each other and contextual information is more likely to be found.

41.   The secondary scatter of a site has less contextual information. It provides a good indication of where to look for the primary cultural deposit, as well as the rest of the site.

42.   The tertiary scatter has even less contextual information to offer. Artifacts are scattered over a wide area. The tertiary site may be miles away from the primary cultural deposit.

43.   The Defendants excavated and recovered a number of artifacts from the sea bottom in Coffins Patch in the course of their treasure-hunting activities. These artifacts were recorded on a Conservation Lab Artifact Report.

44.   Based on the vessel logs completed during the excavation and recovery, Defendants' activities took place within a tertiary scatter, as Defendants were trying to identify whether a site existed in a particular area of Coffins Patch.

45.   Accordingly, the Court concludes that little, if any, contextual information was lost in the course of Defendants' treasure-hunting activities in Coffins Patch.[5]

CONCLUSIONS OF LAW[6]

A.   The Statutory Scheme

1.   Congress enacted the Sanctuaries Act in response to "a growing concern about the increasing degradation of marine habitats." S.Rep. No. 595, 100th Cong., 2d Sess. 1 (1988), reprinted in 1988 U.S.C.C.A.N. 4387.

2.   The Sanctuaries Act provides for the protection of important and sensitive marine areas through the establishment of marine sanctuaries. The purpose of the sanctuaries is to preserve sensitive areas for their conservation, recreational, ecological, or aesthetic value. *Id.*; 16 U.S.C. § 1431. Under the Act, the Secretary of Commerce may designate and manage marine sanctuaries. 16 U.S.C. § 1433. The Secretary has delegated those responsibilities to NOAA.

---

[5][*Orig. fn.*] The United States argues contextual information was lost because Defendants did not record sufficient information about the artifacts during their treasure-hunting activities. The United States contends it is entitled to $68,445 to conduct a scientifically performed analysis of the impacted site and restore part of the lost contextual information.

[6][*Orig. fn.*] To the extent that any Conclusions of Law represent factual findings, they are adopted as Findings of Fact.

3.   The Sanctuaries Act imposes strict liability on "any person who destroys, causes the loss of, or injures any sanctuary resource." 16 U.S.C. § 1443; *United States v. M/V. Miss Beholden*, 856 F. Supp. 668, 670 (S.D. Fla.1994). The Secretary of Commerce may seek damages from and injunctions against anyone who destroys or injures sanctuary resources. 16 U.S.C. §§ 1437 and 1443. A person may avoid liability under Section 1443 only if he can show that the damage was (1) caused by an act of God, an act of war, or the act or omission of a third party, (2) caused by an activity authorized by federal or state law, or (3) negligible. 16 U.S.C. § 1443(a)(1) and (3).

4.   The Sanctuaries Act broadly defines "sanctuary resource" as "any living or nonliving resource of a National Marine Sanctuary that contributes to the conservation, recreational, ecological, historical, research, educational, or aesthetic value of the sanctuary." 16 U.S.C. § 1432(8).

5.   Congress also may designate sanctuaries, as it did in 1990 when it passed the Keys Act. Pub.L. No. 101-605, 104 Stat. 3089 (1990). The Keys Act provides that the Secretary of Commerce shall manage and police the Keys Sanctuary under the Sanctuaries Act. Keys Act § 5(a). Hence, anyone damaging Keys Sanctuary resources is liable to the government in the manner described in 16 U.S.C. § 1443. *Id.*

B.   Seagrass Damage

6.   Among the Congressional findings in the Keys Act were that "spectacular, unique and nationally significant marine environments, including seagrass meadows," need protection through establishment of a marine sanctuary. *Id.* at § 2(2).

7.   Seagrass is distributed in significant amounts along the Florida coast, and, in particular, the Florida Keys. It stabilizes the sea bottom and helps prevent erosion. It provides a habitat and a refuge for numerous small invertebrates, fish, and other organisms. It serves as an important base in the food chain. It helps recycle nutrients into ocean water.

8.   The Court finds that seagrass is a resource within the meaning of both the Keys Act and the Sanctuaries Act. *See United States v. Fisher*, 22 F.3d 262, 265-66 (11th Cir. 1994). Therefore, anyone who destroys or harms seagrass is strictly liable to the United States for damages unless that person has a defense under 16 U.S.C. § 1443(a)(1) or (3).

9.   The Court also finds that Defendants injured and destroyed 1.63 acres of seagrass by using mailboxes to salvage for treasure in Coffins Patch in January, February, and March 1992. The evidence that supports this finding is:

a.   Testimony from Kane Fisher and vessel logs indicating that mailboxes on the three boats made more than 600 blowholes in Coffins Patch during the first three months of 1992.

b.   Testimony from Kane Fisher and Bancroft Thorne that no other salvagers were digging for treasure in Coffins Patch during that time.

c.   Testimony from Bancroft Thorne that despite consistently running dive operations in Coffins Patch from 1987 through 1992, he never saw blowholes of the type at issue in this case until after Kane Fisher and the three boats left the area.

d.   Testimony from Billy Causey that on March 23, 1992, he discovered blowholes with seagrass damage directly below a surface buoy left by Kane Fisher to mark the spot where he had salvaged in Coffins Patch.

e.   Testimony from Billy Causey, Harold Hudson, Curtis Kruer, and Joseph Zieman that the blowholes they saw in Coffins Patch in March, April, and May 1992 had been made within the previous two months because (1) the exposed coral rubble was white and not fouled by algae, and (2) sediment remained on seagrass blades.

f. Testimony from Billy Causey, Harold Hudson, Curtis Kruer, and Joseph Zieman that the freshly made blowholes they observed had been made in the middle of seagrass beds because of the amount of displaced seagrass and the length of the blades of the remaining seagrass.

g. Testimony from Curtis Kruer and Joseph Zieman that the blowholes they observed had not been caused by nature because the holes were more symmetrical, steep, and deep than naturally caused craters.

h. Testimony from Joseph Zieman and the report of McIntosh Marine indicating that the blowholes damaged at least 1.63 acres of seagrass.

i. Testimony from Harold Wanless and Anitra Thorhaug that they did not view the area in question until after the March 1993 "Storm of the Century" had filled in the blowholes. Because the government's expert witnesses had an opportunity to view the damage before that storm, the Court finds their testimony on the nature and scope of the damage more credible than that of Wanless or Thorhaug.

10. For the same reasons as listed in Paragraph 9, the Court finds that the damage in question was not (1) caused by an act of God, an act of war, or the act or omission of a third party[7], (2) caused by an activity authorized by federal or state law[8], or (3) negligible. As a result, none of the liability exceptions listed in 16 U.S.C. § 1443 apply here.

11. Therefore, the Court finds that Defendants are liable to the United States under 16 U.S.C. § 1443(a)(1) for response costs and damages resulting from the destruction, loss, or injury of a Keys Sanctuary resource.

C. Seagrass Restoration

12. Specifically, the United States is entitled to compensation for (1) the cost of replacing, restoring, or acquiring the equivalent of a sanctuary resource, and (2) the value of the lost use of a sanctuary resource pending its restoration or replacement, or the acquisition of an equivalent sanctuary resource. 16 U.S.C. § 1432(6)(A).

13. Because the destroyed seagrass at Coffins Patch cannot be restored or replaced, the public must be compensated by the acquisition of an equivalent sanctuary resource. In order to compensate for the seagrass losses at Coffins Patch, a seagrass restoration project must be performed at another suitable location within the Sanctuary.

14. The Prop Scar Restoration Project developed by NOAA will provide seagrass services equivalent to those lost due to the injuries Defendants caused.

15. The HEA is an appropriate methodology to scale the compensatory restoration project chosenby NOAA in this case.

16. According to the HEA, 1.55 acres of seagrass habitat must be restored under the Prop Scar Restoration Project to compensate for the interim services that will be lost at Coffins Patch as a result of Defendants' actions.

---

[7][*Orig. fn.*] Specifically, the Court rejects the Defendants' arguments that either prior salvage operations or nature made the blowholes and caused the seagrass damage.

[8][*Orig. fn.*] The Court ruled on this issue in its Summary Judgment Order of April 30, 1997.

17.   The estimated cost of implementing the Prop Scar Restoration Project—totaling $351,648—is reasonable and appropriate. Accordingly, the United States is entitled to $351,648 from Defendants to implement the Prop Scar Restoration Project.

18.   Under the Sanctuaries Act, the United States is also entitled to recover the cost of response and damage assessment. 16 U.S.C. § 1432(6)(C) & (7). Therefore, the United States shall recover assessment and response costs in the amount of $211,130 from the Defendants.

19.   The United States is also entitled to recover interest on these assessment and response costs. 16 U.S.C. § 1443(a)(1)(B). Accordingly, the United States shall recover $26,533 in interest accrued on NOAA's assessment and response costs.

D.   Removal of Artifacts

20.   The Court finds that the artifacts Defendants recovered from Coffins Patch in 1992 are a sanctuary resource within the meaning of § 1432(8), as they are nonliving resources that contribute to the historical value of the sanctuary.

21.   By removing these artifacts from the Sanctuary, Defendants caused the loss of sanctuary resources. 16 U.S.C. § 1443(a)(1)(A)

22.   Therefore, under the Sanctuaries Act, the United States is entitled to recover these artifacts. 16 U.S.C. § 1432(6).

23.   This Court finds, however, that the United States is not entitled to receive compensation to professionally evaluate or curate the artifacts.[9]

24.   The Court also concludes that the amount of archeological contextual information lost during Defendants' treasure-hunting activities was negligible. 16 U.S.C. § 1443(a)(3)(C). Accordingly, the Court also declines to award compensation for loss of contextual archeological information.

E.   Injunctive Relief

25.   The Sanctuaries Act empowers district courts to enjoin violations of the Act. 16 U.S.C. § 1437(i).

26.   On July 23, 1992, this Court granted a preliminary injunction restraining the Defendants from using prop wash deflectors in the Keys Sanctuary. The Eleventh Circuit affirmed this Order. *United States v. Fisher*, 22 F.3d 262 (11th Cir. 1994).

27.   The standard for entry of a permanent injunction essentially mirrors that of a preliminary injunction, except the plaintiff must show actual success on the merits rather than likelihood of success. *Amoco Production Co. v. Village of Gambell*, 480 U.S. 531, 546 n. 12, 107 S. Ct. 1396, 1404 n. 12, 94 L. Ed.2d 542 (1987). In addition to success on the

---

[9][*Orig. fn.*] The United States argues that, but for Defendants' activities, NOAA would not be forced to incur these costs. Accordingly, the United States contends it is entitled to $6,385 under 16 U.S.C. § 1432(6)(A)(i)(I). The Court is not persuaded that the statute entitles the United States to this relief.

merits, a plaintiff must prove that it will suffer irreparable harm if the injunction is not granted, that the threatened injury outweighs the harm that granting the injunction would inflict on the defendant, and that the public interest will not be adversely affected if an injunction is granted. *In re Daytona Beach Gen. Hosp.*, 153 B.R. 947, 950 (Bkrtcy. M.D. Fla. 1993).

28. By proving that the Defendants destroyed and lost sanctuary resources, the United States has established success on the merits.

29. The United States has also established that it will suffer irreparable harm if the injunction is not granted. The Court has found that Defendants' treasure-hunting activities in Coffins Patch in 1992, in particular their use of mailboxes, resulted in damage to and loss of Keys Sanctuary resources. Evidence at trial established that regrowth of seagrass damaged and destroyed by mailboxes will take 50 to 100 years. Allowing Defendants to continue to use mailboxes and remove artifacts would likely cause further, irreparable damage to Sanctuary resources.[10]

30. The scale and significance of the harm Defendants' treasure-hunting activities caused outweighs any burden placed on the Defendants.

31. The public interest will not be adversely affected if this injunction is granted. Rather, the public interest will be served by the protection of Sanctuary resources.

32. Accordingly, Defendants are permanently enjoined from using mailboxes and removing artifacts from the Keys Sanctuary without a permit issued by NOAA.[11]

33. The United States shall file a proposed final judgment within ten days from the date stamped on this Order.

Note

As a litigation strategy, linking natural and historic resources damages can strengthen the case against an offender. This strategy was also successful in the matter of *Craft v. National Park Service*, in which the government raised the protection of the seabed in conjunction with penalizing the looters of historic sanctuary resources. Likewise, in a nonsanctuary case, *Lathrop v. The Unidentified, Wrecked and Abandoned Sailing Vessel*, the United States successfully linked Lathrop's treasure-hunting activities with potential damage to turtle nesting grounds.

---

[10][*Orig. fn.*] This activity is now regulated by NOAA through the issuance of permits. See 15 C.F.R. §§ 922.163 and 922.166.

[11][*Orig. fn.*] The Court reminds Defendants that, in addition to complying with this Court order, they are required to follow the law as stated in the Sanctuaries Act and its regulations.

SECTION E.   FEDERAL LAWS THAT GENERALLY APPLY TO PROTECT HERITAGE RESOURCES IN THE MARINE ENVIRONMENT

The federal statutes discussed in Chapter 2, "Federal Compliance Statutes," and in Chapter 3, "Federal Enforcement Statutes," may apply to the protection of heritage resources in the marine environment. In theory, it is of no effect that the heritage resource at issue is terrestrial or submerged. Many of these statutes, however, do not have practical application to submerged heritage resources, principally because the United States does not *own* the submerged lands within its EEZ unless expressly declared. Not even the submerged lands within national marine sanctuaries are owned by the United States. Instead, the United States serves as trustee of sanctuary resources on behalf of the public. Accordingly, federal statutes that require federal land ownership, such as the Archaeological Resources Protection Act, typically cannot be applied to the marine environment, unless the United States owns the submerged lands of a national seashore or other National Park. Furthermore, after the *Treasure Salvors* case, the Antiquities Act appears not to apply to submerged lands absent an express delegation of authority to the United States to exercise control over submerged heritage resources located therein (as was the case in *Lathrop*). While NEPA and the NHPA do have clear application to federal activities occurring in or on the waters of the United States, these statutes do not have enforcement provisions available for unregulated recovery of submerged heritage resources. Consequently, heritage resources in the marine environment are among the resources least protected for the public benefit.

SECTION F.   INTERNATIONAL LAW AND SUBMERGED HERITAGE RESOURCES

1.   An Overview and Brief History

Sources of International Law

There are two sources of international law. The first one is customary international law, which is the custom or conduct of nations that generally has been accepted by the international community of nations (also referred to herein as "States"). Thus, a generally accepted international practice is evidence of customary international law. Treaties, conventions, and other international agreements are the other primary source of international law. While a few international conventions include submerged heritage resources within their purview,[56] currently no treaty exists to comprehensively address submerged heritage resources. Absent a specific international agreement or coastal State domestic legislation, the maritime law of salvage and common law of finds continue to apply to heritage resources in the marine environment.[57]

Treaties, Conventions, and Submerged Heritage Resources

Questions regarding the jurisdiction of a coastal State and the authority of its domestic law over a submerged heritage resource are determined by both the law of the State in question and international law, while the physical location of a resource largely determines the legal protections afforded it. In general, each coastal State may exercise full sovereignty over foreign nationals and vessels within its Territorial Sea. In addition, it may assert sovereign rights by exercising special jurisdiction and authority over foreign nationals and vessels with regard to natural resources on the Continental Shelf and the EEZ. On the High Seas, a State's authority is limited to the activities of its own citizens and others subject to its national jurisdiction and to vessels flying its flag (flag state jurisdiction). If a submerged heritage resource lies outside the territorial waters of a coastal State, the issues of whether, and to what extent, domestic law applies to it arise. For example, if a State's domestic law protects a submerged heritage resource outside its territorial waters, can this law be enforced against a foreign flag vessel or a foreign national? The answer lies in international law.

Treaties and agreements specify how coastal States agree to regulate the signatories' activities in the marine environment. The most comprehensive international convention concerning resources and the conduct of activities in the marine environment is the United Nations Convention on the Law of the Sea (UNCLOS), often referred to as the "Law of the Sea" (LOS). With the exception of the seabed mining provisions and, perhaps, a few other provisions, UNCLOS largely is viewed as a codification of customary international law.

---

[56]Examples include the United Nations Convention on the Law of the Sea (450 U.N.T.S. 82), the World Heritage Convention (1973 World Heritage Convention), and the UNESCO Convention on the Means of Prohibiting and Preventing the Illicit Import, Export and Transfer of Ownership of Cultural Property [823 U.N.T.S. 231 (1972)].

[57]It is worth noting that international law may also be separated into two types: that which governs private activities (such as salvage), which is referred to as "private international law," and that which governs sovereign nations, which is referred to as "public international law."

UNCLOS does not comprehensively address submerged heritage resources, but does provide authority for coastal states to protect submerged heritage resources located in the Territorial Sea and Contiguous Zone up to 24 nautical miles from shore (450 U.N.T.S. 82). It also addresses submerged heritage resources in the Area and under the High Seas. However, the Convention arguably appears to have excluded from its scope submerged heritage resources lying in the zone situated more than 24 miles from shore, on the Continental Shelf, and in the EEZ. Consequently, and for other reasons, the United Nations Educational, Scientific, and Cultural Organization (UNESCO) has drafted a Convention on the Protection of Underwater Cultural Heritage to more specifically address how coastal States will fulfill their LOS duties to protect submerged heritage resources (U.N. Doc. CLT-96/CONF. 202/5), and, particularly, to address the apparent gap created by UNCLOS.

The World Heritage Convention [27 U.S.T. 40 (1973)] applies to natural and cultural resources, including submerged heritage resources, but only to resources located within the Territorial Sea of a coastal State. Thus, this Convention does not provide coastal States with any more authority to protect submerged heritage resources than they already have under UNCLOS and customary international law.

The UNESCO Convention on the Means of Prohibiting and Preventing the Illicit Import, Export and Transfer of Ownership of Cultural Property [823 U.N.T.S. 231 (1972)] may be applied to submerged heritage resources unlawfully removed from the marine environment. However, if the resources are recovered lawfully under the maritime law of salvage and the common law of finds, the Convention may be of limited utility for the purpose of protecting the resources in place.

The International Convention on Salvage [International Convention on Salvage, S. Exec. Rep. No. 102-17, 102nd Cong., 1st Sess. (1991)] applies to navigable vessels. It therefore does not, on its face, apply to submerged heritage resources. However, it does provide for a process whereby States have expressly reserved the right not to apply the Salvage Convention to heritage resources under their jurisdiction and authority. To date, 10 States have made such a reservation. Nevertheless, throughout the world, salvage law is often applied to historic shipwrecks located in all maritime zones.

In addition to entering into a broad convention, such as the proposed UNESCO Convention on the Protection of Underwater Cultural Heritage, States may enter into bilateral or multilateral agreements to protect and recover historic shipwrecks. For example, agreements have been entered for the protection of shipwrecks such as the *Estonia* and the CSS *Alabama*. In addition, an international multilateral agreement to protect the RMS *Titanic* is being pursued by the United States, France, Canada, the United Kingdom, and perhaps others, partially as a result of legislation enacted in 1986 by the Congress of the United States. [16 U.S.C. § 450rr (1994).]

2. The United Nations Convention on the Law of the Sea

The Law of the Sea Convention (450 U.N.T.S. 82) provides a comprehensive framework for the use of the marine environment.[58] It creates a structure for coastal State (sovereign nation) regulation of all uses and areas of the sea, including the airspace above it and the seabed. The LOS also represents a codification of the consensus on the extent of coastal State jurisdiction, and is the legal basis for determining the authority, rights, and responsibilities of coastal States regarding activities in the marine environment.

Two articles of the LOS (Articles 149 and 303) specifically address submerged heritage resources. Other provisions also may apply to heritage resources protection and management, such as the provisions concerning jurisdiction and authority of nations within different marine areas; limitations on coastal State jurisdiction; rights of passage and access; and obligations and duties of coastal States to protect and preserve the marine environment. The LOS designation of maritime zones is particularly important for submerged heritage resources because the extent of coastal State jurisdiction, authority, and rights differs from zone to zone. The closer a zone lies to shore, the more authority the State has with respect to the resources therein.

The four Geneva Conventions on the Law of the Sea of April 29, 1958, were particularly important for the development of the 1982 Montego Bay LOS Convention. They are: the Convention on the Territorial Sea and Contiguous Zone [Territorial Sea Convention, 15 U.S.T. 1606, T.I.A.S. No. 5639, 516 U.N.T.S. 205 (entered into force September 10, 1964)]; the Convention on the Continental Shelf [15 U.S.T. 471, T.I.A.S. No. 5578, 499 U.N.T.S. 311 (entered into force June 10, 1964)]; the Convention on the High Seas [13 U.S.T. 2312, T.I.A.S. No. 5200, 450 U.N.T.S. 82 (entered into force September 30, 1962)]; and the Convention on Fishing and Conservation of the Living Resources of the High Seas [17 U.S.T. 138, T.I.A.S. No. 5969, 559 U.N.T.S. 285 (entered into force March 20, 1966)]. Following these treaties, during the 1960s and 1970s, concerns about the potential develop-

---

[58]The LOS has not yet been ratified by the United States Senate, but it has been signed by the Executive Branch. Moreover, the LOS generally is a codification of the customary international law of the sea, and thus, even though unratified, nearly all of its provisions should be considered customary international law.

ment and use of the marine environment, particularly seabed mining, provided the catalyst for sessions devoted to the development of a more comprehensive law of the sea treaty. In 1979, the Greek delegation submitted an informal proposal addressing antiquities found on the seabed and in the subsoil of the EEZ. Several other coastal States joined Greece in a subsequent proposal to provide each coastal State with sovereign rights over the archeological and historical resources on or in its Continental Shelf. These two proposals also gave the State or country of origin a preferential right over those heritage resources in cases of sale or other disposition. Delegations immediately objected to the expansion of territorial sovereignty into the EEZ and the Continental Shelf, and the proposed assertion of sovereign rights was replaced with an assertion of jurisdiction. The United States, the United Kingdom, and the Netherlands still objected to the proposals, primarily because they were concerned about "creeping jurisdiction" of the sovereign State. Although the 1958 Convention on the Continental Shelf already had granted coastal States limited jurisdiction and authority over natural resources on the Continental Shelf, these countries thought that by agreeing to extend jurisdiction and authority to human-made objects, they might, in effect, be giving coastal States authority to interfere with the freedom of navigation and overflight within that zone, as well as other rights, such as the right to lay cables. The United States delegation instead proposed the establishment of a general duty to protect archeological resources found in the marine environment, and the Greek delegation offered a counter-proposal that adopted the duty to protect, but also clarified that the treaty did not preclude coastal States from enforcing, in an exclusive manner, their own heritage resources laws and regulations out to 200 nautical miles from the shore. Further negotiation resulted in a compromise provision that gave coastal States the authority to protect submerged heritage resources out to 24 miles from the shore. It was adopted, and became Article 303.

General Provisions Affecting Underwater Heritage Resources

The LOS does not, in and of itself, protect, preserve, or dispose of submerged heritage resources, but it does impose duties on coastal States with respect to these activities. It authorizes coastal States to apply domestic heritage resources law to submerged heritage resources located within their Territorial Sea (out to 12 nautical miles from the shore) and Contiguous Zone (12 to 24 nautical miles from the shore), and in the "Area" (the seabed in the international commons, located beyond the Outer Continental Shelf and the 200-nautical-mile EEZ). The LOS also sets forth how and where domestic heritage resources laws may apply to foreign citizens and foreign flag vessels, and provides for future development and application of international treaties dealing with submerged heritage resources.

The LOS designates several maritime zones, each of which delineates the jurisdiction, authority, and rights that a coastal State may assert:

- "Internal Waters" (Article 8(1)): the waters on the landward side of the baseline from which the breadth of the territorial sea is measured, following the definition in Article 5 of the 1958 Territorial Sea Convention. In general, internal waters refers to fresh water and estuarine waters.

- "Normal Baseline" (Article 5): the low water mark along the coast. As coastlines have various geographical features, the rules for drawing straight baselines are contained in Articles 5–11, 13, and 14.

- "Territorial Sea" (Part II, Articles 2–3): the belt of ocean measured from the baseline of the coastal state, not to exceed 12 nautical miles, comprising the seabed, subsoil, water, and corresponding air space. A coastal state may assert full sovereign authority in the 12-mile territorial sea. Thus, a coastal state's domestic laws affecting submerged heritage resources apply even to foreign flag vessels in the territorial sea, and do not conflict with international law, except to the extent that they would prohibit innocent passage. Innocent passage is a continuous or expeditious navigation which is not prejudicial to the peace, order, and security of a nation. Since 1988, the United States has claimed a 12-mile territorial sea pursuant to Presidential Proclamation 5928 [54 Fed. Reg. 777 (1988), reprinted in 43 U.S.C. § 1331 note (1994)].[59]

- "The Contiguous Zone" (Article 33): the belt of ocean adjacent to, or contiguous with, the territorial sea, and extending 24 nautical miles from the baseline, wherein the coastal state may exercise control necessary to prevent or punish infringement of its customs, fiscal, immigration, or sanitary laws and regulations within its territory or territorial sea. It also is an area wherein a coastal state has jurisdiction and authority to protect submerged heritage resources. In 1972, when it had a three-mile territorial sea, the United States claimed a contiguous zone extending twelve miles from the baseline [Dept. of State, Public Notice 358, 37 Fed. Reg. 11,906 (1972)]. Since the 1988 Presidential Proclamation, however, the United States claims identical areas as its territorial sea and contiguous zone.

---

[59]See also Pub. L. No. 104-132, §901, 110 Stat. 1214, 1317 (1996), §901 (a), *reprinted in* 18 U.S.C. § 7 note, and § 901 (b), codified at 18 U.S.C. § 13 (1998) (the territorial sea as defined by Presidential Proclamation 5928 is part of the United States Code for purposes of federal criminal jurisdiction, and is within the special maritime and territorial jurisdiction of the United States for purposes of Title 18 of the United States Code). It should be noted, however, that the United States has recognized a 12-mile territorial sea elsewhere in its domestic legislation. [See, *e.g.,* the National Marine Sanctuaries Act .]

- "The Exclusive Economic Zone (EEZ)" (Part V, Article 55): the belt of ocean extending 200 nautical miles from the baseline, but not including the territorial sea or the contiguous zone. The EEZ regime represents a balancing of the rights of coastal states to protect and develop resources lying off their coasts (for example, fisheries and offshore oil and gas) with the rights and freedoms of all other states on the high seas (such as navigation, overflight, laying and maintenance of pipelines and submarine cables, and related uses compatible with the coastal state's law and other international law. A coastal state does not have sovereignty in the EEZ, but, under Article 56, it may exercise sovereignty for the purpose of exploring and exploiting, conserving, and managing the natural resources of the EEZ. The United States declared its 200-mile EEZ in Presidential Proclamation 5030, in 1983, and Congress incorporated this EEZ into the Magnuson Fishery Conservation and Management Act [16 U.S.C. §§ 1801 & 1811(1994)] and the National Marine Sanctuaries Act [16 U.S.C. §§ 1431 & 1437 (j) (1994)].

- "The High Seas" (Part VII, Article 86): the open ocean waters beyond the EEZ. This zone does not include the EEZ, territorial sea, contiguous zone, archipelagic, or internal waters.

- "The Continental Shelf" (Part VI, Article 76): the seabed and subsoil of the submarine areas beyond the territorial sea, throughout the natural prolongation of a coastal state's land territory, and extending either to the outer edge of the continental margin or, if the continental margin stops short of 200 miles, to a distance of 200 miles from the baseline. The coastal state alone exercises sovereign rights over the Continental Shelf, but only for purposes of exploring it and exploiting its natural resources. Natural resources include oil, gas, minerals, and other non-living resources, as well as living organisms belonging to sedentary species.

- "The Area" (Part XI): the seabed and subsoil beyond national jurisdiction. Exploration and development of mineral resources on or beneath the seabed of the Area must be undertaken pursuant to the international regime established by the LOS, on the premise that these resources are the "common heritage of mankind" (Article 136). The Area is open to use by all states for the exercise of high seas freedoms, defense, scientific research, telecommunications, and other purposes. Article 149 sets forth the duties and responsibilities of states with regard to submerged heritage resources located in the Area.

One of the fundamental tenets of the international law of the sea is that all ships enjoy the right of "innocent passage" throughout the seas, including through another State's Territorial Sea. The term "passage" refers to navigation for the purpose of traversing that sea; it shall be continuous and expeditious [Article 18; see also Article 14(2) and (3) of the 1958 Territorial Sea Convention.] Passage may include stopping and anchoring, but only for the purpose of rendering assistance to persons, ships, or aircraft in danger or distress. Passage is "innocent" as long as it is not prejudicial to the peace, good order, or security of the coastal State [Article 19(1)]. Article 19(2) lists 12 activities considered to be prejudicial to the peace, good order, or security of the coastal State, including: (g) the loading or unloading of any commodity, currency, or person contrary to the customs, fiscal, immigration, or sanitary laws and regulations of the coastal State; (h) any act of willful and serious pollution contrary to this Convention; (j) carrying out research or survey activities; and (l) any other activity not having a direct bearing on passage. Innocent passage does not include a right of overflight or submerged passage (see Articles 17 and 20). Thus, while a sovereign may enforce its domestic laws, including laws affecting the environment and submerged heritage resources, it may not interfere with the right of innocent passage. The salvage of submerged heritage resources, though, is not "passage," nor is it "innocent." Neither is an exploratory survey for submerged heritage resources considered "innocent passage."

Article 25(1) authorizes the coastal State to take appropriate measures in the Territorial Sea to prevent passage that is not innocent. In addition, Article 25(2) allows the coastal State to take measures necessary to prevent the breach of a condition either for admission of a foreign ship to internal waters, or for a call at a port facility outside internal waters.

Although a coastal State may not interfere with the right of innocent passage, under the LOS it has limited authority to regulate that passage. Article 21 allows coastal States to regulate innocent passage: (g) in cases of marine scientific research and hydrographic surveys; and (h) to prevent infringement of the customs, immigration, or sanitary laws and regulations of the coastal State. Also, Articles 218(1) and 220(1) enable States to undertake an investigation and bring an enforcement action against a vessel voluntarily within its port or at an offshore terminal "in respect of any discharge from that vessel outside the internal waters, territorial sea or exclusive economic zone of that State in violation of applicable international rules and standards established through a competent international organization or general diplomatic conference," or "in respect of any violation of its laws and regulations adopted in accordance with this convention or applicable international rules and standards for the prevention, reduction and control of pollution from vessels when the violation has occurred within the territorial sea or the exclusive economic zone of that State." These and other LOS provisions must be considered in regulating the submerged heritage resources to ensure that the rights of others are not infringed upon. LOS provisions may also provide indirect protection of the submerged heritage resources for which there are specific duties and responsibilities under the LOS.

Provisions Specifically Addressing Underwater Heritage Resources

Article 149 (addressing "the Area") and Article 303 (addressing "the Sea") set out some of the coastal States' duties and responsibilities to protect submerged heritage resources. The scope and extent of these duties, however, is unclear. Also, the LOS does not address the duties of coastal States on the Continental Shelf, between the outer limit of the contiguous zone and the outer limit of the EEZ (24–200 nautical miles from the baseline).

Article 149 expressly imposes a duty on coastal States with regard to the preservation or disposition of submerged heritage resources, and sets out a list of stakeholders whose preferential rights must be considered in carrying out that duty:

> All objects of an archaeological and historical nature found in the Area shall be preserved or disposed of for the benefit of mankind as a whole, particular regard being paid to the preferential rights of the State or country of origin, or the State of cultural origin, or the State of historical and archaeological origin.

The Article, however, does not specify the standard governing that duty, nor does it explain the process for executing it. Also, the text does not define "preferential rights of the State or country of origin," "State of cultural origin," or "State of historical or archaeological origin," and it neglects to rank the preferential rights it cites. While Article 149 attempts to address the global community's interest in submerged heritage resources, by failing to provide standards to measure compliance with the duties governing preservation and disposition, it leaves the development of those standards up to the nations working in the Area, their domestic law, customary international law, and other provisions of the LOS.

Article 303 imposes a duty on coastal States to protect underwater heritage resources "at sea":

1)   States have the duty to protect objects of an archaeological and historical nature found at sea and shall co-operate for this purpose.

2)   In order to control traffic in such objects, the coastal State may, in applying article 33 [contiguous zone], presume that their removal from the sea-bed in the zone referred to in that article without its approval would result in an infringement within its territory or territorial sea of the laws and regulations referred to in that article.

3)   Nothing in this article affects the rights of identifiable owners, the law of salvage or other rules of admiralty, or laws and practices with respect to cultural exchanges.

4)   This article is without prejudice to other international agreements and rules of international law regarding the protection of objects of an archaeological and historical nature.

[LOS, Art. 303, 21 I.L.M. 1261 (1982).]

Article 303 does not clarify which resources are protected and what action is required from a State in order to protect them. For example, use of the term "sea" in Article 303 departs from the scheme of maritime zones (Territorial Sea, Contiguous Zone, Exclusive Economic Zone, and the High Seas) set forth elsewhere in the LOS. Thus, "at sea" could be understood to include all zones, with a coastal State having a duty to protect all underwater heritage resources in the marine environment, even though its jurisdiction over foreign flag vessels outside of 24 miles is questionable. Alternatively, since Article 149 addresses underwater heritage resources in the Area, Article 303 might reasonably be read to exclude the Area from its purview. A third possibility would be to read Articles 149 and 303 together, and thereby entrust coastal States with a general duty throughout the marine environment and with specific duties in the Area.

Despite the uncertainty regarding the reach of a coastal State's duty to protect heritage resources, there seems to be a consensus that pursuant to Article 303(2), domestic coastal State regulations may be enforced against foreign flag vessels in the Territorial Sea and the Contiguous Zone. Outside these two zones, coastal State regulation of shipwreck recovery may have to be based on flag State jurisdiction and national jurisdiction, while enforcement of domestic law against foreign flag vessels could be based only on port State jurisdiction. In addition, coastal States have jurisdiction and control over activities that affect their Continental Shelf or the natural resources within their EEZ, and they may use this authority to exert indirect control over submerged heritage resources there. A coastal State can regulate intrusive research on, or recovery of, submerged heritage resources in the EEZ if the activity conflicts with the State's rights concerning authority over natural resources.

Just as it fails to clearly tell coastal States where their duty to protect underwater heritage resources exists, Article 303 also neglects to inform them about what they are supposed to do in order to comply with that duty. One theory is that the duty should be interpreted broadly:

> Article 303(1) may thus be read as: (i) the obligation to report the accidental discovery of archaeological sites to the competent authorities; (ii) the obligation to take the necessary interim protective measures for the preservation of an underwater site before the arrival of marine archaeologists or even to suspend construction projects; (iii) the need to preserve in situ the located remains and to avoid unnecessary excavation; (iv) the need for conservation, proper presentation and restoration of the recovered items.
>
> [Anastasia Strati, "The Protection of the Underwater Cultural Heritage: An Emerging Objective of the Contemporary Law of the Sea" 124 (*Publications on Ocean Development* Vol. 23, 1995).]

Article 303(3), a savings clause, provides that no violation of the LOS occurs even when a coastal State applies the law of salvage to heritage resources. Experts on salvage law and the LOS concur, however, that this savings clause does not prevent parties from placing submerged heritage resources outside the purview of the law of salvage.[60]

According to experts on the LOS, there appears to be a gap in Articles 149 and 303 regarding the duties of a coastal State to protect submerged heritage resources lying outside the Contiguous Zone and within the outer limit of the EEZ. Currently, UNESCO is considering a draft convention to address this gap and to establish submerged heritage resources recovery standards. This draft convention, entitled the "Convention on the Protection of Underwater Cultural Heritage" (U.N. Doc. CLT-96/CONF. 202/5), would, among other things, give coastal States jurisdiction over the submerged heritage resources on their Continental Shelf and in their EEZ.

3. Draft UNESCO Convention on the Protection of the Underwater Cultural Heritage

The initial draft UNESCO Convention, among other things, gave coastal States authority over submerged heritage resources "abandoned" on their Continental Shelf and within their EEZ. It required compliance with the Charter of the International Council on Monuments and Sites (ICOMOS), which sets forth professional scientific guidelines for the research and recovery of these resources. The Charter also seeks to prevent salvage by prohibiting the sale of any of the cultural heritage.

A meeting on the Draft Convention was held in Paris, France, in late June and early July of 1998. The United States delegation supported the underlying objective of protecting submerged heritage resources, but strongly objected to the exercise of coastal State sovereign jurisdiction outside 24 miles from shore, on the Continental Shelf, and in the EEZ. The reason for this objection came out of the same concern over "creeping jurisdiction" that was raised at the LOS Conference. The United States suggested that the goal of protection could be accomplished without disrupting the careful balance accomplished under the LOS by using other means to control the activities that threaten submerged heritage resources, such as the exercise of a State's jurisdiction over its nationals and vessels under its flag. Russia suggested that perhaps there could be some agreement that the activity of research on and recovery of these resources could be regulated by requiring permits. Under this proposal, the coastal State would have the lead on issuing permits for such activities on its Continental Shelf and EEZ in consultation with

---

[60]Comments on Article 3 of the Draft UNESCO Convention on the Protection of Underwater Cultural Heritage, U.N. Doc. CLT-96/CONF. 202/5.

other nations, such as the country of origin, or a State that otherwise has a historical or cultural interest.

The United States delegation also suggested broadening the scope of the Convention to include all historic shipwrecks and other heritage resources that have been underwater for 50 years or more, as opposed to limiting protection only to those which are abandoned and at least 100 years old. The United States noted that the definition of "abandoned" was too vague, and may not protect most of the underwater cultural heritage in deep water. Specifically, the United States expressed its concern that the drafters included in their definition their apparent understanding of the holding in the *Columbus-America Discovery Group* case, which they interpreted as factoring in the availability of deep water technology in making determinations as to whether shipwrecks should be deemed to be abandoned. Accordingly, the United States suggested that the provision regarding abandonment be stricken from the Convention.

The United States also suggested that the draft Convention include among the types of protected resources sovereign immune vessels such as warships, instead of excluding them as proposed in the draft. Toward this end, the United States provided amendments, so that the laws of salvage and finds would not apply to sovereign immune vessels, aircraft, or their associated contents, if they have been underwater for at least 50 years. The United States' amendments also provided that no party should permit such salvage without the express permission of the sovereign State.

The United States also made several suggestions on how to improve the enforcement mechanisms of the Convention, including a suggestion that the Charter be revised to make the enforcement provisions mandatory, rather than advisory. The United States further suggested that these provisions be annexed as rules so that subsequent revisions be subject to an amendment process involving governmental or State parties, as opposed to having such revisions made by ICOMOS, a nongovernmental organization.

It also advocated that the Convention be broadened to cover all submerged heritage resources, including those that are privately owned. To accomplish this, the United States explained that the term "abandoned" should be eliminated from the Convention to increase its scope. By doing so, however, private recovery, public/private partnerships, and the sale of objects of little or no archeological value would have to be accommodated. To provide for such activities, as well as the laying of cables, mineral development, and fishing, the United States suggested that the Convention adopt a multiple use management approach toward submerged heritage resources.

Another meeting will be held by UNESCO in April 1999 to prepare the draft Convention for to the UNESCO Conference, in October 1999. The goal of the next meeting is to reach a consensus on language which best protects the underwater cultural heritage in a manner consistent with the balance of interests embodied by the LOS.

4.   Convention Concerning the Protection of the World Cultural and Natural Heritage

The Convention Concerning the Protection of the World Cultural and Natural Heritage (1973 World Heritage Convention) established a process whereby parties could identify, protect, and conserve for future generations the heritage sites within their territory under a UNESCO program. Parties to the Convention have the authority and responsibility to identify, protect, and conserve for future generations "heritage" sites within their "territory." "Territory" includes terrestrial sites and sites in the Territorial Sea, and "heritage" sites in the marine environment include both cultural heritage sites, such as shipwrecks or sites of prehistoric human existence, and natural heritage sites that have unique or rare natural features. [823 U.N.T.S. 231 (1972).] Australia's Great Barrier Reef is an example of a marine World Heritage Site with both cultural and natural heritage components.

5.   The International Convention on Salvage

There have been uniform international rules regarding maritime salvage since the beginning of commercial shipping. In 1989, the International Convention on Salvage [International Convention on Salvage, S. Exec. Rep. No. 102-17, 102nd Cong., 1st Sess. (1991)] largely replaced the 1910 Convention of Certain Rules of Law Relating to Assistance and Salvage at Sea (37 Stat. 1658, T.I.A.S. No. 576) primarily in order to address increased concern for the protection of the environment as a result of salvage.

The Salvage Convention sets out the duties, rights, rules, conditions, and procedures for salvage, including salvage rewards.

> Salvage operations means any act or activity undertaken to assist a vessel or any other property in danger in navigable waters whatsoever.... Vessel means any ship or craft, or any structure capable of navigation.... Property means any property not permanently and intentionally attached to the shoreline and includes freight at risk.
>   (Article 1.)

The Salvage Convention does not apply to warships or other noncommercial vessels owned or operated by a State that are entitled to sovereign immunity, unless a State party notifies the International Maritime Organization and specifies the terms and conditions of applicability (Article 4). Also, "no provision of this Convention shall be used as a basis for the seizure, arrest or detention by any legal process of, nor any proceeding in rem against, noncommercial cargoes owned by a State and entitled, at the time of the salvage operations, to sovereign immunity" (Article 25). In addition, the Convention "shall not affect any provision of national law or any international convention relating to salvage operations by or under the control of public authorities" (Article 5).

The Salvage Convention applies to recent casualties, and therefore, by its own terms does not apply to submerged heritage resources incapable of navigation for decades or centuries. Nevertheless, in order to accommodate the request for an explicit provision addressing this issue, Article 30(d)(1) of the Convention states that "[a]ny State may, at the time of signature, ratification, acceptance, approval, or accession, reserve the right not to apply the provisions of this Convention... (d) when the property involved is maritime cultural property of prehistoric, archaeological or historic interest and is situated on the sea-bed." Several nations have made reservations pursuant to this provision, including the United Kingdom, Norway, Sweden, China, Canada, Iran, Ireland, Mexico, Spain, and Saudi Arabia.

6. Practical Application of International Law to the Protection of Submerged Heritage Resources

It is important to note that none of these international legal "tools" have been fully tested in United States district courts to protect submerged heritage resources. The proper application and interpretation of these international conventions is, as of yet, still undetermined.

ISSUES FOR DISCUSSION

1. Do States have a duty to return recovered submerged heritage resources to the identifiable State of origin?

2. Do archeological research, recovery, salvage, and other activities affecting submerged heritage resources fall within the meaning of "innocent passage"?

3. Can a coastal State protect submerged heritage resources from unwanted salvage consistent with the LOS, and, if so, in which areas or zones?

4. What is the implication of the LOS Article 303 for coastal States that have certified that the International Convention on Salvage does not apply to their submerged heritage resources?

5. Consider a treaty to protect submerged heritage resources outside the Contiguous Zone and in the Area that would provide for a multiple-use permitting system and be based on flag State jurisdiction. States, in turn, would rely on their domestic law to implement the treaty and determine the management of the submerged heritage resources under their jurisdiction.

INDEX

TABLE OF CASES

CPSIA information can be obtained
at www.ICGtesting.com
Printed in the USA
BVOW05*2057121216
470589BV00014B/141/P